1996 THE COMPLETE HANDBOOK OF BASEBALL

1996
THE COMPLETE HANDBOOK OF BASEBALL

EDITED BY

ZANDER HOLLANDER

AN ASSOCIATED FEATURES BOOK

A SIGNET BOOK

ACKNOWLEDGMENTS

Welcome to '96 and the 26th edition of *The Complete Handbook of Baseball.* And if you can't tell the players without a scorecard, well, put it down as another example of free agency and the money game that make baseball a three-ring circus.

For their contributions, we thank managing editor Howard Blatt, contributing editor Eric Compton, art director Dot Gordineer of Libra Graphics, statistician Lee Stowbridge, the writers and Seymour Siwoff and Bob Rosen of Elias Sports Bureau, Deb Brody, Sandra Mapp, Carl Galian, Linda Spain, Phyllis Hollander, Nat Andriani, Lisa Vaughan, Phyllis Merhige, Katy Feeney, Rickey Clemons, James Kim, Patrick Courtney, Bill Foley, Laura Courtney and the crew at Westchester Book Composition.

Zander Hollander

PHOTO CREDITS: Cover—Dom DeFrisco/MLB Photos. Inside Photos—George Gojkovich, Allen Kee, Vic Milton, Sports Photo Source, Wide World, UPI, ESPN and the major-league team photographers.

SIGNET
Published by the Penguin Group
Penguin Books USA Inc., 375 Hudson Street,
New York, New York 10014, U.S.A.
Penguin Books Ltd, 27 Wrights Lane,
London W8 5TZ, England
Penguin Books Australia Ltd, Ringwood,
Victoria, Australia
Penguin Books Canada Ltd, 10 Alcorn Ave.,
Toronto, Ontario, Canada M4V 3B2
Penguin Books (N.Z.) Ltd, 182-190 Wairau Road,
Auckland 10, New Zealand

Penguin Books Ltd, Registered Offices:
Hamondsworth, Middlesex, England

First Signet Printing, March 1996
10 9 8 7 6 5 4 3 2 1

CONTENTS

Editor's Note: The material herein includes trades and roster up to the final printing deadline.

For masterful Greg Maddux, it's a game of poker.

Maddux-Glavine: The Beauty of Cy-anide!

By I.J. ROSENBERG

It was the day before Game 6 of the World Series, the day before the Braves would win it all, and two of baseball's best

Series MVP Tom Glavine sprays bubbly after title win.

pitchers, Tom Glavine and Greg Maddux, rode to work together, car-pooling from their homes in north Atlanta. And Maddux let his friend and teammate know what he thought about him pitching in what would be the clincher.

"He told me how glad he was that I was getting the chance to win it, that I deserved it, the fact that I had been here longer than anybody," said Glavine. "It's funny, I was thinking the very same thing about him the night before, because of the season he had. What Greg said really made me feel good."

Glavine pitched one of the greatest games in Series history—eight innings of one-hit, shutout ball in a 1-0 victory—and was named MVP as the Braves beat the Indians and gave Atlanta its first major professional sports title.

It capped an incredible five-year ride to the top for Atlanta

---

I.J. Rosenberg covers the Braves for the Atlanta Journal-Constitution. *His latest book is* Bravo, *the story of Atlanta's championship season.*

and for the 30-year-old Glavine and the 29-year-old Maddux, who have won more games than any other pitchers over that stretch.

Glavine has 91 wins.

Maddux has 90.

Maddux went 19-2 in 1995, won his fourth straight Cy Young and became the first pitcher since Walter Johnson in 1918-19 to have an ERA of less than 1.80 in two consecutive seasons. Glavine went 16-7 and his 3.08 ERA paled only when considered in relation to Maddux' 1.63 mark.

"They are both awesome, but they do different things well," said twice-blessed pitching coach Leo Mazzone. "Greg gets most of the attention, but Tommy is right there with him."

And, besides being close in age, they are very different.

Aside from when he is on the mound, the shy, unassuming Maddux tries to blend into the background. Glavine, on the other hand, is a vocal leader of the union, used to have his own radio show and appears in commercials.

The Braves' first encounter with Maddux was in February 1993, as the prize catch in a winter free-agent bidding war reported to West Palm Beach for his first spring training with the Braves after six-plus seasons with the Cubs.

Maddux walked into the clubhouse wearing an old pair of shorts, a wrinkled shirt and no socks. He was skinny and had a small pot belly, and there was a pinch of snuff in his top lip. How could this be the next great pitcher in baseball? He sure didn't look like a $28-million man.

But Greg's astonishing performance since joining the Braves has left no question that he's one of the most amazing pitchers of his generation. He just keeps getting better. Over the past two seasons, he is 35-8 with a 1.60 ERA.

The best thing about Greg, though, is his personality. He's friendly, honest and easy going. How can you not like someone who calls everybody dude? Hey, dude. What's up, dude? It's cool, dude. See ya, dude.

The Las Vegas neighborhood in which Maddux makes his off-season home, called Spanish Trails, is quiet, subtle and a lot like Greg. It is made up of two-story Spanish Tudor homes that all look alike and are only a few feet apart. It's a nice area, but not extravagant.

"We're not out to impress anybody," said his wife, Kathy. "We're not out to say, 'Oh, we've got this much money, we have to make sure everybody knows about it.' I know a lot of people say that. But I think it's one thing to say it and one thing to live it."

Inside the house, you'd never know a great baseball player lives there, except for the Cy Young plaques at the top of the stairs. In the family room, there is a huge television hooked up to a Nintendo, a habit picked up when he was in the minors. Everything is neat, but not because of Greg. Kathy has to pick up after him and sometimes even talk him into taking a shower when he returns from the golf course.

Greg never combs his hair, either.

"He doesn't like how his hair looks when he combs it," Kathy said. "When we go out to dinner and a hockey game, he wears a hat. When we visit friends, he wears a hat. But that's all right. He is not going to try to impress a person that he's Mr. Smooth."

Greg enjoys playing golf at the Tournament Players Club. In fact, he loves the course and plays there at least four times a week during the winter. Sometimes, his party includes his brother, Mike, who pitched for the Red Sox last season and actually has a better golf swing than Greg.

However, Greg is the same way on the golf course as he is on the mound—a tough competitor. For instance, he played in a charity tournament in which, on one hole, everyone had to hit his tee shot with the opposite hand. Maddux normally swings right-handed, so he had to hit his tee shot left-handed. Everyone, including Maddux, dribbled a first shot off the tee. Maddux' ball sat 315 yards from the green. But, swinging righty now, he pulled out a driver, drew it back and whacked the ball just off the front of the green. Then he chipped in for a birdie, the only one on the hole that day.

Greg's family moved to Las Vegas when he was in high school and he loves the area. He can live peacefully there without fans and the media always bugging him. Maddux' dad deals blackjack at one of the local casinos and Greg has been known to visit The Strip. One night when the whole family went to dinner, the bill came to $150. At the end of the meal, Greg went over to a blackjack table, put $150 on one hand and drew a winner.

He has got a reputation for being a terrific poker player. He notices things—such as another player moving his chips around whenever he has a good hand—that help him win.

That comes as no surprise to those who have seen him pitch, because Greg is no dummy on the mound, either. In a game last season against the Mets, he had worked the count to 1-and-2 against Ryan Thompson when the game was halted by rain. About 30 minutes later, the rain stopped and Maddux returned to the dugout. He noticed Thompson taking practice swings and saw that he was swinging as if he were expecting an inside pitch. So when the game resumed, the right-hander threw a slider away and got a strikeout.

Maddux has been known to intentionally throw a ball out of the strike zone on a 2-and-2 pitch because he knows he can come back and get the hitter out on a 3-and-2 changeup. The other Braves pitchers will sometimes bet on whether he'll do it. Maddux' strategy usually works because a major-league hitter just can't believe a pitcher would throw a change-up on a full count.

The best way to describe how Maddux' pitches always seem to miss the hitter's bat is to borrow a few lines from a *Sports Illustrated* story by Tom Verducci:

"Imagine an inclined trough carrying water to home plate. Then imagine a post in front of the center of the plate. The rushing water will flow away from the post and toward the outsides of the plate. That's exactly the flow of Maddux' pitches. Everything moves away from the center of the plate. The nightmare for a hitter is guessing which of Maddux' five pitches is coming and which direction it's flowing. Some hitters try to reduce the permutations by looking for the ball in a certain area, but Maddux defeats that strategy by noticing subtleties that give away whether those hitters are looking for a ball in or a ball away."

Maddux—who went 3-1 in five postseason starts, including a complete-game, two-hitter in World Series Game 1—spends some time before each start studying the lineup card. But he keeps all his information on opposing hitters in his head. He never forgets. If he makes a hitter look bad on a pitch, he remembers it.

"You save it for when you need it again," he says. "It might be late in the game with runners on base. It might not be until the next time you face that team. It might not be for two years."

Even the best hitters are awed by him. Six-time NL batting champion Tony Gwynn says, "He's like a meticulous surgeon in there. Most guys are afraid to pitch inside, because if you make a mistake there, you're going to get hurt big time. But he puts the ball where he wants to. And that cutter (cut fastball) can be a nightmare for me. You see a pitch inside and you wonder, 'Is it the fastball or the cutter?' That's where he's got you."

With each start this season, Maddux seemed to get stronger. And, afterward, he would always attribute his success to his defense or the bullpen or the runs his team scored. He is 18-0, 0.99 over his last 20 road starts, but he never takes full credit.

He keeps a low profile off the field, too. He does no commercials and often goes unnoticed in public.

"I'll be out with him," says teammate John Smoltz, "and people will say, 'Hey, there's John Smoltz,' and nothing else. I've

Glavine won his Cy Young Award in 1991.

seen it happen at home, in Atlanta. He can walk right through a crowd of people.''

More conspicuous by virtue of his Atlanta longevity is Glavine, who won two games in the Series and was named MVP. No player has been in the Braves clubhouse longer than him. He came to the club in 1987, making his way up through the minors after being a hockey and basketball star at a Boston high school and a fourth-round draft pick of the NHL's Los Angeles Kings in 1984. But Glavine chose baseball and, when he first came through the door in Atlanta, then-pitching coach Phil Niekro noted the left-hander has ''that constant mellow feeling.''

Glavine's mellow was severely tested as a young pitcher. He

struggled until 1991, when he had the first of three 20-game seasons. He won the NL Cy Young at 20-11, 2.55 that year, making him the last pitcher to do so before Maddux' current streak.

That was also the season Glavine started turning into a leader. When Dale Murphy left, Glavine had become the players' rep to the union. Braves GM John Schuerholz remembered his first meeting with Tom.

"We started talking about winning, about what we could do about getting a winning attitude in the organization," said Schuerholz. "Just being around him, I could tell he would be a leader in that regard. He had confidence in his ability—and the way his jaw was set—I could tell he was going to have a good season."

Glavine is not a natural like Maddux or Smoltz or Steve Avery. He has relied mostly on a change-up. But, as few pitchers do, he has thrown harder as he has gotten older. He says his fastball has picked up five mph over the last four years.

"I don't have any secret potion," Glavine said. "My arm just feels better."

But his real secret is working so consistently over the outside of the plate. Tom rarely throws any pitch straight over it.

"I have never seen anything like it. He doesn't overpower anybody, but he doesn't give anybody anything to hit," said Indians manager Mike Hargrove after the World Series.

But Glavine has had his share of problems with the fans and the media in Atlanta, like in the winter prior to '95. Glavine got caught up in the talks with the owners, was very vocal and was heavily criticized for it on the airwaves and in the newspapers.

"I was just standing up for what I believed in," said Glavine. "That's all. I wasn't trying to upset everybody and I know what damage the whole thing has done to the game. And I know the players need to change about some things and so do the owners."

But he made offended people forget his strong pro-union stance by what he did on the mound last season. The boos changed to cheers, although he does wonder what would have happened if he had failed.

"Oh, it would have been unbearable," he said. "And I know there are people who probably wish that would have happened to me."

Off the field, Glavine is just a regular guy. He also loves to play golf and has built a 12,000-foot home in the same neighborhood that Maddux lives in when he is in Atlanta.

But, unlike Maddux, he is very media-conscious. Glavine rarely, if ever, turns down a interview. He is always hanging by his locker for anyone that wants to talk. For several years, he had his own radio show, on the town's big FM station, and he was constantly taking abuse from disc jockeys who liked to poke fun at his All-American looks.

Glavine also was victimized by one of the best clubhouse practical jokes of all time, courtesy of Smoltz, back in 1993. Glavine was not hung in effigy, but he was laid to rest in it. On the floor in front of Glavine's locker appeared two big blankets covering a dummy made of bats and catchers mitts. There were a pair of cleats coming out the bottom and a hat on the top, turned as if the faux Glavine were sleeping. On top of it was an article from that day's *Journal-Constitution*, headline in a story about Glavine's second-half troubles the previous two years, with a reading: "Glavine tired of hearing he's tired." On a box next to the dummy was a sign reading "Quiet! It is the second half. I need my rest."

Despite his sometimes rough road as a Brave, Glavine wants to finish his career in Atlanta. He, like Maddux, has two more years on his contract. But he is not worried about what will happen in the future, preferring to focus instead on last year's Game 6 of the World Series.

He had just missed chances to pitch in some huge postseason games before. In the 1992 Series, he was scheduled to be the Game 7 starter against Toronto, but the Braves lost in six. The next year in the NLCS against the Phillies, Glavine again would have started Game 7, but the Braves again lost in six.

Though Maddux had had the better season in '95, many on the club were excited that Glavine was getting the chance to start World Series Game 6.

"Tommy is as competitive and tough-minded as I've seen," said Schuerholz. "If it weren't for Greg Maddux' presence here, Tommy would be regarded as our ace and the leader of our pitching staff—and deservedly so. Beyond how he pitches, he's got a personal toughness and a game toughness. He rises to these kinds of circumstances."

"A lot of people have come up to me and said this is the perfect game for me to pitch," said Glavine before his strong outing in a 1-0 victory. "It would be great to win it, and for David [Justice] and Mark [Lemke] to get some big hits and [Mark] Wohlers to get the save. Those are the guys that have been here the whole time."

And that's exactly what happened. Glavine got the win, Justice the big home run and Wohlers the save.

"It was something I will never forget, an incredible moment," Glavine said. "I have seen the bad times here, the times when there were only 5,000 in the seats. But this is what you remember when you are retired and sit around and talk to the kids."

Meet Jon Miller: Baseball's Funniest Announcer

By JOHN STEADMAN

All the skills that are there in rich abundance, an effusion of talent that only a rare assortment of baseball announcers has ever brought to the microphone: quality of voice, pace of delivery, knowledge of the game and just the right touch of humor—like proper seasoning inside a Baltimore crab cake. No wonder listening to Jon Miller is a grand-slam pleasure.

As the play-by-play voice of the Orioles and ESPN Sunday Night Baseball and a highly-sought banquet speaker, Miller has gained in national prestige and distinction to the point where he's in the league of such other super technicians of past and present as Red Barber, Mel Allen, Vin Scully, Bob Prince and Bob Costas.

But none of the others could justify a seat in the booth carrying the label: "The funniest announcer in baseball."

Listening to him is like watching Mantle or Mays. Effortless. Natural. The humor he projects never comes off as contrived or staged. It just presents itself as kind of a happy interlude to all of the serious goings-on.

Like when an early-season Oriole game a few years ago was accompanied by some snow flurries and Miller told his listeners: "There's some activity in the bullpen. Snow flakes are falling. And out there in the bullpen getting ready are Donder the right-hander, Blitzen the lefty."

When Kansas City was in a 1-11 slump in 1992, Miller was swift with his assessment on a wet day: "The Royals were rained out today. They are holding a victory celebration."

John Steadman, a legendary figure in the Baltimore region, is a sports columnist on the Baltimore Sun.

Jon Miller (left) and Joe Morgan are a winning battery on ESPN's Sunday Night Baseball.

Miller was no less responsive when the Orioles began the 1988 season by dropping 21 straight games. "It's like they started historically bad and then went into a slump," Miller quipped.

In spring-training exhibitions, he has been known to intentionally clip his words, making it sound to listeners that there's a faulty transmission line or a switch that's clicking "on" or "off", interrupting the game account he's delivering. It's as if Miller's sending a subtle message that after a winter respite, the equipment isn't fully warmed up and working properly.

Frequently, he'll be in the middle innings of what amounts to a regular broadcast and he will quickly change into Spanish or Japanese. Just as smoothly, he'll segue into English. Miller has a marvelous touch to his foolishness. It could be temporarily annoying or aggravating, but he has a license to indulge himself without turning off his listeners.

He proved to be the Bard of Baseball when the Queen of

England attended her first major-league game in 1991 at Baltimore's Memorial Stadium. "Her Majesty is at the game today," he told listeners. "But that doesn't mean we're going to call it any differently."

Well, he did.

When Oakland's Rickey Henderson let a pitch go by for a called strike, Miller paraphrased Lady Macbeth: "It was the umpire that shrieked, the fatal bellman, which gives the sternest goodnight."

Miller was ready for Henderson when he was on base en route to a steal. Borrowing again from Shakespeare's *Macbeth*, he quoted Malcolm: "Let us not be dainty of leave-taking, but shift away. There's warrant in that theft which steals itself when there's no mercy left."

The rotund Miller dresses in a tuxedo for Opening Day and special events during the season. It's his own way of signifying to the world around him that baseball means more than merely a livelihood. At all times, he's his own man, an individual who doesn't follow the charted routines. Miller is dedicated to being the best professional communicator he can be.

On and off the air, there's nothing pretentious or stiff about the way he presents himself. His spirited, carefree and light-hearted approach to baseball shows through in every syllable.

"Painting a picture is the essence of this business," he says. "I can't fake my passion for baseball or the enjoyment I derive. I love it all, the contemporary part and also the great history of the game."

Miller is a first-rate reporter, student of baseball and entertainer who holds your attention. And the voice—yes, the voice—is clear as a ladle of spring water. What he describes is presented with clarity and simplicity, tuning in the audience to the mood of the game, whether it's a team trying to end a losing streak or closing in on a pennant.

When things get slow, as they sometimes will, or one team is out of it, Miller might offer a diversion from what's going on between the lines. He's apt to introduce his own lineup of announcers, such as Scully, Keith Jackson, Harry Caray, Chuck Thompson, Phil Rizzuto or even David Brinkley—all expertly mimicked. Scully may be in Los Angeles with the Dodgers but you'd swear he was right there with Miller, making a guest appearance.

Miller has an incredible ability to imitate. He'll even do Babe Ruth, John Wayne and public-address announcers Bob Sheppard in Yankee Stadium, Sherm Feller in Fenway Park and Bob Casey

Miller does hilarious imitations of Dodger announcer Vin Scully (here with Jim Gilliam and Walter Alston).

in the Metrodome. Oh, yes, crowd noise, too.

This all began when Jon started working toward his career ambition at the age of 10, when other children want to become firemen, astronauts or the next Cal Ripken Jr.

Growing up in Hayward, Cal., young Jon saved his allowance, bought a tape recorder for $30 and the Miller household was never the same. Jon was "broadcasting" from every room in the house. He was influenced by three outstanding radio voices and role models: Russ Hodges with the San Francisco Giants, Monte Moore with the Oakland A's and Scully.

At 19, while a student at San Mateo College, Miller was able to get a radio job in Santa Rosa, Cal. Two years later, he sent an audition tape to Moore, who was so impressed he advised Charlie

Finley, owner of the A's, to hire him as a baseball announcer. "He's better than I am," Moore, a gracious man, told Finley.

But, after a year, Finley dropped Miller, which didn't register as an upset since longevity wasn't exactly a characteristic with the owner of the A's. Out of baseball, Miller took assignments calling games for the San Jose Earthquakes and Washington Diplomats of the North American Soccer League. For a time, he covered his bald head with a wig for television appearances, but quickly abandoned the idea. Again, he wanted to be himself.

In 1976, the Rangers were on the hunt for an announcer. Moore again told Miller he was submitting his name, just as he had with Finley, and it worked. He got back to doing what he wanted, calling baseball. Still later, he spent two years with the Red Sox, then came to the Orioles in 1983.

The Cardinals, Cubs and Yankees, among others, have been interested in acquiring his services, but he likes the pace of Baltimore where he's able to do Orioles games on radio and is allowed to work television for ESPN. He teams on TV with Joe Morgan and they make for the best double-play combination any network has put together.

Fred Manfra, who serves as Miller's regular broadcast partner on WBAL radio in Baltimore, says Miller "has an amazing faculty for recall and is tremendously accurate. Of the younger announcers in the business, no one tops Jon. He's superb. Not to borrow a phrase from Howard Cosell, but he also tells it like it is."

That's another endearing quality to Miller. If the hometown Orioles are sleep-walking and failing to execute fundamentals, he quickly informs the audience, which is a refreshingly honest aspect of his work. Being a "homer" isn't for him.

Miller, at age 44, is at the peak of his game. A smooth, modulated baritone, he makes for easy listening. He has the kind of voice that is pleasing, not one that drives the listener to distraction. In idle moments on the air, he will discuss food, one of his weaknesses, with Manfra and has made a celebrity out of WBAL radio engineer, Paul Eicholtz, whom he refers to as a doctor and former agent for the CIA—both fictitious roles.

When visitors come to the booth, he might cup his mouth and offer a whispered advisory that goes something like this: "Be careful what you say. Dr. Eicholtz, as you may or may not know, once worked for the CIA but, somehow, is still involved, so keep your remarks extremely private and confidential."

As for the fun he produces on the air, it's never off-color or suggestive. He's careful and respectful of his responsibilities.

Miller learned early on by listening to Russ Hodges.

Manfra says the reason the fun times play out so well is none of it is pre-arranged. "Humor isn't essential to a good broadcast," Jon insists. "If you just do that and ignore the reporting aspects, or the sound approach to play-by-play, and try to be funny, then the chances are you'll be a buffoon."

In his take-off of Scully, which is so good it might even fool Scully, he frequently taps a line Vin once used in St. Louis when he opened a broadcast by setting the scene and describing the

Harry Caray gets top billing in Miller's mimic lineup.

surroundings thusly: "The Master Painter has painted a Cerulian blue sky around pewter-gray cloudiness." Never before has the start of a baseball game extracted such an eloquent description. Make no mistake, Miller carries only the highest admiration for the man he's imitating.

Miller's calling card, when you often see him on television, is a garish necktie, something that looks as if a bucket of paint was turned upside down. He has established a splendid rapport with Morgan, his ESPN partner. Both know the game and enunciate its nuances and fine points. "If you listen to Joe, you'll learn about baseball," he says.

The same applies to Miller, who has opinions about the game and isn't afraid to express them. He sees nothing wrong with the designated hitter "because it makes the game, the leagues different." He doesn't like what baseball has done with divisional alignments and believes it was a mistake for the League Championship Series to expand from five to seven games, because that put it on equal basis with the World Series.

Jon is not just another pretty voice coming out of the airwaves. At all times, he impresses listeners as an independent thinker, not afraid to inject his personal views, pro or con, on the game he's describing. Plus, a sampling of his humor adds to the mix.

The tradition baseball offers is something he identifies with, which conveys the feeling that he's not some Jon-come-lately in what he believes. Miller is an artist with words, able to extract a smile and a laugh when those listening might be taking things, such as an eight-run rally by the opposition, much too seriously.

He knows the value of a change-of-pace, or when to let empty air provide the border around a dramatic incident, or how to pause and then raise and lower the pitch of his voice for emotional effect.

He'll give an accurate accounting of the hits, runs and errors, of what's happening on the field, but he wins friends and influences listeners because he's truly one of the outstanding personalities and craftsmen in baseball broadcasting. He's never going to be dull.

"I was once paid a great compliment by Bobby Bragan," a self-deprecating Miller revealed. "Bobby said, 'Since Jon Miller has been on ESPN, he has sold a lot of TVs. I know what I'm talking about, because I sold mine.' "

Rating Albert Belle Among Baseball's All-Time Surliest

By JOE GERGEN

In the hours before the final game of the 1995 baseball season, with the Braves poised to realize a five-year mission by winning the World Series for the first time since their move to the Southeast three decades earlier, the general manager of the Cleveland Indians faced an angry tribunal in the interview room at Atlanta-Fulton County Stadium. The journalists gathered underneath the stands were interested less in his team's performance than the stability of the Tribe's cleanup hitter.

During the session, John Hart disclosed that Albert Belle had offered an apology to Hannah Storm for his outburst in advance of Game 3. On that occasion, at Jacobs Field, Belle had unleashed a torrent of verbal abuse at the NBC-TV reporter when he grew disturbed at the media crowd in the Indians' dugout.

For a team that had compiled the best record in baseball and a player whose combination of 50 home runs and 50 doubles had earned comparison with some of the great batting feats in history, the incident had become an unwelcome blot on an otherwise glorious season. Nor was the moment timely for a sport that had sought to mend public relations in the aftermath of a disastrous strike that cancelled the postseason in 1994 and delayed the start of the ensuing campaign.

''We talk to our players in spring training, we have meetings about relationships with our fans and the media,'' testified Hart,

---

From clubhouse to playing field, Newsday's *Joe Gergen has kept book on Albert Belle and other candidates for the Surly Hall of Fame.*

The World Series was not the best of times for Albert.

alluding to the problem. "I think, especially this year, all of major-league baseball has attempted to respond . . .".

Belle, whose past offenses including firing a baseball at a fan, clearly did not embrace the program. As he had done throughout the season, the most fearsome hitter in the American League declined to personally share his innermost thoughts, a tactic also employed by taciturn veteran Eddie Murray. The latter did permit himself to be questioned by a club spokesman after his single drove in the winning run in Game 3 and a written statement was dispersed to the press. But Belle wasn't nearly so accommodating and the language he used on a female representative of the television-rights holder was particularly vile and tasteless, although not out of character.

When it was reported that Belle explained to Storm he hadn't recognized her in Cleveland, at least one newspaperman expressed amusement. "Albert must have thought it was Bud Shaw," decided Shaw, a columnist for the hometown *Plain Dealer* who has been a recipient of Belle's wrath. Shaw happens to be taller than Storm. He also sports a mustache.

Indeed, one man asked Hart before Game 6 of the World Series if Belle was prepared to apologize to everyone on whom "he's dropped the F-bomb." The GM replied, "I'll defer comment on that one." And the interrogation ended with this extraordinary exchange:

Q: "Has [Belle] had any psychiatric evaluations for mood disorder?"

A: "Not that I know of."

This was unchartered territory, even for prying journalists. Alas, Belle's boorishness was not unprecedented. Surly ballplayers have become a media hazard that has grown in direct proportion to escalating salaries.

Of course, there was always the occasional malcontent dating back to the era of Ty Cobb, the patron of baseball curmudgeons, who attacked opponents, teammates and even fans with similar zeal. There were no felons on Murderers' Row, but the most celebrated team in the history of the national pastime, the 1927 Yankees, featured one of the unfriendliest individuals in the major leagues. His name was Bob Meusel and he had little use for conversation until his career was drawing to a close.

The sudden change of heart inspired a famous line from Frank Graham, one of the most respected sports writers of his time. "He's finally saying hello," Graham noted, "when he should be saying goodbye."

Even some of the true legends of the sport were intolerant of the public and their annointed representatives. The great Ted Williams had a long-standing feud with Dave Egan, a Boston columnist who billed himself as "The Colonel" and Ted was observed on at least one occasion expressing his displeasure with the written word by spitting in the direction of the press box. His relationship with the fans was such that, after hitting a home run in the final at-bat of a magnificent career, Williams didn't deign even to tip his cap to the Fenway Park faithful.

Mickey Mantle died a hero's death last year, mourned by millions after a liver transplant failed to save his life. But there was a time early in his career when he was roasted by Yankee fans for not living up to his potential or perhaps for not being as dependable as Joe DiMaggio. Whether for that reason or others,

"The Mick" rarely was outgoing with the public and particularly defensive with newspapermen. Those who covered the team rarely were offered a glimpse of the country humor so prized by teammates. All too often they were greeted by the back of Mantle's neck when they sought an opinion from the superstar.

"People tell me I'm a better guy now than I was when I played," he conceded years later. And, agreed contemporaries, it was true. The product of a small-town upbringing, Mantle recalled that he was terribly shy when he reported to New York and he didn't know how to handle the fame that soon engulfed him. In retirement, however, he grew comfortable with the role fate had handed him, sharing much of his personal life, even his descent into and his rehabilitation from alcohol dependency. At the time of his death, there was nary a child of the '50s who didn't feel he had known Mantle forever and who wasn't moved in some mysterious way.

Perhaps some of the more recent examples of the socially challenged will come to realize they were, at the very least, misguided in their hostility. Fortunately, one of the prime breeding grounds for misbehavior has been disinfected with the rapid turnover of the New York Mets. What had been a cast of veteran malcontents has been transformed into a group of eager youngsters by co-owner Fred Wilpon, general manager Joe McIlvaine and manager Dallas Green.

In the belief the Mets needed only a couple of proven performers to put them over the top a few years ago, rookie GM Al Harazin invested millions in free-agent Bobby Bonilla, a native New Yorker, added the aforementioned Murray and acquired former Cy Young award winner Bret Saberhagen. They joined a team that already featured outfielder Vince Coleman, who had been signed by predecessor Frank Cashen to fill the void created by Darryl Strawberry's defection, and the resulting chemistry was something that hadn't been witnessed since Dr. Frankenstein closed his laboratory in Transylvania.

Not only did the Mets, under the kid-glove care of manager Jeff Torborg, soon sink to the bottom of the National League East but they turned their clubhouse into a little shop of horrors. Murray, who told the press upon his arrival that he might not be available for daily conversations because he had to focus on the games, displayed the personality of a sphinx and, through his acknowledged leadership, encouraged teammates to do the same. A few didn't need much encouragement.

Bonilla, engaging when it was to his advantage, bristled under criticism, even from the electronic scoreboard that displayed the letter E alongside his position too long for his psyche to handle. He threatened one writer with bodily harm, saying "I'll show you the Bronx." Meanwhile, Coleman was so oblivious to his responsibilities he knocked Doc Gooden out of his start one night by clipping the pitcher on the shoulder with the follow-through of his golf swing. Saberhagen joined in the merriment by squirting bleach at a group of reporters in the clubhouse following a game.

The whole dreadful situation came to a head after Torborg had been fired and Harazin had announced his resignation under pressure. Coleman enlivened a West Coast road trip by tossing fireworks at fans gathered around the players' parking lot outside Dodgers Stadium, injuring youngsters in the crowd. For his defense, the ballplayer summoned a Los Angeles celebrity lawyer who soon would gain international recognition for his association with O.J. Simpson. Yes, Robert Shapiro.

It was Wilpon who finally said *enough* and ordered the dismantling of the team. Coleman was the first to go, followed by Murray. Bonilla and Saberhagen finally were unloaded in the course of the 1995 campaign.

Ironically, all but Bonilla, who hit well for the Orioles, reached the postseason last fall. Coleman, who began the season in Kansas City, helped the Mariners to their first division title and a first-round playoff victory over the Yankees. Saberhagen was thoroughly ineffective for the Rockies, but nevertheless rode the team's prodigious displays of power to a wild-card spot in the National League playoffs. And then there was Murray, still remarkably productive in the twilight of his career, still uncommunicative with anyone holding a pen, a microphone or a camera. So consistent was the aging switch-hitter that he even blew off Sparky, the kid wearing the CBS Sports jacket who was filing taped segments of the World Series for David Letterman's late-night follies.

Murray's silence rekindled memories of Steve Carlton at the top of his game 15 years earlier. Carlton was the brilliant left-handed pitcher who led the Phillies to the only world championship in franchise history with a nasty slider and a stony disposition. Carlton, whose views on the world dispensed more than a decade later upon his election to the Baseball Hall of Fame were slightly off-center, declined to acknowledge the media during the tumultuous season of 1980. He delegated Tim McCarver, his personal catcher, as his official spokesman after games.

Such an assignment proved to be terrific practice for McCarver, who went on to an outstanding career as a broadcaster, but it was thoroughly frustrating for writers who sought insights

Cast Ted Williams as manager of the All-Surly team.

from the best pitcher in the sport. Nor was Carlton particularly open with those who shared the uniform. Following the Phillies' World Series victory over the Royals in a stadium ringed with mounted policemen and snarling K-9 dogs, the wine conoisseur known as "Lefty" drank from his own jeraboam of fine champagne at a private party in the trainer's room, occasionally summoning a teammate to join him for a glass of bubbly.

That may have been preferable to the vitriol served by John Tudor of the Cardinals as his team failed in the 1985 World Series, also against the Royals. Along with many of his teammates, Tudor smarted from what he felt was a New York bias in the media, including *USA Today*, and never forgot a slight. His oft-bitter exchanges with journalists foreshadowed a more destructive encounter with an electric fan on his way to the locker room following a disappointing performance in Game 7.

The Cards' defensive posture—although not their defense—was similar to that of the Dodgers' in the mid-to-late 1970s. In counterpoint to the baseball valhalla promoted by Tommy Lasorda, the clubhouse seethed of jealousy, most of it directed at first baseman Steve Garvey. In one memorable episode, Garvey and Don Sutton wrestled in the locker room over the pitcher's description of Garvey's then-wife while the manager was lecturing on the Dodgers' mystique in his office.

While Garvey saved the rest of the infield from numerous errors with his deft glovework, second baseman Davey Lopes, shortstop Bill Russell and third baseman Ron Cey weren't much more accommodating with the first baseman than they were with journalists. They whined about their treatment at the hands of Yankee Stadium fans during losses in the 1977 and 1978 World Series and replied curtly to suggestions they were something less than the best infield of all time. Their futile attempts at snaring hard-hit ground balls were in marked contrast to the glittering success of Craig Nettles, Bucky Dent and even the previously anonymous Brian Doyle, a late substitute for the injured Willie Randolph.

They should have been forced to work for Leo Durocher, whose stint as manager of the Chicago Cubs was a professional embarrassment. Not only did the self-serving Durocher fail to win the National League pennant with the better team in 1969, he turned his own players against him with his heavy-handed tactics. He blasted them in the newspapers as the Cubs began their eventual descent against the Mets and followed that by withdrawing completely to his office, leaving them to explain defeat. Declining to answer questions himself except on a radio show for which he was paid, Durocher appointed coach Hank Aguirre to meet the press.

Some players, such as Jim Rice, have kept journalists and the public at bay with a cold, unblinking stare. Dick ("Don't call me Richie") Allen communicated with his fans in Philadelphia by scrawling "Boo!" or other messages in the dirt around first base. He also honored his teammates by dressing in a separate room of the Phillies' clubhouse.

But perhaps Belle's most memorable predecessor as a merchant of baseball menace was another left fielder, Alex Johnson. The man was talented enough to win an American League batting title while with the Angels and also mean enough to continually foul off pitches in batting practice in an attempt to hit an unsuspecting target. He didn't feel it was necessary to run out ground balls, but he took delight in threatening to run over umpires. He became something of a legend during one spring-training game in Arizona when he positioned himself differently in each succeeding inning so that he was continually standing in the shade.

Reporters weren't the only people afraid of Johnson, whose brother Ron was an excellent and pleasant running back for the New York football Giants. Teammates were terrified, a circumstance that led the extroverted Chico Ruiz to smuggle a gun into the clubhouse for protection. The Indians haven't expressed similar misgivings about Belle. In fact, following the first two games of the World Series in which he was held in check by Atlanta pitchers, they decided he had not been ornery enough.

"He has not gotten as frustrated as I'd like him to," said center fielder Kenny Lofton the day before Game 3. "I'd like to see him break a bat."

Only the previous year, Belle had been suspended by AL president Bobby Brown for suspicion of using a corked bat. Mindful of his record, Boston manager Kevin Kennedy requested that Belle's bat be tested after the man homered in the first game of Cleveland's Division Series against the Red Sox. The slugger subsequently was cleared of all charges, but at a price.

No longer the league president but the man responsible for overseeing the Series, Brown ordered the bat sawed in half. It was returned to Belle in two pieces the following day. "Ever since they cut that bat open," Lofton concluded, "Albert's been down. It was his lucky bat."

The Indians suffered while their most formidable hitter pined over spoiled ash. According to teammates, he was so despondent that he hadn't trashed the clubhouse in at least a couple of weeks.

"Sometimes, he throws coolers out," recounted shortstop

Steve Carlton: No comment.

Omar Vizquel. "Sometimes, he breaks the telephone in the clubhouse. Sometimes, you come in and there's cookies all over the place. He hasn't done that this time. He's controlling himself. I hope he erupts pretty soon."

Well, the Indians didn't have to wait long, about 24 hours to be precise. Belle erupted the following day but he didn't take his frustration out on coolers, the telephone or the cookies baked by a Cleveland nun and delivered daily to team's clubhouse. He took it out on a woman setting up for a television interview with another player in the home-team dugout at Jacobs Field.

As Vizquel had noted only the previous day, "He doesn't snap at us. He doesn't take it out on other players. He's really a sweet guy. It's like talking to a 12-year-old. But when he's on the field and he's 0-for-3, I don't recommend talking to him."

In this particular case, however, the incident occurred in the dugout, where Belle experienced difficulty negotiating his way to the bat rack, and he was the party that initiated the disturbance. Chances are there wouldn't have been quite the fuss if the aggrieved party had worked for a newspaper instead of the network televising the game.

At least, Belle stopped short of the tactics employed by Deion Sanders while a member of the Braves. A media darling and a national merchandizing tool in his alter ego as a professional football player, Sanders didn't take kindly to comments by McCarver during the 1992 NLCS. So while his Atlanta teammates were celebrating their victory over the Pirates and their qualification for a second consecutive appearance in the World Series, Sanders maliciously doused the ABC-TV broadcaster.

While Storm wasn't physically harmed by Belle, she was shaken. The slugger, having relieved his burden, responded with opposite-field homers in Games 4 and 5. But Tom Glavine and Mark Wohlers combined to shut down Belle and his teammates on one hit in Game 6 to close out the Series.

The Indians figure to be on center stage again this season, meaning we haven't heard the last of Belle's transgressions. The acting commissioner, Bud Selig, said he was concerned about the slugger's outburst. Hart made a similar statement. Everyone seemed concerned—except Belle.

"You're talking about a grown man who, if he does make a mistake, it's something he's going to have to live up to," the GM said. "That's still a part of his growth . . . an organization can take whatever action it deems appropriate and ultimately it falls back to the player. That's the nature of this industry."

Clearly, the industry is disturbed.

MADE IN JAPAN

THE STRIKING SAGA OF HIDEO NOMO

By LAWRENCE ROCCA

Even with the advantage of hindsight, Hideo Nomo's first season in the American major leagues still seems only slightly more plausible than a daydream that lasted eight months long.

Considering that Nomo began his journey as a heretofore complete unknown from the Far East, his staggering list of achievements probably exceeded even the fevered imaginings of the most fanciful Hollywood scriptwriter.

Nomo led the NL with 236 strikeouts, including 16 in one game to set a Dodger rookie record. His 2.54 earned-run average was the second-best mark in the league, to Atlanta's Cy Young winner Greg Maddux. He limited opposing hitters to a league-low .182 batting average. He was elected NL Rookie of the Year, becoming the Dodgers' fourth consecutive winner of that award, and finished fourth in the Cy voting.

That's quite a resume for a courageous pioneer who was attempting a transition that had never been made before. In the prime of his career, months before his 27th birthday, Nomo defected from the Japanese leagues and walked away from guaranteed stardom and riches so he could start from scratch in America. The move was the ultimate in high-risk, high-reward gambles. To be sure, the $2-million signing bonus from the Dodg-

---

Lawrence Rocca has been an eyewitness to Nomo-mania as Dodger beat writer for the Orange County Register. *His book,* Nomo in America, *was published last fall in Japan.*

Hideo's heroics have caused an outbreak of Nomo-mania.

ers was an incentive. But so was the desire to perform against the world's best.

Of course, if Nomo had failed, both his reputation and that of Japanese baseball would have been dealt humiliating blows.

The news that Nomo had taken advantage of a loophole in the standard Japanese League player's contract and escaped to the U.S. via "retirement" caused quite a stir in his homeland. Born Aug. 31, 1968 and raised in a blue-collar section of Osaka, with a postal work for a father and a grocery clerk for a mother, Nomo had been a star pitcher for his high-school team and had helped Japan to the silver medal in the 1988 Olympics in Seoul. The Kintetsu Buffaloes, one of Japan's 12 pro teams and a low-budget operation owned by a railroad company, won the rights to draft him in a lottery. As a rookie, Nomo led the six-team Pacific

The Americanization of Nomo.

League in strikeouts and victories and he did the same thing for the next three years before shoulder tendinitis shortened his season in 1994.

Around that time, Nomo did what is the unthinkable in Japan. He hired an agent, which players in Japan do not have. He demanded a multi-year contract, usually accorded to players on the verge of free agency, a status that it takes 10 years to earn. Then he demanded a trade. Finally, he pronounced himself "retired" to gain his freedom. Even his parents did not approve of Nomo's renegade behavior. In Japan, as the proverb states, the nail that sticks up is hammered down.

When Nomo signed with the Dodgers in February 1994, it hardly raised an eyebrow among American baseball fans outside of California, because fans were repulsed by the strike-abbreviated 1994 season and faced with the prospect of replacement players in 1995. But the Dodgers recognized the significance of Nomo's quest immediately, which is largely why they signed him.

Dodgers owner Peter O'Malley has long harbored a dream of a true World Series and he saw Nomo as a potential cornerstone in the construction of a bridge between Japanese and American baseball. To make his new pitcher feel welcome and comfortable in spring training, O'Malley took Nomo for rides up and down the east coast of Florida, pointing out spots where Spanish galleons had perished long before, the way his father, Walter, had done with him when Peter was a child.

After months of physical work with the Dodgers' trainers and coaches to streamline his waist and regain his arm strength after a long winter layoff, Nomo won a spot in the rotation by dominating the Yankees one spring training day in Fort Lauderdale.

The outing vs. the Yankees marked the first time that Nomo's unorthodox windup—he slowly reaches above his head and turns his back completely to the plate before pausing, then whirling through his delivery—baffled American hitters.

"I don't want to see that guy again in my life," said then-Yankee Luis Polonia. "He got me all confused. You can't pick up his release point. You have to wait too long. I only saw him once. I don't want to see him again . . . I couldn't see anything and you can't hit what you can't see."

"You could take a nap during his windup," said Marlins left fielder Gary Sheffield concerning the pitcher whose nickname in Japan was "The Tornado."

Nomo's regular-season debut, May 2 in San Francisco, was trumpeted by both the American and Japanese media. The baseball and football press boxes at Candlestick Park were full. The field was blanketed with still photographers and camera crews during batting practice. The crowd was small (16,099), but spirited. Some people waved signs, in English and Japanese. Others unfurled Japanese flags. When Nomo threw his first pitch, there were more than a few tears of joy.

History was being made, even though Nomo's five innings of one-hit, shutout ball didn't involve him in the decision of what became a 4-3, 15-inning Dodger defeat. Not since Masanori Murakami pitched for San Francisco in 1964 and 1965 had a Japanese-born player appeared in a major-league game. And Nomo brought the grand total to two.

"I was just glad that I could throw over here," said the 6-2, 210-pound wonder. "I don't care about 30 years. I don't care whether I made history or not. I just came to the major leagues so I could go up against the best."

"Anybody who can throw his fastball with such ease and hit the corners with his forkball is tough," said Giants slugger Matt

Williams. "He's going to be very, very good."

Mainstream America was too distracted by Nomo's status as a curiosity, because of his super-slow-motion delivery, his mysterious background and his huge entourage of Japanese reporters, to be much concerned with his ability during May. No widespread assessments of Nomo as a pitcher were made as he went 0-1 in six starts that month.

Then came June 2, when Nomo allowed one run and two hits and defeated the Mets, 2-1, with three outs' worth of relief help from Todd Worrell. As the Dodgers poured out of their dugout to congratulate Worrell on his save, Dodgers manager Tom Lasorda and pitching coach Dave Wallace each embraced Nomo. He smiled broadly. The crowd of 32,002 at Dodger Stadium cheered wildly, chanting "NO-MO! NO-MO! NO-MO!" When he took a curtain call, a Japanese flag was unfurled behind the dugout.

"Our man was outstanding," said Lasorda. "For him to get his first victory like this was just so exciting. The electricity going through this place was something we haven't had around here in quite awhile."

The victory kicked off a six-game June winning streak during which Nomo posted a 0.89 ERA. There was that 16-strikeout game against the Pirates June 14 in which Nomo set the club rookie record. There were back-to-back, 13-strikeout, complete-game shutouts of the Giants June 24 and the Rockies June 29, both at Dodger Stadium. The latter effort gave the right-hander 50 Ks in a span of four starts, exceeding by one the most the great Sandy Koufax ever recorded over a similar period.

"I'm very happy and honored to be compared to Sandy Koufax," said Nomo. "But I don't have records on my mind."

"He's not some gimmick or trick the Dodgers are trying to pull over on you," said Giants manager Dusty Baker. "He is the real thing. The guy comes across just as advertised: a strikeout pitcher."

"There is not too many pitchers who can do what he does," said the Rockies' Andres Galarraga after striking out against him twice. "You think it's a forkball and it's a fastball. Then you think it's a fastball and it's a forkball. You just can't recognize it."

"He made a believer out of me by the third time I saw him," said no-longer-skeptical longtime Mets scout Harry Minor. "He strikes out 13, 14, 15 . . . It doesn't take a rocket scientist to figure out the guy is good."

The spectacular stretch gave credence to comparisons between

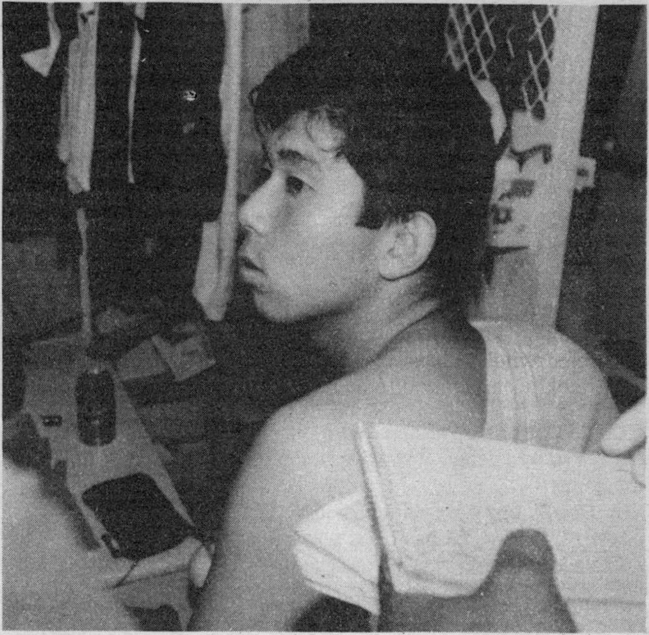

Meeting the press after first shutout, vs. Giants.

Nomo-mania and Fernando-mania, the cultural phenomenon that had accompanied Mexican-born Fernando Valenzuela's arrival in the majors in 1981. Nomo, the NL's Pitcher of the Month of June, had springboarded into a gig as the league's starting pitcher in the All-Star Game and a presence in the national consciousness capable of overcoming widespread fan anger toward the game.

Tickets to Nomo's games became coveted treasures. Adults and children instantly made Nomo memorabilia the hottest-selling souvenir item at Dodger Stadium. There were $150 Nomo Dodgers jackets, $25 Nomo T-shirts, $10 Nomo baseballs, $50 Nomo sweatshirts. The Dodgers' marketing department couldn't dream up new ideas for merchandise fast enough. One front-office employee estimated that the Dodgers recouped that $2-million signing bonus on T-shirt sales alone, by the end of July. Before the season was over, the marketing of Nomo had become a worldwide business.

"Everybody loves Nomo," said Lasorda. "Everybody says,

'Can you get Nomo's autograph?' They don't ask for anybody else. If I asked for everybody, I'd be asking for 50 or 100 a day. Everybody wants a piece of him. Whenever he goes out, wherever he goes, people want his autograph. People want to meet him. People want to see him. I understand that's the price he has to pay because of the success he has had . . . Baseball ought to be so dang grateful for the contributions he has made. Every place he goes, he pulls people in."

Interestingly, Nomo kept his distance from most of the Japanese press corps that reported on his every move, though he read as many articles on him as he could get his hands on. His feud with the Japanese media stemmed from the photographers' persistent pursuit of his wife, Kikuko, every time she left their home in Kobe. But, with the assistance of Michael Okumura, the full-time interpreter whom the Dodgers hired at the start of the season, Nomo dealt with the media horde, too.

If the pressure seemed enormous and the burden of expectations overwhelming, it was impossible to tell from Nomo's demeanor.

"I really think he had envisioned this," said Dodgers GM Fred Claire. "I think this has been played out before his eyes. I think he has seen himself in Dodger Stadium. I think he has seen himself in postseason play, winning big games, winning awards. He envisioned himself an image of success."

"If he is nervous, I can't tell," said his catcher Mike Piazza. "He has just got an outstanding disposition. No matter whether he is having trouble or whether he is throwing well, he has just got a great pitching mentality."

Nomo even tried his best to blend with the other Dodgers in the clubhouse. Though he spoke no English and understood just a little when he arrived in America, he made every effort to be one of the guys and vowed to study English last offseason. He became friendly with Mexican-born right-hander Ismael Valdes, who himself had begun speaking English only a year-and-a-half before. He even joined the Dodgers' fantasy football league.

"He is being judged so much on an individual basis, yet I don't think he has ever seen this as anything other than trying to help a team," said Claire.

Yet, Nomo's star even overshadowed that of Cal Ripken Jr. at the 1995 All-Star Game. Under a media barrage larger and more unrelenting than anybody could recall, Nomo rose to the occasion. He exchanged high fives with hundreds of Little Leaguers on the field for a pregame ceremony. His All-Star teammates greeted him with a playful homage, bowing after he struck out two in the first of his two shutout innings of work.

Japanese prime minister Tomiichi Murayama faxed Nomo a letter of congratulations and encouragement the morning of the game and sumo-wrestling champion Akebono had a congratulatory letter hand-delivered to the pitcher. Actress Hikari Ishada was on the field before the game and said she got "chicken flesh" upon meeting Nomo.

In a season during which baseball attendance was down 20 percent from 1994 pre-strike levels, Nomo was the antidote to apathy.

"Nomo was critical to keeping interest in baseball at the level it is," said Oakland GM Sandy Alderson. "It has transcended the situation in LA. I think it goes beyond the fact that he is Japanese. It has to do with his ability, which is certainly great, but I think it really has to do with his style . . . He's self-effacing. He's the antithesis of what people expect from major leaguers."

Of course, not everyone in America received Nomo with grace.

In Florida, the Marlins' mascot found it humorous to dress in a Godzilla suit. The Marlins' radio station conducted a fake Nomo interview in which a buffoon produced gutteral strains and another provided a translation that derided Florida players and their fans. In Houston, the mascot performed a fake martial arts routine in which he karate-chopped Styrofoam boards in half the day Nomo pitched there.

Even Hall of Fame announcer Harry Caray indulged in offensive behavior, asking Cubs manager Jim Riggleman in a pregame radio interview Sept. 12, the day Nomo posted his 11th victory, "Well, my eyes are slanty enough, how 'bout yours?" Riggleman changed the subject and the station apologized, but not before members of the Japanese-American League expressed their outrage.

Nomo never even allowed that he noticed the slights. There were other things he found disconcerting in the season's second half: a recurring cracked fingernail that limited his effectiveness; a tender elbow that surfaced in a start vs. the Cards Aug. 12; the persistent rumors that weariness was taking a toll on his stuff and, finally, the persistent Nomo-maniacs, who followed him home so often that the club hired an off-duty police officer to escort him from Dodger Stadium each night.

However, Nomo put aside all the distractions down the Dodgers' stretch run and ended his first regular season in America the only way it seemed appropriate. On the next-to-last day of the season, Nomo pitched one of his finest games to propel the Dodg-

From Japan to the U.S., fans await Nomo's next pitch.

ers to a 7-2 victory over the Padres that clinched their first division title since 1988 as he allowed one earned run and struck out 11 in eight innings.

"I gave him the ball," said Delino DeShields, who caught a popup for the final out in the taking of the NL West. "If anyone deserved it, this game or this year, it was him."

Though he was manhandled by the Reds in Game 3 of the Division Series as Cincinnati completed its sweep of the Dodgers, Nomo lost none of the luster off his rookie year. In fact, the Reds' Ron Gant made a point at a postgame press conference to shake the pitcher's hand and thank him "for helping to save our game."

"What he has done already is legendary stuff," said Claire.

"He's already part of Dodger folklore, never to be taken away."

And what Nomo did made him part of Japanese folklore as well.

"During my era, I couldn't even start to imagine playing in the majors," said former Tokyo Giants star Isao Shibata. "Physically, we had no chance. It's really exciting to see what he did. The gap between levels of play had been quite substantial before. We feel that Nomo reflects that the level of play (in Japan) has been raised."

Claire believes that Nomo accomplished more in a strike-shortened season than all but a relative handful of big leaguers do in their entire careers. The most mythic of figures need be referred to by only one name. Babe. Willie. Mickey. Hank. And now, Nomo.

"They are up there, among the stars—and he's there with them," said Claire.

But he will remain there only if the Nomo name withstands the test of time—and not everyone thinks it will.

"The first year he came up [in Japan], nobody hit him," said Orestes Destrade, a marginal major leaguer who faced Nomo overseas. "He dominated the Pacific League in 1990. But by the second or third year, we started figuring him out. I had several home runs off him and several strikeouts . . . He will have continued success, but they will study the films and begin to catch up. We did."

On the other hand, Minor figures that Nomo should have a long run of success.

"If he stays healthy, I don't think he will (slip)," said the scout. "The secret of trying to hit him is to not swing at the split-finger, because most of the time they're not strikes. But that is a lot easier said than done. For years and years, they said the secret to hitting the knuckleball was to never ever swing at it. But it's just too hard to lay off it."

For now, there is just one glorious season to make one recall the sentiments expressed by the eloquent Vin Scully, the Dodgers' Hall of Fame radio and television announcer, at the news conference that the Dodgers called to announce the Nomo signing.

"Over the years, the Dodgers have had some remarkable pitchers," he said. "A great black pitcher in Don Newcombe. A great Jewish pitcher in Sandy Koufax. A great Mexican pitcher by the name of Fernando Valenzuela. So, in retrospect, it's only right that we should have, hopefully, a great Japanese pitcher."

It was silly, sweet optimism at the time. Now it seems like a perfect prognostication.

INSIDE THE NATIONAL LEAGUE

By FRANK ISOLA and TONY DeMARCO
N.Y. Daily News *Denver Post*

PREDICTED ORDER OF FINISH

East	Central	West
Atlanta	Chicago	Colorado
N.Y. Mets	Cincinnati	Los Angeles
Philadelphia	Houston	San Diego
Montreal	St. Louis	San Francisco
Florida	Pittsburgh	

Wild Card: Los Angeles
Playoffs Winner: Atlanta

EAST DIVISION

	Team	Colors	Owner	1995	Morning Line / Manager
1	**BRAVES** Who says there are no dynasties?	Royal blue & white	Ted Turner	W 90 L 54	2-1 Bobby Cox
2	**METS** Young and dangerous	Orange, white & blue	N. Doubleday/F. Wilpon	W 69 L 75	10-1 Dallas Green
3	**PHILLIES** Aging and ailing	Crimson & white	William Y. Giles	W 69 L 75	15-1 Jim Fregosi
4	**EXPOS** Only a longshot	Scarlet, white & royal blue	Claude Brochu	W 66 L 78	20-1 Felipe Alou
5	**MARLINS** Bottom of the pack	Blue, silver, orange & black	Wayne Huizenga	W 67 L 76	50-1 Rene Lachemann

Brave Classic

120th Running. National League Race. Distance 162 games plus playoffs. Payoff (based on '95): $206,608.95 per winning player, World Series; $121,945 per losing player, World Series. A field of 14 entered in three divisions.

Track Record: 116 wins—Chicago, 1906

CENTRAL DIVISION

	Team	Owner / Colors	1995	Morning Line / Manager
1	**CUBS** A Ryne revival	Andy MacPhail; Royal blue & white	W 73 L 71	5-1 Jim Riggle-man
2	**REDS** Misses in photo finish	Marge Schott; Red & white	W 85 L 59	7-1 Ray Knight
3	**ASTROS** Biggio's return a boon	Drayton McLane Jr.; Orange & white	W 76 L 68	15-1 Terry Collins
4	**CARDINALS** Good jockey can take you so far	August A. Busch III; Red & white	W 62 L 81	30-1 Tony La Russa
5	**PIRATES** Saddest in the field	Kevin McClatchy; Old gold, white & black	W 58 L 86	100-1 Jim Leyland

WEST DIVISION

	Team	Owner / Colors	1995	Morning Line / Manager
1	**ROCKIES** Mile-high expectations	Jerry McMorris; Purple, silver & black	W 77 L 67	5-1 Don Baylor
2	**DODGERS** Swan song for Lasorda?	Peter O'Malley; Royal blue & white	W 78 L 66	6-1 Tommy Lasorda
3	**PADRES** Building once again	John Moores; Brown, gold & white	W 70 L 74	15-1 Bruce Bochy
4	**GIANTS** Little hope at 3COM Park	Peter Magowan; White, orange & black	W 67 L 77	Dusty Baker

ATLANTA BRAVES

TEAM DIRECTORY: Owner: Ted Turner; Chairman: Bill Bartholomay; Pres.: Stan Kasten; Sr. VP/Asst. to Pres.: Hank Aaron; Exec. VP/GM: John Schuerholz; Dir. Scouting: Paul Snyder; Dir. Pub. Rel.: Jim Schultz; Med. Rel. Mgr.: Glen Serra; Trav. Sec.: Bill Acree; Mgr.: Bobby Cox; Coaches: Jim Beauchamp, Pat Corrales, Clarence Jones, Leo Mazzone, Jimy Williams, Ned Yost. Home: Atlanta-Fulton County Stadium (52,709). Field distances: 330, l.f. line; 402, c.f.; 330, r.f. line. Spring training: West Palm Beach, Fla.

SCOUTING REPORT

HITTING: Atlanta won the World Series, at last. How did the Braves do it? With pitching, of course. But they also have power. They produced 168 home runs, second in the NL behind Colorado, and generated 645 runs.

Atlanta figures to hit better in '96 because Marquis Grissom (.258, 12, 42, 29 steals) should hit better. Of course, Fred McGriff remains the heart and soul of the lineup as the Braves' leader in home runs (27) and RBI (93). David Justice (.253, 24, 78) slipped a little in 1995.

In Chipper Jones, Ryan Klesko and Javier Lopez, the Braves have a trio of terrific young hitters. Jones (.265, 23, 86) is on the verge of stardom. Klesko (.310, 23, 70) is a potential 40-home-run hitter and Lopez (.315, 14, 51) is among the best-hitting catchers in the game.

PITCHING: It's so good, it's frightening. NL Cy Young magnet Greg Maddux (19-2, 1.63) is in a world of his own and, next to Randy Johnson, Tom Glavine (16-7, 3.08) is the best lefty in baseball. Oh yeah, don't forget about John Smoltz (12-7, 3.18) and Steve Avery (7-13, 4.67).

Glavine, the World Series MVP, is baseball's winningest pitcher the last five years with 91 victories and Maddux is second with 90. Smoltz, the hardest thrower among the starters, rebounded from a mediocre 1994 season. Avery was a puzzle during the regular season, but won both of his postseason starts.

The Braves even have a strong bullpen, led by closer Mark Wohlers (7-3, 2.09), who converted 25-of-29 save opportunities

Mark Wohlers finally ended Brave search for closer.

and added four saves in the postseason. Pedro Borbon Jr. (2-2, 3.09), Greg McMichael (7-2, 2.79) and sinkerballer Brad Clontz (8-1, 3.65) are reliable setup men.

FIELDING: The Braves' 100 errors were the third-fewest total of any team in the NL. Manager Bobby Cox swears Gold Glove winner Grissom is the best center fielder he's ever seen. He had better be with the lumbering Klesko in left and the erratic Justice in right. Mark Lemke may be the most underrated second baseman in baseball while Jeff Blauser is more than adequate at shortstop. Jones committed 25 errors in his first season at third base. But Maddux is a Gold Glover plus Lopez is solid behind the plate.

OUTLOOK: The Braves, 90-54 en route to the NL East title in '95, want more than just one World Series title and, with their pitching staff, they'll have a chance to repeat. They should run away with the division again and, if they avoid major injuries, the Braves will be the favorites to return to the Fall Classic for the fourth time in six years.

BRAVE PROFILES

MARQUIS GRISSOM 28 5-11 190 Bats R Throws R

One of the game's best defensive center fielders . . . Struggled offensively for most of '95 season, but he was a force in postseason . . . Set a postseason record with 25 hits . . . Batted .360 (9-for-25) in World Series . . . Played final 91 games without making an error . . . Leadoff hitter batted .366 with three home runs and nine RBI in June . . . Had five hits and reached base safely six straight times vs. Expos Aug. 5 . . . Batted .543 against his Montreal ex-mates . . . Has six career leadoff home runs, including one in Game 2 of Division Series against Rockies . . . Matched a career best with 14-game hitting streak from June 5-20 . . . Tied for ninth among NL outfielders with nine assists . . . Was NL's 10th-hardest batter to strike out, fanning once per 9.9 plate appearances . . . Acquired by Braves from Expos for Roberto Kelly, Tony Tarasco and Esteban Yan prior to last season . . . Ranked second in NL in runs and at-bats and third in steals in '94 . . . Won second Gold Glove in 1995 . . . Led NL in stolen bases in 1991 and 1992 . . . Expos' third-round pick of 1988 draft . . . Born April 17, 1967, in Atlanta . . . Earned $4.9 million last season.

Year	Club	Pos.	G	AB	R	H	2B	3B	HR	RBI	SB	Avg.
1989	Montreal	OF	26	74	16	19	2	0	1	2	1	.257
1990	Montreal	OF	98	288	42	74	14	2	3	29	22	.257
1991	Montreal	OF	148	558	73	149	23	9	6	39	76	.267
1992	Montreal	OF	159	653	99	180	39	6	14	66	78	.276
1993	Montreal	OF	157	630	104	188	27	2	19	95	53	.298
1994	Montreal	OF	110	475	96	137	25	4	11	45	36	.288
1995	Atlanta	OF	139	551	80	142	23	3	12	42	29	.258
	Totals		837	3229	510	889	153	26	66	318	295	.275

CHIPPER JONES 23 6-3 195 Bats S Throws R

A budding star . . . Batted .365 (20-for-55) with three home runs and eight RBI in post-season . . . Committed 25 errors at third base in '95, but he was outstanding with glove in October . . . Made impressive return from major left knee surgery which forced him to miss 1994 season . . . Led all rookies in RBI (86), runs (87) and games (140) while ranking second among first-year players in homers (23), hits (139) and walks (73) . . . Fell one RBI shy of tying Earl Williams' Atlanta rookie record, set in 1971 . . . Batted .274 with 10 homers and 38 RBI after All-Star break . . . Cracked first home run May 9, off Mets' Josias Manzanillo . . . Tore anterior cruciate ligament in left knee running to first base, March 3, 1994 . . . In '93, he led International League in hits (174), runs (97), total bases (268) and triples (12) in his first Triple-A season with Richmond . . . Braves made him first overall selection in 1990 draft . . . Born April 24, 1972, in Deland, Fla. . . . Earned $114,000 last season.

Year	Club	Pos.	G	AB	R	H	2B	3B	HR	RBI	SB	Avg.
1993	Atlanta	SS	8	3	2	2	1	0	0	0	0	.667
1994	Atlanta					Injured						
1995	Atlanta	3B-OF	140	524	87	139	22	3	23	86	8	.265
	Totals		148	527	89	141	23	3	23	86	8	.268

DAVE JUSTICE 29 6-3 197 **Bats L Throws L**

Hero in Game 6 of World Series . . . Hit solo home run, which accounted for only run in clincher . . . Won back hearts of Braves fans after criticizing them as fickle . . . Did not have an extra-base hit in 42 postseason at-bats before collecting double and homer in Game 6 . . . Has hit 20-or-more homers in every full season except strike year . . . Was on DL from June 2-16 with torn ligaments in right shoulder . . . Braves' all-time left-handed home-run hitter with 154 . . . Had four game-winning hits in Braves' final at-bat, including three home runs . . . Hit 20 of 24 homers after June 21 . . . Set career highs in homers (40) and RBI (120) in '93 and finished third in NL MVP voting . . . 1990 NL Rookie of Year . . . Married to actress Halle Berry . . . Born April 14, 1966, in Cincinnati . . . Selected by Braves in fourth round of 1985 draft . . . Earned $5.2 million last year.

Year	Club	Pos.	G	AB	R	H	2B	3B	HR	RBI	SB	Avg.
1989	Atlanta	OF	16	51	7	12	3	0	1	3	2	.235
1990	Atlanta	1B-OF	127	439	76	124	23	2	28	78	11	.282
1991	Atlanta	OF	109	396	67	109	25	1	21	87	8	.275
1992	Atlanta	OF	144	484	78	124	19	5	21	72	2	.256
1993	Atlanta	OF	157	585	90	158	15	4	40	120	3	.270
1994	Atlanta	OF	104	352	61	110	16	2	19	59	2	.313
1995	Atlanta	OF	120	411	73	104	17	2	24	78	4	.253
	Totals		777	2718	452	741	118	16	154	497	32	.273

MARK LEMKE 30 5-9 167 Bats S Throws R

Perfect complementary player for a team loaded with stars . . . Underrated defensive second baseman made five errors all of last season . . . Went 78 games, from May 26, 1994 to May 10, 1995, without a miscue . . . Stole his first base since 1993 and finished with career-high two steals . . . Began hitting in No. 2 spot in early August and finished with a .301 average in that role . . . Seventh-hardest player in NL to strike out, fanning once per 11.3 plate appearances in '95 . . . Batted just .220 in postseason, but he was a rock at second . . . Set franchise record for highest fielding percentage by a second baseman (.994) in '94 as he committed only three errors . . . Selected by Braves in 27th round of 1983 draft . . . Born Aug. 13, 1965, in Utica, N.Y. . . . Earned $1.25 million last year.

Year	Club	Pos.	G	AB	R	H	2B	3B	HR	RBI	SB	Avg.
1988	Atlanta	2B	16	58	8	13	4	0	0	2	0	.224
1989	Atlanta	2B	14	55	4	10	2	1	2	10	0	.182
1990	Atlanta	3B-2B-SS	102	239	22	54	13	0	0	21	0	.226
1991	Atlanta	2B-3B	136	269	36	63	11	2	2	23	1	.234
1992	Atlanta	2B-3B	155	427	38	97	7	4	6	26	0	.227
1993	Atlanta	2B	151	493	52	124	19	2	7	49	1	.252
1994	Atlanta	2B	104	350	40	103	15	0	3	31	0	.294
1995	Atlanta	2B	116	399	42	101	16	5	5	38	2	.253
	Totals		794	2290	242	565	87	14	25	200	4	.247

RYAN KLESKO 24 6-3 220 Bats L Throws L

Swings as if he's trying to hit the longest home run ever recorded . . . Likely to be shifted from left field to first base . . . Set career highs in homers (23) and RBI (70) in '95 . . . Hit a homer in Games 4, 5 and 6 of World Series . . . Hit first career grand slam and had career-high six RBI June 6 vs. Cubs . . . Missed two weeks in May with sprained left thumb . . . His homer off Pirates' Dan Plesac July 24 was his first against lefty . . . Finished last season with three home runs off left-handers . . . Finished '95 with team-high .608 slugging percentage . . . Homered once per 14.3 at-bats and had one RBI per 4.7 at-bats . . . Would have finished in top 10 in both categories but didn't have enough at-bats (329) to qualify . . . Finished third in race for NL Rookie of the Year Award in '94 . . . Braves' sixth selection in

1989 draft . . . Born June 12, 1971, in Westminster, Cal. . . . Earned $150,000 last season.

Year	Club	Pos.	G	AB	R	H	2B	3B	HR	RBI	SB	Avg.
1992	Atlanta	1B	13	14	0	0	0	0	0	1	0	.000
1993	Atlanta	1B-OF	22	17	3	6	1	0	2	5	0	.353
1994	Atlanta	OF-1B	92	245	42	68	13	3	17	47	1	.278
1995	Atlanta	OF-1B	107	329	48	102	25	2	23	70	5	,310
	Totals		234	605	93	176	39	5	42	123	6	.291

FRED McGRIFF 32 6-3 216 Bats L Throws L

One of the game's most feared hitters . . . His bat more than makes up for his mediocre defensive skills at first base . . . Batted .333 with four home runs and nine RBI in postseason . . . Hit first World Series homer in Game 1 off Indians' Orel Hershiser on first pitch he saw . . . Led Braves in home runs (27) and RBI (93) . . . Shortened '95 season halted his string of consecutive seasons of 30-or-more home runs at seven . . . Eight other players have accomplished the feat and all are Hall of Famers . . . Has hit 20-or-more homers in nine straight years since rookie season in '87 . . . Selected to All-Star team for third time . . . Has 24 career two-homer games . . . Has missed only one game since joining Braves in July 1993 . . . Acquired by Braves from financially strapped Padres for prospects Melvin Nieves, Vince Moore and Donnie Elliott, July 18, 1993, and sparked Braves to 51-17 closing kick and NL West title . . . Led majors in homers in '89 with Blue Jays and in '92 with Padres, becoming first player in history to win home-run titles in both leagues . . . Drafted in ninth round by Yankees in 1981 . . . Born Oct. 31, 1963, in Tampa . . . Earned $4.25 million last year . . . Re-signed to four-year, $20-million deal as free agent last winter.

Year	Club	Pos.	G	AB	R	H	2B	3B	HR	RBI	SB	Avg.
1986	Toronto	1B	3	5	1	1	0	0	0	0	0	.200
1987	Toronto	1B	107	295	58	73	16	0	20	43	3	.247
1988	Toronto	1B	154	536	100	151	35	4	34	82	6	.282
1989	Toronto	1B	161	551	98	148	27	3	36	92	7	.269
1990	Toronto	1B	153	557	91	167	21	1	35	88	5	.300
1991	San Diego	1B	153	528	84	147	19	1	31	106	4	.278
1992	San Diego	1B	152	531	79	152	30	4	35	104	8	.286
1993	S.D.-Atl.	1B	151	557	111	162	29	2	37	101	5	.291
1994	Atlanta	1B	113	424	81	135	25	1	34	94	7	.318
1995	Atlanta	1B	144	528	85	148	27	1	27	93	3	.280
	Totals		1291	4512	788	1284	229	17	289	803	48	.285

JAVIER LOPEZ 25 6-3 185 **Bats R Throws R**

Terrific young catcher . . . Set career highs in homers (14), RBI (51), doubles (11) and triples (4) in '95 . . . Became first catcher to hit .300 or better for Braves since Joe Torre hit .315 in 1966 . . . Six of his homers came either in or after seventh inning . . . Batted .361 with seven homers and 26 RBI after All-Star break . . . Hit two-run homer in Game 2 of World Series and picked off Manny Ramirez, the potential tying run at first base, in eighth inning . . . Tied Fred McGriff for most postseason RBI with nine . . . Hit three-run homer in Game 2 of NLCS vs. Reds . . . Caught Kent Mercker's no-hitter, April 6, 1994 vs. Dodgers, in just his 10th major-league start . . . Became youngest backstop in NL to catch a no-hitter since 22-year-old Ted Simmons caught Bob Gibson's no-hitter in 1991 . . . Named an International League All-Star with Richmond in '93 . . . Signed by Atlanta as non-drafted free agent in November 1987 . . . Born Nov. 5, 1970, in Ponce, P.R. . . . Earned $115,000 last year.

Year	Club	Pos.	G	AB	R	H	2B	3B	HR	RBI	SB	Avg.
1992	Atlanta	C	9	16	3	6	2	0	0	2	0	.375
1993	Atlanta	C	8	16	1	6	1	1	1	2	0	.375
1994	Atlanta	C	80	277	27	68	9	0	13	35	0	.245
1995	Atlanta	C	100	333	37	105	11	4	14	51	0	.315
	Totals		197	642	68	185	23	5	28	90	0	.288

JEFF BLAUSER 30 6-1 183 **Bats R Throws R**

Plagued by injury throughout '95 season and postseason . . . Bruised thigh kept him off World Series roster . . . Played just one game in NLCS . . . Sixteen of his 31 RBI came via long ball . . . Reached double figures in home runs for fifth time in last seven seasons, despite career-low .211 batting average . . . Eleven of his 12 home runs came off right-handers . . . Tied for fourth in NL in getting hit by a pitch (12 times) . . . Matched his Braves record with .970 fielding percentage in '94 . . . Posted career highs in batting average, home runs, RBI, hits, runs, walks and steals in '93, his first full season at shortstop . . . Became first shortstop to hit over .300 for Braves since Alvin Dark batted .322 in 1948 . . . Batted .280 with two homers vs. Phillies in 1993 NLCS . . . Braves' first selection in secondary phase of 1984 draft . . . Born Nov. 8, 1965, in Los Gatos, Cal. . . . Earned $3 million last year.

Year	Club	Pos.	G	AB	R	H	2B	3B	HR	RBI	SB	Avg.
1987	Atlanta	SS	51	165	11	40	6	3	2	15	7	.242
1988	Atlanta	2B-SS	18	67	7	16	3	1	2	7	0	.239
1989	Atlanta	3B-2B-SS-OF	142	456	63	123	24	2	12	46	5	.270
1990	Atlanta	SS-2B-3B-OF	115	386	46	104	24	3	8	39	3	.269
1991	Atlanta	SS-2B-3B	129	352	49	91	14	3	11	54	5	.259
1992	Atlanta	SS-2B-3B	123	343	61	90	19	3	14	46	5	.262
1993	Atlanta	SS	161	597	110	182	29	2	15	73	16	.305
1994	Atlanta	SS	96	380	56	98	21	4	6	45	1	.258
1995	Atlanta	SS	115	431	60	91	16	2	12	31	8	.211
	Totals		950	3177	463	835	156	23	82	356	50	.263

TOM GLAVINE 30 6-1 185 Bats L Throws L

The best No. 2 starter in baseball . . . Named MVP of World Series . . . Won two games, allowing one hit over eight shutout innings in Series-clinching Game 6 victory . . . Winningest pitcher in majors over past five seasons with 91, one more than Greg Maddux . . . Hit double figures in victories (16) for seventh straight season . . . Notched his 1,000th career strikeout, Aug. 21 vs. Astros . . . His ERA after first inning was 2.28 while his first-inning ERA was 7.76 in '95 . . . Finished fourth in NL in wins, sixth in innings (198⅔), and tied for fifth in ERA (3.08) in '95 . . . In '93, he became first NL pitcher to win 20 games for three straight years since Ferguson Jenkins won 20 from 1967-72 . . . Recorded career-high five shutouts in 1992 . . . Won NL Cy Young in 1991 . . . Braves' second-round pick in 1984 draft . . . Was also fourth-round pick of NHL's Los Angeles Kings . . . Born March 25, 1966, in Concord, Mass. . . . Earned $4,750,000 last season.

Year	Club	G	IP	W	L	Pct.	SO	BB	H	ERA
1987	Atlanta	9	50⅓	2	4	.333	20	33	55	5.54
1988	Atlanta	34	195⅓	7	17	.292	84	63	201	4.56
1989	Atlanta	29	186	14	8	.636	90	40	172	3.68
1990	Atlanta	33	214⅓	10	12	.455	129	78	232	4.28
1991	Atlanta	34	246⅔	20	11	.645	192	69	201	2.55
1992	Atlanta	33	225	20	8	.714	129	70	197	2.76
1993	Atlanta	36	239⅓	22	6	.786	120	90	236	3.20
1994	Atlanta	25	165⅓	13	9	.591	140	70	173	3.97
1995	Atlanta	29	198⅔	16	7	.696	127	66	182	3.08
	Totals	262	1721	124	82	.602	1031	579	1649	3.52

GREG MADDUX 29 6-0 175 Bats R Throws R

Perhaps the greatest pitcher of his generation . . . Won unprecedented fourth straight NL Cy Young . . . Winningest pitcher in majors over the last eight years (142) . . . Became first pitcher since Walter Johnson (1918-19) to post ERA of less than 1.80 in consecutive seasons . . . Went 3-1 in five postseason starts, including a complete-game, two-hitter in Game 1 of World Series . . . Pitched his first career one-hitter, May 28 vs. Astros . . . Had career-best, 10-game winning streak, from May 23-Aug. 4 . . . Set major-league record with 17 straight road wins . . . Has gone 18-0, 0.99 in his last 20 road starts . . . Ranked tied for first in NL in innings (209⅔), shutouts (3) and third in strikeouts (181) . . . Had major-league-high 10 complete games for second straight season . . . Has amassed 200-plus innings for eight straight years . . . Won fifth Gold Glove in 1995 . . . Set major-league record in 1994 by finishing 1.09 ahead of Athletics' Steve Ontiveros, who posted majors' second-best ERA at 2.65 . . . Born April 14, 1966, in San Angelo, Tex. . . . Cubs' second pick in 1984 draft . . . Earned $5.5 million last year . . . Braves signed him as free agent prior to 1993 season.

Year	Club	G	IP	W	L	Pct.	SO	BB	H	ERA
1986	Chicago (NL)	6	31	2	4	.333	20	11	44	5.52
1987	Chicago (NL)	30	155⅔	6	14	.300	101	74	181	5.61
1988	Chicago (NL)	34	249	18	8	.692	140	81	230	3.18
1989	Chicago (NL)	35	238⅓	19	12	.613	135	82	222	2.95
1990	Chicago (NL)	35	237	15	15	.500	144	71	242	3.46
1991	Chicago (NL)	37	263	15	11	.577	198	66	232	3.35
1992	Chicago (NL)	35	268	20	11	.645	199	70	201	2.18
1993	Atlanta	36	267	20	10	.667	197	52	228	2.36
1994	Atlanta	25	202	16	6	.727	156	31	150	1.56
1995	Atlanta	28	209⅔	19	2	.905	181	23	147	1.63
	Totals	301	2120⅔	150	93	.617	1471	561	1877	2.88

JOHN SMOLTZ 28 6-3 185 Bats R Throws R

Proved that 1994 was an aberration . . . Enjoyed fifth winning season in last six years . . . Finished second in NL with 193 strikeouts and has finished in top two in strikeouts three of last four seasons . . . Did not allow more than four earned runs in any of his 29 starts . . . Struck out 12 vs. Dodgers July 5 . . . Hurled back-to-back complete games, June 14 at Montreal and June 19 at Cincinnati, and the win against Reds was his first shutout in two years . . . Was 0-0, 6.60 in three postseason starts, after carrying 5-1, 1.93 career postseason numbers into '95 . . . Underwent arthroscopic surgery to remove bone chips from right elbow, Sept. 8, 1994 . . . Selected to third All-Star team in 1993, when he matched career high with 15 wins and finished second in NL in strikeouts with 208 . . . Led NL with 215 strikeouts in '92 . . . Born May 15, 1967, in Warren, Mich. . . . Signed by Tigers as non-drafted free agent in September 1985 . . . Traded to Braves for Doyle Alexander, Aug. 12, 1987 . . . Earned $4.75 million last season.

Year	Club	G	IP	W	L	Pct.	SO	BB	H	ERA
1988	Atlanta	12	64	2	7	.222	37	33	74	5.48
1989	Atlanta	29	208	12	11	.522	168	72	160	2.94
1990	Atlanta	34	231⅓	14	11	.560	170	90	206	3.85
1991	Atlanta	36	229⅔	14	13	.519	148	77	206	3.80
1992	Atlanta	35	246⅔	15	12	.556	215	80	206	2.85
1993	Atlanta	35	243⅔	15	11	.577	208	100	208	3.62
1994	Atlanta	21	134⅔	6	10	.375	113	48	120	4.14
1995	Atlanta	29	192⅔	12	7	.632	193	72	166	3.18
	Totals	231	1550⅔	90	82	.523	1252	572	1346	3.53

STEVE AVERY 25 6-4 190 Bats L Throws L

Was better pitcher than his 7-13 record in '95 indicates . . . Received total of 16 runs of support in his first seven starts . . . Matched a career mark with three complete games . . . Was outstanding in his two postseason starts, going 2-0 with 1.42 ERA . . . Was winning pitcher in Game 4 of World Series . . . Tied career mark with 11 strikeouts vs. Expos Sept. 23 . . . All of his 22 home runs allowed were hit by right-handers . . . Braves were 15-9 in games that this guy started in 1994 . . . Won career-high eight straight games while matching career best with 18 wins in '93 . . . Youngest pitcher in Braves history to reach 50 career wins . . . Braves scored total of 25 runs in his 11 losses in 1992 . . . Captured 1991 NLCS MVP honors vs. Pirates, when he won two games while hurling 16⅓ shutout innings . . . Braves made him third overall selection in 1988 draft . . . Born April 14, 1970, in Trenton, Mich. . . . Earned $4 million last year.

Year	Club	G	IP	W	L	Pct.	SO	BB	H	ERA
1990	Atlanta	21	99	3	11	.214	75	45	121	5.64
1991	Atlanta	35	210⅓	18	8	.692	137	65	189	3.38
1992	Atlanta	35	233⅔	11	11	.500	129	71	216	3.20
1993	Atlanta	35	223⅓	18	6	.750	125	43	216	2.94
1994	Atlanta	24	151⅔	8	3	.727	122	55	127	4.04
1995	Atlanta	29	173⅓	7	13	.350	141	52	165	4.67
	Totals	179	1091⅓	65	52	.556	729	331	1034	3.75

MARK WOHLERS 26 6-4 207 **Bats R Throws R**

Finally, Braves have a closer . . . This hard-throwing righty led team and finished 10th in NL with career-high 25 saves . . . Recorded four saves in postseason, including two in World Series . . . Retired Indians in order in ninth inning of Game 6 to clinch series . . . Teamed with Tom Glavine for first combined one-hitter in World Series history . . . Didn't become full-time closer until June . . . Blew four save opportunities during regular season . . . Allowed 9-of-28 inherited runners to score . . . Prior to '95, he had a total of seven saves in his first 146 appearances with Braves . . . Set an Atlanta record with 21 consecutive saves, from May 15-Sept. 3 . . . Posted lowest ERA of career (2.09) . . . Pitched team-high 22⅓ consecutive scoreless innings . . . Went 2-0 with nine saves and 0.00 ERA in 13 games in August . . . Fastball has been clocked at 102 mph . . . Braves' eighth-round pick in 1988 draft . . . Born Jan. 23, 1970, in Holyoke, Mass. . . . Earned $202,500 last season.

Year	Club	G	IP	W	L	Pct.	SO	BB	H	ERA
1991	Atlanta	17	19⅔	3	1	.750	13	13	17	3.20
1992	Atlanta	32	35⅓	1	2	.333	17	14	28	2.55
1993	Atlanta	46	48	6	2	.750	45	22	37	4.50
1994	Atlanta	51	51	7	2	.778	58	33	51	4.59
1995	Atlanta	65	64⅔	7	3	.700	90	24	51	2.09
	Totals	211	218⅔	24	10	.706	223	106	184	3.38

TOP PROSPECTS

ANDRUW JONES 18 6-1 170 **Bats R Throws R**

Baseball America's Minor League Player of the Year . . . Outfield prospect batted .277 for Macon (A), led minors in extra-base hits (71) and was named South Atlantic League MVP . . . Became first minor leaguer to total 25 homers, 100 RBI and 50-plus steals (56) since Jose Cardenal in 1961 . . . Struck out 122 times in 537 at-bats . . . Signed as non-drafted free agent in July 1993 . . . Born April 23, 1977, in Curacao, Netherlands Antilles.

JERMAINE DYE 22 6-0 195 **Bats R Throws R**

Batted .285 with 15 home runs and 71 RBI for Greenville (AA) . . . Teamed with Damon Hollins to form two-thirds of best outfield in Southern League . . . Produced 26 doubles, four triples, 27 walks and 50 runs in 403 at-bats . . . Attended Cosumnes River JC in California . . . Braves' 17th-round pick in 1993 draft . . . Born Jan. 28, 1974, in Oakland.

DAMON HOLLINS 21 5-11 180 Bats R Throws L
Outfielder batted .247 with 18 home runs and 77 RBI for Greenville (AA) . . . Also collected 155 hits, including 26 doubles and two triples, in 466 at-bats . . . Selected by Braves in fourth round of 1992 draft . . . Born June 12, 1974, in Fairfield, Cal.

BRAD WOODALL 26 6-0 175 Bats S Throws L
Candidate for fifth spot in rotation . . . Went 1-1 with 6.10 ERA in nine relief appearances, covering 10.1 innings, for Braves . . . Was 4-4, 5.10 in 13 games, including 11 starts, for Richmond (AAA), for whom he struck out 44 batters in 65 innings . . . Went 15-6, 2.38 in 27 starts for Richmond in '94, when he led International League in victories . . . Signed by Braves as non-drafted free agent in June 1991 . . . Born June 25, 1969, in Atlanta.

MANAGER BOBBY COX: Finally was rewarded with World

Series title after winning pennants in 1991 and 1992 . . . Has managed winningest team in baseball the last five years (454-290) . . . Respected by his players . . . Showed confidence in closer Mark Wohlers and Wohlers responded by saving four games in postseason, including Game 6 of World Series . . . Was second-guessed for starting Steve Avery in Game 4, but Avery picked up victory . . . Finished with 90-54 record in '95, tops in NL . . . His Braves captured first NL East title, then went 11-3 in postseason . . . Atlanta finished 68-46 in '94, with a rookie catcher and rookie left fielder . . . Guided club to franchise-record 104 wins in '93, when Braves became first NL West team to win three straight titles . . . Named NL Manager of the Year twice (1991, 1993) . . . Only manager other than Sparky Anderson to win title in both leagues as he also won award with Blue Jays in '85 . . . Joined Braves as GM in October

1985 . . . Took over managerial reins from Russ Nixon during 1990 season . . . In '91, Braves went from worst to first and lost to Twins in Game 7 of World Series . . . Managed Blue Jays from 1982-85 . . . A year after Toronto finished seventh, he took Blue Jays to within one game of World Series in 1985 . . . Compiled 266-323 record as Braves skipper from 1978-81 . . . Infielder played 12 professional seasons, two with Yankees and 10 in minors, before bad knees ended his playing career . . . Born May 21, 1941, in Tulsa, Okla. . . . Overall managerial record is 1,115-962.

ALL-TIME BRAVE SEASON RECORDS

BATTING: Rogers Hornsby, .387, 1928
HRs: Eddie Mathews, 47, 1953
Hank Aaron, 47, 1971
RBI: Eddie Mathews, 135, 1953
STEALS: Otis Nixon, 72, 1991
WINS: Vic Willis, 27, 1902
Charles Pittinger, 27, 1902
Dick Rudolph, 27, 1914
STRIKEOUTS: Phil Niekro, 262, 1977

FLORIDA MARLINS

TEAM DIRECTORY: Owner: H. Wayne Huizenga; Pres.: Don Smiley; Exec. VP/GM: Dave Dombrowski; VP-Player Pers.: Gary Hughes; VP-Broadcasting: Dean Jordan; VP/Asst. GM: Frank Wren; VP-Player Dev.: John Boles; Dir. Media Rel.: Chuck Pool; Mgr.: Rene Lachemann; Coaches: Rusty Kuntz, Jose Morales, Cookie Rojas, Larry Rothschild, Rick Williams. Home: Joe Robbie Stadium (47,226). Field distances: 335, l.f. line; 380, l.c.; 410, c.f.; 380, r.c.; 345, r.f. line. Spring training: Viera, Fla.

SCOUTING REPORT

HITTING: It's mind-boggling to imagine the run-production numbers that Gary Sheffield could generate if he ever stays healthy. Sheffield belted 16 home runs and had 46 RBI in just 63 games in 1995. His bat could carry the Marlins—who generated a middling 673 runs last year—for weeks at a time.

All-Star MVP Jeff Conine (.302, 25, 105) never gets hurt,

All-Star MVP Jeff Conine did Marlins proud.

which is why Florida can count on him producing another big year following his career season in '95. Isn't Terry Pendleton supposedly on the down side of his career? You couldn't tell by his .290 batting average last season.

Pendleton also serves an important role as a pseudo hitting coach for promising young Marlins such as Quilvio Veras (.261, 86 runs, a league-leading 56 steals) and Charles Johnson (.251, 11, 39). Two underrated Marlins—Greg Colbrunn (.277, 23, 89) and Kurt Abbott (.255, 17, 60)—plus free-agent imports Devon White (.283, 10, 53 with Blue Jays) and Joe Orsulak (.283, 1, 37 with Mets) offer balance to the attack.

PITCHING: The Marlins certainly pitch like an expansion team. Florida's staff ranked 11th in the NL in ERA (4.27), fifth in most home runs allowed (139) and first in walks yielded (562).

John Burkett (14-14, 4.30) is the Marlins' ace, but Pat Rapp (14-7, 3.44) is the emerging force on the staff. The Marlins used 26 different pitchers last season and, other than Chris Hammond (9-6, 3.80) and David Weathers (4-5, 5.98), couldn't seem to find anyone to stick in the rotation. So they signed free-agent lefty Al Leiter (11-11, 3.64 with the Blue Jays) and Kevin Brown (10-9, 3.60 with the Orioles) to provide quality innings. Oft-injured Ryan Bowen (2-0, 3.78) remains a candidate for the No. 5 spot.

Although the Marlins ranked 13th in saves with only 29, they found a quality closer in Robb Nen (0-7, 3.29, 23 saves) to replace ailing ex-closer Bryan Harvey. Yorkis Perez (2-6, 5.21), who led Marlins pitchers in games with 69, will be joined by ex-Brave Alejandro Pena (2-0, 2.61).

FIELDING: The arrival of third baseman Pendleton gave the Marlins' infield some stability, but there's still a long way to go. Abbott has good range, but the shortstop committed 19 errors. Second baseman Veras made only nine errors in his rookie year, which is a good sign. Gold Glove winner Johnson is an exceptional defensive catcher with a gun for an arm. The outfield is suspect, with Sheffield and Conine guarding the lines, but White is without peer in center field and has seven Gold Gloves to prove it.

OUTLOOK: The Rockies have made life difficult for South Florida's expansion team. How do you tell your fans to be patient when Colorado has already been to the playoffs? Rene Lachemann's Marlins have the resources, just not the players. After finishing 67-76 in '95, they'll be lucky to reach .500 this year.

MARLIN PROFILES

JEFF CONINE 29 6-1 220 Bats R Throws R

One of the best players no one knows about ... MVP of the '95 All-Star Game in Texas, when he homered off Oakland's Steve Ontiveros ... Outfielder set career highs in home runs (25), RBI (105), extra-base hits (53) and total bases (251) ... Tied with Dodgers' Eric Karros for fourth in NL in RBI as he became first player in club history to reach 100 mark ... Had eighth-highest slugging percentage (.520) in NL ... Led league with 12 sacrifice flies ... Finished 10th in NL in batting average in '94 ... Set an expansion record by appearing in all 162 games in '93, when he was named to All-Rookie team ... Marlins made him their 11th pick of expansion draft, out of Royals' organization ... Originally drafted by Kansas City in 58th round of '87 draft, out of UCLA ... Born June 27, 1966, in Tacoma, Wash. ... Earned $290,000 in '95 ... World-class racquetball player.

Year	Club	Pos.	G	AB	R	H	2B	3B	HR	RBI	SB	Avg.
1990	Kansas City ...	1B	9	20	3	5	2	0	0	2	0	.250
1992	Kansas City ...	OF-1B	28	91	10	23	5	2	0	9	0	.253
1993	Florida	OF-1B	162	595	75	174	24	3	12	79	2	.292
1994	Florida	OF-1B	115	451	60	144	27	6	18	82	1	.319
1995	Florida	OF-1B	133	483	72	146	26	2	25	105	2	.302
	Totals		447	1640	220	492	84	13	55	277	5	.300

GARY SHEFFIELD 27 5-11 190 Bats R Throws R

Imagine what he would have done if he had stayed healthy ... Hit 16 home runs and had 46 RBI despite missing 80 games ... Suffered torn ligaments in his right thumb June 10. He slipped rounding second and hurt thumb while attempting to brace himself ... Had 10 homers and 27 RBI after returning from disabled list Sept. 10. His 27 RBI in one month are club record and he tied his own club mark with 10 homers in one month ... In his first game back, he hit a 426-foot homer off Astros' Greg Swindell on first pitch he saw ... Tied club record and career high with five hits Sept. 17 vs. Colorado ... Set club record with 27 home runs in '94, despite missing 28 games with bruised rotator-cuff muscle . . . Played 580 straight games in infield before switching to outfield in '94 . . . Acquired from Padres with Rich Rodriguez for Trevor Hoffman, Andres Berumen and Jose Martinez, June 24, 1993 . . . Youngest defending batting champ ever traded . . . Became first expansion player to start All-Star Game in '93 . . . Started his Marlins' career with 12-game hitting streak . . . Born Nov. 18, 1968, in Tampa . . . Nephew of Yankees' Dwight Gooden . . . Florida's highest-paid player earned $5.625 million last season . . . Brewers drafted him sixth overall in 1986.

Year	Club	Pos.	G	AB	R	H	2B	3B	HR	RBI	SB	Avg.
1988	Milwaukee	SS	24	80	12	19	1	0	4	12	3	.238
1989	Milwaukee	SS-3B	95	368	34	91	18	0	5	32	10	.247
1990	Milwaukee	3B	125	487	67	143	30	1	10	67	25	.294
1991	Milwaukee	3B	50	175	25	34	12	2	2	22	5	.194
1992	San Diego	3B	146	557	87	184	34	3	33	100	5	.330
1993	S.D.-Fla.	3B	140	494	67	145	20	5	20	73	17	.294
1994	Florida	OF	87	322	61	89	16	1	27	78	12	.276
1995	Florida	OF	63	213	46	69	8	0	16	46	19	.324
	Totals		730	2696	399	774	139	12	117	430	96	.287

KURT ABBOTT 26 6-0 185 Bats R Throws R

Established career highs in nearly every offensive category . . . Finished third on team in home runs (17) and fourth in RBI (60) in '95 . . . He and Quilvio Veras shared team lead with club-record seven triples . . . Shortstop committed a team-high 19 errors . . . Tied for sixth in NL with 110 strikeouts . . . Became first NL player in eight years to have two inside-the-park home runs in one season . . . Inherited shortstop job from Walt Weiss in '94 . . . Set club record by homering in four consecutive games, June 14-17, 1994 . . . Acquired from Oakland for Kerwin Moore prior to '94 season . . . Started 14 games for Athletics after being promoted to majors, Sept. 7, 1993 . . . In his first major-league start and second at-bat, he homered off Toronto's Jack Morris . . . Selected by Oakland in 15th round of '89 draft . . . Born June 2, 1969, in Zanesville, Ohio . . . Earned $119,000 last season.

Year	Club	Pos.	G	AB	R	H	2B	3B	HR	RBI	SB	Avg.
1993	Oakland	OF-SS-2B	20	61	11	15	1	0	3	9	2	.246
1994	Florida	SS	101	345	41	86	17	3	9	33	3	.249
1995	Florida	SS	120	420	60	107	18	7	17	60	4	.255
	Totals		241	826	112	208	36	10	29	102	9	.252

TERRY PENDLETON 35 5-9 195 Bats S Throws R

Third baseman acquired via free agency prior to '95 became leader the Marlins desperately needed . . . Proved he still has some miles left . . . At .290, he batted 18 points higher than previous career average . . . Played in 133 games, second-highest total on team . . . Led Florida in hits (149) and set club record with 32 doubles . . . His 18 errors were second-highest total on team . . . Finished 10th in NL with 46 multi-hit games . . . Has below-average speed, but he was the 10th-hardest player in NL to double up, grounding into a double play once per 73.3 at-bats . . . Raised batting average 78 points after May 29 . . . Hit 11 of 14 home runs batting left-handed . . . Three-time Gold Glove winner . . . Was named NL MVP in '91 . . . Career .306 hitter in 23 World Series games . . . Holds NLCS record with 129 at-bats . . . Spent four years in Atlanta after leaving Cardinals as free agent prior to '91 season . . . Originally selected by St. Louis in seventh round of '82 draft . . . Born July 16, 1960, in Los Angeles . . . Earned $1.5 million last season.

Year	Club	Pos.	G	AB	R	H	2B	3B	HR	RBI	SB	Avg.
1984	St. Louis	3B	67	262	37	85	16	3	1	33	20	.324
1985	St. Louis	3B	149	559	56	134	16	3	5	69	17	.240
1986	St. Louis	3B-OF	159	578	56	138	26	5	1	59	24	.239
1987	St. Louis	3B	159	583	82	167	29	4	12	96	19	.286
1988	St. Louis	3B	110	391	44	99	20	2	6	53	3	.253
1989	St. Louis	3B	162	613	83	162	28	5	13	74	9	.264
1990	St. Louis	3B	121	447	46	103	20	2	6	58	7	.230
1991	Atlanta	3B	153	586	94	187	34	8	22	86	10	.319
1992	Atlanta	3B	160	640	98	199	39	1	21	105	5	.311
1993	Atlanta	3B	161	633	81	172	33	1	17	84	5	.272
1994	Atlanta	3B	77	309	25	78	18	3	7	30	2	.252
1995	Florida	3B	133	513	70	149	32	1	14	78	1	.290
	Totals		1611	6114	772	1673	311	38	125	825	122	.274

QUILVIO VERAS 24 5-9 170 Bats S Throws R

Established himself as a quality second baseman in first season in majors . . . Dangerous leadoff hitter . . . Led NL in stolen bases with 56 . . . Was also caught stealing a league-leading 21 times . . . Finished tied for third in league with 80 walks . . . Led Marlins in runs with 86 and tied Kurt Abbott for team lead with seven triples . . . Committed just nine errors in 124 games . . . Acquired from Mets for Carl Everett prior to last season . . . Batted .249 with 22 doubles, 43 RBI and 40 steals for Norfolk (AAA) in 1994 . . . In '93, he batted .306 with a league-high 91 walks for Binghamton (AA) . . . Signed by Mets as non-drafted free agent in November 1989 . . . Born April 3, 1971, in Santo Domingo, D.R. . . . Earned major-league minimum of $109,000 last season.

Year	Club	Pos.	G	AB	R	H	2B	3B	HR	RBI	SB	Avg.
1995	Florida	2B-OF	124	440	86	115	20	7	5	32	56	.261

CHARLES JOHNSON 24 6-2 215 Bats R Throws R

One of top rookies in baseball in '95 . . . Impressive young catcher . . . Committed six errors in first full season in majors and won Gold Glove . . . Hit a home run in three of final four games . . . On disabled list from Aug. 8-Sept. 1 with fractured bone in right hand . . . Suffered injury when he was hit by a Bret Saberhagen pitch . . . Gunned down 36-of-87 would-be base-stealers (41.4%) . . . Fourteen of his first 16 hits were singles . . . Batted .310 after the All-Star break . . . In 1994, he became the first player from Marlins' farm system to reach majors . . . Began season at Portland (AA) and was called up to majors on May 6, when Benito Santiago began to serve four-game suspension . . . That same night, he homered in second major-league at-bat, off the Phillies' Curt Schilling . . . Was returned to Portland May 10 . . . Selected to Double-A All Star Game and tied for Double-A lead in home runs with 28 in '94 . . . Florida's first-round pick and 28th player chosen overall in '92 draft . . . Born July 20, 1971, in Ft. Pierce, Fla. . . . Earned $113,000 last season.

Year	Club	Pos.	G	AB	R	H	2B	3B	HR	RBI	SB	Avg.
1994	Florida	C	4	11	5	5	1	0	1	4	0	.455
1995	Florida	C	97	315	40	79	15	1	11	39	0	.251
	Totals		101	326	45	84	16	1	12	43	0	.258

GREG COLBRUNN 26 6-0 200 Bats R Throws R

First baseman set career highs in nearly every offensive category . . . Ranked second on Marlins behind Jeff Conine in homers (23) and RBI (89) . . . Led team in games played (138) and at-bats (528) . . . Swiped 11 bases in 14 attempts . . . Set club record with seven RBI July 18 vs. Giants. Gary Sheffield later tied mark . . . Committed five errors . . . Made Opening

Day roster in '94, just nine months after having surgery to repair a torn ligament in right elbow . . . Had two stints on disabled list in '94 and had arthroscopic surgery on left knee . . . Played in just 70 games for Expos in '93 due to elbow problems . . . Claimed by Florida off waivers prior to '94 season . . . Montreal's sixth-round pick in '87 draft . . . Born July 26, 1969, in Fontana, Cal. . . . Earned $225,000 last season.

Year	Club	Pos.	G	AB	R	H	2B	3B	HR	RBI	SB	Avg.
1992	Montreal	1B	52	168	12	45	8	0	2	18	3	.268
1993	Montreal	1B	70	153	15	39	9	0	4	23	4	.255
1994	Florida	1B	47	155	17	47	10	0	6	31	1	.303
1995	Florida	1B	138	528	70	146	22	1	23	89	11	.277
	Totals		307	1004	114	277	49	1	35	161	19	.276

DEVON WHITE 33 6-2 190 Bats S Throws R

Injuries cut into brilliant center fielder's playing time in '95 and held down all of his offensive numbers . . . But still scored 61 runs for Blue Jays and homered in double figures (10) for ninth straight season . . . Not bad for everyday leadoff man . . . Marlins signed him to three-year, $9.9-million deal as free agent last winter . . . Had 24 homers, 87 RBI and 32 stolen bases for Angels in 1987 season, but finished behind Mark McGwire in AL Rookie of Year balloting . . . Resisted efforts to make him leadoff hitter in California, but embraced that role under Blue Jays manager Cito Gaston . . . Stole 30-or-more bases in each of first three seasons with Blue Jays, but did not even notch a total of 30 attempts the past two seasons combined . . . Born Dec. 29, 1962, in Kingston, Jamaica . . . Salary for '95 season was $4,000,000 . . . Angels sixth-round pick in 1981.

Year	Club	Pos.	G	AB	R	H	2B	3B	HR	RBI	SB	Avg.
1985	California	OF	21	7	7	1	0	0	0	0	3	.143
1986	California	OF	29	51	8	12	1	1	1	3	6	.235
1987	California	OF	159	639	103	168	33	5	24	87	32	.263
1988	California	OF	122	455	76	118	22	2	11	51	17	.259
1989	California	OF	156	636	86	156	18	13	12	56	44	.245
1990	California	OF	125	443	57	96	17	3	11	44	21	.217
1991	Toronto	OF	156	642	110	181	40	10	17	60	33	.282
1992	Toronto	OF	153	641	98	159	26	7	17	60	37	.248
1993	Toronto	OF	146	598	116	163	42	6	15	52	34	.273
1994	Toronto	OF	100	403	67	109	24	6	13	49	11	.270
1995	Toronto	OF	101	427	61	121	23	5	10	53	11	.283
	Totals		1268	4942	789	1284	246	58	131	515	249	.260

JOHN BURKETT 31 6-3 211 **Bats R Throws R**

Ace of the staff . . . Won 12 or more games for fifth time in six years . . . He and Pat Rapp tied for team lead by winning club-record 14 games . . . Lost three of his final four starts . . . Led pitching staff in starts (30), losses (14), innings (188⅓), hits (208), runs (95) and home runs (22) . . . Finished fourth in NL in hits allowed . . . Tied Expos' Jeff Fassero for second-highest loss total in NL . . . Ranked sixth in home runs allowed . . . Signed two-year deal with Florida as free agent prior to '95 season . . . Was the Marlins' Opening Day starter . . . Set career high and club record with four complete games . . . Induced league-high 26 double plays . . . Finished fourth in NL Cy Young voting in 1993, when he became third Giant in 20 years to win 20 games with 22 victories . . . Traded by Giants to Rangers for Desi Wilson and Rich Aurilla after '94 season and then Texas didn't offer him a contract . . . Selected by Giants in sixth round of '83 draft . . . Born Nov. 28, 1964, in New Brighton, Pa. . . . Earned $3.350 million last season.

Year	Club	G	IP	W	L	Pct.	SO	BB	H	ERA
1987	San Francisco	3	6	0	0	.000	5	3	7	4.50
1990	San Francisco	33	204	14	7	.667	118	61	201	3.79
1991	San Francisco	36	206⅔	12	11	.522	131	60	223	4.18
1992	San Francisco	32	189⅔	13	9	.591	107	45	194	3.84
1993	San Francisco	34	231⅔	22	7	.759	145	40	224	3.65
1994	San Francisco	25	159⅓	6	8	.429	85	36	176	3.62
1995	Florida	30	188⅓	14	14	.500	126	57	208	4.30
	Totals	193	1185⅔	81	56	.591	717	302	1233	3.90

ROBB NEN 26 6-4 190 **Bats R Throws R**

Who needs Bryan Harvey? . . . Notched a career-high 23 saves in his first full season as Florida's closer . . . Fastball has been clocked at 98 mph . . . Converted 12 consecutive save opportunities from July 22-Aug. 28 before blowing a save against Astros Sept. 3 . . . Owns an .864 career save percentage (38-for-44) . . . Had 18 saves in final 31 outings in '95 . . . Second on team with career-high 62 appearances last year . . . Marlins' career leader in games among pitchers with 130 . . . Became closer in '94, following season-ending injuries to Harvey and Jeremy Hernandez . . . Converted first 15 save opportunities in '94 . . . Rangers chose him in 32nd round of 1987 draft . . . Made major-league debut in '93 with Rangers . . . Dealt by Texas to Marlins along with Kurt Miller for Cris Carpenter, July 17, 1993 . . . Son of former major-league first baseman Dick Nen . . . Born Nov. 28, 1969, in San Pedro, Cal. . . . Earned $180,000 last season.

Year	Club	G	IP	W	L	Pct.	SO	BB	H	ERA
1993	Texas	9	22⅔	1	1	.500	12	26	28	6.35
1993	Florida	15	33⅓	1	0	1.000	27	20	35	7.02
1994	Florida	44	58	5	5	.500	60	17	46	2.95
1995	Florida	62	65⅔	0	7	.000	68	23	62	3.29
	Totals	130	179⅔	7	13	.350	167	86	171	4.26

PAT RAPP 28 6-3 215 Bats R Throws R

A developing force . . . Ended season with a nine-game winning streak, second-longest in NL to Greg Maddux (10) . . . Tossed a one-hitter in 17-0 rout of Rockies Sept. 17 . . . Shut out the Mets five days later in rain-shortened game to become the first Marlins' pitcher to toss back-to-back shutouts . . . Tied Maddux with 11 wins after All-Star break . . . Marlins' all-time winningest pitcher with 25 . . . Tied John Burkett for team lead with 14 wins . . . Marlins were shut out in six of his 12 road starts in '95 . . . Posted lowest ERA in club history by Marlins starter, breaking his own mark set in 1994 . . . Led staff in strikeouts, walks and complete games in '94 . . . Won first major-league game, July 21, 1993 vs. Colorado . . . Marlins got him from Giants with fifth pick of expansion draft . . . Selected by San Francisco in 15th round of '89 draft, out of Southern Miss. . . . Born July 13, 1967, in Jennings, La. . . . Earned $161,500 last season . . . Named son after Nolan Ryan.

Year	Club	G	IP	W	L	Pct.	SO	BB	H	ERA
1992	San Francisco	3	10	0	2	.000	3	6	8	7.20
1993	Florida	16	94	4	6	.400	57	39	101	4.02
1994	Florida	24	133⅓	7	8	.467	75	69	132	3.85
1995	Florida	28	167⅓	14	7	.667	102	76	158	3.44
	Totals	71	404⅔	25	23	.521	237	190	399	3.80

KEVIN BROWN 31 6-4 195 Bats R Throws R

As Oriole free agent, he signed three-year, $12.9-million contract with Marlins last winter . . . Signed by Orioles before start of '95 season, this former Ranger quickly established himself as one of club's top starting pitchers . . . However, his season was interrupted and upended by injury, when he dislocated a finger trying to barehand a ball in June . . . Went two months without a victory before getting back on track in September . . . Sinkerballer has great stuff and sometimes volatile temperament . . . Won 21 games for Texas in 1992, but never more than 15 in any other season . . . Best home run-to-inning ratio on Orioles pitching staff, allowing only 10 in 172⅓ . . . Born March 14, 1965, in McIntyre, Ga. . . . Salary was $4,225,000 last year . . . Rangers drafted him fourth overall in 1986.

Year	Club	G	IP	W	L	Pct.	SO	BB	H	ERA
1986	Texas	1	5	1	0	1.000	4	0	6	3.60
1988	Texas	4	23⅓	1	1	.500	12	8	33	4.24
1989	Texas	28	191	12	9	.571	104	70	167	3.35
1990	Texas	26	180	12	10	.545	88	60	175	3.60
1991	Texas	33	210⅔	9	12	.429	96	90	233	4.40
1992	Texas	35	265⅔	21	11	.656	173	76	262	3.32
1993	Texas	34	233	15	12	.556	142	74	228	3.59
1994	Texas	26	170	7	9	.438	123	50	218	4.82
1995	Baltimore	26	172⅓	10	9	.526	117	48	155	3.60
	Totals	213	1451	88	73	.547	859	476	1477	3.78

TOP PROSPECTS

BILLY McMILLON 24 5-11 172 Bats L Throws L

The Marlins' Minor League Player of the Year . . . Promising outfielder is probably still a year away from majors . . . Should start season in Triple-A . . . Batted .313 with 14 home runs, 93 RBI and 15 stolen bases for Portland (AA) . . . Hit .252 with 17 home runs, 101 RBI and 88 runs for Kane County (A) in '94 . . . Marlins made him eighth-round pick in '93 draft . . . Born Nov. 17, 1971, in Otero, N.M.

EDGAR RENTERIA 20 6-1 172 Bats R Throws R

Regarded as one of Marlins' top hitting prospects . . . Shortstop batted .289 with seven home runs, 68 RBI, 15 doubles and 30 steals last season for Portland (AA) . . . Batted .253 with 36 RBI for Brevard County (A) in '94 . . . Signed by Florida as non-drafted free agent in 1992 . . . Born Aug. 7, 1975, in Barranquilla, Colombia.

MARC VALDES 24 6-0 187 **Bats R Throws R**

Candidate for Florida's rotation in 1996 . . . Made three starts for Marlins in '95, compiling 14.14 ERA (11 earned runs in seven innings), but did not have a decision . . . Went 9-13 with 4.86 ERA in 27 starts for Edmonton in his first season at Triple-A last year . . . Struck out 104 batters in 170 innings . . . Named Marlins Minor League Pitcher of the Year in '94 . . . Finished combined 15-8 with 2.72 ERA in 26 starts for Kane County (A) and Portland (AA) . . . Marlins chose him 27th overall in '93 draft . . . Born Dec. 20, 1971, in Dayton, Ohio.

JESUS TAVAREZ 25 6-0 170 **Bats S Throws R**

Outfielder batted .300 with one home run and eight RBI in 140 at-bats for Charlotte (AAA) . . . In 63 games with Marlins, he batted .289 with two home runs, 13 RBI and 31 runs . . . Became first Florida player to have two triples in one game, Sept. 28 . . . Marlins made him 13th pick of expansion draft, from Seattle . . . Collected first major-league hit and RBI, May 23, 1994 . . . Went 7-for-39 (.179) in 17 games with Marlins and batted .286 in 89 games with Portland (AA) in '94 . . . Signed by Seattle as non-drafted free agent in November 1989 . . . Born March 26, 1971, in Santo Domingo, D.R.

MANAGER RENE LACHEMANN: His Marlins didn't enjoy

the same success as their expansion brothers in Colorado, but it was still a record year in Florida . . . Finished with best record in club history (67-76) after having worst record in baseball through 35 games . . . Placed fourth in NL East, despite losing Gary Sheffield for 80 games and having closer Bryan Harvey for only one game . . . Still finished 22½ games behind Braves. . . . Went 37-34 at home . . . Received two-year extension in October 1994 through the '97 season . . . Named first Marlins manager, Oct. 23, 1992 . . . Posted 64-98 record in club's inaugural season, the fifth-best expansion record in history . . .

Served as coach for Tony La Russa with Athletics from 1987-92 . . . Became youngest manager in majors when he replaced Maury Wills in Seattle, May 6, 1981 . . . Managed Mariners for three seasons, finishing with a 140-180 mark . . . Recorded 67-94 record as Brewers manager in '84 . . . This former catcher batted .210 during 118-game major-league career . . . Former Dodgers bat boy . . . Born May 4, 1945, in Los Angeles . . . Overall managerial record is 389-512.

ALL-TIME MARLIN SEASON RECORDS

BATTING: Jeff Conine, .319, 1994
HRs: Gary Sheffield, 27, 1994
RBI: Jeff Conine, 105, 1995
STEALS: Chuck Carr, 58, 1993
WINS: Pat Rapp, 14, 1995
John Burkett, 14, 1995
STRIKEOUTS: Charlie Hough, 126, 1993
John Burkett, 126, 1995
Chris Hammond, 126, 1995

MONTREAL EXPOS

TEAM DIRECTORY: Pres.-General Partner: Claude Brochu; VP-Baseball Oper.: Bill Stoneman; GM: Jim Beattie; Dir. Media Rel.: Peter Loyello; Dir. Media Services: Monique Giroux; Mgr.: Felipe Alou; Coaches: Pierre Arsenault, Tommy Harper, Joe Kerrigan, Jerry Manuel, Luis Pujols, Jim Tracy. Home: Olympic Stadium (46,500). Field distances: 325, l.f. line; 375, l.c.; 404, c.f.; 375, r.c.; 325, r.f. line. Spring training: West Palm Beach, Fla.

SCOUTING REPORT

HITTING: Montreal ranked near the bottom in every major offensive category in '95, including 12th in runs (621). But what did you expect? The Expos traded Marquis Grissom, said goodbye to free-agent defector Larry Walker and lost Moises Alou to injury the final two months. Things should change in '96.

Alou (.273, 14, 58) is healthy, as is Cliff Floyd (.130, 1, 8),

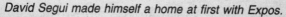

David Segui made himself a home at first with Expos.

who missed almost the entire '95 season with a wrist injury. Floyd and Alou should lend support to David Segui (.309, 12, 68), who will have to prove that he wasn't just a one-year wonder.

Rondell White (.295, 13, 57, 25 steals) played like a young Grissom. Mike Lansing (.255, 10, 62) is a solid No. 2 hitter. Wil Cordero (.286, 10, 49) was moved from shortstop to left field and starting hitting like a shortstop. Despite his .249 showing last year, Montreal still thinks Tony Tarasco's lefty bat will be a force in its lineup. Darrin Fletcher (.286, 11, 45) gives the Expos power at the bottom of the lineup, but the team will miss Sean Berry (.318, 14, 55), traded to the Astros.

PITCHING: There is a good reason the Expos lost 25 of their last 34 games last season—Montreal's pitching collapsed and the Expos' team ERA swelled to 4.11.

Jeff Fassero (13-14, 4.33) and Carlos Perez (10-8, 3.69) were not the same pitchers in August and September as they were in May and June. Fassero was the first in the majors to seven wins, but wound up going 0-4 in his final six starts. Perez was challenging Hideo Nomo for top rookie honors before slumping in the stretch. The Expos need Fassero and Perez to last an entire season.

At least, manager Felipe Alou can rely on Pedro Martinez (14-10, 3.51), one of the NL's top power pitchers. But, after that, Montreal will be counting on several youngsters—Kirk Rueter (5-3, 3.23) and Gil Heredia (5-6, 4.31)—to provide depth and innings.

If the Expos can somehow get to the ninth inning with a lead, more often than not, Mel Rojas (1-4, 4.12, 30 saves) will hold it. For more relief, the Expos traded for Dave Veres (5-1, 2.26, 72 appearances with the Astros).

FIELDING: The Expos could be one of the NL's better defensive teams. Segui is a Gold Glove-caliber first baseman while Lansing is more than adequate at second. Fletcher is an exceptional defensive catcher and Alou and White can chase down balls in the outfield. Shortstop and third, with Berry gone, are weak spots. The Expos may decide to shift Cordero back there now that Floyd seems headed to the outfield.

OUTLOOK: Despite their financial woes, the Expos, coming off a 66-78 finish, have talent at all positions—but not much depth. You just know Moises Alou is in for a big year and, if Floyd lives up to his promise, Montreal could compete for a wild-card spot.

EXPO PROFILES

MOISES ALOU 29 6-3 190 Bats R Throws R

His '95 season was marred by injury and tragedy . . . His father-in-law and brother-in-law were murdered at a Brooklyn bodega in June . . . Outfielder's shoulder problems limited him to career-low 93 games . . . Still tied for team lead with 14 home runs and was third on club with 58 RBI . . . Batted .273, 28 points lower than his previous career average . . . Appeared in only one game after Aug. 19 . . . Was placed on disabled list twice in final two months . . . Underwent surgery on his right shoulder in September and, one month later, had the same procedure on his left shoulder . . . Was expected to be fully recovered by spring training . . . Finished third in NL in batting, sixth in runs, hits, extra-base hits (58) and slugging percentage (.592) in '94 . . . Clubhouse leader in mold of father Felipe, the Expos' highly respected manager . . . Suffered dislocated ankle, fractured fibula and ligament damage rounding first base at St. Louis, Sept. 16, 1993 . . . Was runnerup to Dodgers' Eric Karros for '92 NL Rookie of the Year honors . . . Acquired by Montreal from Pirates for Zane Smith, Aug. 8, 1990 . . . Pirates picked him second overall in 1986 draft . . . Cousin Mel Rojas is a teammate . . . Born July 3, 1966, in Atlanta . . . Earned $3 million last season.

Year	Club	Pos.	G	AB	R	H	2B	3B	HR	RBI	SB	Avg.
1990	Pitt.-Mont.	OF	16	20	4	4	0	1	0	0	0	.200
1991	Montreal					Injured						
1992	Montreal	OF	115	341	53	96	28	2	9	56	16	.282
1993	Montreal	OF	136	482	70	138	29	6	18	85	17	.286
1994	Montreal	OF	107	422	81	143	31	5	22	78	7	.339
1995	Montreal	OF	93	344	48	94	22	0	14	58	4	.273
	Totals		467	1609	256	475	110	14	63	277	44	.295

WIL CORDERO 24 6-2 185 Bats R Throws R

No longer an adequate shortstop, he is now a marginally acceptable outfielder . . . Shifted to left field when Moises Alou got injured . . . Made major-league debut in left Aug. 26 . . . Batted .286, despite hitting just .222 after move to outfield . . . Enjoyed first career two-homer game against the Marlins' John Burkett on Sept. 25 . . . Had 11 three-hit games . . . Led team in hits (147) and strikeouts (88) and ranked second in total bases (216) . . . Finished fifth in NL with 35 doubles . . . Went 109 plate appearances without an RBI before driving in two Sept. 15 . . . In '94, he led all NL shortstops in batting average, home runs and RBI and was named to first All-Star team . . . Recorded a team-record 36 errors as a rookie shortstop in '93 . . . Signed by Expos as a non-drafted free agent in May 1988 . . . Born Oct. 3, 1971, in Mayaguez, P.R. . . . Earned $315,000 last year.

Year	Club	Pos.	G	AB	R	H	2B	3B	HR	RBI	SB	Avg.
1992	Montreal	SS-2B	45	126	17	38	4	1	2	8	0	.302
1993	Montreal	SS-3B	138	475	56	118	32	2	10	58	12	.248
1994	Montreal	SS	110	415	65	122	30	3	15	63	16	.294
1995	Montreal	SS-OF	131	514	64	147	35	2	10	49	9	.286
	Totals		424	1530	202	425	101	8	37	178	37	.278

DAVID SEGUI 29 6-1 202 **Bats S Throws L**

Unwanted by Mets, he was unstoppable in Montreal . . . Enjoyed best all-around season . . . Established career marks in batting average (.309), home runs (12), RBI (68), hits (141) and runs (68) . . . His average was seventh-best in NL . . . Had 18-game hitting streak from June 17-Aug. 8, the fifth-longest streak in NL . . . Struck out once per 10.9 at-bats, making him eighth-toughest batter to fan in league . . . Outstanding defensive first baseman . . . Acquired from Mets for Reid Cornelius June 8 . . . Was hitting .329 with two home runs and 11 RBI before trade . . . Top-fielding first baseman in NL in '94, but he was moved to outfield in late July to make room for Rico Brogna . . . Came to Mets late in spring training '94 from Baltimore for Kevin Baez and Tom Wegmann . . . Batted .263 in three-plus seasons with Orioles . . . Lists Cal Ripken Jr. as his favorite teammate . . . Father Diego pitched in majors for 15 seasons . . . Originally selected by Orioles in 18th round of '87 draft . . . Born July 19, 1966, in Kansas City, Mo. . . . Earned $600,000 last season.

Year	Club	Pos.	G	AB	R	H	2B	3B	HR	RBI	SB	Avg.
1990	Baltimore	1B	40	123	14	30	7	0	2	15	0	.244
1991	Baltimore	OF-1B	86	212	15	59	7	0	2	22	1	.278
1992	Baltimore	1B-OF	115	189	21	44	9	0	1	17	1	.233
1993	Baltimore	1B	146	450	54	123	27	0	10	60	2	.273
1994	New York (NL)	1B-OF	92	336	46	81	17	1	10	43	0	.241
1995	NY (NL)-Mont.	1B-OF	130	456	68	141	25	4	12	68	2	.309
	Totals		609	1766	218	478	92	5	37	225	6	.271

CLIFF FLOYD 23 6-4 220 Bats L Throws L

This can't-miss prospect had nearly all of '95 wiped out because of injury . . . Suffered potentially career-threatening injury when he shattered his left wrist in collision at first base with the Mets' Todd Hundley May 15 . . . Placed on 60-day disabled list . . . Activated Sept. 11, after missing 118 days and 108 games . . . Had just one hit in his final 17 at-bats . . . Will probably be moved from first to outfield . . . Rated No. 1 prospect by *Baseball America* in '94 . . . Started 63 games at first base and 16 in outfield in '94 . . . Power hitter with deceptive speed . . . Ranked third on Expos with 15 infield hits along with 10 steals in '94 . . . Hit first big-league homer, Sept. 26, 1993 vs. Mets, and became second-youngest player in team history to hit one, at age 20 . . . Expos drafted him 14th overall in 1991 . . . Born Dec. 5, 1972, in Chicago . . . Earned $145,000 last season.

Year	Club	Pos.	G	AB	R	H	2B	3B	HR	RBI	SB	Avg.
1993	Montreal	1B	10	31	3	7	0	0	1	2	0	.226
1994	Montreal	1B-OF	100	334	43	94	19	4	4	41	10	.281
1995	Montreal	1B-OF	29	69	6	9	1	0	1	8	3	.130
	Totals		139	434	52	110	20	4	6	51	13	.253

RONDELL WHITE 24 6-1 205 Bats R Throws R

Endless potential . . . Softened blow of having to trade Marquis Grissom . . . Center fielder finished fourth on club in home runs (13) and RBI (57) in his first full major-league season . . . His 25 steals were second-best on Expos . . . Has speed to track down any ball . . . Set a franchise record by collecting six hits June 11 against San Francisco . . . Also became fourth player in club history to hit for the cycle that day . . . Hit homer to lead off a game twice . . . Batted .331 in August . . . Hit a home run out of Wrigley Field on April 28 against Kevin Foster . . . Prize product of Expos' talented minor-league system . . . Split time between Montreal and Ottawa (AAA) in '94 as he started 20 games in right for Expos after Larry Walker was switched to first . . . Drove in career-high seven runs, July 24, 1994 vs. Dodgers, falling one RBI short of major-league record . . . Smacked first home run off Greg Swindell in Astrodome, Sept. 4, 1993 . . . Expos drafted him 24th overall in 1990 as compensation pick for

Angels signing free-agent Mark Langston . . . Born Feb. 23, 1972, in Milledgeville, Ga. . . . Earned $130,000 last year.

Year	Club	Pos.	G	AB	R	H	2B	3B	HR	RBI	SB	Avg.
1993	Montreal	OF	23	73	9	19	3	1	2	15	1	.260
1994	Montreal	OF	40	97	16	27	10	1	2	13	1	.278
1995	Montreal	OF	130	474	87	140	33	4	13	57	25	.295
	Totals		193	644	112	186	46	6	17	85	27	.289

DARRIN FLETCHER 29 6-1 198 Bats L Throws R

One of NL's best catchers . . . Batted a career-high .286 . . . His 11 home runs and 21 doubles were both career highs . . . Enjoyed first career four-hit game June 11 vs. Giants, including three-run homer off William VanLandingham . . . Batted .300 after All-Star break . . . Threw out 25-of-106 would-be base-stealers (23.6%) . . . Made 92 starts behind the plate . . . Still waiting to steal his first base . . . Appeared in first All-Star Game in 1994 . . . Had career-high five RBI May 24 vs. Marlins . . . Know primarily as a quality handler of pitchers . . . Started 105 games in 1993, his first full season in the majors . . . Acquired by Expos from Phillies for Barry Jones prior to '92 season . . . Former sixth-round pick of Dodgers in 1987 draft . . . Father Tom pitched for Tigers in 1962 . . . Born Oct. 3, 1966, in Elmhurst, Ill. . . . Earned $900,000 last season.

Year	Club	Pos.	G	AB	R	H	2B	3B	HR	RBI	SB	Avg.
1989	Los Angeles	C	5	8	1	4	0	0	1	2	0	.500
1990	L.A.-Phil	C	11	23	3	3	1	0	0	1	0	.130
1991	Philadelphia	C	46	136	5	31	8	0	1	12	0	.228
1992	Montreal	C	83	222	13	54	10	2	2	26	0	.243
1993	Montreal	C	133	396	33	101	20	1	9	60	0	.255
1994	Montreal	C	94	285	28	74	18	1	10	57	0	.260
1995	Montreal	C	110	350	42	100	21	1	11	45	0	.286
	Totals		482	1420	125	367	78	5	34	203	0	.258

JEFF FASSERO 33 6-1 195 Bats L Throws L

Quality pitcher, but he is dreadfully inconsistent . . . Was first pitcher in the NL to win seven games in '95 . . . Went 7-1 in first eight starts before dropping his next four decisions . . . Went 8-6 before the All-Star break, but was 5-8 in final 16 starts . . . Finished tied with the Marlins' John Burkett for most losses in NL with 14 . . . Ranked sixth in NL with 164 strikeouts . . . Allowed 207 hits, fifth-highest total in NL . . . Averaged 7.8 strikeouts per nine innings . . . Finished second on team in wins . . . Tossed his first complete game in two years June 23, when he beat the Pirates . . . Had fourth-best ERA in NL in 1994 . . . Came within one strike of tossing no-hitter, June 13, 1994, before the Pirates' Carlos Garcia singled off his glove . . . Made first major-league start, July 10, 1993 against the Padres, after 161 consecutive relief appearances . . . Originally selected by Cardinals in 22nd round of '84 draft . . . Signed by Expos as minor-league free agent in 1991 . . . Born Jan. 5, 1963, in Springfield, Ill. . . . Earned $1.5 million last year.

Year	Club	G	IP	W	L	Pct.	SO	BB	H	ERA
1991	Montreal	51	55⅔	2	5	.286	42	17	39	2.44
1992	Montreal	70	85⅔	8	7	.533	63	34	81	2.84
1993	Montreal	56	149⅔	12	5	.706	140	54	119	2.29
1994	Montreal	21	138⅔	8	6	.571	119	40	119	2.99
1995	Montreal	30	189	13	14	.481	164	74	207	4.33
	Totals	228	618⅓	43	37	.538	528	219	565	3.16

PEDRO MARTINEZ 24 5-11 170 Bats R Throws R

Don't be fooled by choir-boy looks, he is a fearless competitor who is not afraid to pitch inside . . . Totaled 11 hit batsmen for second straight year . . . Held opponents to a .227 batting average, third-best mark in NL . . . Averaged eight strikeouts per nine innings . . . Younger brother of the Dodgers' Ramon . . . Led Expos in wins (14), innings (194⅔) and strikeouts (174) . . . Had lowest ERA among Expos' starters at 3.51 . . . Retired 27 straight batters June 3 against the Padres before Bip Roberts led off 10th inning with a double in the Expos' 1-0 win . . . Became the first pitcher to lose a perfect game but win in extra innings . . . On April 13, 1994, he had a perfect game through 7⅓ before plunking Reds' Reggie Sanders, who charged the mound . . . Sixteen days later, he ignited another bench-clearing brawl vs. San Diego by grooving a fastball under Derek Bell's chin . . . Traded to Expos by Dodgers for Delino DeShields after the 1993 season . . . Started 1993 with Albuquerque (AAA), but was promoted to Los Angeles after one start . . . In 63 relief appearances, he stranded 26-of-33 inherited runners, holding opponents to a .187 batting average . . . Broke Steve Howe's rookie record for most games . . . Underwent 1992 postseason reconstructive surgery on non-pitching shoulder . . . Signed by Dodgers as non-drafted free agent in June 1988 . . . Born July 25, 1971, in Santo Domingo, D.R. . . . Earned $270,000 last year.

Year	Club	G	IP	W	L	Pct.	SO	BB	H	ERA
1992	Los Angeles	2	8	0	1	.000	8	1	6	2.25
1993	Los Angeles	65	107	10	5	.667	119	57	76	2.61
1994	Montreal	24	144⅔	11	5	.688	142	45	115	3.42
1995	Montreal	30	194⅔	14	10	.583	174	66	158	3.51
	Totals	121	454⅓	35	21	.625	443	169	355	3.25

MEL ROJAS 29 5-11 195 Bats R Throws R

Always wanted to be a stopper . . . Finally got his wish when the Expos traded John Wetteland to Yankees last spring . . . Finished seventh in NL with 30 saves . . . Blew nine save opportunities . . . Ranks fifth in Expos history with 73 career saves . . . Saved 16 of the Expos' last 34 wins after the All-Star break . . . Allowed 14 runs in final 21 appearances, spanning 23⅓ innings . . . Allowed eight of 21 inherited runners to score . . . Hard thrower . . . Recorded a career-high 16 saves in 1994 as mainly a setup man . . . Ranked second in NL in games (58) . . . Only setup man to record 10-plus saves in three straight seasons . . . Led majors with 84 relief innings . . . Converted 10-of-11 save opportunities and stranded 48-of-58 inherited runners in 1993 . . . Signed by Expos scout Jesus Alou, his uncle, as non-drafted free agent in November 1985 . . . Born Dec. 10, 1966, in Santo Domingo, D.R. . . . Earned $1.3 million last year.

Year	Club	G	IP	W	L	Pct.	SO	BB	H	ERA
1990	Montreal	23	40	3	1	.750	26	24	34	3.60
1991	Montreal	37	48	3	3	.500	37	13	42	3.75
1992	Montreal	68	100⅔	7	1	.875	70	34	71	1.43
1993	Montreal	66	88⅓	5	8	.385	48	30	80	2.95
1994	Montreal	58	84	3	2	.600	84	21	71	3.32
1995	Montreal	59	67⅔	1	4	.200	61	29	69	4.12
	Totals	311	428⅔	22	19	.537	326	151	367	3.00

CARLOS PEREZ 25 6-2 168 Bats L Throws L

Charismatic rookie lefty got off to a blazing start, but closed out season with problems on and off the mound . . . Was arrested in September by Atlanta police on a rape charge . . . Younger sibling of Pascual and Melido won his first five starts . . . Was 7-2 with 3.26 ERA before being named an All-Star . . . Went 3-6 in final 11 starts . . . Expos averaged only 2.1 runs in his eight losses . . . Never won again after beating the

Braves Aug. 6 . . . No-hit the Giants for 6⅔ innings Sept. 4, but he was removed due to a tired arm . . . Went 9-3 at home . . . Gyrates every time he strikes out a batter . . . Allowed three or fewer runs in 18 starts . . . Went 7-2 with 1.94 ERA in 12 games with Harrisburg (AA) in 1994 before going 7-5 with a 3.33 ERA in 17 starts for Ottawa (AAA) . . . Led California League in ERA (3.44) in 1993 . . . Signed as non-drafted free agent in January 1988 . . . Born Jan. 14, 1971, in Nigua, D.R. . . . Earned $109,000 last season . . . Only southpaw among the Perez pitching family.

Year	Club	G	IP	W	L	Pct.	SO	BB	H	ERA
1995	Montreal	28	141⅓	10	8	.556	106	28	142	3.69

Moises Alou is geared for a fresh start in '96.

Hitters ducked to Pedro Martinez' chin-music beat.

TOP PROSPECTS

VLADIMIR GUERRERO 20 6-0 165 Bats R Throws R
Top outfield prospect was named the organization's Minor League Player of the Year . . . Batted .333 with 16 home runs, 63

RBI, 21 doubles, 10 triples, 77 runs and 12 stolen bases in 421 at-bats for Albany (A) . . . Rated as having best arm in South Atlantic League . . . Regarded as a better prospect than Rondell White at this stage in career . . . Signed by Expos as non-drafted free agent in March 1993 . . . Born Feb. 9, 1976, in Mizao Bani, D.R.

CHRIS WEIDERT 21 6-3 210 Bats R Throws R
Top-rated pitcher in New York-Penn League . . . Went 11-1 with 1.79 ERA in 15 starts for Vermont (R), allowing 67 hits, 21 walks and striking out 52 in 95 innings . . . Control pitcher who throws fastball, breaking ball and change-up . . . Attended Butler County CC in Kansas . . . Drafted by Expos in 40th round of 1993 draft . . . Was 5-3 with 2.83 in Gulf Coast League in '94 . . . Born April 13, 1974, in Emporia, Kan.

TAVO ALVAREZ 24 6-3 245 Bats R Throws R
Candidate for starting rotation . . . Went 1-5 with 6.75 ERA in eight starts for Expos . . . Made his major-league debut on Aug. 21 vs. Dodgers . . . Picked up first win Sept. 6, holding the Giants to two runs on two hits over seven innings . . . Went 2-1, 2.49 for Ottawa (AAA) and 2-1, 2.25 for Harrisburg (AA) . . . Pitched on three different levels of pro ball within 32 days after not pitching an inning in '94 . . . Missed entire 1994 season after having surgery on right rotator cuff on March 1 . . . Went 7-10 with 4.22 ERA for Ottawa in 1993 . . . Expos made him second-round pick in 1990 draft . . . Born Nov. 25, 1971, in Obregon, Mexico.

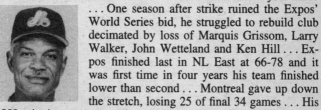

MANAGER FELIPE ALOU: What a difference a year made

. . . One season after strike ruined the Expos' World Series bid, he struggled to rebuild club decimated by loss of Marquis Grissom, Larry Walker, John Wetteland and Ken Hill . . . Expos finished last in NL East at 66-78 and it was first time in four years his team finished lower than second . . . Montreal gave up down the stretch, losing 25 of final 34 games . . . His .558 winning percentage is second among active managers, behind Davey Johnson . . . Well-respected by his players and peers . . . Named NL Manager of the Year in '94, when he guided club to major-league-best 74-40 record . . . Expos won 94 games, second-highest total in club history, in his first full season as skipper in '93 . . . Became ninth manager in club history, May 22, 1992, taking over a team that started 17-20 under Tom Runnells . . . That season the Expos finished 87-75 in second place . . . First Dominican-born manager in major-league history . . . Has served in Expos organization for 20 years . . . Paid his dues by managing 12 seasons in minors and 12 in winter leagues . . . Fifth manager in history to manage his son (Moises) in majors . . . Outfielder enjoyed impressive 17-year playing career, batting .286 with 206 home runs and 852 RBI . . . Born May 12, 1935, in Haina, D.R. . . . Overall managerial record is 304-241.

ALL-TIME EXPO SEASON RECORDS

BATTING: Moises Alou, .339, 1994
HRs: Andre Dawson, 32, 1983
RBI: Tim Wallach, 123, 1987
STEALS: Ron LeFlore, 97, 1980
WINS: Ross Grimsley, 20, 1978
STRIKEOUTS: Bill Stoneman, 251, 1971

NEW YORK METS

TEAM DIRECTORY: Chairman: Nelson Doubleday; Pres./CEO: Fred Wilpon; Sr. VP-Consultant: Frank Cashen; Exec. VP-Baseball Oper.: Joe McIlvaine; VP-Business Affairs: Dave Howard; Asst. GM: Steve Phillips; Dir. Minor Leagues: Jack Zduriencik; Dir. Scouting: John Barr; Dir. Media Rel.: Jay Horwitz; Mgr.: Dallas Green; Coaches: Mike Cubbage, Frank Howard, Tom McCraw, Greg Pavlick, Steve Swisher, Bobby Wine. Home: Shea Stadium (55,601). Field distances: 338, l.f. line; 371, l.c.; 410, c.f.; 371, r.c.; 338, r.f. line. Spring training: Port St. Lucie, Fla.

SCOUTING REPORT

HITTING: The Mets, seventh in the NL in runs (657) in '95, are in need of a cleanup hitter. With the exile of Bobby Bonilla, Rico Brogna (.289, 22, 76), Jeff Kent (.278, 20, 65), Todd Hundley (.280, 15, 51) and Carl Everett (.260, 12, 54) were the only Mets to to hit 12-or-more home runs last season.

At least, the team that ranked last in steals with 58 in '95 solved its long-standing leadoff problem by signing Lance Johnson (.306, 10, 57, 10 triples, 40 steals for the White Sox) as a free agent last winter.

Jason Isringhausen threw NL hitters nasty knuckle curve.

And the Mets do have a collection of good young hitters. Brogna led the team in home runs and RBI, but needs to be more consistent, especially against lefties. Everett's 12 home runs in just 289 at-bats were a professional high for him. Kent is one of the game's few power-hitting second basemen. If Hundley stays healthy, he can be a 20-homer, 75-RBI catcher. Ex-Oriole prospect Alex Ochoa will get the chance to live up to his blue-chip billing.

That second-half surge by Jose Vizcaino (.287, 3, 56) could have been a contract push or a sign that he is finally coming into his own.

PITCHING: This organization, with a storied history of developing pitchers, now boasts the best set of young arms in baseball. Jason Isringhausen (9-2, 2.81) and Bill Pulsipher (5-7, 3.98) showed they are the real deal as the Mets posted the NL's third-best ERA at 3.88 in '95.

Paul Wilson, expected to make the jump from Triple-A to the majors this season, is regarded as the best of the lot. Even without Bret Saberhagen, this staff can dominate the league for the next five to eight years.

Veteran Pete Harnisch (2-8, 3.68), who missed most of the second half of '95 following shoulder surgery, will be looked upon for leadership and innings. Bobby Jones (10-10, 4.19) never found his groove last season, but should be able to win 15. Dave Mlicki (9-7, 4.26) can start or relieve and John Franco (5-3, 2.44, 29 saves) is still a quality closer.

FIELDING: Dallas Green's goal the last two seasons was to improve the Mets' defense and, to a large degree, the Mets have done just that. Brogna is the team's best-fielding first baseman since Keith Hernandez. Shortstop Vizcaino has never been better. Promising Edgardo Alfonzo can play three infield positions and play them well. In the outfield, Johnson eats up the ground in center and Everett and Ochoa will dare anyone to take an extra base. Hundley, no longer a liability vs. the steal, had his best all-around season last year.

OUTLOOK: The youngest team in the majors last season is ready to take the next step, to improve on 69-75. The playoffs may still be a year away, but the Mets will give their fans something they've missed the last four years—a competitive team that will fight for a wild-card berth in September. If the pitching is as good as advertised, watch out.

MET PROFILES

RICO BROGNA 25 6-2 205 Bats L Throws L

Best all-around first baseman Mets have had since Keith Hernandez . . . Led club in home runs (22), RBI (76) and batting average (.289) in first full season . . . Also struck out team-high 111 times . . . Had best fielding percentage among NL first basemen as he committed just three errors in 134 games . . . Hit safely in 53 of final 76 games . . . Had first grand slam, first multiple home-run game and drove in five runs for first time, Sept. 17 vs. Phillies . . . Batted just .222 with only two home runs against left-handers . . . Promoted from Norfolk (AAA), June 20, 1994, and made 33 starts at first base . . . In '94, he committed one error in 336 total chances . . . Began his career with Mets with an 0-for-7, but later went on 15-game hitting streak . . . Acquired from Tigers for Alan Zinter in deal of former No. 1 picks prior to 1994 season, a trade that ranks as one of GM Joe McIlvaine's best . . . Former Detroit manager Sparky Anderson tried to make him into a dead pull hitter . . . Coaches football at Taft School, a private school in Connecticut, during offseason . . . Drafted 26th overall by Tigers in 1988 . . . Born April 18, 1970, in Turner Falls, Mass. . . . Earned $125,000 last season.

Year	Club	Pos.	G	AB	R	H	2B	3B	HR	RBI	SB	Avg.
1992	Detroit	1B	9	26	3	5	1	0	1	3	0	.192
1994	New York (NL)	1B	39	131	16	46	11	2	7	20	1	.351
1995	New York (NL)	1B	134	495	72	143	27	2	22	76	0	.289
	Totals		182	652	91	194	39	4	30	99	1	.298

TODD HUNDLEY 26 5-11 185 Bats S Throws R

Finally blossomed into All-Star caliber catcher in '95 . . . Enjoyed his best all-around season, despite missing five weeks with sprained left wrist . . . Played in just 90 games and fell one home run short and two RBI shy of matching career highs with 15 and 51 respectively . . . At .280, he batted 61 points higher than previous career average . . . Injured wrist in home-plate collision with Colorado's Eric Young July 23 . . . On disabled list from July 24-Sept. 1 . . . Batted .288 after returning from DL . . . Threw out 16-of-66 would-be base-stealers (24.2%) . . . Worked well with young pitching staff . . . In '94, he hit career-high 16 homers and threw out 20-of-63 would-be base-stealers (31.7%), including four in one game . . . Struggled with throwing mechanics in '93 . . . Made major-league debut, May 18, 1990, as 19-year-old . . . Father Randy was former big-league catcher with Giants, Cubs, Twins and Padres and also wore No. 9 . . . Born May 27, 1969, in Martinsville, Va. . . . Earned $975,000 last season . . . Mets picked him in second round of 1987 draft.

Year	Club	Pos.	G	AB	R	H	2B	3B	HR	RBI	SB	Avg.
1990	New York (NL)	C	36	67	8	14	6	0	0	2	0	.209
1991	New York (NL)	C	21	60	5	8	0	1	1	7	0	.133
1992	New York (NL)	C	123	358	32	75	17	0	7	32	3	.209
1993	New York (NL)	C	130	417	40	95	17	2	11	53	1	.228
1994	New York (NL)	C	91	291	45	69	10	1	16	42	2	.237
1995	New York (NL)	C	90	275	39	77	11	0	15	51	1	.280
	Totals		491	1468	169	338	61	4	50	187	7	.230

CARL EVERETT 24 6-0 190 Bats S Throws R

Who says you can never get out of Dallas Green's doghouse? . . . His relationship with the manager got off to rocky start. But, by the end of '95 season, this speedy outfielder was one of Green's favorites . . . Looms as Mets' likely everyday right fielder in '96 . . . Was club's most productive player down stretch, after spending five weeks in Norfolk (AAA) . . . Recalled July 24, he had 34 RBI in last 39 games . . . Finished season with 12 home runs and 54 RBI after totaling 38 home runs and 187 RBI in first five seasons of pro ball . . . Cracked first grand slam, off Padres' Willie Blair, Aug. 25 . . . Drove in career-high five runs vs. Phillies, Aug. 8 . . . Owns second-best outfield arm on team, better than all but Alex Ochoa . . . Acquired from Marlins for Quilvio Veras prior to '95 season . . . Played in just 27 games over two seasons with Marlins and batted .186 with two home runs and six RBI . . . Attended Hillsborough High School in Tampa, which also produced Gary Sheffield and Dwight Gooden . . . Born June 3, 1971, in Tampa . . . Earned $109,000 last season . . . Yanks picked him 10th overall in 1990 draft, then Florida plucked him in expansion draft.

Year	Club	Pos.	G	AB	R	H	2B	3B	HR	RBI	SB	Avg.
1993	Florida	OF	11	19	0	2	0	0	0	0	1	.105
1994	Florida	OF	16	51	7	11	1	0	2	6	4	.216
1995	New York (NL)	OF	79	289	48	75	13	1	12	54	2	.260
	Totals		106	359	55	88	14	1	14	60	7	.245

LANCE JOHNSON 32 5-11 160 Bats L Throws L

Moved into leadoff role for White Sox in '95 . . . Has hit better than .300 in two of the past three seasons after posting .306 mark in '95 . . . Reached double figures in home runs (10) for first time in his career . . . His 57 RBI were also a career high . . . His 12 triples were second in AL to Cleveland's Kenny Lofton (13), marking first time in five seasons that he didn't lead league in that department . . . Stole 40 bases in '95 and has stolen more than 25 for six consecutive seasons, becoming first White Sox player to do that since Luis Aparicio (1957-62) . . . Good defensive center fielder . . . His only weakness is weak arm . . . Earned $2.66 million in '95 . . . Signed two-year, $5-million deal with Mets as free agent last winter . . . Cards drafted him in sixth round in 1984 . . . Born July 6, 1963, in Cincinnati . . . Was teammate of Kirby Puckett at Triton (Ill.) Community College.

Year	Club	Pos.	G	AB	R	H	2B	3B	HR	RBI	SB	Avg.
1987	St. Louis	OF	33	59	4	13	2	1	0	7	6	.220
1988	Chicago (AL) . .	OF	33	124	11	23	4	1	0	6	6	.185
1989	Chicago (AL) . .	OF	50	180	28	54	8	2	0	16	16	.300
1990	Chicago (AL) . .	OF	151	541	76	154	18	9	1	51	36	.285
1991	Chicago (AL) . .	OF	159	588	72	161	14	13	0	49	26	.274
1992	Chicago (AL) . .	OF	157	567	67	158	15	12	3	47	41	.279
1993	Chicago (AL) . .	OF	147	540	75	168	18	14	0	47	35	.311
1994	Chicago (AL) . .	OF	106	412	56	114	11	14	3	54	26	.277
1995	Chicago (AL) . .	OF	142	607	98	186	18	12	10	57	40	.306
	Totals		978	3618	487	1031	108	78	17	334	232	.285

EDGARDO ALFONZO 22 5-11 187 Bats R Throws R

Another home-grown prospect who is a cornerstone in club's future . . . Can play third base as well as shortstop, but is best suited for second base . . . Played well as rookie until injuring his back Aug. 10 . . . Played in just 101 games . . . Was placed on disabled list Aug. 11 after MRI revealed herniated disc . . . Activated from DL Sept. 1 and made seven starts at third . . . Batted .278 with four home runs and 41 RBI . . . Committed seven errors . . . Made 1995 Opening Day roster out of spring training following one season at Double-A . . . At Binghamton in '94, he batted .293 with 15 home runs and 75 RBI and he hit .308 in seven playoff games to help club win Eastern League Championship . . . Signed by Mets as non-drafted free agent in February 1991 . . . Born Aug. 11, 1973, in St. Teresa, Venezuela and now resides in Caracas . . . Earned big-league minimum of $109,000 last year.

Year	Club	Pos.	G	AB	R	H	2B	3B	HR	RBI	SB	Avg.
1995	New York (NL)	3B-2B-SS	101	335	26	93	13	5	4	41	1	.278

JOSE VIZCAINO 28 6-1 180 Bats R Throws R

"Viz" enjoyed his best all-around season . . . Was the Mets' unofficial MVP . . . Was superb defensively at shortstop, committing just 10 errors but could wind up at second in '96 . . . Drove in career-best 56 runs in 135 games . . . His .287 batting average tied a career high he set in '93 with Cubs . . . Even stole eight bases in 11 attempts one season after stealing only one base in 11 tries . . . Had first 5-for-5 game, Sept. 23 vs. Marlins . . . Batted .304 (117-384) in final 101 games . . . Acquired by Mets from Cubs for Anthony Young and Ottis Smith prior to '94 season . . . Signed by Dodgers as non-drafted free agent in February 1986 and traded four years later to Cubs for Greg Smith . . . Born March 26, 1968, in Palenque de San Cristobal, D.R. . . . Earned $1,335,000 last year and signed two-year contract in December.

Year	Club	Pos.	G	AB	R	H	2B	3B	HR	RBI	SB	Avg.
1989	Los Angeles . . .	SS	7	10	2	2	0	0	0	0	0	.200
1990	Los Angeles . . .	SS-2B	37	51	3	14	1	1	0	2	1	.275
1991	Chicago (NL) . .	3B-SS-2B	93	145	7	38	5	0	0	10	2	.262
1992	Chicago (NL) . .	SS-3B-2B	86	285	25	64	10	4	1	17	3	.225
1993	Chicago (NL) . .	SS-3B-2B	151	551	74	158	19	4	4	54	12	.287
1994	New York (NL)	SS	103	410	47	105	13	3	3	33	1	.256
1995	New York (NL)	SS-2B	135	509	66	146	21	5	3	56	8	.287
	Totals		612	1961	224	527	69	17	11	172	27	.269

BILL PULSIPHER 22 6-3 208 Bats L Throws L

Great arm, great stare, great future . . . The "Pulse" of the Mets' new-breed pitching staff didn't disappoint Met fans after being called up in late June . . . Lasted at least 6⅔ innings in 16 of 17 starts . . . Made debut June 17 vs. Astros and lost, 7-3, giving up five runs on four hits in first inning, but he still lasted seven innings . . . Notched first win June 27 against Pirates, when he pitched 7⅓ scoreless innings, allowed three hits and set career high with nine strikeouts . . . Matched that strikeout mark, July 3 against Cubs . . . Missed final three weeks of season with strained ligaments in left elbow . . . Was 6-4 with 3.14 ERA in 13 starts for Norfolk (AAA) . . . Hard thrower went 14-9 with 3.22 ERA in 28 starts with league-leading 171 strikeouts for Binghamton (AA) in 1994 . . . Tossed first no-hitter in Eastern League since 1937, against Harrisburg during playoffs . . . Mets made him second-round pick in '91 . . . Born Oct. 9, 1973, in Fort Benning, Ga. . . . Earned $109,000 last season.

Year	Club	G	IP	W	L	Pct.	SO	BB	H	ERA
1995	New York (NL)	17	126⅔	5	7	.417	81	45	122	3.98

JASON ISRINGHAUSEN 23 6-3 196 Bats R Throws R

One of rising pitching stars in baseball . . . Has ability to be 20-game winner . . . Throws a vicious knuckle curve . . . Won seven straight starts, but fell one victory shy of club mark held by Tom Seaver and David Cone when he got no-decision in final start, despite holding the Braves to four hits and no runs over eight innings . . . Started last season with Binghamton (AA) and stopped at Norfolk (AAA) on way to Mets . . . Made major-league debut July 17 at Wrigley and held Cubs to two runs on two hits over seven innings . . . Finished with overall record of 20-4 in '95 . . . Picked up his first major-league win by beating the Pirates July 30 . . . Missed one start in early September due to inflammation of right elbow . . . Gave up 17 earned runs in final 10 starts (69⅓ innings) for 2.21 ERA . . . Went 9-1 with 1.55 ERA in 12 starts for Norfolk last year . . . Started 1994 at St. Lucie (A) and finished that season at Binghamton (AA) . . . Wears No. 44, because he was picked by Mets in 44th round of the '91 draft . . . Born Sept. 7, 1972, in Brighton, Ill. . . . Earned $109,000 last season.

Year	Club	G	IP	W	L	Pct.	SO	BB	H	ERA
1995	New York (NL)	14	93	9	2	.818	55	31	88	2.81

PETE HARNISCH 29 6-0 205 Bats R Throws R

Will be called upon to be anchor of the Mets' young and talented staff, but he must stay healthy . . . Arm troubles ruined his season for second straight year . . . Underwent surgery Aug. 18 to repair a torn labrum in right shoulder . . . Went 1-2, despite allowing only seven earned runs in final five starts (33 innings) for 1.91 ERA . . . Tossed four-hitter in beating Padres, 8-0, May 30 . . . His Aug. 1 loss to Reds was his final start of season . . . Was 1-7 with six no-decisions in first 14 starts . . . Acquired by Mets from Astros for Juan Castillo and Andy Beckerman prior to last season . . . Spent month on DL in '94 with partially torn right biceps tendon . . . Enjoyed best season in '93, when he won a career-high 16 games, led NL with four shutouts and held opponents to a league-low .214 batting average . . . Part of one of the more lopsided deals of last five years when he, Steve Finley and Curt Schilling were traded by Orioles to Astros for Glenn Davis prior to 1991 season . . . Born Sept. 23, 1966, in Commack, N.Y. . . . Was the Mets' highest-paid survivor of last season, earning $3 million on first year of three-year deal.

Year	Club	G	IP	W	L	Pct.	SO	BB	H	ERA
1988	Baltimore	2	13	0	2	.000	10	9	13	5.54
1989	Baltimore	18	103⅓	5	9	.357	70	64	97	4.62
1990	Baltimore	31	188⅔	11	11	.500	122	86	189	4.34
1991	Houston	33	216⅔	12	9	.571	172	83	169	2.70
1992	Houston	34	206⅔	9	10	.474	164	64	182	3.70
1993	Houston	33	217⅔	16	9	.640	185	79	171	2.98
1994	Houston	17	95	8	5	.615	62	39	100	5.40
1995	New York (NL)	18	110	2	8	.200	82	24	111	3.68
	Totals	186	1151	63	63	.500	867	448	1032	3.72

BOBBY JONES 26 6-4 225 Bats R Throws R

Endured disappointing second season . . . Led Mets in both wins (10) and losses (10) . . . His 4.19 ERA was highest of his five seasons in organization . . . Did strike out career-high 127 . . . Started 30 games, most of any pitcher on staff . . . Went 4-3 with 2.60 ERA in first 10 starts . . . Finished eighth in NL with 3.15 ERA and tied for sixth in victories with 12 in '94 . . . Was 8-1 with a 1.77 ERA in 10 road starts that season . . . Tossed first career shutout and complete game, May 7, 1994, in St. Louis . . . Won his major-league debut, Aug. 14, 1993, in Philadelphia . . . Selected by Mets as a compensation sandwich pick in '91 draft for losing free-agent Darryl Strawberry to Dodgers . . . Attended Fresno High School, the school that produced Hall of Famer Tom Seaver . . . Born Feb. 10, 1970, in Fresno, Cal. . . . Earned $220,000 last season.

Year	Club	G	IP	W	L	Pct.	SO	BB	H	ERA
1993	New York (NL)	9	61⅔	2	4	.333	35	22	61	3.6
1994	New York (NL)	24	160	12	7	.632	80	56	157	3.1
1995	New York (NL)	30	195⅔	10	10	.500	127	53	209	4.1
	Totals	63	417⅓	24	21	.533	242	131	427	3.7

JOHN FRANCO 35 5-10 185 **Bats L Throws L**

Somehow survived the Great Met Purge of '95 . . . Struggled early, but only the strike-shortened season prevented the fiery closer from recording his seventh 30-save season . . . Finished with 29 saves, eighth-best total in NL . . . Had 22 saves and three victories in his last 30 outings . . . Blew seven save chances . . . Allowed 5-of-19 inherited runners to score . . . His 294 career saves are most by any left-hander in history . . . Led NL in saves (30) in '94 for third time in career and ranked second in baseball to Orioles' Lee Smith (33) . . . Ranks as Mets' all-time saves leader with 146 . . . His surgically repaired left elbow forced him to DL twice during 1993 season as he converted just 10-of-17 save opportunities . . . In '92, he was disabled twice and eventually underwent surgery Sept. 29 to repair a torn flexor tendon in his elbow . . . Best season was in '88, when he posted saves in 39 of 42 opportunities . . . Dodgers drafted him in fifth round in 1981, out of St. John's . . . Acquired by Mets from Reds with Don Brown for Randy Myers and Kip Gross prior to 1990 season . . . Born Sept. 17, 1960, in Brooklyn, N.Y. . . . Earned $2.5 million last season.

Year	Club	G	IP	W	L	Pct.	SO	BB	H	ERA
1984	Cincinnati	54	79⅓	6	2	.750	55	36	74	2.61
1985	Cincinnati	67	99	12	3	.800	61	40	83	2.18
1986	Cincinnati	74	101	6	6	.500	84	44	90	2.94
1987	Cincinnati	68	82	8	5	.615	61	27	76	2.52
1988	Cincinnati	70	86	6	6	.500	46	27	60	1.57
1989	Cincinnati	60	80⅔	4	8	.333	60	36	77	3.12
1990	New York (NL)	55	67⅔	5	3	.625	56	21	66	2.53
1991	New York (NL)	52	55⅓	5	9	.357	45	18	61	2.93
1992	New York (NL)	31	33	6	2	.750	20	11	24	1.64
1993	New York (NL)	35	36⅓	4	3	.571	29	19	46	5.20
1994	New York (NL)	47	50	1	4	.200	42	19	47	2.70
1995	New York (NL)	48	51⅔	5	3	.625	41	17	48	2,44
	Totals	661	822⅓	68	54	.557	600	315	752	2.62

TOP PROSPECTS

PAUL WILSON 23 6-5 235 **Bats R Throws R**

Considered even better prospect than Bill Pulsipher and Jason Isringhausen . . . Hard thrower will join the Mets' rotation in '96 . . . His total of 194 strikeouts were most by any minor-league pitcher in '95 . . . Went 6-3 with 2.17 ERA and 127 strikeouts in

16 starts for Binghamton (AA) and 5-3 with 2.85 ERA for Norfolk (AAA) . . . Named Eastern League Pitcher of the Year . . . Mets made him top overall pick of '94 draft . . . Went 0-7 first year of pro ball . . . All-American at Florida State . . . Born March 28, 1973, in Orlando.

ALEX OCHOA 24 6-0 185 Bats S Throws R

Future is now for gifted right fielder . . . Owns best outfield arm in organization . . . Considered a five-tool player, but he hit just 10 home runs in 459 at-bats in Triple-A last season . . . Hit .283 with 61 RBI and 24 steals for Rochester and Norfolk . . . Acquired July 28 from Orioles with Damon Buford for Bobby Bonilla and Jimmy Williams . . . Batted .297 (11-37) with no homers and no RBI for Mets after being promoted from Norfolk Sept. 15 . . . Orioles made him third overall pick in '91 draft . . . Born March 29, 1972, in Miami Lakes, Fla.

REY ORDONEZ 24 5-10 170 Bats R Throws R

Makes plays at shortstop that leave people shaking their heads in wonderment . . . Will have a chance to win major-league job this season . . . Has yet to hit much . . . Batted .214 with two homers and 50 RBI in 439 at-bats for Norfolk (AAA) last year . . . Committed 21 errors . . . In 1992, he defected from Cuba during World University Games in Buffalo by scaling a 10-foot fence . . . Became a Met through weighted lottery in October 1993 . . . Born Jan. 11, 1972, in Havana, Cuba.

JUAN ACEVEDO 25 6-2 195 Bats R Throws R

Will compete for spot on Met staff in 1996 . . . Acquired from Rockies with Arnold Gooch for Bret Saberhagen and Dennis Swanson, July 31 of last season . . . Pitched just three innings for Norfolk (AAA), due to inflammation in right elbow and a right rib-cage injury . . . Went 4-6 with a 6.44 ERA in 17 games (11 starts) with Colorado in '95 . . . Was 1-1 with 6.14 ERA in three starts for Colorado Springs (AAA) . . . Will probably start season in bullpen . . . Went 17-6 for New Haven (AA) in 1994 . . . Born May 5, 1970, in Juarez, Mexico.

MANAGER DALLAS GREEN: Some have called him Comeback Manager of the Year . . . Mets' horrible start seemed to seal his fate, but impressive second-half turnaround earned him a one-year contract with a club option on '97 . . . Mets were 25-44 at All-Star break, but closed out season with 44-31 run to second-place tie with Phils. Only the Dodgers had a better second-half record in NL . . . Adjusted to shake tag as manager who can't work with young players . . . Made effort to become more visible in clubhouse . . . Mets were 40-32 at home, including a franchise-record-tying, 11-game home winning streak to close out season . . . He turned 61 last year . . . Inherited club from Jeff Torborg, May 21, 1993. Mets were 13-25 when he took over and finished with baseball's worst record (59-103) . . . Managed Phillies from 1979-81, winning a World Series in 1980 . . . Served as Cubs general manager from 1982-87 . . . Named Executive of the Year when Cubs won divisional title in 1984 . . . Managed Yankees for 121 games in 1989 and spent most of those days fighting with owner George Steinbrenner . . . He, Casey Stengel, Yogi Berra and Joe Torre are only four men to manage both Mets and Yankees . . . A right-handed pitcher, he compiled lifetime 20-22 record during eight seasons spent with Phillies, Senators and Mets . . . Born Aug. 4, 1934, in Newport, Del. . . . Lives on farm in Chester County, Pa. . . . Overall managerial record is 395-406.

ALL-TIME MET SEASON RECORDS

BATTING: Cleon Jones, .340, 1969
HRs: Darryl Strawberry, 39, 1987, 1988, 1990
RBI: Howard Johnson, 117, 1991
STEALS: Mookie Wilson, 58, 1982
WINS: Tom Seaver, 25, 1969
STRIKEOUTS: Tom Seaver, 289, 1971

PHILADELPHIA PHILLIES

TEAM DIRECTORY: Pres.: William Y. Giles; Exec. VP/COO: David Montgomery; VP/GM: Lee Thomas; Asst. GM: Ed Wade; VP-Pub. Rel.: Larry Shenk; Mgr. Media Rel.: Gene Dias; Publicity Mgr.: Leigh Tobin; Trav. Sec.: Eddie Ferenz; Mgr.: Jim Fregosi; Coaches: Larry Bowa, Dave Cash, Denis Menke, Johnny Podres, John Vukovich. Home: Veterans Stadium (64,538). Field distances: 330, l.f. line; 408, c.f.; 330, r.f. line. Spring training: Clearwater, Fla.

SCOUTING REPORT

HITTING: Two years after nearly setting a major-league record for runs, the Phillies ranked 13th in runs (615) and last in home runs (94) in '95. What happened? Well, Darren Daulton appeared in only 98 games and Lenny Dykstra was limited to 62.

The Phillies suffered from a severe case of slow feet (they ranked 13th in steals with 72) and bad timing (second in runners left on base with 1,114). A healthy Dykstra (.264, 2, 18, 37 runs) and Daulton (.249, 9, 55) can change all that. Those two and Japanese re-import Pete Incaviglia should also enhance Gregg Jefferies' presence in the order. Jefferies batted .306, but drove in only 56 runs.

The Phillies replaced free-agent defector Charlie Hayes (.276, 11, 85) with Todd Zeile (.246, 14, 52 with the Cubs). They re-signed Jim Eisenreich (.316, 10, 55) and, if they can find a way to get him 400 at-bats, it would help. Maybe the biggest offensive surprise for the Phillies in '95 was All-Star Mickey Morandini (.283, 6, 49).

PITCHING: Things can only get better following last season's disaster, when Paul Quantrill (11-12, 4.67), who has been traded to the Blue Jays, was the only Phillies pitcher to win 10 games. Philadelphia used 26 pitchers en route to a 4.21 team ERA and 14 pitchers started at least two games.

Curt Schilling (7-5, 3.57) still figures prominently in the Phillies' plans, if he stays healthy. Sid Fernandez (6-1, 3.34 as a Phillie) provided a spark after being released by the Orioles in '95, but he's another pitcher with a history of breaking down.

With the loss of Quantrill, who led the team with 29 starts, the Phillies hope young Tyler Greene (8-9, 5.31) grows up quickly. The best developments for the Phillies came in their bull-

Sticky-fingered Mickey Morandini showed he can hit, too.

pen, namely Ricky Bottalico (5-3, 2.46, 62 games) and Heathcliff Slocumb (5-6, 2.89, 32 saves).

FIELDING: Jim Fregosi spent last season shuffling his players around the field and yet only the Reds committed fewer errors than the Phillies (97). Even the defensively challenged Jefferies, who began '95 in the outfield before settling at first base, committed just three errors. Shortstop Kevin Stocker, charged with a team-high 17 errors, and second baseman Morandini are a dependable double-play team and the Phils have Zeile to take over for Hayes at third. Dykstra, when he's not crashing into walls, is a solid center fielder.

OUTLOOK: Can anyone guarantee that Dykstra or Daulton will stay healthy? Does anyone know whether the Phillies' suspect pitching staff will hold up over 162 games? The answer to both questions is no, which should tell you something about the Phillies' chances. Even a wild-card berth is an unattainable dream for a team that sagged to a 69-75 finish in '95.

PHILLIE PROFILES

GREGG JEFFERIES 28 5-10 185 Bats S Throws R

Has always been a pure hitter—and he is no longer a disaster in the field . . . Started last season in left field after signing a four-year, $20-million contract with Phils as free agent, but was moved to first base after Dave Hollins was traded . . . Committed just three errors . . . His .306 batting average was ninth-highest in NL . . . Great compact swing . . . Was the second-hardest batter to strike out in the league in '95, fanning once per 20 at-bats . . . Led Phillies in hits (147) and runs (69), despite playing in only 114 games . . . Had more walks (35) than strikeouts (26) . . . Still in prime of his career . . . Acquired by Cards from Royals with Ed Gerald for Felix Jose and Craig Wilson prior to '93 season . . . Originally selected by Mets with 20th overall pick of '85 draft . . . Born Aug. 1, 1967, in Burlingame, Cal. . . . Earned $3 million last season.

Year	Club	Pos.	G	AB	R	H	2B	3B	HR	RBI	SB	Avg.
1987	New York (NL)	PH	6	6	0	3	1	0	0	2	0	.500
1988	New York (NL)	3B-2B	29	109	19	35	8	2	6	17	5	.321
1989	New York (NL)	2B-3B	141	508	72	131	28	2	12	56	21	.258
1990	New York (NL)	2B-3B	153	604	96	171	40	3	15	68	11	.283
1991	New York (NL)	2B-3B	136	486	59	132	19	2	9	62	26	.272
1992	Kansas City . . .	3B-2B	152	604	66	172	36	3	10	75	19	.285
1993	St. Louis	1B-2B	142	544	89	186	24	3	16	83	46	.342
1994	St. Louis	1B	103	397	52	129	27	1	12	55	12	.325
1995	Philadelphia . . .	1B-OF	114	480	69	147	31	2	11	56	9	.306
	Totals		796	3738	522	1106	214	18	91	474	149	.296

DARREN DAULTON 34 6-2 202 Bats L Throws R

All-Star catcher had season cut short by injury for second straight year . . . Started 93 of first 112 games before tearing anterior cruciate ligament in right knee while rounding second base . . . Underwent surgery on right knee for the eighth time Aug. 29 . . . Also had surgery to repair torn rotator cuff in right shoulder . . . His nine homers raised his career total to 123, which ties him for 10th place on club's all-time list . . . This reliable backstop finished second among catchers in fielding percentage (.994) . . . Led team with 55 walks . . . Was named to third All-Star team . . . "Dutch" was on pace to set career highs in several offensive categories in '94 before fracturing his right clavicle June 28 and missing final 38 games . . . Phillies drafted him in 25th round in 1980 . . . Born Jan. 3, 1962, in Arkansas City, Kan. . . . Earned $5.25 million last season.

Year	Club	Pos.	G	AB	R	H	2B	3B	HR	RBI	SB	Avg.
1983	Philadelphia . . .	C	2	3	1	1	0	0	0	0	0	.333
1985	Philadelphia . . .	C	36	103	14	21	3	1	4	11	3	.204
1986	Philadelphia . . .	C	49	138	18	31	4	0	8	21	2	.225
1987	Philadelphia . . .	C-1B	53	129	10	25	6	0	3	13	0	.194
1988	Philadelphia . . .	C-1B	58	144	13	30	6	0	1	12	2	.208
1989	Philadelphia . . .	C	131	368	29	74	12	2	8	44	2	.201
1990	Philadelphia . . .	C	143	459	62	123	30	1	12	57	7	.268
1991	Philadelphia . . .	C	89	285	36	56	12	0	12	42	5	.196
1992	Philadelphia . . .	C	145	485	80	131	32	5	27	109	11	.270
1993	Philadelphia . . .	C	147	510	90	131	35	4	24	105	5	.257
1994	Philadelphia . . .	C	69	257	43	77	17	1	15	56	4	.300
1995	Philadelphia . . .	C	98	342	44	85	19	3	9	55	3	.249
	Totals		1020	3223	440	785	176	17	123	525	44	.244

LENNY DYKSTRA 33 5-10 185 Bats L Throws L

"Nails" continues to hammer his body . . . Two-time All-Star is one of game's most exciting players—if he stays healthy . . . Played in career-low 62 games in '95 and Phillies desperately missed his fire . . . Missed 22 games with a sore lower back . . . Placed on disabled list July 28 with a sore right knee and missed remainder of season . . . Had arthroscopic surgery to relieve arthritis of the patella Aug. 8 . . . Batted .264, 23 points lower than his previous career average . . . Center fielder made nine starts in left . . . His home run July 21 vs. St. Louis was his first since May 22, 1994 . . . Last season marked fourth time in five years he has played in 85 or fewer games . . . Diminutive sparkplug led Phils in runs, on-base percentage, walks, steals and doubles in '94 . . . Has hit 18 career leadoff home runs, including 11 as a Phillie . . . Ranks seventh on the Phillies' all-time stolen-base list with 166 . . . Scored 143 runs in '93, most in NL since Chuck Klein's 152 in 1932 . . . Became first player in NL history to lead league in walks (129) and at-bats (637) in same season, in '93 . . . A career .320 hitter with 6 homers and 11 RBI in 13 World Series games . . . Acquired by Phils from Mets with Roger McDowell for Tom Edens and Juan Samuel, June 18, 1989 . . . Mets drafted him in 12th round in 1981 . . . Born Feb. 10, 1963, in Santa Ana, Cal. . . . Earned $6.2 million last year.

Year	Club	Pos.	G	AB	R	H	2B	3B	HR	RBI	SB	Avg.
1985	New York (NL)	OF	83	236	40	60	9	3	1	19	15	.254
1986	New York (NL)	OF	147	431	77	127	27	7	8	45	31	.295
1987	New York (NL)	OF	132	431	86	123	37	3	10	43	27	.285
1988	New York (NL)	OF	126	429	57	116	19	3	8	33	30	.270
1989	N.Y. (NL)-Phil.	OF	146	511	66	121	32	4	7	32	30	.237
1990	Philadelphia . . .	OF	149	590	106	192	35	3	9	60	33	.325
1991	Philadelphia . . .	OF	63	246	48	73	13	5	3	12	24	.297
1992	Philadelphia . . .	OF	85	345	53	104	18	0	6	39	30	.301
1993	Philadelphia . . .	OF	161	637	143	194	44	6	19	66	37	.305
1994	Philadelphia . . .	OF	84	315	68	86	26	5	5	24	15	.273
1995	Philadelphia . . .	OF	62	254	37	67	15	1	2	18	10	.264
	Totals		1238	4425	781	1263	275	40	78	391	282	.285

JIM EISENREICH 36 5-11 195 Bats L Throws L

Where would the Phillies have been without him last season? . . . Steady pro . . . Veteran outfielder belted career-high 10 home runs and fell four RBI short of career mark set in 1989 with 55 . . . His .316 batting average was highest among regulars . . . Played in 129 games, second-most on team to Charlie Hayes' 141 . . . Led NL outfielders with a 1.000 fielding percentage . . . Has a 181-game errorless streak dating back to May 1994 . . . Had NL's leading batting average for most of June, but did not have enough plate appearances until July 1, when he was hitting .352 . . . Still has good speed . . . Went 10-for-10 in stolen-base attempts in '95 and is 21-for-23 in three years as a Phil . . . Had a pinch-hit grand slam Aug. 8 vs. Padres . . . Has batted .300 or better in four of last five seasons . . . Signed with Phils as free agent prior to '93 season . . . Started all six games of 1993 World Series and had one homer and seven RBI . . . Twins drafted him in 16th round in 1980 . . . Claimed off waivers by Royals in 1984 . . . Made successful return to baseball in the mid-'80s, conquering effects of Tourette Syndrome, a neurological disorder . . . Born April 18, 1959, in St. Cloud, Minn. . . . Earned $1.2 million last year and was re-signed to one-year, $1.2-million deal last winter.

Year	Club	Pos.	G	AB	R	H	2B	3B	HR	RBI	SB	Avg.
1982	Minnesota	OF	34	99	10	30	6	0	2	9	0	.303
1983	Minnesota	OF	2	7	1	2	1	0	0	0	0	.286
1984	Minnesota	OF	12	32	1	7	1	0	0	3	2	.219
1987	Kansas City . . .	DH	44	105	10	25	8	2	4	21	1	.238
1988	Kansas City . . .	OF	82	202	26	44	8	1	1	19	9	.218
1989	Kansas City . . .	OF	134	475	64	139	33	7	9	59	27	.293
1990	Kansas City . . .	OF	142	496	61	139	29	7	5	51	12	.280
1991	Kansas City . . .	OF-1B	135	375	47	113	22	3	2	47	5	.301
1992	Kansas City . . .	OF	113	353	31	95	13	3	2	28	11	.269
1993	Philadelphia . . .	OF-1B	153	362	51	115	17	4	7	54	5	.318
1994	Philadelphia . . .	OF	104	290	42	87	15	4	4	43	6	.300
1995	Philadelphia . . .	OF	129	377	46	119	22	2	10	55	10	.316
	Totals		1084	3173	390	915	175	33	46	389	88	.288

MICKEY MORANDINI 29 5-11 171 Bats L Throws R

Underrated second baseman continues to improve each year . . . Selected to first All-Star team . . . Reached career highs in at-bats (494), runs (65), hits (140), doubles (34), home runs (6) and RBI (49) . . . Had career-high five hits, June 24 vs. Cardinals . . . Batted .346 with runners in scoring position, fifth-best mark in NL . . . Tied for sixth in NL in triples (7) and led Phils in that category for fourth straight season . . . Committed just seven errors . . . Has a .989 career fielding percentage . . . Had surgery to remove bone spurs from right elbow Oct. 6 . . . Finished second among NL second basemen with .990 fielding percentage in 1993, when he had a 66-game errorless streak . . . Phillies made him fifth-round pick in '88 draft . . . Born April 22, 1966, in Leechburg, Pa. . . . Earned $975,000 last season.

Year	Club	Pos.	G	AB	R	H	2B	3B	HR	RBI	SB	Avg.
1990	Philadelphia . . .	2B	25	79	9	19	4	0	1	3	3	.241
1991	Philadelphia . . .	2B	98	325	38	81	11	4	1	20	13	.249
1992	Philadelphia . . .	2B-SS	127	422	47	112	8	8	3	30	8	.265
1993	Philadelphia . . .	2B	120	425	57	105	19	9	3	33	13	.247
1994	Philadelphia . . .	2B	87	274	40	80	16	5	2	26	10	.292
1995	Philadelphia . . .	2B	127	494	65	140	34	7	6	49	9	.283
	Totals		584	2019	256	537	92	33	16	161	56	.266

KEVIN STOCKER 26 6-1 178 **Bats S Throws R**

Established himself as solid shortstop in first full season . . . Set career highs in games (125), at-bats (412), hits (90), doubles (14), RBI (32) and stolen bases (6) . . . Stole home May 13 vs. Astros . . . Knocked in career-high four runs, May 20 against the Mets . . . Had a pair of three-hit games for first time in career . . . Led Phillies with 10 sacrifices . . . Hit by a pitch nine times . . . Committed 17 errors . . . Missed 27 games in '94, following wrist surgery May 5 . . . Reached base via hit or walk in 25 straight games in '94 (July 1-29), when his .383 on-base percentage was third on club . . . Began '93 season with Scranton-Wilkes Barre (AAA), then became Phillies everyday shortstop July 7 . . . Made major-league debut by playing all 20 innings of 7-6 victory over Dodgers . . . Phillies drafted him with their second pick in '91 . . . Born Feb. 13, 1970, in Spokane, Wash. . . . Earned $205,000 last season.

Year	Club	Pos.	G	AB	R	H	2B	3B	HR	RBI	SB	Avg.
1993	Philadelphia . . .	SS	70	259	46	84	12	3	2	31	5	.324
1994	Philadelphia . . .	SS	82	271	38	74	11	2	2	28	2	.273
1995	Philadelphia . . .	SS	125	412	42	90	14	3	1	32	6	.218
	Totals		277	942	126	248	37	8	5	91	13	.263

TODD ZEILE 30 6-1 190 **Bats R Throws R**

Cub free agent signed one-year, $2.5 million pact with Phils last winter . . . Third baseman never got into a groove last season . . . Acquired from Cardinals June 16 for Mike Morgan and minor leaguers Paul Torres and Francisco Morales . . . Crushed two-run homer off Dodgers' Ramon Martinez in his Cubs debut June 17 . . . Missed three weeks in September with bruised right thumb . . . Had just eight hits in his final 47 at-bats . . . Batted .291 with five home runs and 22 RBI in 34 games with Cardinals . . . Began career as catcher, but was moved to third during his rookie year . . . Cards' third-round pick in 1986 draft . . . Born Sept. 9, 1965, in Van Nuys, Cal. . . . Earned $3.7 million last year.

Year	Club	Pos.	G	AB	R	H	2B	3B	HR	RBI	SB	Avg.
1989	St. Louis	C	28	82	7	21	3	1	1	8	0	.256
1990	St. Louis	C-3B-1B-OF	144	495	62	121	25	3	15	57	2	.244
1991	St. Louis	3B	155	565	76	158	36	3	11	81	17	.280
1992	St. Louis	3B	126	439	51	113	18	4	7	48	7	.257
1993	St. Louis	3B	157	571	82	158	36	1	17	103	5	.277
1994	St. Louis	3B	113	415	62	111	25	1	19	75	1	.267
1995	St.L.-Chi. (NL)	3B-1B-OF	113	426	50	105	22	0	14	52	1	.246
	Totals		836	2993	390	787	165	13	84	424	33	.263

HEATHCLIFF SLOCUMB 29 6-3 220 Bats R Throws R

Emerged as one of the premier closers in the majors after being given job in Phillies' third game of '95 season . . . Recorded a save in his first eight opportunities and finished the season with 32, tying him with Dodgers' Todd Worrell for fourth-best total in NL . . . Selected to first All-Star team and was the winning pitcher . . . Named NL Pitcher of the Month in May, going 1-0 with 1.76 ERA and 12 saves in 14 games . . . Struck out 63 in 65⅓ innings . . . His 32 saves were third-best total in a season in club history . . . Appeared in a career-high 61 games . . . Went 5-1 in 52 games in '94 . . . Traded to Phillies from Indians for Ruben Amaro Jr. prior to '94 season . . . Originally signed with Mets as non-drafted free agent in July 1984 . . . Born June 7, 1966, in Jamaica, N.Y. . . . Earned $200,000 last year.

Year	Club	G	IP	W	L	Pct.	SO	BB	H	ERA
1991	Chicago (NL)	52	62⅔	2	1	.667	34	30	53	3.45
1992	Chicago (NL)	30	36	0	3	.000	27	21	52	6.50
1993	Chicago (NL)	10	10⅔	1	0	1.000	4	4	7	3.38
1993	Cleveland	20	27⅓	3	1	.750	18	16	28	4.28
1994	Philadelphia	52	72⅓	5	1	.833	58	28	75	2.86
1995	Philadelphia	61	65⅓	5	6	.455	63	35	64	2.89
	Totals	225	274⅓	16	12	.571	204	134	279	3.64

SID FERNANDEZ 33 6-1 225 Bats L Throws L

"El Sid" salvaged his season and possibly his career after being released by Orioles July 9 . . . He's a quality pitcher if he can stay healthy . . . Still struggles to keep his weight down . . . As an Oriole, he spent two weeks on disabled list with sore left shoulder and went 0-4, 7.39 . . . Was unhappy being moved to the bullpen and was later waived by Baltimore . . . Suffered only loss in first start with Phillies, then won six of final 10 outings . . . Beat the Cardinals July 21 for his first win since July 15, 1994 . . . Struck out season-high 11 against the Reds, Aug. 6 . . . Has struck out 10-or-more 34 times in career . . . Was NL Pitcher of the Month in August, going 5-0 with 2.88 ERA . . . Left last three starts early due to left shoulder soreness . . . Left-handers hit just .103 against him . . . Hasn't been the same pitcher since '89, when he went 14-5 with 2.83 ERA . . . Spent 10 seasons with the Mets before signing with Orioles as free agent prior to '94 season . . . Two-time All-Star . . . Drafted by Dodgers in third round of 1981 draft . . . Born Oct. 12, 1962, in Honolulu, Hawaii . . . Earned $2,333,333 last year and re-signed with Phils as free agent for one-year, $250,000 deal with another $1.4 million in incentives last winter.

Year	Club	G	IP	W	L	Pct.	SO	BB	H	ERA
1983	Los Angeles	2	6	0	1	.000	9	7	7	6.00
1984	New York (NL)	15	90	6	6	.500	62	34	74	3.50
1985	New York (NL)	26	170⅓	9	9	.500	180	80	108	2.80
1986	New York (NL)	32	204⅓	16	6	.727	200	91	161	3.52
1987	New York (NL)	28	156	12	8	.600	134	67	130	3.81
1988	New York (NL)	31	187	12	10	.545	189	70	127	3.03
1989	New York (NL)	35	219⅓	14	5	.737	198	75	157	2.83
1990	New York (NL)	30	179⅓	9	14	.391	181	67	130	3.46
1991	New York (NL)	8	44	1	3	.250	31	9	36	2.86
1992	New York (NL)	32	214⅔	14	11	.560	193	67	162	2.73
1993	New York (NL)	18	119⅔	5	6	.455	81	36	82	2.93
1994	Baltimore	19	115⅓	6	6	.500	95	46	109	5.15
1995	Baltimore	8	28	0	4	.000	31	17	36	7.39
1995	Philadelphia	11	64⅔	6	1	.857	79	21	48	3.34
	Totals	295	1798⅔	110	90	.550	1663	687	1367	3.35

CURT SCHILLING 29 6-4 225 — Bats R Throws R

Tough, gritty competitor has seen last two seasons cut short by injury . . . Went on disabled list July 25 after making 17 starts and later underwent season-ending arthroscopic surgery on his right rotator cuff . . . Was 4-0 after nine starts . . . Walked one or fewer batters in 10 starts . . . Struck out career-high 12 batters, May 17 against Marlins . . . Tossed complete-game two-hitter vs. Padres, June 7 . . . Pitched into the seventh inning in 12 starts . . . Was among NL leaders in innings, strike-outs and opponents' batting average before getting hurt . . . In '94, he started season 0-7 in nine starts . . . Placed on DL for first time in career, May 17, 1994, with tender right elbow . . . Underwent elbow surgery May 20 and knee surgery June 10 that season . . . Finished tied for second in NL in complete games (7), tied for third in shutouts (2) and fourth in strikeouts (186) in '93 . . . Acquired from Astros for Jason Grimsley prior to 1992 season . . . Red Sox drafted him in second round in January 1986 . . . Born Nov. 14, 1966, in Anchorage, Alaska . . . Earned $2.3 million.

Year	Club	G	IP	W	L	Pct.	SO	BB	H	ERA
1988	Baltimore	4	14⅔	0	3	.000	4	10	22	9.82
1989	Baltimore	5	8⅔	0	1	.000	6	3	10	6.23
1990	Baltimore	35	46	1	2	.333	32	19	38	2.54
1991	Houston	45	75⅔	3	5	.375	71	39	79	3.81
1992	Philadelphia	42	226⅓	14	11	.560	147	59	165	2.35
1993	Philadelphia	34	235⅓	16	7	.696	186	57	234	4.02
1994	Philadelphia	13	82⅓	2	8	.200	58	28	87	4.48
1995	Philadelphia	17	116	7	5	.583	114	26	96	3.57
	Totals	206	805	43	42	.506	618	241	731	3.56

TOP PROSPECTS

RICKY BOTTALICO 26 6-1 200 — Bats L Throws R

Solidified himself as dependable reliever in first full season in majors . . . Went 5-3 with 2.46 ERA in 62 relief appearances for Phils . . . Struck out 87 in 87⅓ innings . . . Earned first win, May 13 vs. Houston . . . Picked up first save, June 12 against Mets . . . Had a 15-inning scoreless streak and 14-inning scoreless streak . . . Led bullpen in games (62) and strikeouts (87) . . . Held opposing batters to .167 average . . . Signed by Phils as non-drafted free agent in July 1991 . . . Born Aug. 26, 1969, in New Britain, Conn.

GENE SCHALL 25 6-3 190 — Bats R Throws R

One of the organization's top hitting prospects . . . Will compete for an outfield job on Phillies . . . Led Scranton-Wilkes Barre (AAA) in batting (.313) and home runs (12) and was second on the team in RBI (63) in '95 . . . Batted .231 with no homers and five RBI in 24 games with Philadelphia . . . Was named the Phillies Minor League Player of the Year in '94 . . . Hit combined total of 19 home runs and drove in 76 runs for Spartanburg (A) and Clearwater (A) in 1993 . . . Attended Villanova . . . Phillies drafted him in fourth round in 1991 . . . Born June 5, 1970, in Abington, Pa.

SCOTT ROLEN 20 6-4 195 — Bats R Throws R

Power-hitting third-base prospect . . . Batted .289 with three home runs and 15 RBI in 76 at-bats for Reading (AA) . . . Began last

Phils hope for full campaign from Darren Daulton.

season in Florida State League, where he batted .290 with 10 home runs, 39 RBI and 13 doubles for Clearwater (A) . . . Played in just 66 games before being promoted . . . Very strong . . . Great attitude . . . Phillies made him second-round pick in '93 draft . . . Born April 4, 1975, in Evansville, Ind.

RICH HUNTER 21 6-1 185 **Bats R Throws R**
Named the Phillies' Minor League Player of the Year . . . Finished impressive season with combined 19-2 record and 2.74 ERA . . .

Struck out 143 in 184 innings . . . Started '95 season with Piedmont (A) before jumping to Clearwater (A) and Reading (AA) . . . Went 3-0, 2.05 in three starts for Reading . . . Was 6-0, 2.93 in nine starts for Clearwater . . . Was 3-2, 4.50 and five saves for Martinsville (R) in '94 . . . Phillies made him 14th-round pick in '83 draft . . . Born Sept. 25, 1974, in Pasadena, Cal.

MANAGER JIM FREGOSI: Did a decent job holding team

together while his star players were falling apart . . . Suffered second straight losing season (69-75) after falling two victories short of winning World Series in '93 . . . Last year, Phils led division by five games June 26, but one month later, they trailed Braves by 15½ games . . . Set club records by using 50 players, including 26 pitchers . . . NL All-Star manager . . . Was credited with turning last-place club in '92 into first-place team in '93, when Phillies finished 97-65 and upset heavily-favored Braves in NLCS . . . Runs loose clubhouse, but gets his players to produce . . . Replaced Nick Leyva as Philadelphia manager, April 23, 1991, and guided team to third-place finish, Phils' best since 1986 . . . Managed Angels from 1978-81, winning divisional title in 1979 . . . Skipper of Louisville (AAA) from 1983-86, winning two divisional crowns . . . Returned to majors to manage White Sox from 1986-88 . . . Enjoyed 18-year playing career with Angels, Mets, Rangers and Pirates . . . Batted .265 with 151 homers . . . Went to six All-Star Games as shortstop . . . Overall major-league managerial record is 795-843.

ALL-TIME PHILLIE SEASON RECORDS

BATTING: Frank O'Doul, .398, 1929
HRs: Mike Schmidt, 48, 1980
RBI: Chuck Klein, 170, 1930
STEALS: Juan Samuel, 72, 1984
WINS: Grover Alexander, 33, 1916
STRIKEOUTS: Steve Carlton, 310, 1972

CHICAGO CUBS

TEAM DIRECTORY: Pres./CEO: Andy MacPhail; GM: Ed Lynch; Dir. Scouting: Jim Hendry; Dir. Media Rel.: Sharon Pannozzo; Media Inf. Coordinator: Chuck Wasserstrom; Trav. Sec.: Jimmy Bank; Mgr.: Jim Riggleman; Coaches: Billy Williams, Tony Muser, Dan Radison, Dave Bialas, Ferguson Jenkins, Mako Oliveras. Home: Wrigley Field (38,765). Field distances: 355, l.f. line; 400, c.f.; 353, r.f. line. Spring training: Mesa, Ariz.

SCOUTING REPORT

HITTING: It's like 1989 again, sort of. With Ryne Sandberg back, the Cubs are looking to recapture the magic of their last playoff team. Sandberg may need a little magic to hit .300 again, but, hey, it won't be tough for him to do better than the now-departed Todd Zeile's '95 batting average of .246.

Shawon Dunston (.296, 14, 69) recaptured some of his old magic from the '80s, but he was allowed to escape via free agency. Mark Grace (.326, 16, 92), coming off one of his best years, was re-signed, much to the relief of the Wrigley faithful.

Sandberg looked like he was slipping when he quit baseball midway through 1994. But he won't be asked to carry the Cubs like he did during the '80s. Instead, that job will fall on the broad shoulders of Sammy Sosa, who led the Cubs in home runs (36), RBI (119) and steals (34) last year. In Sosa and Brian McRae (.288, 12, 48, 92 runs), the Cubs have a dangerous combination of speed and power. Luis Gonzalez (.276, 13, 69), Rey Sanchez (.278) and Scott Servais (.265, 13, 47) form a strong supporting cast for a team that ranked fourth in the league in runs (693) a year ago.

PITCHING: This group holds the key to the Cubs' season. While there is no clearcut ace, the Cubs have a starting staff of five competent pitchers capable of 15 wins. Jamie Navarro (14-6, 3.28), who re-signed as a free agent, Kevin Foster (12-11, 4.51), Jim Bullinger (12-8, 4.14) and Frank Castillo (11-10, 3.21) all won at least 11 last season. The Cubs are hoping Steve Trachsel (7-13, 5.15) was only experiencing a sophomore jinx in 1995.

Castillo is coming off his best year, while Foster throws smoke, but also has a tendency to get smoked. He struck out 146

Sammy Sosa became two-time 30-30 man for Cubs.

and gave up 32 home runs last season.

Randy Myers (1-2, 3.88, NL-leading 38 saves) left a huge hole in the bullpen when he left via free agency. Larry Casian (1-0, 1.93) and rookie Terry Adams (1-1, 6.50) are the setup men.

FIELDING: Sandberg, who will likely play third base this time around, gives the Cubs another strong defensive presence. Grace earned another Gold Glove at first and has an uncanny knack of turning errant throws into assists. Center fielder McRae is good for one Play of the Week catch every three games. Sosa sometimes looks lost in right, but possesses one of the NL's best arms.

OUTLOOK: The Cubs' September push to a 73-71 finish is a sign of things to come. Yes, they have a lot of aging players, but there is also a lot a talent at Jim Riggleman's disposal at Wrigley Field. And if Castillo or Bullinger or Navarro wins 18-20 games, the Cubs will compete for the NL Central title in '96.

CUB PROFILES

SAMMY SOSA 27 6-0 185 Bats R Throws R

Lethal combination of power and speed . . . Finished second in NL to Rockies' Dante Bichette in home runs (36) and RBI (119), establishing career marks in both categories . . . Produced second career 30-30 season and remains only player in Cubs history to accomplish feat even one time . . . Played in all 144 games . . . Struck out 134 times, second to Colorado's Andres Galarraga in NL . . . Hit 16 homers and had 46 RBI over final 42 games . . . Hit 10 homers in 13-game span from Aug. 17-30 . . . Hit 10,000th homer in franchise history, off Dodgers' Tom Candiotti Aug. 14 . . . Improving defensive player . . . His 13 outfield assists ranked second-best in NL in '95 . . . Signed as non-drafted free agent by Texas in July 1985 . . . Acquired by Cubs from White Sox for Ken Patterson and George Bell prior to 1992 season . . . Born Nov. 12, 1968, in San Pedro de Macoris, D.R. . . . Earned $4.3 million last season.

Year	Club	Pos.	G	AB	R	H	2B	3B	HR	RBI	SB	Avg.
1989	Tex.-Chi. (AL) . .	OF	58	183	27	47	8	0	4	13	7	.257
1990	Chicago (AL) . .	OF	153	532	72	124	26	10	15	70	32	.233
1991	Chicago (AL) . .	OF	116	316	39	64	10	1	10	33	13	.203
1992	Chicago (NL) . .	OF	67	262	41	68	7	2	8	25	15	.260
1993	Chicago (NL) . .	OF	159	598	92	156	25	5	33	93	36	.261
1994	Chicago (NL) . .	OF	105	426	59	128	17	6	25	70	22	.300
1995	Chicago (NL) . .	OF	144	564	89	151	17	3	36	119	34	.268
	Totals		802	2881	419	738	110	27	131	423	159	.256

MARK GRACE 31 6-2 190 Bats L Throws L

"Amazing Grace" produced his finest all-around season . . . Established career highs in batting average (.326) and home runs (16) . . . Fell six RBI short of career mark with 92 . . . One of slickest-fielding first basemen in game, he committed just seven errors in 143 games in '95 . . . Lashed NL-leading 51 doubles, becoming first NL player to reach 50-double mark since Reds' Pete Rose in 1978 . . . Finished among NL's top six in batting average, runs, hits, multi-hit games, total bases and extra-base hits . . . Was NL's third-hardest batter to strike out, fanning once per 13.6 at-bats . . . Had a pair of four-hit games, giving him 13 for his career . . . Had 15-game hitting streak, from May 19-June 3 . . . His .994 career fielding percentage is highest in club history for a first baseman (minimum 500 games) . . . Won third Gold Glove in 1995 . . . Born June 28, 1964, in Winston-Salem, N.C. . . . Cubs' 24th-round selection in 1985 draft . . . Earned $4.05 million last season . . . Was re-signed to two-year, $9.05-million pact as free agent last season.

Year	Club	Pos.	G	AB	R	H	2B	3B	HR	RBI	SB	Avg.
1988	Chicago (NL) . .	1B	134	486	65	144	23	4	7	57	3	.296
1989	Chicago (NL) . .	1B	142	510	74	160	28	3	13	79	14	.314
1990	Chicago (NL) . .	1B	157	589	72	182	32	1	9	82	15	.309
1991	Chicago (NL) . .	1B	160	619	87	169	28	5	8	58	3	.273
1992	Chicago (NL) . .	1B	158	603	72	185	37	5	9	79	6	.307
1993	Chicago (NL) . .	1B	155	594	86	193	39	4	14	98	8	.325
1994	Chicago (NL) . .	1B	106	403	55	120	23	3	6	44	0	.298
1995	Chicago (NL) . .	1B	143	552	97	180	51	3	16	92	6	.326
	Totals		1155	4356	608	1333	261	28	82	589	55	.306

BRIAN McRAE 28 6-0 185 Bats S Throws R

One of game's best all-around center fielders . . . Came to Cubs after five seasons in Kansas City and instantly became a fan favorite at Wrigley . . . Posted a career-high batting average (.288) and tied career mark in home runs (12) . . . His 38 doubles ranked second in NL to teammate Mark Grace's 50 . . . Hit second career grand slam, off Pirates' Mike Dyer June 28 . . . Led off a game with a home run three times . . . Had 52 multi-hit games . . . Stole 27 bases, one short of his career high set in '94 with Royals . . . Father Hal, a former Kansas City player and manager, is Reds hitting coach . . . Royals selected him 17th overall in 1985 draft . . . Born Aug. 27, 1967, in Bradenton, Fla. . . . Earned $2.65 million last season . . . Cubs got him from Royals for Derek Wallace and Gene Morones just prior to start of '95 season.

Year	Club	Pos.	G	AB	R	H	2B	3B	HR	RBI	SB	Avg.
1990	Kansas City . . .	OF	46	168	21	48	8	3	2	23	4	.286
1991	Kansas City . . .	OF	152	629	86	164	28	9	8	64	20	.261
1992	Kansas City . . .	OF	149	533	63	119	23	5	4	52	18	.223
1993	Kansas City . . .	OF	153	627	78	177	28	9	12	69	23	.282
1994	Kansas City . . .	OF	114	436	71	119	22	6	4	40	28	.273
1995	Chicago (NL) . .	OF	137	580	92	167	38	7	12	48	27	.288
	Totals		751	2973	411	794	147	39	42	296	120	.267

RYNE SANDBERG 36 6-2 190 Bats R Throws R

So much for enjoying life without baseball . . . One of the most popular players in Cubs history signed a one-year deal to return last fall for guaranteed $1.5 million, with another $2.5 million in possible incentive bonuses . . . Had been away from the game since June 13, 1994, when he retired in the middle of four-year contract worth $28.4 million . . . "Ryno" could play either second or third base in '95 . . . His skills appeared to have diminished in '94 . . . Was batting .238 with five home runs and 24 RBI when he quit . . . Named NL MVP in 1984 . . . Became first Cub to win award since Ernie Banks . . . He's a 10-time All-Star and nine-time Gold Glove winner at second base . . . His .990 fielding percentage is highest in major-league history for a second baseman . . . Originally drafted by Phillies in 20th round in 1978 . . . Traded to Cubs with Larry Bowa for Ivan DeJesus prior to '82 season . . . Led NL with career-high 40 home runs in 1990 . . . Also set career high with 100 RBI and matched that feat in 1991 . . . Leading All-Star vote getter from 1990-92 . . . Born Sept. 18, 1959, in Spokane, Wash.

Year	Club	Pos.	G	AB	R	H	2B	3B	HR	RBI	SB	Avg.
1981	Philadelphia . . .	SS-2B	13	6	2	1	0	0	0	0	0	.167
1982	Chicago (NL) . .	3B-2B	156	635	103	172	33	5	7	54	32	.271
1983	Chicago (NL) . .	2B-SS	158	633	94	165	25	4	8	48	37	.261
1984	Chicago (NL) . .	2B	156	636	114	200	36	19	19	84	32	.314
1985	Chicago (NL) . .	2B-SS	153	609	113	186	31	6	26	83	54	.305
1986	Chicago (NL) . .	2B	154	627	68	178	28	5	14	76	34	.284
1987	Chicago (NL) . .	2B	132	523	81	154	25	2	16	59	21	.294
1988	Chicago (NL) . .	2B	155	618	77	163	23	8	19	69	25	.264
1989	Chicago (NL) . .	2B	157	606	104	176	25	5	30	76	15	.290
1990	Chicago (NL) . .	2B	155	615	116	188	30	3	40	100	25	.306
1991	Chicago (NL) . .	2B	158	585	104	170	32	2	26	100	22	.291
1992	Chicago (NL) . .	2B	158	612	100	186	32	8	26	87	17	.304
1993	Chicago (NL) . .	2B	117	456	67	141	20	0	9	45	9	.309
1994	Chicago (NL) . .	2B	57	223	36	53	9	5	5	24	2	.238
	Totals		1879	7384	1179	2133	349	72	245	905	325	.289

LUIS GONZALEZ 28 6-2 180 Bats L Throws R

Overlooked part of strong outfield . . . Made Cubs debut June 29 vs. St. Louis, after being acquired from Houston with Scott Servais for Rick Wilkins the previous day . . . Had 11-game hitting streak snapped on final day of '95 season . . . Batted .327 in last 30 games . . . Notched career-high six RBI Aug. 18 against Rockies, the first-six RBI game by Cub since

Shawon Dunston did it, Aug. 12, 1989 . . . Made first career starts in center field and in leadoff spot, Aug. 29 vs. Marlins . . . Hit homer to start a game for first time in career, Sept. 27 off Cardinals' Allen Watson . . . In 56 games with Astros, he batted .258 with six homers, 35 RBI, 10 doubles and four triples . . . Attended South Alabama University . . . Astros' fourth-round pick in 1988 draft . . . Born Sept. 3, 1967, in Tampa . . . Earned $1.4 million last year.

Year	Club	Pos.	G	AB	R	H	2B	3B	HR	RBI	SB	Avg.
1990	Houston	3B-1B	12	21	1	4	2	0	0	0	0	.190
1991	Houston	OF	137	473	51	120	28	9	13	69	10	.254
1992	Houston	OF	122	387	40	94	19	3	10	55	7	.243
1993	Houston	OF	154	540	82	162	34	3	15	72	20	.300
1994	Houston	OF	112	392	57	107	29	4	8	67	15	.273
1995	Hou.-Chi. (NL)	OF	133	471	69	130	29	8	13	69	6	.276
	Totals		670	2284	300	617	141	27	59	332	58	.270

The best news is that Mark Grace didn't defect.

Wrigley welcomes back long-lost Ryno named Sandberg.

JAMIE NAVARRO 28 6-4 225 Bats R Throws R

Cubs' top free-agent addition prior to '95 . . . Led team in wins (14) . . . Ranked fifth in NL in innings (200⅓) and 10th in ERA (3.28) . . . Was third on staff in strikeouts (128) . . . His .700 winning percentage was sixth-best in league . . . Last Cubs starter to finish a season with a .700-plus winning percentage was Mike Bielecki (.720 in 1989) . . . Has pitched 200-plus innings in four of last five seasons . . . Went 1-1 with three no-decisions in final five starts . . . Tossed his seventh career shutout, Aug. 12 vs. Giants . . . Went 62-59 in six seasons with Brewers . . . Pitched out of the bullpen 19 times in '94 . . . Set career highs in wins, shutouts and innings in 1992 . . . Selected by Brewers in third round of 1987 draft . . . Born March 27, 1968, in Bayamon, P.R. . . . Earned $850,000 last season . . . Re-signed with Cubs for one-year, $3.4-million deal last winter.

Year	Club	G	IP	W	L	Pct.	SO	BB	H	ERA
1989	Milwaukee	19	109⅔	7	8	.467	56	32	119	3.12
1990	Milwaukee	32	149⅓	8	7	.533	75	41	176	4.46
1991	Milwaukee	34	234	15	12	.556	114	73	237	3.92
1992	Milwaukee	34	246	17	11	.607	100	64	224	3.33
1993	Milwaukee	35	214⅓	11	12	.478	114	73	254	5.33
1994	Milwaukee	29	89⅔	4	9	.308	65	35	115	6.62
1995	Chicago (NL)	29	200⅓	14	6	.700	128	56	194	3.28
	Totals	212	1243⅓	76	65	.539	652	374	1319	4.13

FRANK CASTILLO 27 6-1 190 Bats R Throws R

Enjoyed best season of career in '95 . . . Second on club in innings (188) behind Jamie Navarro . . . Tied career high with 135 strikeouts . . . Posted lowest ERA (3.21) since breaking into majors in 1991 and the eighth-best mark in NL . . . Came within one out of pitching no-hitter, Sept. 25 vs. Cardinals, but Bernard Gilkey hit opposite-field triple with two outs in ninth . . . Struck out career-high 13 in that one-hitter . . . Tossed his first career shutout, Sept. 4 vs. Rockies . . . Went 5-6 at Wrigley, despite having a 2.78 home ERA . . . Was 8-2, 2.67 in 12 starts vs. NL West . . . Allowed 22 home runs . . . Walked two-or-fewer batters in 21 of his 29 starts . . . Experienced injury-riddled season in '94 . . . Set career marks in starts and innings in 1992 . . . Earned first major-league win and first complete game by beating Cardinals, July 5, 1991 . . . Cubs' sixth-round pick in

1987 draft . . . Born April 1, 1969, in El Paso, Tex. . . . Earned $225,000 last year.

Year	Club	G	IP	W	L	Pct.	SO	BB	H	ERA
1991	Chicago (NL)	18	111⅔	6	7	.462	73	33	107	4.35
1992	Chicago (NL)	33	205⅓	10	11	.476	135	63	179	3.46
1993	Chicago (NL)	29	141⅓	5	8	.385	84	39	162	4.84
1994	Chicago (NL)	4	23	2	1	.667	19	5	25	4.30
1995	Chicago (NL)	29	188	11	10	.524	135	52	179	3.21
	Totals	113	669⅓	34	37	.479	446	192	652	3.86

JIM BULLINGER 30 6-2 185 **Bats R Throws R**

Emerged as promising starter in his first full season . . . Slumped down the stretch . . . His 12 victories matched his high as a professional . . . Won seven straight decisions between July 18, 1994 and June 22, 1995 . . . Was on DL from May 21-June 22 with tendinitis in right elbow . . . Was leading NL in ERA with 1.95 mark at time of injury . . . Won four straight starts from July 24-Aug. 11, allowing four earned runs in 30 innings . . . Worked 25 scoreless innings during streak . . . Went 2-6, 6.97 in his final eight starts . . . Tossed his first complete-game shutout in 8-0 victory over Phillies July 30 . . . Game was his 100th major-league appearance . . . Beat Reds on Opening Day, allowing five hits over six innings . . . Former minor-league shortstop had perfect 1.000 fielding percentage . . . Held opponents to .235 batting average . . . Allowed just six homers in 100 innings . . . Made 23 relief appearances in '94 . . . Made major-league debut, May 26, 1992 . . . Recorded four saves in first five outings . . . Homered in first career at-bat, on first pitch he saw, June 8, 1992, becoming 10th pitcher in major-league history to accomplish feat . . . Cubs' ninth-round pick in 1986 draft . . . Born Aug. 21, 1965, in New Orleans . . . Earned $182,500 last season.

Year	Club	G	IP	W	L	Pct.	SO	BB	H	ERA
1992	Chicago (NL)	39	85	2	8	.200	36	54	72	4.66
1993	Chicago (NL)	15	16⅔	1	0	1.000	10	9	18	4.32
1994	Chicago (NL)	33	100	6	2	.750	72	34	87	3.60
1995	Chicago (NL)	24	150	12	8	.600	93	65	152	4.14
	Totals	111	351⅔	21	18	.538	211	162	329	4.12

KEVIN FOSTER 27 6-1 160 **Bats R Throws R**

Rookie power pitcher led Cubs with 146 strikeouts . . . Averaged 7.8 strikeouts per nine innings, fifth-best ratio in NL . . . Held opponents to .240 batting average, eighth-best mark in league . . . Gave up league-high 32 home runs, including 25 solo shots . . . Struck out career-high 13 Cards in final start of season Sept. 27 . . . Led NL pitchers with nine RBI . . . Acquired by Cubs from Phillies for Shawn Boskie, April 12, 1994 . . . Won first major-league game, June 19, 1994, at San Francisco . . . Had consecutive 10-strikeout outings against Reds, July 17 and 23 . . . Expos' 31st-round pick in 1987 . . . Born Jan. 13, 1969, in Evanston, Ill. . . . Earned $140,000 last year.

Year	Club	G	IP	W	L	Pct.	SO	BB	H	ERA
1993	Philadelphia	2	6⅔	0	1	.000	6	7	13	14.85
1994	Chicago (NL)	13	81	3	4	.429	75	35	70	2.89
1995	Chicago (NL)	30	167⅔	12	11	.522	146	65	149	4.51
	Totals	45	255⅓	15	16	.484	227	107	232	4.27

TOP PROSPECTS

BROOKS KIESCHNICK 23 6-4 228 **Bats L Throws R**

Cubs' Minor League Player of the Year . . . Will compete for an outfield job on major-league roster in '96 . . . All-around talent . . . Power hitter who uses the entire field . . . Did struggle against left-handers . . . Batted .295 with 23 home runs, 73 RBI, 30 doubles and 61 runs for Iowa (AAA) in '95 . . . In first pro season in '94, he batted .282 with 14 homers and 55 RBI for Orlando (AA) . . . Struck out 91 times in 505 at-bats last season . . . Cubs' first-round pick in 1991 draft . . . Born June 6, 1972, in Robstown, Tex.

PEDRO VALDES 22 6-1 170 **Bats L Throws L**

Outfield prospect batted .300 with seven home runs, 68 RBI, 28 doubles, 57 runs for Orlando (AA) of Southern League in '95 . . . Has raised power numbers each year . . . Batted .282 with one home run and 14 doubles for Orlando in '94 . . . Made his pro debut at age 17 in 1991 . . . Cubs' 12th-round pick in 1990 draft . . . Born June 29, 1973, in Fajardo, P.R.

TERRY ADAMS 23 6-3 205 **Bats R Throws R**

Could become Randy Myers' successor as closer . . . Made his major-league debut Aug. 10 vs. Padres . . . Earned first major-league save, Aug. 14 vs. Dodgers, and picked up first win Sept. 13 against Los Angeles . . . Went 1-1, 6.50 with one save in 18 appearances for Cubs and struck out 15 in 18 innings . . . Earned five saves in seven games and didn't allow a run for Iowa (AAA) before being promoted to majors . . . Started '95 season with Orlando (AA) and was 2-3 with 1.43 ERA and 19 saves in 37 games . . . Was 9-10 with 4.38 ERA for Daytona (A) in '94 before being moved to bullpen . . . Cubs' fourth-round pick in 1991 draft . . . Born March 6, 1973, in Mobile, Ala.

ROBIN JENNINGS 23 6-2 200 **Bats L Throws L**

Had breakthrough season in '95 . . . Owns one of best outfield arms in organization . . . Batted .296 with 17 home runs, 79 RBI, 71 runs, 27 doubles and seven triples for Orlando (AA) of Southern League . . . Batted .279 with eight homers and 60 RBI for Daytona (A) in '94 . . . Cubs' 32nd-round pick in 1991 draft . . . Born April 11, 1972, in Singapore.

MANAGER JIM RIGGLEMAN: His club remained in playoff hunt until final week of '95 season . . . Cubs finished 73-71 in his first year in Chicago, 12 games behind Reds in NL Central . . . That represented improvement of 24 games from 1994 . . . Named Chicago's 12th manager in 12 years after '94 season . . . Took reins from Tom Trebelhorn . . . This guy was only man whom new GM Ed Lynch interviewed . . . Both had worked together in San Diego . . . Padres finished 47-70 and in last place in NL West in '94, his second full season at helm . . . Padres went 61-101 in 1993 . . . A Whitey Herzog disciple . . . Spent nine years in Cardinals organization as a coach . . . Managed Las Vegas (AAA) for two years before moving to majors . . . Began managerial career at St. Petersburg (A) from 1982-84 before moving on to Arkansas (AA) for three years . . . Played eight seasons in St. Louis organization as infielder-outfielder . . . Had 558-554 record as minor-league manager . . .

Fourth-round pick of Dodgers in 1976 . . . Born Nov. 9, 1952, in Fort Dix, N.J. . . . Overall major-league managerial record is 185-250.

ALL-TIME CUB SEASON RECORDS

BATTING: Rogers Hornsby, .380, 1929
HRs: Hack Wilson, 56, 1930
RBI: Hack Wilson, 190, 1930
STEALS: Frank Chance, 67, 1903
WINS: Mordecai Brown, 29, 1908
STRIKEOUTS: Ferguson Jenkins, 274, 1970

CINCINNATI REDS

TEAM DIRECTORY: Principal Owner/Pres.: Marge Schott; GM: James Bowden IV; Dir. Scouting: Julian Mock; Dir. Player Development: Sheldon (Chief) Bender; Publicity Dir.: Mike Ringering; Trav. Sec.: Joel Pieper; Mgr.: Ray Knight; Coaches: Marc Bombard, Mike Griffin, Don Gullett, Jim Lett, Hal McRae, Joel Youngblood. Home: Riverfront Stadium (52,952). Field distances: 330, l.f. line; 404, c.f.; 330, r.f. line. Spring training: Plant City, Fla.

SCOUTING REPORT

HITTING: If new manager Ray Knight is smart, he'll leave well enough alone and let this unit keep on doing what it did for Davey Johnson in 1995. The Reds led the NL in stolen bases (190),

Reds' classy leader Barry Larkin never comes up short.

finished tied for second in runs (747), ranked third in homers (161) and fourth in batting average (.270).

There is a blend of power and speed that few teams possess. Barry Larkin (.319, 15, 66, 98 runs, 51 steals) is the league's best offensive shortstop. Before his terrible NLCS, Reggie Sanders (.306, 28, 99, 36 steals) enjoyed a breakthrough regular season. Ron Gant (.276, 29, 88), unsigned at press time, re-established himself as one of the NL's most dangerous hitters.

Bret Boone (.267, 15, 68) has more power than most second basemen. Hal Morris (.279, 11, 51) re-signed, but Benito Santiago (.286, 11, 44) was not.

PITCHING: GM Jim Bowden loaded up his staff for a run at the Braves in the NLCS and it fell short. But that doesn't mean Bowden didn't make some good moves that helped Cincinnati post a fourth-ranked 4.03 ERA in '95. Claiming Pete Schourek (18-7, 3.22) on waivers from the Mets in '94 was the best one.

Otherwise, John Smiley (12-5, 3.46) and Mark Portugal (11-10, 4.01) can go south at any time and nobody knows if Jose Rijo (5-4, 4.17) can bounce back from serious surgery to be effective this season. David Wells (16-8 overall), another late-season pickup, is coming off his best season.

The sweep at the hands of Atlanta in the NLCS exposed a weakness in the setup corps in front of closer Jeff Brantley (3-2, 2.82, 28 saves). Dave Burba (10-4, 3.97) is versatile and dependable. Mike Jackson (6-1, 2.39), unsigned at press time, is overpowering when healthy. But Hector Carrasco (2-7, 4.12) and Xavier Hernandez (7-2, 4.60) were inconsistent.

FIELDING: The Reds led the NL in fielding percentage (.986) and in the fewest errors (79) and did so by wide margins.

Talk about strong up the middle. Shortstop Larkin has won two Gold Gloves and second baseman Boone committed only four errors last season. But the Reds must replace Darren Lewis, one of the NL's best defensive center fielders. Sanders was one of the NL leaders in assists from his spot in right.

OUTLOOK: With so much money committed to the top half of the roster, Bowden was expected to have to bite the bullet on the other half. That could keep the Reds from matching their relatively easy 85-59 run to the NL Central title last season. It could be more interesting this time around, but you can expect the Reds to be in the race.

Met castoff Pete Schourek seeks encore to 18-7, 3.22.

RED PROFILES

BARRY LARKIN 31 6-0 190 **Bats R Throws R**

Another banner year for league's best shortstop earned him NL MVP award in '95 . . . Another .300-plus batting average (.319) plus a career-high 51 steals to lead league's fastest team . . . Ranked second among NL shortstops with .980 fielding percentage and won Gold Glove . . . Drove in 500th career run and stole 200th career base . . . Only Reds hitter who had a successful NLCS, he batted .389 in four-game sweep at hands of Atlanta . . . Salary was $5.7 million in '95 . . . Ended Ozzie Smith's streak of 10 consecutive All-Star starts in '94 and also won first Gold Glove that year, but he didn't hit .300 for the first time in six years . . . His five consecutive .300-plus seasons from 1989-93 marked first time in 40 years an NL shortstop had accomplished that feat . . . Reds drafted him fourth overall in 1985 . . . Was Big 10 MVP twice at University of Michigan . . . Born April 29, 1964, in Cincinnati.

Year	Club	Pos.	G	AB	R	H	2B	3B	HR	RBI	SB	Avg.
1986	Cincinnati	SS-2B	41	159	27	45	4	3	3	19	8	.283
1987	Cincinnati	SS	125	439	64	107	16	2	12	43	21	.244
1988	Cincinnati	SS	151	588	91	174	32	5	12	56	40	.296
1989	Cincinnati	SS	97	325	47	111	14	4	4	36	10	.342
1990	Cincinnati	SS	158	614	85	185	25	6	7	67	30	.301
1991	Cincinnati	SS	123	464	88	140	27	4	20	69	24	.302
1992	Cincinnati	SS	140	533	76	162	32	6	12	78	15	.304
1993	Cincinnati	SS	100	384	57	121	20	3	8	51	14	.315
1994	Cincinnati	SS	110	427	78	119	23	5	9	52	26	.279
1995	Cincinnati	SS	131	496	98	158	29	6	15	66	51	.319
	Totals		1176	4429	711	1322	222	44	102	537	239	.298

HAL MORRIS 30 6-4 215 **Bats L Throws L**

It took a late rush for him to get season average to a disappointing .279 . . . Career average was .313 entering 1995 . . . Batted only .221 against lefties in '95 . . . As a result, he was platooned at first base and played in only 100 games . . . Hit .309 after the All-Star break . . . Struggled to .167 mark vs. Atlanta in NLCS . . . Salary was $3,300,000 in '95 . . . First baseman hit .335 in 1994 and as high as .340 in 1990 . . . His .318 mark in

1991 left him just shy of NL batting title . . . Has smooth swing despite highly unusual habit of moving both feet in his approach . . . Reds stole him from Yankees for Tim Leary and Van Snider prior to 1990 season . . . Yanks' eighth-round pick in 1986 draft . . . Played with Barry Larkin at University of Michigan . . . Born April 9, 1965, in Fort Rucker, Ala. . . . Re-signed to two-year, $5-million free-agent contract in December.

Year	Club	Pos.	G	AB	R	H	2B	3B	HR	RBI	SB	Avg.
1988	New York (AL)	OF	15	20	1	2	0	0	0	0	0	1.00
1989	New York (AL)	OF-1B	15	18	2	5	0	0	0	4	0	.278
1990	Cincinnati	1B-OF	107	309	50	105	22	3	7	36	9	.340
1991	Cincinnati	1B-OF	136	478	72	152	33	1	14	59	10	.318
1992	Cincinnati	1B	115	395	41	107	21	3	6	53	6	.271
1993	Cincinnati	1B	101	379	48	120	18	0	7	49	2	.317
1994	Cincinnati	1B	112	436	60	146	30	4	10	78	6	.335
1995	Cincinnati	1B	101	359	53	100	25	2	11	51	1	.279
	Totals		702	2394	327	737	149	13	55	330	34	.308

REGGIE SANDERS 28 6-1 190 Bats R Throws R

Breakthrough season was spoiled by postseason slide . . . Reached another level with .306 average, 28 homers and 99 RBI, all career highs . . . Also stole 36 bases in 48 tries . . . Pounded lefties, hitting .365 against them . . . But his '95 season ended on bitter note . . . Hit .125 with 10 strikeouts in 16 at-bats in NLCS . . . Also struck out in last five at-bats in Division Series against LA . . . Salary was $1,975,000 in 1995 . . . Signed three-year extension following '95 regular season . . . Led Reds in hitting, runs, RBI and stolen bases in '93 . . . Former shortstop is adjusting well to outfield . . . Strong arm led to 12 assists from right field, fourth-most in NL . . . Reds made him seventh-round pick in 1987 draft . . . Born Dec. 1, 1967, in Florence, S.C.

Year	Club	Pos.	G	AB	R	H	2B	3B	HR	RBI	SB	Avg.
1991	Cincinnati	OF	9	40	6	8	0	0	1	3	1	.200
1992	Cincinnati	OF	116	385	62	104	26	6	12	36	16	.270
1993	Cincinnati	OF	138	496	90	136	16	4	20	83	27	.274
1994	Cincinnati	OF	107	400	66	105	20	8	17	62	21	.263
1995	Cincinnati	OF	133	484	91	148	36	6	28	99	36	.306
	Totals		503	1805	315	501	98	24	78	283	101	.278

Only NLCS spoiled Reggie Sanders' fine season.

BRET BOONE 26 5-10 185 Bats R Throws R

Proved he was more than a free swinger . . . Also developed into one of the league's better defensive second basemen . . . Committed only four errors . . . Led NL second basemen with .994 fielding percentage . . . Made first error of season July 8 . . . Last one came 79 games earlier, back in 1994 season . . . Average fell from .320 in 1994 to .267 in '95 . . . Went 193 at-bats between homers, from July 29-Oct. 1 . . . Still finished with career-high 15 . . . Hit .214 in NLCS . . . Earned $400,000 in 1994 . . . Part of three-generation, big-league family . . . Father Bob is Royals manager and former catcher . . . Grandfather Ray was an All-Star infielder during a 13-year career . . . Brother Aaron is on his way to big leagues, in Reds system . . . Acquired by Reds from Seattle with Erik Hanson for Bobby Ayala and Dan Wilson prior to 1994 season . . . Mariners' fifth-round pick in 1990 draft . . . Born April 6, 1969, in El Cajon, Cal.

Year	Club	Pos.	G	AB	R	H	2B	3B	HR	RBI	SB	Avg.
1992	Seattle	2B-3B	33	129	15	25	4	0	4	15	1	.194
1993	Seattle	2B	76	271	31	68	12	2	12	38	2	.251
1994	Cincinnati	2B-3B	108	381	59	122	25	2	12	68	3	.320
1995	Cincinnati	2B	138	513	63	137	34	2	15	68	5	.267
	Totals		355	1294	168	352	75	6	43	189	11	.272

PETE SCHOUREK 26 6-5 210 Bats L Throws L

Emerged as one of league's best pitchers after disappointing first four big-league seasons . . . Finished second in NL in wins (18) and winning percentage (.720), fifth in opponents' average (.228), seventh in strikeouts (160) and ninth in ERA (3.22) . . . Was deadly in Riverfront Stadium, where he went 13-2 with 1.85 ERA in 15 regular-season starts . . . Made two strong starts in NLCS, going 0-1 despite 1.26 ERA against Braves ... Earned $725,000 in 1995 ... Reds claimed him on waivers before 1994 season ... Mets, particularly manager Dallas Green, gave up him ... Was 16-24 in parts of three seasons for them, including 5-12 mark with 5.96 ERA in 1993 ... Mets' second-round pick in 1987 draft ... Born May 10, 1969, in Austin, Tex.

Year	Club	G	IP	W	L	Pct.	SO	BB	H	ERA
1991	New York (NL)	35	86⅓	5	4	.556	67	43	82	4.27
1992	New York (NL)	22	136	6	8	.429	60	44	137	3.64
1993	New York (NL)	41	128⅓	5	12	.294	72	45	168	5.96
1994	Cininnati	22	81⅓	7	2	.778	69	29	90	4.09
1995	Cininnati	29	190⅓	18	7	.720	160	45	158	3.22
	Totals	149	622⅓	41	33	.554	428	206	635	4.14

JOSE RIJO 30 6-2 205 Bats R Throws R

Elbow finally gave out on him after years of throwing one of the game's nastiest sliders ... Had "Tommy John surgery" and is expected to miss a good portion of this season ... Went 5-4 with 4.17 ERA in 14 starts before pain wouldn't let him continue ... Salary was $5,750,000 in 1995 ... In previous seven seasons, he was 87-53 and had an ERA above 3.00 only once (3.08 in 1994) ... Had big year in 1993, leading NL in strikeouts and finishing second in ERA and innings ... Reds got him from Athletics with Tim Birtsas for Dave Parker following 1987 season ... Went 17-22 in three seasons in Oakland ... Athletics got him from Yankees in Rickey Henderson deal prior to 1985 season ... Went 2-8 in only season in New York, at age 20 ... Signed by Yanks as non-drafted free agent in August 1980 ... Born May 13, 1965, in San Cristobal, D.R.

Year	Club	G	IP	W	L	Pct.	SO	BB	H	ERA
1984	New York (AL)	24	62⅓	2	8	.200	47	33	74	4.76
1985	Oakland	12	63⅔	6	4	.600	65	28	57	3.53
1986	Oakland	39	193⅔	9	11	.450	176	108	172	4.65
1987	Oakland	21	82⅓	2	7	.222	67	41	106	5.90
1988	Cincinnati	49	162	13	8	.619	160	63	120	2.39
1989	Cincinnati	19	111	7	6	.538	86	48	101	2.84
1990	Cincinnati	29	197	14	8	.636	152	78	151	2.70
1991	Cincinnati	30	204⅓	15	6	.714	172	55	165	2.51
1992	Cincinnati	33	211	15	10	.600	171	44	185	2.56
1993	Cincinnati	36	257⅓	14	9	.609	227	62	218	2.48
1994	Cincinnati	26	172⅓	9	6	.600	171	52	177	3.08
1995	Cincinnati	14	69	5	4	.556	62	22	76	4.17
	Totals	332	1786	111	87	.561	1556	634	1602	3.16

JOHN SMILEY 31 6-4 220 **Bats L Throws L**

Veteran turned in his best season since 1992 ... Went 12-5 for fourth-best winning percentage (.706) in NL ... Walked only 39 in 176⅔ innings ... Allowed two runs in five innings in a no-decision in NLCS start ... Earned $4,975,000 in 1995 ... Has 102-75 record in 10 big-league seasons ... Reds signed him as free agent before 1993 season ... Gave them only three wins that year and 11 in 1994 ... Pirates dealt him in salary-dumping deal to Twins for Denny Neagle and Midre Cummings before 1992 season ... Won 20 games for division-winning Pirates in 1991 before making two horrible starts in NLCS against Atlanta ... Pirates' 12th-round pick in 1983 ... Born March 17, 1965, in Phoenixville, Pa.

Year	Club	G	IP	W	L	Pct.	SO	BB	H	ERA
1986	Pittsburgh	12	11⅔	1	0	1.000	9	4	4	3.86
1987	Pittsburgh	63	75	5	5	.500	58	50	69	5.76
1988	Pittsburgh	34	205	13	11	.542	129	46	185	3.25
1989	Pittsburgh	28	205⅓	12	8	.600	123	49	174	2.81
1990	Pittsburgh	26	149⅓	9	10	.474	86	36	161	4.64
1991	Pittsburgh	33	207⅔	20	8	.714	129	44	194	3.08
1992	Minnesota	34	241	16	9	.640	163	65	205	3.21
1993	Cincinnati	18	105⅔	3	9	.250	60	31	117	5.62
1994	Cincinnati	24	158⅔	11	10	.524	112	37	169	3.86
1995	Cincinnati	28	176⅔	12	5	.706	124	39	173	3.46
	Totals	300	1536	102	75	.576	993	401	1451	3.67

DAVID WELLS 32 6-4 230 **Bats L Throws L**

Big guy put together his best season in '95 ... Went 16-8 with 3.24 ERA in 203 innings, splitting season between Detroit (10-3) and Cincinnati (6-5) ... Reds got him for C.J. Nitkowski, Dave Tuttle and a player to be named July 31 ... Won 14 of his last 20 starts ... Was 9-0 in last 15 outings with sad-sack Tigers ... Lost his NLCS start ... Salary was $2 million in 1995 ... Was only 5-7 in 1994, when season was interrupted by elbow surgery ... Tigers signed him as free agent before 1993 season ... Still a free spirit, but he has cleaned up reputation somewhat from days in Toronto ... Has tattoo of young son on right arm . . . Won 15 games in 1991 with Blue Jays . . . Prior to that, he bounced between bullpen and rotation for three seasons . . . Born May 20, 1963, in Torrance, Cal. . . . Blue Jays drafted him in second round in 1982.

Year	Club	G	IP	W	L	Pct.	SO	BB	H	ERA
1987	Toronto	18	29⅓	4	3	.571	32	12	37	3.99
1988	Toronto	41	64⅓	3	5	.375	56	31	65	4.62
1989	Toronto	54	86⅓	7	4	.636	78	28	66	2.40
1990	Toronto	43	189	11	6	.647	115	45	165	3.14
1991	Toronto	40	198⅓	15	10	.600	106	49	188	3.72
1992	Toronto	41	120	7	9	.438	62	36	138	5.40
1993	Detroit	32	187	11	9	.550	139	42	183	4.19
1994	Detroit	16	111⅓	5	7	.417	71	24	113	3.96
1995	Detroit	18	130⅓	10	3	.769	83	37	120	3.04
1995	Cincinnati	11	72⅔	6	5	.545	50	16	74	3.59
	Totals	314	1188⅔	79	61	.564	792	320	1149	3.77

JEFF BRANTLEY 32 5-10 190 Bats R Throws R

Underrated closer . . . Doesn't overpower people, just he gets them out . . . Saved career-best 28 games in 33 tries . . . Had sub-3.00 ERA (2.82) for fifth time in last six years . . . Reds won 49 of 56 games in which he appeared . . . Allowed only 53 hits in 70⅓ innings . . . Salary was $1 million in 1995 . . . Signed with Reds as free agent before 1994 season . . . Went 29-20 with 3.24 ERA in five-plus seasons with Giants . . . In 1993, the year his ERA rose to 4.28, he started 12 games . . . Posted microscopic 1.56 ERA with 19 saves in 1990 . . . Saved 15 games in 1991 and 1994 . . . Giants made him sixth-round pick in 1985 draft . . . Teammate of Will Clark and Rafael Palmeiro at Mississippi State . . . Born Sept. 5, 1963, in Florence, Ala. . . . Has 85 career saves.

Year	Club	G	IP	W	L	Pct.	SO	BB	H	ERA
1988	San Francisco	9	20⅔	0	1	.000	11	6	22	5.66
1989	San Francisco	59	97⅓	7	1	.875	69	37	101	4.07
1990	San Francisco	55	86⅔	5	3	.625	61	33	77	1.56
1991	San Francisco	67	95⅓	5	2	.714	81	52	78	2.45
1992	San Francisco	56	91⅔	7	7	.500	86	45	67	2.95
1993	San Francisco	53	113⅔	5	6	.455	76	46	112	4.28
1994	Cincinnati	50	65⅓	6	6	.500	63	28	46	2.48
1995	Cincinnati	56	70⅓	3	2	.600	62	20	53	2.82
	Totals	405	641	38	28	.576	509	267	556	3.12

TOP PROSPECTS

POKEY REESE 22 5-11 180 Bats R Throws R

Being groomed as shortstop Barry Larkin's successor . . . Hit only .239 in first season with Indianapolis (AAA), but will return there this season . . . Did hit 10 homers and drive in 46 runs in '95 . . . Real name is Calvin . . . Reds made him first-round pick in 1991 draft . . . Born June 10, 1973, in Columbia, S.C.

CHAD MOTTOLA 24 6-3 220 Bats R Throws R

Big outfielder has power potential . . . Hit 18 homers and drove in 76 runs while splitting season between Chattanooga (AA) and Indianapolis (AAA) in '95 . . . Led Carolina League with 91 RBI for Winston Salem (A) in '93 . . . Reds made him first-round pick in 1992, out of University of Central Florida . . . Born Oct. 15, 1971, in Augusta, Ga.

ERIC OWENS 25 6-1 185 Bats R Throws R

Enjoyed big year with Indianapolis (AAA) in '95 . . . Hit .314 and stole 33 bases . . . Also had 12 homers, 63 RBI and 44 extra-base hits, including eight triples . . . Originally was a shortstop . . . Was moved to second base . . . Reds made him fourth-round pick in 1992, out of Ferrum (Va.) College . . . Born Feb. 3, 1971, in Danville, Va.

GABE WHITE 24 6-2 200 Bats L Throws L

Acquired from Expos for Jhonny Carvajal last winter . . . Made 19 appearances, but only one start in 1995 and went 1-2 with 7.01 ERA for Montreal . . . Struck out 25 in 25⅔ innings, but also yielded seven home runs . . . In 12 starts for Ottawa (AAA), he was 2-3 with a 3.90 ERA . . . Went 1-1 with a 6.08 ERA in seven games with Expos in '94 . . . Spent most of '94 season with Ottawa, finishing with a 8-3 record and 5.05 ERA in 14 starts . . . Struck out 63 in 73 innings . . . Led organization with 176 strikeouts for Rockford (A) in '92 . . . Expos' sandwich-round pick in 1990 draft as compensation for the Angels signing free-agent Mark Langston . . . Born Nov. 20, 1971, in Sebring, Fla.

SCOTT SULLIVAN 25 6-4 215 **Bats R Throws R**

Closer prospect made big-league debut with Reds, posting 4.91 ERA in three games . . . Was 4-3 with 3.53 ERA for Indianapolis (AAA) . . . Struck out 54 and allowed 51 hits in 59 innings . . . Reds made him second-round pick in 1993, out of Auburn . . . Born March 13, 1971, in Tuscaloosa, Ala.

MANAGER RAY KNIGHT: Marge Schott's kind of guy . . .

Reds owner didn't want Davey Johnson back and told him so before '95 season . . . Never mind the fact that the Reds went on to win 85 games and division title and reached NLCS . . . At least he and Johnson were able to make the uncomfortable situation work, a tribute to their friendship . . . Johnson brought him in when he took over for Tony Perez in May 1993 . . . Had been working for ESPN since 1989 . . . Has no managerial experience, unless you count two games in Colorado in August, when Johnson was serving a suspension . . . Served as bench coach and hitting instructor under Johnson . . . Retired after 1988 season following solid 13-year career . . . Hit .271 with 84 homers in 1,495 games . . . Hard-nosed player . . . Played first six seasons in Cincinnati and also wore uniforms of Astros, Mets, Orioles and Tigers . . . Named to two NL All-Star teams . . . Was World Series MVP for Mets in 1986, hitting .391 . . . Also was NL Comeback Player of the Year in 1986 . . . Reds made him 10th-round draft choice in 1970 . . . Wife is golfing great Nancy Lopez . . . Born Dec. 28, 1952, in Albany, Ga.

ALL-TIME RED SEASON RECORDS

BATTING: Cy Seymour, .377, 1905
HRs: George Foster, 52, 1977
RBI: George Foster, 149, 1977
STEALS: Bob Bescher, 81, 1911
WINS: Adolfo Luque, 27, 1923
Bucky Walters, 27, 1939
STRIKEOUTS: Mario Soto, 274, 1982

HOUSTON ASTROS

TEAM DIRECTORY: Owner: Drayton McLane Jr.; GM: Gerry Hunsicker; Dir. Scouting: Dan O'Brien; Dir. Pub. Rel.: Rob Matwick; Trav. Sec.: Barry Waters; Mgr.: Terry Collins; Coaches: Matt Galante, Steve Henderson, Julio Linares, Rick Sweet, Brent Strom. Home: Astrodome (54,313). Field distances: 325, l.f. line; 375, l.c.; 400, c.f.; 375, r.c.; 325, r.f. line. Spring training: Kissimmee, Fla.

SCOUTING REPORT

HITTING: Even without Jeff Bagwell (.290, 21, 87) for 30 games and Derek Bell (.334, 8, 86) for 32 games, Terry Collins'

Broken hands are only things that stop Jeff Bagwell.

aggressive attack finished second in the NL in batting average (.275) and steals (176) and tied for second in runs (747).

The Astros dug deep into their pockets to make sure free-agent Craig Biggio (.302, 22, 77, 33 steals) didn't escape last winter. It's a good thing because 123 runs scored are not easy to replace for a team lacking in power, even with Biggio in the mix.

What Collins is going to need are dramatic improvements from young players Brian Hunter (.302, 2, 28, 24 steals), Orlando Miller (.262, 5, 36), Tony Eusebio (.299, 6, 58) and James Mouton (.262, 4, 27, 25 steals) to ignite his lineup in '96. The Astros also should get a boost from Sean Berry (.318, 14, 55 with the Expos).

PITCHING: The Astros have a built-in advantage here because they play their home games in the pitcher-friendly Astrodome. That translated into the NL's fifth-best team ERA (4.06) in 1995.

There is the basis for a solid rotation in Doug Drabek (10-9, 4.77), Shane Reynolds (10-11, 3.47), Mike Hampton (9-8, 3.35), Darryl Kile (4-12, 4.96), Greg Swindell (10-9, 4.47) and youngsters Donnie Wall and Billy Wagner. But any of the high-salaried guys might well be traded.

The bullpen could be aided by a return to health and form by 1994 closer John Hudek (2-2, 5.40, 7 saves), who had a circulatory problem. Todd Jones (6-5, 3.07, 15 saves) didn't grab the finisher's role, so veteran Mike Henneman was acquired for the '95 stretch run and then was not re-signed. Dave Veres (5-1, 2.26, 72 appearances) was a busy setup man, but he's now an Expo.

FIELDING: With several young players and so few everyday players, the Astros suffered from defensive inconsistencies. They dropped to a tie for ninth in the NL in fielding percentage and only the Pirates and Dodgers committed more errors.

On the plus side, Bagwell has made himself into one of the league's better first basemen, Biggio is remarkable at second, Berry will be adequate at third and Bell is rangy and has a strong arm in center field. Hunter and Mouton have plenty of speed to cover ground in left and right. The addition of Berry fills a hole at third.

OUTLOOK: The financial woes of owner Drayton McLane are so severe, he was seriously negotiating to sell the club following a 76-68 finish in '95. Former GM Bob Watson saw the red-ink writing on the wall and bailed out. Another anticipated result is a big downsizing of the Astros' payroll and record. Fortunately, the Astros are in a division with the rebuilding Cardinals and Pirates, so there always is the chance of a wild-card spot.

ASTRO PROFILES

CRAIG BIGGIO 30 5-11 180 Bats R Throws R

Came up big in Jeff Bagwell's absence, solidifying status as one of game's best all-around players . . . Stepped up home-run production to career-high 22 as he spent part of '95 season in No. 3 spot . . . Hit above .300 for second consecutive season (.302) and established career-best RBI total (77) . . . On-base percentage was lofty .406 . . . Has made four All-Star Game appearances in last five years . . . Only player to make it as both a catcher and second baseman . . . His conversion to second occurred in 1992 . . . Has stolen 30-plus bases in three of last four seasons since making the switch . . . Won Gold Gloves in '94 and '95 . . . Earned $4.6 million in 1994 and was re-signed to four-year, $22.4-million deal last winter. . . . Attended Seton Hall . . . Astros made him 22nd player chosen overall in 1987 draft . . . Born Dec. 14, 1965, in Smithtown, N.Y.

Year	Club	Pos.	G	AB	R	H	2B	3B	HR	RBI	SB	Avg.
1988	Houston	C	50	123	14	26	6	1	3	5	6	.211
1989	Houston	C-OF	134	443	64	114	21	2	13	60	21	.257
1990	Houston	C-OF	150	555	53	153	24	2	4	42	25	.276
1991	Houston	C-3B-OF	149	546	79	161	23	4	4	46	19	.295
1992	Houston	2B	162	613	96	170	32	3	6	39	38	.277
1993	Houston	2B	155	610	98	175	41	5	21	64	15	.287
1994	Houston	2B	114	437	88	139	44	5	6	56	39	.318
1995	Houston	2B	141	553	123	167	30	2	22	77	33	.302
	Totals		1055	3880	615	1105	221	24	79	389	196	.285

JEFF BAGWELL 27 6-0 205 Bats R Throws R

Another tough break of his left hand cost him and Astros dearly . . . This one happened same way as last one in '94, the result of being hit by a pitch . . . Astros swooned in his absence and just missed a wild-card spot . . . Despite missing 30 games, first baseman still hit 21 homers and drove in 87 runs . . . But those were big comedowns from '94, when he was unanimous choice for NL MVP . . . Batting average also dropped from .368 in 1994 to .290 last season . . . In '94, he was first player to finish first or second in his league in average, runs, RBI and homers since Carl Yastrzemski 27 years earlier . . . Also named to first All-Star Game and won first Gold Glove in '94 . . . Earned $6,875,000 in '95, first year of four-year, $27.5-million extension . . . Born May 27, 1968, in Boston . . . Chosen by Red

Sox in fourth round of 1989 draft, but sent to Astros in deal for Larry Andersen, Aug. 31, 1990.

Year	Club	Pos.	G	AB	R	H	2B	3B	HR	RBI	SB	Avg.
1991	Houston	1B	156	554	79	163	26	4	15	82	7	.294
1992	Houston	1B	162	586	87	160	34	6	18	96	10	.273
1993	Houston	1B	142	535	76	171	37	4	20	88	13	.320
1994	Houston	1B-OF	110	400	104	147	32	2	39	116	15	.368
1995	Houston	1B	114	448	88	130	29	0	21	87	12	.290
	Totals		684	2523	434	771	158	16	113	469	57	.306

DEREK BELL 27 6-2 205 Bats R Throws R

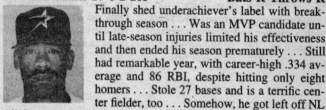

Finally shed underachiever's label with breakthrough season . . . Was an MVP candidate until late-season injuries limited his effectiveness and then ended his season prematurely . . . Still had remarkable year, with career-high .334 average and 86 RBI, despite hitting only eight homers . . . Stole 27 bases and is a terrific center fielder, too . . . Somehow, he got left off NL All-Star team . . . Hit .410 against left-handers . . . Saving grace for Astros in huge 11-player deal with Padres that cost them Ken Caminiti and Steve Finley prior to last season . . . Astros have little else to show for that one . . . Went to Padres from Blue Jays prior to 1993 season . . . Was Little League World Series teammate of Gary Sheffield . . . Earned $1.45 million in 1995 . . . Born Dec. 11, 1968, in Tampa . . . Signed by Toronto as second-round pick in 1987 draft.

Year	Club	Pos.	G	AB	R	H	2B	3B	HR	RBI	SB	Avg.
1991	Toronto	OF	18	28	5	4	0	0	0	1	3	.143
1992	Toronto	OF	61	161	23	39	6	3	2	15	7	.242
1993	San Diego	OF-3B	150	542	73	142	19	1	21	72	26	.262
1994	San Diego	OF	108	434	54	135	20	0	14	54	24	.311
1995	Houston	OF	112	452	63	151	21	2	8	86	27	.334
	Totals		449	1617	218	471	66	6	45	228	87	.291

TONY EUSEBIO 28 6-2 200 Bats R Throws R

Unheralded catcher has developed into a legitimate offensive force . . . Hit his way into regular job, batting .299 with 58 RBI in 368 at-bats . . . Threw out 30.5 percent of would-be base-stealers (29-of-95) . . . Hit .307 against right-handers and .312 on the road . . . Split time with Rick Wilkins and Pat Borders . . . Salary was $150,000 in 1995 . . . Split duties with Scott Servais in '94 . . . Batted .426 against lefties and .338

with runners on base that year . . . Rose slowly through Astros' chain . . . Spent seven seasons in minors before sticking in big leagues . . . Signed by Houston as non-drafted free agent in May 1985 . . . Born April 27, 1967, in San Jose de Los Llamos, D.R.

Year	Club	Pos.	G	AB	R	H	2B	3B	HR	RBI	SB	Avg.
1991	Houston	C	10	19	4	2	1	0	0	0	0	.105
1994	Houston	C	55	159	18	47	9	1	5	30	0	.296
1995	Houston	C	113	368	46	110	21	1	6	58	0	.299
	Totals		178	546	68	159	31	2	11	88	0	.291

SEAN BERRY 30 5-11 200 Bats R Throws R

Came to Astros from Expos in December trade for Dave Veres and Raul Chavez . . . Underrated third baseman . . . Set career high with 55 RBI and tied a personal best with 14 homers last year . . . Had a 12-game hitting streak in August, going 22-for-47 . . . Belted two home runs and tied a career high with six RBI against San Francisco Aug. 25 . . . Batted everywhere in lineup, except second, third or ninth . . . Hit leadoff for first time in career May 11 . . . Batted .300 with five home runs and 28 RBI in first half of the season . . . His .529 slugging percentage was best on the team . . . Committed 12 errors . . . Originally selected by Kansas City in first round of secondary phase in January 1986 draft . . . Born March 22, 1966, in Santa Monica, Cal. . . . Earned $285,000 last season.

Year	Club	Pos.	G	AB	R	H	2B	3B	HR	RBI	SB	Avg.
1990	Kansas City ...	3B	8	23	2	5	1	1	0	4	0	.217
1991	Kansas City ...	3B	31	60	5	8	3	0	0	1	0	.133
1992	Montreal	3B	24	57	5	19	1	0	1	4	2	.333
1993	Montreal	3B	122	299	50	78	15	2	14	49	12	.261
1994	Montreal	3B	103	320	43	89	19	2	11	41	14	.278
1995	Montreal	3B–1B	103	314	38	100	22	1	14	55	3	.318
	Totals		391	1073	143	299	61	6	40	154	31	.279

DOUG DRABEK 33 6-1 190 Bats R Throws R

Last season was a tough one for this durable veteran . . . ERA was highest of his fine 10-year career at 4.77, 1.60 runs per game higher than his career mark entering last season . . . Reached double figures in wins (10) for eighth time in nine years, but just barely . . . Three-year record in Houston is 31-33 . . . Not a very good return for Astros, who signed this free agent to a four-year, $19.5-million deal after '92 season . . .

Earned $5 million in 1995 . . . Endured 18-loss season in '93, when he deserved a better fate . . . Rebounded in '94, posting 2.84 ERA and finishing among NL's top 10 in five other categories . . . Was Pirates ace during their glory years of early 1990's . . . Named NL Cy Young Award winner in 1990, when he went 22-6 with 2.76 ERA . . . White Sox made him 11th-round pick in 1983 draft . . . Born July 25, 1962, in Victoria, Tex.

Year	Club	G	IP	W	L	Pct.	SO	BB	H	ERA
1986	New York (AL)	27	131⅔	7	8	.467	76	50	126	4.10
1987	Pittsburgh	29	176⅓	11	12	.478	120	46	165	3.88
1988	Pittsburgh	33	219⅓	15	7	.682	127	50	194	3.08
1989	Pittsburgh	35	244⅓	14	12	.538	123	69	215	2.80
1990	Pittsburgh	33	231⅓	22	6	.786	131	56	190	2.76
1991	Pittsburgh	35	234⅔	15	14	.517	142	62	245	3.07
1992	Pittsburgh	34	256⅔	15	11	.577	177	54	218	2.77
1993	Houston	34	237⅔	9	18	.333	157	60	242	3.79
1994	Houston	23	164⅔	12	6	.667	121	45	132	2.84
1995	Houston	31	185	10	9	.526	143	54	205	4.77
	Totals	314	2081⅔	130	103	.558	1317	546	1932	3.32

GREG SWINDELL 31 6-3 230 Bats R Throws L

Big lefty got to 10-win mark with two in last week of season . . . Found himself on trading block in midseason, as Astros were trying to shed salaries . . . There were no takers, not at the hefty price . . . His salary was $4,450,000 in '95, as part of four-year, $16-million deal he got as free agent after '92 season . . . Has gone 30-31 in Astros uniform . . . Allowed 180 hits in 153 innings last season and landed in bullpen for seven appearances . . . Strikeout-to-walk ratio (96-to-39) also fell off . . . Served up 21 homers . . . Has winning record in 10-year, big-league career, but nobody will say he overachieved . . . Only All-Star Game appearance came in 1989 . . . Won career-high 18 games for Cleveland in 1988 . . . Indians made him second pick overall in 1986 draft . . . Born Jan. 2, 1965, in Fort Worth, Tex.

Year	Club	G	IP	W	L	Pct.	SO	BB	H	ERA
1986	Cleveland	9	61⅔	5	2	.714	46	15	57	4.23
1987	Cleveland	16	102⅓	3	8	.273	97	37	112	5.10
1988	Cleveland	33	242	18	14	.563	180	45	234	3.20
1989	Cleveland	28	184⅓	13	6	.684	129	51	170	3.37
1990	Cleveland	34	214⅔	12	9	.571	135	47	245	4.40
1991	Cleveland	33	238	9	16	.360	169	31	241	3.48
1992	Cincinnati	31	213⅔	12	8	.600	138	41	210	2.70
1993	Houston	31	190⅓	12	13	.480	124	40	215	4.16
1994	Houston	24	148⅓	8	9	.471	74	26	175	4.37
1995	Houston	33	153	10	9	.526	96	39	180	4.47
	Totals	272	1748⅓	102	94	.520	1188	372	1839	3.80

SHANE REYNOLDS 28 6-3 210 Bats R Throws R

The record (10-11) doesn't say so, but he was Astros' best pitcher in '95 . . . Struck out 175 in 189⅓ innings, fourth-highest total in NL . . . His 8.3 strikeouts per nine innings ranked third in NL . . . Walked only 1.76 per nine innings, second in league to the Braves' Greg Maddux . . . Earned $175,000 in 1995 . . . Finished fifth in NL in ERA in '94, his first full season in majors . . . Went 8-5 splitting time between rotation and bullpen . . . In first start that year, he retired first 15 batters he faced . . . Made big-league debut in 1992 and went 1-3 in eight appearances . . . Astros made him third-round pick in 1989 draft . . . Pitched one season for University of Texas . . . Born March 26, 1968, in Bastrop, La.

Year	Club	G	IP	W	L	Pct.	SO	BB	H	ERA
1992	Houston	8	25⅓	1	3	.250	10	6	42	7.11
1993	Houston	5	11	0	0	.000	10	6	11	0.82
1994	Houston	33	124	8	5	.615	110	21	128	3.05
1995	Houston	30	189⅓	10	11	.476	175	37	196	3.47
	Totals	76	349⅔	19	19	.500	305	70	377	3.50

JOHN HUDEK 29 6-1 200 Bats S Throws R

Injury ended hard-throwing closer's season early . . . Went on disabled list June 23 and had surgery to fix blocked vein in right arm . . . Is expected to recover in time for start of '96 season . . . Converted 7-of-9 save opportunities in '95 before injury . . . Struck out 29 and walked only five in 20 innings . . . Right-handers hit only .159 against him . . . Salary was $185,000 in 1995 . . . Rags-to-riches story of 1994 . . . Became only the fifth player in big-league history to start a season in the minors and be named to the All-Star team, joining Don Newcombe, Don Schwall, Bill Dawley and Alvin Davis . . . Claimed by Houston off waivers from Detroit, June 29, 1993 . . . Bounced around White Sox chain for five years . . . Born Aug. 8, 1966, in Tampa . . . White Sox drafted him in 10th round in 1988, out of Florida Southern . . . Has career total of 23 saves.

Year	Club	G	IP	W	L	Pct.	SO	BB	H	ERA
1994	Houston	42	39⅓	0	2	.000	39	18	24	2.97
1995	Houston	19	20	2	2	.500	29	5	19	5.40
	Totals	61	59⅓	2	4	.667	68	23	43	3.78

DARRYL KILE 27 6-5 195 **Bats R Throws R**

If there is a more exasperating pitcher in big leagues, Terry Collins doesn't want to manage him . . . Great stuff, especially a wicked breaking ball, but has had command in only one season, 1993, when he went 15-8 . . . Landed in minors last season, bottoming out at 4-12, 4.96 . . . Walked 73 in 127 innings . . . Also threw 11 wild pitches and was second in league with 12 hit batsmen . . . Salary was $1,272,500 in '95 . . . Led NL with 82 walks in 1994 . . . Allowed only 152 hits in 171⅔ innings in '93, when he also pitched a no-hitter on Sept. 8 against New York . . . Also had nine-game winning streak that year and was Astros' lone All-Star representative . . . Astros' 30th-round pick in 1987 draft . . . Born Dec. 2, 1968, in Garden Grove, Cal.

Year	Club	G	IP	W	L	Pct.	SO	BB	H	ERA
1991	Houston	37	153⅔	7	11	.389	100	84	144	3.69
1992	Houston	22	125⅓	5	10	.333	90	63	124	3.95
1993	Houston	32	171⅔	15	8	.652	141	69	152	3.51
1994	Houston	24	147⅔	9	6	.600	105	82	153	4.57
1995	Houston	25	127	4	12	.250	113	73	114	4.96
	Totals	140	725⅓	40	47	.460	539	371	687	4.09

MIKE HAMPTON 23 5-10 180 **Bats R Throws L**

Promising youngster is about to blossom into front-line starter . . . Has command of pitches and savvy beyond the norm . . . Allowed only 141 hits in 150⅔ innings . . . Opponents hit only .247 against him, 11th-lowest mark in NL . . . Earned $135,000 in '95 . . . Spent all of 1994 with Astros at age 21 . . . Pitched only in relief . . . Allowed only 8-of-27 inherited runners to score . . . Astros stole him from Mariners with Mike Felder for Eric Anthony prior to 1994 season . . . First surfaced with Mariners at age 20 in 1993, when he struggled miserably . . . Had 9.53 ERA and allowed 35 base-runners in 17 innings . . . Mariners' sixth-round pick in 1990 draft . . . Born Sept. 9, 1972, in Brooksville, Fla.

Year	Club	G	IP	W	L	Pct.	SO	BB	H	ERA
1993	Seattle	13	17	1	3	.250	8	17	28	9.53
1994	Houston	44	41⅓	2	1	.667	24	16	46	3.70
1995	Houston	24	150⅔	9	8	.529	115	49	141	3.35
	Totals	81	209	12	12	.500	147	82	215	3.92

TOP PROSPECTS

BILLY WAGNER 24 5-11 180 **Bats L Throws L**
Hard thrower is a prospect everybody would like to have . . . Was 7-5 combined for Jackson (AA) and Tucson (AAA) in '95 before late-season promotion to Astros . . . Struck out 157 in 146 minor-league innings in '95 . . . Fanned 204 in 153 innings for Quad City (A) in 1994, his first full minor-league season . . . Astros made him their first pick in 1993 draft, out of tiny Ferrum College . . . Born June 25, 1971, in Tannersville, Va.

BOB ABREU 22 6-0 170 **Bats L Throws R**
Hit .304 with 10 homers, 75 RBI and 17 triples for Tucson (AAA) in '95 . . . Has been one of youngest players in his league each of last two years . . . Speedy outfielder also hit 17 triples for Osceola (A) in '93 . . . Born March 11, 1974, in Aragua, Venezuela . . . Signed by Astros as non-drafted free agent in August 1990.

DONNIE WALL 28 6-1 185 **Bats R Throws R**
Veteran minor leaguer was big winner for Tucson (AAA) in '95 . . . Went 17-6 with 3.30 ERA before late-season recall . . . Went 3-1, 5.55 for Astros . . . Not overpowering, he relies on control . . . Has posted double-figure win totals in four of last five minor-league seasons . . . Astros' 18th-round pick in 1989 draft . . . Born July 11, 1967, in Potosi, Mo.

RICHARD HIDALGO 20 6-2 175 **Bats R Throws R**
Quick-rising young outfielder has loads of potential . . . Hit .266 with 14 homers and 59 RBI for Jackson (AA), playing most of the season at age 19 . . . Set Midwest League record with 47 doubles for Quad City (A) in 1994 . . . Signed by Astros as non-drafted free agent in July 1991, the day he turned 16 . . . Born July 2, 1975, in Caracas, Venezuela.

MANAGER TERRY COLLINS: Tough year for manager caught in tough spot . . . Ownership is losing tons of money and trying to shed salaries, but still expecting postseason appearances . . . Had to mix-and-match lineup because of injuries, particularly one to Jeff Bagwell . . . Followed up 66-49 finish in '94 with 76-68 mark, falling one game short of wild-card spot . . . His big-league managerial record is 142-117 . . . Spunky little guy who isn't afraid to speak his mind . . . Criticized the home-run propensity of Coors Field, calling the Rockies' new park "a joke" . . . Jim Leyland recommended him for the Astros' job, and as usual, Leyland was right . . . Worked his way up to Leyland's staff with long and successful minor-league managing career . . . His Triple-A record was 824-736 . . . Posted three consecutive 80-win seasons for Buffalo from 1989-91 . . . Served as Pirates bullpen coach in 1992 . . . Also managed in Dodgers system for eight seasons . . . Was named PCL Manager of the Year in 1988 at Albuquerque (AAA) . . . Former infielder never played in big leagues . . . Born May 27, 1949, in Midland, Mich. . . . Was 19th-round pick of Dodgers in 1971 draft, out of Eastern Michigan.

ALL-TIME ASTRO SEASON RECORDS

BATTING: Jeff Bagwell, .368, 1994
HRs: Jeff Bagwell, 39, 1994
RBI: Jeff Bagwell, 116, 1994
STEALS: Gerald Young, 65, 1988
WINS: Joe Niekro, 21, 1979
STRIKEOUTS: J. R. Richard, 313, 1979

PITTSBURGH PIRATES

TEAM DIRECTORY: Owner: Kevin McClatchy; Pres/CEO: Mark Sauer; GM: Cam Bonifay; Dir. Media Rel.: Jim Trdinich; Trav. Sec. Greg Johnson; Mgr.: Jim Leyland; Coaches: Rich Donnelly, Gene Lamont, Milt May, Ray Miller, Tommy Sandt, Spin Williams. Home: Three Rivers Stadium (49,972). Field distances: 335, l.f. line; 375, l.c.; 400, c.f.; 375, r.c.; 335, r.f. line. Spring training: Bradenton, Fla.

SCOUTING REPORT

HITTING: The division-winning days of Barry Bonds and Bobby Bonilla have never seemed so distant. Today, the Pirates are about Jacob Brumfield and Midre Cummings—and it could get uglier. Pittsburgh, ranked 11th in the NL with 629 runs in '95, still has some talent.

Jeff King played three infield positions while hitting a career-high 18 home runs last season. Don Slaught hit a career-high .304, but escaped via free agency. Carlos Garcia batted .294 and was third on the club with 50 RBI. Orlando Merced batted .300 with 15 home runs and drove in a career-high 83 RBI and Jay Bell (.262, 13, 55) is a pro's pro.

But, after King, Garcia, Merced and Bell, there isn't much else. The Pirates don't have enough power or speed to compete with the big boys. Brumfield (.271, 22 steals) has good speed, free-agent addition Mike Kingery (.269, 8, 37 with Colorado) makes contact and Al Martin (.282, 13, 41) has power potential. Still, Pittsburgh doesn't have enough stars in its lineup, its bench is weak and its best players are aging quickly.

PITCHING: The Pirates' pitching staff makes it so the offense has to score five runs a game just to stay close. Stick Denny Neagle on, say, the Indians and he could win 20 games. The fact that he went 13-8 with his 3.43 ERA last year for the Pirates is nothing short of a miracle. He was the only Pirate to win more than eight games. The Pirates' staff ranked 12th in the NL in ERA at 4.70 and second in most hits allowed (1,407).

Paul Wagner (5-16, 4.80) was perhaps the Pirates' second-best pitcher and, if he had not been pulled from the starting rotation twice during the year, he would have probably lost 20 games. Esteban Loaiza (8-9, 5.16) is emerging as a solid starter and Jon Lieber (4-7, 6.32), the Pirates' Opening Day starter in 1995, will

Workhorse Denny Neagle won 13 of Bucs' 58 last season.

be given another chance to win a job in the rotation. Closer Dan Miceli (4-4, 4.66, 21 saves) may be the Pirates' best pitcher, but he needs opportunities to work at his craft.

FIELDING: Bad hitting, bad pitching and yes, weak fielding. Only the Dodgers committed more errors than the Pirates (122) last season. Three of the Pirates' best players—shortstop Bell, first baseman King and second baseman Garcia—combined for 46 miscues. They are better than that—especially Bell. On the plus side, Pittsburgh has plenty of speed in the outfield.

OUTLOOK: There is hope on the way, in the form of new ownership. But until the Pirates spend money, they simply can't expect to be more competitive than last year's 58-86 edition. Jim Leyland is a great manager, but even a great manager can't get a .500 record out of a dreadfully bad team.

PIRATE PROFILES

JAY BELL 30 6-0 181 Bats R Throws R

Backbone of the Pirates . . . Was Pittsburgh's Opening Day shortstop for seventh straight season . . . Ranked third among NL shortstops with .978 fielding percentage . . . Was batting as low as .198 after 50 games, but went 102-for-343 (.297) over his final 88 games . . . Had a career-best, 44-game errorless streak from May 27-July 19 . . . Made first career start at third base June 27 and started three games there in '95 . . . Collected 1,000th career hit July 25, off the Braves' Tom Glavine . . . Batted .306 vs. lefties . . . Led club with 42 multi-hit games . . . Was second on team in hits (139), behind Orlando Merced . . . His 110 strikeouts were sixth-highest total in NL . . . Won only Gold Glove in '93, snapping Ozzie Smith's 13-year reign, and he batted career-high .310 that season . . . Owns a lifetime .282 batting average in three NLCS . . . Acquired by Pirates from Indians for Felix Fermin prior to '89 season . . . Twins drafted him eighth overall in 1984 . . . Born Dec. 11, 1965, at Eglin AFB, Fla. . . . Earned $4.4 million last season.

Year	Club	Pos.	G	AB	R	H	2B	3B	HR	RBI	SB	Avg.
1986	Cleveland	2B	5	14	3	5	2	0	1	4	0	.357
1987	Cleveland	SS	38	125	14	27	9	1	2	13	2	.216
1988	Cleveland	SS	73	211	23	46	5	1	2	21	4	.218
1989	Pittsburgh	SS	78	271	33	70	13	3	2	27	5	.258
1990	Pittsburgh	SS	159	583	93	148	28	7	7	52	10	.254
1991	Pittsburgh	SS	157	608	96	164	32	8	16	67	10	.270
1992	Pittsburgh	SS	159	632	87	167	36	6	9	55	7	.264
1993	Pittsburgh	SS	154	604	102	187	32	9	9	51	16	.310
1994	Pittsburgh	SS	110	424	68	117	35	4	9	45	2	.276
1995	Pittsburgh	SS-3B	138	530	79	139	28	4	13	55	2	.262
	Totals		1071	4002	598	1070	220	43	70	390	58	.267

CARLOS GARCIA 28 6-1 193 Bats R Throws R

Versatile infielder emerged as one of the Pirates' most consistent offensive threats . . . Set career marks in batting average (.294) and RBI (50) . . . Made 89 starts at second base and 12 at shortstop . . . Made debut at short June 11 vs. Marlins . . . Had career-best, 21-game hitting streak from June 5-27 . . . It was second-longest streak in NL, behind 23-gamer of Colorado's Dante Bichette . . . Began September with 15-game hitting streak . . . Had a career-best six RBI, vs. Dodgers June 15 . . . Batted safely in 23 of 26 games in June . . . Batted in the cleanup spot for the first time, Aug. 19 vs. Florida . . . Hit .315 at Three Rivers Stadium . . . Became an All-Star in 1994 . . . In '93, he ranked third among NL rookies with 147 hits and ranked fifth among NL second basemen with .983 fielding percentage . . . Signed as non-drafted free agent by Pirates in January 1987 . . . Born Oct. 15, 1967, in Tachira, Venezuela . . . Earned $250,000 last year.

Year	Club	Pos.	G	AB	R	H	2B	3B	HR	RBI	SB	Avg.
1990	Pittsburgh	SS	4	4	1	2	0	0	0	0	0	.500
1991	Pittsburgh	SS-3B-2B	12	24	2	6	0	2	0	1	0	.250
1992	Pittsburgh	2B-SS	22	39	4	8	1	0	0	4	0	.205
1993	Pittsburgh	2B-SS	141	546	77	147	25	5	12	47	18	.269
1994	Pittsburgh	2B	98	412	49	114	15	2	6	28	18	.277
1995	Pittsburgh	2B-SS	104	367	41	108	24	2	6	50	8	.294
	Totals		381	1392	174	385	65	11	24	130	44	.277

JEFF KING 31 6-1 187 Bats R Throws R

Finally flexed a little muscle . . . His 18 home runs led Pirates and were a career high . . . Made 80 starts at third base, but also played first, second and short . . . Collected at least one RBI in seven consecutive games from May 5-12 . . . Was batting .310 with six homers and 34 RBI after his first 32 games . . . Went on disabled list June 16 with sprained left wrist . . . Became 16th National League player to hit two home runs in the same inning, Aug. 8 against the Giants . . . Matched career best with four hits, Aug. 31 vs. the Reds . . . Ranked second in NL with eight sacrifice flies . . . Averaged one RBI per 5.1 at-bats, the ninth-best ratio in league . . . Committed 10 fielding errors and seven throwing errors . . . In '94, it took him 136 at-bats before producing his first home run . . . Was demoted to Buffalo (AAA) for seven games in 1992 . . . Pirates made him top overall pick in 1986 draft, out of Arkansas . . . Born Nov. 26, 1964, in Marion, Ind. . . . Earned $2.16 million last season and re-signed with Pirates for two years at $5 million last winter.

Year	Club	Pos.	G	AB	R	H	2B	3B	HR	RBI	SB	Avg.
1989	Pittsburgh	1B-3B-2B-SS	75	215	31	42	13	3	5	19	4	.195
1990	Pittsburgh	3B-1B	127	371	46	91	17	1	14	53	3	.245
1991	Pittsburgh	3B	33	109	16	26	1	1	4	18	3	.239
1992	Pittsburgh	3B-2B-1B-SS-OF	130	480	56	111	21	2	14	65	4	.231
1993	Pittsburgh	3B-2B-SS	158	611	82	180	35	3	9	98	8	.295
1994	Pittsburgh	3B-2B	94	339	36	89	23	0	5	42	3	.263
1995	Pittsburgh	3B-1B-2B-SS	122	445	61	118	27	2	18	87	7	.265
	Totals		739	2570	328	657	137	12	69	382	32	.256

AL MARTIN 28 6-2 215 **Bats L Throws L**

Steady outfielder with promising bat . . . Batted .329 in 66 games following All-Star break . . . Hit .231 in 58 first-half games . . . Made 73 starts in left field and 32 in center . . . Had eight outfield assists . . . Swiped a career-high 20 bases in 31 attempts . . . Finished last year with four leadoff home runs . . . Hit safely in 50 of final 70 games (.335) and scored 42 runs . . . Had a career-best, 12-game hitting streak from July 4-25 . . . Suffered season-ending left wrist injury, July 11, 1994, and underwent surgery to repair ligament and cartilage damage . . . Led all NL rookies in runs in '93 and ranked second among NL rookies in home runs, behind the Dodgers' Mike Piazza . . . Braves drafted him in eighth round in 1985 . . . Nicknamed "Little Hurt" . . . Signed by Pirates as minor-league free agent prior to 1992 season . . . Born Nov. 24, 1967, in West Covina, Cal. . . . Earned $375,000 last season.

Year	Club	Pos.	G	AB	R	H	2B	3B	HR	RBI	SB	Avg.
1992	Pittsburgh	OF	12	12	1	2	0	1	0	2	0	.167
1993	Pittsburgh	OF	143	480	85	135	26	8	18	64	16	.281
1994	Pittsburgh	OF	82	276	48	79	12	4	9	33	15	.286
1995	Pittsburgh	OF	124	439	70	124	25	3	13	41	20	.282
	Totals		361	1207	204	340	63	16	40	140	51	.282

MIDRE CUMMINGS 24 6-0 199 **Bats L Throws R**

Pirates want him to win an outfield job . . . Drove in 15 runs in two tours with Bucs . . . Began last season in Pittsburgh, but was optioned to Calgary (AAA) after seven games . . . Batted .277 with one homer and 16 RBI in 45 games with Calgary . . . Was recalled July 26 . . . Hit safely in career-best six straight games from Sept. 17-25 . . . Made 19 starts in center field, nine in right and five in left . . . Was 8-for-23 (.348) as a pinch-hitter . . . Blasted first major-league homer, July 31, 1994, off Mets' Juan Castillo . . . Acquired by Pirates from Twins with Denny Neagle for John Smiley prior to 1992 season . . . Minnesota drafted him in first round in 1990 . . . Born Oct. 14, 1971, in St. Croix, V.I. . . . Earned pro-rated $109,000 last year.

Year	Club	Pos.	G	AB	R	H	2B	3B	HR	RBI	SB	Avg.
1993	Pittsburgh	OF	13	36	5	4	1	0	0	3	0	.111
1994	Pittsburgh	OF	24	86	11	21	4	0	1	12	0	.244
1995	Pittsburgh	OF	59	152	13	37	7	1	2	15	1	.243
	Totals		96	274	29	62	12	1	3	30	1	.226

Orlando Merced, veteran Pirate survivor, is thriving.

ORLANDO MERCED 29 5-11 191 Bats L Throws R

One of Pirates' most consistent performers . . . Enjoyed career year in '95 . . . Posted career highs in home runs (15), RBI (83), hits (146), doubles (29) and at-bats (487) . . . Batted .300 for second time in three years . . . Made 100 starts in right field . . . Hit safely in 12 straight games from April 28-May 18 . . . Matched career high with four hits, May 21 vs. Padres and Sept. 19 vs. St. Louis . . . Had first career two-homer game, June 1 vs. Reds . . . Batted .336 with runners in scoring position and

.417 (5-for-12) with the bases loaded . . . Committed all six of his errors in right . . . In '94, he led Pirates in RBI . . . Finished ninth in NL in batting average and ranked fourth with .414 on-base percentage in 1993 . . . Signed by Pirates as non-drafted free agent in February 1985 . . . Born Nov. 2, 1966, in San Juan, P.R. . . . Earned $2 million in 1995 and was re-signed to two-year, $5.4-million deal last winter.

Year	Club	Pos.	G	AB	R	H	2B	3B	HR	RBI	SB	Avg.
1990	Pittsburgh	OF-C	25	24	3	5	1	0	0	0	0	.208
1991	Pittsburgh	1B-OF	120	411	83	113	17	2	10	50	8	.275
1992	Pittsburgh	1B-OF	134	405	50	100	28	5	6	60	5	.247
1993	Pittsburgh	OF-1B	137	447	68	140	26	4	8	70	3	.313
1994	Pittsburgh	OF-1B	108	386	48	105	21	3	9	51	4	.272
1995	Pittsburgh	OF-1B	132	487	75	146	29	4	15	83	7	.300
	Totals		656	2160	327	609	122	18	48	314	27	.282

ESTEBAN LOAIZA 24 6-4 190 Bats R Throws R

Grew up hard way, as decent pitcher on mediocre staff in '95 . . . Led NL in runs allowed (115) and earned runs (99) surrendered . . . Tied for sixth in wins (8) among NL rookies . . . Tied for NL lead in games started (31) . . . Picked up win in major-league debut, April 29 against Phillies . . . Did not win again until June 10 . . . Won four straight decisions from June 20-July 9 . . . Tossed first complete game July 9 vs. Mets . . . Was 6-3 with 5.12 ERA in 16 games prior to the All-Star break . . . Beat Rockies Aug. 22, but lost his final four decisions . . . Began '94 season on disabled list while recovering from shoulder surgery and finished it 10-5 with 3.79 ERA in 24 starts for Carolina (AA) . . . Signed by Pirates as non-drafted free agent in March 1991 . . . Born Dec. 31, 1971, in Tijuana, Mexico . . . Earned major-league minimum of $109,000 last season.

Year	Club	G	IP	W	L	Pct.	SO	BB	H	ERA
1995	Pittsburgh	32	172⅔	8	9	.471	85	55	205	5.16

DENNY NEAGLE 27 6-2 216 Bats L Throws L

The Pirates' best pitcher posted career highs in nearly every category . . . Tied for NL lead in games started (31) and innings (209⅔) . . . Gave up league-high 221 hits . . . Led staff in strikeouts (150) for second straight season and ranked eighth in league . . . Ranked fourth in NL in complete games (5) . . . Was league's first 10-game winner . . . Named to his first

All-Star team and pitched scoreless inning . . . Tossed his first major-league shutout by holding the Expos to two hits, June 23 . . . Won career-best five straight games from May 12-June 1 . . . Went 4-4 with 3.63 ERA in his final 15 starts . . . Set career high with 10 strikeouts vs. Giants, Sept. 16 . . . Pirates were 18-13 when he started . . . Posted third-best walks-per-nine-inning ratio in NL at 1.9 . . . Allowed 24 first-inning runs . . . Acquired by Pirates from Twins with Midre Cummings for John Smiley prior to '92 season . . . Born Sept. 13, 1968, in Gambrills, Md. . . . Earned $720,000 last year . . . Twins chose him in third round of 1989 draft.

Year	Club	G	IP	W	L	Pct.	SO	BB	H	ERA
1991	Minnesota	7	20	0	1	.000	14	7	28	4.05
1992	Pittsburgh	55	86⅓	4	6	.400	77	43	81	4.48
1993	Pittsburgh	50	81⅓	3	5	.375	73	37	82	5.31
1994	Pittsburgh	24	137	9	10	.474	122	49	135	5.12
1995	Pittsburgh	31	209⅔	13	8	.619	150	45	221	3.43
	Totals	167	534⅓	29	30	.492	436	181	547	4.35

DAN MICELI 25 6-0 207 — Bats R Throws R

Emerged as club's most dependable reliever . . . Led team with 21 saves, most by Pirate since Bill Landrum saved 26 games in 1989 . . . Allowed 11-of-25 inherited runners to score and blew six save opportunities . . . Posted seven saves in eight chances and 1.42 ERA in first 14 appearances . . . Picked up a save in four consecutive games from July 12-18 . . . Surrendered five home runs in first 27 games . . . Made 27 straight appearances (26⅔ innings) without giving up a home run from July 12-Sept. 17 . . . Began to tire in final month . . . Was scored upon in seven of last nine outings . . . Pitched 58 games . . . Acquired by Pirates from Kansas City with Jon Lieber for Stan Belinda, July 31, 1993 . . . Signed as non-drafted free agent by Royals in March 1990 . . . Born Sept. 9, 1970, in Newark, N.J. . . . Earned $125,000 last year.

Year	Club	G	IP	W	L	Pct.	SO	BB	H	ERA
1993	Pittsburgh	9	5⅓	0	0	.000	4	3	6	5.06
1994	Pittsburgh	28	27⅓	2	1	.667	27	11	28	5.93
1995	Pittsburgh	58	58	4	4	.500	56	28	61	4.66
	Totals	95	90⅔	6	5	.545	87	42	95	5.06

PAUL WAGNER 28 6-1 202 **Bats R Throws R**

Pitched better than 5-16 record indicated . . . Had third-lowest ERA (4.80) among Pirates starters . . . Was 1-10 by Aug. 1 . . . Finished second on club in strikeouts (120) for second straight year . . . Came within one out of tossing no-hitter, Aug. 29 vs. Rockies . . . Andres Galarraga broke it up with infield single . . . Allowed 96 runs, eighth-highest total in NL . . . Set career high with three complete games . . . Collected one save in eight relief appearances . . . Pirates' 12th-round pick in 1989 draft . . . Born Nov. 14, 1967, in Milwaukee . . . Earned $225,000 last season.

Year	Club	G	IP	W	L	Pct.	SO	BB	H	ERA
1992	Pittsburgh	6	13	2	0	1.000	5	5	9	0.69
1993	Pittsburgh	44	141⅓	8	8	.500	114	42	143	4.27
1994	Pittsburgh	29	119⅔	7	8	.467	86	50	136	4.59
1995	Pittsburgh	33	165	5	16	.238	120	72	174	4.80
	Totals	112	439	22	32	.407	325	169	462	4.45

TOP PROSPECTS

JASON KENDALL 21 6-0 170 **Bats R Throws R**

Pittsburgh's catcher of the future . . . Was organization's Minor League Player of the Year . . . All-around talent was top-rated prospect in Southern League . . . Finished second in batting with .326 average for Carolina (AA) with eight home runs, 71 RBI, 26 doubles and 10 stolen bases . . . Terrific arm . . . Father Fred is former major-league catcher . . . Set since-broken national record with 43-game hitting streak in high school . . . Batted .318 with seven home runs and 66 RBI for Salem (A) in '94 . . . Pirates drafted him 23rd overall in 1992 draft . . . Born June 16, 1974, in San Diego.

TREY BEAMON 22 6-3 195 **Bats L Throws R**

Gifted outfielder will compete for a job in 1996 . . . Raw talent . . . Mostly a singles and doubles hitter . . . Needs to improve defensively . . . Rated as one of top 10 players in Pacific Coast League as he batted .334 with five home runs, 62 RBI, 29 doubles and 39 walks for Calgary (AAA) . . . Led Southern League in batting with .323 average in '94, when he finished with five home runs, 47 RBI and 69 runs for Carolina (AA) . . . Pirates' second-round pick in 1992 draft . . . Born Feb. 11, 1974, in Dallas.

JERMAINE ALLENSWORTH 24 5-11 180 B: R T: R
Solid outfielder and emerging hitter . . . Split time between Carolina (AA) and Calgary (AAA) last season . . . Batted .269 with one homer and 14 RBI for Carolina and .316 with three home runs and 11 RBI in 190 at-bats for Calgary . . . Dangerous on basepaths . . . Stole total of 26 bases and scored 83 runs . . . Batted .241 for Carolina in 1994 . . . Pirates made him first-round supplemental pick in 1993 draft . . . Born Jan. 11, 1972, in Anderson, Ind.

RICH AUDE 24 6-5 209 Bats R Throws R
Power-hitting first baseman began last season with Pirates . . . Hit first major-league home run, May 18 off Dodgers' Todd Williams . . . Batted .248 with two home runs and 19 RBI in 42 games with Pirates . . . Optioned to Calgary (AAA) July 1 . . . Batted .333 with nine home runs and 42 RBI there . . . Recalled Sept. 5 . . . Led Calgary with 15 home runs and 79 RBI in first full season in Triple-A, in '94 . . . Started '93 season at Carolina (AA), but was promoted after belting 18 home runs and driving in 73 runs in 120 games . . . Collected his first hit and RBI with a pinch-hit single off Cardinals' Tom Urbani, Sept. 17, 1993 . . . Pirates made him second-round pick in 1989 draft . . . Born July 13, 1971, in Van Nuys, Cal.

MANAGER JIM LEYLAND: Regarded as one of the top managers in baseball and the epitome of a players' manager . . . Doesn't have the players to compete, but would never use that as an excuse . . . In his 11th season as Pittsburgh skipper, he finished 58-86, worst record in the NL and third worst in majors . . . Signed long-term contract extension after last season . . . Passed Chuck Tanner to become third-winningest manager in Pirate history behind Fred Clarke (1,422) and Danny Murtaugh (1,115) . . . Named NL Manager of the Year in 1990 and 1992 . . . Pirates won three straight Eastern Division

crowns from 1990-92 . . . Won division title after losing Bobby Bonilla to free agency prior to 1992 season . . . Was minor-league catcher . . . Started managing in the Tigers' farm system in 1971 . . . Became Pirates manager in 1986, after serving four seasons as White Sox coach under Tony La Russa . . . Born Dec. 15, 1944, in Toledo, Ohio . . . Overall managerial record is 778-774.

ALL-TIME PIRATE SEASON RECORDS

BATTING: Arky Vaughan, .385, 1935
HRs: Ralph Kiner, 54, 1949
RBI: Paul Waner, 131, 1927
STEALS: Omar Moreno, 96, 1980
WINS: Jack Chesbro, 28, 1902
STRIKEOUTS: Bob Veale, 276, 1965

(St. Louis awaited approval of new ownership at press time.)

ST. LOUIS CARDINALS

TEAM DIRECTORY: Chairman: August A. Busch III; Pres.: Mark Lamping; GM: Walt Jocketty; Spec. Asst. to GM: Red Schoendienst; Dir. Player Dev.: Mike Jorgensen; Dir. Media Services: Brian Bartow; Trav. Sec.: C.J. Cherre; Mgr.: Tony La Russa; Coaches: Dave Duncan, Mark DeJohn, George Hendrick, Ron Hassey, Dave McKay, Tommie Reynolds. Home: Busch Stadium (57,700). Field distances: 330, l.f. line; 402, c.f.; 330, r.f. line. Spring training: St. Petersburg, Fla.

SCOUTING REPORT

HITTING: If you want to know the biggest reason for the Cardinals' fall, look here. They were last in the NL in batting average (.247) and runs (563), the latter by a huge margin, and were next-to-the-bottom in home runs (107). The power problem

Bernard Gilkey bounced back to reach .300 for third time.

was addressed with the signing of free-agent Ron Gant (.276, 29, 85, 23 steals with the Reds) and free-agent Gary Gaetti (.261, 35, 96 with the Royals) last winter.

The outfield trio of Ray Lankford (.277, 25, 82, 24 steals), Brian Jordan (.296, 22, 81, 24 steals) and Bernard Gilkey (.298, 17, 69) offers a good combination of power and speed. The problem was, they combined for 64 of the Cards' 107 homers and 60 of the team's 79 steals.

The measly stolen-base total is the biggest difference between this team and Whitey Herzog's Cardinal teams that reached the World Series in the 1980s. Adding Royce Clayton (24 steals with the Giants) should help some, but the re-enlisting of aging former Card Willie McGee (.285 with the Red Sox) is an exercise in nostalgia.

PITCHING: Ken Hill was dealt to the Indians last summer and Allen Watson was sent to the Giants last winter, but there is a semblance of a competitive rotation with Andy Benes (11-9, 4.76, 171 strikeouts with the Padres and Mariners), the re-signed Mike Morgan (7-7, 3.56), Mark Petkovsek (6-6, 4.00), a healthy Danny Jackson (2-12, 5.90) and Donovan Osborne (4-6, 3.81). There also is top prospect Alan Benes (1-2, 8.44), who surfaced late last season.

Veteran closer Tom Henke (1-1, 1.82, 36 saves) was every bit as good of a free-agent signing in '95 as Jackson was bad. But Henke was unsigned at press time. John Habyan (3-2, 2.88) and Jeff Parrett (4-7, 3.64), who re-signed as a free agent, are quality setup men and so is AL import Rick Honeycutt (5-1, 2.96 with the Athletics and Yankees), the lefty specialist. Brian Barber (2-1, 5.22) and John Frascatore (1-1, 4.41) are promising young right-handers.

FIELDING: Jordan's development as an everyday right fielder gives the Cards a speedy outfield with strong throwing arms all around. John Mabry hit .307 as a rookie and could fit in at first base or in the outfield. Shortstop Ozzie Smith's run of Gold Glove awards has ended and he could wind up caddying for the newly acquired Clayton. David Bell took over the second-base job late last season and adjusted fairly well, considering he had been a third baseman in the minors. Tom Pagnozzi is one of the league's better defensive catchers.

OUTLOOK: Even with Tony La Russa, one of the game's best managers at the helm in '96, it's tough to be too optimistic about this franchise on the block. August Busch III, son of the great

August Busch Jr., is treating this St. Louis institution like a poor-selling product and is anxious to unload it.

At least the payroll hasn't been chopped too far for the Cards, 62-81 in '95, to be competitive.

CARDINAL PROFILES

OZZIE SMITH 41 5-10 170 Bats S Throws R

The end is near for "The Wizard", but there's no denying his place in history . . . The finest-fielding shortstop of his generation and arguably of all time . . . Shoulder injury cost him most of 1995 season . . . Played in only 44 games . . . Ended streak of consecutive 100-plus-hit seasons at 17 . . . Hit a career-low .199, just .143 against left-handers . . . His 31 hits brought his career total to 2,396—not bad for a guy who many said would never make it because of a weak bat . . . All-time assist leader among shortstops and one of only four players with more than 8,000 assists . . . Nobody has made more acrobatic and artistic plays at shortstop . . . Streak of All-Star Game appearances ended at 13 . . . Salary was $3 million in 1995 . . . Padres' fourth-round pick in 1977 draft . . . Traded to Cards for Garry Templeton prior to 1982 season . . . Born Dec. 26, 1954, in Mobile, Ala.

Year	Club	Pos.	G	AB	R	H	2B	3B	HR	RBI	SB	Avg.
1978	San Diego	SS	159	590	69	152	17	6	1	46	40	.258
1979	San Diego	SS	156	587	77	124	18	6	0	27	28	.211
1980	San Diego	SS	158	609	67	140	18	5	0	35	57	.230
1981	San Diego	SS	110	450	53	100	11	2	0	21	22	.222
1982	St. Louis	SS	140	488	58	121	24	1	2	43	25	.248
1983	St. Louis	SS	159	552	69	134	30	6	3	50	34	.243
1984	St. Louis	SS	124	412	53	106	20	5	1	44	35	.257
1985	St. Louis	SS	158	537	70	148	22	3	6	54	31	.276
1986	St. Louis	SS	153	514	67	144	19	4	0	54	31	.280
1987	St. Louis	SS	158	600	104	182	40	4	0	75	43	.303
1988	St. Louis	SS	153	575	80	155	27	1	3	51	57	.270
1989	St. Louis	SS	155	593	82	162	30	8	2	50	29	.273
1990	St. Louis	SS	143	512	61	130	21	1	1	50	32	.254
1991	St. Louis	SS	150	550	96	157	30	3	3	50	35	.285
1992	St. Louis	SS	132	518	73	153	20	2	0	31	43	.295
1993	St. Louis	SS	141	545	75	157	22	6	1	53	21	.288
1994	St. Louis	SS	98	381	51	100	18	3	3	30	6	.262
1995	St. Louis	SS	44	156	16	31	5	1	0	11	4	.199
	Totals		2491	9169	1221	2396	392	67	26	775	573	.261

RAY LANKFORD 28 5-11 200 Bats L Throws L

Not much went right in St. Louis last season, but there wasn't much wrong with his season . . . Speedy center fielder led team in homers (25) and RBI (82), and tied for club lead in stolen bases (24) . . . Tied for fifth in NL with 35 doubles . . . Ninth in NL with 62 extra-base hits . . . If only he could cut down on strikeouts as his 110 Ks tied him for sixth-most in NL . . . Led club with 49 extra-base hits in 1994, when he bounced back from injury-plagued 1993 season . . . Salary was $2.8 million in 1995 . . . Led club in 13 offensive categories in 1992, his breakthrough season . . . Cards' third-round pick in 1987 draft . . . Born June 5, 1967, in Los Angeles.

Year	Club	Pos.	G	AB	R	H	2B	3B	HR	RBI	SB	Avg.
1990	St. Louis	OF	39	126	12	36	10	1	3	12	8	.286
1991	St. Louis	OF	151	566	83	142	23	15	9	69	44	.251
1992	St. Louis	OF	153	598	87	175	40	6	20	86	42	.293
1993	St. Louis	OF	127	407	64	97	17	3	7	45	14	.238
1994	St. Louis	OF	109	416	89	111	25	5	19	57	11	.267
1995	St. Louis	OF	132	483	81	134	35	2	25	82	24	.277
	Totals		711	2596	416	695	150	32	83	351	143	.268

BRIAN JORDAN 29 6-1 205 Bats R Throws R

Cards made room for him as everyday outfielder by trading away Mark Whiten and he responded with breakthrough season . . . Set career highs in almost every major offensive category—at-bats (490), hits (145), homers (22), RBI (81) and steals (24) . . . Hit .304 against right-handers . . . Could be a bit more patient at the plate . . . Walked only 22 times . . . Three-year, $9-million deal signed late last season removed threat he would return to the National Football League . . . Salary was $725,000 in 1994 . . . Former All-Pro defensive back with Atlanta Falcons . . . Shares NFL record for most safeties in a season (two) . . . Cards used 30th overall pick on him in 1988 draft, a compensation choice for loss of Type-A free-agent Jack Clark . . . Born March 29, 1967, in Baltimore.

Year	Club	Pos.	G	AB	R	H	2B	3B	HR	RBI	SB	Avg.
1992	St. Louis	OF	55	193	17	40	9	4	5	22	7	.207
1993	St. Louis	OF	67	223	33	69	10	6	10	44	6	.309
1994	St. Louis	OF-1B	53	178	14	46	8	2	5	15	4	.258
1995	St. Louis	OF	131	490	83	145	20	4	22	81	24	.296
	Totals		306	1084	147	300	47	16	42	162	41	.277

BERNARD GILKEY 29 6-0 190 Bats R Throws R

Bounced back with a solid season after a poor 1994 . . . Just missed hitting .300 for the third time while setting a career high in homers (17) . . . Hit .311 against left-handers and .318 on the road . . . Committed only three errors in left field and totalled 10 assists, tied for sixth in NL . . . Has speed to steal more bases . . . Swiped only 12 in 1995 and career high is 18 in 1992 . . . Batting average fell off 52 points in 1994 after breakthrough 1993 season . . . Reached career highs in homers, RBI and batting average in 1993, his second season as an everyday player . . . Salary was $975,000 in 1995 . . . Hometown product was signed by Cards as non-drafted free agent in August 1984 . . . Born Sept. 24, 1966, in St. Louis.

Year	Club	Pos.	G	AB	R	H	2B	3B	HR	RBI	SB	Avg.
1990	St. Louis	OF	18	64	11	19	5	2	1	3	6	.297
1991	St. Louis	OF	81	268	28	58	7	2	5	20	14	.216
1992	St. Louis	OF	131	384	56	116	19	4	7	43	18	.302
1993	St. Louis	OF-1B	137	557	99	170	40	5	16	70	15	.305
1994	St. Louis	OF	105	380	52	96	22	1	6	45	15	.253
1995	St. Louis	OF	121	480	73	143	33	4	17	69	12	.298
	Totals		593	2133	319	602	126	18	52	250	80	.282

TOM PAGNOZZI 33 6-1 190 Bats R Throws R

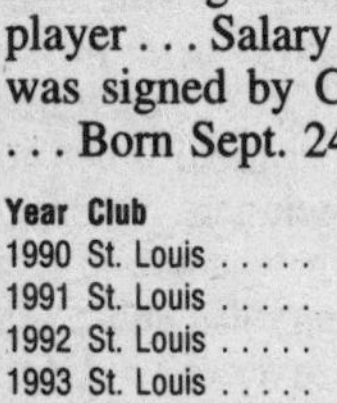

Catcher can't seem to shake injury problems . . . Knee injury was part of his worst season . . . Hit just .215 in 219 at-bats—42 points below his career average entering 1995 . . . Had only 11 more at-bats than backup Danny Sheaffer . . . Drove in only 15 runs and had only 17 extra-base hits . . . Caught 36 percent of would-be base-stealers, an average percentage, but a dropoff for him . . . Played in only 70 games in 1994, when he suffered a knee injury . . . But when he played, he was impressive enough to win his third Gold Glove as he made just one error and threw out 51 percent of would-be base-stealers . . . Salary was $2,675,000 in 1995 . . . Cards' eighth-round pick in 1983 draft, out of Arkansas . . . Born July 30, 1962, in Tucson, Ariz.

Year	Club	Pos.	G	AB	R	H	2B	3B	HR	RBI	SB	Avg.
1987	St. Louis	C-1B	27	48	8	9	1	0	2	9	1	.188
1988	St. Louis	1B-C-3B	81	195	17	55	9	0	0	15	0	.282
1989	St. Louis	C-1B-3B	52	80	3	12	2	0	0	3	0	.150
1990	St. Louis	C-1B	69	220	20	61	15	0	2	23	1	.277
1991	St. Louis	C-1B	140	459	38	121	24	5	2	57	9	.264
1992	St. Louis	C	139	485	33	121	26	3	7	44	2	.249
1993	St. Louis	C	92	330	31	85	15	1	7	41	1	.258
1994	St. Louis	C-1B	70	243	21	66	12	1	7	40	0	.272
1995	St. Louis	C	62	219	17	47	14	1	2	15	0	.215
	Totals		732	2279	188	577	118	11	29	247	14	.253

RON GANT 31 6-0 200 Bats R Throws R

NL's Comeback Player of the Year in '95 with Reds, he converted free agency into five-year pact with Cardinals last winter . . . Muscular slugger bounced back in a big way after missing all of 1994 with a broken leg . . . Led Reds in homers (29) and hit many of them when it counted, including four game-winners . . . Also stole 23 bases, proving his leg was sound . . . Hit only .188 in NLCS, however, and that was his third sub-.200 NLCS performance . . . Salary was $3.5 million in 1995 . . . Outfielder hit 30-plus homers in three of four years with Braves before the injury, including career-high 36 in '93 . . . Named to NL All-Star team in 1992 . . . Won Silver Slugger Award in 1991, when he hit 32 homers and drove in 105 runs . . . Braves made him fourth-round pick in 1983 draft . . . Born March 2, 1965, in Victoria, Tex.

Year	Club	Pos.	G	AB	R	H	2B	3B	HR	RBI	SB	Avg.
1987	Atlanta	2B	21	83	9	22	4	0	2	9	4	.265
1988	Atlanta	2B-3B	146	563	85	146	28	9	19	60	19	.259
1989	Atlanta	3B-OF	75	260	26	46	8	3	9	25	9	.177
1990	Atlanta	OF	152	575	107	174	34	3	32	84	33	.303
1991	Atlanta	OF	154	561	101	141	35	3	32	105	34	.251
1992	Atlanta	OF	153	544	74	141	22	6	17	80	32	.259
1993	Atlanta	OF	157	606	113	166	27	4	36	117	26	.274
1994	Cincinnati			Injured								
1995	Cincinnati	OF	119	410	79	113	19	4	29	88	23	.276
	Totals		977	3602	594	949	177	31	176	568	180	.263

GARY GAETTI 37 6-0 200 **Bats R Throws R**

Royals free agent turned a productive season into a one-year, $2-million contract with the Cards last winter . . . Was a legitimate AL MVP candidate for much of the summer while Kansas City surprisingly stayed in the wild-card race . . . His career-high 35 home runs were one short of the club record, set by Steve Balboni in 1985 . . . Also finished with 96 RBI, third-highest total of his career . . . A two-time All-Star who played on 1987 Twins world championship team . . . Four-time Gold Glove winner at third base . . . Team leader in the clubhouse . . . This guy was hitting .180 in 20 games with Angels when they released him in '93 . . . Hit .300 in 1987 ALCS vs. Detroit and .259 in '87 World Series vs. St. Louis . . . Had base salary of $700,000 in '95 . . . Signed by Royals as free agent, June 19, 1993, after California had released him . . . Born Aug. 19, 1958, in Centralia, Ill. . . . Twins drafted him in first round of secondary phase in 1979.

Year	Club	Pos.	G	AB	R	H	2B	3B	HR	RBI	SB	Avg.
1981	Minnesota	3B	9	26	4	5	0	0	2	3	0	.192
1982	Minnesota	3B-SS	145	508	59	117	25	4	25	84	0	.230
1983	Minnesota	3B-SS	157	584	81	143	30	3	21	78	7	.245
1984	Minnesota	3B-OF-SS	162	588	55	154	29	4	5	65	11	.262
1985	Minnesota	3B-OF-1B	160	560	71	138	31	0	20	63	13	.246
1986	Minnesota	3B-SS-OF-2B	157	596	91	171	34	1	34	108	14	.287
1987	Minnesota	3B	154	584	95	150	36	2	31	109	10	.257
1988	Minnesota	3B-SS	133	468	66	141	29	2	28	88	7	.301
1989	Minnesota	3B-1B	130	498	63	125	11	4	19	75	6	.251
1990	Minnesota	3B-1B-SS-OF	154	577	61	132	27	5	16	85	6	.229
1991	California	3B	152	586	58	144	22	1	18	66	5	.246
1992	California	3B-1B	130	456	41	103	13	2	12	48	3	.226
1993	Cal.-KC	3B-1B	102	331	40	81	20	1	14	50	1	.245
1994	Kansas City . . .	3B-1B	90	327	53	94	15	3	12	57	0	.287
1995	Kansas City . . .	3B-1B	137	514	76	134	27	0	35	96	3	.261
	Totals		1972	7203	914	1832	349	32	292	1075	86	.254

JOHN MABRY 25 6-4 205 **Bats L Throws R**

Put together promising rookie season . . . Hit .307 in 399 at-bats . . . Not much power, however . . . He's more in the Dave Magadan-Mark Grace mold, but there's nothing wrong with that . . . Hit .330 against left-handed pitching, .299 against righties and .324 at Busch Stadium, where spacious gaps suit his line-drive stroke . . . Free swinger walked only 24 times . . . Played mostly at first base, but is capable in left or right field as well . . . Possesses strong throwing arm in outfield, but he may not play there much this season . . . Hit .083 in 12 at-bats for Louisville (AAA) last year . . . Hit above .300 only once in minors (.310 for Hamilton in Rookie League in 1991) . . . Cards' sixth-round pick in 1991 draft . . . Born Oct. 17, 1970, in Wilmington, Del.

Year	Club	Pos.	G	AB	R	H	2B	3B	HR	RBI	SB	Avg.
1994	St. Louis	OF	6	23	2	7	3	0	0	3	0	.304
1995	St. Louis	1B-OF	129	388	35	119	21	1	5	41	0	.307
	Totals		135	411	37	126	24	1	5	44	0	.307

ROYCE CLAYTON 26 6-0 185 — Bats R Throws R

Still not the offensive player he was in breakthrough 1993 season, so Giants dealt him to Cards for Allen Watson, Rich DeLucia and Doug Creek last winter . . . Hit only .244, but did drive in 58 runs hitting near the bottom of the order . . . Struck out 109 times in 509 at-bats . . . Stole a career-high 24 bases . . . Shortstop committed 20 errors in 136 games, up from 14 in strike-shortened 1994 season . . . Salary was $475,000 in 1995 . . . Offense took a big dip in 1994 from rookie year . . . Average fell from .282 to .236, RBI from 70 to 30 in 45 fewer games . . . In his first full season, he tied Chris Speier's club record for RBI by a shortstop with 70 . . . Giants' first-round pick in 1988, 15th player selected overall . . . Was named top minor-league prospect by *The Sporting News* in 1991 . . . Born Jan. 2, 1970, in Burbank, Cal.

Year	Club	Pos.	G	AB	R	H	2B	3B	HR	RBI	SB	Avg.
1991	San Francisco	SS	9	26	0	3	1	0	0	2	0	.115
1992	San Francisco	SS-3B	98	321	31	72	7	4	4	24	8	.224
1993	San Francisco	SS	153	549	54	155	21	5	6	70	11	.282
1994	San Francisco	SS	108	385	38	91	14	6	3	30	23	.236
1995	San Francisco	SS	138	509	56	124	29	3	5	58	24	.244
	Totals		506	1790	179	445	72	18	18	184	66	.249

ANDY BENES 28 6-6 240 — Bats R Throws R

Mariner free agent became Cardinal with two-year, $8.1-million deal last winter . . . Went 7-2 for Seattle after being acquired from San Diego for Ron Villone and Marc Newfield July 31 last season . . . Didn't pitch as well as his record indicated, though, given his 5.86 ERA . . . Was 4-7 with 4.17 ERA for Padres in '95 . . . Was rocked for six runs in 2⅓ innings by

Indians in only ALCS start . . . Has reached double figures in wins in five of past six seasons, but he just hasn't developed into No. 1 starter . . . Led NL in strikeouts in 1994 . . . Padres' all-time strikeout leader with 1,036 . . . Joins younger brother Alan on Cards' staff . . . Made $3.4 million in '95 . . . Padres made him No. 1 overall pick in '88 draft . . . Born Aug. 20, 1967, in Evansville, Ind.

Year	Club	G	IP	W	L	Pct.	SO	BB	H	ERA
1989	San Diego	10	66⅔	6	3	.667	66	31	51	3.51
1990	San Diego	32	192⅓	10	11	.476	140	69	177	3.60
1991	San Diego	33	223	15	11	.577	167	59	194	3.03
1992	San Diego	34	231⅓	13	14	.481	169	61	230	3.35
1993	San Diego	34	230⅔	15	15	.500	179	86	200	3.78
1994	San Diego	25	172⅓	6	14	.300	189	51	155	3.86
1995	San Diego	19	118⅔	4	7	.364	126	45	121	4.17
1995	Seattle	12	63	7	2	.778	45	33	72	5.86
	Totals	199	1298	76	77	.497	1081	435	1200	3.68

DANNY JACKSON 34 6-0 220 Bats R Throws L

One of last season's biggest free-agent busts . . . Had worst season since 1991, when he won only once and was injured . . . Big disappointment after signing three-year, $11-million deal . . . Also had cancer scare early in the season . . . Strong 1994 season got him the big contract . . . Went 14-6 with Philadelphia and was named to All-Star team . . . His 14 wins were tops among NL lefties . . . Also was second in NL in starts . . . Career year was 1988 . . . Went 23-8 with Cincinnati and finished second in Cy Young balloting . . . Hasn't come anywhere close since . . . Is 3-1 with 2.35 ERA in six LCS appearances . . . A below-.500 pitcher in his 13-year career . . . Salary was $2.1 million in 1995 . . . Cards are his sixth major-league team, fifth in NL . . . Born Jan. 5, 1962, in San Antonio, Tex.

Year	Club	G	IP	W	L	Pct.	SO	BB	H	ERA
1983	Kansas City	4	19	1	1	.500	9	6	26	5.21
1984	Kansas City	15	76	2	6	.250	40	35	84	4.26
1985	Kansas City	32	208	14	12	.538	114	76	209	3.42
1986	Kansas City	32	185⅔	11	12	.478	115	79	177	3.20
1987	Kansas City	36	224	9	18	.333	152	109	219	4.02
1988	Cincinnati	35	260⅔	23	8	.742	161	71	206	2.73
1989	Cincinnati	20	115⅔	6	11	.353	70	57	122	5.60
1990	Cincinnati	22	117⅓	6	6	.500	76	40	119	3.61
1991	Chicago (NL)	17	70⅔	1	5	.167	31	48	89	6.75
1992	Chi (NL)-Pitt.	34	201⅓	8	13	.381	97	77	211	3.84
1993	Philadelphia	32	210⅓	12	11	.522	120	80	214	3.77
1994	Philadelphia	25	179⅓	14	6	.700	129	46	183	3.26
1995	St. Louis	19	100⅔	2	12	.143	52	48	120	5.90
	Totals	323	1968⅔	109	121	.474	1166	772	1979	3.88

MIKE MORGAN 36 6-2 225 **Bats R Throws R**

Cards drew criticism for June 16 deal that brought him and two minor leaguers from Cubs for Todd Zeile . . . Pitched respectably, posting 3.56 ERA in 21 starts overall . . . Bounced back from horrible 1994 season, when he was 2-10 with 6.69 ERA . . . Had reached double figures in wins from 1990-93, including first winning season in majors (14-10 in 1991 with Los Angeles) . . . Cards are his eighth big-league team . . . Athletics selected him fourth overall in 1978 draft and brought him to the big leagues not long after his high-school graduation . . . Many think he was rushed, hurting his development . . . Numbers support that theory as he struggled to 9-27 record in first four seasons . . . Seven wins finally got him over 100 (102) for his career . . . Salary was $3,375,000 in 1995 . . . Born Oct. 8, 1959, in Tulare, Cal. . . . Was re-signed to one-year, $1.25-million deal last winter.

Year	Club	G	IP	W	L	Pct.	SO	BB	H	ERA
1978	Oakland	3	12	0	3	.000	0	8	19	7.50
1979	Oakland	13	77	2	10	.167	17	50	102	5.96
1982	New York (AL)	30	150⅓	7	11	.389	71	67	167	4.37
1983	Toronto	16	45⅓	0	3	.000	22	21	48	5.16
1985	Seattle	2	6	1	1	.500	2	5	11	12.00
1986	Seattle	37	216⅓	11	17	.393	116	86	243	4.53
1987	Seattle	34	207	12	17	.414	85	53	245	4.65
1988	Baltimore	22	71⅓	1	6	.143	29	23	70	5.43
1989	Los Angeles	40	152⅔	8	11	.421	72	33	130	2.53
1990	Los Angeles	33	211	11	15	.423	106	60	216	3.75
1991	Los Angeles	34	236⅓	14	10	.583	140	61	197	2.78
1992	Chicago (NL)	34	240	16	8	.667	123	79	203	2.55
1993	Chicago (NL)	32	207⅔	10	15	.400	111	74	206	4.03
1994	Chicago (NL)	15	80⅔	2	10	.167	57	35	111	6.69
1995	Chi. (NL)-St.L.	21	131⅓	7	7	.500	61	34	133	3.56
	Totals	366	2045	102	144	.415	1012	689	2101	3.98

TOP PROSPECTS

ALAN BENES 24 6-5 215 **Bats R Throws R**

Could end up in starting rotation this year, after going 4-2, 2.41 for Louisville (AAA) and 1-2, 8.44 for Cards in '95 . . . How about the pitching genes in his family? Brother is Andy . . . Blistered through three levels of minors in 1994, compiling 17-3 mark . . . St. Louis' first-round pick in 1993 draft, out of Creighton . . . Born Jan. 21, 1972, in Evansville, Ind.

BRIAN BARBER 23 6-1 175 Bats R Throws R

Got first big-league exposure, making four starts and nine appearances for Cards and going 2-1, 5.22 . . . Struck out 27 in 29 innings . . . Started season at Louisville (AAA), where he went 6-5, 4.70 . . . In 1994, he was 4-7 for Louisville after 1-6 start . . . Cards selected him 22nd overall in 1991 draft . . . Born March 4, 1973, in Hamilton, Ohio.

JOHN FRASCATORE 26 6-1 210 Bats R Throws R

Hard thrower got two big-league looks, going 1-1, 4.41 with Cards in '95 . . . Went 2-8, 3.95 for Louisville (AAA) last year . . . Made four starts for Cards, but could end up as a closer . . . Still battling control problems . . . Breakthrough season was 1994, when he went 15-6 combined for Louisville and Arkansas (AA) . . . Cards selected him in 24th round in 1991 draft . . . Born Feb. 4, 1970, in Queens, N.Y.

AARON HOLBERT 23 6-0 165 Bats R Throws R

Cards patiently waiting for him to become shortstop successor to Ozzie Smith . . . They picked him 18th overall in 1990 draft . . . Slowly has climbed organization ladder, hitting .257 with nine homers and 40 RBI for Louisville (AAA) in '95 . . . Born Jan. 9, 1973, in Torrance, Cal. . . . Brother Ray is infielder in Padres organization.

MANAGER TONY La RUSSA: One of best managers in history . . . Arrives in St. Louis after parting of ways with new ownership of Athletics . . . Succeeds interim manager Mike Jorgensen following 62-81 finish . . . Three-time AL Manager of Year . . . His lifetime record stands at 1,320-1,183 after 67-77 finish in '95 . . . In eight-plus seasons in Oakland, his record was 798-673 . . . Became Oakland manager, July 1, 1986, only two weeks after being fired by White Sox owner Jerry Reinsdorf, who regrets the decision to this day . . . Has a law degree from Florida State . . . Passed the bar exam in 1979 . . . One of five managers in major-league history to have law degree—and

the other four are in Hall of Fame . . . One of game's most respected managers by his peers . . . Wasn't much of a player, batting only .199 with no homers and seven RBI in 132 major-league games . . . Became 40th manager in major-league history to win 1,000 games, July 14, 1991 . . . Born Oct. 4, 1944, in Tampa, Fla.

ALL-TIME CARDINAL SEASON RECORDS

BATTING: Rogers Hornsby, .424, 1924
HRs: Johnny Mize, 43, 1940
RBI: Joe Medwick, 154, 1937
STEALS: Lou Brock, 118, 1974
WINS: Dizzy Dean, 30, 1934
STRIKEOUTS: Bob Gibson, 274, 1970

COLORADO ROCKIES

TEAM DIRECTORY: Chairman/CEO: Jerry McMorris; Exec. VP-GM: Bob Gebhardt; Sr. VP-Bus. Oper.: Keli McGregor; VP-Player Pers.: Dick Balderson; Dir. Scouting: Pat Daugherty; Dir. Pub. Rel.: Mike Swanson; Trav. Sec.: Peter Durso; Mgr.: Don Baylor; Coaches: Frank Funk, Gene Glynn, Ken Griffey Sr., Jackie Moore, Paul Zuvella. Home: Coors Field (50,000). Field distances: 347, l.f. line; 415, c.; 350, r.f. line. Spring training: Tucson, Ariz.

SCOUTING REPORT

HITTING: No problems here, especially when the Rockies are playing in mile-high, hitter-friendly Coors Field. Name an important offensive category and the Rockies led the NL in it: av-

Rockies didn't let Dante's infernal bat slip away.

erage (.282), runs (785), home runs (200) and RBI (749).

The Blake Street Bombers—Dante Bichette (.340, 40, 128), Andres Galarraga (.280, 31, 106), Larry Walker (.306, 36, 101) and Vinny Castilla (.309, 32, 90)—did most of the damage. They became only the second foursome in history to hit 30 homers apiece and, with Bichette's re-signing last winter, they will be in the Nos. 3-6 spots in manager Don Baylor's order once again.

Eric Young (.317, 68 runs, 35 steals) will have a full season to build on his impressive totals after taking over the leadoff spot in late June. And Ellis Burks (.266, 14, 49) will get another chance to stay healthy and put up big numbers.

PITCHING: If Bill Swift (9-3, 4.94) and Bret Saberhagen (7-6, 4.18) can stay healthy, the burden on an overworked but effective bullpen could be eased. Both veteran right-handers underwent arthroscopic surgery in the offseason.

Kevin Ritz (11-11, 4.21) was the most dependable starter on a staff that posted a league-worst 4.97 ERA last season. And from a group that includes Armando Reynoso, Bryan Rekar, Marvin Freeman, David Nied and Mark Thompson, solid fourth and fifth starters should emerge.

GM Bob Gebhard chose to re-sign veterans Bruce Ruffin (0-1, 2.12, 11 saves) and Darren Holmes (6-1, 3.24, 14 saves), keeping intact one of the best bullpen foursomes in the league. Curtis Leskanic (6-3, 3.40, 10 saves) will get a chance as the closer and Steve Reed (5-2, 2.14) returns in a setup role.

FIELDING: The Rockies finished fourth in team fielding percentage in '95 and, if that up-the-middle defense adage is true, could be in trouble. Center fielder Burks is slipping. Young's forte is offense, although he should get better with a full spring training at second base. At least re-signed shortstop Walt Weiss is solid and catcher Joe Girardi has been replaced by the defensively sound Jeff Reed.

Bichette needs to improve in left, but right fielder Walker and third baseman Castilla had Gold Glove-caliber seasons, plus Galarraga is above average at first.

OUTLOOK: There will be no more sneaking up on anybody for the fourth-year Rockies. After becoming the expansion team to reach the playoffs fastest, Colorado will be expected to do it again. But that's not to say it won't. The Rockies still have all the offense you could want and, if the starting pitching is healthy and effective, it should come as no surprise if they improve on their 77-67 record of '95 and win the NL West.

ROCKIE PROFILES

DANTE BICHETTE 32 6-3 240 Bats R Throws R

Say what you want about Coors Field inflating offensive numbers; this guy's year was huge . . . Led NL in home runs (40) and RBI (128) while hitting .340, third best in league . . . Also led league in total bases (359), slugging percentage (.620), extra-base hits (80), and tied for lead in hits (197) . . . Scored 102 runs and had hitting streaks of 23 and 19 games . . . Also hit .588 in Division Series vs. Braves . . . Only black mark was below-average defense in left field . . . Salary was $3.1 million in 1995 . . . Rockies got him from Milwaukee in lopsided expansion-draft day trade for Kevin Reimer prior to 1993 season . . . Studies hitting like his hero, Ted Williams, did . . . Traded to Milwaukee from California for Dave Parker prior to 1991 season . . . Angels took him in 17th round of 1984 draft . . . Club's impatience and his immaturity led to his departure . . . Born Nov. 18, 1963, in West Palm Beach, Fla. . . . Re-signed to three-year, $11.1-million deal last fall.

Year	Club	Pos.	G	AB	R	H	2B	3B	HR	RBI	SB	Avg.
1988	California	OF	21	46	1	12	2	0	0	8	0	.261
1989	California	OF	48	138	13	29	7	0	3	15	3	.210
1990	California	OF	109	349	40	89	15	1	15	53	5	.255
1991	Milwaukee	OF-3B	134	445	53	106	18	3	15	59	14	.238
1992	Milwaukee	OF	112	387	37	111	27	2	5	41	18	.287
1993	Colorado	OF	141	538	93	167	43	5	21	89	14	.310
1994	Colorado	OF	116	484	74	147	33	2	27	95	21	.304
1995	Colorado	OF	139	579	102	197	38	2	40	128	13	.340
	Totals		820	2966	413	858	183	15	126	488	88	.289

LARRY WALKER 29 6-3 220 Bats L Throws R

Signed four-year, $22.5-million deal as free agent prior to '95 and then proved he was worth it with his best season . . . Set career highs with 36 homers, 101 RBI . . . Also hit .306 and scored 96 runs . . . Second to Dante Bichette in NL in slugging percentage (.607), total bases (300) and extra-base hits (72) . . . Home-run total is single-season high by a native Canadian . . . Slumped to .214 in Division Series . . . One of NL's best right fielders . . . Tied for second in league in assists with 13 . . . Won Gold Gloves in 1992 and 1993 . . . Left Expos after averaging .280 with 20 homers and 80 RBI and 20 steals from 1990-94 . . . Expos signed him as non-drafted free agent in November 1984 . . . Raw talent who had to learn the game in minor leagues . . . Was a goalie in amateur hockey days . . . Born Dec. 1, 1966, in Maple Ridge, B.C. . . . Earned $4,744,302 in 1995.

Year	Club	Pos.	G	AB	R	H	2B	3B	HR	RBI	SB	Avg.
1989	Montreal	OF	20	47	4	8	0	0	0	4	1	.170
1990	Montreal	OF	133	419	59	101	18	3	19	51	21	.241
1991	Montreal	OF-1B	137	487	59	141	30	2	16	64	14	.290
1992	Montreal	OF	143	528	85	159	31	4	23	93	18	.301
1993	Montreal	OF-1B	138	490	85	130	24	5	22	86	29	.265
1994	Montreal	OF-1B	103	395	76	127	44	2	19	86	15	.322
1995	Colorado	OF	131	494	96	151	31	5	36	101	16	.306
	Totals		805	2860	464	817	178	21	135	485	114	286

ANDRES GALARRAGA 34 6-3 235 Bats R Throws R

Last of the four Blake Street Bombers to reach 30-homer mark, winding up with 31 . . . Set career high with 106 RBI . . . Numbers were helped by fact "The Big Cat" stayed healthy for first time in four seasons . . . Missed only one game . . . Hit .278 in Division Series . . . Alarming strikeout total of 146 is sign of some slippage . . . First baseman's usually sparkling defense wasn't consistent . . . Fractured right hand ended his 1994 season on July 28 . . . Rockies skidded to 3-10 finish without him . . . Signed four-year, $16.4-million deal after leading NL in hitting with .370 mark in 1993 . . . Salary was $3.85 million in 1995 . . . Signed as a free agent before Rockies' first season on manager Don Baylor's recommendation . . . Expos signed him as non-drafted free agent in January 1979 . . . Born June 18, 1961, in Caracas, Venezuela.

Year	Club	Pos.	G	AB	R	H	2B	3B	HR	RBI	SB	Avg.
1985	Montreal	1B	24	75	9	14	1	0	2	4	1	.187
1986	Montreal	1B	105	321	39	87	13	0	10	42	6	.271
1987	Montreal	1B	147	551	72	168	40	3	13	90	7	.305
1988	Montreal	1B	157	609	99	184	42	8	29	92	13	.302
1989	Montreal	1B	152	572	76	147	30	1	23	85	12	.257
1990	Montreal	1B	155	579	65	148	29	0	20	87	10	.256
1991	Montreal	1B	107	375	34	82	13	2	9	33	5	.219
1992	St. Louis	1B	95	325	38	79	14	2	10	39	5	.243
1993	Colorado	1B	120	470	71	174	35	4	22	98	2	.370
1994	Colorado	1B	103	417	77	133	21	0	31	85	8	.319
1995	Colorado	1B	143	554	89	155	29	3	31	106	12	.280
	Totals		1308	4848	669	1371	267	23	200	761	81	.283

VINNY CASTILLA 28 6-1 190 Bats R Throws R

Unknown to many, he zoomed into prominence with 32 homers and All-Star Game start in first season as an everyday player . . . Did that after having to win regular job in spring training . . . Big benefactor of mile-high air at Coors Field . . . Hit .383 at home and .229 on road . . . Hit .388 against lefties . . . Also had Gold Glove-caliber season defensively at third . . . Possesses a strong and very accurate arm . . . Former shortstop went to instructional league to polish third-base play . . . Hit .467 with two homers in Division Series . . . Had been a very productive reserve in prior two seasons . . . Hit .331 in 130 at-bats in 1994 and .255 with nine homers in 337 at-bats in 1993 . . . Rockies picked him off Braves roster in expansion draft prior to '93 . . . Born July 4, 1967, in Oaxaca, Mexico . . . Made $240,000 in 1995, then was signed to two-year deal last winter.

Year	Club	Pos.	G	AB	R	H	2B	3B	HR	RBI	SB	Avg.
1991	Atlanta	SS	12	5	1	1	0	0	0	0	0	.200
1992	Atlanta	3B-SS	9	16	1	4	1	0	0	1	0	.250
1993	Colorado	SS	105	337	36	86	9	7	9	30	2	.255
1994	Colorado	INF	52	130	16	43	11	1	3	18	2	.331
1995	Colorado	3B-SS	139	527	82	163	34	2	32	90	2	.309
	Totals		317	1015	136	297	55	10	44	139	6	.293

WALT WEISS 32 6-0 180 Bats S Throws R

Valuable and underrated veteran shortstop did exactly what Rockies needed him to do: solidify their defense . . . Made 16 errors, three on a totally out-of-character night in Los Angeles . . . Also was a threat in No. 8 spot, with .403 on-base percentage and 98 walks, second to only Barry Bonds in NL . . . Hit .167 in Division Series . . . Rockies signed him as free agent prior to '94, after he spent one year with expansion Marlins . . . Only player to play for last two NL expansion teams . . . Salary was $1.6 million in 1995 . . . Was AL Rookie of the Year in 1988, when he had 58-game errorless streak and batted .333 in ALCS against Red Sox . . . Spent five-plus seasons with A's, but two were cut short by injuries . . . First-round pick of Athletics in

1985, out of North Carolina . . . Born Nov. 28, 1963, in Tuxedo, N.Y. . . . Re-signed to two-year, $4.1-million deal last winter.

Year	Club	Pos.	G	AB	R	H	2B	3B	HR	RBI	SB	Avg.
1987	Oakland	SS	16	26	3	12	4	0	0	1	1	.462
1988	Oakland	SS	147	452	44	113	17	3	3	39	4	.250
1989	Oakland	SS	84	236	30	55	11	0	3	21	6	.233
1990	Oakland	SS	138	445	50	118	17	1	2	35	9	.265
1991	Oakland	SS	40	133	15	30	6	1	0	13	6	.226
1992	Oakland	SS	103	316	36	67	5	2	0	21	6	.212
1993	Florida	SS	158	500	50	133	14	2	1	39	7	.266
1994	Colorado	SS	110	423	58	106	11	4	1	32	12	.251
1995	Colorado	SS	137	427	65	111	17	3	1	25	15	.260
	Totals		933	2958	351	745	102	16	11	226	66	.252

ELLIS BURKS 31 6-2 205 — Bats R Throws R

Rockies ignored his history and gave him a three-year, $9-million deal as free agent before 1994 season, but injuries have followed him to Colorado . . . Started last season on disabled list following offseason wrist surgery . . . Also suffered from ulcers . . . When healthy, he couldn't wrestle the everyday center-field job from Mike Kingery . . . Salary was $3 million in 1995 . . . Was on his way to terrific 1994 season when he suffered wrist injury and missed the next 70 games . . . Signed with White Sox as free agent prior to 1993 season . . . Made AL All-Star team and won Gold Glove in 1990 . . . Red Sox' first pick in secondary phase of January 1983 draft . . . Born Sept. 11, 1964, in Vicksburg, Miss.

Year	Club	Pos.	G	AB	R	H	2B	3B	HR	RBI	SB	Avg.
1987	Boston	OF	133	558	94	152	30	2	20	59	27	.272
1988	Boston	OF	144	540	93	159	37	5	18	92	25	.294
1989	Boston	OF	97	399	73	121	19	6	12	61	21	.303
1990	Boston	OF	152	588	89	174	33	8	21	89	9	.296
1991	Boston	OF	130	474	56	119	33	3	14	56	6	.251
1992	Boston	OF	66	235	35	60	8	3	8	30	5	.255
1993	Chicago (AL) . .	OF	146	499	75	137	24	4	17	74	6	.275
1994	Colorado	OF	42	149	33	48	8	3	13	24	3	.322
1995	Colorado	OF	103	278	41	74	10	6	14	49	7	.266
	Totals		1013	3720	589	1044	202	40	137	534	109	.281

Vinny Castilla was shock Rock with 32 HRs, 90 RBI.

BILL SWIFT 34 6-0 190 Bats R Throws R

Sinkerballer accepted risk of pitching in mile-high altitude, signing three-year, $13.15-million deal as free agent last April . . . Season unraveled because of shoulder woes . . . Had arthroscopic surgery to repair torn labrum immediately after Rockies' postseason ended . . . Managed to win nine games, despite two stints on the disabled list . . . Won points for pitching in pain down stretch . . . ERA didn't fall below 5.00 until last regular-season start . . . Entered '96 season with 3.62 career mark and 78-62 record . . . Salary was $3,933,333 in 1995 . . . Big year was 1993 with San Francisco, when he went 21-8 with 2.82 ERA . . . Led NL in ERA with 2.08 mark in 1992 . . . Went to Giants from Mariners with Dave Burba and Mike Jackson for Kevin Mitchell before 1992 season . . . Saved 17 games and had 1.99

ERA with Mariners in 1991 . . . Seattle picked him second overall in 1984 draft . . . Born Oct. 27, 1961, in South Portland, Me.

Year	Club	G	IP	W	L	Pct.	SO	BB	H	ERA
1985	Seattle	23	120⅔	6	10	.375	55	48	131	4.77
1986	Seattle	29	115⅓	2	9	.182	55	55	148	5.46
1988	Seattle	38	174⅔	8	12	.400	47	65	199	4.59
1989	Seattle	37	130	7	3	.700	45	38	140	4.43
1990	Seattle	55	128	6	4	.600	42	21	135	2.39
1991	Seattle	71	90⅓	1	2	.333	48	26	74	1.99
1992	San Francisco	30	164⅔	10	4	.714	77	43	144	2.08
1993	San Francisco	34	232⅔	21	8	.724	157	55	195	2.82
1994	San Francisco	17	109⅓	8	7	.533	62	31	109	3.38
1995	Colorado	19	105⅔	9	3	.750	68	43	122	4.94
	Totals	353	1371⅓	78	62	.557	656	425	1397	3.62

BRET SABERHAGEN 31 6-1 195 Bats R Throws R

Another veteran right-hander whose shoulder didn't hold up . . . Underwent arthroscopic surgery after season . . . Won only two of eight starts after being acquired from Mets with David Swanson July 31 for Juan Acevedo and Arnold Gooch . . . Was bombed by Braves in his Division Series outing, too . . . Salary was $5,362,990 in 1995 . . . Was 5-5 with 3.35 ERA in 16 starts for Mets before trade . . . Won Cy Young Award at age 21 in 1985, going 20-6 with 2.87 ERA for Kansas City . . . Won another AL Cy in 1989 with 23-6 mark and 2.16 ERA . . . Injuries limited him to 28 victories over next four seasons . . . Went to Mets with Bill Pecota from KC for Gregg Jefferies, Kevin McReynolds and Keith Miller prior to 1992 season . . . Rebounded to 14-4 season in 1994 . . . Royals picked him in 19th round of 1982 draft . . . Born April 11, 1964, in Chicago Heights, Ill.

Year	Club	G	IP	W	L	Pct.	SO	BB	H	ERA
1984	Kansas City	38	157⅔	10	11	.476	73	36	138	3.48
1985	Kansas City	32	235⅓	20	6	.769	158	38	211	2.87
1986	Kansas City	30	156	7	12	.368	112	29	165	4.15
1987	Kansas City	33	257	18	10	.643	163	53	246	3.36
1988	Kansas City	35	260⅔	14	16	.467	171	59	271	3.80
1989	Kansas City	36	262⅓	23	6	.793	193	43	209	2.16
1990	Kansas City	20	135	5	9	.357	87	28	146	3.27
1991	Kansas City	28	196⅓	13	8	.619	136	45	165	3.07
1992	New York (NL)	17	97⅔	3	5	.375	81	27	84	3.50
1993	New York (NL)	19	139⅓	7	7	.500	93	17	131	3.29
1994	New York (NL)	24	177⅓	14	4	.778	143	13	169	2.74
1995	NY (NL)-Col.	25	153	7	6	.538	100	33	165	4.18
	Totals	337	2227⅔	141	100	.585	1510	421	2100	3.26

BRUCE RUFFIN 32 6-2 220 Bats S Throws L

Veteran did something in '95 he hadn't done in nine previous seasons—he went on the disabled list . . . Elbow and upper forearm troubles put him on DL twice . . . When healthy, he was effective as ever . . . Had seven saves in first 12 appearances through May 28 . . . Converted 11-of-12 opportunities . . . Salary was $1 million in 1995 . . . Found niche as closer in 1994, when he saved 16 in place of Darren Holmes . . . Pitched in 59 games, including 12 starts, in Rockies' inaugural 1993 season . . . Signed with Rockies as a free agent after going 1-6 with 6.67 ERA with Milwaukee in 1992 . . . Went 42-58 in six seasons with Phillies . . . Phillies' second-round pick in 1985 draft . . . Born Oct. 4, 1963, in Lubbock, Tex. . . . Made $1,000,000 in '95 and was re-signed to two-year deal last winter.

Year	Club	G	IP	W	L	Pct.	SO	BB	H	ERA
1986	Philadelphia	21	146⅓	9	4	.692	70	44	138	2.46
1987	Philadelphia	35	204⅔	11	14	.440	93	73	236	4.35
1988	Philadelphia	55	144⅓	6	10	.375	82	80	151	4.43
1989	Philadelphia	24	125⅔	6	10	.375	70	62	152	4.44
1990	Philadelphia	32	149	6	13	.316	79	62	178	5.38
1991	Philadelphia	31	119	4	7	.364	85	38	125	3.78
1992	Milwaukee	25	58	1	6	.143	45	41	66	6.67
1993	Colorado	59	139⅔	6	5	.545	126	69	145	3.87
1994	Colorado	56	55⅔	4	5	.444	65	30	55	4.04
1995	Colorado	37	34	0	1	.000	23	19	26	2.12
	Totals	375	1176⅓	53	75	.414	738	518	1272	4.19

KEVIN RITZ 30 6-4 220 Bats R Throws R

Went to spring training as a question mark and ended '95 season as staff ace . . . Only Rockies starter to win in double figures (11) . . . Also led staff in starts (26), innings (173⅔) and strikeouts (120) . . . Started Game 1 of Division Series . . . Slumped to 0-5 with 6.12 ERA in August and temporarily landed in bullpen . . . Pitched his way out with two four-inning saves and finished strong . . . Salary was $350,000 in 1995 . . . Rockies picked him off Tigers roster in second round of expansion draft prior to '93 . . . Did not pitch at all in 1993 after undergoing ligament reconstruction surgery . . . Made 15 starts in 1994, going 5-6 . . . Had little success in Detroit, going 6-18 in parts of four seasons from 1989-92 . . . Tigers picked him in fourth round of 1985 draft . . . Born June 8, 1965, in Eatontown, N.J.

Year	Club	G	IP	W	L	Pct.	SO	BB	H	ERA
1989	Detroit	12	74	4	6	.400	56	44	75	4.38
1990	Detroit	4	7⅓	0	4	.000	3	14	14	11.05
1991	Detroit	11	15⅓	0	3	.000	9	22	17	11.74
1992	Detroit	23	80⅓	2	5	.286	57	44	88	5.60
1993	Colorado					Injured				
1994	Colorado	15	73⅔	5	6	.455	53	35	88	5.62
1995	Colorado	31	173⅓	11	11	.500	120	65	171	4.21
	Totals	96	424	22	35	.386	298	224	453	5.14

CURTIS LESKANIC 28 5-11 180 Bats R Throws R

Former starter was moved permanently to bullpen last season—and the shift paid huge dividends . . . Emerged as closer of the future . . . Saved 10 games, including wild-card clincher on final day of season . . . Led NL in appearances (76) and strikeouts by a relief pitcher . . . Fanned 107 in 98 innings . . . Allowed only 83 hits . . . Right-handers hit only .213 against him . . . Blew six save opportunities . . . Salary was $130,000 in 1995 . . . Bounced between Rockies and Colorado Springs (AAA) in 1993 and 1994 . . . Tried starting and middle relief, but prefers late-inning role . . . Was Rockies' seventh pick in third round of expansion draft prior to '93 . . . Eighth-round pick of Cleveland in 1989 draft, out of Louisiana State . . . Born April 2, 1968, in Homestead, Pa. . . . Made $130,000 in 1995.

Year	Club	G	IP	W	L	Pct.	SO	BB	H	ERA
1993	Colorado	18	57	1	5	.167	30	27	59	5.37
1994	Colorado	8	22⅓	1	1	.500	17	10	27	5.64
1995	Colorado	76	98	6	3	.667	107	33	83	3.40
	Totals	102	177⅓	8	9	.471	154	70	169	4.21

TOP PROSPECTS

QUINTON McCRACKEN 26 5-7 175 Bats S Throws R

Speedy little outfielder in Tim Raines mold . . . Hit .362 at New Haven (AA), then .361 at Colorado Springs (AAA) . . . Stole 17 bases for Colorado Springs and 26 for New Haven, scoring total of 88 runs . . . Rockies picked him in 25th round of 1992 draft . . . Born March 16, 1970, in Wilmington, N.C. . . . Struck out in his only at-bat with Rockies last year.

CRAIG COUNSELL 25 6-0 180 Bats L Throws R

Solid shortstop has climbed the Rockies' chain since being picked in 11th round in 1992 draft . . . Hit .218 with five homers and 53 RBI for Colorado Springs (AAA) in '95 after hitting .280 in each of his previous two minor-league seasons . . . Played collegiately at Notre Dame . . . Born Aug. 21, 1970, in South Bend, Ind. . . . Went 0-for-1 with Rockies last season.

JOHN BURKE 26 6-4 220 Bats R Throws R

Rockies' patience is wearing thin with their first-ever draft pick in 1992 . . . Won first six decisions for Colorado Springs (AAA) but wound up 7-1 with a 4.65 ERA because of succession of injuries . . . Hometown kid as product of Denver suburb of Englewood . . . Born Feb. 9, 1970, in Durango, Colo.

GARVIN ALSTON 24 6-1 180 Bats R Throws R

Started last season in majors, but was sent down when rosters shrunk from 28 to 25 . . . Had strong season at New Haven (AA), where he went 4-4, 2.84 . . . Saved six games and allowed only 47 hits in 67 innings . . . Rockies' 10th-round pick in 1992 draft . . . Born Dec. 8, 1971, in Mt. Vernon, N.Y.

MANAGER DON BAYLOR: Won NL Manager of the Year

honors for getting a pitching-short team into postseason play . . . Asked a lot of his overworked bullpen, because of ineffective starting pitching . . . Has the secret to managing 81 games a year at mile-high altitude: use plenty of relievers and only in situations where they have best chance to succeed . . . Physical presence and mental toughness have earned him respect in the clubhouse . . . With 77-67 regular-season finish in 1995, his career record is 197-216 . . . Not bad considering his only experience is with the three-year-old Rockies . . . Spent four years as a hitting instructor—two in St. Louis and two in Milwaukee—before being named Rockies manager . . . Draws from experience of playing for both Earl Weaver and Gene Mauch . . . Hit .260 with 338 homers and 1,276 RBI in distinguished big-league career . . . Won 1979 AL MVP award by hitting .296 with 36 homers, 139 RBI and 120 runs . . . Holds major-league record for being hit by a pitch: 267 times . . . Played in three World Series and seven playoffs, finishing with three in a row with Boston, Minnesota and Oakland from 1986-88 . . . Had his best years with Angels from 1977-82 . . . Began career with Orioles . . . Also played for Yankees . . . Born June 28, 1949, in Austin, Tex.

ALL-TIME ROCKIE SEASON RECORDS

BATTING: Andres Galarraga, .370, 1993
HRs: Dante Bichette, 40, 1995
RBI: Dante Bichette, 128, 1995
STEALS: Eric Young, 42, 1993
WINS: Armando Reynoso, 12, 1993
STRIKEOUTS: Bruce Ruffin, 126, 1993

LOS ANGELES DODGERS

TEAM DIRECTORY: Pres.: Peter O'Malley; Exec. VP-Player Pers.: Fred Claire; VP-Marketing: Barry Stockhamer; VP-Communications: Tommy Hawkins; Dir. Minor League Oper.: Charlie Blaney; Dir. Scouting: Terry Reynolds; Publicity Dir.: Jay Lucas; Trav. Sec.: Billy DeLury; Mgr.: Tom Lasorda; Coaches: Joe Amalfitano, Mark Cresse, Manny Mota, Bill Russell, Reggie Smith, Dave Wallace. Home: Dodger Stadium (56,000). Field distances: 330, l.f. line; 370, l.c.; 395, c.f.; 370, r.c.; 330, r.f. line. Spring training: Vero Beach, Fla.

SCOUTING REPORT

HITTING: Tommy Lasorda's team isn't lacking for middle-of-the-lineup threats, with Mike Piazza (.346, 32, 93), Eric Karros (.298, 32, 105) and Raul Mondesi (.285, 26, 88). The question is: Who will be in the lineup with that powerful trio?

The Dodgers, who scored only 634 runs in '95, are expected to have a younger look in '96, with outfielders Todd Hollandsworth (.233, 5, 13), Billy Ashley (.237, 8, 27) and Roger Cedeno

Mike Piazza, Tom Lasorda's godson, remains LA godsend.

(.238, 0, 3), perhaps getting chances to fit in with Mondesi. But this time LA made sure it kept Brett Butler (.300, 32 steals) around as insurance by re-signing him to a one-year deal.

The left side of the infield also will have a new look, with free-agent signee Greg Gagne (.256, 6, 49 with the Royals) replacing Jose Offerman at short and trade import Mike Blowers (.257, 23, 96 with the Mariners) assuming third base from Tim Wallach. Factor in Chad Fonville (.278, 20 steals) and Delino DeShields (.256, 8, 37, 39 steals) and it should add up to plenty of power, a middle-of-the-pack batting average and more runs.

PITCHING: The re-enlistment of Ramon Martinez (17-7, 3.66) was achieved, much to the Dodgers' relief. NL Rookie of the Year Hideo Nomo (13-6, 2.54, NL-leading 236 strikeouts) got the ink, but it was Martinez who was the No. 1 starter on a staff that posted a second-ranked 3.66 ERA in '95.

Ismael Valdes (13-11, 3.05) is about to emerge as one of the NL's best pitchers, potentially giving the Dodgers a trio of starters unmatched anywhere except Atlanta. Pedro Astacio (7-8, 4.24) could move back in the rotation after spending most of last season in the bullpen and knuckleballer Tom Candiotti (7-14, 3.50) was re-signed.

Closer Todd Worrell (4-1, 2.02, 32 saves) was brought back for '96 and he is joined by hard-throwers Antonio Osuna (2-4, 4.43), Rudy Seanez (1-3, 6.75) and Jose Parra (0-0, 4.35) plus former Kansas City lefty Billy Brewer (2-4, 5.56 with the Royals).

FIELDING: You had to ask. Brutal is the best way to describe the Dodgers' defense in 1995, and really, over the last several years. Once again, they were last in team fielding percentage (.976) and led the NL with 130 errors and hope the additions of Gagne at shortstop and Blowers at third will stabilize the infield.

Mondesi is the lone jewel in the outfield alignment. He led the NL's outfielders with 16 assists despite teams not taking many chances against his powerful right arm. He also has tremendous range in right field. Cedeno has even more speed in center and is better-equipped to play there than Hollandsworth.

OUTLOOK: The defending NL West champions, at 78-66 in '95, have undergone many changes, but the heart of this team is intact. Still, there are plenty of young players—maybe too many for LA to progress any further than the first round of the playoffs in '96. In what could be Lasorda's final season, the Dodgers could return to the playoffs, but don't expect much more.

DODGER PROFILES

MIKE PIAZZA 27 6-3 220 Bats R Throws R

Is this guy scary, or what? . . . Belted 32 homers and drove in 93 runs in just 112 games . . . Imagine what he would do in a 162-game season . . . And he almost won a batting title (.346), finishing second to the incomparable Tony Gwynn . . . All that from a catcher . . . Hit .384 on the road . . . Earned $900,000 in 1995 . . . Unanimous NL Rookie of the Year in 1993 . . . Keeps getting better . . . Hit .318 with 35 homers and 112 RBI in first full major-league season . . . Average was highest by any NL Rookie of the Year . . . Was on pace for similar numbers in strike-shortened 1994 season . . . Hit one home run per 16.9 at-bats and drove in one run per 4.4 at-bats in '94 . . . His father is a friend of Dodger manager Tom Lasorda . . . Dodgers took him as a courtesy in 62nd round of 1988 draft as he was the 1,389th player picked . . . Born Sept. 4, 1968, in Norristown, Pa.

Year	Club	Pos.	G	AB	R	H	2B	3B	HR	RBI	SB	Avg.
1992	Los Angeles . . .	C	21	69	5	16	3	0	1	7	0	.232
1993	Los Angeles . . .	C-1B	149	547	81	174	24	2	35	112	3	.318
1994	Los Angeles . . .	C	107	405	64	129	18	0	24	92	1	.319
1995	Los Angeles . . .	C	112	434	82	150	17	0	32	93	1	.346
	Totals		389	1455	232	469	62	2	92	304	5	.322

ERIC KARROS 28 6-4 210 Bats R Throws R

Took his game to another level . . . As good as Mike Piazza was, some considered this guy the team MVP in '95 . . . Set career highs in average (.298), homers (32) and RBI (105) . . . Clutch hitter, too . . . First baseman batted .315 against lefties . . . Clubhouse leader . . . Takes media pressure off Piazza with engaging personality . . . Earned $2,350,000 in 1995 . . . Has 107 doubles in last four seasons . . . Was solid player, but not a star, in first three full seasons . . . Named NL Rookie of the Year in 1992, when he hit 20 homers and drove in 88 runs . . . Entered 1995 with .256 career batting average . . . Overachiever . . . Walked on at UCLA and became All-American before he left campus . . . Dodgers made him sixth-round pick in 1988 draft . . . Born Nov. 4, 1967, in Hackensack, N.J.

Year	Club	Pos.	G	AB	R	H	2B	3B	HR	RBI	SB	Avg.
1991	Los Angeles . . .	1B	14	14	0	1	1	0	0	1	0	.071
1992	Los Angeles . . .	1B	149	545	63	140	30	1	20	88	2	.257
1993	Los Angeles . . .	1B	158	619	74	153	27	2	23	80	0	.247
1994	Los Angeles . . .	1B	111	406	51	108	21	1	14	46	2	.266
1995	Los Angeles . . .	1B	143	551	83	164	29	3	32	105	4	.298
	Totals		575	2135	271	566	108	7	89	320	8	.265

RAUL MONDESI 25 5-11 215 Bats R Throws R

His star keeps rising . . . Nothing he can't do on a baseball field . . . Right fielder won Gold Glove last season, leading league in outfield assists with 16, even though teams stopped running on him . . . Hit 26 homers and stole 27 bases . . . Should join 30-30 club in a full season . . . Hitting in front of Mike Piazza and Eric Karros, he drove in 88 runs and scored 91—and did it all in only 139 games . . . Earned $435,000 in 1995 . . . Named NL Rookie of the Year in '94, when he hit .306 with 16 homers and 56 RBI . . . His success was a long time coming . . . Dodgers signed him as non-drafted free agent in June 1988 . . . Spent six years in minors before sticking . . . Injuries and immaturity held him back . . . Born March 12, 1971, in San Cristobal, D.R. . . . Underwent surgery to repair knee ligaments torn during final weekend of regular season in '95.

Year	Club	Pos.	G	AB	R	H	2B	3B	HR	RBI	SB	Avg.
1993	Los Angeles . . .	OF	42	86	13	25	3	1	4	10	4	.291
1994	Los Angeles . . .	OF	112	434	63	133	27	8	16	56	11	.306
1995	Los Angeles . . .	OF	139	536	91	153	23	6	26	88	27	.285
	Totals		293	1056	167	311	53	15	46	154	42	.295

BRETT BUTLER 38 5-10 160 Bats L Throws L

Center fielder came back to Dodgers from Mets for prospects Dwight Maness and Scott Hunter Aug. 18 and provided his usual pesky spark . . . Dodgers had let him go to Mets as free agent prior to '95 . . . His outspokenness during labor strife played a part in that parting of the ways . . . Dodgers got the best of his season . . . Was hitting .256 at the All-Star break and finished season at exactly .300 . . . Still has some speed left . . . Stole 32 bases in 40 tries . . . Suffered loss of mother to brain tumor during last season . . . Salary was $2 million in 1995 . . . Posted career-high .314 average in '94 . . . Scored 100 or more runs six times and 90-plus two other years . . . Braves made him 23rd-round pick in 1979 draft . . . Born June 15, 1967, in Los Angeles . . . Re-signed with Dodgers for one year at $2 million last fall.

Year	Club	Pos.	G	AB	R	H	2B	3B	HR	RBI	SB	Avg.
1981	Atlanta	OF	40	126	17	32	2	3	0	4	9	.254
1982	Atlanta	OF	89	240	35	52	2	0	0	7	21	.217
1983	Atlanta	OF	151	549	84	154	21	13	5	37	39	.281
1984	Cleveland	OF	159	602	108	162	25	9	3	49	52	.269
1985	Cleveland	OF	152	591	106	184	28	14	5	50	47	.311
1986	Cleveland	OF	161	587	92	163	17	14	4	51	32	.278
1987	Cleveland	OF	137	522	91	154	25	8	9	41	33	.295
1988	San Francisco	OF	157	568	109	163	27	9	6	43	43	.287
1989	San Francisco	OF	154	594	100	168	22	4	4	36	31	.283
1990	San Francisco	OF	160	622	108	192	20	9	3	44	51	.309
1991	Los Angeles ...	OF	161	615	112	182	13	5	2	38	38	.296
1992	Los Angeles ...	OF	157	553	86	171	14	11	3	39	41	.309
1993	Los Angeles ...	OF	156	607	80	181	21	10	1	42	39	.298
1994	Los Angeles ...	OF	111	417	79	131	13	9	8	33	27	.314
1995	NY (NL)-LA ...	OF	129	513	78	154	18	9	1	38	32	.300
	Totals		2074	7706	1285	2243	268	127	54	552	535	.291

GREG GAGNE 34 5-11 180 Bats R Throws R

Veteran shortstop signed one-year, $2.6-million deal with Dodgers as free agent last winter . . . Was steady performer for Kansas City . . . Finished with 49 RBI in '95, marking first time in three years he didn't drive home at least 50 . . . Was the shortstop on both Twins World Series winners, in '87 and '91 . . . Hit game-winning homer in Game 2 of '91 World Series . . . Signed by Royals as free agent prior to '93 season . . . Originally was fifth-round pick in 1979 draft by Yankees . . . Made $4.366 million in '95 . . . Born Nov. 12, 1961, in Fall River, Mass.

Year	Club	Pos.	G	AB	R	H	2B	3B	HR	RBI	SB	Avg.
1983	Minnesota	SS	10	27	2	3	1	0	0	3	0	.111
1984	Minnesota	PR-PH	2	1	0	0	0	0	0	0	0	.000
1985	Minnesota	SS	114	293	37	66	15	3	2	23	10	.225
1986	Minnesota	SS-2B	156	472	63	118	22	6	12	54	12	.250
1987	Minnesota	SS-OF-2B	137	437	68	116	28	7	10	40	6	.265
1988	Minnesota	SS-OF-2B-3B	149	461	70	109	20	6	14	48	15	.236
1989	Minnesota	SS-OF	149	460	69	125	29	7	9	48	11	.272
1990	Minnesota	SS-OF	138	388	38	91	22	3	7	38	8	.235
1991	Minnesota	SS-3B	139	408	52	108	23	3	8	42	11	.265
1992	Minnesota	SS	146	439	53	108	23	0	7	39	6	.246
1993	Kansas City ...	SS	159	540	66	151	32	3	10	57	10	.280
1994	Kansas City ...	SS	107	375	39	97	23	3	7	51	10	.259
1995	Kansas City ...	SS	120	430	58	110	25	4	6	49	3	.256
	Totals		1526	4731	615	1202	263	45	92	492	102	.254

MIKE BLOWERS 30 6-2 210 **Bats R Throws R**

Became a Dodger in November when Mariners traded him for minor leaguers Miguel Cairo and Willis Otanez . . . This was after a breakthrough season in which he set career highs in hits (113), doubles (24), home runs (23) and RBI (96) . . . Was hitting only .118 with no homers and seven RBI in first 18 games . . . Then he went 4-for-5 against Boston May 24 and picked up steam from there . . . Third baseman is a career .316 batter against left-handers . . . Also has 25 of his 54 career homers against lefties . . . Expos picked him in 10th round of 1986 draft . . . Sent by Montreal to Yankees in John Candelaria trade, Aug. 27, 1989 . . . Seattle acquired him from Yanks for Jim Blueberg, May 17, 1991 . . . Made $500,000 in '95 . . . Born April 24, 1965, in Wurzburg, Germany.

Year	Club	Pos.	G	AB	R	H	2B	3B	HR	RBI	SB	Avg.
1989	New York (AL)	3B	13	38	2	10	0	0	0	3	0	.263
1990	New York (AL)	3B	48	144	16	27	4	0	5	21	1	.188
1991	New York (AL)	3B	15	35	3	7	0	0	1	1	0	.200
1992	Seattle	3B-1B	31	73	7	14	3	0	1	2	0	.192
1993	Seattle	3B-OF-1B-C	127	379	55	106	23	3	15	57	1	.280
1994	Seattle	3B-1B-OF	85	270	37	78	13	0	9	49	2	.289
1995	Seattle	3B-1B-OF	143	439	59	113	24	1	23	96	2	.257
	Totals		453	1378	179	355	67	4	54	229	6	.258

CHAD FONVILLE 25 5-6 160 **Bats S Throws R**

Spunky little guy came out of nowhere and became important player down the stretch . . . Hit .278 with 20 steals in 27 attempts . . . Took over at shortstop for Jose Offerman late in season . . . Also played second, left and center . . . Had only seven extra-base hits (six doubles, one triple) among his 89 hits . . . Dodgers got him on waivers May 31 from Expos, who wanted to send him to minors . . . Expos had picked him in Rule V draft from Giants . . . Played in Class-A ball in 1994 . . . Salary was $109,000 in 1995 . . . Giants made him 11th-round pick in 1982 . . . Hit above .300 in each of last two minor-league seasons . . . Had total of 110 steals in three minor-league seasons . . . Born March 5, 1971, in Jacksonville, N.C.

Year	Club	Pos.	G	AB	R	H	2B	3B	HR	RBI	SB	Avg.
1995	Los Angeles ...	SS-2B-OF	102	320	43	89	6	1	0	16	20	.278

HIDEO NOMO 27 6-2 210 Bats R Throws R

Japanese import proved to be far more than a novelty . . . Put up some mind-boggling numbers in first season in our major leagues and won NL Rookie of the Year honors over Braves' Chipper Jones . . . Became fourth straight Dodger to win award . . . Led league with 236 strikeouts, in 191⅓ innings . . . Also posted league-low .182 opponents' batting average . . . Tied the Braves' Greg Maddux for league lead with three shutouts and was second to Maddux in ERA (2.54) . . . Also led league in wild pitches (19) and balks (5) . . . Funky, twisting windup earned him nickname "Tornado" from Japanese press . . . Earned $109,000 in salary plus $2-million signing bonus in '95 . . . Left Japan's major-league Kintetsu Buffaloes team after five seasons . . . Posted 78-46 record there, including two 17-win seasons . . . Dodgers signed him as non-drafted free agent in February 1995 . . . Born Aug. 31, 1968, in Osaka, Japan . . . Became close friends with Ismael Valdes, despite language gap.

Year	Club	G	IP	W	L	Pct.	SO	BB	H	ERA
1995	Los Angeles	28	191⅓	13	6	.684	236	78	124	2.54

RAMON MARTINEZ 28 6-5 175 Bats L Throws R

Proved again he was ace of the staff . . . Had best season since 1991, when he last won 17 . . . Won nine of his last 10 decisions . . . Allowed only 176 hits in 206⅓ innings . . . Finished third in NL in wins (17) and innings, fourth in winning percentage (.708), tied for fifth in complete games (9) and sixth in opponents' average (.231) . . . Also pitched a no-hitter against Florida . . . Earned $3,925,000 in '95 . . . Bothered by elbow problems in 1991 and 1992 . . . Won 20 with 2.92 ERA and tied Sandy Koufax's single-game club record with 18 strikeouts in 1990 . . . Signed by Dodgers as non-drafted free agent, at age 16, in September 1984 . . . Younger brother and ex-LA teammate Pedro pitches for Expos . . . Born March 22, 1968, in Santo

Domingo, D.R. . . . Re-signed with Dodgers as free agent in four-year, $15-million deal last winter.

Year	Club	G	IP	W	L	Pct.	SO	BB	H	ERA
1988	Los Angeles	9	35⅔	1	3	.250	23	22	27	3.79
1989	Los Angeles	15	98⅔	6	4	.600	89	41	79	3.19
1990	Los Angeles	33	234⅓	20	6	.769	223	67	191	2.92
1991	Los Angeles	33	220⅓	17	13	.567	150	69	190	3.27
1992	Los Angeles	25	150⅔	8	11	.421	101	69	141	4.00
1993	Los Angeles	32	211⅔	10	12	.455	127	104	202	3.44
1994	Los Angeles	24	170	12	7	.632	119	56	160	3.97
1995	Los Angeles	30	206⅓	17	7	.708	138	81	176	3.66
	Totals	201	1327⅔	91	63	.591	970	509	1166	3.48

ISMAEL VALDES 22 6-3 210 Bats R Throws R

Future looks bright for this hard thrower . . . Won 13 games and posted 3.05 ERA in '95 . . . Led staff with six complete games . . . Allowed only 168 hits in 197⅔ innings . . . Lefties and righties both hit .228 against him . . . Finished fourth in NL in ERA and opponents' batting average . . . Salary was $136,000 in 1995 . . . Went 3-1 with Dodgers in 1994, when he jumped from San Antonio (AA) to Albuquerque (AAA) to big leagues . . . At 20, he was youngest player in NL when promoted . . . Another Mexican find of Dodgers scout Mike Brito, who also discovered Fernando Valenzuela . . . Signed by Dodgers as non-drafted free agent in June 1991 . . . Went 17-8 and threw 13 complete games for Mexico City (A) in 1993 . . . Born Aug. 21, 1973, in Victoria Tamaulipas, Mexico.

Year	Club	G	IP	W	L	Pct.	SO	BB	H	ERA
1994	Los Angeles	21	28⅓	3	1	.750	28	10	21	3.18
1995	Los Angeles	33	197⅔	13	11	.542	150	51	168	3.05
	Totals	54	226	16	12	.571	178	61	189	3.07

TODD WORRELL 36 6-5 225 Bats R Throws R

Hard-throwing closer stabilized a shaky bullpen . . . Saved 32 games in 36 tries . . . Allowed only 50 hits and struck out 61 in 62⅓ innings . . . Salary was $4,666,667 in 1995 . . . Save total was his best since 1988, when he saved 32 for St. Louis . . . Racked up 101 saves in three-year period from 1986-88 . . . First two seasons in Los Angeles weren't pretty . . . Blew 8-of-19 save opportunities and had 4.29 ERA in '94, when his eight blown saves were most in NL . . . Elbow and forearm trouble slowed him in 1993, when he posted 6.05 ERA . . . NL All-Star in 1988 . . . Pitched in two World Series with St. Louis, in 1985 and 1987 . . . Did not pitch at all after elbow surgery in 1990 . . . Cards made him 22nd overall pick in 1982 draft, out of Biola (Cal.) College . . . Born Sept. 28, 1959, in Arcadia, Cal. . . . Has 177 career saves.

Year	Club	G	IP	W	L	Pct.	SO	BB	H	ERA
1985	St. Louis	17	21⅓	3	0	1.000	17	7	17	2.91
1986	St. Louis	74	103⅔	9	10	.474	73	41	86	2.08
1987	St. Louis	75	94⅔	8	6	.571	92	34	86	2.66
1988	St. Louis	68	90	5	9	.357	78	34	69	3.00
1989	St. Louis	47	51⅔	3	5	.375	41	26	42	2.96
1990	St. Louis			Injured						
1991	St. Louis			Injured						
1992	St. Louis	67	64	5	3	.625	64	25	45	2.11
1993	Los Angeles	35	38⅔	1	1	.500	31	11	46	6.05
1994	Los Angeles	38	42	6	5	.545	44	12	37	4.29
1995	Los Angeles	59	62⅓	4	1	.800	61	19	50	2.02
	Totals	480	568⅔	44	40	.524	501	209	478	2.86

TOP PROSPECTS

ROGER CEDENO 21 6-1 170 Bats S Throws R

Speedy outfielder could be ready to take over in center field . . . Hit .305 and stole 23 bases for Albuquerque (AAA) in '95 . . . Batted .321 and stole 30 bases there in '94 . . . Hit .238 in 42 at-bats for Dodgers in '95 . . . Born Aug. 16, 1974, in Valencia Estado, Venezuela . . . Signed by Dodgers as non-drafted free agent in March 1991.

KARIM GARCIA 20 6-0 175 Bats L Throws L

Had big season for Albuquerque (AAA) at age 19 . . . Hit .319 with 20 homers and drove in 90 runs . . . Can only get better . . . Skipped Double-A level after big season (.265, 21 homers, 84 RBI) for Vero Beach (A) in 1994 . . . Outfielder possesses very strong arm . . . Born Oct. 29, 1975, in Ciudad Obregon, Mexico . . . Signed by Dodgers as non-drafted free agent in July 1992.

PAUL KONERKO 20 6-3 205 Bats S Throws R

Big catcher could be Mike Piazza's successor in a few years . . . Hit .277 with 19 homers and 77 RBI for San Bernardino (AA) in '95 . . . Dodgers made him first catcher taken in 1994 draft and the 13th player chosen overall . . . Batted .288 with 58 RBI in 257 at-bats for Yakima (A) in 1994 . . . Born March 5, 1976, in Providence, R.I.

CHAN HO PARK 22 6-2 195 **Bats R Throws R**

He's not Hideo Nomo, but he has a promising future . . . First Korean to play in majors . . . Went 6-7 with 4.19 ERA for Albuquerque (AAA) in '95 and allowed only 93 hits in 110 innings . . . Made big-league debut in 1994, when he went 0-0, 11.25 in four innings for LA . . . Went 0-0, 4.50 in another four innings for Dodgers in '95 . . . Born June 30, 1973, in Kong Ju City, Korea . . . Dodgers signed him as non-drafted free agent in January 1994.

MANAGER TOM LASORDA: Back for his 20th season . . .

But only after a year in which he came under criticism for everything from napping on the bench to the handling of his bullpen . . . Putting quick end to speculation, Dodgers extended his contract through '96 season days after club's disappointing exit from Division Series . . . Still one of baseball's best ambassadors . . . With 78-66 finish in '95, his career big-league mark is 1,558-1,404 . . . Passed Clark Griffith and moved into 14th place on all-time win list . . . Can pass Dick Williams, Fred Clark and Ralph Houk with 62 more victories . . . Has won seven division titles, three pennants and two World Series since replacing Walter Alston in 1977 . . . Only Alston has won more games as Dodgers manager (2,042) . . . Talk about bleeding Dodger Blue. This will be his 47th year in the Dodgers organization . . . Office in Dodger Stadium is littered with pictures of Frank Sinatra, Don Rickles and other stars . . . His schtick ranks with anybody's . . . Had short stay in big leagues as pitcher, 1954 with Dodgers and 1955 with Kansas City, and was 0-4 in 26 games . . . Indefatigable spirit and energy . . . Still throws batting practice . . . Born Sept. 22, 1927, in Norristown, Pa.

ALL-TIME DODGER SEASON RECORDS

BATTING: Babe Herman, .393, 1930
HRs: Duke Snider, 43, 1956
RBI: Tommy Davis, 153, 1962
STEALS: Maury Wills, 104, 1962
WINS: Joe McGinnity, 29, 1900
STRIKEOUTS: Sandy Koufax, 382, 1965

SAN DIEGO PADRES

TEAM DIRECTORY: Principal Owner: John Moores; CEO: Larry Lucchino; GM: Kevin Towers; Dir. Minor League Adm.: Priscilla Oppenheimer; Dir. Media Rel. and Team Travel: Roger Riley; Mgr.: Bruce Bochy; Coaches: Tim Flannery, Davey Lopes, Grady Little, Rob Picciolo, Merv Rettenmund. Home: San Diego Jack Murphy Stadium (47,750). Field distances: 327, l.f. line; 405, c.f.; 327, r.f. line. Spring training: Peoria, Ariz.

SCOUTING REPORT

HITTING: Any lineup that has Tony Gwynn (.368, 9, 90) in it can't be bad. Mr. Padre did it again last season, winning his sixth

Tony Gwynn comes off .368 in search of 7th batting title.

batting title and helping the Padres toward a total of 668 runs, sixth-best in the NL.

Ken Caminiti (.302, 26, 94) got out of the Astrodome and turned into a slugger, giving the Padres at least one legitimate home-run threat. Steve Finley (.297, 10, 44, 104 runs, 36 steals) is a force in either the No. 1 or No. 2 spots. He had to flip-flop because of the usual assortment of injuries to Bip Roberts (.304 in 296 at-bats, 20 steals). Now Roberts is gone in the trade for Wally Joyner (.310, 12, 83 with the Royals).

The Padres' problem isn't so much run production, but power as they mustered only 116 homers in '95. Melvin Nieves (.205, 14, 38) has power, but must cut down on his strikeouts (88 in 234 at-bats) to play more regularly.

PITCHING: Even without the traded Andy Benes, the Padres have a promising young rotation, capable of engineering an improvement on the staff's 4.13 ERA of last season. Right-handers Joey Hamilton (6-9, 3.08), Andy Ashby (12-10, 2.94) and Scott Sanders (5-5, 4.30) all figure to improve and lefty Glenn Dishman (4-8, 5.01) showed promise. Veteran Bob Tewksbury (8-7, 4.58 with the Rangers) was signed to provide experience and there are enough fifth-starter candidates in the re-signed Fernando Valenzuela and Brian Williams.

Closer Trevor Hoffman (7-4, 3.88, 31 saves) seems capable of 40 saves. With him in the bullpen are more quality, young hard throwers in Doug Bochtler (4-4, 3.57), Bryce Florie (2-2, 3.01), Andres Berumen (2-3, 5.68), Dustin Hermanson (3-1, 6.82) and Ron Villone (2-1, 4.21).

FIELDING: The plusses are numerous: Gwynn, a former Gold Glove winner in right; re-signed second baseman Jody Reed, who committed only four errors all year; and Finley, an acrobatic center fielder with a strong arm.

Caminiti also has the league's best throwing arm at third, but suffered through a first-half throwing slump that led to his alarmingly high total of 27 errors. Brad Ausmus is above average behind the plate. Shortstop Andujar Cedeno remains too inconsistent for comfort. The slick-fielding Joyner (three errors last season) takes over at first.

OUTLOOK: Bruce Bochy's Padres could emerge as the surprise in the NL West, and perhaps the league, coming off a 70-74 finish in '95. The likelihood of that occurring depends upon the development of many young pitchers in the rotation and bullpen. The

Padres won't be able to pound on too many people offensively, but they do have enough quality hitters to get by.

Most likely, everything won't come together, and the Padres will be closer to the .500 mark than to a postseason appearance.

PADRE PROFILES

TONY GWYNN 35 5-11 225 Bats L Throws L

Ho-hum . . . Added another batting title—his sixth during a Hall-of-Fame-caliber career . . . Overtook Los Angeles' Mike Piazza down the stretch and finished at .368 . . . Also drove in career-high 90 runs . . . Hit .389 against righties and .387 in Jack Murphy Stadium . . . Once again, he was hardest to strike out in NL, with one whiff per 38.5 at-bats . . . Was making a serious run at .400 when strike hit in August 1994 . . . His .394 mark was the highest in the NL since Bill Terry hit .401 in 1930 . . . Dedicated 1994 season to his father, who died the previous November . . . Knee injuries ended his three previous seasons prematurely, bringing on criticism of his bulging middle . . . Has hit .300 or more for 13 consecutive seasons, longest streak since Stan Musial did it 16 years in a row . . . Brother Chris plays for the Dodgers, but this guy got the good-hitting genes . . . Padres' third-round pick in 1981, out of San Diego State, where he also played basketball . . . Right fielder earned $4 million last season . . . Born May 9, 1960, in Los Angeles.

Year	Club	Pos.	G	AB	R	H	2B	3B	HR	RBI	SB	Avg.
1982	San Diego	OF	54	190	33	55	12	2	1	17	8	.289
1983	San Diego	OF	86	304	34	94	12	2	1	37	7	.309
1984	San Diego	OF	158	606	88	213	21	10	5	71	33	.351
1985	San Diego	OF	154	622	90	197	29	5	6	46	14	.317
1986	San Diego	OF	160	642	107	211	33	7	14	59	37	.329
1987	San Diego	OF	157	589	119	218	36	13	7	54	56	.370
1988	San Diego	OF	133	521	64	163	22	5	7	70	26	.313
1989	San Diego	OF	158	604	82	203	27	7	4	62	40	.336
1990	San Diego	OF	141	573	79	177	29	10	4	72	17	.309
1991	San Diego	OF	134	530	69	168	27	11	4	62	8	.317
1992	San Diego	OF	128	520	77	165	27	3	6	41	3	.317
1993	San Diego	OF	122	489	70	175	41	3	7	59	14	.358
1994	San Diego	OF	110	419	79	165	35	1	12	64	5	.394
1995	San Diego	OF	135	535	82	197	33	1	9	90	17	.368
	Totals		1830	7144	1073	2401	384	80	87	804	285	.336

STEVE FINLEY 31 6-2 180 Bats L Throws L

Center fielder put together best season after being part of the 12-player mega-deal between Padres and Astros prior to '95 . . . Set career highs in average (.297) and runs (104) . . . Got red-hot when put in leadoff spot in midseason, hitting .390 with 49 runs in 47-game stretch . . . Hit .326 against lefties . . . Salary was $4,450,000 in 1995 . . . Signed two-year deal last offseason . . . Previous two seasons were interrupted by injuries . . . Broke a bone in his right hand in June 1994 and broke his wrist in 1993, when he also suffered from a case of Bell's Palsy in spring training . . . Traded to Houston from Baltimore along with Pete Harnisch and Curt Schilling for Glenn Davis prior to 1991 season . . . Orioles' 14th-round pick in 1987 draft . . . Born March 12, 1965, in Union City, Tenn.

Year	Club	Pos.	G	AB	R	H	2B	3B	HR	RBI	SB	Avg.
1989	Baltimore	OF	81	217	35	54	5	2	2	25	17	.249
1990	Baltimore	OF	142	464	46	119	16	4	3	37	22	.256
1991	Houston	OF	159	596	84	170	28	10	8	54	34	.285
1992	Houston	OF	162	607	84	177	29	13	5	55	44	.292
1993	Houston	OF	142	545	69	145	15	13	8	44	19	.266
1994	Houston	OF	94	373	64	103	16	5	11	33	13	.276
1995	San Diego	OF	139	562	104	167	23	8	10	44	36	.297
	Totals		919	3364	486	935	132	55	47	292	185	.278

KEN CAMINITI 32 6-0 205 Bats S Throws R

Another reason Astros have to regret that 12-player blockbuster with Padres prior to '95 . . . Set career highs in average (.302), homers (26) and RBI (94), filling No. 4 spot in lineup behind Tony Gwynn . . . Became first major-leaguer to hit home runs from both sides of the plate three times in one season. Actually, he did it within four-game span from Sept. 16-19 . . . Third baseman's cannon arm deserted him last season, when he committed career-high 25 errors, mostly on errant throws, but he won first Gold Glove . . . Salary was $4,550,000 in 1995 . . . Pittsburgh manager Jim Leyland intentionally walked him three times in a game in 1994 . . . Astros' third-round pick in 1984 draft, out of San Jose State . . . Born April 21, 1963, in Hanford, Cal. . . . Was re-signed to two-year deal last winter.

Year	Club	Pos.	G	AB	R	H	2B	3B	HR	RBI	SB	Avg.
1987	Houston	3B	63	203	10	50	7	1	3	23	0	.246
1988	Houston	3B	30	83	5	15	2	0	1	7	0	.181
1989	Houston	3B	161	585	71	149	31	3	10	72	4	.255
1990	Houston	3B	153	541	52	131	20	2	4	51	9	.242
1991	Houston	3B	152	574	65	145	30	3	13	80	4	.253
1992	Houston	3B	135	506	68	149	31	2	13	62	10	.294
1993	Houston	3B	143	543	75	142	31	0	13	75	8	.262
1994	Houston	3B	111	406	63	115	28	2	18	75	4	.283
1995	San Diego	3B	143	526	74	159	33	0	26	94	12	.302
	Totals		1091	3967	483	1055	213	13	101	539	51	.266

WALLY JOYNER 33 6-2 200 Bats L Throws L

Royals traded him to Padres with Aaron Dorlarque for Bip Roberts and Bryan Wolff last winter . . . Doesn't have much power anymore, but is productive . . . Consistently hits for high average and drives in good number of runs . . . Batting average in '95 was just one point lower than career-high .311 in '94 . . . Was definition of a power-hitting first baseman in '87, when he slugged 34 home runs and drove in 117 runs for Angels . . . Had an emotional parting of the ways with Angels after the '91 season, crying when he left . . . Signed by Kansas City as free agent prior to '92 season . . . Finished second to Jose Canseco in 1986 AL Rookie of the Year voting . . . Batted .455 for Angels vs. Boston in 1986 ALCS . . . Was the highest-paid Royal in '95 at $4.8 million . . . Born June 16, 1962, in Atlanta . . . Angels made him third-round pick in 1983, out of Brigham Young.

Year	Club	Pos.	G	AB	R	H	2B	3B	HR	RBI	SB	Avg.
1986	California	1B	154	593	82	172	27	3	22	100	5	.290
1987	California	1B	149	564	100	161	33	1	34	117	8	.285
1988	California	1B	158	597	81	176	31	2	13	85	8	.295
1989	California	1B	159	593	78	167	30	2	16	79	3	.282
1990	California	1B	83	310	35	83	15	0	8	41	2	.268
1991	California	1B	143	551	79	166	34	3	21	96	2	.301
1992	Kansas City ...	1B	149	572	66	154	36	2	9	66	11	.269
1993	Kansas City ...	1B	141	497	83	145	36	3	15	65	5	.292
1994	Kansas City ...	1B	97	363	52	113	20	3	8	57	3	.311
1995	Kansas City ...	1B	131	465	69	144	28	0	12	83	3	.310
	Totals		1364	5105	725	1481	290	19	158	789	50	.290

JODY REED 33 5-9 165 **Bats R Throws R**

Padres' last-minute free-agent signee was well worth the price in '95 . . . Stepped in and solidified infield defense, committing only four errors in 130 games . . . Hit .256, but was valuable in No. 2 spot, moving over runners and doing the little things . . . Signed out of Homestead, Fla., free-agent camp . . . Salary was $200,000 in 1995 . . . Padres were his fourth club in as many years . . . Played with Milwaukee in 1994 and Los Angeles in 1993 after five seasons as starter in Boston . . . Foolishly turned down huge multi-year offer from Dodgers, who then traded for Delino DeShields . . . Selected by Rockies in first round of expansion draft and immediately dealt to Los Angeles for Rudy Seanez . . . Red Sox' eighth-round pick in 1984 draft . . . Born July 26, 1962, in Tampa . . . Re-signed two-year, $1.4-million contract in December.

Year	Club	Pos.	G	AB	R	H	2B	3B	HR	RBI	SB	Avg.
1987	Boston	SS-2B-3B	9	30	4	9	1	1	0	8	1	.300
1988	Boston	SS-2B-3B	109	338	60	99	23	1	1	28	1	.293
1989	Boston	SS-2B-3B-OF	146	524	76	151	42	2	3	40	4	.288
1990	Boston	2B-SS	155	598	70	173	45	0	5	51	4	.289
1991	Boston	2B	153	618	87	175	42	2	5	60	6	.283
1992	Boston	2B	143	550	64	136	27	1	3	40	7	.247
1993	Los Angeles . . .	2B	132	445	48	123	21	2	2	31	1	.276
1994	Milwaukee	2B	108	399	48	108	22	0	2	37	5	.271
1995	San Diego	2B-SS	131	445	58	114	18	1	4	40	6	.256
	Totals		1086	3947	515	1088	241	10	25	335	35	.276

BRAD AUSMUS 26 5-11 190 **Bats R Throws R**

Promising young catcher developed offensively in second full season . . . Hit career-best .293 with 34 RBI . . . Also stole 16 bases . . . Batted .314 against lefties and .323 on the road . . . Defense still is best part of his game . . . Strong thrower nailed 39-of-94 would-be basestealers, a 42-percent rate . . . Made only six errors in 100 games . . . Salary was $197,000 in 1995 . . . Dartmouth product is one-half of brainy catching duo, along with backup Brian Johnson from Stanford . . . Part of Padres' steal from Rockies as they acquired Andy Ashby and Doug Bochtler for Greg Harris and Bruce Hurst, July 26, 1993 . . .

Yanks' 47th-round pick in 1987 draft . . . Born April 14, 1969, in New Haven, Conn.

Year	Club	Pos.	G	AB	R	H	2B	3B	HR	RBI	SB	Avg.
1993	San Diego	C	49	160	18	41	8	1	5	12	2	.256
1994	San Diego	C-1B	101	327	45	82	12	1	7	24	5	.251
1995	San Diego	C-1B	103	328	44	96	16	4	5	34	16	.293
	Totals		253	815	107	219	36	6	17	70	23	.269

JOEY HAMILTON 25 6-4 225 Bats R Throws R

Durable, bulldog-type pitcher could only register six victories despite otherwise impressive numbers . . . Led staff with 204⅓ innings, during which he allowed only 189 hits . . . Pitched two shutouts . . . ERA was 3.08, just a tad higher than 1994, when he went 9-6 as a rookie . . . Posted ninth-best opponents' average in NL (.246) . . . Lefties hit only .229 against him . . . Issued only 2.47 walks per nine innings . . . Allowed one or fewer earned runs in seven of his 16 starts in 1994 . . . Offensive woes are becoming legendary . . . Went 57 at-bats before getting his first major-league hit . . . Salary was $170,000 in 1995 . . . Padres' first-round pick in 1991 draft, the eighth player taken overall . . . Starred at Georgia Southern University . . . Born Sept. 9, 1970, in Statesboro, Ga.

Year	Club	G	IP	W	L	Pct.	SO	BB	H	ERA
1994	San Diego	16	108⅔	9	6	.600	61	29	98	2.98
1995	San Diego	31	204⅓	6	9	.400	123	56	189	3.08
	Totals	47	313	15	15	.500	184	85	287	3.05

ANDY ASHBY 28 6-5 195 Bats R Throws R

Finally turned potential into success . . . Led staff with 12 victories and his 2.94 ERA was third-lowest in NL . . . Allowed only 180 hits in 192⅔ innings . . . Tied for league lead with 31 starts . . . Tied for eighth in league with 150 strikeouts . . . Salary was $755,000 in 1995 . . . Padres got him in one-sided deal with Rockies . . . Went west with Brad Ausmus and Doug Bochtler for Greg Harris and Bruce Hurst, July 26, 1993 . . . Went 9-17 in one-plus seasons with Padres before emerging last year . . . Stay in Colorado was positively dreadful . . . Went 0-4 with 8.50 ERA, allowing 89 hits and 32 walks in 54 innings . . . Rockies took him off Phillies' roster in expansion draft prior to '93 . . . Phillies signed him as non-drafted free agent in May 1986 . . . Born July 11, 1967, in Kansas City, Mo.

Year	Club	G	IP	W	L	Pct.	SO	BB	H	ERA
1991	Philadelphia	8	42	1	5	.167	26	19	41	6.00
1992	Philadelphia	10	37	1	3	.250	24	21	42	7.54
1993	Col.-SD	32	123	3	10	.231	77	56	168	6.80
1994	San Diego	24	164⅓	6	11	.353	121	43	145	3.40
1995	San Diego	31	192⅔	12	10	.545	150	62	180	2.94
	Totals	105	559	23	39	.371	398	201	576	4.46

FERNANDO VALENZUELA 35 5-11 220 B: L T: L

Still hanging around, although his presence is probably more because of his gate appeal than effectiveness . . . Did have best season last year, at least record-wise, in nearly a decade . . . Went 8-3 despite allowing 101 hits, including 16 homers, in 90⅓ innings . . . Made 15 starts and 14 relief appearances . . . In 10-year run with Dodgers, highlights included sparking them to World Series in 1981 as well as four LCS appearances . . . Phenomenal rookie season in '81 spawned Fernando-mania . . . Signed by Padres as free agent before beginning of '95 . . . Earned $1,000,000 last season and re-signed for $500,000 in December . . . Born Nov. 1, 1960, in Sonora, Mexico.

Year	Club	G	IP	W	L	Pct.	SO	BB	H	ERA
1980	Los Angeles	10	18	2	0	1.000	16	5	8	0.00
1981	Los Angeles	25	192	13	7	.650	180	61	140	2.48
1982	Los Angeles	37	285	19	13	.594	199	83	247	2.87
1983	Los Angeles	35	257	15	10	.600	189	99	245	3.75
1984	Los Angeles	34	261	12	17	.414	240	106	218	3.03
1985	Los Angeles	35	272⅓	17	10	.630	208	101	211	2.45
1986	Los Angeles	34	269⅓	21	11	.656	242	85	226	3.14
1987	Los Angeles	34	251	14	14	.500	190	124	254	3.98
1988	Los Angeles	23	142⅓	5	8	.385	64	76	142	4.24
1989	Los Angeles	31	196⅔	10	13	.435	116	98	185	3.43
1990	Los Angeles	33	204	13	13	.500	115	77	223	4.59
1991	California	2	6⅔	0	2	.000	5	3	14	12.15
1993	Baltimore	32	178⅔	8	10	.444	78	79	179	4.94
1994	Philadelphia	8	45	1	2	.333	19	7	42	3.00
1995	San Diego	29	90⅓	8	3	.727	57	34	101	4.98
	Totals	402	2669⅓	158	133	.543	1918	1038	2435	3.49

TREVOR HOFFMAN 28 6-2 200 Bats R Throws R

Hard-throwing closer had an inconsistent season . . . Set career high with 31 saves, but blew eight other opportunities . . . Allowed 6-of-18 inherited runners to score . . . ERA rose to 3.88 from 2.57 in 1994 . . . Also surrendered 10 homers in 53⅓ innings . . . Traded to Padres with Andres Berumen and Jose Martinez by Marlins for Gary Sheffield and Rich Rodriguez, June 24, 1993 . . . Didn't allow any of 17 inherited runners to score after his arrival . . . Marlins chose him from Reds in the expansion draft prior to '93 . . . His 1995 salary was $315,000 . . . Reds' 11th-round pick in 1989 draft . . . Born Oct. 13, 1967, in Bellflower, Cal. . . . Brother Glenn played for Red Sox, Dodgers and Angels . . . Father was known as the Singing Usher at Anaheim Stadium.

Year	Club	G	IP	W	L	Pct.	SO	BB	H	ERA
1993	Fla.-S.D.	67	90	4	6	.400	79	39	80	3.90
1994	San Diego	47	56	4	4	.500	68	20	39	2.57
1995	San Diego	55	53⅓	7	4	.636	52	14	48	3.88
	Totals	169	199⅓	15	14	.517	199	73	167	3.52

SCOTT SANDERS 27 6-4 220 Bats R Throws R

Injury ended his season prematurely . . . Went 5-5 despite allowing only 79 hits in 90 innings . . . Struck out just under nine batters per nine innings . . . Fanned 10 and 12 in back-to-back starts in July . . . He's no easy out with a bat in his hands . . . Batted .296 . . . Went 4-8 in 23 appearances in first full season in 1994 . . . Tough-luck pitcher allowed two or fewer runs in six of his last 10 starts that year, but went 2-4 . . . Split 1993 between Padres and Las Vegas (AAA) . . . Struck out a league-leading 161 in 152⅓ innings at Las Vegas . . . Went 3-3 with 4.13 ERA in nine starts with Padres . . . Padres made him a supplemental pick between first and second rounds in 1990 draft . . . Born March 25, 1969, in Hannibal, Mo.

Year	Club	G	IP	W	L	Pct.	SO	BB	H	ERA
1993	San Diego	9	52⅓	3	3	.500	37	23	54	4.13
1994	San Diego	23	111	4	8	.333	109	48	103	4.78
1995	San Diego	17	90	5	5	.500	88	31	79	4.30
	Totals	49	253⅓	12	16	.429	234	102	236	4.48

TOP PROSPECTS

DUSTIN HERMANSON 23 6-2 195 Bats R Throws R
Padres' top pick in 1994 draft surfaced as setup man last season . . . Went 3-1, but had lofty 6.82 ERA in 31⅔ innings for Padres . . . Had 11 saves, 0-1 record and 3.50 ERA for Las Vegas (AAA) before promotion . . . Third player picked in 1994 draft . . . Saved eight games, struck out 30 and had 0.43 ERA in 21 innings for Wichita (AA) before moved to Las Vegas in '94 . . . Born Dec. 21, 1972, in Hamilton, Ohio.

RAY McDAVID 24 6-3 195 Bats L Throws R
Outfielder has lots of talent, but still hasn't reached potential . . . Slowed by injury . . . Hit .271 with five homers and 27 RBI in 166 at-bats for Las Vegas (AAA) . . . Went 3-for-17 (.176) in seven games with Padres . . . Also hit .271 in 1994 for Las Vegas . . . Stole 33 bases for Wichita (AA) in 1993 . . . Padres' ninth-round pick in 1989 draft . . . Born July 20, 1971, in San Diego.

MARC NEWFIELD 23 6-4 210 Bats R Throws R
Outfield prospect came to Padres from Seattle with Ron Villone for Andy Benes last July . . . Power numbers fell off after big 1994 season . . . Hit .309 with one homer and seven RBI in 55 at-bats with Padres after posting .189 mark in 85 at-bats with Mariners in '95 . . . Hit .343 with three homers and 12 RBI for Las Vegas (AAA) and .278 with five homers and 30 RBI for Tacoma (AAA) last year . . . Batted .349 with 19 homers and 83 RBI for Calgary in 1994 . . . Mariners made him sixth overall pick in 1990 draft . . . Born Oct. 19, 1972, in Sacramento, Cal.

RAUL CASANOVA 23 5-11 205 Bats S Throws R
Switch-hitting catcher with arm strong enough to stop running game . . . Injuries limited him to .271 average, 12 homers and 44 RBI in 306 at-bats for Wichita (AA) . . . Had big year for Rancho Cucamonga (A) in 1994, hitting .340 with 23 homers and 120 RBI . . . Padres got him from Mets with Wally Whitehurst and D.J. Dozier for Tony Fernandez prior to '93 . . . Mets picked him in eighth round in 1990 draft . . . Born Aug. 23, 1972, in Humacao, P.R.

MANAGER BRUCE BOCHY: After much speculation about

his departure, he is back for another season . . . Tony Gwynn, for one, publicly endorsed this guy's return when it was in doubt . . . Popular with players . . . Got his break when then-GM Randy Smith named him manager after the 1994 season, hours after Jim Riggleman left for the manager's job with the Cubs . . . Now Smith is gone, but he remains . . . Received a one-year extension . . . Padres' 70-74 mark in 1995 represented major-league managerial debut of Padres' 15th manager in 27-year club history . . . Won minor-league titles at Spokane (A), High Desert (A) and Wichita (AA) in four years of managing in Padres system . . . Joined Riggleman's staff in 1993 . . . Was third-base coach in 1994 . . . Began pro career in 1975, when he was drafted in first round by Astros . . . Made major-league debut in 1978 . . . Your basic backup catcher during big-league career that spanned nine seasons . . . His most at-bats (154) came in 1978 rookie season . . . Hit .239 in 333 major-league games . . . Joined Padres in 1983 and played five seasons, including pennant-winning 1984 season . . . Delivered pinch-hit single in only World Series at-bat (vs. Tigers in 1984) . . . Born April 16, 1955, in Landes de Boussac, France.

ALL-TIME PADRE SEASON RECORDS

BATTING: Tony Gwynn, .394, 1994
HRs: Fred McGriff, 35, 1992
RBI: Dave Winfield, 118, 1979
STEALS: Alan Wiggins, 70, 1984
WINS: Randy Jones, 22, 1976
STRIKEOUTS: Clay Kirby, 231, 1971

SAN FRANCISCO GIANTS

TEAM DIRECTORY: Pres./Managing General Partner: Peter Magowan; Sr. VP/Gen. Mgr.: Bob Quinn; Exec. VP: Larry Baer; Sr. VP-Business Oper.: Pat Gallagher; Sr. VP-Player Pers.: Brian Sabean; Dir. Pub. Rel.: Bob Rose; Dir. Team Travel: Reggie Younger; Mgr.: Dusty Baker; Coaches: Bobby Bonds, Bob Brenly, Wendell Kim, Bob Lillis, Dick Pole, Denny Sommers. Home: Candlestick Park (62,000). Field distances: 335, l.f. line; 365 l.c.; 400, c.f.; 365, l.c.; 328, r.f. line. Spring training: Scottsdale, Ariz.

SCOUTING REPORT

HITTING: Dusty Baker doesn't ask for much—just a healthy Matt Williams (.336, 23, 65). After two injury-marred seasons, that is likely to occur, if the law of averages takes hold. And that will mean the Giants will have a more potent attack than the one that generated only 652 runs and 152 homers in '95.

Barry Bonds (.294, 33, 104) put together another great season despite being pitched around frequently and leading the league in walks (120). With the help of Baker's guidance and a full season of at-bats, Glenallen Hill (.264, 24, 86) emerged as a force.

Deion Sanders (.268, 24 steals) was quickly deemed not worth the trouble by the Giants, who signed free-agent Stan Javier (.278, 8, 56 with the Athletics) to play center. But can Robby Thompson (.223, 8, 23) bounce back and will J.R. Phillips (.195, 9, 28) improve or fade away?

PITCHING: If the Giants are to be any factor in the West, things are going to have to get dramatically better here. Last year, San Francisco ranked 13th in the NL with a 4.86 ERA.

Mark Leiter (10-12, 3.82) is the closest thing to an ace—and he was signed off the scrap heap in the spring of '95. Allen Watson (7-9, 4.96 with the Cards) was acquired in the Royce Clayton deal last winter, Trevor Wilson (3-4, 3.92) was not re-signed and William VanLandingham (6-3, 3.67) must bounce back from injuries. Youngsters Jamie Brewington (6-4, 4.54), Sergio Valdez (4-5, 4.75), Shawn Estes (0-3, 6.75) and Joe Rosselli (2-1, 8.70) must step up.

Rod Beck (5-6, 4.45, 33 saves in 43 opportunities) characterized an inconsistent bullpen that was weakened by the departure of Dave Burba in the Sanders trade last summer and strengthened

Giant hopes were crippled when Matt Williams broke his foot.

by the addition of Rich DeLucia (8-7, 3.39 with the Cards) last winter.

FIELDING: Williams and Bonds—both multiple Gold Glove winners—are the stars, at third and in left respectively. In fact, the Giants have one of the league's better defenses, as second baseman Thompson and catcher Kirt Manwaring are outstanding. But Hill is a liability in right field.

OUTLOOK: Baker stepped in and won 103 games in his first season, winning NL Manager of the Year honors in '93. Since then, however, it has gone all downhill in the City by the Bay—to a 67-77 finish in '95—as ownership doesn't have the financial wherewithal to compete with the Dodgers and Rockies. The payroll has been cut and attendance has fallen dramatically. That isn't the combination that will lead the Giants back into contention in the league's toughest division.

GIANT PROFILES

BARRY BONDS 31 6-1 190 **Bats L Throws L**

Five-time All-Star and five-time Gold Glove winner now is in two-year drought in MVP department . . . But he did reach the 30-30 club for the third time with 33 homers and 31 steals . . . The last Giant player to do that was his father, Bobby, the Giants' current hitting coach . . . Had to do it without Matt Williams behind him in the order . . . Led NL in intentional walks (22) . . . Was on pace to hit 52 homers and drive in 114 runs in strike-shortened '94 season . . . Ranked near the top in nearly every offensive category in 1993 . . . Best left fielder in the game . . . Only black mark on career is .191 average, one homer and three RBI in 68 postseason at-bats . . . In fourth year of six-year, $43.75-million contract he signed as free agent before 1993 season . . . Salary was $8 million in 1995 . . . The father-son home-run record he and his father share now totals 624 . . . Pirates drafted him sixth overall in 1985, out of Arizona State . . . Born July 24, 1964, in Riverside, Cal.

Year	Club	Pos.	G	AB	R	H	2B	3B	HR	RBI	SB	Avg.
1986	Pittsburgh	OF	113	413	72	92	26	3	16	48	36	.223
1987	Pittsburgh	OF	150	551	99	144	34	9	25	59	32	.261
1988	Pittsburgh	OF	144	538	97	152	30	5	24	58	17	.283
1989	Pittsburgh	OF	159	580	96	144	34	6	19	58	32	.248
1990	Pittsburgh	OF	151	519	104	156	32	3	33	114	52	.301
1991	Pittsburgh	OF	153	510	95	149	28	5	25	116	43	.292
1992	Pittsburgh	OF	140	473	109	147	36	5	34	103	39	.311
1993	San Francisco	OF	159	539	129	181	38	4	46	123	29	.336
1994	San Francisco	OF	112	391	89	122	18	1	37	81	29	.312
1995	San Francisco	OF	144	506	109	149	30	7	33	104	31	.294
	Totals		1425	5020	999	1436	306	48	292	864	340	.286

MATT WILLIAMS 30 6-2 215 **Bats R Throws R**

Maybe this is the year he stays healthy and plays a full season . . . If so, NL pitchers beware . . . Broken foot interrupted what could have been another monster year for the game's best third baseman . . . Hit .336 with 23 homers in only 76 games . . . Forty-one of his 95 hits were for extra bases . . . Giants took a tumble in the standings once he went out . . . Hit .377 against left-handers and .344 on the road . . . Had 43 homers when strike hit in August 1994 . . . His 40 homers through July of that year set an NL record . . . Also won first Gold Glove in 1994 . . . Finished among league leaders in six offensive categories in 1993 . . . Has hit 33-or-more homers and driven in 96-or-more runs in four of the last six years . . . Salary was $5.8 million in 1995 . . . Giants picked him third overall in 1986 draft, out of Nevada-Las Vegas . . . Born Nov. 28, 1965, in Bishop, Cal.

Year	Club	Pos.	G	AB	R	H	2B	3B	HR	RBI	SB	Avg.
1987	San Francisco	SS-3B	84	245	28	46	9	2	8	21	4	.188
1988	San Francisco	3B-SS	52	156	17	32	6	1	8	19	0	.205
1989	San Francisco	3B-SS	84	292	31	59	18	1	18	50	1	.202
1990	San Francisco	3B	159	617	87	171	27	2	33	122	7	.277
1991	San Francisco	3B-SS	157	589	72	158	24	5	34	98	5	.268
1992	San Francisco	3B	146	529	58	120	13	5	20	66	7	.227
1993	San Francisco	3B	145	579	105	170	33	4	38	110	1	.294
1994	San Francisco	3B	112	445	74	119	16	3	43	96	1	.267
1995	San Francisco	3B	76	283	53	95	17	1	23	65	2	.336
	Totals		1015	3735	525	970	163	24	225	647	28	.260

GLENALLEN HILL 31 6-2 225 Bats R Throws R

It took him seven seasons to become an everyday player and he earned his keep . . . Free-agent signee from Cubs prior to '95 posted career highs in homers (24), RBI (86), steals (25) and doubles (29) . . . Hit .308 vs. lefties . . . Pet project of manager Dusty Baker . . . Free swinger with power and speed . . . Not the greatest right fielder around, however . . . Committed 10 errors . . . Giants are fourth team in what had been an underachieving career . . . One-time big prospect for Toronto . . . Salary was $500,000 in 1995 . . . Got on track in second half of 1994 with Cubs . . . From June 18 through end of season, he hit .316 with eight homers and 30 RBI . . . Cubs got him from Indians for Candy Maldonado, Aug. 20, 1993 . . . Blue Jays' ninth-round pick in 1983 draft . . . Born March 22, 1965, in Santa Cruz, Cal.

Year	Club	Pos.	G	AB	R	H	2B	3B	HR	RBI	SB	Avg.
1989	Toronto	OF	19	52	4	15	0	0	1	7	2	.288
1990	Toronto	OF	84	260	47	60	11	3	12	32	8	.231
1991	Tor.-Clev.	OF	72	221	29	57	8	2	8	25	6	.258
1992	Cleveland	OF	102	369	38	89	16	1	18	49	9	.241
1993	Cleveland	OF	66	174	19	39	7	2	5	25	7	.224
1993	Chicago (NL) . .	OF	31	87	14	30	7	0	10	22	1	.345
1994	Chicago (NL) . .	OF	89	269	48	80	12	1	10	38	19	.297
1995	San Francisco	OF	132	497	71	131	29	4	24	86	25	.264
	Totals		595	1929	270	501	90	13	88	284	77	.260

ROBBY THOMPSON 33 5-11 175 Bats R Throws R

Gutsy team leader can't shake injury problems ... His '95 season ended prematurely because of arthroscopic surgery ... Struggled when he was able to play, hitting just .223 in 336 at-bats ... That followed .209 mark in only 35 games in 1994 ... Spent two stints on the DL that year because of shoulder trouble and underwent surgery July 8 ... Career year was 1993, when he set Giants records for second baseman in average, homers and RBI ... That was the last of five consecutive seasons in which he hit at least 13 homers and drove in at least 48 runs ... Outstanding defensive player ... Made only three errors in 91 starts last season ... Earned $3,333,333 in 1995 ... Giants' first-round pick in secondary phase of 1983 draft ... Born May 10, 1962, in West Palm Beach, Fla.

Year	Club	Pos.	G	AB	R	H	2B	3B	HR	RBI	SB	Avg.
1986	San Francisco	2B-SS	149	549	73	149	27	3	7	47	12	.271
1987	San Francisco	2B	132	420	62	110	26	5	10	44	16	.262
1988	San Francisco	2B	138	477	66	126	24	6	7	48	14	.264
1989	San Francisco	2B	148	547	91	132	26	11	13	50	12	.241
1990	San Francisco	2B	144	498	67	122	22	3	15	56	14	.245
1991	San Francisco	2B	144	492	74	129	24	5	19	48	14	.262
1992	San Francisco	2B	128	443	54	115	25	1	14	49	5	.260
1993	San Francisco	2B	128	494	85	154	30	2	19	65	10	.312
1994	San Francisco	2B	35	129	13	27	8	2	2	7	3	.209
1995	San Francisco	2B	95	336	51	75	15	0	8	23	1	.223
	Totals		1241	4385	636	1139	227	38	114	437	101	.260

KIRT MANWARING 30 5-11 205 Bats R Throws R

Completed another solid season, his fourth as Giants' everyday catcher ... Regarded as one of the league's best throwers and receivers ... Threw out 29-of-99 would-be base-stealers ... And that was despite playing with five broken ribs on his right side for more than two months ... Injured in July 18 game against Florida, but kept playing ... Offense is consistently ordinary ... Hit .251 in 379 at-bats, following up on .250 mark in

1994 . . . Did increase home-run (4) and RBI (36) production . . . Hit two home runs July 14 off Houston's Greg Swindell, his first multi-homer game in majors . . . Had career-high, 10-game hitting streak from July 20-Aug. 2 . . . Salary was $1.8 million in 1995 . . . Won Gold Glove in 1993 . . . Giants' second-round pick in 1986 draft . . . Born July 15, 1965, in Elmira, N.Y.

Year	Club	Pos.	G	AB	R	H	2B	3B	HR	RBI	SB	Avg.
1987	San Francisco	C	6	7	0	1	0	0	0	0	0	.143
1988	San Francisco	C	40	116	12	29	7	0	1	15	0	.250
1989	San Francisco	C	85	200	14	42	4	2	0	18	2	.210
1990	San Francisco	C	8	13	0	2	0	1	0	1	0	.154
1991	San Francisco	C	67	178	16	40	9	0	0	19	1	.225
1992	San Francisco	C	109	349	24	85	10	5	4	26	2	.244
1993	San Francisco	C	130	432	48	119	15	1	5	49	1	.275
1994	San Francisco	C	97	316	30	79	17	1	1	29	1	.250
1995	San Francisco	C	118	379	21	95	15	2	4	36	1	.251
	Totals		660	1990	165	492	77	12	15	193	8	.247

ALLEN WATSON 25 6-3 190 Bats L Throws L

Left-hander with promise still hasn't harnessed his talent, but Giants sent Royce Clayton to Cards for him, Rich DeLucia and Doug Creek last winter . . . Went 7-9, but his ERA was 4.96 . . . Gopher-ball prone . . . Gave up 17 homers in 114⅓ innings in 1995 . . . Allowed 130 hits and 81 walks in 115⅓ innings in rough 1994 season, when control failed him . . . Reached big leagues in 1993, only his second pro season . . . Had 2.91 ERA for Louisville (AAA) to earn July promotion . . . Won his first six big-league decisions, then lost his next seven . . . Was 21st player taken in 1991 draft, by Cards . . . Was 14-9 with 1.99 ERA at three levels in Cards system in 1992 . . . Was named New York City Player of the Year in high school . . . Born Nov. 18, 1970, in Jamaica, N.Y. . . . Made $144,000 last season.

Year	Club	G	IP	W	L	Pct.	SO	BB	H	ERA
1993	St. Louis	16	86	6	7	.462	49	28	90	4.60
1994	St. Louis	22	115⅔	6	5	.545	74	53	130	5.52
1995	St. Louis	21	114⅓	7	9	.438	49	41	126	4.96
	Totals	59	316	19	21	.475	172	122	346	5.07

MARK LEITER 32 6-3 210 **Bats R Throws R**

Plucked off scrap heap by Giants, who got their money's worth . . . Signed for $350,000 base salary as free agent prior to '95, he led staff with 10 wins . . . Had .500 record until last week of season, when he lost twice to Rockies . . . Final loss came in relief in season finale . . . Also led staff in starts (29), innings (195⅔) and strikeouts (129) . . . Giants rewarded him with $1-million deal for 1996 . . . Led NL in hit batsmen with 17 . . . Suffered through tragic death of young son two springs ago, then was released by Detroit . . . Went 23-18 for Tigers in two-plus seasons from 1991-93 . . . Brother Al has pitched for Yankees and Blue Jays . . . Another brother, Kurt, pitched in minors . . . Fourth-round pick of Orioles in 1983 draft . . . Did not pitch professionally from 1986-88, because of injury . . . Born April 13, 1963, in Joliet, Ill.

Year	Club	G	IP	W	L	Pct.	SO	BB	H	ERA
1990	New York (AL)	8	26⅓	1	1	.500	21	9	33	6.84
1991	Detroit	38	134⅔	9	7	.563	103	50	125	4.21
1992	Detroit	35	112	8	5	.615	75	43	116	4.18
1993	Detroit	27	106⅔	6	6	.500	70	44	111	4.73
1994	California	40	95⅓	4	7	.364	71	35	99	4.72
1995	San Francisco	30	195⅔	10	12	.455	129	55	185	3.82
	Totals	178	670⅔	38	38	.500	469	236	669	4.35

ROD BECK 27 6-1 240 **Bats R Throws R**

Big, mustachioed closer saved 33 games to tie Gary Lavelle for all-time club record with 127 . . . But he needed 43 chances to notch his 33 in '95 . . . His 10 blown saves were an NL high . . . Last one came on Aug. 21 . . . Was unscored upon in 11 of last 12 outings . . . Converted all 28 of his save opportunities in 1994, finishing second in the league for second year in a row . . . Has converted 74 of last 84 chances and 104-of-115 dating back to 1993 . . . Career save percentage is 87.6 . . . Had streak of consecutive saves snapped at 41, May 3, 1995, when he allowed four runs in ninth inning of loss to Los Angeles . . . Acquired from Athletics for the forgettable Charlie Corbell before 1988 season . . . Took three more years to reach the big leagues

. . . Oakland chose him in 13th round in 1986 draft . . . Born Aug. 3, 1968, in Burbank, Cal.

Year	Club	G	IP	W	L	Pct.	SO	BB	H	ERA
1991	San Francisco	31	52⅓	1	1	.500	38	13	53	3.78
1992	San Francisco	65	92	3	3	.500	87	15	62	1.76
1993	San Francisco	76	79⅓	3	1	.750	86	13	57	2.16
1994	San Francisco	48	48⅔	2	4	.333	39	13	49	2.77
1995	San Francisco	60	58⅔	5	6	.455	42	21	60	4.45
	Totals	280	331	14	15	.483	292	75	281	2.80

WILLIAM VanLANDINGHAM 25 6-2 210 B: R T: R

Injuries interrupted development of one of Giants' top young arms . . . In parts of two seasons, he has 14-5 record and 3.61 ERA . . . Right-handers hit only .230 against him in 1995 . . . But lefties batted .304 . . . Missed 38 games with left rib-cage strain . . . Has distinction of longest name in big-league history . . . Rose quickly through Giants' system, and made splashy debut in 1994 . . . Went 8-2 in 16 games, allowing only 70 hits in 84 innings . . . Returned to minors just before Aug. 12 strike . . . Made jump from Shreveport (AA) to Giants May 19 . . . Giants' fifth-round pick in 1991 draft, out of University of Kentucky . . . Born July 16, 1970, in Columbia, Tenn. . . . Made $142,500 last season.

Year	Club	G	IP	W	L	Pct.	SO	BB	H	ERA
1994	San Francisco	16	84	8	2	.800	56	43	70	3.54
1995	San Francisco	18	122⅔	6	3	.667	95	40	124	3.67
	Totals	34	206⅔	14	5	.737	151	83	194	3.61

TOP PROSPECTS

JOE ROSSELLI 23 6-1 175 Bats R Throws L

Young lefty had two stints with Giants in 1995 . . . Won first big-league game May 5, vs. San Diego . . . Started five games and wound up 2-1 with 8.70 ERA . . . Went 4-3 with 4.99 ERA for Phoenix (AAA) in '95 . . . Was 7-2 with 1.89 ERA in 1994 with Shreveport (AA) before moving to Phoenix . . . Missed most of 1993 due to shoulder surgery . . . Giants' fifth pick in 1990 draft . . . Born May 28, 1972, in Burbank, Cal.

SHAWN ESTES 23 6-2 185 **Bats S Throws L**

Made three big-league starts and lost them all for 0-3, 6.75 numbers as a Giant in '95 . . . Rose from Single-A to majors in same season . . . Was 7-2 with 2.11 ERA in 12 minor-league starts for Burlington (A), San Jose (A), and Shreveport (AA) before promotion . . . Giants got him from Mariners for Salomon Torres prior to '95 . . . Was Seattle's first pick, 11th overall, in 1991 draft . . . Born Feb. 28, 1973, in San Bernardino, Cal.

MARVIN BENARD 26 5-9 180 **Bats L Throws L**

Outfielder is longshot overachiever . . . Giants' 50th-round pick in 1992 draft . . . Made impressive late September showing in San Francisco, hitting .382 in 34 at-bats, including one homer and four RBI . . . Batted .304 with six homers and 32 RBI in 378 at-bats for Phoenix (AAA), his third consecutive .300-plus season . . . Born Jan. 20, 1970, in Bluefields, Nicaragua.

DAN CARLSON 26 6-1 185 **Bats R Throws R**

Went 9-5, 4.27 for Phoenix (AAA), bringing minor-league mark to 67-43 . . . Won at least 12 games each year from 1991-94 . . . Led Pacific Coast League with 13 wins for Phoenix in 1994 . . . Giants' 33rd-round pick in 1989 draft . . . Born Jan. 26, 1970, in Portland, Ore.

MANAGER DUSTY BAKER: Tough '95 season for one of the game's great communicators . . . Couldn't make up for loss of Matt Williams, multiple injuries to pitching staff and salary-dumping trade of Mark Portugal, Darren Lewis and Dave Burba to Reds for Deion Sanders and Scott Service . . . His strength is relating to players . . . Worked wonders with Glenallen Hill, getting him to be a productive everyday player . . . Former slugger won more games than any other rookie manager in NL history (103), as fifth manager to win 100-or-more games in rookie year . . . Yankees' Ralph Houk (109 in

1961) was only rookie manager to win more . . . Named NL Manager of the Year in 1993 . . . Last year's 67-77 finish, Giants' second straight sub-.500 mark, left career major-league managerial record at 225-196 . . . Replaced Roger Craig following 1992 season . . . Spent 16 years as outfielder with Braves, Dodgers, Giants and Athletics, compiling .278 average, 242 home runs and 1,013 RBI before retiring in 1986 . . . Was out of baseball in 1987, working as an investment broker . . . Was Giants' hitting instructor for four years before becoming their manager . . . Born June 15, 1949, in Riverside, Cal. . . . Was boyhood friend of current Giants hitting coach Bobby Bonds.

ALL-TIME GIANT SEASON RECORDS

BATTING: Bill Terry, .401, 1930
HRs: Willie Mays, 52, 1965
RBI: Mel Ott, 151, 1929
STEALS: George Burns, 62, 1914
WINS: Christy Mathewson, 37, 1908
STRIKEOUTS: Christy Mathewson, 267, 1903

INSIDE THE AMERICAN LEAGUE

By PETER SCHMUCK and SCOTT MILLER
Baltimore Sun *St. Paul Pioneer Press*

PREDICTED ORDER OF FINISH

East	*Central*	*West*
Baltimore	Cleveland	Seattle
Boston	Kansas City	Texas
N.Y. Yankees	Chicago	California
Toronto	Minnesota	Oakland
Detroit	Milwaukee	

Wild Card: Boston
Playoffs Winner: Cleveland

EAST DIVISION

	Team	Owner		Morning Line Manager
1	**ORIOLES** Black & orange Bobby Bo will lead 'em home	Peter Angelos	1995 W 73 L 73	8-5 Davey Johnson
2	**RED SOX** Red, white & blue Nailed in the stretch	John Harrington	1995 W 86 L 58	5-1 Kevin Kennedy
3	**YANKEES** Navy blue pinstripes Turmoil in the barn	George Steinbrenner III	1995 W 79 L 65	8-1 Joe Torre
4	**BLUE JAYS** Blue & white Left at the starting gate	Paul Beeston	1995 W 56 L 88	15-1 Cito Gaston
5	**TIGERS** Navy, orange & white No Bell-ringer	Mike Ilitch	1995 W 79 L 65	30-1 Buddy Bell

Tribal Derby

96th Running. American League Race. Distance: 162 games plus playoffs. Payoff (based on '95): $206,608.95 per winning player, World Series; $121,945 per losing player, World Series. A field of 14 entered in three divisions.

Track Record: 111 wins—Cleveland, 1954

CENTRAL DIVISION

	Team	Owner		Morning Line Manager
1	**INDIANS** Black & orange Raring for a repeat	Richard Jacobs	1995 W 100 L 44	6-5 Mike Hargrove
2	**ROYALS** Royal blue & white Ready to move up	David Glass	1995 W 70 L 74	10-1 Bob Boone
3	**WHITE SOX** Navy, white & scarlet Not enough gallop	J. Reinsdorf/E. Einhorn	1995 W 68 L 76	15-1 Terry Bevington
4	**TWINS** Scarlet, white & black Wide of the field	Carl Pohlad	1995 W 56 L 88	50-1 Tom Kelly
5	**BREWERS** Blue, gold & white Out of the running	Bud Selig	1995 W 65 L 79	100-1 Phil Garner

WEST DIVISION

	Team	Owner		Morning Line Manager
1	**MARINERS** Blue, gold & white One Big Unit and all else	John Ellis	1995 W 79 L 66	3-2 Lou Piniella
2	**RANGERS** Red, white & blue Hemmed in on the rail	T. Schieffer/E. Rose	1995 W 74 L 70	8-1 Johnny Oates
3	**ANGELS** Red, white & navy Need more oats	Gene Autry	1995 W 78 L 67	20-1 Marcel Lache-mann
4	**ATHLETICS** Forest green, gold & white Art can't show 'em Howe	Steve Schott	1995 W 67 L 77	40-1 Art Howe

BALTIMORE ORIOLES

TEAM DIRECTORY: Managing Gen. Partner: Peter Angelos; Vice Chairman/Bus.-Fin.: Joe Foss; GM: Pat Gillick; Dir. Player Dev.: Syd Thrift; Dir. Pub. Rel.: John Maroon; Trav. Sec.: Phil Itzoe; Mgr.: Davey Johnson; Coaches: To be announced. Home: Oriole Park at Camden Yards (48,000). Field distances: 335, l.f. line; 410, l.c.; 400, c.f.; 386, r.c.; 318, r.f. line. Spring training: Ft. Lauderdale, Fla.

SCOUTING REPORT

HITTING: The Orioles were surprisingly unimposing at the plate in '95, ranking 11th in the league in batting average (.262) and ninth in runs (704). But the figures should mount with addition of Roberto Alomar (.300, 13, 66 with the Blue Jays) and B.J. Surhoff (.320, 13, 73 with the Brewers).

Just the presence of Bobby Bonilla in the order for the entire season will make a big difference. Bonilla batted .333 with 10 home runs and 46 RBI after he was acquired from the Mets July 31 and his overall numbers (28 homers, 99 RBI) showed again what kind of offensive impact he can wield. New manager Davey Johnson rates the club's 3-4-5 hitters—Rafael Palmeiro, Bonilla and Cal Ripken Jr.—as one of the game's most explosive combinations. Palmeiro (.310, 39, 104) just keeps getting better and Ripken (.262, 17, 88) remains one of the game's most productive shortstops. Chris Hoiles (.250, 19, 58) and Jeffrey Hammonds (.242, 4, 23) are capable of more.

Add Brady Anderson (.262, 108 runs) and Curtis Goodwin (.263, 22 steals) to what figures as the best offense in the division.

PITCHING: Despite ranking second in ERA at 4.31 in '95, the pitching staff was riddled with uncertainty last winter. Right-hander Mike Mussina (19-9, 3.29) is a constant—write in 18-20 victories by his name—but the rest of the rotation needed work.

Scott Erickson (13-10, 4.81) made great strides after he was acquired from the Twins. The club figures to gamble on 23-year-old right-hander Jimmy Haynes, who was 2-1 in three late-season starts and struck out 22 batters in 24 innings. Kent Mercker (7-8, 4.15 with the Braves) is a solid replacement for Jamie Moyer.

Another coup was the addition of free-agent Randy Myers

Rafael Palmeiro salutes his favorite iron horse, Ripken.

(1-2, 3.88, 38 saves with the Cubs) as a replacement for closer Doug Jones (0-4, 5.01, 22 saves). Meyers' setup men will include his ex-Met teammates Roger McDowell (7-4, 4.02, 4 saves for the Rangers) and Jesse Orosco (2-4, 3.26).

FIELDING: This is an area where the Orioles have always been solid. Last year, the Orioles again led the AL in fielding percentage (.986) and committed the fewest errors (72). Ripken is the centerpiece of a steady infield that will now have the peerless Alomar at second base.

OUTLOOK: The organization is anxious to bounce back from a very disappointing '95 season in which the Orioles had one of baseball's highest payrolls and finished below .500 at 71-73. A commitment to a '96 turnaround was evident by the choice of Johnson, whose teams have never finished under .500 in a season he managed from start to finish. There is enough talent here to assure that he keeps that impressive career record intact.

ORIOLE PROFILES

CAL RIPKEN Jr. 35 6-4 220 **Bats R Throws R**

Became baseball immortal, Sept. 6, 1995, when he played in his 2,131st consecutive game and broke Lou Gehrig's supposedly unbreakable record . . . Has 2,153-game streak coming into '96 . . . Apparently has no intention of taking a day off any time soon, so he could play every game for 14th straight season in '96 . . . Slumped for two weeks after breaking record, but he finished well to amass run-production numbers (17 homers, 88 RBI) that would have been among his best if projected over a 162-game season . . . Most dependable shortstop in league . . . Made just seven errors last year to lead all full-time shortstops . . . Finished '95 season with string of 70 straight errorless games, 25 short of his own major-league record . . . Only Oriole to win AL MVP award twice, in 1983 and 1991 . . . Holds all-time record for home runs by a shortstop (319) . . . Has two years remaining on current contract . . . Born Aug. 24, 1960, in Havre de Grace, Md. . . . Salary was $6.6 million last year . . . Drafted by Orioles in second round in 1978 . . . Father Cal Sr. coached and managed Orioles and brother Billy is ex-teammate.

Year	Club	Pos.	G	AB	R	H	2B	3B	HR	RBI	SB	Avg.
1981	Baltimore	SS-3B	23	39	1	5	0	0	0	0	0	.128
1982	Baltimore	SS-3B	160	598	90	158	32	5	28	93	3	.264
1983	Baltimore	SS	162	663	121	211	47	2	27	102	0	.318
1984	Baltimore	SS	162	641	103	195	37	7	27	86	2	.304
1985	Baltimore	SS	161	642	116	181	32	5	26	110	2	.282
1986	Baltimore	SS	162	627	98	177	35	1	25	81	4	.282
1987	Baltimore	SS	162	624	97	157	28	3	27	98	3	.252
1988	Baltimore	SS	161	575	87	152	25	1	23	81	2	.264
1989	Baltimore	SS	162	646	80	166	30	0	21	93	3	.257
1990	Baltimore	SS	161	600	78	150	28	4	21	84	3	.250
1991	Baltimore	SS	162	650	99	210	46	5	34	114	6	.323
1992	Baltimore	SS	162	637	73	160	29	1	14	72	4	.251
1993	Baltimore	SS	162	641	87	165	26	3	24	90	1	.257
1994	Baltimore	SS	112	444	71	140	19	3	13	75	1	.315
1995	Baltimore	SS	144	550	71	144	33	2	17	88	0	.262
	Totals		2218	8577	1272	2371	447	42	327	1267	34	.276

RAFAEL PALMEIRO 31 6-0 188 Bats L Throws L

There was some trepidation when Orioles signed him to five-year, $30.5-million contract as free agent after breakthrough year with Rangers in 1993 . . . However, he has been one of the most productive hitters in baseball his first two years with Orioles . . . Rang up career high in home runs (39) in '95, in spite of shortened season . . . Has had 30-or-more doubles in six of his eight full major-league seasons . . . Averages about one strikeout per seven at-bats, very good for player who has averaged a home run per 16 at-bats the past three years . . . Durable player and solid defensive first baseman . . . Born Sept. 24, 1964, in Havana, Cuba . . . Salary was $4,906,603 last year . . . Cubs drafted him in first round in 1985.

Year	Club	Pos.	G	AB	R	H	2B	3B	HR	RBI	SB	Avg.
1986	Chicago (NL) . .	OF	22	73	9	18	4	0	3	12	1	.247
1987	Chicago (NL) . .	OF-1B	84	221	32	61	15	1	14	30	2	.276
1988	Chicago (NL) . .	OF-1B	152	580	75	178	41	5	8	53	12	.307
1989	Texas	1B	156	559	76	154	23	4	8	64	4	.275
1990	Texas	1B	154	598	72	191	35	6	14	89	3	.319
1991	Texas	1B	159	631	115	203	49	3	26	88	4	.322
1992	Texas	1B	159	608	84	163	27	4	22	85	2	.268
1993	Texas	1B	160	597	124	176	40	2	37	105	22	.295
1994	Baltimore	1B	111	436	82	139	32	0	23	76	7	.319
1995	Baltimore	1B	143	554	89	172	30	2	39	104	3	.310
	Totals		1300	4857	758	1455	296	27	194	706	60	.300

BOBBY BONILLA 33 6-3 240 Bats S Throws R

Traded by Mets to Orioles July 28 with Jimmy Williams for outfield prospects Alex Ochoa and Damon Buford . . . Immediately added power (10 homers) and run production (46 RBI) to lineup, although rest of club was slow to respond to his offensive leadership . . . Has hit 20-or-more home runs in six of last eight years . . . Figures to bat cleanup behind Rafael Palmeiro for all of '96 . . . Will benefit from full year of Cal Ripken hitting behind him, so MVP-type numbers are not out of the question . . . Continues to be error-prone at third base, but he could end up starting there for outfield-rich Orioles this season . . . Originally signed as non-drafted free agent by Pirates in July 1981 . . . Born Feb. 23, 1963, in New York, N.Y. . . . Salary was

$4,600,950 last year . . . Tangled with Mets' third-base coach Mike Cubbage and New York media during sometimes stormy stay.

Year	Club	Pos.	G	AB	R	H	2B	3B	HR	RBI	SB	Avg.
1986	Chicago (AL) . .	OF-1B	75	234	27	63	10	2	2	26	4	.269
1986	Pittsburgh	OF-1B-3B	63	192	28	46	6	2	1	17	4	.240
1987	Pittsburgh	3B-OF-1B	141	466	58	140	33	3	15	77	3	.300
1988	Pittsburgh	3B	159	584	87	160	32	7	24	100	3	.274
1989	Pittsburgh	3B-1B-OF	163	616	96	173	37	10	24	86	8	.281
1990	Pittsburgh	OF-3B-1B	160	625	112	175	39	7	32	120	4	.280
1991	Pittsburgh	OF-3B-1B	157	577	102	174	44	6	18	100	2	.302
1992	New York (NL)	OF-1B	128	438	62	109	23	0	19	70	4	.249
1993	New York (NL)	OF-3B-1B	139	502	81	133	21	3	34	87	3	.265
1994	New York (NL)	3B	108	403	60	117	24	1	20	67	1	.290
1995	New York (NL)	3B-OF	80	317	49	103	25	4	18	53	0	.325
1995	Baltimore	OF-1B	61	237	47	79	12	4	10	46	0	.333
	Totals		1434	5191	809	1472	306	49	217	849	36	.284

CHRIS HOILES 31 6-0 213 Bats R Throws R

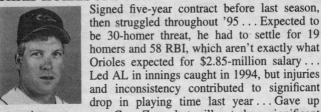

Signed five-year contract before last season, then struggled throughout '95 . . . Expected to be 30-homer threat, he had to settle for 19 homers and 58 RBI, which aren't exactly what Orioles expected for $2.85-million salary . . . Led AL in innings caught in 1994, but injuries and inconsistency contributed to significant drop in playing time last year . . . Gave up some time to prospect Greg Zaun, but will not share significant time with anyone in '96 . . . Best season was '93, when he hit .310 with 29 homers and 82 RBI and nearly became first AL catcher ever to hit .300 or better with 30 homers . . . Born March 20, 1965, in Bowling Green, Ohio . . . Drafted by Detroit in 19th round in 1986 . . . Obtained by Orioles from Tigers with Robinson Garces and Cesar Mejia in deal for Fred Lynn, Aug. 31, 1988.

Year	Club	Pos.	G	AB	R	H	2B	3B	HR	RBI	SB	Avg.
1989	Baltimore	C	6	9	0	1	1	0	0	1	0	.111
1990	Baltimore	C-1B	23	63	7	12	3	0	1	6	0	.190
1991	Baltimore	C-1B	107	341	36	83	15	0	11	31	0	.243
1992	Baltimore	C	96	310	49	85	10	1	20	40	0	.274
1993	Baltimore	C	126	419	80	130	28	0	29	82	1	.310
1994	Baltimore	C	99	332	45	82	10	0	19	53	2	.247
1995	Baltimore	C	114	352	53	88	15	1	19	58	1	.250
	Totals		571	1826	270	481	82	2	99	271	4	.263

BRADY ANDERSON 32 6-1 195 Bats L Throws L

Solid combination of speed and power at top of the lineup, but there is some question whether he'll be the full-time leadoff guy in '96 . . . Outfielder has been in leadoff role full-time since 1992, when he had breakthrough season and drew comparisons to Oakland lead-off man Rickey Henderson . . . Numbers have not been quite so spectacular the past two years . . . Home runs, RBI and steals have dropped, though there are still plenty of each to remain in everyday leadoff role . . . Scored more than 100 runs for only second time in career (108) . . . Born Jan. 18, 1964, in Silver Spring, Md. . . . Salary was $3,333,333 last year . . . Drafted by Red Sox in 10th round in 1985 . . . Acquired by Orioles with Curt Schilling for Mike Boddicker, July 30, 1988.

Year	Club	Pos.	G	AB	R	H	2B	3B	HR	RBI	SB	Avg.
1988	Bos.-Balt.	OF	94	25	31	69	13	4	1	21	10	.212
1989	Baltimore	OF	94	266	44	55	12	2	4	16	16	.207
1990	Baltimore	OF	89	234	24	54	5	2	3	24	15	.231
1991	Baltimore	OF	113	256	40	59	12	3	2	27	12	.230
1992	Baltimore	OF	159	623	100	169	28	10	21	80	53	.271
1993	Baltimore	OF	142	560	87	147	36	8	13	66	24	.263
1994	Baltimore	OF	111	453	78	119	25	5	12	48	31	.263
1995	Baltimore	OF	143	554	108	145	33	10	16	64	26	.262
	Totals		945	3271	512	817	164	44	72	346	187	.250

B. J. SURHOFF 31 6-1 200 Bats L Throws R

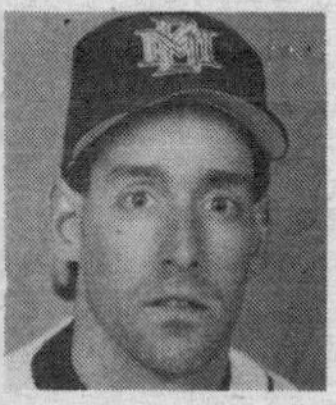

Versatile veteran left Brewers as free agent for three-year, $3.7-million deal with Orioles last winter . . . Disenfranchised temporarily after 1994 season, but he eventually signed cut-rate contract with Brewers and was one of their top offensive performers . . . Led club in batting average (.320), RBI (73) and runs (72) in '95 . . . Posted highest batting average of his nine major-league seasons . . . Despite shortened season, he compiled second-highest RBI total of career and third-highest hit total (133) . . . Broke into professional baseball as a catcher, but he now can play almost any position . . . Born Aug. 4, 1964, in Bronx, N.Y.

. . . Salary last year was $250,000 . . . Brewers drafted him in first round in 1985.

Year	Club	Pos.	G	AB	R	H	2B	3B	HR	RBI	SB	Avg.
1987	Milwaukee	C-3B-1B	115	395	50	118	22	3	7	68	1	.299
1988	Milwaukee	C-3B-1B-SS-OF	139	493	47	121	21	0	5	38	21	.245
1989	Milwaukee	C-3B-OF	126	436	42	108	17	4	5	55	14	.248
1990	Milwaukee	C-3B	135	474	55	131	21	4	6	59	8	.276
1991	Milwaukee	C-3B-OF-2B	143	505	5	146	19	4	5	68	5	.289
1992	Milwaukee	C-1B-OF-3B	139	480	63	121	19	1	4	62	14	.252
1993	Milwaukee	3B-OF-1B-C	148	552	66	151	38	3	7	79	12	.274
1994	Milwaukee	3B-C-1B-OF	40	134	20	35	11	2	5	22	0	.261
1995	Milwaukee	1B-OF-C	117	415	72	133	26	3	13	73	7	.320
	Totals		1102	3884	472	1064	194	24	57	524	102	.274

ROBERTO ALOMAR 28 6-0 185 Bats S Throws R

Toronto free agent signed three-year, $18-million deal with Orioles last winter . . . Second baseman is one of best all-around players in the game, but his overall offensive numbers have been in decline the past couple of years . . . Still, he hits for average (.300), plays great defense, steals bases (30) and drives in runs (66), so what's not to like? . . . Stole 30-or-more bases for fifth time in eight major-league seasons . . . Improved base-stealing efficiency to better than 90 percent last year with 30 in 33 attempts . . . In just five seasons with Blue Jays, he ranked among club's all-time leaders in stolen bases (206) and triples (36) . . . Son of former major leaguer Sandy Alomar and brother of current Indians catcher Sandy Alomar Jr. . . . Born Feb. 5, 1968, in Ponce, P.R. . . . Salary was $5,500,000 last year . . . Signed as non-drafted free agent by Padres in February 1985.

Year	Club	Pos.	G	AB	R	H	2B	3B	HR	RBI	SB	Avg.
1988	San Diego	2B	143	545	84	145	24	6	9	41	24	.266
1989	San Diego	2B	158	623	82	184	27	1	7	56	42	.295
1990	San Diego	2B-SS	147	586	80	168	27	5	6	60	24	.287
1991	Toronto	2B	161	637	88	188	41	11	9	69	53	.295
1992	Toronto	2B	152	571	105	177	27	8	8	76	49	.310
1993	Toronto	2B	153	589	109	192	35	6	17	93	55	.326
1994	Toronto	2B	107	392	78	120	25	4	8	38	19	.306
1995	Toronto	2B	130	517	71	155	24	7	13	66	30	.300
	Totals		1151	4460	697	1329	230	48	77	499	296	.298

MIKE MUSSINA 27 6-2 185 Bats R Throws R

In just four full seasons, he has established himself as one of AL's top five starters... Would have likely won 20 games in '94 and '95 if seasons had gone the distance... His 16-5 record in '94 projected to 23-7. Last year, he would have gotten five more starts to improve on 19-9 mark... Always ranks among league leaders in fewest walks per nine innings (2.03 last year)... Narrowly missed winning Cy Young Award with 18-5, 2.54 performance in first full major-league season in 1992... Continues to rank among top active pitchers in career winning percentage (.703), but ERA jumped to 4.46 in '93 and has been above 3.00 the last couple of years... Had never lost more than six decisions at any professional level before last season... Born Dec. 8, 1968, in Williamsport, Pa., site of the Little League World Series... Salary was $2,925,000 last year... Orioles drafted him 20th overall in 1990, out of Stanford, after failing to sign him three years earlier.

Year	Club	G	IP	W	L	Pct.	SO	BB	H	ERA
1991	Baltimore	12	87⅔	4	5	.444	52	21	77	2.87
1992	Baltimore	32	241	18	5	.783	130	48	212	2.54
1993	Baltimore	25	167⅔	14	6	.700	117	44	163	4.46
1994	Baltimore	24	176⅓	16	5	.762	99	42	163	3.06
1995	Baltimore	32	221⅔	19	9	.679	158	50	187	3.29
	Totals	125	894⅓	71	30	.703	556	205	802	3.22

RANDY MYERS 332 6-1 230 Bats L Throws L

Re-established himself as NL's premier closer with Cubs in '95, then signed two-year, $6.3-million deal with Orioles as free agent last winter.... Finished first in NL in saves for second time in three seasons with 38... Struck out 59 batters in 55⅔ innings... Selected to third All-Star team and earned save in NL's 3-2 victory as he pitched scoreless ninth... Ranks 11th on all-time saves list with 243... Ranks third in career saves among lefties, behind John Franco and Dave Righetti... Became fourth left-handed reliever to reach 200-save mark June 27, 1994 vs. Pirates... Ranks third on Cubs' all-time save list (112), behind Lee Smith (180) and Bruce Sutter (133)... Saved 21 games for lowly Cubs in '94... Tied for fifth in NL in saves... Holds club record of 20 straight converted saves... Set NL record with 53 saves in '93, falling four short of Bobby Thigpen's major-league mark... Signed by Cubs as free agent prior to 1993 season . . . Born Sept. 19, 1962, in Vancouver, Wash. . . . Earned $3,833,334 last season . . . Explored free agency last winter.

Year	Club	G	IP	W	L	Pct.	SO	BB	H	ERA
1985	New York (NL)	1	2	0	0	.000	2	1	0	0.00
1986	New York (NL)	10	10⅔	0	0	.000	13	9	11	4.22
1987	New York (NL)	54	75	3	6	.333	92	30	61	3.96
1988	New York (NL)	55	68	7	3	.700	69	17	45	1.72
1989	New York (NL)	65	84⅓	7	4	.636	88	40	62	2.35
1990	Cincinnati	66	86⅔	4	6	.400	98	38	59	2.08
1991	Cincinnati	58	132	6	13	.316	108	80	116	3.55
1992	San Diego	66	79⅔	3	6	.333	66	34	84	4.29
1993	Chicago (NL)	73	75⅓	2	4	.333	86	26	65	3.11
1994	Chicago (NL)	38	40⅓	1	5	.167	32	16	40	3.79
1995	Chicago (NL)	57	55⅔	1	2	.333	59	28	49	3.88
	Totals	543	709⅔	34	49	.410	713	319	592	3.17

SCOTT ERICKSON 28 6-4 234 Bats R Throws R

Acquired from Twins in July for stretch run in exchange for prospects Scott Klingenbeck and Kimera Bartee . . . Pitched very well for Orioles in second half, finishing year at 13-10, 4.81, after several disappointing seasons with Twins . . . Should be third starter this year . . . Has potential to win 20 games and did so in 1991, but he has not won more than 13 in any other major-league season . . . High hits-to-innings ratio has plagued him past three seasons . . . Averaged more than five earned runs per nine innings for two straight years, but showed dramatic improvement after arrival in Baltimore . . . Change of scenery apparently made a difference . . . Born Feb. 2, 1968, in Long Beach, Cal. . . . Salary last year was $1,862,500 . . . Twins drafted him in fourth round in 1989.

Year	Club	G	IP	W	L	Pct.	SO	BB	H	ERA
1990	Minnesota	19	113	8	4	.667	53	51	108	2.87
1991	Minnesota	32	204	20	8	.714	108	71	189	3.18
1992	Minnesota	32	212	13	12	.520	101	83	197	3.40
1993	Minnesota	34	218⅔	8	19	.296	116	71	266	5.19
1994	Minnesota	23	144	8	11	.421	104	59	173	5.44
1995	Minn.-Balt.	32	196⅓	13	10	.565	106	67	213	4.81
	Totals	172	1088	70	64	.522	588	402	1146	4.19

TOP PROSPECTS

ARMANDO BENITEZ 23 6-4 180 Bats R Throws R

Hard-throwing prospect is considered to be the Orioles' closer of the future, but he barely survived up-and-down '95 season . . .

Very vulnerable to long ball at major-league level, surrendering eight in 47⅔ innings . . . Also very vulnerable to emotional outbursts . . . Averaged more than a strikeout an inning with 56 . . . Went 1-5 with 5.66 ERA and two saves for Orioles . . . Was 2-2, 1.25 with eight saves for Rochester (AAA) before recall in '95 . . . Born Nov. 3, 1972, in Ramon Santana, D.R. . . . Signed as non-drafted free agent by Orioles in April 1990.

CURTIS GOODWIN 23 5-11 180 Bats L Throws L

Speedy leadoff candidate got a lot of playing time at the major-league level last year, hitting .263 with one homer, 24 RBI and 22 steals in 26 attempts for Orioles . . . Burst into majors with .500 average through first two weeks in starting lineup . . . Center fielder impressed club with aggressive style at the plate and on the bases . . . Hit .264 with no homers, seven RBI and 17 steals for Rochester (AAA) in '95 . . . Born Sept. 30, 1972, in Oakland . . . Orioles drafted him in 12th round in 1991 . . . Stole 215 bases in five minor-league seasons.

JIMMY HAYNES 23 6-4 185 Bats R Throws R

Orioles auditioned a number of young starting pitchers at end of '95 season and he was among the most impressive . . . Gave up only three runs on eight hits and struck out 15 over 14⅓ innings in first two major-league starts . . . Wound up 2-1 with 2.25 ERA for Orioles . . . Went 12-8, 3.29 for Rochester (AAA) . . . Will get a serious look in spring training . . . Born Sept. 5, 1972, in La Grange, Ga. . . . Orioles drafted him in seventh round in 1991 . . . Struck out 191 in 187 innings in minors during 1994.

RICK KRIVDA 26 6-1 180 Bats R Throws L

Got more than a September look . . . Spent final two months of '95 season in starting rotation and pitched better than his 2-7, 4.54 record . . . Went 6-5, 3.19 for Rochester (AAA) in '95 . . . One of winningest pitchers in minor-league system with mark of 49-27 over five seasons . . . Born Jan. 19, 1970, in McKeesport, Pa. . . . Orioles selected him 23rd overall in 1991 draft.

Control artist Mike Mussina's motto: Thou shalt not pass.

MANAGER DAVEY JOHNSON: Second time around was the charm for newest Orioles manager, who was prominent in club's managerial search a year ago, but didn't get the call . . . Now, as the possessor of a three-year contract estimated at $2.25 million, he replaces Phil Regan and returns to team he broke in with as a second baseman in 1965 . . . Is baseball's winningest active manager in terms of percentage (.576) with 799-589 career record . . . Managed Mets from 1984-90 and never finished lower than second before he was fired 42 games into '90 season . . . Won World Series with Mets in 1986 and won NL East title in 1988 before losing to Dodgers in playoffs . . . Replaced Tony Perez in Cincinnati, May 24, 1993 . . . Managed Reds to two first-place finishes in NL Central, but was lame duck last year after owner Marge Schott let it be known early on that he would be replaced by Ray Knight . . . Still had great year, bringing Reds back from 1-8 start to second-best record in NL at 85-59 . . . Reds defeated Dodgers in Division Series, but were no match for eventual world champion Braves in NLCS . . . Born Jan. 30, 1943, in Orlando, Fla. . . . Hit 43 homers for 1973 Braves and played two seasons in Japan with Yomiuri Giants.

ALL-TIME ORIOLE SEASON RECORDS

BATTING: Ken Singleton, .328, 1977
HRs: Frank Robinson, 49, 1966
RBI: Jim Gentile, 141, 1961
STEALS: Luis Aparicio, 57, 1964
WINS: Steve Stone, 25, 1980
STRIKEOUTS: Dave McNally, 202, 1968

BOSTON RED SOX

TEAM DIRECTORY: Gen. Partners: Jean Yawkey Trust; Trustees: John Harrington, William Gutfarb; VP-Baseball Oper.: Lou Gorman; Exec. VP-GM: Daniel Duquette; Exec. VP-Adm.: John Buckley; VP-Baseball: Ed Kasko; Dir. Scouting: Wayne Britton; Dir. Player Dev. and Adm.: Ed Kenney; VP-Pub. Rel.: Dick Bresciani; Pub. Mgr.: Kevin Shea; Trav. Sec.: Steve August; Mgr.: Kevin Kennedy; Coaches: Dave Carlucci, Mike Easler, Tim Johnson, Dave Oliver. Home: Fenway Park (34,171). Field distances: 315, l.f. line; 379, l.c.; 390, c.f.; 420, deep c.f.; 380 r.f.; 302, r.f. line. Spring training: Fort Myers, Fla.

SCOUTING REPORT

HITTING: The Red Sox were the AL's surprise team last year, but their solid offensive production was no surprise. It was a given, with a lineup that included AL MVP Mo Vaughn (.300, 39, 126) and Jose Canseco (.306, 24, 81). But Boston also took advantage of a career year from shortstop John Valentin (.298, 27, 102) to hit .280, generate 175 homers and score 791 runs. Only the Indians, Angels and Mariners scored more.

No one can say for sure the offensive chemistry in '96 will be as good, but the addition of free-agent Mike Stanley (.268, 18, 63 with the Yankees) should give Boston more pop at catcher's position. Canseco's numbers, though very solid, could rise significantly if he can remain healthy all season. Vaughn has become the superstar everyone knew he would be and there is no reason he shouldn't continue to put up tremendous numbers. The big question, however, is whether the Red Sox can keep the hits coming after a year in which Troy O'Leary (.308, 10, 49) Tim Naehring (.307, 10, 57) and Mike Greenwell (.297, 15, 76) joined Vaughn, Canseco and Valentin in hitting .297 or higher.

PITCHING: Expectations are high after a '95 season in which the Red Sox ranked third in the AL in ERA (4.39) and the staff allowed a league-low 127 homers in spite of the cozy dimensions of Fenway Park. Boston fans could be in for a disappointment, because it will be hard to duplicate that success unless virtually everything goes right again this year.

Mo Vaughn didn't whiff when it came down to MVP.

Knuckleballer Tim Wakefield (16-8, 2.95) came out of nowhere to win 14 of his first 15 decisions last year, but what if he continues to throw like he did while going 2-7 the rest of the way? With Erik Hanson (15-5, 4.24) gone to Toronto via free agency, the Red Sox signed curveballer Tom Gordon (12-12, 4.43 with the Royals) and Jamie Moyer (8-6, 5.21 with the Orioles). And Vaughn Eshelman (6-3, 4.85) could better his rookie season.

General manager Dan Duquette hopes former Expo Butch Henry (7-9, 2.84) bounces back from elbow surgery. Roger Clemens (10-5, 4.18) has to re-establish himself as a dominant pitcher.

The bullpen shouldn't be a major problem. The Red Sox have good depth, although the closer's job is open again with the defection of Rick Aguilera (3-3, 2.60, 32 saves).

Tim Wakefield's 16 Ws made Fenway fans' hearts flutter.

FIELDING: Somehow, the Red Sox won the AL East with the worst-fielding team in the AL. They ranked 14th in fielding percentage (.987) and led the league with 120 errors. The four regular infielders—Naehring, Valentin, Luis Alicia and Vaughn from third to first—combined to make 61 in a shortened season, only 11 fewer than the entire Orioles team. The area of least concern is the outfield, where left fielder Greenwell can play the Green Monster with his eyes closed and the Red Sox have just enough speed to handle the rest.

OUTLOOK: It will be very tough to repeat an 86-58 run to the AL East title. Too much went right last year to predict that Kevin Kennedy's Red Sox will get back to the postseason, but don't count them out.

RED SOX PROFILES

MO VAUGHN 28 6-1 230 Bats L Throws R

Big first baseman won MVP laurels over Indians' Albert Belle last year, hitting .300 and leading the Red Sox with 39 homers and 126 RBI . . . No one had a greater impact on the success of his team, despite 150 strikeouts during regular season . . . Got in a fracas at nightspot last season, but showed tremendous class by apologizing to Red Sox fans even though incident apparently was not his fault . . . Could not carry big season into October . . . Ran into tough Cleveland pitching and went hitless in 14 at-bats (seven strikeouts) in Division Series, which Indians won in three games . . . Boston's second pick in 1989 draft . . . Born Dec. 15, 1967, in Norwalk, Conn. . . . Salary was $2,675,000 last year.

Year	Club	Pos.	G	AB	R	H	2B	3B	HR	RBI	SB	Avg.
1991	Boston	1B	74	219	21	57	12	0	4	32	2	.260
1992	Boston	1B	113	355	42	83	16	2	13	57	3	.234
1993	Boston	1B	152	539	86	160	34	1	29	101	4	.297
1994	Boston	1B	111	394	65	122	25	1	26	82	4	.310
1995	Boston	1B	140	550	98	165	28	3	39	126	11	.300
	Totals		590	2057	312	587	115	7	111	398	24	.285

JOSE CANSECO 31 6-4 240 Bats R Throws R

Once considered most dangerous hitter in the game, this DH-outfielder could return to that stature if he could stay healthy . . . Hit 24 homers and had 81 RBI, but probably would have had normal 30-plus HR, 100-plus RBI season if he had gotten 500 or more at-bats . . . Batted .306, his highest average since career performance in 1988 with Oakland, when he batted .307 with 42 homers and 124 RBI . . . Oakland chose him in 15th round of 1982 draft . . . Has played for three teams in last four years after stellar seven-plus seasons with Athletics . . . Acquired prior to '95 season in much-debated trade with Rangers for center fielder Otis Nixon and infielder Luis Ortiz . . . Always controversial . . . Predicted before season that favored Yankees would have pitching problems and struggle in AL East. Turned out to be right . . . Went 0-for-13 in Division Series vs. Indians . . . Born July 2,

. . . Re-signed two-year contract in December estimated at $9 million.

Year	Club	Pos.	G	AB	R	H	2B	3B	HR	RBI	SB	Avg.
1985	Oakland	OF	29	96	16	29	3	0	5	13	1	.302
1986	Oakland	OF	157	600	85	144	29	1	33	117	15	.240
1987	Oakland	OF	159	630	81	162	35	3	31	113	15	.257
1988	Oakland	OF	158	610	120	187	34	0	42	124	40	.307
1989	Oakland	OF	65	227	40	61	9	1	17	57	6	.269
1990	Oakland	OF	131	481	83	132	14	2	37	101	19	.274
1991	Oakland	OF	154	572	115	152	32	1	44	122	26	.266
1992	Oak-Tex	OF	119	439	74	107	15	0	26	87	6	.244
1993	Texas	OF-P	60	231	30	59	14	1	10	46	6	.255
1994	Texas	DH	111	429	88	121	19	2	31	90	15	.282
1995	Boston	OF	102	396	64	121	25	1	24	81	4	.306
	Totals		1245	4711	796	1275	229	12	300	951	153	.271

JOHN VALENTIN 29 6-0 185 Bats R Throws R

Breakthrough season put him in upper echelon of major-league shortstops . . . Batted .298 with 27 homers and 102 RBI in first season with 500-plus at-bats . . . Missed 27 games in 1994 with knee injury, but still batted .316 with nine homers and 49 RBI in what amounted to a half-season . . . Also missed time in '93 with broken finger . . . Hit one of three Red Sox homers in Division Series last fall as he had three hits in 12 at-bats against Indians . . . Broke into majors in 1992, four years after Red Sox made him fifth-round pick in 1988 draft . . . Born Feb. 18, 1967, in Mineola, N.Y. . . . Salary last year was $612,500.

Year	Club	Pos.	G	AB	R	H	2B	3B	HR	RBI	SB	Avg.
1992	Boston	SS	58	185	21	51	13	0	5	25	1	.276
1993	Boston	SS	144	468	50	130	40	3	11	66	3	.278
1994	Boston	SS	84	301	53	95	26	2	9	49	3	.316
1995	Boston	SS	135	520	108	155	37	2	27	102	20	.298
	Totals		421	1474	232	431	116	7	52	242	27	.292

MIKE GREENWELL 32 6-0 200 Bats L Throws R

Dean of Red Sox position players . . . Only Roger Clemens has been with the team longer . . . Once one of top run producers in game, he never has matched level of performance attained in first three full seasons at major-league level, when he batted a combined .320 and averaged 19 home runs and 101 RBI . . . Still solid and plays left field well in shadow of Green Monster . . . Shut down like everybody else in Division Series against Indians, batting .200 with just three singles and no RBI in 15 at-bats . . . Boston's third-round pick in 1982 draft . . . Born July 18, 1963, in Louisville, Ky. . . . Salary last year was $3,600,000.

Year	Club	Pos.	G	AB	R	H	2B	3B	HR	RBI	SB	Avg.
1985	Boston	OF	17	31	7	10	1	0	4	8	1	.323
1986	Boston	OF	31	35	4	11	2	0	0	4	0	.314
1987	Boston	OF-C	125	412	71	135	31	6	19	89	5	.328
1988	Boston	OF	158	590	86	192	39	8	22	119	16	.325
1989	Boston	OF	145	578	87	178	36	0	14	95	13	.308
1990	Boston	OF	159	610	71	181	30	6	14	73	8	.297
1991	Boston	OF	147	544	76	163	26	6	9	83	15	.300
1992	Boston	OF	49	180	16	42	2	0	2	18	2	.233
1993	Boston	OF	146	540	77	170	38	6	13	72	5	.315
1994	Boston	OF	95	327	60	88	25	1	11	45	2	.269
1995	Boston	OF	120	481	67	143	25	4	15	76	9	.297
	Totals		1192	4328	622	1313	255	37	123	682	76	.303

TROY O'LEARY 26 6-0 198 — Bats L Throws L

Came out of nowhere to play significant role . . . Well, actually, came from Milwaukee on a waiver claim April 14 and batted .308 in first season as major-league regular . . . Right fielder had appeared in just 46 games before coming to Red Sox, but was considered a big reason why club got moving early in the season . . . Did not appear in Division Series . . . Late developer . . . Broke into pro ball in '87, after Brewers made him 13th-round choice in that year's draft . . . Was Texas League MVP with El Paso (AA) in 1993 . . . Homered in double figures only once in seven-plus minor-league seasons, then did it this year in part-time, major-league role . . . Born Aug. 4, 1969, in Compton, Cal. . . . Salary last year was $125,000.

Year	Club	Pos.	G	AB	R	H	2B	3B	HR	RBI	SB	Avg.
1993	Milwaukee	OF	19	41	3	12	3	0	0	3	0	.293
1994	Milwaukee	OF	27	66	9	18	1	1	2	7	1	.273
1995	Boston	OF	112	399	60	123	31	6	10	49	5	.308
	Totals		158	506	72	153	35	7	12	59	6	.302

TIM NAEHRING 29 6-2 205 — Bats R Throws R

Veteran Red Sox third baseman has had trouble staying healthy, but set career high with 433 at-bats in 1995 and that led to highs in every other offensive category . . . His .307 batting average last year was 46 points over previous career mark . . . Always a tough hitter with men on base, especially with bases loaded . . . Was one of rare bright spots in dismal Division Series, batting .308 with one home run. Was only Boston player to score more than one run, with two . . . Was Red Sox' eighth pick in 1988 draft . . . Born Feb. 1, 1967, in Cincinnati . . . Salary in 1995 was $562,500.

Year	Club	Pos.	G	AB	R	H	2B	3B	HR	RBI	SB	Avg.
1990	Boston	SS-3B-2B	24	85	10	23	6	0	2	12	0	.271
1991	Boston	SS-3B-2B	20	55	1	6	1	0	0	3	0	.109
1992	Boston	SS-2B-3B-OF	72	186	12	43	8	0	3	14	0	.231
1993	Boston	2B-3B-SS	39	127	14	42	10	0	1	17	1	.331
1994	Boston	INF	80	297	41	82	18	1	7	42	1	.276
1995	Boston	3B	126	433	61	133	27	2	10	57	0	.307
	Totals		361	1183	139	329	70	3	23	145	2	.278

LUIS ALICEA 30 5-9 177 — Bats S Throws R

If only the rest of the Red Sox had stepped up in the postseason like he did, they might have made a better account of themselves . . . Second baseman had six hits in 10 at-bats against Indians, including a double and a home run for 1.000 slugging percentage . . . Acquired from Cardinals for Nat Minchey and Jeff McNeely prior to '95 season . . . Cards drafted him in first round in 1986 . . . Set career high with 419 at-bats in '95 . . . Batting average (.270) was in line with previous two years in St. Louis, but is deceptive . . . Has good eye at the plate, as evidenced by 63 walks and .367 on-base percentage . . . Born July 29, 1965, in Santurce, P.R. . . . Salary last year was $800,000.

Year	Club	Pos.	G	AB	R	H	2B	3B	HR	RBI	SB	Avg.
1988	St. Louis	2B	93	297	20	63	10	4	1	24	1	.212
1991	St. Louis	2B-3B-SS	56	68	5	13	3	0	0	0	0	.191
1992	St. Louis	2B-SS	85	265	26	65	9	11	2	32	2	.245
1993	St. Louis	2B-OF-3B	115	362	50	101	19	3	3	46	11	.279
1994	St. Louis	2B-OF	88	205	32	57	12	5	5	29	4	.278
1995	Boston	2B	132	419	64	113	20	3	6	44	13	.270
	Totals		569	1616	197	412	73	26	17	175	31	.255

MIKE STANLEY 32 6-0 190 — Bats R Throws R

Red Sox were thrilled to sign top power-hitting catcher in AL to one-year, $2.3-million deal as free agent last winter . . . Yankees spurned him in favor of Joe Girardi . . . Had tough act to follow after 1993 season, when he and Baltimore's Chris Hoiles joined select club of catchers to hit .300 with 25-or-more home runs . . . Might have done it again in 1994, when he was batting .300 and was on pace to hit 25 homers when strike wiped out final two months . . . Though 1995 numbers were not as impressive, he still was league's most productive catcher with 18 homers and 83 RBI . . . Batted .313 in Division Series against Mariners . . . Signed by Yankees as free agent prior to '92 season, after six years with Rangers . . . Texas chose him in 16th round in 1985 draft . . . Born June 25, 1963, in Fort Lauderdale, Fla. . . . Salary last year was $562,000.

Year	Club	Pos.	G	AB	R	H	2B	3B	HR	RBI	SB	Avg.
1986	Texas	3B-C-OF	15	30	4	10	3	0	1	1	1	.333
1987	Texas	C-1B-OF	78	216	34	59	8	1	6	37	3	.273
1988	Texas	C-1B-3B	94	249	21	57	8	0	3	27	0	.229
1989	Texas	C-1B-3B	67	122	9	30	3	1	1	11	1	.246
1990	Texas	C-1B-3B	103	189	21	47	8	1	2	19	1	.249
1991	Texas	C-1B-3B-OF	5	181	25	45	13	1	3	25	0	.249
1992	New York (AL)	C-1B	68	173	24	43	7	0	8	27	0	.249
1993	New York (AL)	C	130	423	70	129	17	1	26	84	1	.305
1994	New York (AL)	C-1B	82	290	54	87	20	0	17	57	0	.300
1995	New York (AL)	C	118	399	63	107	29	1	18	83	1	.268
	Totals		850	2272	325	614	116	6	85	371	8	.270

TIM WAKEFIELD 29 6-2 204 Bats R Throws R

Floundering knuckleball pitcher was signed as a minor-league free agent by Red Sox prior to '95 and then proceeded to reconstruct his career with a tremendous season that included 16 victories and All-Star Game selection . . . Could not keep up early pace, but that was no surprise . . . Received aid from Phil Niekro . . . Got off to 14-1 start before going 2-7 the rest of the way . . . Late fold cost him a chance to rank higher in Cy Young balloting . . . Struggles continued in postseason . . . Experienced control problems and gave up seven earned runs in 5⅓ innings in Division Series start against Indians . . . Born Aug. 2, 1966, in Melbourne, Fla. . . . Salary last year was $170,000 . . . Pirates chose him in eighth round of 1988 draft, as first baseman out of Florida Tech.

Year	Club	G	IP	W	L	Pct.	SO	BB	H	ERA
1992	Pittsburgh	13	92	8	1	.889	51	35	76	2.15
1993	Pittsburgh	24	128⅓	6	11	.353	59	75	145	5.61
1995	Boston	27	195⅓	16	8	.667	119	68	163	2.95
	Totals	64	415⅔	30	20	.600	229	178	384	3.59

ROGER CLEMENS 33 6-4 227 Bats R Throws R

Dean of Red Sox roster, but not nearly the overpowering pitcher he was earlier in his career . . . Numbers still solid, though ERA was over 4.00 for second time in three years . . . His 10-5 record gave him best percentage (.667) since 1990, but he has a combined 30-26 (.536) mark over past three seasons . . . Won back-to-back Al Cy Youngs in 1986 and 1987 . . . Still able to step up for big games . . . Pitched seven good innings in Division Series against Indians, giving up three runs on five hits . . . Red Sox career leader in games started (348) and strikeouts (2,333) . . . Boston picked him 19th overall in 1983 draft . . . Born Aug. 4, 1962, in Dayton, Ohio . . . Salary last year was $5,655,250.

Year	Club	G	IP	W	L	Pct.	SO	BB	H	ERA
1984	Boston	21	133⅓	9	4	.692	126	29	146	4.32
1985	Boston	15	98⅓	7	5	.583	74	37	83	3.29
1986	Boston	33	254	24	4	.857	238	67	179	2.48
1987	Boston	36	281⅔	20	9	.690	256	83	248	2.97
1988	Boston	35	264	18	12	.600	291	62	217	2.93
1989	Boston	35	253⅓	17	11	.607	230	93	215	3.13
1990	Boston	31	228⅓	21	6	.778	209	54	193	1.93
1991	Boston	35	271⅓	18	10	.643	241	65	219	2.62
1992	Boston	32	246⅔	18	11	.621	208	62	203	2.41
1993	Boston	29	191⅔	11	14	.440	160	67	175	4.46
1994	Boston	24	170⅔	9	7	.563	168	71	124	2.85
1995	Boston	23	140	10	5	.667	132	60	141	4.18
	Totals	349	2533⅓	182	98	.650	2333	750	2143	3.00

TOP PROSPECTS

VAUGHN ESHELMAN 26 6-3 205 Bats L Throws L
Selected from Orioles in Rule V draft prior to '95, he got off to a solid start at major-league level . . . Finished with 6-3 record and 4.85 ERA in swing role. Made 14 starts and nine relief appearances . . . Born May 22, 1969, in Philadelphia . . . Orioles' fourth-round pick in 1991 draft, out of Houston.

NOMAR GARCIAPARRA 22 6-0 165 Bats R Throws R
Promising shortstop was Boston's first choice in 1994 draft, out of Georgia Tech . . . Fifth-round pick by Brewers out of high school . . . Still a couple years away, but that's okay because the Red Sox have John Valentin just coming into his own . . . Hit .267

More missions for The Rocket, after 2,333 career Ks.

with eight homers, 47 RBI and 35 stolen bases in '95 with Trenton (AA) in Eastern League . . . Born July 23, 1973, in Whittier, Cal.

TROT NIXON 21 6-2 196 Bats L Throws L
Solidly built outfielder was drafted by Red Sox as seventh choice overall in 1993 . . . Has had back problems, but club is still high on him after season in which he hit .303 with five homers and 39 RBI in 264 at-bats with Sarasota (A) in the Florida State League and .160 with two homers and eight RBI in 94 at-bats with Trenton (AA) in Eastern League . . . Born April 11, 1974, in Durham, N.C.

DWAYNE HOSEY 29 5-10 175 **Bats S Throws R**

Minor-league journeyman spent eight years trying to get to the big leagues . . . Finally made it last year and hit well in very limited playing time with Red Sox . . . Batted .338 in 68 at-bats . . . Scored 20 runs . . . Stole six bases in six attempts . . . Earned role in Division Series against Cleveland, but went hitless in 12 at-bats . . . Born March 11, 1967, in Sharon, Pa. . . . White Sox picked him in 13th round in 1987 draft . . . Red Sox claimed him on waivers from Royals, Aug. 31 of last season.

MANAGER KEVIN KENNEDY: Followed strange 1994 season with Texas with breakthrough campaign in Boston, where surprising Red Sox posted 86-58 record and ran away with AL East title . . . Gambled on a couple of marginal free-agent pitchers—Tim Wakefield and Erik Hanson—and came up a big winner when both delivered comeback seasons . . . Indians cut down Red Sox in postseason, but he received extension through '97 . . . With Texas, he finished in first place in AL West in 1994, the season killed by the strike, and he wound up being fired . . . Though he's a tough, strong communicator, he's also known for coddling his star performers . . . Career record is 224-196 . . . Born May 26, 1954, in Los Angeles . . . Hit .238 in eight minor-league seasons as a catcher . . . Managed in Dodgers farm system from 1984-91 . . . Was Felipe Alou's bench coach with Expos in 1992 and took over as Rangers manager in 1993.

ALL-TIME RED SOX SEASON RECORDS

BATTING: Ted Williams, .406, 1941
HRs: Jimmie Foxx, 50, 1938
RBI: Jimmie Foxx, 175, 1938
STEALS: Tommy Harper, 54, 1973
WINS: Joe Wood, 34, 1912
STRIKEOUTS: Roger Clemens, 291, 1988

DETROIT TIGERS

TEAM DIRECTORY: Owner: Michael Ilitch; Pres.: John McHale; GM: Randy Smith; Asst. GM: Gary Vitto; Sr. Dir. Pub. Rel.: Dan Ewald; Trav. Sec.: Bill Brown; Mgr.: Buddy Bell; Coaches: Glenn Ezell, Terry Francona, Larry Herndon, Fred Kenall, Jon Matlack, Ron Oester. Home: Tiger Stadium (52,416). Field distances: 340, l.f. line; 365, l.c.; 440, c.f.; 370, r.c.; 325, r.f. line. Spring training: Lakeland, Fla.

SCOUTING REPORT

HITTING: The AL's worse offensive club last year doesn't figure to get a lot better in 1996, which looks like a rebuilding year

With a hitter like Fielder, will wonders ever Cec?

for new GM Randy Smith and new manager Buddy Bell.

The Tigers ranked last in the AL with a .247 batting average and 12th in runs (654) and Detroit could be without two of the three top hitters for average from last year's club. Second baseman Lou Whitaker (.293, 14, 44), a free agent at press time, was doubtful about returning and his partner Alan Trammell (.269, 2, 23) seemed headed for the front office.

At least the heart of the lineup remains intact, with Cecil Fielder (.243, 31, 82) a lock to hit 30-or-more home runs and Travis Fryman (.275, 15, 81) likely to improve on last year's numbers. Much will depend on the development of young hitters Chris Gomez (.223, 11, 50), John Flaherty (.243, 11, 40) and Phil Nevin (.219, 2, 12 as a Tiger), a possible boost from free-agent addition Mark Parent (.234, 18, 38 with the Pirates and the Cubs) and the continued productivity of Chad Curtis, who had 21 homers and 27 stolen bases last year. The Tigers look for a comeback year from Phil Plantier (.255, 9, 34 with the Padres).

PITCHING: Detroit was one of two AL teams to surrender an average of more than five earned runs per game (5.49), so it is little wonder that the Tigers are not considered a serious contender in '96. There are some promising young arms in the organization, but the club traded away its only impact pitcher, David Wells, last July and doesn't figure to spend much to patch up its rotation.

The young nucleus of the rotation—Felipe Lira (9-13, 4.31), Sean Bergman (7-10, 5.12) and Jose Lima (3-9, 6.11)—was a combined 13-under-.500 last year. The bullpen, headed by John Doherty (5-9, 5.10, 6 saves) and Joe Boever (5-7, 6.39), does not have a returning pitcher who saved more than six games in '95.

FIELDING: Not great. Only two teams in the AL made more errors than the Tigers (106) last year and only three had a worse combined fielding percentage. There is nothing glaringly wrong in an outfield anchored by Bobby Higginson. But Fielder lacks range at first and the left side of the infield, Fryman and Gomez, will make their share of miscues. The porous pitching will be the club's major weakness, but a good defensive club might be able to smooth some of the rough edges. No such luck here.

OUTLOOK: The front office has a fresh new look, but it will take more than that to pull the Tigers, 60-84 in 1995, out of a long organizational slump. Look for Smith and Bell to embark on a bottom-to-top rebuilding plan that could have the team in contention by '98, but not much sooner than that.

TIGER PROFILES

TRAVIS FRYMAN 27 6-1 194 Bats R Throws R

Big offensive threat who can play either third base or shortstop . . . Has become cornerstone of the Tigers' rebuilding effort . . . Did not have big home-run (15) and RBI (81) numbers last year, but teams with Cecil Fielder to give Tigers one of AL's best three-four hitting combinations . . . Biggest weakness is the strikeout . . . After leading AL with 128 Ks in 1994, he improved marginally last year (100), but home-run ratio went down concurrently . . . Came into '95 averaging home run per 28 at-bats and strikeout per 4.2 at-bats. Last season, home-run frequency dropped to about one per 38 at-bats and strikeout ratio improved to one per 5.7 . . . Posted higher batting average (.275), but his run production slipped . . . Experienced no power shortage against division-winning Red Sox in '95, hitting four homers against Boston, two of them grand slams . . . Born March 25, 1969, in Lexington, Ky. . . . Salary was $4,150,000 last year and two years remain on five-year, $25-million deal . . . Tigers drafted him in third round in 1987.

Year	Club	Pos.	G	AB	R	H	2B	3B	HR	RBI	SB	Avg.
1990	Detroit	3B-ss	66	232	32	69	11	1	9	27	3	.297
1991	Detroit	3B-SS	149	557	65	144	36	3	21	91	12	.259
1992	Detroit	SS-3B	161	659	87	175	31	4	20	96	8	.266
1993	Detroit	SS-3B	151	607	98	182	37	5	22	97	9	.300
1994	Detroit	3B	114	464	66	122	34	5	18	85	2	.263
1995	Detroit	3B	144	567	79	156	21	5	15	81	4	.275
	Totals		785	3086	427	848	170	23	105	477	38	.275

CECIL FIELDER 32 6-3 250 Bats R Throws R

First baseman is still one of baseball's biggest boppers, in both size and impact . . . Hit 30-or-more home runs for fifth time in six seasons with Tigers (31) and almost certainly would have done it in all six if players' strike had not held him to 28 in 1994 . . . Became only Tiger ever to hit 25-or-more homers six straight seasons . . . No other player in Tiger history has hit as many over a six-year period (219) . . . No other major-league player has more homers over the same period . . . Had string of seasons with 90-or-more RBI snapped at five when he finished with team-leading 82 in '95 . . . Strikes out about once per four at-bats and homers once per 15 at-bats . . . Born Sept. 21, 1963, in Los Angeles . . . Salary last year was $9,237,500, including pro-rated bonuses and deferrals, with two seasons left on five-year, $36-million deal . . . Royals' fourth-round pick in 1982 draft . . . Tigers bought him home after he hit 38 homers for Hanshin of Japanese League in 1989.

Year Club	Pos.	G	AB	R	H	2B	3B	HR	RBI	SB	Avg.
1985 Toronto	1B	30	74	6	23	4	0	4	16	0	.311
1986 Toronto	1B-3B-OF	34	83	7	13	2	0	4	13	0	.157
1987 Toronto	1B-3B	82	175	30	47	7	1	14	32	0	.269
1988 Toronto	1B-3B-2B	74	174	24	40	6	1	9	23	0	.230
1990 Detroit	1B	159	573	104	159	25	1	51	132	0	.277
1991 Detroit	1B	162	624	102	163	25	0	44	133	0	.261
1992 Detroit	1B	155	594	80	145	22	0	35	124	0	.244
1993 Detroit	1B	154	573	80	153	23	0	30	117	0	.267
1994 Detroit	1B	109	425	67	110	16	2	28	90	0	.259
1995 Detroit	1B	136	494	70	120	18	1	31	82	0	.243
Totals		1095	3789	570	973	148	6	250	762	0	.257

CHAD CURTIS 27 5-10 175 — Bats R Throws R

Acquired by Tigers from Angels for veteran outfielder Tony Phillips prior to last season, he made the deal look good, setting career highs in every run-production category (21 homers, 67 RBI) and establishing himself as a regular . . . Good speed on bases . . . Stole 43 and 48 bases respectively his first two years in majors . . . His stolen-base numbers dropped last two years, partly because of shortened schedules . . . Base-stealing efficiency is a problem, though, as he was thrown out more than one-third of the time last year (27 steals in 42 attempts) . . . Good outfielder who led league in putouts in 1994 . . . Born Nov. 6, 1968, in Marion, Ind. . . . Salary last year was $1,900,000 . . . Beat long odds as Angels' 45th-round pick in 1989 after being named NAIA All-American at Grand Canyon College.

Year Club	Pos.	G	AB	R	H	2B	3B	HR	RBI	SB	Avg.
1992 California	OF	139	441	59	114	16	2	10	46	43	.259
1993 California	OF-2B	152	583	94	166	25	3	6	59	48	.285
1994 California	OF	114	453	67	116	23	4	11	50	25	.256
1995 Detroit	OF	144	586	96	157	29	3	21	67	27	.268
Totals		549	2063	316	553	93	12	48	222	143	.268

CHRIS GOMEZ 24 6-1 183 **Bats R Throws R**

Former Long Beach State All-American was chosen by Tigers in third round of 1992 draft . . . Spent parts of only two seasons in minors before making big-league debut in 1993 . . . Spent all of strike-shortened '94 season in majors and was on pace to drive in 75 runs over full schedule . . . Struggled with batting average (.223) last year and saw run-production numbers (11 homers, 50 RBI) lag considerably behind '94 pace . . . Still considered Alan Trammell's successor as the Tigers' everyday shortstop of present and future, though he could play second if future roster situation dictates . . . Born June 16, 1971, in Los Angeles . . . Salary last year was $215,000.

Year	Club	Pos.	G	AB	R	H	2B	3B	HR	RBI	SB	Avg.
1993	Detroit	SS-2B	46	128	11	32	7	1	0	11	2	.250
1994	Detroit	SS-2B	84	296	32	76	19	0	8	53	5	.257
1995	Detroit	SS-2B	123	431	49	96	20	2	11	50	4	.223
	Totals		253	855	92	204	46	3	19	114	11	.239

PHIL NEVIN 25 6-2 180 **Bats R Throws R**

Averaged 86 RBI in two minor-league seasons after Astros made him No. 1 pick in nation, out of Cal State Fullerton, in 1992 draft . . . But apparently Houston was not impressed enough to stick with plans to make him an integral part of club's future . . . Traded to Detroit for aging all-time Tiger saves leader Mike Henneman Aug. 10 of last season in salary dumping that could be a steal for Tigers if he pans out . . . Did not make good first impression . . . Batted just .219 in 96 AL at-bats with two homers and 12 RBI . . . Previously hit woeful .117 with one RBI and 13 Ks in 60 at-bats for Astros, then popped off about demotion to Tucson (AAA) . . . Struggled defensively in left field at quirky Tiger Stadium, after being converted from third base, but should adjust . . . Born Jan. 19, 1971, in Fullerton, Cal. . . . Hit .291 with seven homers and 41 RBI in 223 at-bats for Tucson before Tigers rescued him.

Year	Club	Pos.	G	AB	R	H	2B	3B	HR	RBI	SB	Avg.
1995	Houston	3B-OF	18	60	4	7	1	0	0	1	1	.117
1995	Detroit	OF	29	96	9	21	3	1	2	12	0	.219
	Totals		47	156	13	28	4	1	2	13	1	.179

Travis Fryman is key Tiger rebuilding block.

JOHN FLAHERTY 28 6-1 200 Bats R Throws R

Took his time developing into major-league player . . . Was 25th-round pick of Red Sox in 1988 and came into '95 season with just 82 games under his belt at major-league level . . . Was only catcher on the Tigers' 40-man roster when spring training began . . . Played regularly and performed solidly behind the plate . . . Not regarded as big offensive threat—he came into last year with .168 batting average and no home runs in 131 big-league at-bats—but he did reach double figures in home runs (11) and ranked fifth in slugging percentage (.404) among Tiger regulars . . . Born Oct. 21, 1967, in New York, N.Y. . . . Salary last year was $172,500 . . . Tigers acquired him from Boston for Rich Rowland prior to '94 season.

Year	Club	Pos.	G	AB	R	H	2B	3B	HR	RBI	SB	Avg.
1992	Boston	C	35	66	3	13	2	0	0	2	0	.197
1993	Boston	C	13	25	3	3	2	0	0	2	0	.120
1994	Detroit	C	34	40	2	6	1	0	0	4	0	.150
1995	Detroit	C	112	354	39	86	22	1	11	40	0	.243
	Totals		194	485	47	108	27	1	11	48	0	.223

BOBBY HIGGINSON 25 5-11 180 Bats L Throws R

Not a high draft choice (12th round by Tigers in 1992), but outfielder has become a major part of the Tigers' rebuilding effort . . . Struggled to make contact in first season at major-league level, averaging a strikeout per 3.7 at-bats, and did not hit for average (.224), but he displayed enough power (14 homers, 43 RBI) to rate a place in '96 starting lineup . . . Hit just nine homers in 679 at-bats over first two years in low minor leagues, but he had 23 for Toledo (AAA) in 1994 to emerge as legitimate power prospect . . . Will need to produce more runs to stay in lineup this year . . . Born Aug. 18, 1970, in Philadelphia . . . Made minimum major-league salary of $109,000 last season . . . Was Temple's all-time leading home-run hitter.

Year	Club	Pos.	G	AB	R	H	2B	3B	HR	RBI	SB	Avg.
1995	Detroit	OF	131	410	61	92	17	5	14	43	6	.224

FELIPE LIRA 23 6-0 170 Bats R Throws R

Rookie was winningest (9) and losingest (13) pitcher still on the Tigers' roster when '95 season ended . . . Pitched as member of starting rotation for most of season, but also made 15 relief appearances and even recorded a save . . . Averaged five strikeouts and three walks per nine innings . . . Vulnerable to the long ball, he gave up one home run per eight innings for a total of 17 . . . Figures to be big part of very youthful Detroit rotation in '96 . . . Born April 26, 1972, in Miranda, Venezuela . . . Earned minimum major-league salary of $109,000 last year . . . Tigers signed him as non-drafted free agent in February 1990.

Year	Club	G	IP	W	L	Pct.	SO	BB	H	ERA
1995	Detroit	37	146⅓	9	13	.409	89	56	151	4.31

SEAN BERGMAN 26 6-4 230 Bats R Throws R

Finished last season with most starts by any Tiger pitcher (28), but he needs to improve ratios if he is going to be a winning major leaguer . . . Gave up 33 more hits than innings pitched and averaged nearly a walk every two innings . . . Also very vulnerable to long ball (19 homers), which shouldn't be surprising considering number of hits he gives up and the cozy dimensions of Tiger Stadium . . . Detroit's sixth-round draft choice, out of Southern Illinois, in 1991 . . . Born April 11, 1970, in Joliet, Ill. . . . Salary last year was $137,500.

Year	Club	G	IP	W	L	Pct.	SO	BB	H	ERA
1993	Detroit	9	39⅔	1	4	.200	19	23	47	5.67
1994	Detroit	3	17⅔	2	1	.667	12	7	22	5.60
1995	Detroit	28	135⅓	7	10	.412	86	67	169	5.12
	Totals	40	192⅔	10	15	.400	117	97	238	5.28

JOHN DOHERTY 28 6-4 215 Bats R Throws R

Selected by Tigers in 19th round of 1989 draft, he rose quickly through organization and won 14 games as a starter in 1993 . . . Moved to bullpen after ERA ballooned to 6.48 in '94 and spent almost all of last season in middle and setup relief roles . . . Not overpowering . . . Walks-to-strikeouts ratio virtually even . . . Hits-to-innings ratio also contributed to another high ERA (5.10) . . . Had six saves, but he doesn't figure to compete for wide-open role of closer . . . Born June 11, 1967, in Bronx, N.Y. . . . Salary last year was $375,000.

Year	Club	G	IP	W	L	Pct.	SO	BB	H	ERA
1992	Detroit	47	116	7	4	.636	37	25	131	3.88
1993	Detroit	32	184⅔	14	11	.560	63	48	205	4.44
1994	Detroit	18	101⅓	6	7	.462	28	26	139	6.48
1995	Detroit	48	113	5	9	.357	46	37	130	5.10
	Totals	145	515	32	31	.508	174	136	605	4.86

JOE BOEVER 35 6-1 200 **Bats R Throws R**

Veteran middle reliever, signed by Detroit after being released by Athletics in '93 and re-signed as free agent prior to '95, ended up being most-used arm in the Tigers' bullpen, for better or worse . . . His 6.39 ERA was nearly twice as high as his career number, inflated by average of one home run per five innings for total of 17 . . . His hits-to-innings and walks-to-strikeouts ratios don't bode well for a significant role this year . . . Has pitched for 12 teams in majors and minors since professional career began in 1982 as non-drafted signee by Cardinals . . . Born Oct. 4, 1960, in St. Louis . . . Salary last year was $500,000 . . . Three saves in '95 boosted career total to 47, with 21 of those recorded for Atlanta in 1989.

Year	Club	G	IP	W	L	Pct.	SO	BB	H	ERA
1985	St. Louis	13	16⅓	0	0	.000	20	4	17	4.41
1986	St. Louis	11	21⅔	0	1	.000	8	11	19	1.66
1987	Atlanta	14	18⅓	1	0	1.000	18	12	29	7.36
1988	Atlanta	16	20⅓	0	2	.000	7	1	12	1.77
1989	Atlanta	66	82⅓	4	11	.267	68	34	78	3.94
1990	Atl.-Phil.	67	88⅓	3	6	.333	75	51	77	3.36
1991	Philadelphia	68	98⅓	3	5	.375	89	54	90	3.84
1992	Houston	81	111⅓	3	6	.333	67	45	103	2.51
1993	Oak.-Det.	61	102⅓	6	3	.667	63	44	101	3.61
1994	Detroit	46	81⅓	9	2	.818	49	37	80	3.98
1995	Detroit	60	98⅔	5	7	.417	71	44	128	6.39
	Totals	503	739⅓	34	43	.442	535	337	734	3.90

TOP PROSPECTS

ANTHONY CLARK 23 6-7 240 **Bats S Throws R**

Did not perform particularly well in brief major-league tryout last year (.238, three homers, 11 RBI), but is expected to be solid power prospect . . . Had total of 23 home runs and 99 RBI while splitting 1994 season between Trenton (AA) and Toledo (AAA) in '94 . . . Hit .242 with 14 homers, 63 RBI and 129 strikeouts in 405 at-bats for Toledo last season . . . Plays first base, which could be a problem with Cecil Fielder around . . . Born June 15, 1972, in Newton, Kan. . . . Tigers made him second overall choice in 1990 draft . . . Played basketball for Arizona and San Diego State.

TODD STEVERSON 25 6-2 200 Bats R Throws R

Outfielder was obtained from Blue Jays organization in the Rule V draft prior to '95 . . . Appeared in only 30 games at major-league level and performed well (.262, two homers, six RBI) . . . Hit .107 with one homer and five RBI in 28 at-bats for Toledo (AAA) in '95 . . . Club hopes speed and power will make him a candidate for regular playing time this year . . . Born Nov. 15, 1971, in Los Angeles . . . Hit .263 with nine homers and 38 RBI for Knoxville (AA) in 1994 . . . Had total of 58 steals in three minor-league seasons after Toronto drafted him in first round in 1992, out of Arizona State . . . Cousin of former Tiger Ron LeFlore.

CLINT SODOWSKY 23 6-3 180 Bats L Throws R

Pitched well (2-2, 5.01) in September tryout . . . Had 2-1 record and 3.63 ERA over first four starts, but was hit hard on final day of '95 season (4 runs, 1⅔ innings) . . . Control was minor problem as he walked 18 in 23⅓ major-league innings . . . Tigers drafted him in 11th round in 1991 . . . Born July 13, 1972, in Ponca City, Okla. . . . Went 5-1 with 2.85 ERA in nine starts for Toledo (AAA) in '95.

GREG GOHR 28 6-3 205 Bats R Throws R

First-round draft choice by Tigers in 1989 has been hampered by shoulder and rib-cage injuries the past four years . . . But he gave indications late last season that he might be about to arrive as a solid major-league pitcher . . . Gave up just one run in string of 10 relief appearances as he went 1-0, 0.87 with 12 Ks in 10⅓ innings for Tigers in September . . . Always worked as a starter in minor leagues, so could get a chance to compete for place in rotation if he's healthy . . . Born Oct. 29, 1967, in Santa Clara, Cal. . . . Was 0-2, 2.87 in six games for Toledo (AAA) last year . . . Notched first major-league victory, June 14, 1994, at Milwaukee . . . Carries 3-2 mark and 4.43 career ERA as Tiger into 1996 . . . Did not begin to pitch until attending college at Santa Clara.

MANAGER BUDDY BELL: Former All-Star third baseman will be making his major-league managing debut with Tigers this year, though he has a wide range of experience as a player, coach and minor-league instructor . . . Chosen by new GM Randy Smith to replace Sparky Anderson as Detroit manager after a 60-84 finish last season in a surprising announcement . . . Former Yankee manager Buck Showalter was expected to get the job . . . Spent the past two seasons as infield coach of Indians . . . Before that, he spent three seasons as director of minor-league instruction for White Sox . . . During 18-year, major-league playing career (Indians, Rangers, Reds), he was chosen to All-Star team four times and won six consecutive Gold Gloves from 1979-84 . . . Finished his playing career ranked among baseball's all-time leaders at third base in total chances, games played, assists and double plays . . . Along with father Gus, he owns major-league record for hits by a father-son combination (4,337) and soon could have at least one third-generation major leaguer in family. Son David is with Cardinals and son Michael was first pick of Rangers in 1993 draft . . . Played ball at Xavier and Miami (Ohio) . . . Born Aug. 27, 1951, in Pittsburgh, Pa.

ALL-TIME TIGER SEASON RECORDS

BATTING: Ty Cobb, .420, 1911
HRs: Hank Greenberg, 58, 1938
RBI: Hank Greenberg, 183, 1937
STEALS: Ty Cobb, 96, 1915
WINS: Denny McLain, 31, 1968
STRIKEOUTS: Mickey Lolich, 308, 1971

NEW YORK YANKEES

TEAM DIRECTORY: Principal Owner: George Steinbrenner III; General Partner: Joseph Malloy; GM: Bob Watson; Dir. Player Dev. and Scouting: Jack Hubbard; Dir. Minor League Oper.: Mitch Lukevics; Sr. Advisor: Arthur Richman; Dir. Media Rel.: Rob Butcher; Trav. Sec.: David Szen; Mgr.: Joe Torre; Coaches: Jose Cardenal, Chris Chambliss, Tony Cloninger, Willie Randolph, Mel Stottlemyre, Don Zimmer. Home: Yankee Stadium (57,545). Field distances: 312, l.f. line; 379 l.f.; 411, l.c.; 410, c.f.; 385, r.c.; 310, r.f. line. Spring training: Tampa, Fla.

SCOUTING REPORT

HITTING: The Yankees ended up in the playoffs last year at 79-65, but didn't get there on their offensive numbers. They ranked sixth in the AL in runs (749), sixth in batting average (.276) and 12th in home runs (122).

The makeup of the lineup should change dramatically. Don Mattingly, a free agent at press time, was headed elsewhere or into retirement and he will be replaced by Tino Martinez (.293, 31, 111 with the Mariners). Free-agent Mike Stanley was ditched in favor of ex-Rockie Joe Girardi (.262, 8, 55), who offers none of Stanley's punch. But the rest of the offensive nucleus should remain intact, including the re-enlisted Wade Boggs (.324, 5, 63), Paul O'Neill (.300, 22, 96), Bernie Williams (.307, 18, 82) and Ruben Sierra (.263, 19, 86).

And Mariano Duncan (.287, 6, 36 with the Phillies and Reds) could fill the utility role left by new Angel Randy Velarde.

PITCHING: Don't look here for an explanation for the Yankees' solid 1995 season. They were in the middle of the pack in combined ERA (4.56) after injuries to Jimmy Key and Melido Perez decimated the rotation, but did rank second in complete games (18) and had the AL's third-best hits-to-innings ratio.

The club did build a solid rotation by the end of last season, thanks to acquiring 1994 Cy Young winner David Cone (18-8, 3.57) from the Blue Jays July 28 and getting a solid season from rookie Andy Pettitte (12-9, 4.17). If Key can beat the odds and come all the way back from rotator-cuff surgery, if Scott Kamieniecki (7-6, 4.01) can stay healthy or if free-agent addition Dwight Gooden, suspended since mid-1994, can resurrect his ca-

Andy Pettitte was Stadium stalwart, at 8-2 with 2.61 ERA.

reer, the Yankees may be able to weather the defection of Jack McDowell (15-10, 3.93) to the Indians.

There is also uncertainty in the bullpen. Stopper John Wetteland is coming back from a strong season (1-5, 2.93, 31 saves) and Mariano Rivera (5-3, 5.51) and Jeff Nelson (7-3, 2.17 with the Mariners) are among the youngsters who will audition for setup roles alongside Bob Wickman (2-4, 4.05).

FIELDING: The Yankees finished in a virtual tie with the Orioles for the AL's top combined fielding percentage, committing just 74 errors. The infield defense will be hurt by the loss of perennial Gold Glove winner Mattingly at first. However, Girardi throws better than Stanley and the Gold Glove-winning Boggs made only five errors in 276 chances at third. However, young Derek Jeter figures to be far more erratic than Tony Fernandez at short and the outfield defense could be unpredictable.

OUTLOOK: The Yankees took advantage of a depressed AL East last year, recovering from a poor first half to finish strong and win a place in the Division Series. The competition should be much tougher for new manager Joe Torre's team in 1996, which doesn't bode well.

YANKEE PROFILES

Paul O'Neill has become best bet for .300 and 20-plus HRs.

PAUL O'NEILL 33 6-4 215 **Bats L Throws L**

Once again the most dependable all-around player on the Yankee roster, with big offensive numbers (.300, 22 HR, 96 RBI) and steady outfield play . . . Led club with .526 slugging percentage . . . Batted .333 with three homers and six RBI in Division Series against Mariners . . . Won American League batting championship in shortened 1994 season with .359 average . . . Led NL outfielders in fielding percentage (.997) in

1992 before being traded from Reds to Yankees with Joe DeBerry for Roberto Kelly . . . Originally looked like Reds got better end of that deal, but this guy has batted .300-plus with at least 20 home runs and a progressively increasing RBI total in three years with Yankees . . . Born Feb. 25, 1963, in Columbus, Ohio . . . Salary last year was $2,800,000 . . . Reds' fourth-round pick in 1981 draft.

Year	Club	Pos.	G	AB	R	H	2B	3B	HR	RBI	SB	Avg.
1985	Cincinnati	OF	5	12	1	4	1	0	0	1	0	.333
1986	Cincinnati	PH	3	2	0	0	0	0	0	0	0	.000
1987	Cincinnati	OF-1B-P	84	160	24	41	14	1	7	28	2	.256
1988	Cincinnati	OF-1B	145	485	58	122	25	3	16	73	8	.252
1989	Cincinnati	OF	117	428	49	118	24	2	15	74	20	.276
1990	Cincinnati	OF	145	503	59	136	28	0	16	78	13	.270
1991	Cincinnati	OF	152	532	71	136	36	0	28	91	12	.256
1992	Cincinnati	OF	148	496	59	122	19	1	14	66	6	.246
1993	New York (AL)	OF	141	498	71	155	34	1	20	75	2	.311
1994	New York (AL)	OF	103	368	68	132	25	1	21	83	5	.359
1995	New York (AL)	OF	127	460	82	138	30	4	22	96	1	.300
	Totals		1170	3944	542	1104	236	13	159	665	69	.280

BERNIE WILLIAMS 27 6-2 205 Bats S Throws R

Smashing season for Yankee center fielder, who had averaged only 12 homers and 62 RBI in first two full seasons in the big leagues . . . Posted career highs in average (.307), homers (18), RBI (82) and runs (93) . . . Batted .429 with two homers and five RBI in Division Series against Mariners. Walked four times in final game and scored two big runs, but Mariners came back to win . . . Committed eight errors last year to rank among league leaders . . . Had AL's highest average by a leadoff hitter (.364) in 1994, but finished at .289 overall . . . Signed by Yankees as non-drafted free agent in September 1985 . . . Born Sept. 13, 1968, in San Juan, P.R. . . . Salary last year was $400,000.

Year	Club	Pos.	G	AB	R	H	2B	3B	HR	RBI	SB	Avg.
1991	New York (AL)	OF	85	320	43	76	19	4	3	34	10	.238
1992	New York (AL)	OF	62	261	39	73	14	2	5	26	7	.280
1993	New York (AL)	OF	139	567	67	152	31	4	12	68	9	.268
1994	New York (AL)	3B-1B	108	408	80	118	29	1	12	57	16	.289
1995	New York (AL)	OF	144	563	93	173	29	9	18	82	8	.307
	Totals		538	2119	322	592	122	20	50	267	50	.279

JOE GIRARDI 31 5-11 210 Bats R Throws R

Acquired by Yanks from Rockies for Mike DeJean and Steve Shoemaker last winter . . . Veteran catcher set career highs in homers and RBI for Colorado in '95, but he's no Mike Stanley with the bat . . . Stayed healthy and caught 122 games, most since 1990 . . . Home-run total of eight was two short of big-league total in six previous seasons . . . Threw out 25-of-99 (25.3%) would-be base-stealers . . . Committed 10 errors . . . Hit .125 in Division Series vs. Braves . . . Salary was $1,750,000 in 1995 . . . Has one year remaining on three-year deal signed after 1993 season . . . Rockies used 10th pick in first round of expansion draft to take him off Cubs roster prior to '93 . . . Owns industrial engineering degree from Northwestern . . . Picked by Cubs in fifth round of 1986 draft . . . Born Oct. 14, 1964, in Peoria, Ill.

Year	Club	Pos.	G	AB	R	H	2B	3B	HR	RBI	SB	Avg.
1989	Chicago (NL) . .	C	59	157	15	39	10	0	1	14	2	.248
1990	Chicago (NL) . .	C	133	419	36	113	24	2	1	38	8	.270
1991	Chicago (NL) . .	C	21	47	3	9	2	0	0	6	0	.191
1992	Chicago (NL) . .	C	91	270	19	73	3	1	1	12	0	.270
1993	Colorado	C	86	310	35	90	14	5	3	31	6	.290
1994	Colorado	C	93	330	47	91	9	4	4	34	3	.276
1995	Colorado	C	125	462	63	121	17	2	8	55	3	.262
	Totals		608	1995	218	536	79	14	18	190	22	.269

WADE BOGGS 37 6-2 197 Bats L Throws R

Five-time AL batting champion was thought by many to be in decline after batting average dropped to .259 in 1992, his final year with Boston . . . But he has climbed back to previous status as one of baseball's best pure hitters with three straight solid seasons as Yankees third baseman . . . Led Yankees with .324 average last season . . . Batted .342 the year before . . . His .334 lifetime average ranks second-highest among active players, behind Tony Gwynn's .336 mark . . . Batted .350 over last 82 games of '95 season and .366 in last 46 games . . . Batted .263 with three RBI in Division Series against Seattle . . . Boston drafted him in seventh round of 1976 draft . . . Signed by Yankees as free agent prior to '93 season . . . Born June 15, 1958, in Omaha, Neb. . . . Salary last year was $4,624,316, on third season of $11-million deal that lured him from Red Sox . . . Has achieved Gold Glove status at third, winning his first two the last wo seasons . . . Won four straight batting titles from 1985-88 . . . Re-signed with Yankees last winter for two-year, $4.1-million deal with club option on '98.

Year	Club	Pos.	G	AB	R	H	2B	3B	HR	RBI	SB	Avg.
1982	Boston	1B-3B-OF	104	338	51	118	14	1	5	44	1	.349
1983	Boston	3B	153	582	100	210	44	7	5	74	3	.361
1984	Boston	3B	158	625	109	203	31	4	6	55	3	.325
1985	Boston	3B	161	653	107	240	42	3	8	78	2	.368
1986	Boston	3B	149	580	107	207	47	2	8	71	0	.357
1987	Boston	3B-1B	147	551	108	200	40	6	24	89	1	.363
1988	Boston	3B	155	584	128	214	45	6	5	58	2	.366
1989	Boston	3B	156	621	113	205	51	7	3	54	2	.330
1990	Boston	3B	155	619	89	187	44	5	6	63	0	.302
1991	Boston	3B	144	546	93	181	42	2	8	51	1	.332
1992	Boston	3B	143	514	62	133	22	4	7	50	1	.259
1993	New York (AL)	3B	143	560	83	169	26	1	2	59	0	.302
1994	New York (AL)	3B-1B	97	366	61	125	19	1	11	55	2	.342
1995	New York (AL)	3B-1B	126	460	76	149	22	4	5	63	1	.324
	Totals		1991	7599	1287	2541	489	53	103	864	19	.334

TINO MARTINEZ 28 6-2 210 Bats L Throws R

Enjoyed big-time breakthrough season as he set career highs in every offensive category for Mariners in '95 before being dealt to Yanks with Jeff Nelson and minor leaguer Jim Mecir for Russ Davis and Sterling Hitchcock last winter . . . Set Seattle record for homers by a first baseman with 31, surpassing Alvin Davis' 29 in 1987 . . . Hit .370 through first 15 games and never looked back . . . Became only the eighth player since 1973 to homer into the black seats in Yankee Stadium, June 11 off Bob MacDonald . . . Made his first All-Star team when he was added late, in place of injured Mark McGwire . . . Moved into seventh place on the Mariners' all-time home-run list with 88 . . . Made $1 million in '95 . . . Hit .136 vs. Indians in ALCS . . . Seattle made him 14th player taken overall in 1988 draft . . . Yanks showered him with five-year, $20.25-million contract following trade . . . Played on 1988 U.S. Olympic team . . . Born Dec. 7, 1967, in Tampa, and went to same high school as Fred McGriff.

Year	Club	Pos.	G	AB	R	H	2B	3B	HR	RBI	SB	Avg.
1990	Seattle	1B	24	68	4	15	4	0	0	5	0	.221
1991	Seattle	1B	36	112	11	23	2	0	4	9	0	.205
1992	Seattle	1B	136	460	53	118	19	2	16	66	2	.257
1993	Seattle	1B	109	408	48	108	25	1	17	60	0	.265
1994	Seattle	1B	97	329	42	86	21	0	20	61	1	.261
1995	Seattle	1B	141	519	92	152	35	3	31	111	0	.293
	Totals		543	1896	250	502	106	6	88	312	3	.265

RUBEN SIERRA 30 6-1 200 Bats S Throws R

Veteran outfielder-DH came to Yankees from Athletics with Jason Beverlin for Danny Tartabull in July 28 trade that simply gave each slugger a change of scenery . . . Had fallen out of favor with then-Oakland manager Tony La Russa . . . Hit .260 with seven homers and 44 RBI in 56 games as Yankee . . . Batted disappointing .174 in Division Series against Mariners . . . Defensively, he has good arm, but led AL outfielders with nine errors in 1994 . . . Originally signed by Rangers as non-drafted free agent in November 1982 . . . After six-plus seasons that made him Texas' all-time leader in six offensive categories, he landed in Oakland with Bobby Witt and Jeff Russell for Jose Canseco, Aug. 31, 1992 . . . Born Oct. 6, 1965, in Rio Piedras, P.R. . . . Salary last year was $6,200,000 and his contract runs through '97.

Year	Club	Pos.	G	AB	R	H	2B	3B	HR	RBI	SB	Avg
1986	Texas	OF	113	382	50	101	13	10	16	55	7	.264
1987	Texas	OF	158	643	97	169	35	4	30	109	16	.263
1988	Texas	OF	156	615	77	156	32	2	23	91	18	.254
1989	Texas	OF	162	634	101	194	35	14	29	119	8	.306
1990	Texas	OF	159	608	70	170	37	2	16	96	9	.280
1991	Texas	OF	161	661	110	203	44	5	25	116	16	.307
1992	Tex.-Oak.	OF	151	601	83	167	34	7	17	87	14	.278
1993	Oakland	OF	158	630	77	147	23	5	22	101	25	.233
1994	Oakland	OF	110	426	71	114	21	1	23	92	8	.268
1995	Oak.-NY (AL)	OF	126	479	73	126	32	0	19	86	5	.26
	Totals		1454	5679	809	1547	306	50	220	952	126	.27

ANDY PETTITTE 23 6-5 235 Bats L Throws L

Made a big impression in first season in the starting rotation, finishing third in AL top rookie balloting . . . Had 26 starts and recorded 12 victories . . . Pitched particularly well at Yankee Stadium, where he was 8-2 with a 2.61 ERA . . . His performance bought him a starting assignment against Mariners in Game 2 of Division Series at home. Gave up four runs over seven innings but was not involved in decision . . . Signed by Yankees as non-drafted free agent in May 1991 . . . Born June 15, 1972, in Baton Rouge, La. . . . Salary last year was major-league minimum of $109,000.

Year	Club	G	IP	W	L	Pct.	SO	BB	H	ERA
1995	New York (AL)	31	175	12	9	.429	114	63	183	4.1

DAVID CONE 33 6-1 190 Bats L Throws R

Blue Jays may have put the Yankees into the postseason by dumping him last July 28 for Marty Janzen, Jason Jarvis and Mike Gordon . . . One of the top right-handers in the game, he came through with some big ones down the stretch, going 9-2, 3.82 in 13 starts as Yankee . . . Finished with stellar numbers again, winning 18 games—just one off AL lead . . . Added one more win in Division Series, but let one-run lead get away in decisive fifth game, later won by Mariners in extra innings . . . Won Cy Young Award with 16-5, 2.94 performance for Kansas City in 1994, then was traded twice within one year . . . Royals' third-round pick in 1981 draft . . . Has played for KC twice, Toronto twice, Mets and Yankees . . . Born Jan. 2, 1963, in Kansas City . . . Salary of $8,000,000 last year included prorated signing bonus and deferrals . . . Re-signed to three-year, $19.5-million contract as free agent last winter. Pact includes no-trade clause.

Year	Club	G	IP	W	L	Pct.	SO	BB	H	ERA
1986	Kansas City	11	22⅔	0	0	.000	21	13	29	5.56
1987	New York (NL)	21	99⅓	5	6	.455	68	44	87	3.71
1988	New York (NL)	35	231⅓	20	3	.870	213	80	178	2.22
1989	New York (NL)	34	219⅔	14	8	.636	190	74	183	3.52
1990	New York (NL)	31	211⅔	14	10	.583	233	65	177	3.23
1991	New York (NL)	34	232⅔	14	14	.500	241	73	204	3.29
1992	New York (NL)	27	196⅔	13	7	.650	214	82	162	2.88
1992	Toronto	8	53	4	3	.571	47	29	39	2.55
1993	Kansas City	34	254	11	14	.440	191	114	205	3.33
1994	Kansas City	23	171⅔	16	5	.762	132	54	130	2.94
1995	Tor.-NY (AL)	30	229⅓	18	8	.692	191	88	195	3.57
	Totals	288	1922	129	78	.623	1741	716	1589	3.17

DWIGHT GOODEN 31 6-3 210 Bats S Throws R

Troubled former Cy Young winner has been granted another chance to rescue career ravaged by drugs . . . Reinstated by commissioner's office Oct. 2 after being suspended 16 months for twice violating baseball's drug policy . . . Yanks outbid Marlins and White Sox for him, giving him three-year deal for potential $6 million, beginning with $850,000 salary in '96 . . . Scouts believe once-feared right arm has some miles left in it . . . Working on a slider . . . Coached son Dwight Jr.'s Little League team in St. Petersburg last summer . . . Was pitching poorly in '94 with Mets before being suspended 60 days June 2 for testing positive for drugs . . . Suspended for entire '95 seaso after testing positive again in August, following a brief stay a the Betty Ford Center . . . Last four seasons have been marked b injury and mediocrity . . . In '94, he was placed on disabled lis for third time in four years April 26 . . . Gave up nine home run in 41⅓ innings . . . Only Met pitcher other than Tom Seaver t win as many as 150 games (157) . . . Underwent surgery on hi shoulder and rotator cuff, Sept. 7, 1991 . . . Became younges pitcher ever to win Cy Young in '85 . . . Was 1984 NL Rooki of the Year, setting major-league rookie record with 276 strike outs . . . Born Nov. 16, 1964, in Tampa . . . Mets drafted him fift overall in 1982.

Year	Club	G	IP	W	L	Pct.	SO	BB	H	ER
1984	New York (NL)	31	218	17	9	.654	276	73	161	2.6
1985	New York (NL)	35	276⅔	24	4	.857	268	69	198	1.5
1986	New York (NL)	33	250	17	6	.739	200	80	197	2.8
1987	New York (NL)	25	179⅔	15	7	.682	148	53	162	3.2
1988	New York (NL)	34	248⅓	18	9	.667	175	57	242	3.1
1989	New York (NL)	19	118⅓	9	4	.692	101	47	93	2.8
1990	New York (NL)	32	232⅔	19	7	.731	223	70	229	3.8
1991	New York (NL)	27	190	13	7	.650	150	56	185	3.6
1992	New York (NL)	31	206	10	13	.435	145	70	197	3.6
1993	New York (NL)	29	208⅓	12	15	.556	149	61	188	3.4
1994	New York (NL)	7	41⅓	3	4	.429	40	15	46	6.3
1995	New York (NL)					Suspended				
	Totals	305	337⅓	157	85	.648	1875	651	1898	3.1

JOHN WETTELAND 29 6-2 215 Bats R Throws

One of three pitching acquisitions that helpe put Yankees in playoffs as he struck out 66 i just 61⅓ innings in '95 . . . Yankees outbid th Orioles and several other teams for him, get ting him from Expos for Roberto Seguigno and cash just prior to last season . . . If Oriole had gotten him, they might have been the wild card winner . . . He saved 31 games and le Yankees with a 2.93 ERA . . . Did not have great postseason . . Was 0-1 with ugly 14.54 ERA against Seattle, giving up fou earned runs during Mariners' dramatic Game 4 victory . . . Dodg ers drafted him in secondary round of secondary phase in Januar

1985 . . . Born Aug. 21, 1966, in San Mateo, Cal. . . . Salary last year was $3,375,000 . . . Has 137 career saves.

Year	Club	G	IP	W	L	Pct.	SO	BB	H	ERA
1989	Los Angeles	31	102⅔	5	8	.385	96	34	81	3.77
1990	Los Angeles	22	43	2	4	.333	36	17	44	4.81
1991	Los Angeles	6	9	1	0	1.000	9	3	5	0.00
1992	Montreal	67	83⅓	4	4	.500	99	36	64	2.92
1993	Montreal	70	85⅓	9	3	.750	113	28	58	1.37
1994	Montreal	52	63⅔	4	6	.400	68	21	46	2.83
1995	New York (AL)	60	61⅓	1	5	.167	66	14	40	2.93
	Totals	308	448⅓	26	30	.464	487	153	338	2.93

TOP PROSPECTS

DEREK JETER 21 6-3 185 Bats R Throws R

Yankees' first-round pick (sixth overall) in 1992 draft . . . Got a quick look at major-league level last year, batting .250 with no homers and seven RBI in 48 at-bats . . . Hit .317 with two homers, 45 RBI and 20 steals for Columbus (AAA) in the International League . . . Was named *Baseball America's* 1994 Minor League Player of the Year after batting .344 and stealing 50 bases at three minor-league levels . . . Yankee shortstop of the future . . . Born June 26, 1974, in Pequannock, N.J.

MARIANO RIVERA 26 6-4 168 Bats R Throws R

Tall, thin right-hander got a decent look at major-league level last year . . . Made 19 appearances and 10 starts for Yankees . . . Finished with 5-3 record, but ERA was up there (5.51) . . . Pitched twice in tough situations in Division Series and did not give up a run in four innings . . . Was 2-2 with 2.10 ERA with Columbus (AAA) before callup . . . In first professional season (1990), he led Gulf Coast League (R) with a 0.17 ERA in 22 appearances for Tampa . . . Born Nov. 29, 1969, in Panama City, Panama . . . Signed by Yankees as non-drafted free agent in February 1990.

BRIEN TAYLOR 24 6-3 220 Bats L Throws L

Yankees still waiting for return on big investment ($1.8-million signing bonus) in No. 1 overall pick of 1991 draft, but it may never come . . . Hard-throwing left-hander had two good minor-league seasons before undergoing reconstructive shoulder surgery and missing entire 1994 season . . . Road back has been slow . . . Last year, he started 11 games and posted 2-5 record with 6.08 ERA with Tampa (R) in the Gulf Coast League . . . Born Dec. 26, 1971, in Beaufort, N.C.

MANAGER JOE TORRE: Experienced major-league manager who will be making AL debut after 14 seasons managing in NL . . . Fired last June by Cardinals after club got off to 20-27 start and replaced by Mike Jorgensen . . . Hired by Yankees last fall to replace Buck Showalter, who turned down unacceptable offer from George Steinbrenner and chose not to return after leading club into Division Series against Seattle . . . Made managerial debut with Mets in 1977, after stellar playing career that featured .297 career batting average, 252 career home runs and 1,185 RBI . . . Catcher-third baseman played for Braves, Cardinals and Mets . . . Had little success managing struggling Mets, posting 286-420 mark from 1977-81 . . . Led Braves to NL West title in first season as their manager, in 1982, then finished second twice before being replaced after '84 season . . . Spent six years in broadcast booth before coming back to manage Cardinals for 4½ seasons . . . Posted 351-354 mark with Cards, finishing second once and third three times before being replaced last year . . . Has never reached World Series as either a player or manager, but he inherits contending club coming off 79-65 year . . . Signed two-year contract worth reported $1.05 million . . . Lifetime record as manager is 894-1,003 . . . Born July 18, 1940, in Brooklyn, N.Y.

ALL-TIME YANKEE SEASON RECORDS

BATTING: Babe Ruth, .393, 1923
HRs: Roger Maris, 61, 1961
RBI: Lou Gehrig, 184, 1931
STEALS: Rickey Henderson, 93, 1988
WINS: Jack Chesbro, 41, 1904
STRIKEOUTS: Ron Guidry, 248, 1978

David Cone ended guessing game, re-signing as Yank.

TORONTO BLUE JAYS

TEAM DIRECTORY: Pres./CEO: Paul Beeston; VP-GM: Gord Ash; VP-Baseball: Al LaMacchia, Bob Mattick; Dir. Pub. Rel.: Howard Starkman; Trav. Sec.: John Brioux; Mgr.: Cito Gaston; Coaches: Alfredo Griffin, Nick Leyva, Mel Queen, Gene Tenace, Willie Upshaw. Home: SkyDome (50,300). Field distances: 330, l.f. line; 375, l.c.; 400, c.f.; 375, r.c.; 330, r.f. line. Spring training: Dunedin, Fla.

SCOUTING REPORT

HITTING: In two seasons, the Blue Jays have gone from one of the most imposing offensive teams to a shadow of their former selves. En route to a 56-88 finish in '95, they ranked 13th in the AL in runs (642) and batting average (.260).

If it seemed like every big hitter in the lineup had an off year, well, that's about what happened. Joe Carter (.253, 25, 76), Rob-

With eight years of 100-plus, Joe Carter has 1,173 RBI.

erto Alomar (.300, 13, 66), Paul Molitor (.270, 15, 60), John Olerud (.291, 8, 54) and Devon White (.283, 10, 53, 11 steals) all had sub-par years. The good news is, the law of averages suggest they'll bounce back. The bad news is, some won't be with the Blue Jays when that happens. The club bought out Molitor's 1996 contract, White fled to Florida via free agency and Alomar took off as a free agent for Baltimore.

At least free-agent signee Otis Nixon (.295, 87 runs, 50 steals with the Rangers) will take White's place in center.

The organization is downsizing, so promising youngsters like Shawn Green (.288, 15, 54), Carlos Delgado (.165, 3, 11) and Alex Gonzalez (.243, 10, 42) will have to step up and support carryovers like Ed Sprague (.244, 18, 74) for the Blue Jays to rebound from their offensive slump.

PITCHING: If somebody can figure out how to get Juan Guzman (4-14, 6.32) back on track, then maybe the Blue Jays can think about having a decent rotation in '96. He used to be one of the league's most dominating pitchers, but last year ranked among the league's worst starting pitchers.

The performance of Pat Hentgen (10-14, 5.11) also was a disappointment. But Eric Hanson (15-5, 4.24 with the Red Sox) and Paul Quantrill (11-12, 4.67 with the Phillies) give some hope to a rotation without free-agent defector Al Leiter this season.

The bullpen used to be a major strength for the Blue Jays, but they were unable to replace injured Duane Ward again last year and ranked last in the AL with only 22 saves. Newcomer Bill Risley (2-1, 3.13 with the Mariners) gets a shot at closing in '96, with Mike Timlin (4-3, 2.14, 5 saves) and Danny Cox (1-3, 7.40) setting him up.

FIELDING: The left side of the everyday infield—shortstop Gonzalez and third baseman Sprague—committed 36 errors last year, but the Blue Jays remained among the AL's better fielding clubs. That could change if the club winds up losing both of its top middle defense guys, second baseman Alomar and center fielder White. Ex-Brave Charlie O'Brien can catch with the best of them.

OUTLOOK: Not very good. The team is for sale and the front office has been slashing the payroll for the past year. It would take some amazing good fortune for manager Cito Gaston to assemble a decent pitching staff, but the 1995 Red Sox proved that it is possible to sign a couple of struggling veterans and make a silk purse out of a sour year.

BLUE JAY PROFILES

OTIS NIXON 37 6-2 180 — Bats S Throws R

Ranger free agent signed two-year, $4.4-million contract with Blue Jays in December . . . The consummate leadoff hitter . . . Tied Kansas City's Tom Goodwin for second in AL with 50 stolen bases . . . Also finished ninth with 50 multi-hit games . . . Consistently ranks at the top of league in bunt hits . . . His .295 batting average was his highest since '91 . . . Center fielder drives defenses nuts with his ability to slap at ball . . . Stole 160 bases from 1991-93 . . . Made $3.15 milllion in '95 . . . Led Texas with 589 at-bats . . . Obtained by Texas with Luis Ortiz from Boston in big Jose Canseco deal prior to last season . . . Born Jan. 9, 1959, in Evergreen, N.C. . . . Began career with Angels, who chose him in secondary phase of January 1979 draft.

Year	Club	Pos.	G	AB	R	H	2B	3B	HR	RBI	SB	Avg.
1983	New York (AL)	OF	13	14	2	2	0	0	0	0	2	.143
1984	Cleveland	OF	49	91	16	14	0	0	0	1	12	.154
1985	Cleveland	OF	104	162	34	38	4	0	3	9	20	.235
1986	Cleveland	OF	105	95	33	25	4	1	0	8	23	.263
1987	Cleveland	OF	19	17	2	1	0	0	0	1	2	.059
1988	Montreal	OF	90	271	47	66	8	2	0	15	46	.244
1989	Montreal	OF	126	258	41	56	7	2	0	21	37	.217
1990	Montreal	OF-SS	119	231	46	58	6	2	1	20	50	.251
1991	Atlanta	OF	124	401	81	119	10	1	0	26	72	.297
1992	Atlanta	OF	120	456	79	134	14	2	2	22	41	.294
1993	Atlanta	OF	134	461	77	124	12	3	1	24	47	.269
1994	Boston	OF	103	398	60	109	15	1	0	25	42	.274
1995	Texas	OF	139	589	87	174	21	2	0	45	50	.295
	Totals		1245	3444	605	920	101	16	7	217	444	.267

JOE CARTER 36 6-3 225 — Bats R Throws R

Somewhat off-peak numbers in '95 (.253, 25 homers, 76 RBI) certain to raise question of whether years are beginning to catch up with him . . . Still managed 27 homers and 103 RBI in just 111 games in '94 . . . Last year, outfielder's run-production numbers projected over 162 games would have worked out to very decent 28 home runs and 84 RBI . . . Set Blue Jays record for most consecutive games reaching base (37) in 1994 . . . Should be solid bet to hit 400 career homers, if he plays at least three more seasons . . . Has averaged 30 homers per season over 11 full seasons in major leagues . . . Born March 7, 1960, in Oklahoma City, Okla. . . . Salary for 1995 was $7,500,000, including deferred compensation . . . Cubs drafted him second overall in 1981 . . . Came from Padres with Roberto Alomar for Fred McGriff and Tony Fernandez prior to 1991 season . . . Posted 100-or-more RBI eight times.

Year	Club	Pos.	G	AB	R	H	2B	3B	HR	RBI	SB	Avg.
1983	Chicago (NL) . .	OF	23	51	6	9	1	1	0	1	1	.176
1984	Cleveland	OF-1B	66	244	32	67	6	1	13	41	2	.275
1985	Cleveland	OF-1B-2B-3B	143	489	64	128	27	0	15	59	24	.262
1986	Cleveland	OF-1B	162	663	108	200	36	9	29	121	29	.302
1987	Cleveland	OF-1B	149	588	83	155	27	2	32	106	31	.264
1988	Cleveland	OF	157	621	85	168	36	6	27	98	27	.271
1989	Cleveland	OF-1B	162	651	84	158	32	4	35	105	13	.243
1990	San Diego	OF-1B	162	634	79	147	27	1	24	115	22	.232
1991	Toronto	OF	162	638	89	174	42	3	33	108	20	.273
1992	Toronto	OF-1B	158	622	97	164	30	7	34	119	12	.264
1993	Toronto	OF	155	603	92	153	33	5	33	121	8	.254
1994	Toronto	OF	111	435	70	118	25	2	27	103	11	.271
1995	Toronto	OF-1B	139	558	70	141	23	0	25	76	12	.253
	Totals		1749	6797	959	1782	345	41	327	1173	212	.262

JOHN OLERUD 27 6-5 218 Bats L Throws L

First baseman had career year in '93 with .363 average, 24 home runs and 107 RBI, but hasn't touched that kind of performance in either of last two seasons . . . In fact, his combined homer (20) and RBI totals (121) for shortened '94 and '95 schedules suggest '93 season was fluke . . . Though '93 early-summer run at .400 was tough act to follow, he is still hitting for high batting average . . . Broke virtually every major record for a pitcher or hitter at Washington State and was drafted in third round by Blue Jays in 1989 . . . Despite so-so numbers, he still ranked among the Blue Jays' leaders in batting average (.291) and on-base percentage (.398) in '95 . . . Finished above career average in runs (72) . . . Born Aug. 5, 1968, in Seattle . . . Salary last year was $5,750,000 . . . Overcame brain aneurism suffered as collegian in January 1989.

Year	Club	Pos.	G	AB	R	H	2B	3B	HR	RBI	SB	Avg.
1989	Toronto	1B	6	8	2	3	0	0	0	0	0	.375
1990	Toronto	1B	111	358	43	95	15	1	14	48	0	.265
1991	Toronto	1B	139	454	64	116	30	1	17	68	0	.256
1992	Toronto	1B	138	458	68	130	28	0	16	66	1	.284
1993	Toronto	1B	158	551	109	200	54	2	24	107	0	.363
1994	Toronto	1B	108	384	47	114	29	2	12	67	1	.297
1995	Toronto	1B	135	492	72	143	32	0	8	54	0	.291
	Totals		795	2705	405	801	188	6	91	410	2	.296

ED SPRAGUE 28 6-2 210 Bats R Throws R

Solid third baseman who can hit for power and drive in runs . . . Had biggest offensive season of career in '95, competing with Joe Carter for team RBI lead (74), but overall numbers (.244, 18 homers) were not spectacular . . . Was Blue Jays' No. 1 pick in 1988 draft and was playing for Syracuse at Triple-A level one year later . . . Broke in with Blue Jays in 1991, just in time to enjoy three division titles and two World Series . . . Father Ed Sr. was eight-year major-league veteran pitcher and now is West Coast scout for Orioles . . . Born July 25, 1967, in Castro Valley, Cal. . . . Salary last year was $760,000.

Year	Club	Pos.	G	AB	R	H	2B	3B	HR	RBI	SB	Avg.
1991	Toronto	3B-1B-C	61	160	17	44	78	0	4	20	0	.275
1992	Toronto	C-1B-3B	22	47	6	11	2	0	1	7	0	.234
1993	Toronto	3B	150	546	50	142	31	1	12	73	1	.260
1994	Toronto	3B-1B	109	405	38	97	19	1	11	44	1	.240
1995	Toronto	3B	144	521	77	127	27	2	18	74	0	.244
	Totals		486	1679	188	421	86	4	46	218	2	.251

ALEX GONZALEZ 22 6-0 182 Bats R Throws R

Shortstop is one of cornerstones of the Blue Jays' rebuilding project . . . Played first full major-league season in '95 and appears to be here to stay, although Blue Jays are looking for more run production (.243, 10 homers, 42 RBI) and fewer strikeouts (114) than he produced last year . . . No hurry . . . Was youngest player in AL (20) to start the season in 1994 and had just turned 21 when 1995 season began . . . Big stolen-base guy in minor leagues, notching high of 38 for Knoxville (AA) in '93, but hardly ran at all last year (4 in 8 attempts) . . . Selected by Blue Jays in 14th round of 1991 draft . . . Born April 8, 1973, in Miami . . . Salary last year was $130,000.

Year	Club	Pos.	G	AB	R	H	2B	3B	HR	RBI	SB	Avg.
1994	Toronto	SS	15	53	7	8	3	1	0	1	3	.151
1995	Toronto	SS-3B	111	367	51	89	19	4	10	42	4	.243
	Totals		126	420	58	97	22	5	10	43	7	.231

SHAWN GREEN 23 6-4 190 Bats L Throws L

Promising rookie outfielder opened some eyes with solid '95 season . . . Ranked among club leaders in batting average (.288) and had solid run-production numbers (15 homers, 54 RBI) in less-than-full-time role . . . Blue Jays made him 16th player taken overall in 1991 draft . . . Passed up baseball scholarship at Stanford to sign with Jays . . . Batted .344 with 13 homers and 19 steals for Syracuse (AAA) in 1994 . . . Averaged an extra-base hit per seven at-bats for Blue Jays last year en route to .509 slugging percentage . . . Should be lock for full-time job this season . . . Born Nov. 10, 1972, in Des Plaines, Ill. . . . Salary was $130,000 last year.

Year	Club	Pos.	G	AB	R	H	2B	3B	HR	RBI	SB	Avg.
1993	Toronto	OF	3	6	0	0	0	0	0	0	0	.000
1994	Toronto	OF	14	33	1	3	1	0	0	1	1	.091
1995	Toronto	OF	121	379	52	109	31	4	15	54	1	.288
	Totals		138	418	53	112	32	4	15	55	2	.268

PAUL QUANTRILL 27 6-1 185 Bats L Throws R

Joined Blue Jays in December trade with Phils for Howard Battle and Rickey Jordan . . . Led Phillies in wins (11), losses (12), starts (29) and innings (179⅓) . . . His 93 earned runs allowed were fourth-highest total in NL . . . Finished seventh in NL with 2.2 walks per nine innings . . . Did not issue a walk in seven starts . . . Has yet to toss a complete game, but he did pitch eight innings three times . . . A terrific fielding pitcher . . . Acquired by Phillies from Red Sox with Billy Hatcher for Wes Chamberlain and Mike Sullivan, May 31, 1994 . . . Red Sox chose him in sixth round in '89 draft . . . Born Nov. 3, 1968, in Ontario, Can. . . . Earned $235,000 last season.

Year	Club	G	IP	W	L	Pct.	SO	BB	H	ERA
1992	Boston	27	49⅓	2	3	.400	24	15	55	2.19
1993	Boston	49	138	6	12	.333	66	44	151	3.91
1994	Boston	17	23	1	1	.500	15	5	25	3.52
1994	Philadelphia	18	30	2	2	.500	13	10	39	6.00
1995	Philadelphia	33	179⅓	11	12	.478	103	44	212	4.67
	Totals	144	419⅔	22	30	.423	221	118	482	4.16

ERIK HANSON 30 6-6 210 — Bats R Throws R

Red Sox free agent signed three-year, 9.5-million deal with Blue Jays last winter . . . Rescued by Red Sox from free-agent camp at Homestead, Fla., prior to '95, he won 15 games to rank second on surprising pitching staff . . . Did not have outstanding ERA (4.24), but didn't need to on club with big offensive attack . . . Pitched decently in Division Series, giving up four runs on four hits over eight innings against Indians in first career postseason start, but was charged with loss . . . Born May 18, 1965, in Kinnelon, N.J. . . . Salary last year was $1,125,000 . . . Mariners' second-round pick in 1986 draft.

Year	Club	G	IP	W	L	Pct.	SO	BB	H	ERA
1988	Seattle	6	41⅔	2	3	.400	36	12	35	3.24
1989	Seattle	17	113⅓	9	5	.643	75	32	103	3.18
1990	Seattle	33	236	18	9	.667	211	68	205	3.24
1991	Seattle	27	174⅔	8	8	.500	143	56	182	3.81
1992	Seattle	31	186⅔	8	17	.320	112	57	209	4.82
1993	Seattle	31	215	11	12	.478	163	60	215	3.47
1994	Cincinnati	22	122⅔	5	5	.500	101	23	137	4.11
1995	Boston	29	186⅔	15	5	.750	139	59	187	4.24
	Totals	196	1276⅔	76	64	.543	980	367	1273	3.81

PAT HENTGEN 27 6-2 200 — Bats R Throws R

Late developer has more victories than any other Blue Jays pitcher over last three years (42), but suffered through frustrating '95 season like everyone else on Toronto staff . . . Finished below .500 for first time in major-league career at 10-14 with 5.11 ERA . . . Allowed more hits (236) than innings pitched (200⅔) for first time in pro career . . . Has had higher ERA in only one other professional season (5.36 in 1992) . . . Made AL All-Star team in '93 and '94 . . . Won only World Series start with six-inning, five-hit performance against Phillies in 1993 . . . Born Nov. 13, 1968, in Detroit . . . Salary in 1995 was $1,250,000 . . . Drafted in fifth round by Toronto in 1986.

Year	Club	G	IP	W	L	Pct.	SO	BB	H	ERA
1991	Toronto	3	7⅓	0	0	.000	3	3	5	2.45
1992	Toronto	28	50⅓	5	2	.714	39	32	49	5.36
1993	Toronto	34	216⅓	19	9	.679	122	74	215	3.87
1994	Toronto	24	174⅔	13	8	.619	147	59	158	3.40
1995	Toronto	30	200⅔	10	14	.417	135	90	236	5.11
	Totals	119	649⅓	47	33	.588	446	258	663	4.20

JUAN GUZMAN 29 6-0 190 **Bats R Throws R**

Blue Jays still trying to figure out what went wrong with one of top pitchers in organization ... Has gone 16-25 with 5.99 ERA over last two seasons following 4-14, 6.32 disaster in '95 ... Broke into majors with 10-3 record and 2.99 ERA during division title run in 1991 and was combined 30-8 over next two seasons ... Finished second in 1991 AL Rookie of Year balloting ... Is 5-0 with 2.27 lifetime ERA in ALCS play ... Also pitched well in three World Series starts (0-1, 2.70) in '92 and '93 ... Control has ruined him, as indicated by 73 walks in 135⅓ innings last year ... Also surrendered 151 hits ... Born Oct. 28, 1966, in Santo Domingo, D.R. ... Salary last year was $2,800,000 ... Obtained from Dodgers for Mike Sharperson in September 1987.

Year	Club	G	IP	W	L	Pct.	SO	BB	H	ERA
1991	Toronto	23	138⅔	10	3	.769	123	66	98	2.99
1992	Toronto	28	180⅔	16	5	.762	165	72	135	2.64
1993	Toronto	33	221	14	3	.824	194	110	211	3.99
1994	Toronto	25	147⅓	12	11	.522	124	76	165	5.68
1995	Toronto	24	135⅓	4	14	.222	94	73	151	6.32
	Totals	133	823	56	36	.609	700	397	760	4.21

TOP PROSPECTS

CARLOS DELGADO 23 6-3 220 **Bats L Throws R**

Listed as catcher on the Blue Jays' 40-man roster, but he plays mostly outfield and some first base ... Big power prospect who flirted with breakthrough season in 1994 ... Tied major-league rookie record with eight home runs in April, but scouts figured out he was vulnerable to the curveball ... Hit only one more homer at major-league level before returning to minor leagues ... Still has some growing to do, but has plenty of time to do it ... Hit .318 with 22 homers and 74 RBI for Syracuse (AAA) in '95 ... Played only sparingly in big leagues (.165, three homers, 11 RBI in 91 at-bats) last year, but should be ready to move up this spring ... Born June 25, 1972, in Aguadilla, P.R. ... Signed as non-drafted free agent in October 1988.

ANGEL MARTINEZ 23 6-4 200 **Bats L Throws R**

Got a couple months of valuable experience at major-league level last year, getting 191 at-bats and holding his own at the plate (.241, two homers, 25 RBI) ... Hit .229 with two homers and 22 RBI for Knoxville (AA) in '95 ... Solid defensive catcher ...

Threw out 41 percent of potential base-stealers during full season for Dunedin (A) in 1994 . . . Born Oct. 3, 1972, in Villa Mella, D.R. . . . Signed by Blue Jays as non-drafted free agent in January 1990.

JEFF WARE 25 6-3 190 **Bats R Throws R**

Worked as part of Blue Jays starting rotation late last year and pitched effectively (2-1, 5.47) . . . Will go to spring training with a chance to make the team . . . Not bad considering he missed all of 1993 with shoulder injury and went 0-7, 6.87 for Knoxville (AA) in 1994 . . . Went 7-0 with 3.00 for Syracuse (AAA) last season . . . Born Nov. 11, 1970, in Norfolk, Va. . . . Drafted by Blue Jays in first round in 1991, out of Old Dominion . . . Pitched in 1991 Pan American Games.

MANAGER CITO GASTON: Suffered through worst season of major-league managerial career last year as Blue Jays slipped into last place for first time since post-expansion seasons . . . Club finished with 56-88 record . . . Could not work miracle with dismal bullpen and thin starting rotation, but still is known as steady manager who gets the best out of good players . . . Has led Blue Jays to two world championships (1992, 1993) with quiet, easy-going managerial style . . . Does not get recognition as great manager because he has always had clubs with great offensive talent and a front office willing to make big moves with the pennant on the line, but bottom line should be most important measuring stick . . . Even after last year, he has 537-463 career mark . . . Nearly turned down opportunity to manage Blue Jays at the beginning, but would go on to become the first African-American to lead a team into the World Series . . . Known as Clarence Gaston during 12-year playing career as an outfielder with San Diego, Atlanta and Pittsburgh . . . Born March 17, 1944, in San Antonio.

ALL-TIME BLUE JAY SEASON RECORDS

BATTING: John Olerud, .363, 1993
HRs: George Bell, 47, 1987
RBI: George Bell, 134, 1987
STEALS: Dave Collins, 60, 1984
WINS: Jack Morris, 21, 1992
STRIKEOUTS: Dave Stieb, 198, 1984

CHICAGO WHITE SOX

TEAM DIRECTORY: Chairman: Jerry Reinsdorf; Vice Chairman: Eddie Einhorn; Exec. VP: Howard Pizer; Sr. VP-Baseball: Jack Gould; Sr. VP-Major League Oper.: Ron Schueler; VP-Free-Agent/Major League Scouting: Larry Monroe; Dir. Baseball Oper.: Dan Evans; Dir. Pub. Rel.: Doug Abel; Trav. Sec.: Glen Rosenbaum; Mgr.: Terry Bevington; Coaches: Ruby de Armas, Ron Jackson, Doug Masolino, Joe Nossek, Mike Pazik, Bill Buckner. Home: Comiskey Park (44,321). Field distances: 347, l.f. line; 375, l.c.; 400, c.f.; 375, r.c., 347, r.f. line. Spring training: Sarasota, Fla.

SCOUTING REPORT

HITTING: The White Sox ranked second in the AL with a .280 batting average and fifth in runs (755) last year. Although Frank

The Big Hurt has averaged 35 HRs and 112.8 RBI since '91.

Thomas (.308, 40, 111) didn't win another MVP award, he finished second in home runs and tied for fifth in RBI. He gives the White Sox that unusual combination of power and walks (136).

Lance Johnson (.306, 10, 57, 40 steals) was allowed to exit when the White Sox declined to pick up his option last winter, but Harold Baines (.299, 24, 63 with the Orioles) was brought back to be the DH. The re-signed Dave Martinez (.307, 5, 37), Robin Ventura (.295, 26, 93) and Ozzie Guillen (.248, 1, 41) give the club stability and Ray Durham (.257, 7, 51) will help add juice.

The White Sox re-signed catcher Ron Karkovice (.217, 13, 51), but Tim Raines (.285, 12, 67, 13 steals) figured to be elsewhere before the snows melted.

PITCHING: The departures of Jack McDowell and Jim Abbott over the past year weakened the depth of what once was perhaps the league's finest pitching staff. The decline of Jason Bere (8-15, 7.19) also hurt and contributed to the White Sox' 10th-ranked 4.85 ERA last season.

What the White Sox can count on in 1996 is another steady season from Alex Fernandez (12-8, 3.80), whose work down the stretch last summer would have been even more terrific if Chicago had been in a pennant race. They should be able to count on some improvement from lefty Wilson Alvarez (8-11, 4.32) and more saves from fireballer Roberto Hernandez (3-7, 3.92, 32 saves).

The key to '96, though, is whether young pitchers such as Rodney Bolton (0-2, 8.18) can develop and help out.

FIELDING: Defense was one of the biggest disappointments for the White Sox in '95 and it simply has to be better this season. The troubles started with third baseman Ventura, a three-time Gold Glover who committed 19 of Chicago's 108 errors.

Second baseman Durham and shortstop Guillen give the White Sox solid up-the-middle defense. Otherwise, this is a team that needs to work overtime on defensive drills in spring training.

OUTLOOK: With thin pitching and questionable defense, the prospects don't look too good for Terry Bevington's club, especially with Cleveland lurking in the AL Central. The White Sox finished 32 games behind the Indians at 68-76 last summer and, without an aggressive approach both on and off the field, that gap is too large to close in one year.

WHITE SOX PROFILES

FRANK THOMAS 27 6-5 257 Bats R Throws R

"The Big Hurt" . . . Missed out on AL MVP award in 1995 for the first time since 1992, but it wasn't exactly like he slipped . . . Became only player in major-league history to bat .300 or better with 20 home runs, 100 RBI, 100 walks and 100 runs for five consecutive seasons . . . Slugging percentage was better than .600 (.606) again . . . First baseman's 40 homers left him one shy of his own club-record total of 41, set in 1993 . . . Was unanimous AL MVP in '93 when he finished among league's top 10 in 10 offensive categories . . . Became only 11th player in major-league history to earn consecutive MVP awards in '94 . . . Former football star at Auburn . . . Expanded his off-field activities in 1994 by starting Big Hurt Enterprises to handle marketing, fan mail and charitable activities . . . Made $7.15 million in 1995, in second year of four-year, $29-million extension . . . Born May 27, 1968, in Columbus, Ga. . . . Selected seventh overall by White Sox in 1989 draft.

Year	Club	Pos.	G	AB	R	H	2B	3B	HR	RBI	SB	Avg.
1990	Chicago (AL) . .	1B	60	191	39	63	11	3	7	31	0	.330
1991	Chicago (AL) . .	1B	158	559	104	178	31	2	32	109	1	.318
1992	Chicago (AL) . .	1B	160	573	108	185	46	2	24	115	6	.323
1993	Chicago (AL) . .	1B	153	549	106	174	36	0	41	128	4	.317
1994	Chicago (AL) . .	1B	113	399	106	141	34	1	38	101	2	.353
1995	Chicago (AL) . .	1B	145	493	102	152	27	0	40	111	3	.308
	Totals		789	2764	565	893	185	8	182	595	16	.323

ROBIN VENTURA 28 6-1 200 Bats L Throws R

White Sox' slow start in '95 was mirrored by his . . . Third baseman's uncharacteristic rash of early-season errors helped grease skids . . . Finished with 19 errors after being charged with 20 in '94, so maybe this three-time Gold Glover's defensive prime is past . . . Still, he bounced back offensively . . . His .295 average and 26 home runs were career highs and his 93 RBI tied for his third-highest total . . . Became first White Sox player to be regular third baseman for five consecutive seasons since Willie Kamm (1923-1930) . . . Member of 1988 U.S. Olympic team . . . Named 1987 College Player of the Year by *Baseball America* while at Oklahoma State . . . Made $5.1 million in '95 and is signed through '97, with an option for '98 . . . Born July 14, 1967, in Santa Monica, Cal. . . . Selected 10th overall by White Sox in 1988 draft.

Year	Club	Pos.	G	AB	R	H	2B	3B	HR	RBI	SB	Avg.
1989	Chicago (AL) . .	3B	16	45	5	8	3	0	0	7	0	.178
1990	Chicago (AL) . .	3B-1B	150	493	48	123	17	1	5	54	1	.249
1991	Chicago (AL) . .	3B-1B	157	606	92	172	25	1	23	100	2	.284
1992	Chicago (AL) . .	3B-1B	157	592	85	167	38	1	16	93	2	.282
1993	Chicago (AL) . .	3B-1B	157	554	85	145	27	1	22	94	1	.262
1994	Chicago (AL) . .	3B-1B-SS	109	401	57	113	15	1	18	78	3	.282
1995	Chicago (AL) . .	3B-1B	135	492	79	145	22	0	26	93	4	.295
	Totals		881	3183	451	873	147	5	110	519	13	.274

OZZIE GUILLEN 32 5-11 164 Bats L Throws R

Rough season for this stylish shortstop . . . Missed a few games early to return to Venezuela after the murder of a friend and then finished season with lowest batting average for a full season (.248) in his career . . . The decline followed two consecutive seasons in which he increased his average, including a career-high .288 mark in 1994 . . . As usual, he went up there swinging in '95, drawing just 13 walks in 415 at-bats . . . A pretty darn good player, especially considering his comeback after missing nearly the entire 1992 season with major knee surgery . . . Padres signed him as non-drafted free agent in December 1980 . . . Obtained from San Diego in the LaMarr Hoyt deal prior to '85 season . . . Made $3.5 million in '94 and is signed through '97, with an option year in '98 . . . Spends winters in Venezuela, where he is a celebrity . . . He even starred in Venezuelan soap opera in winter of 1989 . . . White Sox have pretty good history of Venezuelan shortstops as Chico Carrasquel and Luis Aparicio came before this guy . . . Born Jan. 20, 1964, in Ocumare del Tuy, Venezuela.

Year	Club	Pos.	G	AB	R	H	2B	3B	HR	RBI	SB	Avg.
1985	Chicago (AL) . .	SS	150	491	71	134	21	9	1	33	7	.273
1986	Chicago (AL) . .	SS	159	547	58	137	19	4	2	47	8	.250
1987	Chicago (AL) . .	SS	149	560	64	156	22	7	2	51	25	.279
1988	Chicago (AL) . .	SS	156	566	58	148	16	7	0	39	25	.261
1989	Chicago (AL) . .	SS	155	597	63	151	20	8	1	54	36	.253
1990	Chicago (AL) . .	SS	160	516	61	144	21	4	1	58	13	.279
1991	Chicago (AL) . .	SS	154	524	52	143	20	3	3	49	21	.273
1992	Chicago (AL) . .	SS	12	40	5	8	4	0	0	7	1	.200
1993	Chicago (AL) . .	SS	134	457	44	128	23	4	4	50	5	.280
1994	Chicago (AL) . .	SS	100	365	46	105	9	5	1	39	5	.288
1995	Chicago (AL) . .	SS	122	415	50	103	20	3	1	41	6	.248
	Totals		1451	5078	572	1357	195	54	16	468	152	.267

HAROLD BAINES 37 6-2 195 Bats L Throws L

Hit his 300th career home run, Sept. 22, 1995 . . . Orioles' everyday designated hitter the past three seasons signed one-year, $1.5-million deal to return to White Sox as free agent last winter. . . . Chronic knee problems have plagued him throughout career, but he failed to reach 400 at-bats last two years because of baseball labor trouble, not injuries . . . Hit 20-or-more homers for the ninth time in his career (24) . . . Born March 15, 1959, in St. Michael's, Md., and still lives there . . . Salary was $1,600,000 last year . . . White Sox drafted him No. 1 overall in 1977 . . . Acquired by Orioles from Oakland for Rob Chiounard and Allen Plaster prior to '93 season.

Year	Club	Pos.	G	AB	R	H	2B	3B	HR	RBI	SB	Avg.
1980	Chicago (AL) . .	OF	141	491	55	125	23	6	13	49	2	.255
1981	Chicago (AL) . .	OF	82	280	42	80	11	7	10	41	6	.286
1982	Chicago (AL) . .	OF	161	608	89	165	29	8	25	105	10	.271
1983	Chicago (AL) . .	OF	156	596	76	167	33	2	20	99	7	.280
1984	Chicago (AL) . .	OF	147	569	72	173	28	10	29	94	1	.304
1985	Chicago (AL) . .	OF	160	640	86	198	29	3	22	113	1	.309
1986	Chicago (AL) . .	OF	145	570	72	169	29	2	21	88	2	.296
1987	Chicago (AL) . .	OF	132	505	59	148	26	4	20	93	0	.293
1988	Chicago (AL) . .	OF	158	599	55	166	39	1	13	81	0	.277
1989	Chi. (AL)-Tex. . .	OF	146	505	73	156	29	1	16	72	0	.309
1990	Tex.-Oak.	OF	135	415	52	118	15	1	16	65	0	.284
1991	Oakland	OF	141	488	76	144	25	1	20	90	0	.295
1992	Oakland	OF	140	478	58	121	18	0	16	76	1	.253
1993	Baltimore	DH	118	416	64	130	22	0	20	78	0	.313
1994	Baltimore	DH	94	326	44	96	12	1	16	54	0	.294
1995	Baltimore	DH	127	385	60	115	19	1	24	63	0	.299
	Totals		2183	7871	1033	2271	387	48	301	1261	30	.289

RAY DURHAM 24 5-8 170 Bats S Throws R

Solid rookie season for White Sox second baseman in '95 . . . Was AL Rookie of Year candidate early last season before Twins' Marty Cordova and Angels' Garret Anderson started putting up big power numbers . . . Still, for a little guy, his seven homers and 51 RBI weren't bad . . . Was White Sox organization's Minor League Player of the Year in '94 . . . Led American Association in total bases (261) playing for Nashville (AAA) that year and tied for league lead with 12 triples . . . Was second in Southern League with 39 steals for Birmingham

(AA) in 1993 . . . Fifth-round pick by White Sox in 1990 draft . . . Made major-league minimum of $109,000 in '95 . . . Born Nov. 30, 1971, in Charlotte, N.C.

Year	Club	Pos.	G	AB	R	H	2B	3B	HR	RBI	SB	Avg.
1995	Chicago (AL) . .	2B	125	471	68	121	27	6	7	51	18	.257

Alex Fernandez is ready to fill void as White Sox ace.

ALEX FERNANDEZ 26 6-1 215 Bats R Throws R

Turned into the ace of White Sox staff in '95 with departures of Jack McDowell and Jim Abbott . . . Will be legitimate ace if he continues to throw like he did toward end of last season . . . Went 7-0 with 1.35 ERA in his last 11 starts . . . Has double-figure win totals in each of past three seasons and he is still young . . . Cut down on his home runs allowed in '95, giving up 19 in 203⅔ innings after surrendering 25 in 170⅓ in '94 . . . Had five complete games, not including a 10-inning effort against Minnesota on season's final day that White Sox won in 11th . . . Finished sixth in AL with 159 strikeouts and second with two shutouts . . . Was impressive in '93 ALCS against Toronto, yielding only three earned runs in 15 innings, but still was 0-2 in series . . . Made $3.25 million in '95 . . . Picked fourth overall by White Sox in 1990 draft . . . Born Aug. 13, 1969, in Miami Beach, Fla.

Year	Club	G	IP	W	L	Pct.	SO	BB	H	ERA
1990	Chicago (AL)	13	87⅔	5	5	.500	61	34	89	3.80
1991	Chicago (AL)	34	191⅔	9	13	.409	145	88	186	4.51
1992	Chicago (AL)	29	187⅔	8	11	.421	95	50	199	4.27
1993	Chicago (AL)	34	247⅓	18	9	.667	169	67	221	3.13
1994	Chicago (AL)	24	170⅓	11	7	.611	122	50	163	3.86
1995	Chicago (AL)	30	203⅔	12	8	.600	159	65	200	3.80
	Totals	164	1088⅓	63	53	.543	751	354	1058	3.86

ROBERTO HERNANDEZ 31 6-4 235 Bats R Throws R

Back to form after a rough 1994 . . . Ranked third in AL with 32 saves in 1995 and boosted career total to 96 . . . Had only 14 in 1994 . . . His ERA also dropped, from 4.91 in '94 to 3.92 in '95 . . . Big, imposing presence on mound . . . Underwent surgery to relieve life-threatening, blood-clotting problem in right arm in 1991 after feeling numbness in his hand . . . Became White Sox closer in 1992, taking role from Bobby Thigpen . . . Converted 38-of-44 save opportunities in 1993 . . . Made $975,000 in '95 . . . Angels drafted him 16th overall in

1986 . . . Obtained from California for outfielder Mark Davis, Aug. 3, 1989 . . . Born Nov. 11, 1964, in Santurce, P.R., he grew up in New York City.

Year	Club	G	IP	W	L	Pct.	SO	BB	H	ERA
1991	Chicago (AL)	9	15	1	0	1.000	6	7	18	7.80
1992	Chicago (AL)	43	71	7	3	.700	68	20	45	1.65
1993	Chicago (AL)	70	78⅔	3	4	.429	71	20	66	2.29
1994	Chicago (AL)	45	47⅔	4	4	.500	50	19	44	4.91
1995	Chicago (AL)	60	59⅔	3	7	.300	84	28	63	3.92
	Totals	227	272	18	18	.500	279	94	236	3.24

JASON BERE 24 6-3 185 — Bats R Throws R

One of the biggest disappointments on White Sox staff last year . . . Entered '95 season as the winningest active AL pitcher age 25 or under (.774 at 24-7) . . . White Sox spent last season trying to figure out what was wrong as he compiled his worst winning percentage at any level of pro ball (.348 at 8-15) . . . This is a guy who led AL with a .857 winning percentage in '94 . . . Opponents hit .277 against him in '95 . . . His ERA of 7.19 was by far worst of his career . . . Allowed 151 hits in 137⅔ innings . . . Salary was $205,000 in '95 . . . Was losing pitcher in his first All-Star Game in Pittsburgh in '94 . . . Selected in 36th round of 1990 draft by White Sox . . . Born May 26, 1971, in Cambridge, Mass.

Year	Club	G	IP	W	L	Pct.	SO	BB	H	ERA
1993	Chicago (AL)	24	142⅔	12	5	.706	129	81	109	3.47
1994	Chicago (AL)	24	141⅔	12	2	.857	127	80	119	3.81
1995	Chicago (AL)	27	137⅔	8	15	.348	110	106	151	7.19
	Totals	75	422	32	22	.593	366	267	379	4.80

WILSON ALVAREZ 26 6-1 235 — Bats L Throws L

Slumped some in '95 after winning 27 games during previous two seasons . . . Won eight in '95 with 4.32 ERA, his highest since 5.20 mark in 1992 . . . Still, he is one of the AL's better left-handers . . . Won 15 consecutive decisions from Aug. 24, 1993 through May 27, 1994, tying LaMarr Hoyt for the longest White Sox winning streak since 1970 . . . Opponents hit only .258 against him in '95 . . . Had three complete games in 29 starts . . . With 43 career victories, he is closing in on Luis Leal (51) for distinction as the all-time winningest Venezuelan pitcher

. . . Won Game 3 of the '93 ALCS against Toronto . . . Became the eighth-youngest pitcher in major-league history to throw a no-hitter when he did it at 21, Aug. 11, 1991, at Baltimore . . . Made $2.2 million in 1995 . . . Texas signed him as non-drafted free agent in September 1986 . . . How about this trade: Rangers shipped this guy, Sammy Sosa and Scott Fletcher to White Sox for Harold Baines and Fred Manrique, July 29, 1989 . . . Born March 24, 1970, in Maracaibo, Venezuela.

Year	Club	G	IP	W	L	Pct.	SO	BB	H	ERA
1989	Texas	1	0	0	1	.000	0	2	3	—
1991	Chicago (AL)	10	56⅓	3	2	.600	32	29	47	3.51
1992	Chicago (AL)	34	100⅓	5	3	.625	66	65	103	5.20
1993	Chicago (AL)	31	207⅔	15	8	.652	155	122	168	2.95
1994	Chicago (AL)	24	161⅔	12	8	.600	108	62	147	3.45
1995	Chicago (AL)	29	175	8	11	.421	118	93	171	4.32
	Totals	129	701	43	33	.566	479	373	639	3.81

TOP PROSPECTS

RODNEY BOLTON 27 6-2 190 Bats R Throws R
Should be ready for White Sox any day now . . . Went 14-3 with 2.88 ERA in '95 for Nashville (AAA) . . . Struck out 76 and walked only 23 in 131 innings . . . Got into eight games, starting three, for White Sox and went 0-2 with 8.18 ERA . . . Was Chicago's 13th-round pick in 1990 draft . . . Born Sept. 23, 1968, in Chattanooga, Tenn.

CHRIS SNOPEK 25 6-1 185 Bats R Throws R
Another late-season call-up, this third baseman will eventually succeed Robin Ventura . . . Batted an impressive .324 with one homer, seven RBI and a .426 slugging percentage in 22 games for Chicago . . . Batted .323 with 12 homers and 55 RBI for Nashville (AAA) while playing both third and shortstop . . . Chicago's sixth-round pick in 1992 draft . . . Born Sept. 20, 1970, in Cynthiana, Ky.

CHRIS TREMIE 26 6-0 200 Bats R Throws R
Batted only .200 for Nashville (AAA) after establishing career bests in virtually every category for Birmingham (AA) in 1994 . . . Suspect bat, good glove . . . Chicago's 39th-round pick in 1992 draft . . . Hit .167 in 10 games during late-season call-up . . . Born Oct. 17, 1969, in Houston.

NORBERTO MARTIN 29 5-10 165 Bats R Throws R
Versatile shortstop who can play other positions . . . Hit respectable .269 with two homers and 17 RBI in 72 games for Chicago . . . Committed only seven errors . . . Scrappy player in Joey Cora mold . . . Chicago's fifth-round pick in 1990 draft . . . Born Dec. 10, 1966, in Santo Domingo, D.R.

MANAGER TERRY BEVINGTON: Took over White Sox

reins June 2 of last season, replacing Gene Lamont when club got off to 11-20 start . . . White Sox stabilized with 57-56 record under him . . . Was surprisingly rewarded with a multi-year contract on last day of season . . . Is popular with White Sox players . . . Frank Thomas spoke out in his support as late-season controversy raged concerning White Sox pursuit of Tony La Russa . . . Was in his seventh season as White Sox coach and sixth as third-base coach last year . . . Got into a much-publicized shoving match with Milwaukee manager Phil Garner . . . Won division titles in five of his eight seasons as minor-league manager . . . Managed Vancouver (AAA) to PCL Northern Division title in both halves of 1988 . . . Coached in Brewers system for seven years before joining White Sox in 1988 . . . Began managerial career at Burlington (A) of Midwest League in 1981 . . . Was catcher in Yankees system from 1974-80, but never made it to majors . . . Born July 27, 1956, in Akron, Ohio.

ALL-TIME WHITE SOX SEASON RECORDS

BATTING: Luke Appling, .388, 1936
HRs: Frank Thomas, 41, 1993
RBI: Zeke Bonura, 138, 1936
STEALS: Rudy Law, 77, 1983
WINS: Ed Walsh, 40, 1908
STRIKEOUTS: Ed Walsh, 269, 1908

CLEVELAND INDIANS

TEAM DIRECTORY: Owner: Richard Jacobs; GM: John Hart; Dir. Baseball Oper./Asst. GM: Dan O'Dowd; VP-Pub. Rel: Bob DiBiasio; Mgr. Media Rel.: Bart Swain; Trav. Sec.: Mike Seghi; Mgr.: Mike Hargrove; Coaches: Luis Isaac, Charles Manuel, Dave Nelson, Jeff Newman, Mark Wiley. Home: Jacobs Field (42,865). Field distances: 325, l.f. line; 368, l.c.; 400, c.f.; 375, r.c.; 320, r.f. line. Spring training: Winter Haven, Fla.

SCOUTING REPORT

HITTING: Forget the World Series. The Indians have the AL's most explosive offensive lineup, scoring a league-leading 840 runs with a .291 average and 207 homers, both AL bests.

Albert Belle (.317, 50, 126) became the first player ever to

Tribe's terrific troika: Martinez, Hershiser and Nagy.

have 50-or-more homers and 50-or-more doubles in the same season. Kenny Lofton (.310, 7, 53, 54 steals) is the best leadoff man in the game. Young Manny Ramirez broke through with 31 homers and 107 RBI and may have room for improvement. Four Indians had at least 25 homers, including Jim Thome (.314, 25, 73) and Eddie Murray (.323, 21, 82), who re-signed. Carlos Baerga ranked among the AL leaders in hits (175), batting average (.314) and multi-hit games (52). Julio Franco is back from Japan to replace Paul Sorrento at first.

There's no guarantee all these Indians will play at that level this year, but they have thunder to spare in the weak AL Central.

PITCHING: Cleveland's pitching staff was nearly as impressive as its lineup last year, leading the league with a 3.83 ERA and tying for the top spot with 10 shutouts. However, the rotation is no lock to reproduce its '95 numbers.

Re-signed Dennis Martinez (12-5, 3.08) had very solid numbers, but he'll be 40 Opening Day. Orel Hershiser (16-6, 3.87) had a great season and postseason, but he's 37 and his repaired right shoulder is coming off a very strenuous season. Hence there was a need to recruit free-agent stud Jack McDowell (15-10, 3.93 with the Yankees) last winter.

Fortunately, the Indians expect another big season from Charles Nagy (16-6, 4.55). Promising Chad Ogea (8-3, 3.05) figures to get a shot since the Indians did not re-sign Ken Hill.

The bullpen figures to be outstanding again, with closer Jose Mesa (3-0, 1.13, 46 saves) coming off his breakthrough season and young Julian Tavarez (10-2, 2.44) as the primary setup man. Tavarez, Eric Plunk (6-2, 2.67), Paul Assenmacher (6-2, 2.82) and Jim Poole (3-3, 3.75), the main four middle and setup guys, had a record of 25-9 and a 1.84 ERA.

FIELDING: The Indians' other strengths gloss over their average play in the field. They ranked sixth in the league with a .982 fielding percentage and seventh with 101 errors. Sandy Alomar Jr. is solid behind the plate. Lofton is a blur in center. Second baseman Baerga led the club with 19 errors, but was not a liability. Belle does some frightening things in left field, but more than compensates with his bat.

OUTLOOK: The Indians' impressive 100-44 record in '85 makes Mike Hargrove's team a solid favorite to win the AL Central and return to the World Series in '96. The only team that can beat the Indians is the Indians themselves, who could falter if the volatile behavior of the boorish Belle becomes disruptive.

INDIAN PROFILES

ALBERT BELLE 29 6-2 210 Bats R Throws R

In a league of his own last year . . . Became first player ever to notch 50 home runs and 50 doubles in the same season—and didn't need a full season to do it . . . Left fielder's tremendous late-season rush was large reason that Indians were able to win 100 games in strike-shortened 144-game schedule . . . Led AL in homers (50), runs (121), RBI (126), slugging percentage (.690), doubles (52) and total bases (377) . . . Intimidating both physically and psychologically . . . No Mr. Nice Guy attitude seems to work for him, but raises unanswered question: What has this guy got to be so ticked off about? . . . Very difficult with media and got himself in trouble at World Series for using abusive language to network sportscaster Hannah Storm . . . Batted .239 in postseason with four homers and eight RBI in 14 games . . . Can be defensive liability in outfield . . . Selected by Indians in second round of 1987 draft . . . Born Aug. 25, 1966, in Shreveport, La. . . . Salary last year was $4,300,000.

Year	Club	Pos.	G	AB	R	H	2B	3B	HR	RBI	SB	Avg.
1989	Cleveland	OF	62	218	22	49	8	4	7	37	2	.225
1990	Cleveland	OF	9	23	1	4	0	0	1	3	0	.174
1991	Cleveland	OF	123	461	60	130	31	2	28	95	3	.282
1992	Cleveland	OF	153	585	81	152	23	1	34	112	8	.260
1993	Cleveland	OF	159	594	93	172	36	3	38	129	23	.290
1994	Cleveland	OF	106	412	90	147	35	2	36	101	9	.357
1995	Cleveland	OF	143	546	121	173	52	1	50	126	5	.317
	Totals		755	2839	468	827	185	13	194	603	50	.291

KENNY LOFTON 28 6-0 180 Bats L Throws L

Speedy leadoff hitter gets on base and makes things happen . . . Batted .310, stole 54 bases and scored 93 runs last year, numbers that are consistent with his career averages when shortened schedule is factored in . . . His on-base percentage was down slightly at .362, but he would likely have scored more than 100 runs for third straight year if season had run normal course . . . Good center fielder . . . Indians' offensive star of postseason, with .290 average, 11 runs and 10 steals . . . Came from Houston with Dave Rohde in steal of trade for Willie Blair and Eddie Taubensee prior to '92 . . . Astros chose him in 12th round in 1988 draft, out of Arizona . . . Played for Final Four basketball squad in 1988 . . . Born May 31, 1967, in East Chicago, Ind. . . . Salary last year was $1,875,000.

Year	Club	Pos.	G	AB	R	H	2B	3B	HR	RBI	SB	Avg.
1991	Houston	OF	20	74	9	15	1	0	0	0	2	.203
1992	Cleveland	OF	148	576	96	164	15	8	5	42	66	.285
1993	Cleveland	OF	148	569	116	185	28	8	1	42	70	.325
1994	Cleveland	OF	112	459	105	160	32	9	12	57	60	.349
1995	Cleveland	OF	118	481	93	149	22	13	7	53	54	.310
	Totals		546	2159	419	673	98	38	25	194	252	.312

JIM THOME 25 6-4 220 Bats L Throws R

Big, quiet third baseman has developed into a big and anything-but-quiet hitter . . . Set career highs with .314 average, 25 homers and 73 RBI . . . Played big role in the Indians' early-season dominance with couple of dramatic, ninth-inning home runs . . . Solid defensive player . . . Not afraid to take a walk, he took 97 last year to lead team . . . Ranked first among Indians regulars with .438 on-base percentage . . . Also led club in strikeouts (113), but may grow out of that tendency . . . Batted just .213 in postseason, but had some very big hits, including four home runs, and he led club with 10 postseason RBI . . . Selected by Indians in 13th round of 1989 draft . . . Born Aug. 27, 1970, in Peoria, Ill. . . . Salary last year was $825,000.

Year	Club	Pos.	G	AB	R	H	2B	3B	HR	RBI	SB	Avg.
1991	Cleveland	3B	27	98	7	25	4	2	1	9	1	.255
1992	Cleveland	3B	40	117	8	24	3	1	2	12	2	.205
1993	Cleveland	3B	47	154	28	41	11	0	7	22	1	.266
1994	Cleveland	3B	98	321	58	86	20	1	20	52	3	.268
1995	Cleveland	3B	137	452	92	142	29	3	25	73	4	.314
	Totals		349	1142	193	318	67	7	55	168	12	.278

CARLOS BAERGA 27 5-11 200 Bats S Throws R

Solid second baseman hits for power and average, although his 15 homers in '95 was a four-year low . . . His 90 RBI were consistent with his career RBI-to-AB ratio . . . It was rumored during winter that he might be moved to third base if Indians were able to secure free-agent Roberto Alomar . . . No surprise . . . He's a team player who has enjoyed winning the past two years . . . Struck out just 31 times in 557 at-bats in

'95, which is great for a guy who swings freely enough to hit 20-plus home runs . . . Acquired with Sandy Alomar Jr. and Chris James in deal that sent Joe Carter to Padres prior to '90 season . . . Originally signed as non-drafted free agent by Padres in November 1985 . . . Another example of contribution that Indians scouting department made to club's current success . . . Batted .292 in postseason with nine RBI, but only .192 in World Series . . . Born Nov. 4, 1968, in San Juan, P.R. . . . Salary last year was $3,625,000.

Year	Club	Pos.	G	AB	R	H	2B	3B	HR	RBI	SB	Avg.
1990	Cleveland	3B-SS-2B	108	312	46	81	17	2	7	47	0	.260
1991	Cleveland	3B-2B-SS	158	593	80	171	28	2	11	69	3	.288
1992	Cleveland	2B	161	657	92	205	32	1	20	105	10	.312
1993	Cleveland	2B	154	624	105	200	28	6	21	114	15	.321
1994	Cleveland	2B	103	442	81	139	32	2	19	80	8	.314
1995	Cleveland	2B	135	557	87	175	28	2	15	90	11	.314
	Totals		819	3185	491	971	165	15	93	505	47	.305

SANDY ALOMAR Jr. 29 6-5 215 Bats R Throws R

Big catcher made solid contributions to Indians' 100-win season, but again was unable to answer the bell on an everyday basis . . . Batted .300, but played in only 66 games after missing first two months of season recovering from arthroscopic surgery on his left knee . . . Batted .348 in first 30 games with five home runs, 18 RBI . . . Hit 10 homers in 203 at-bats after having hit career-high 14 in 282 in 1994 . . . Very effective against left-handers (.364 last year) . . . Threw out 26.5 percent of runners trying to steal . . . Batted .267 in ALCS against Seattle, only .200 against Atlanta in World Series . . . Son of ex-major leaguer Sandy Sr. and brother of Roberto . . . Padres signed him as undrafted free agent in October 1983 . . . Came from Padres to Cleveland with Carlos Baerga and Chris James in Joe Carter deal before '90 season . . . Born June 18, 1966, in Salinas, P.R. . . . Salary last year was $2.55 million.

Year	Club	Pos.	G	AB	R	H	2B	3B	HR	RBI	SB	Avg.
1988	San Diego	PH	1	1	0	0	0	0	0	0	0	.000
1989	San Diego	C	7	19	1	4	1	0	1	6	0	.211
1990	Cleveland	C	132	445	60	129	26	2	9	66	4	.290
1991	Cleveland	C	51	184	10	40	9	0	0	7	0	.217
1992	Cleveland	C	89	299	22	75	16	0	2	26	3	.251
1993	Cleveland	C	64	215	24	58	7	1	6	32	3	.270
1994	Cleveland	C	80	292	44	84	15	1	14	43	8	.288
1995	Cleveland	C	66	203	32	61	6	0	10	35	3	.300
	Totals		490	1658	193	451	80	4	42	215	21	.272

MANNY RAMIREZ 23 6-0 190 Bats R Throws R

Where do the Indians keep getting these guys? ... Was one of two Indians with more than 100 RBI (107) and one of six everyday players to hit better than .300 (.308) ... Indians made him 13th player taken overall in 1991 draft and now we know why ... Finished second in AL Rookie of the Year balloting after hitting 17 homers and driving in 60 runs in '94 ... Those numbers would have worked out to be about 25 homers and 90 RBI over full season—and he bettered that pace last year, when his full-season production would have translated to 35 homers and 120 RBI over 162 games ... Batted just .196 in postseason, but did hit three home runs ... Still looks like raw project sometimes in right field ... Born May 30, 1972, in Santo Domingo, D.R. ... Salary last year was $150,000 ... Was arguably biggest bargain in baseball and he received four-year, $10.15-million deal last winter.

Year	Club	Pos.	G	AB	R	H	2B	3B	HR	RBI	SB	Avg.
1993	Cleveland	OF	22	53	5	9	1	0	2	5	0	.170
1994	Cleveland	OF	91	290	51	78	22	0	17	60	4	.269
1995	Cleveland	OF	137	484	85	149	26	1	31	107	6	.308
	Totals		250	827	141	236	49	1	50	172	10	.285

EDDIE MURRAY 40 6-2 220 Bats S Throws R

Made history last summer, collecting his 3,000th career hit ... If all goes well, he'll join baseball's exclusive 500-homer club this season ... Quiet superstar had second-highest batting average (.323) of his 19-year major-league career at age 39 in '95 ... Big leader on 100-win club, even though Indians had three offensive players who put up bigger production numbers ... Had about 100 fewer plate appearances than other regulars because of late-season injury ... Owns major-league record with 19 consecutive seasons of 75-or-more RBI ... That's why they call this designated hitter and first baseman "Steady Eddie" ... Certain Hall of Famer ... Signed as free agent by Indians prior to '94 season ... Orioles drafted him in third round in 1973 ... Batted just .236 in postseason and only .105 in World

Series . . . Born Feb. 24, 1956, in Los Angeles . . . Salary last year was $3,000,000 . . . Re-signed to one-year, $2-million deal last winter.

Year	Club	Pos.	G	AB	R	H	2B	3B	HR	RBI	SB	Avg.
1977	Baltimore	OF-1B	160	611	81	173	29	2	27	88	0	.283
1978	Baltimore	1B-3B	161	610	85	174	32	3	27	95	6	.285
1979	Baltimore	1B	159	606	90	179	30	2	25	99	10	.295
1980	Baltimore	1B	158	621	100	186	36	2	32	116	7	.300
1981	Baltimore	1B	99	378	57	111	21	2	22	78	2	.294
1982	Baltimore	1B	151	550	87	174	30	1	32	110	7	.316
1983	Baltimore	1B	156	582	115	178	30	3	33	111	5	.306
1984	Baltimore	1B	162	588	97	180	26	3	29	110	10	.306
1985	Baltimore	1B	156	583	111	173	37	1	31	124	5	.297
1986	Baltimore	1B	137	495	61	151	25	1	17	84	3	.305
1987	Baltimore	1B	160	618	89	171	28	3	30	91	1	.277
1988	Baltimore	1B	161	603	75	171	27	2	28	84	5	.284
1989	Los Angeles . . .	1B-3B	160	594	66	147	29	1	20	88	7	.247
1990	Los Angeles . . .	1B	155	558	96	184	22	3	26	95	8	.330
1991	Los Angeles . . .	1B-3B	153	576	69	150	23	1	19	96	10	.260
1992	New York (NL)	1B	156	551	64	144	37	2	16	93	4	.261
1993	New York (NL)	1B	154	610	77	174	28	1	27	100	2	.285
1994	Cleveland	1B	108	433	57	110	21	1	17	76	8	.254
1995	Cleveland	1B	113	436	68	141	21	0	21	82	5	.323
	Totals		2819	10603	1545	3071	532	34	479	1820	105	.290

OMAR VIZQUEL 28 5-9 165 Bats S Throws R

This spectacular defensive shortstop won his third Gold Glove last year . . . Like rest of Indians, his batting average in World Series was miserable .174, but, hey, in regular season he had career highs in home runs (6) and RBI (56) . . . Little difference on the switch. He batted .262 from the left side, .267 from the right . . . Born April 24, 1967, in Caracas, Venezuela . . . Was acquired from Seattle in trade for Felix Fermin, Reggie Jefferson and cash prior to '94 season . . . Mariners signed him as undrafted free agent in April 1984 . . . Made $2,850,000 last year . . . Received five-year, $15.35-million deal with club option on 2002 last winter.

Year	Club	Pos.	G	AB	R	H	2B	3B	HR	RBI	SB	Avg.
1989	Seattle	SS	143	387	45	85	7	3	1	20	1	.220
1990	Seattle	SS	81	255	19	63	3	2	2	18	4	.247
1991	Seattle	SS-2B	142	426	42	98	16	4	1	41	7	.230
1992	Seattle	SS	136	483	49	142	20	4	0	21	15	.294
1993	Seattle	SS	158	560	68	143	14	2	2	31	12	.255
1994	Cleveland	SS	69	286	39	78	10	1	1	33	13	.273
1995	Cleveland	SS	136	542	87	144	28	0	6	56	29	.266
	Totals		865	2939	349	753	98	16	13	220	81	.256

JOSE MESA 29 6-3 225 Bats R Throws R

Orioles have to be kicking themselves... They gave up on him after several so-so seasons as a starting pitcher and watched from deep in the standings while he set a major-league record for consecutive successful save opportunities (38) in '95... Finished with unbelievable season numbers of 46 saves and a 1.13 ERA as Indians closer... Was 1-0 with two saves in postseason... One of hardest throwers in game, despite undergoing "Tommy John" reconstructive elbow surgery early in career... Indians gambled by giving him long-term contract and now have him for bargain price the next three years... Acquired by Indians from Baltimore for Kyle Washington, July 14, 1992... Originally signed by Blue Jays as non-drafted free agent in October 1981... Born May 22, 1966, in Azua, D.R.... Salary in '95 was $900,000... Had only two major-league saves in 149 games prior to last season.

Year	Club	G	IP	W	L	Pct.	SO	BB	H	ERA
1987	Baltimore	6	31⅓	1	3	.250	17	15	38	6.03
1990	Baltimore	7	46⅔	3	2	.600	24	27	37	3.86
1991	Baltimore	23	123⅔	6	11	.353	64	62	151	5.97
1992	Balt.-Clev.	28	160⅔	7	12	.368	62	70	169	4.59
1993	Cleveland	34	208⅔	10	12	.455	118	62	232	4.92
1994	Cleveland	51	73	7	5	.583	63	26	71	3.82
1995	Cleveland	62	64	3	0	1.000	58	17	49	1.13
	Totals	211	708	37	45	.451	406	279	747	4.55

DENNIS MARTINEZ 40 6-1 180 Bats R Throws R

Apparently, age has nothing to do with it... Opened '95 season by winning his first eight decisions and went on to register another solid year... Total of 12 regular-season victories is deceptive... Made 28 starts and had very good numbers... Just didn't get a lot of decisions... Pitched better in postseason than 1-2 record indicates as he had 2.73 postseason ERA for five starts, in spite of shoulder stiffness... Classy veteran came back from an alcohol problem early in career to establish himself as one of game's elder statesman... So respected that he has been talked about as presidential candidate in native Nicaragua... Is one of only seven major-league pitchers to win

100-or-more games in each league en route to 231 total ... Signed by Indians as a free agent prior to '94 season ... Originally signed by Orioles as non-drafted free agent in December 1973 ... Born May 14, 1955, in Granada, Nicaragua ... Salary last year was $4,500,000.

Year	Club	G	IP	W	L	Pct.	SO	BB	H	ERA
1976	Baltimore	4	28	1	2	.333	18	8	23	2.57
1977	Baltimore	42	167	14	7	.667	107	64	157	4.10
1978	Baltimore	40	276	16	11	.593	142	93	257	3.25
1979	Baltimore	40	292	15	16	.484	132	78	279	3.67
1980	Baltimore	25	100	6	4	.600	42	44	103	3.96
1981	Baltimore	25	179	14	5	.737	88	62	173	3.32
1982	Baltimore	40	252	16	12	.571	111	87	262	4.21
1983	Baltimore	32	153	7	16	.304	71	45	209	5.53
1984	Baltimore	34	141⅔	6	9	.400	77	37	145	5.02
1985	Baltimore	33	180	13	11	.542	68	63	203	5.15
1986	Baltimore	4	6⅔	0	0	.000	2	2	11	6.75
1986	Montreal	19	98	3	6	.333	63	28	103	4.59
1987	Montreal	22	144⅔	11	4	.733	84	40	133	3.30
1988	Montreal	34	235⅓	15	13	.536	120	55	215	2.72
1989	Montreal	34	232	16	7	.696	142	49	227	3.18
1990	Montreal	32	226	10	11	.476	156	49	191	2.95
1991	Montreal	31	222	14	11	.560	123	62	187	2.39
1992	Montreal	32	226⅓	16	11	.593	147	60	172	2.47
1993	Montreal	35	224⅔	15	9	.625	138	64	211	3.85
1994	Cleveland	24	176⅔	11	6	.647	92	44	166	3.52
1995	Cleveland	28	187	12	5	.706	99	46	174	3.08
	Totals	610	3748	231	176	.568	2022	1080	3601	3.60

CHARLES NAGY 28 6-3 200 — Bats L Throws R

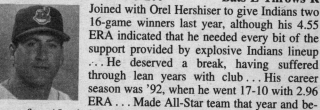

Joined with Orel Hershiser to give Indians two 16-game winners last year, although his 4.55 ERA indicated that he needed every bit of the support provided by explosive Indians lineup ... He deserved a break, having suffered through lean years with club ... His career season was '92, when he went 17-10 with 2.96 ERA ... Made All-Star team that year and became first AL pitcher since 1963 to register a hit. Also pitched scoreless inning ... Tough to figure out his 1994 numbers ... Went 10-8 with 3.45 ERA, but should have been bigger winner considering strong run support. Offense averaged 6.75 runs in his games and only six AL pitchers had more runs to work with ... Pitched well in postseason last fall, going 1-0 with 2.86 ERA ... Selected by Indians as 17th player taken overall in 1988 draft ... Born May 5, 1967, in Fairfield, Conn. ... Salary last year was

$1,800,000 . . . Received two-year, $6.75-million deal last winter that included club option on '98.

Year	Club	G	IP	W	L	Pct.	SO	BB	H	ERA
1990	Cleveland	9	45⅔	2	4	.333	26	21	58	5.91
1991	Cleveland	33	211⅓	10	15	.400	109	66	228	4.13
1992	Cleveland	33	252	17	10	.630	169	57	245	2.96
1993	Cleveland	9	48⅔	2	6	.250	30	13	66	6.29
1994	Cleveland	23	169⅓	10	8	.556	108	48	175	3.45
1995	Cleveland	29	178	16	6	.727	139	61	194	4.55
	Totals	136	905	57	49	.538	581	266	966	3.97

OREL HERSHISER 37 6-3 195 Bats R Throws R

Signed by Cleveland as a free agent prior to '95 season, after stellar career with Dodgers . . . Regained velocity last year . . . Set major-league record with 59 consecutive scoreless innings during 1988 dream season . . . Went on to be playoff and World Series MVP that year . . . Was one of most dependable starters in NL during late 1980s, but had to overcome 1990 shoulder surgery to re-emerge as big winner . . . Finished '95 with 16-6 record to rank fifth among league leaders in victories and post .727 winning percentage, but impressive field of candidates made him fade into woodwork in AL Cy Young voting . . . No wallflower in postseason . . . Went 4-1 with 1.53 ERA to improve career postseason record to 8-1 . . . Was named MVP in ALCS vs. Mariners . . . Nickname of "Bulldog" was given to him by former manager Tom Lasorda when he was wispy, unimposing rookie, but it turned out to be appropriate measure of his competitiveness . . . Born Sept. 16, 1958, in Buffalo, N.Y. . . . Dodgers drafted him in 17th round in 1979 . . . Salary last year was $1,450,000 and he received $2.7-million extension through '97 last winter.

Year	Club	G	IP	W	L	Pct.	SO	BB	H	ERA
1983	Los Angeles	8	8	0	0	.000	5	6	7	3.38
1984	Los Angeles	45	189⅔	11	8	.579	150	50	160	2.66
1985	Los Angeles	36	239⅔	19	3	.864	157	68	179	2.03
1986	Los Angeles	35	231⅓	14	14	.500	153	86	213	3.85
1987	Los Angeles	37	264⅔	16	16	.500	190	74	247	3.06
1988	Los Angeles	35	267	23	8	.742	178	73	208	2.26
1989	Los Angeles	35	256⅔	15	15	.500	178	77	226	2.31
1990	Los Angeles	4	25⅓	1	1	.500	16	4	26	4.26
1991	Los Angeles	21	112	7	2	.778	73	32	112	3.46
1992	Los Angeles	33	210⅔	10	15	.400	130	69	209	3.67
1993	Los Angeles	33	215⅔	12	14	.462	141	72	201	3.59
1994	Los Angeles	21	135⅓	6	6	.500	72	42	146	3.79
1995	Cleveland	26	167⅓	16	6	.727	111	51	151	3.87
	Totals	369	2323⅓	150	108	.581	1554	704	2085	3.06

JACK McDOWELL 30 6-5 188 Bats R Throws R

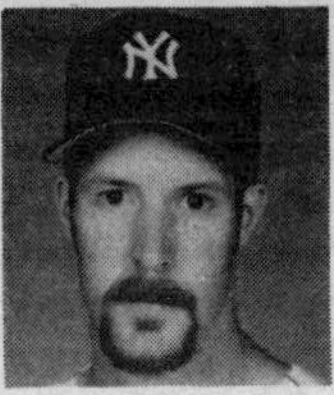

Signed by Indians to two-year, $10.15-million deal as free agent last winter . . . Yankees pulled off the steal of offseason last year when they traded minor leaguers Keith Heberling and Lyle Mouton to White Sox for one of the top winners in the AL . . . Did what he always does, pitching more than 200 innings (217⅔) and ranking among league's big winners (15) . . . New York fans were hard on him early in the season, but all was forgiven when he helped club get back to postseason . . . Lost twice in Division Series, once in late relief on short rest in decisive game . . . Was 20-game winner in both 1992 and '93 for White Sox and won Cy Young in '93 . . . Born Jan. 16, 1966, in Van Nuys, Cal. . . . Salary last year was team-high $5,400,000 . . . White Sox drafted him fifth overall in 1987.

Year	Club	G	IP	W	L	Pct.	SO	BB	H	ERA
1987	Chicago (AL)	4	28	3	0	1.000	15	6	16	1.93
1988	Chicago (AL)	26	158⅔	5	10	.333	84	68	147	3.97
1990	Chicago (AL)	33	205	14	9	.609	165	77	189	3.82
1991	Chicago (AL)	35	253⅔	17	10	.630	191	82	212	3.41
1992	Chicago (AL)	34	260⅔	20	10	.667	178	75	247	3.18
1993	Chicago (AL)	34	256⅔	22	10	.688	158	69	261	3.37
1994	Chicago (AL)	25	181	10	9	.526	127	42	186	3.73
1995	New York (AL)	30	217⅔	15	10	.600	157	78	211	3.93
	Totals	221	1561⅓	106	68	.609	1075	497	1469	3.56

TOP PROSPECTS

ALAN EMBREE 26 6-2 185 Bats L Throws L

Made 23 appearances in middle and late relief for major-league club last year (3-2, 5.11, one save) . . . Worked as a full-time starter in the minors until '95, when he went 3-4 with 0.89 ERA and five saves for Buffalo (AAA) . . . Appeared in five postseason games with Indians and had 2.70 ERA . . . Was Indians' fifth-round choice in 1989 draft . . . Two years removed from elbow surgery, he could be ready to step up in class . . . Born Jan. 23, 1970, in Vancouver, Wash.

EINAR DIAZ 23 5-10 165 Bats R Throws R

Seemingly undersized catching prospect can swing the bat . . . Hit .263 with six homers and 43 RBI for Kinston (A) in '95 . . . Broke through for 16 homers and 71 RBI for Columbus (A) in '94 . . .

May have to beef up some to be Ivan Rodriguez-type major-league catcher . . . Born Dec. 28, 1972, in Chiriqui, Panama . . . Signed by Indians as non-drafted free agent in October 1990.

BARTOLO COLON 20 6-0 185 **Bats R Throws R**
Hard-throwing right-hander was on the way to another strong minor-league season with a 13-3 record, 1.96 ERA and 152 strike-outs in 129 innings for Kingston (A) in '95, when a bruised elbow forced him to sidelines . . . Could jump to Triple-A sometime this season . . . Born May 24, 1975, in Puerta Plata, D.R. . . . Signed by Indians as non-drafted free agent in June 1993 . . . Has three-year pro record of 26-8.

MANAGER MIKE HARGROVE: Weathered tremendous adversity to build Indians into super team of '95 . . . Tribe won 100 games in 144-game season, blowing away all competition in AL Central and reaching World Series, only to lose in six games to Braves . . . Managed club during lean years, then had promising team devastated in '93, when relievers Steve Olin and Tim Crews were killed in spring-training boating accident and Cliff Young died in separate incident . . . Indians came back to post 66-47 record during '94 and finally lifted a 40-year jinx when they won Central title last year . . . His career won-loss mark is now above .500, at 350-316, in four-plus seasons since replacing John McNamara, July 6, 1991 . . . Former first baseman was solid major-league hitter who played for Texas, San Diego and Cleveland . . . Compiled a .290 career batting average over 14 seasons . . . Nicknamed "The Human Rain Delay" for his deliberate routine at the plate, but Indians don't waste any time disposing of opponents . . . First name is "Dudley" . . . Born Oct. 26, 1949, in Perrytown, Tex.

ALL-TIME INDIAN SEASON RECORDS

BATTING: Joe Jackson, .408, 1911
HRs: Albert Belle, 50, 1995
RBI: Hal Trosky, 162, 1936
STEALS: Kenny Lofton, 70, 1993
WINS: Jim Bagby, 31, 1920
STRIKEOUTS: Bob Feller, 348, 1946

KANSAS CITY ROYALS

TEAM DIRECTORY: Chairman/CEO: David D. Glass; Exec. VP/GM: Herk Robinson; VP-Adm.: Dennis Cryder; VP-Baseball Oper.: George Brett; Dir. Scouting: Art Stewart; Dir. Minor League Oper.: Bob Hegman; Dir. Player Pers.: Larry Doughty; VP-Communications/Marketing: Mike Levy; Dir. Team Travel: David Witty; Mgr.: Bob Boone; Coaches: Tim Foli, Guy Hansen, Bruce Kison, Greg Luzinski, Mitchell Page, Jamie Quirk. Home: Kauffman Stadium (40,625). Field distances: 330, l.f. line; 375, l.c.; 400, c.f.; 375, r.c.; 330, r.f. line. Spring training: Baseball City Stadium, Orlando, Fla.

SCOUTING REPORT

HITTING: Most people figured that the Royals didn't have much pop in their lineup last season—they generated the fewest number of runs in the AL with 629—and the same could probably be said about '96. Certainly the loss of Gary Gaetti to the Dodgers via free agency won't help.

Gaetti's MVP-type year (.261, 35, 96) and Wally Joyner's

Tom Goodwin's larcenous legs rang up 50 steals.

strong showing (.310, 12, 83) helped carry the Royals in '95. Now reborn Royal Mike Macfarlane (.225, 15, 5 with the Red Sox) must help pick up the slack for Gaetti, along with youngsters like ex-Dodger Jose Offerman (.287, 4, 33 with LA), Tom Goodwin (.288, 4, 28, 50 steals) and Johnny Damon (.282, 3, 22). Goodwin was second in the AL in stolen bases last year and Damon now has a full season ahead in which to strut his stuff.

Jon Nunnally (.244, 14, 42) was in the AL Rookie of the Year race through the All-Star break before his numbers dropped off. Michael Tucker (.260, 4, 17) should improve with experience.

And what ever happened to Bob Hamelin (.168, 7, 25)?

PITCHING: Few teams have a better one-two punch in their rotation than Kevin Appier (15-10, 3.89) and the re-signed Mark Gubicza (12-14, 3.75). Tom Gordon (12-12, 4.43) was not re-signed, but the Royals ranked fourth in the AL with a 4.49 ERA in '95 and there's no reason they shouldn't rank in the top half again.

Chris Haney (3-4, 3.65) will contribute. Tom Browning (0-2, 8.10) gets another shot to recapture his former form. Plus premier closer Jeff Montgomery (2-3, 3.43, 31 saves) was re-enlisted to anchor the bullpen.

Manager Bob Boone went with a four-man rotation last year with mixed results. Appier was outstanding before running into late-season arm problems. More starts for your top pitchers sounds like a good idea. Whether the four-man scheme will work in 1996 will be interesting to see.

FIELDING: If nothing else, the Royals are usually fundamentally sound. Their 90 errors last year were the third-lowest figure in the AL.

Free-agent defector Greg Gagne's defense at shortstop will be missed, because Offerman (35 errors) is a liability. Second baseman Keith Lockhart is solid. Damon is outstanding in center field with the total package: speed, talent, smarts and arm strength. Goodwin, in left, is certainly better with the glove than predecessor Vince Coleman.

OUTLOOK: The Royals, 70-74 in '95, are just two years removed from being named Organization of the Year by everyone but *Farmer's Almanac*. This is an exciting team, loaded with young prospects. Kansas City's wild-card run in 1995 was wholly unexpected but, with some experience now, don't be surprised if the Royals make another playoff run in '96.

ROYAL PROFILES

BIP ROBERTS 32 5-7 170 Bats S Throws R

Padres traded him to Royals with Bryan Wolff for Wally Joyner and Aaron Dorlarque last winter . . . When this infielder-outfielder is healthy, he's a devastating leadoff hitter . . . But he can't stay healthy for a whole season . . . Injuries limited him to just 73 games . . . Hit .304, had .346 on-base percentage and stole 20 bases . . . Hit .323 against righties and only .253 against lefties . . . Last year was his third .300-plus season in last four . . . Salary was $2.3 million in 1995 . . . Hit .320 in 1994 and .323 in 1992 . . . Left team for several days in May 1994 because of personal problems . . . Came back strong with 23-game hitting streak, longest in NL in five years . . . In second stint with Padres, who signed him as free agent prior to '94 season . . . Traded to Reds for closer Randy Myers prior to 1992 season, he became Reds' MVP that year . . . Pirates took him in first round of secondary phase of 1982 draft . . . Born Oct. 27, 1963, in Berkeley, Cal.

Year	Club	Pos.	G	AB	R	H	2B	3B	HR	RBI	SB	Avg.
1986	San Diego	2B	101	241	34	61	5	2	1	12	14	.253
1988	San Diego	2B-3B	5	9	1	3	0	0	0	0	0	.333
1989	San Diego	OF-3B-SS-2B	117	329	81	99	15	8	3	25	21	.301
1990	San Diego	OF-3B-SS-2B	149	556	104	172	36	3	9	44	46	.309
1991	San Diego	2B-OF	117	424	66	119	13	3	3	32	26	.281
1992	Cincinnati	OF-2B-3B	147	532	92	172	34	6	4	45	44	.323
1993	Cincinnati	2B-OF-3B-SS	83	292	46	70	13	0	1	18	26	.240
1994	San Diego	2B-OF	105	403	52	129	15	5	2	31	21	.320
1995	San Diego	OF-2B-SS	73	296	40	90	14	0	2	25	20	.304
	Totals		897	3082	516	915	145	27	25	232	218	.297

TOM GOODWIN 27 6-1 170 Bats L Throws R

Outfielder tied for second in AL with Texas' Otis Nixon with 50 stolen bases in '95 . . . Is a threat on the bases, but doesn't have much power for an outfielder . . . Spent first full season in the majors in '95 after splitting time between Los Angeles and Albuquerque (AAA) from 1991-93 and between Kansas City and Omaha (AAA) in '94 . . . Started last season with major-league lifetime average of only .232 in 105 games . . . Two-time All-American selection while at Fresno State . . . Made $145,000 in '95 . . . Claimed by Royals on waivers from Dodgers prior to '94 season . . . Los Angeles drafted him 22nd overall in 1989 draft . . . Born July 27, 1968, in Fresno, Cal.

Year	Club	Pos.	G	AB	R	H	2B	3B	HR	RBI	SB	Avg.
1991	Los Angeles . . .	OF	16	7	3	1	0	0	0	0	1	.143
1992	Los Angeles . . .	OF	57	73	15	17	1	1	0	3	7	.233
1993	Los Angeles . . .	OF	30	17	6	5	1	0	0	1	1	.294
1994	Kansas City . . .	OF	2	2	0	0	0	0	0	0	0	.000
1995	Kansas City . . .	OF	133	480	72	138	16	3	4	28	50	.288
	Totals		238	579	96	161	18	4	4	32	59	.278

MIKE MACFARLANE 31 6-1 210 Bats R Throws R

Red Sox free-agent catcher came back to Royals with two-year, $1.6-million contract in December . . . He'd signed as a free agent with Boston at the beginning of '95 season, hitting .225 with 15 homers and 51 RBI . . . Had played for Royals from 1987-94 . . . In '94 he led AL in being hit by pitch with 18 and added 14 more last year for a total of 61 in last five seasons . . . Gunned down 34 percent of would-be base-stealers . . . Was Royals' first-round pick in 1985 draft . . . Born April 12, 1964, in Stockton, Cal. . . . Earned $1,725,000 in '95.

Year	Club	Pos.	G	AB	R	H	2B	3B	HR	RBI	SB	Avg.
1987	Kansas City . . .	C	8	19	0	4	1	0	0	3	0	.211
1988	Kansas City . . .	C	70	211	25	56	15	0	4	26	0	.265
1989	Kansas City . . .	C	69	157	13	35	6	0	2	19	0	.223
1990	Kansas City . . .	C	124	400	37	102	24	4	6	58	1	.255
1991	Kansas City . . .	C	84	267	34	74	18	2	13	41	1	.277
1992	Kansas City . . .	C	129	402	51	94	28	3	17	48	1	.234
1993	Kansas City . . .	C	117	388	55	106	27	0	20	67	2	.273
1994	Kansas City . . .	C	92	314	53	80	17	3	14	47	1	.255
1995	Boston	C	115	364	45	82	18	1	15	51	2	.225
	Totals		808	2522	313	633	154	13	91	360	8	.251

MICHAEL TUCKER 24 6-2 185 Bats L Throws R

Made major-league debut in '95 . . . His numbers were respectable after a somewhat disappointing minor-league season in '94, when he hit .276 with 21 homers and 77 RBI for Omaha (AAA) . . . Attended Longwood College and was member of United States' 1992 Olympic team . . . Was Division II Player of the Year . . . Was a shortstop in college, a second baseman as a first-year pro and is now a left fielder . . . Made major-league minimum of $109,000 in '95 . . . Was invited to Royals big-league camp in spring of 1994 . . . Selected by Kansas City in first round of '92 draft . . . Born June 25, 1971, in South Boston, Va.

Year	Club	Pos.	G	AB	R	H	2B	3B	HR	RBI	SB	Avg.
1995	Kansas City . . .	OF	62	177	23	46	10	0	4	17	2	.260

JOSE OFFERMAN 27 6-0 170 Bats S Throws R

Dodgers traded dispensable shortstop to Royals for Billy Brewer last winter. . . . Had a bizarre year in '95, even by his standards . . . Enjoyed outstanding first two months, hitting above .300 . . . But Dodger Stadium fans booed announcement of his spot on NL All-Star team . . . Lost job late in the season to rookie Chad Fonville . . . Salary was $1.6 million in 1995 . . . Finished with 35 errors, far and away the most by any shortstop in league . . . Did hit a career-high .287, which was 41 points above his career average entering '95 . . . Great prospect who hasn't panned out . . . Went back to minors in midst of terrible 1994 season . . . Signed by Dodgers as non-drafted free agent in July 1986 . . . Born Nov. 8, 1968, in the cradle of shortstops, San Pedro de Macoris, D.R.

Year	Club	Pos.	G	AB	R	H	2B	3B	HR	RBI	SB	Avg.
1990	Los Angeles . . .	SS	29	58	7	9	0	0	1	7	1	.155
1991	Los Angeles . . .	SS	52	113	10	22	2	0	0	3	3	.195
1992	Los Angeles . . .	SS	149	534	67	139	20	8	1	30	23	.260
1993	Los Angeles . . .	SS	158	590	77	159	21	6	1	62	30	.269
1994	Los Angeles . . .	SS	72	243	27	51	8	4	1	25	2	.210
1995	Los Angeles . . .	SS	119	429	69	123	14	6	4	33	2	.287
	Totals		579	1967	257	503	65	24	8	160	61	.256

JON NUNNALLY 24 5-10 190 Bats L Throws R

Average slipped as the season got deeper, but this outfielder still had a pretty good rookie year . . . Selected by Kansas City in Rule V draft from Cleveland organization prior to last season . . . Was Cleveland's third-round pick in '92 draft . . . Played three seasons in Indians' minor-league system . . . Best year was '94 at Kinston (A), where he batted .267 with 22 homers and 74 RBI . . . Played two years at Miami Dade South Community College and was named Junior College Conference Player of the Year in the Southern Division after hitting .410 as

Royals hope Kevin Appier is free of arm ails.

a sophomore . . . Made major-league minimum of $109,000 in '95 . . . Born Nov. 9, 1971, in Pelham, N.C.

Year	Club	Pos.	G	AB	R	H	2B	3B	HR	RBI	SB	Avg.
1995	Kansas City . . .	OF	119	303	51	74	15	6	14	42	6	.244

JOHNNY DAMON 22 6-0 175 Bats L Throws L

Was given his chance on that fateful weekend of Aug. 11 last year, when Royals made 11 player moves . . . They decided to go with youth, released Vince Coleman and inserted this speedster into center field . . . Funny thing happened, as Royals unexpectedly stayed in wild-card race . . . His .282 average with three homers and 23 RBI in 47 games wasn't bad . . . Major-league scouts say he's the real deal . . . Stole total of 103 bases in minor leagues in '93 and '94 . . . Talented center fielder . . . Made pro-rated portion of major-league minimum of $109,000 for 47 games he played . . . Selected by Royals as sandwich pick between first and second rounds in '92 draft . . . Born Nov. 5, 1973, in Fort Riley, Kan.

Year	Club	Pos.	G	AB	R	H	2B	3B	HR	RBI	SB	Avg.
1995	Kansas City . . .	OF	47	188	32	53	11	5	3	23	7	.282

KEVIN APPIER 28 6-2 195 **Bats R Throws R**

Got off to hot start in '95, but then ran into arm trouble . . . Was it unavoidable or did it have something to do with manager Bob Boone's four-man rotation? . . . Pitcher said it had nothing to do with short rest . . . Finished fifth in AL with 185 strikeouts and ninth with 201⅓ innings . . . Opponent hit only .221 against him, second-lowest mark in AL . . . Has won in double figures in five of past six years . . . His 3.89 ERA was highest of career for full season . . . Second year in a row he posted career-high ERA . . . Workhorse . . . Has averaged almost 200 innings per season for his career . . . Kansas City's Opening Day pitcher for four consecutive seasons . . . Made $4.337 million in '95 . . . Ranks among Royals' all-time top 10 in several pitching categories . . . Selected by Royals ninth overall in '87 draft . . . Born Dec. 6, 1967, in Lancaster, Cal.

Year	Club	G	IP	W	L	Pct.	SO	BB	H	ERA
1989	Kansas City	6	21⅔	1	4	.200	10	12	34	9.14
1990	Kansas City	32	185⅔	12	8	.600	127	54	179	2.76
1991	Kansas City	34	207⅔	13	10	.565	158	61	205	3.42
1992	Kansas City	30	208⅓	15	8	.652	150	68	167	2.46
1993	Kansas City	34	238⅔	18	8	.692	186	81	183	2.56
1994	Kansas City	23	155	7	6	.538	145	63	137	3.83
1995	Kansas City	31	201⅓	15	10	.600	185	80	163	3.89
	Totals	190	1218⅓	81	54	.600	961	419	1068	3.22

MARK GUBICZA 33 6-5 230 **Bats R Throws R**

"Goobie" . . . When you think of Cal Ripken, you think Baltimore. When you think of Alan Trammell and Lou Whitaker, you think Detroit. When you think of this guy, you think of Royals . . . He's only player remaining from Kansas City's 1985 World Series winner . . . Has been stalwart on Royals staff since '84 . . . Led AL with 33 games started, was third in innings (213⅓) and ranked 10th in ERA (3.75) in '95 . . . Last year was his best since early 1990s . . . Successfully came back from rotator-cuff surgery in '94 . . . A two-time All-Star . . . Set club record with 14 strikeouts against Minnesota, Aug. 27, 1988 . . . Did not pitch in 1985 World Series, but was 1-0 with 3.24 ERA in '85 ALCS . . . A bargain at a salary of $650,000 in '95

. . . Selected by Royals in second round of '81 draft . . . Born Aug. 14, 1962, in Philadelphia . . . Re-signed to two-year, $3.2-million deal last winter.

Year	Club	G	IP	W	L	Pct.	SO	BB	H	ERA
1984	Kansas City	29	189	10	14	.417	111	75	172	4.05
1985	Kansas City	29	177⅓	14	10	.583	99	77	160	4.06
1986	Kansas City	35	180⅔	12	6	.667	118	84	155	3.64
1987	Kansas City	35	241⅔	13	18	.419	166	120	231	3.98
1988	Kansas City	35	269⅔	20	8	.714	183	83	237	2.70
1989	Kansas City	36	255	15	11	.577	173	63	252	3.04
1990	Kansas City	16	94	4	7	.364	71	38	101	4.50
1991	Kansas City	26	133	9	12	.429	89	42	168	5.68
1992	Kansas City	18	111⅓	7	6	.538	81	36	110	3.72
1993	Kansas City	49	104⅓	5	8	.385	80	43	128	4.66
1994	Kansas City	22	130	7	9	.438	59	26	158	4.50
1995	Kansas City	33	213⅓	12	14	.462	81	62	222	3.75
	Totals	363	2099⅓	128	123	.510	1311	749	2094	3.85

JEFF MONTGOMERY 34 5-11 180 Bats R Throws R

Another solid year . . . His 31 saves tied him for fifth in AL with Yankees' John Wetteland . . . It was his sixth consecutive year with 24-or-more saves, boosting career total to 218 . . . Royals' all-time career ERA leader at 2.60 . . . Increased his saves total for six straight seasons between 1988-93, joining Sammy Stewart as only pitchers to accomplish that feat . . . Two-time All-Star . . . Tied Toronto's Duane Ward for AL saves lead with 45 in '93 and won Rolaids Relief Award that year . . . Has now made 488 consecutive relief appearances since his only major-league start, Aug. 11, 1987, for Cincinnati against Los Angeles . . . Royals traded outfielder Van Snider to Reds for him prior to '88 season . . . Cincinnati's ninth-round pick in '83 draft . . . Made $4.166 million in '95 . . . Born Jan. 7, 1962, in Wellston, Ohio . . . Re-signed to two-year, $4.75-million deal last winter.

Year	Club	G	IP	W	L	Pct.	SO	BB	H	ERA
1987	Cincinnati	14	19⅓	2	2	.500	13	9	25	6.52
1988	Kansas City	45	62⅔	7	2	.778	47	30	54	3.45
1989	Kansas City	63	92	7	3	.700	94	25	66	1.37
1990	Kansas City	73	94⅓	6	5	.545	94	34	81	2.39
1991	Kansas City	67	90	4	4	.500	77	28	83	2.90
1992	Kansas City	65	82⅔	1	6	.143	69	27	61	2.18
1993	Kansas City	69	87⅓	7	5	.583	66	23	65	2.27
1994	Kansas City	42	44⅔	2	3	.400	50	15	48	4.03
1995	Kansas City	54	65⅔	2	3	.400	49	25	60	3.43
	Totals	492	638⅔	38	33	.535	559	216	543	2.72

TOP PROSPECTS

JOE VITIELLO 25 6-2 215 Bats R Throws R

Played well after recall in '95, hitting seven homers, collecting 21 RBI and hitting .254 in 53 games . . . Also had .446 slugging percentage for Royals . . . Hit .279 with 12 homers and 42 RBI for Omaha (AAA) in '95 . . . Up-and-comer . . . American Association Rookie of the Year in '94, when he hit .344 with 10 homers and 61 RBI for Omaha . . . Can play first base or outfield . . . Royals chose him seventh overall in 1991 draft . . . Born April 11, 1970, in Cambridge, Mass.

KEITH LOCKHART 31 5-10 170 Bats L Throws R

Infielder bounced around minors for nine years before finally getting a legitimate chance in Kansas City last season and running with it . . . Hit .321 with six homers, 33 RBI and eight steals in 94 games . . . Hit .378 with five homers and 19 RBI for Omaha (AAA) in '95 . . . Signed as minor-league free agent prior to last season . . . Originally an 11th-round pick by Cincinnati in '86 draft . . . Born Nov. 10, 1964, in Whittier, Cal.

JIM PITTSLEY 22 6-7 215 Bats R Throws R

Went 4-1 with 3.21 ERA in eight games for Omaha (AAA) before being sidelined and eventually undergoing elbow surgery . . . Good news was he had only a slight tear and didn't need Tommy John surgery . . . Royals chose him 17th overall in 1992 draft . . . Threw only 3⅓ innings for Royals in '95 . . . Born April 3, 1974, in DuBois, Pa. . . . Led Carolina League with 171 strikeouts for Wilmington (A) in 1994.

MIKE SWEENEY 22 6-1 195 Bats R Throws R

Hit .250 in four games for Kansas City following a September callup . . . Led Carolina League in hitting with .310 mark and also added 18 homers and 53 RBI for Wilmington (A) in '95 . . . Royals' 10th-round selection in '91 draft . . . Signed when he was still only 17 . . . Catcher has now batted over .300 in two consecutive minor-league seasons . . . Born July 22, 1973, in Ontario, Cal.

MANAGER BOB BOONE: Wasted no time in taking charge in his debut season . . . Instituted a four-man rotation . . . Move was somewhat controversial, but he was tremendously successful, keeping Royals in wild-card race until last two weeks . . . His team finished 70-74, even after dumping several veterans, including Vince Coleman, and deciding to embark on youth movement in mid-August . . . Named to replace Hal McRae after '94 season, in which Royals finished 64-51 . . . Was Davey Johnson's bench coach in Cincinnati in '94 . . . Wooed former manager Gene Mauch back into uniform to serve as his bench coach with Royals . . . Father Ray was former major-league infielder and son Bret plays for Cincinnati . . . Ranks second all-time in games caught behind Carlton Fisk at 2,225 over 18-year career . . . Retired after playing for Royals in '90 . . . Played nine years with Phillies and seven more with Angels . . . Played in four NLCS with Phils and two ALCS with Angels . . . Was four-time All-Star . . . Born Nov. 19, 1947, in San Diego . . . Became 11th full-time manager of Royals and third straight former Kansas City player to serve as their field boss, following John Wathan and McRae.

ALL-TIME ROYAL SEASON RECORDS

BATTING: George Brett, .390, 1980
HRs: Steve Balboni, 36, 1985
RBI: Hal McRae, 133, 1982
STEALS: Willie Wilson, 83, 1979
WINS: Bret Saberhagen, 23, 1989
STRIKEOUTS: Dennis Leonard, 244, 1977

MILWAUKEE BREWERS

TEAM DIRECTORY: Pres./CEO: Allan (Bud) Selig; Sr. VP-Baseball Oper.: Sal Bando; Dir. Player Dev.: Fred Stanley; VP-Corp. Affairs: Laurel Prieb; Dir. Media Rel.: Jon Greenberg; Dir. Publications: Mario Ziino; Trav. Sec.: Steve Ethier; Mgr.: Phil Garner; Coaches: Chris Bando, Bill Castro, Jim Gantner, Larry Johnson, Don Rowe. Home: Milwaukee County Stadium (53,192). Field distances: 315, l.f. line; 362, l.f.; 392, l.c.; 402, c.f.; 392, r.c.; 362, r.f.; 315, r.f. line. Spring training: Chandler, Ariz.

SCOUTING REPORT

HITTING: This small-market team developed a surprising amount of bang for Bud Selig's buck last year and remained in

John Jaha's .579 slugging percentage led Milwaukee.

the wild-card race until late in the season, but the Brewers do not pose a major offensive threat. Ranked eighth in the league in batting average (.266), they were in the upper half of the rankings with 740 runs, but ranked 10th in on-base percentage (.336) and displayed little power (11th in home runs with 128).

Still, three regulars batted above .310, headed by B.J. Surhoff (.320, 13, 73), who left via free agency. A down year from Greg Vaughn (.224, 17, 59) hurt. But the Brewers could be more explosive this year if Vaughn bounces back, the re-signed Kevin Seitzer (.311, 5, 69) sustains his pace, John Jaha (.313, 20, 65) continues to progress and Chuck Carr (.227, 25 steals with the Marlins) finds a way to get on first.

Milwaukee needs more of an offensive lift from Dave Nilsson (.278, 12, 53), Jeff Cirillo (.277, 9, 39) and Matt Mieske (.251, 12, 48). The Brewers remained competitive largely on evenly distributed run production, getting 47-or-more RBI from 11 players. But that isn't enough.

PITCHING: Milwaukee finished in the middle of the AL rankings with a 4.82 ERA, but that was deceptive. This inexperienced staff had the third-worst opponents' batting average (.280) and ranked ahead of only Detroit with seven complete games. The bullpen's 31 saves were the third-worst total in the AL and the Brewers' staff struck out a league-low 699 batters.

The most effective pitcher on the staff was closer Mike Fetters (0-3, 3.38), but he was limited to 40 appearances and 22 saves. Right-hander Steve Sparks (9-11, 4.63) could be on verge of big things. Left-hander Scott Karl (6-7, 4.14) performed well enough in 18 starts last year to arrive in spring training with a place set aside in the '96 rotation. To be truly competitive, the Brewers need Ricky Bones (10-12, 4.63) to realize his potential.

FIELDING: Manager Phil Garner stresses defensive fundamentals, but the Brewers ranked ninth in fielding percentage (.981) and 11th with 105 errors in '95. There are no glaring weaknesses. Jaha made just two errors at first base. Second baseman Cirillo and shortstop Jose Valentin made 15 each.

OUTLOOK: It's tough to be a small-market club in the same division with the Indians. The Brewers, 65-79 in '95, have to that the Tribe suffers a major reversal this year just to dream about contending for an AL Central title—and that's without factoring in a likely recovery by the White Sox from a disappointing '95 season. Milwaukee probably won't finish higher than fourth.

BREWER PROFILES

GREG VAUGHN 30 6-0 205 Bats R Throws R

The Brewers' big bopper has watched power numbers decline past two seasons, mostly because of drop in playing time due to injury and labor unrest . . . Designated hitter averaged one home run per 23 at-bats last year, not far off career pace of one per 20 at-bats . . . It was first time since 1990 that he was not the Brewers' home-run leader as his 17 ranked second to John Jaha's 20 . . . One of only six right-handed hitters in Brewer history to hit 30-or-more homers in a season (30 in 1993) . . . Struck out once per 4.5 at-bats last year, slightly better than career ratio . . . Batting average in '95 was .224, 23 points below previous career mark . . . Born July 3, 1965, in Sacramento, Cal. . . . Salary in 1995 was $4,875,000 . . . Brewers drafted him in first round in 1986 . . . Rarely plays in outfield any more because of injuries.

Year	Club	Pos.	G	AB	R	H	2B	3B	HR	RBI	SB	Avg.
1989	Milwaukee	OF	38	113	18	30	3	0	5	23	4	.265
1990	Milwaukee	OF	120	382	51	84	26	2	17	61	7	.220
1991	Milwaukee	OF	145	542	81	132	24	5	27	98	2	.244
1992	Milwaukee	OF	141	501	77	114	18	2	23	78	15	.228
1993	Milwaukee	OF	154	569	97	152	28	2	30	97	10	.267
1994	Milwaukee	OF	95	370	59	94	24	1	19	55	9	.254
1995	Milwaukee	DH	108	392	67	88	19	1	17	59	10	.224
	Totals		801	2869	450	694	142	13	138	471	57	.242

JOHN JAHA 29 6-1 222 Bats R Throws R

Heavy hitter who averaged a home run per 16 at-bats last year, nearly double his previous ratio . . . Led the Brewers in home runs with 20 . . . If he had not homered on last day of season, Brewers would have gone back-to-back years without a 20-homer hitter . . . Tied club mark when he was hit by pitches 10 times in '94 . . . Has hovered around .300 batting average since he was recalled by Brewers in September 1994 . . . Ranked third on the club with 65 RBI in '95 . . . Led Brewers with .579 slugging percentage . . . Is not known for his speed, but once had four stolen bases in game against Orioles in 1992 . . . Born May 27, 1966, in Portland, Ore. . . . Salary in 1995 was

$229,000 . . . First baseman was drafted by Brewers in 14th round of 1984 draft . . . Bounced back from surgery to repair torn anterior cruciate ligament in right knee prior to 1990 season . . . Hit .344 with 31 homers and 134 RBI for El Paso (AA) in '91.

Year	Club	Pos.	G	AB	R	H	2B	3B	HR	RBI	SB	Avg.
1992	Milwaukee	1B-OF	47	133	17	30	3	1	2	10	10	.226
1993	Milwaukee	1B-3B-2B	153	515	78	136	21	0	19	70	13	.264
1994	Milwaukee	1B	84	291	45	70	14	0	12	39	3	.241
1995	Milwaukee	1B	88	316	59	99	20	2	20	65	2	.313
	Totals		372	1255	199	335	58	3	53	184	28	.267

KEVIN SEITZER 34 5-11 193 — Bats R Throws R

Scrappy third baseman has given Brewers fans their money's worth, though he's another veteran who has been forced to settle for less in baseball's brave new economic world . . . Led Brewers in hits (153), ranked third in batting average (.311) and second in RBI (69) . . . Scored 105 runs and tied for league lead with 207 hits as a member of Royals in '87 . . . Only Brewer to finish '95 season with more than 30 doubles (33) . . . Good contact hitter who usually ends up with more walks than strikeouts (64-57 in '95) . . . Born March 26, 1962, in Springfield, Ill. . . . Salary in 1995 was $550,000 . . . Royals drafted him in 11th round in 1983 . . . Brewers signed him a free agent after KC aived him prior to 1992 season . . . Re-signed to one-year, $1-million deal as free agent last winter.

Year	Club	Pos.	G	AB	R	H	2B	3B	HR	RBI	SB	Avg.
1986	Kansas City . . .	1B-OF-3B	28	96	16	31	4	1	2	11	0	.323
1987	Kansas City . . .	3B-OF-1B	161	641	105	207	33	8	15	83	12	.323
1988	Kansas City . . .	3B-OF	149	559	90	170	32	5	5	60	10	.304
1989	Kansas City . . .	3B-SS-OF-1B	160	597	78	168	17	2	4	48	17	.281
1990	Kansas City . . .	3B-2B	158	622	91	171	31	5	6	38	7	.275
1991	Kansas City . . .	3B	85	234	28	62	11	3	1	25	4	.265
1992	Milwaukee	3B-2B-1B	148	540	74	146	35	1	5	71	13	.270
1993	Oak.-Mil.	INF-OF	120	417	45	112	16	2	11	57	7	.269
1994	Milwaukee	3B-1B	80	309	44	97	24	2	5	49	2	.314
1995	Milwaukee	3B-1B	132	492	56	153	33	3	5	69	2	.311
	Totals		1221	4507	627	1317	236	32	59	511	74	.292

Brewers await more wins Rickey Bones.

DAVE NILSSON 26 6-3 231 Bats L Throws R

One of two native Australians on the Brewers' roster in '95 as Graeme Lloyd was the other . . . Signed by Milwaukee as non-drafted free agent in January 1987 and spent five years in minors before making major-league debut in 1992 . . . Named the Brewers' Most Valuable Player in 1994 (12 homers, 69 RBI) . . . Catcher improved power and run-production ratios last year . . . At last year's pace, his 12 homers and 53 RBI in 263 at-bats would have projected to 26 home runs and 111 RBI over 550 at-bats . . . Part owner of Australian professional baseball team . . . Born Dec. 14, 1969, in Brisbane, Australia . . . Salary last year was $200,000.

Year	Club	Pos.	G	AB	R	H	2B	3B	HR	RBI	SB	Avg.
1992	Milwaukee	C-1B	51	164	15	38	8	0	4	25	2	.232
1993	Milwaukee	C-1B	100	296	35	76	10	2	7	40	3	.257
1994	Milwaukee	C-1B	109	397	51	109	28	3	12	69	1	.275
1995	Milwaukee	OF-1B-C	81	263	41	73	12	1	12	53	2	.278
	Totals		341	1120	142	296	58	6	35	187	8	.264

JEFF CIRILLO 26 6-2 190 Bats R Throws R

Infielder spent first year as a major-league regular and batted a respectable .277 as only four Brewers hit for a higher average in '95 . . . On-base average (.371) and slugging percentage (.442) also ranked among top five on Milwaukee roster . . . Said to sleep with his bat when he is slumping, but he hit well enough last year to sustain more conventional sleeping arrangement . . . Brewers selected him in 11th round of 1991 draft, out of USC . . . Hits particularly well against Twins, but who doesn't? . . . Born Sept. 23, 1969, in Pasadena, Cal. . . . Made minimum major-league salary of $109,000 last year.

Year	Club	Pos.	G	AB	R	H	2B	3B	HR	RBI	SB	Avg.
1994	Milwaukee	3B-2B	39	126	17	30	9	0	3	12	0	.238
1995	Milwaukee	INF	125	328	57	91	19	4	9	39	7	.277
	Totals		164	454	74	121	28	4	12	51	7	.267

MATT MIESKE 28 6-0 192 Bats R Throws R

Jury is still out on outfielder acquired from Padres with Ricky Bones and Jose Valentin in Gary Sheffield deal prior to 1992 season . . . Still waiting to show what he can do over full season, but he has proven he can hit for power . . . Has averaged a home run per 23.4 at-bats in parts of three major-league seasons, so he could be a 20-25-homer guy if he ever gets 550-600 at-bats . . . Selected by Padres in 17th round of 1990 draft . . . Born Feb. 13, 1968, in Midland, Mich. . . . Salary in 1995 was $135,000.

Year	Club	Pos.	G	AB	R	H	2B	3B	HR	RBI	SB	Avg.
1993	Milwaukee	OF	23	58	9	14	0	0	3	7	0	.241
1994	Milwaukee	OF	84	259	39	67	13	1	10	38	3	.259
1995	Milwaukee	OF	117	267	42	67	13	1	12	48	2	.251
	Totals		224	584	90	148	26	2	25	93	5	.253

RICKY BONES 26 6-0 193 Bats R Throws R

Winningest pitcher on Brewers staff over last two years, though that is not saying all that much . . . Posted total of 20 victories over that period, including 10-12 mark in '95 . . . But decent 4.07 ERA since start of '94 provides evidence that he could have been a bigger winner with better club . . . Has several major weaknesses, beginning with poor strikeout-to-walk ratio (77-83 last year) . . . Also averages more than a hit per inning at major-league level . . . Gave up 26 homers last year . . . Durable . . . Pitched 200-or-more innings for second time in four full major-league seasons and has pitched at least 163 innings in each . . . Born April 7, 1969, in Salinas, P.R. . . . Salary last year was $487,500 . . . Obtained from Padres with Matt Mieske and Jose Valentin in Gary Sheffield deal prior to 1992 season . . . San Diego signed him as non-drafted free agent in May 1986.

Year	Club	G	IP	W	L	Pct.	SO	BB	H	ERA
1991	San Diego	11	54	4	6	.400	31	18	57	4.83
1992	Milwaukee	31	163⅓	9	10	.474	65	48	169	4.57
1993	Milwaukee	32	203⅔	11	11	.500	63	63	222	4.86
1994	Milwaukee	24	170⅔	10	9	.526	57	45	166	3.43
1995	Milwaukee	32	200⅓	10	12	.455	77	83	218	4.63
	Totals	130	792	44	48	.478	293	257	832	4.43

STEVE SPARKS 30 6-0 187 **Bats R Throws R**

Despite losing record at 9-11, this knuckleballer was one of cornerstones of pitching staff ... Led club in innings (202) and ranked second to Ricky Bones in victories ... Tough final start pushed ERA up and made hits-to-innings ratio look worse ... Allowed 17 home runs ... Late developer spent eight years in minor leagues after Brewers drafted him in fifth round in 1987 ... Posted 77-75 record and 3.96 ERA in minors ... Born July 2, 1965, in Tulsa, Okla. ... Made minimum major-league salary of $109,000 last year.

Year	Club	G	IP	W	L	Pct.	SO	BB	H	ERA
1995	Milwaukee	33	202	9	11	.450	96	86	210	4.63

MIKE FETTERS 31 6-4 224 **Bats R Throws R**

Has served as the Brewers' top closer the past two years, ranking fifth in AL in saves (17) in 1994 and eighth (22) last year ... ERA of 3.38 was right in line with career mark, but he registered worst hits-to-innings ratio since Brewers acquired him from Angels with Glenn Carter for Chuck Crim prior to '92 season ... Was once top pitching prospect in California organization, but he only emerged briefly from the Angels' minor-league system ... First full major-league season was 1992, when he made 50 appearances—mostly in middle relief—and finished with an impressive 1.87 ERA ... Had elbow surgery before '93 season, but he still pitched well ... Born Dec. 19, 1964, in Van Nuys, Cal. ... Salary in 1995 was $900,000 ... Angels drafted him in first round in 1986 ... Career save total is 42.

Year	Club	G	IP	W	L	Pct.	SO	BB	H	ERA
1989	California	1	3⅓	0	0	.000	4	1	5	8.10
1990	California	26	67⅔	1	1	.500	35	20	77	4.12
1991	California	19	44⅔	2	5	.286	24	28	53	4.84
1992	Milwaukee	50	62⅔	5	1	.833	43	24	38	1.87
1993	Milwaukee	45	59⅓	3	3	.500	23	22	59	3.34
1994	Milwaukee	42	46	1	4	.200	31	27	41	2.54
1995	Milwaukee	40	34⅔	0	3	.000	33	20	40	3.38
	Totals	223	318⅓	12	17	.414	193	142	313	3.36

TOP PROSPECTS

SCOTT KARL 24 6-2 195 Bats L Throws L

Got serious look at major-league level in '95 and did enough (6-7, 4.14) to catch on with young pitching staff . . . Pitched six-hit shutout against Red Sox on final day of '95 season, holding Mo Vaughn, John Valentin, Jose Canseco and Mike Greenwell to a combined 1-for-11 . . . Went 3-4, 3.30 for New Orleans (AAA) in '95 . . . Born Aug. 9, 1971, in Fontana, Cal. . . . Brewers drafted him in sixth round in 1992, out of University of Hawaii . . . Went 30-14, 2.69 in three minor-league seasons before '95.

JEFF BRONKEY 30 6-3 211 Bats R Throws R

Acquired from Rangers for minor-league pitcher Dave Pike prior to '94 season . . . Made big first impression with Brewers in '94 with 13⅓ straight scoreless innings out of gate, but he underwent elbow surgery June 1 of that season and pitched only seven more innings . . . Spent time on DL again in '95, but he returned to majors briefly and pitched well in middle relief (0-0, 3.65 in 12⅓ innings) . . . Went 0-1, 2.25 in two games with New Orleans (AAA) . . . Born Sept. 18, 1965, in Kabul, Afghanistan . . . Twins drafted him in second round in 1986 . . . Went 1-1, 4.00 for Texas during major-league debut in '93 and finished at 1-1, 4.35 for Milwaukee in '94.

MIKE MATHENY 25 6-3 205 Bats R Throws R

Milwaukee's eighth-round choice in 1991 draft has moved up organizational ladder . . . Catcher was summoned to Brewers each of last two seasons . . . Got longer look in '95, playing regularly in final weeks and batting .247 with no homers and 21 RBI in 166 at-bats . . . Hit .353 in 17 at-bats for New Orleans (AAA) last year . . . Decent defensive catcher made four errors in '95 . . . Born Sept. 22, 1970, in Columbus, Ohio . . . Hit .226 with one homer and two RBI in 53 at-bats for Brewers in '94 . . . Attended Michigan.

JAMIE McANDREW 28 6-2 190 Bats R Throws R

Went 2-3, 4.71 in 36⅓ innings for Brewers and was 7-5, 3.97 for New Orleans (AAA) in '95 . . . Acquired from Marlins for Tom McGraw prior to 1993 season, he missed entire '94 season with injury . . . Journeyman minor-league starter went 11-6, 3.94 for New Orleans in '93 . . . Made 10 appearances, including four starts, for Brewers in brief look last year . . . Born Sept. 2, 1967, in Williamsport, Pa. . . . Father Jim pitched for Mets and Padres from 1968-74 . . . Dodgers drafted him in third round in 1989 . . . Posted 10-3, 2.27 mark for Bakersfield (A) in 1990.

MANAGER PHIL GARNER: Solid tactical manager is entering fifth season with struggling Brewers, who hung around the wild-card race for awhile last year, but eventually sagged to fourth place, 14 games under .500, at 65-79 . . . Considering circumstances, not a bad performance by a manager working with the limited resources of the smallest of small-market teams . . . Nickname is ''Scrap Iron'' because of scrappy style of play during lengthy career as infielder with A's, Pirates, Astros, Dodgers and Giants . . . Had .260 career batting average and played on division champions in three different cities . . . Batted .417 in 1979 NLCS for Pittsburgh, then hit .500 in World Series with 12 hits in seven games against Orioles . . . Brewers exhibit his trademark scrappy, no-nonsense attitude, but low payroll makes postseason appearance this year very unlikely . . . Born April 30, 1949, in Jefferson City, Tenn. . . . Career record is 279-304.

ALL-TIME BREWER SEASON RECORDS

BATTING: Paul Molitor, .353, 1987
HRs: Gorman Thomas, 45, 1979
RBI: Cecil Cooper, 126, 1983
STEALS: Pat Listach, 54, 1992
WINS: Mike Caldwell, 22, 1978
STRIKEOUTS: Ted Higuera, 240, 1987

MINNESOTA TWINS

TEAM DIRECTORY: Owner: Carl Pohlad; Pres.: Jerry Bell; VP/GM Terry Ryan; VP/Asst. GM: Bill Smith; Dir. Media Rel.: Rob Antony; Trav. Sec.: Remzi Kiratli; Mgr.: Tom Kelly; Coaches: Terry Crowley, Ron Gardenhire, Rick Stelmaszek, Dick Such, Scott Ullger. Home: Hubert H. Humphrey Metrodome (55,883). Field distances: 343, l.f. line; 408, c.f.; 327, r.f. line. Spring training: Fort Myers, Fla.

SCOUTING REPORT

HITTING: As bad as the 1995 Twins were, their hitting was deceptively good at times. The Twins' .279 batting average ranked fourth in the AL, but their 703 runs ranked 10th. As long as the steady bats of Chuck Knoblauch (.333, 11, 63, 46 steals) and the re-committed Kirby Puckett (.314, 23, 99) anchor the

Marty Cordova was AL Rookie of the Year.

lineup, there will certainly be worse offenses in the AL.

The lineup's biggest weakness is clutch hitting. The Twins ranked last in the AL much of the year in batting average with runners on base. They got a total of only 15 home runs from their left-handed hitters. That's why GM Terry Ryan added Paul Molitor (.270, 15, 60 with the Blue Jays) to his lineup via a free-agent signing.

Pedro Munoz (.301, 18, 58) is coming off a strong year. Alex Cole (.342, 1, 14) was hampered by injury. Marty Cordova (.277, 24, 84) won AL Rookie of the Year honors. More offense from Matt Walbeck (.257, 1, 44), Pat Meares (.269, 12, 49) and Scott Stahoviak (.266, 3, 23) would help.

PITCHING: This is the department that has caused the Twins to fall into the abyss. Last year's team ERA of 5.76 meant the Twins had the worst in the majors for a second consecutive year and their 210 homers allowed were the most in the majors.

The good news is most of the cast has changed heading into this year. Last year's trades of Rick Aguilera, Kevin Tapani and Scott Erickson helped yield a decent crop of arms. The Twins hope Frank Rodriguez (5-8, 6.13) and Jose Parra (1-5, 7.59) will be two cornerstones to their rotation, along with free-agent returnee and former closer Aguilera (3-3, 2.60, 32 saves with the Twins and Red Sox). Brad Radke (11-14, 5.32) had a decent rookie season, even though he allowed 32 home runs.

If Dave Stevens (5-4, 5.07, 10 saves) develops into the closer the Twins think he can be, the staff should be in better shape than it has been in recent years.

FIELDING: One of the hallmarks of a Tom Kelly-managed team has always been solid defense. Although that is still true, the Twins slipped a bit in '95. The retirement of first baseman Kent Hrbek, an underrated fielder, hurt some, even though Stahoviak was decent there in 1995. The Twins are just OK, instead of superlative, defensively at the corners now. Center field, after Cole's injury, was also mediocre.

The Twins have a solid double-play combination, though, in second baseman Knoblauch and shortstop Meares.

OUTLOOK: The inclusion of a wild-card team in the playoffs gives the Twins something to shoot for, although, coming off an AL-worst 56-88 finish, they are probably two or three years away from that. This is a team that finished 44 games behind Cleveland in the AL Central. There is much work still to be done, even with Puckett choosing to remain in Minnesota.

TWIN PROFILES

KIRBY PUCKETT 35 5-9 223 Bats R Throws R

The Artist Formerly Known as Prince and fishing have nothing on this guy when it comes to popularity in Minnesota . . . He's The Franchise . . . One of few remaining star players to spend entire career with one team . . . His contract runs through '97 . . . Chose to not exercise clause that permitted him to declare himself a free agent after last season . . . Outfielder suffered the first serious injury of his career when he was hit in the mouth by a Dennis Martinez fastball Sept. 28 . . . The pitch broke his upper jaw and he missed the season's final three games, but he is expected to be ready for spring training . . . Played in his 10th consecutive All-Star Game in '95 . . . Finished with a .314 average, the eighth time in 10 years he batted above .300 . . . Finished strong, batting .321 with six homers and 22 RBI in his final 30 games . . . Made $6 million in 1995 . . . Twins drafted him third overall in January 1982 . . . Born March 14, 1961, in Chicago.

Year	Club	Pos.	G	AB	R	H	2B	3B	HR	RBI	SB	Avg.
1984	Minnesota	OF	128	557	63	165	12	5	0	31	14	.296
1985	Minnesota	OF	161	691	80	199	29	13	4	74	21	.288
1986	Minnesota	OF	161	680	119	223	37	6	31	96	20	.328
1987	Minnesota	OF	157	624	96	207	32	5	28	99	12	.332
1988	Minnesota	OF	158	657	109	234	42	5	24	121	6	.356
1989	Minnesota	OF	159	635	75	215	45	4	9	85	11	.339
1990	Minnesota	OF-2B-SS-3B	146	551	82	164	40	3	12	80	5	.298
1991	Minnesota	OF	152	611	92	195	29	6	15	89	11	.319
1992	Minnesota	OF-2B-3B-SS	160	639	104	210	38	4	19	110	17	.329
1993	Minnesota	OF	156	622	89	184	39	3	22	89	8	.296
1994	Minnesota	OF	108	439	79	139	32	3	20	112	6	.317
1995	Minnesota	OF-2B-3B-SS	137	538	83	169	39	0	23	99	3	.314
	Totals		1783	7244	1071	2304	414	57	207	1085	134	.318

CHUCK KNOBLAUCH 27 5-9 181 Bats R Throws R

Scouts who questioned the Twins when they picked this scrapper 25th overall in the 1989 draft are on the bandwagon now . . . Every year, this second baseman's future appears more and more unlimited . . . Collected career highs last year in batting average (.333), stolen bases (46), home runs (11), RBI (63), triples (8) and runs (107) . . . Ranked first in AL in multi-hit games with 56 and eighth in AL in runs . . . Stolen-base total was second-best ever by a Twin, behind Rod Carew's 49 in 1976 . . . Got married during last offseason . . . Was AL Rookie of the Year in '91, when he batted .281 with 25 stolen bases . . . Made $2.987 million in '95 . . . Twins were negotiating a multi-year contract with him last winter, because they would like to make him cornerstone of rebuilding effort . . . Born July 7, 1968, in Houston.

Year	Club	Pos.	G	AB	R	H	2B	3B	HR	RBI	SB	Avg.
1991	Minnesota	2B-SS	151	565	78	159	24	6	1	50	25	.281
1992	Minnesota	2B-SS	155	600	104	178	19	6	2	56	34	.297
1993	Minnesota	2B-SS-OF	153	602	82	167	27	4	2	41	29	.277
1994	Minnesota	2B-SS	109	445	85	139	45	3	5	51	35	.312
1995	Minnesota	2B-SS	136	538	107	179	34	8	11	63	46	.333
	Totals		704	2750	456	822	149	27	21	261	169	.299

MARTY CORDOVA 26 6-0 193 Bats R Throws R

On the way to becoming AL Rookie of the Year, he smacked home runs in five consecutive games during one mid-May stretch . . . That feat tied him with Harmon Killebrew for club record . . . Outfielder finished with 24 homers and 20 stolen bases, becoming only third Twin in history to join the 20-20 club (Kirby Puckett in 1986 and Larry Hisle in 1977) . . . Few things that he cannot do . . . A couple of early base-running gaffes in '95 caused him to concentrate in that department and improve as season went along . . . Has worked for a friend at a Las Vegas casino during each of the past two off-seasons . . . Made the major-league minimum $109,000 in '95 . . . Born July 10, 1969, in Las Vegas, Nev. . . . Chosen by Twins in 10th round of 1989 draft.

Year	Club	Pos.	G	AB	R	H	2B	3B	HR	RBI	SB	Avg.
1995	Minnesota	OF	137	512	81	142	27	4	24	84	20	.277

PAT MEARES 27 6-0 188 Bats R Throws R

He and Chuck Knoblauch became only the second Twins keystone combination to hit double figures in home runs. He had 12 and Knoblauch had 11 . . . Had entered last season with only two career home runs to his credit . . . Has developed into a solid all-around shortstop after feeling the heat from prospect Denny Hocking in the spring of '94 . . . Compiled a career-high, 12-game hitting streak in September '95 . . . Collected 35 extra-base hits in '95 after getting only 17 and 15 respectively in his first two seasons . . . Member of Wichita State's 1989 College World Series championship team . . . Hit first two major-league home runs in the same game in Baltimore June 19, 1994, after going homerless in his first 498 at-bats . . . Made $165,000 last year . . . Picked by Twins in 12th round of 1990 draft . . . Born Sept. 6, 1968, in Salina, Kan.

Year	Club	Pos.	G	AB	R	H	2B	3B	HR	RBI	SB	Avg.
1993	Minnesota	SS	111	346	33	87	14	3	0	33	4	.251
1994	Minnesota	SS	80	229	29	61	12	1	2	24	5	.266
1995	Minnesota	SS-OF	116	390	57	105	19	4	12	49	10	.269
	Totals		307	965	119	253	45	8	14	106	19	.262

MATT WALBECK 26 5-11 188 Bats S Throws R

Increased batting average 53 points over '94 mark, but still needs to show more power . . . Raised his average from .226 to .257 over last season's final 65 games . . . Threw out 25% of base-runners attempting to steal in '95 after throwing out 31% in '94 . . . This catcher has stayed away from injuries . . . Caught 115 games in '95 . . . Was handed starting job as a rookie two years ago and has always been adept behind the plate . . . Made Cubs' roster out of spring training in '93, hitting .333 in five games before being optioned to Iowa (AAA) . . . Made $175,000 in '95 . . . Born Oct. 2, 1969, in Sacramento . . . Cubs drafted him in eighth round in '87 . . . Traded by Cubs to Twins with Dave Stevens for Willie Banks prior to '94 season.

Year	Club	Pos.	G	AB	R	H	2B	3B	HR	RBI	SB	Avg.
1993	Chicago (NL) . .	C	11	30	2	6	2	0	1	6	0	.200
1994	Minnesota	C	97	338	31	69	12	0	5	35	1	.204
1995	Minnesota	C	115	393	40	101	18	1	1	44	3	.257
	Totals		223	761	73	176	32	1	7	85	4	.231

PEDRO MUNOZ 27 5-10 208 Bats R Throws R

When they invented the designated hitter, they did it for guys like him . . . A classic streak hitter for most of his career who became more consistent in '95, evidenced by his career-high .301 average . . . Actually, it was the best season of his career as he quietly went about putting up 18 homers and 58 RBI . . . Has five career two-homer games . . . Hit the longest home run ever to center in the Metrodome, April 5, 1994, a blast that carried 473 feet . . . Still doesn't play every day against right-handers in manager Tom Kelly's platoon system . . . One of the Twins' slowest runners, he is a liability in the outfield . . . Born Sept. 19, 1968, in Ponce, P.R. . . . Made $700,000 in '95 . . . Obtained by Twins from Toronto with Nelson Liriano for John Candelaria, July 27, 1990 . . . Blue Jays signed him as non-drafted free agent in May 1985.

Year	Club	Pos.	G	AB	R	H	2B	3B	HR	RBI	SB	Avg.
1990	Minnesota	OF	22	85	13	23	4	1	0	5	3	.271
1991	Minnesota	OF	51	138	15	39	7	1	7	26	3	.283
1992	Minnesota	OF	127	418	44	113	16	3	12	71	4	.270
1993	Minnesota	OF	104	326	34	76	11	1	13	38	1	.233
1994	Minnesota	OF	75	244	35	72	15	2	11	36	0	.295
1995	Minnesota	OF-1B	104	376	45	113	17	0	18	58	0	.301
	Totals		483	1587	186	436	70	8	61	234	11	.275

SCOTT STAHOVIAK 26 6-5 222 Bats L Throws R

Might have been most surprising rookie position player in a Twins season filled with youngsters . . . Batted .266 with three homers and 23 RBI in 94 games after early-season recall . . . His numbers weren't great but were encouraging enough to earn look for '96 . . . Needs to develop power because of Metrodome's short 327-foot, right-field fence . . . One of many candidates to replace Kent Hrbek at first base as Twins used 11 different first basemen in '95 . . . Made major-league minimum of $109,000 in '95 . . . Born March 6, 1970, in Waukegan, Ill. . . . Played in 1991 College World Series and led Creighton that season in batting (.456) that topped the nation in hitting . . . Drafted by Twins as a first-round sandwich pick, 27th overall, in 1991 draft.

Year	Club	Pos.	G	AB	R	H	2B	3B	HR	RBI	SB	Avg.
1993	Minnesota	3B	20	57	1	11	4	0	0	1	0	.193
1995	Minnesota	1B-2B	94	263	28	70	19	0	3	23	5	.266
	Totals		114	320	29	81	23	0	3	24	5	.253

PAUL MOLITOR 39 6-0 180 Bats R Throws R

Free agent DH comes back to home state with one-year, $2-million Twins contract with $2-million option for '97 . . . Blue Jays chose to not exercise $4-million option on him for '96 . . . Batted below .280 (.270) for first time since 1984 . . . Fifth straight season free of serious injury pushed him within 211 hits of becoming 21st player to amass 3,000 . . . Rates as likely

Hall of Famer . . . Age may be an issue, but, from 1991-94, he had more hits (777) and runs (429) than any other major-league player . . . Born Aug. 22, 1966, in St. Paul, Minn. . . . Salary last year was $4,500,000 . . . Spent 15 seasons with Milwaukee, which drafted him third overall in 1977, then went to Toronto as free agent prior to '93 season.

Year	Club	Pos.	G	AB	R	H	2B	3B	HR	RBI	SB	Avg.
1978	Milwaukee	2B-SS-3B	125	521	73	142	26	4	6	45	30	.273
1979	Milwaukee	2B-SS	140	584	88	188	27	16	9	62	33	.322
1980	Milwaukee	2B-SS-3B	111	450	81	137	29	2	9	37	34	.304
1981	Milwaukee	OF	64	251	45	67	11	0	2	19	10	.267
1982	Milwaukee	3B-SS	160	666	136	201	26	8	19	71	41	.302
1983	Milwaukee	3B	152	608	95	164	28	6	15	47	41	.269
1984	Milwaukee	3B	13	46	3	10	1	0	0	6	1	.217
1985	Milwaukee	3B	140	576	93	171	28	3	10	48	21	.297
1986	Milwaukee	3B-OF	105	437	62	123	24	6	9	55	20	.281
1987	Milwaukee	3B-2B	118	465	114	164	41	5	16	75	45	.353
1988	Milwaukee	3B-2B	154	609	115	190	34	6	13	60	41	.312
1989	Milwaukee	3B-2B	155	615	84	194	35	4	11	56	27	.315
1990	Milwaukee	2B-1B-3B	103	418	64	119	27	6	12	45	18	.285
1991	Milwaukee	1B	158	665	133	216	32	13	17	75	19	.325
1992	Milwaukee	1B	158	609	89	195	36	7	12	89	31	.320
1993	Toronto	1B	160	636	121	211	37	5	22	111	22	.332
1994	Toronto	1B	115	454	86	155	30	4	14	75	20	.341
1995	Toronto	DH	130	525	63	142	31	2	15	60	12	.270
	Totals		2261	9135	1545	2789	503	97	211	1036	466	.305

BRAD RADKE 23 6-2 186 Bats R Throws R

How does a young, inexperienced rookie become the best pitcher on a major-league staff? . . . Well, by throwing the ball over the plate and by moving it inside and out . . . Struck out 75 and walked only 47 in his debut season . . . Opponents' batting average against was .275, one of the best marks on Twins staff . . . Showed terrific composure on the mound . . . Only drawback was that he led AL pitchers in home runs allowed with 32 . . . Made Twins out of spring training after going 12-9 with 2.66 ERA for Nashville (AA) in '94 . . . Learned he had made the club when pitching coach Dick Such asked him if he owned a suit and tie (the dress code for team flights) . . . Made major-league minimum of $109,000 in '95 . . . Born Oct. 27, 1972, in Eau Claire, Wis. . . . Picked by Twins in eighth round of 1991 draft.

Year	Club	G	IP	W	L	Pct.	SO	BB	H	ERA
1995	Minnesota	29	181	11	14	.440	75	47	195	5.32

FRANK RODRIGUEZ 23 6-0 195 **Bats R Throws R**

Sports terrific fastball and decent curve, the stuff to be a dominating major-league pitcher ... Has a tendency to be wild, but Twins are hoping to fix that ... Really, he is still learning how to pitch ... Was drafted by Boston in second round in 1990 as a shortstop and converted into a pitcher in '92 ... Bounced back and forth between Red Sox rotation and bullpen in '95 before being traded to Twins July 6 with Jermaine Johnson as part of package for closer Rick Aguilera ... It was uncomfortable for him at first in Twins clubhouse because he came as part of deal that signalled the dismantling of Twins last year ... Voted top major-league prospect as a shortstop by managers in New York-Penn League in 1991 ... Was 1991 Junior College Player of the Year as a shortstop ... Led Howard Junior College to '91 national title with a 12-1 record, 2.51 ERA, .464 batting average, 25 home runs and 83 RBI ... Made major-league minimum of $109,000 in '95 ... Born Dec. 11, 1972, in Brooklyn, N.Y.

Year	Club	G	IP	W	L	Pct.	SO	BB	H	ERA
1995	Bos.-Minn.	25	105⅔	5	8	.385	59	57	114	6.13

DAVE STEVENS 25 6-3 205 **Bats R Throws R**

Bright lights are on him in '96 ... Inherited closer's role when Twins traded Rick Aguilera to Boston and converted his first seven save opportunities before blowing two of his next five chances ... Finished with 10 saves, but gave up 14 home runs in 65⅔ innings ... First batters hit .395 against him ... Twins were reluctant to officially name him as their closer for fear of putting too much pressure on him ... Twins received him and Matt Walbeck in trade with Cubs for Willie Banks prior to '94 season ... Cubs drafted him in 20th round in 1989 ... Had 6.80 ERA in '94, during his first tour of majors, before being sent back to Salt Lake (AAA) just before strike started ... Born March 4, 1970, in La Habra, Cal. ... Made $125,000 in '95.

Year	Club	G	IP	W	L	Pct.	SO	BB	H	ERA
1994	Minnesota	24	45	5	2	.714	24	23	55	6.80
1995	Minnesota	56	65⅔	5	4	.556	47	32	74	5.07
	Totals	80	110⅔	10	6	.625	71	55	129	5.77

RICK AGUILERA 34 6-5 203 Bats R Throws R

Free agent left Boston to return to Minnesota for three-year, $9-million contract in December . . . Acquired by Red Sox from Minnesota for pitching prospect Frank Rodriguez and Jermaine Johnson July 6 of last season, he helped Boston nail down AL East title . . . Solid veteran stopper who played big role in Twins' surprising 1991 world championship drive . . . Ranked among league save leaders again last year with 32 and lowered ERA (2.60) significantly from 1994 (3.63) . . . Didn't really get to show his stuff in postseason . . . Figures as starter in Tom Kelly's plans this time around . . . Born Dec. 31, 1961, in San Gabriel, Cal. . . . Salary last year was $4,300,000 . . . Mets' third-round pick in 1983 draft . . . Has 211 career saves.

Year	Club	G	IP	W	L	Pct.	SO	BB	H	ERA
1985	New York (NL)	21	122⅓	10	7	.588	74	37	118	3.24
1986	New York (NL)	28	141⅔	10	7	.588	104	36	145	3.88
1987	New York (NL)	18	115	11	3	.786	77	33	124	3.60
1988	New York (NL)	11	24⅔	0	4	.000	16	10	29	6.93
1989	New York (NL)	36	69⅓	6	6	.500	80	21	59	2.34
1989	Minnesota	11	75⅔	3	5	.375	57	17	71	3.21
1990	Minnesota	56	65⅓	5	3	.625	61	19	55	2.76
1991	Minnesota	63	69	4	5	.444	61	30	44	2.35
1992	Minnesota	64	66⅔	2	6	.250	52	17	60	2.84
1993	Minnesota	65	72⅓	4	3	.571	59	14	60	3.11
1994	Minnesota	44	44⅔	1	4	.200	46	10	57	3.63
1995	Minn.-Bos.	52	55⅓	3	3	.500	52	13	46	2.60
	Totals	469	922	59	56	.513	739	257	868	3.25

TOP PROSPECTS

LaTROY HAWKINS 23 6-5 193 Bats R Throws R

Whizzed through Twins farm system, but stumbled last year in major-league debut . . . Sent back to Salt Lake (AAA) after three rough early starts . . . Went 9-7 with a 3.55 ERA in 22 starts in minors, then returned to win two September starts and finish 2-3 with 8.67 ERA for Twins . . . Has good fastball and potential to be dominating . . . Twins' seventh-round pick in 1991 draft . . . Born Dec. 21, 1972, in Gary, Ind.

TODD WALKER 22 6-0 170 Bats L Throws R

Owns one of quickest bats in Twins organization . . . Has hit everywhere he has played . . . Batted .290 with 21 homers and 85 RBI for New Britain (AA) in '95 . . . Twins sent this second baseman to Arizona Fall League to work on third-base skills . . . A good fall and a good spring could win him spot on Twins' Opening Day roster . . . Twins drafted him seventh overall in 1994 . . . Born May 25, 1973, in Bakersfield, Cal.

MANAGER TOM KELLY: Twins' .389 winning percentage in '95 was lowest of his nine-year managerial reign . . . His skills haven't diminished. He has just gotten caught in a downward talent draft and financial squeeze . . . Twins pared payroll dramatically in '94 . . . Loss of outfielder Shane Mack, who signed to play in Japanese League, and first baseman Kent Hrbek, who retired, devastated club . . . Twins' 56-88 finish in '95 caused his career record to fall to .500, at 707-707 . . . Maneuvers role players as well as any manager in game . . . Named AL Manager of Year in '91, when Twins won second World Series in five years . . . Players still have a difficult time getting out of his doghouse . . . Replaced Ray Miller as manager, Sept. 12, 1986 . . . Had been Twins' third-base coach since 1983 . . . Three-time Manager of Year in minors from 1979-81 . . . Spent all but 49 games of 11-year playing career in minors . . . Hit .181 in 127 at-bats for Twins at end of '75 season . . . Only major-league homer came off Detroit's Vern Ruhle in Tiger Stadium in 1975 . . . Born Aug. 15, 1950, in Graceville, Minn.

ALL-TIME TWIN SEASON RECORDS

BATTING: Rod Carew, .388, 1977
HRs: Harmon Killebrew, 49, 1964, 1969
RBI: Harmon Killebrew, 140, 1969
STEALS: Rod Carew, 49, 1976
WINS: Jim Kaat, 25, 1966
STRIKEOUTS: Bert Blyleven, 258, 1973

CALIFORNIA ANGELS

TEAM DIRECTORY: Chairman: Gene Autry; Pres./CEO: Richard Brown; Exec. VP: Jackie Autry; VP-Oper.: Kevin Uhlich; GM: Bill Bavasi; Dir. Minor League Oper.: Ken Forsch; VP-Civic Affairs: Tom Seeberg; VP-Media Relations: John Sevano; Dir. Baseball Inf.: Larry Babcock; Trav. Sec.: Frank Sims; Mgr.: Marcel Lachemann; Coaches: Mick Billmeyer, Rick Burleson, Rod Carew, Chuck Hernandez, Bobby Knoop, Bill Lachemann, Joe Maddon. Home: Anaheim Stadium (64,593). Field distances: 333, l.f. line; 386, l.c.; 404, c.f.; 386, r.c.; 333, r.f. line. Spring training: Tempe, Ariz.

SCOUTING REPORT

HITTING: In a stunning development, the Angels led baseball in runs last July en route to ranking second to the Indians with

Near-perfect Angel Tim Salmon had 34 doubles, 34 HRs.

801. But, in the final two months, the roof caved in and it will be mighty interesting to see what '96 brings.

Tim Salmon (.330, 34, 105), Chili Davis (.318, 20, 86) and Jim Edmonds (.290, 33, 107) provide an excellent heart of the lineup, even though, during the Angels' historic slide, Edmonds found RBI as common as snow in Southern California. Young Garret Anderson (.321, 16, 69) has promise, but needs to prove his worth over an entire season. The defection of Tony Phillips (.261, 27, 61) via free agency doesn't help.

Gary DiSarcina (.307, 5, 41) missed significant time with a hand injury and Damion Easley was injury-prone, too, so ex-Yank Randy Velarde (.278, 2, 46) was recruited as a free agent to play the middle infield. Is DiSarcina a .300 hitter? Many think not. J.T. Snow (.289, 24, 102) had a monster year, contributing to the Angels' second-ranked total of 186 homers, but must do it again. Tim Wallach (.266, 9, 38 with the Dodgers) must prove he's not done at 38.

PITCHING: Southpaws Jim Abbott (11-8, 3.70) and Chuck Finley (15-12, 4.21)—both unsigned at press time—and Mark Langston (15-7, 4.63) were the muscle of a staff that could lose heart this year.

What's left? The Angels have been waiting for what seems like forever for Brian Anderson (6-8, 5.87) to develop. If he doesn't do anything this year, stamp him with the word "bust."

With closer Lee Smith (0-5, 3.47, 37 saves) and setup man Troy Percival (3-2, 1.95), the Angels are set in the pen. But they decided to bring back comebacking former Angel Bryan Harvey as a free agent in the hope he'll prove sound.

FIELDING: The Angels' 95 errors were the fourth-lowest total in the AL last year and that good glove work should continue.

Snow is a master at first and DiSarcina is splendid at shortstop. Easley and Velarde are more than capable at second and Wallach is dependable at third. The outfield is in good shape too, particularly with Edmonds in center and the rifle-armed Salmon in right.

OUTLOOK: This will be a difficult year. The Angels will have to live with their "choke" label left over from last year's 78-67 finish until they win something and Seattle's playoff run will give the Mariners confidence heading into this year. Unless Marcel Lachemann's Angels come up with pitching replacements, they can't expect to be a contender.

ANGEL PROFILES

TIM SALMON 27 6-3 220 Bats R Throws R

Has established himself as one of AL's premier players over past three seasons . . . Enjoyed sensational AL Rookie of the Year season in '93, but his breakthrough season came last summer, when he established career highs in average (.330), home runs (34), and RBI (105) . . . Was third in AL in batting, eighth in home runs, second in multi-hit games (55), fourth in total bases (319) and fourth in hits (177) . . . Had slugging percentage of .594 . . . Good defensive outfielder with strong arm . . . Was Angels' first-ever Rookie of the Year . . . Had 31 homers and 95 RBI in '93 despite missing final three weeks with fractured finger . . . Made $900,000 in '95 . . . Angels' third-round pick in '89 draft . . . Selected as Minor League Player of the Year in 1992 by both *The Sporting News* and *Baseball America* . . . Born Aug. 24, 1968, in Long Beach, Cal.

Year	Club	Pos.	G	AB	R	H	2B	3B	HR	RBI	SB	Avg.
1992	California	OF	23	79	8	14	1	0	2	6	1	.177
1993	California	OF	142	515	93	146	35	1	31	95	5	.283
1994	California	OF	100	373	67	107	18	2	23	70	1	.287
1995	California	OF	143	537	111	177	34	3	34	105	5	.330
	Totals		408	1504	279	444	88	6	90	276	12	.295

JIM EDMONDS 25 6-1 190 Bats L Throws L

Established himself in '95, but found himself square in the middle of Angels' historic late-season collapse . . . Was sailing along as a legitimate MVP candidate into August, then suddenly went nearly three weeks without an RBI . . . Still finished with impressive numbers (33 homers, 107 RBI), particularly in power departments . . . Strikes out too much as evidenced by 130 Ks in '95 . . . Angels cleared the way for him to take the center-field job when they traded Chad Curtis to Detroit in spring training of '95 . . . Was only Angels rookie to spend entire season on roster in '94 . . . Quite a bargain at a $117,500 salary in '95 . . . A Southern California native . . . Selected by Angels in seventh round of '88 draft . . . Born June 27, 1970, in Fullerton, Cal.

Year	Club	Pos.	G	AB	R	H	2B	3B	HR	RBI	SB	Avg.
1993	California	OF	18	61	5	15	4	1	0	4	0	.246
1994	California	OF-1B	94	289	35	79	13	1	5	37	4	.273
1995	California	OF	141	558	120	162	30	4	33	107	1	.290
	Totals		253	908	160	256	47	6	38	148	5	.282

GARY DiSARCINA 28 6-1 178 Bats R Throws R

Was having a career year, both offensively and defensively, when he suffered torn thumb ligaments shortly after the All-Star Game . . . Was limited to 99 games because of that and, although he was activated at tail end of last season, he watched helplessly while Angels let 11-game lead in AL West evaporate . . . His .307 batting average was a career high, up 47 points from his '94 mark . . . Had career average of .242 when '95 began . . . Committed only six errors in 99 games at shortstop last year . . . Made first All-Star team . . . Made $900,000 in '95 . . . Had played in 221 games in a row before pitch from Baltimore's Ben McDonald broke his thumb in '93 . . . Born Nov. 19, 1967, in Malden, Mass. . . . Boyhood hero was Larry Bird, which is why he wears No. 33 . . . Angels' sixth-round pick in '88 draft.

Year	Club	Pos.	G	AB	R	H	2B	3B	HR	RBI	SB	Avg.
1990	California	SS-2B	18	57	8	8	1	1	0	0	1	.140
1991	California	SS-2B-3B	18	57	5	12	2	0	0	3	0	.211
1992	California	SS	157	518	48	128	19	0	3	42	9	.247
1993	California	SS	126	416	44	99	20	1	3	45	5	.238
1994	California	SS	112	389	53	101	14	2	3	33	3	.260
1995	California	SS	99	362	61	111	28	6	5	41	7	.307
	Totals		530	1799	219	459	84	10	14	164	25	.255

CHILI DAVIS 36 6-3 217 Bats S Throws R

One of baseball's most popular players . . . Appears to have found eternal youth . . . His batting average in '95 was a career-high .318 . . . Has put together quite a career . . . Three-time All-Star . . . Helped lead 1991 Twins to World Series title . . . His power numbers dwindled in '92, leading Twins and most other clubs to figure he was finally slowing down . . . Wrong . . . Signed contract with Angels last summer that will take him through 1997 . . . Designated hitter was signed as free agent prior to '93 season for second go-round with California . . . He is one of eight switch-hitters in history to reach 1,000 RBI. Eddie Murray, Mickey Mantle, Ted Simmons, Pete Rose, Frankie Frisch, Reggie Smith and Ken Singleton are the others . . . Was San Francisco's 11th-round pick in '77 draft . . . Played his first six full major-league seasons with Giants . . . Made $3.8 million in '95 . . . Born Jan. 17, 1960, in Kingston, Jamaica.

Year	Club	Pos.	G	AB	R	H	2B	3B	HR	RBI	SB	Avg.
1981	San Francisco	OF	8	15	1	2	0	0	0	0	2	.133
1982	San Francisco	OF	154	641	86	167	27	6	19	76	24	.261
1983	San Francisco	OF	137	486	54	113	21	2	11	59	10	.233
1984	San Francisco	OF	137	499	87	157	21	6	21	81	12	.315
1985	San Francisco	OF	136	481	53	130	25	2	13	56	15	.270
1986	San Francisco	OF	153	526	71	146	28	3	13	70	16	.278
1987	San Francisco	OF	149	500	80	125	22	1	24	76	16	.250
1988	California	OF	158	600	81	161	29	3	21	93	9	.268
1989	California	OF	154	560	81	152	24	1	22	90	3	.271
1990	California	OF	113	412	58	109	17	1	12	58	1	.265
1991	Minnesota	OF	153	534	84	148	34	1	29	93	5	.277
1992	Minnesota	OF-1B	138	444	63	128	27	2	12	66	4	.288
1993	California	DH	153	573	74	139	32	0	27	112	4	.243
1994	California	OF	108	392	72	122	18	1	26	84	3	.311
1995	California	DH	119	424	81	135	23	0	20	86	3	.318
	Totals		1970	7087	1026	1934	348	29	270	1100	127	.273

J.T. SNOW 28 6-2 202 **Bats S Throws L**

Everything finally came together for him in '95 . . . After inconsistent previous two seasons that included stints in minors, he finally kept his average up there (.289), whacked his share of home runs (24) and nearly doubled his career RBI high of 57 in '93 with 102 . . . Terrific defensive first baseman who committed only four errors in 143 games . . . Slugging percentage was .465 last year . . . Broke onto the scene in a big way in '93, homering on Opening Day in Anaheim, but his average dipped badly and he found himself at Vancouver (AAA) before season's end . . . Son of former Los Angeles Ram receiver Jack Snow . . . Made $200,000 in '95 . . . Acquired by Angels from Yankees with Russ Springer and Jerry Nielsen for Jim Abbott prior to '93 season . . . Yankees' fifth-round pick in 1989 draft . . . Born Feb. 26, 1968, in Long Beach, Cal. . . . Won first Gold Glove last year.

Year	Club	Pos.	G	AB	R	H	2B	3B	HR	RBI	SB	Avg.
1992	New York (AL)	1B	7	14	1	2	1	0	0	2	0	.143
1993	California	1B	129	419	60	101	18	2	16	57	3	.241
1994	California	1B	61	223	22	49	4	0	8	30	0	.220
1995	California	1B	143	544	80	157	22	1	24	102	2	.289
	Totals		340	1200	163	309	45	3	48	191	5	.258

GARRET ANDERSON 23 6-3 190 Bats L Throws L

Remained in AL Rookie of the Year race all summer . . . Opened season on roster, didn't play much and was optioned to Vancouver (AAA), where he hit .311 with no homers and 12 RBI in 61 at-bats . . . Was recalled in May and immediately won left-field job . . . Slumped toward end of last season as Angels swooned, but still finished with .321 average, 16 homers and 69 RBI . . . His 16 home runs were career high at any professional level . . . Was erratic defensively at times last summer . . . Has tendency to let mind wander . . . Angels are expecting big things from him in '96, which should be his first full season in majors . . . Made major-league minimum of $109,000 in '95 . . . Angels' fourth-round pick in '90 draft . . . Born June 30, 1972, in Los Angeles.

Year	Club	Pos.	G	AB	R	H	2B	3B	HR	RBI	SB	Avg.
1994	California	OF	5	13	0	5	0	0	0	1	0	.385
1995	California	OF	106	374	50	120	19	1	16	69	6	.321
	Totals		111	387	50	125	19	1	16	70	6	.323

DAMION EASLEY 26 5-11 185 Bats R Throws R

Has a lot of promise but, unfortunately, the Angels can never keep him in lineup . . . More fragile than an egg . . . Subbed at shortstop while Gary DiSarcina was out and helped, but he will remain at second base if he can ward off challenge from Randy Velarde . . . Played in career-high 114 games . . . Has hit .216 and .215 in the past two seasons . . . Appeared in 47 of California's first 51 games in '94 before being placed on disabled list with inflamed right shoulder . . . Missed much of '93 because of severe shin splint . . . Best stretch of his career was in '92, when he hit .258 with 12 RBI and nine stolen bases in 47 late-season games . . . Made $170,000 in '95 . . . Angels' 30th-round pick in '88 draft, out of Long Beach City College . . . Born Nov. 11, 1969, in New York City.

Year	Club	Pos.	G	AB	R	H	2B	3B	HR	RBI	SB	Avg.
1992	California	3B-SS	47	151	14	39	5	0	1	12	9	.258
1993	California	2B-3B	73	230	33	72	13	2	2	22	6	.313
1994	California	3B-2B	88	316	41	68	16	1	6	30	4	.215
1995	California	2B-SS	114	357	35	77	14	2	4	35	5	.216
	Totals		322	1054	123	256	48	5	13	99	24	.243

Jim Edmonds was tops among three 100-RBI Angels with 107.

RANDY VELARDE 33 6-1 198 Bats L Throws R

Yankees wouldn't give him a full-time job, so this versatile free agent accepted three-year, $2.45-million contract to play second base for Angels . . . Started 104 games at four positions, including 53 at second last season . . . Made 10 errors . . . Batted .293 in final 35 games . . . Was 19th-round pick by White Sox in 1985 draft . . . Was traded to Yankees with Pete Filson for Scott Nielsen and Mike Soper in January 1987 . . . Born Nov. 24, 1962, in Lubbock, Tex . . . Earned $350,000 last year.

Year	Club	Pos.	G	AB	R	H	2B	3B	HR	RBI	SB	Avg.
1987	New York (AL)	SS	8	22	1	4	0	0	0	1	0	.182
1988	New York (AL)	SS-2B-3B	48	115	18	20	6	0	5	12	1	.174
1989	New York (AL)	3B-SS	33	100	12	34	4	2	2	11	0	.340
1990	New York (AL)	SS-SB-OF-3B	95	229	21	48	6	2	5	19	0	.210
1991	New York (AL)	3B-SS-OF	80	184	19	45	11	1	1	15	3	.245
1992	New York (AL)	SS-3B-OF-2B	121	412	57	112	24	1	7	46	7	.272
1993	New York (AL)	OF-SS-2B	85	226	28	68	13	2	7	24	2	.301
1994	New York (AL)	SS-2B-3B-OF	77	280	47	78	16	1	9	34	4	.279
1995	New York (AL)	SS-2B-3B-OF	111	367	60	102	19	1	7	46	5	.278
	Totals		658	1935	263	511	99	10	43	208	22	.264

MARK LANGSTON 35 6-2 184 Bats R Throws L

Last year was heartbreaking for this veteran, who is running out of time to pitch in postseason . . . Was Angels' starter and loser in memorable one-game playoff with Seattle to determine AL West champion . . . Last year was first time in his 12-year major-league career he pitched for team that finished above .500 . . . Has posted ERA of more than 4.00 for two consecutive years . . . Stumbled down the stretch, partly, he said, because of tendinitis in throwing arm . . . Workhorse . . . Has pitched 200-or-more innings in nine of last 10 years . . . Was highest-salaried player on Angels last year at $5 million . . . Signed as free agent with Angels prior to '90 season and his current contract runs through '97 . . . Mariners drafted him in third round in 1981 . . . Traded from Seattle to Montreal for Randy Johnson, Gene Harris and Brian Holman, May 25, 1989 . . . Born Aug. 20, 1960, in San Diego . . . Added seventh Gold Glove last year.

Year	Club	G	IP	W	L	Pct.	SO	BB	H	ERA
1984	Seattle	35	225	17	10	.630	204	118	188	3.40
1985	Seattle	24	126⅔	7	14	.333	72	91	122	5.47
1986	Seattle	37	239⅓	12	14	.452	245	123	234	4.85
1987	Seattle	35	272	19	13	.594	262	114	242	3.84
1988	Seattle	35	261⅓	15	11	.577	235	110	222	3.34
1989	Seattle	10	73⅓	4	5	.444	60	19	60	3.56
1989	Montreal	24	176⅔	12	9	.571	175	93	138	2.39
1990	California	33	223	10	17	.370	195	104	215	4.40
1991	California	34	246⅓	19	8	.704	183	96	190	3.00
1992	California	32	229	13	14	.481	174	74	206	3.66
1993	California	35	256⅓	16	11	.593	196	85	220	3.20
1994	California	18	119⅓	7	8	.467	109	54	121	4.68
1995	California	31	200⅓	15	7	.682	142	64	212	4.63
	Totals	383	2648⅔	166	141	.541	2252	1145	2370	3.81

LEE SMITH 38 6-6 269 Bats R Throws R

Ranked second in AL with 37 saves in '95 . . . Hasn't had fewer than 33 since 1990 . . . Owns major-league record with 473 saves . . . Has arguably the slowest walk from the bullpen to the mound in major-league history. It has been timed at nearly two minutes . . . One of only two closers in history to collect at least 40 saves in three consecutive seasons (1991-93). Dennis Eckersley is the other . . . A certain Hall of Famer . . . An expert on how to pack as he has now worked for six organizations . . . Made $1.9 million in '95, on first year of two-year contract which he signed as free agent . . . Born Dec. 4, 1957, in Jamestown, La. . . . An all-state high school basketball player, he played guard at Northwestern (La.) State . . . Was Cubs' second-round pick in '75 draft.

Year	Club	G	IP	W	L	Pct.	SO	BB	H	ERA
1980	Chicago (NL)	18	22	2	0	1.000	17	14	21	2.86
1981	Chicago (NL)	40	67	3	6	.333	50	31	57	3.49
1982	Chicago (NL)	72	117	2	5	.286	99	37	105	2.69
1983	Chicago (NL)	66	103⅓	4	10	.286	91	41	70	1.65
1984	Chicago (NL)	69	101	9	7	.563	86	35	98	3.65
1985	Chicago (NL)	65	97⅔	7	4	.636	112	32	87	3.04
1986	Chicago (NL)	66	90⅓	9	9	.500	93	42	69	3.09
1987	Chicago (NL)	62	83⅔	4	10	.286	96	32	84	3.12
1988	Boston	64	83⅔	4	5	.444	96	37	72	2.80
1989	Boston	64	70⅔	6	1	.857	96	33	53	3.57
1990	Boston	11	14⅓	2	1	.667	17	9	13	1.88
1990	St. Louis	53	68⅔	3	4	.429	70	20	58	2.10
1991	St. Louis	67	73	6	3	.667	67	13	70	2.34
1992	St. Louis	70	75	4	9	.308	60	26	62	3.12
1993	St. Louis	55	50	2	4	.333	49	9	49	4.50
1993	New York (AL)	8	8	0	0	.000	11	5	4	0.00
1994	Baltimore	41	38⅓	1	4	.200	42	11	34	3.29
1995	California	52	49⅓	0	5	.000	43	25	42	3.47
	Totals	943	1213	68	87	.439	1195	452	1048	2.95

TOP PROSPECTS

TODD GREENE 24 5-9 195 **Bats R Throws R**

Ranks as third-leading home-run hitter in NCAA history . . . This catcher was named league MVP in each of his first two seasons in minors . . . Hit total of 40 homers for Midland (AA) and Vancouver (AAA) in '95, most of any player in minors since Danny Tartabull hit 40 in '85 . . . Hit .327 with 26 homers and 57 RBI for Midland and .250 with 14 homers and 35 RBI for Vancouver . . . Angels' 12th-round selection in '93 draft, out of Georgia Southern . . . Born May 8, 1971, in Augusta, Ga.

GEORGE ARIAS 24 5-11 190 Bats R Throws R

Strong third-base prospect . . . Hit .279 with 30 homers and 104 RBI for Midland (AA) in '95 . . . Not only that, he is a slick fielder . . . Has hit 53 homers over past two minor-league seasons . . . Angels' seventh-round selection in '93 draft, out of Arizona . . . Born March 12, 1972, in Tucson, Ariz.

EDUARDO PEREZ 26 6-4 215 Bats R Throws R

Angels' Opening Day first baseman in '94, but his career so far has been a study in frustration . . . Played in only 29 games for Angels in '95, batting .169 with one home run and seven RBI . . . Hit .325 with six homers and 37 RBI for Vancouver (AAA) in '95 . . . Can play first, third and the outfield and has good bloodlines as the son of former great Tony . . . Angels' first-round pick in '91 draft, out of Florida State . . . Born Sept. 11, 1969, in Cincinnati.

JORGE FABREGAS 26 6-3 205 Bats L Throws R

Has spent parts of past two seasons with Angels . . . Bats left-handed, which can be a plus for a catcher . . . Hit .247 with one homer and 22 RBI for Angels in '95, after hitting .283 with no homers and 16 RBI for them in '94 . . . Hit .247 with four homers and 10 RBI for Vancouver (AAA) last season. . . . Angels' first-round pick in '91 draft, out of Miami . . . Born March 13, 1970, in Miami.

MANAGER MARCEL LACHEMANN: Couldn't right the Angels' sinking ship in '95 and watched huge 11-game lead in August disappear . . . Still, he gained respect of peers by transforming a poor '94 club into contender last year with mostly the same talent . . . Longtime major-league pitching coach . . . Left that role with his brother Rene's Florida club to take over as manager of Angels, May 17, 1994 . . . Became California's 15th different manager and eighth to assume club leadership with no previous managerial experience . . . Replaced Buck Rodgers . . . He and Rene are first set of brothers to manage in majors since Harry and George Wright managed against each other in 1879. Harry managed Providence and George managed

Boston in NL . . . Brother Bill is bullpen coach, marking first time three brothers have been either major-league coaches or managers somewhere in same season since Boyer trio in '80. Ken was St. Louis manager, Cloyd was Atlanta coach and Clete was Oakland coach . . . Angels' 78-66 mark in '95 leaves him with lifetime record of 108-110 . . . Had been with Angels' organization for 11 years, including nine as major-league pitching coach, before leaving for Florida . . . Born June 13, 1941, in Los Angeles.

ALL-TIME ANGEL SEASON RECORDS

BATTING: Rod Carew, .339, 1983
HRs: Reggie Jackson, 39, 1982
RBI: Don Baylor, 139, 1979
STEALS: Mickey Rivers, 70, 1975
WINS: Clyde Wright, 22, 1970
Nolan Ryan, 22, 1974
STRIKEOUTS: Nolan Ryan, 383, 1973

OAKLAND ATHLETICS

TEAM DIRECTORY: Pres.: Steve Schott; Pres. Strategic Planning: Ken Hoffman; Exec. VP-Adm.: Ed Alvarez; GM: Sandy Alderson; Dir. Player Dev.: Keith Lieppman; Dir. Scouting: Grady Fuson; Dir. Pub. Rel.; Jim Bloom; Media Rel. Mgr.: Ted Santiago; Baseball Inf. Mgr.: Mike Selleck; Trav. Sec.: Mickey Morabito; Mgr.: Art Howe; Coaches: Bob Clack, Duffy Dyer, Brad Fischer, Denny Walling, Ron Washington. Home: Oakland Coliseum (47,313). Field distances: 330, l.f. line; 375, l.c.; 400, c.f.; 375, r.c.; 330, r.f. line. Spring training: Phoenix, Ariz.

SCOUTING REPORT

HITTING: The Swingin' Athletics don't swing quite as well nowadays as their predecessors did in the 1980s. They managed a middle-of-the-pack 730 runs in '95. Still, they have the sticks to make things interesting.

Consider a lineup that might feature a healthy Mark McGwire (.274, 39, 90) and Danny Tartabull (.236, 8, 35), a fearless Geronimo Berroa (.278, 22, 88), a steady Terry Steinbach (.278, 15, 65) and the offensively solid double-play combination of Mike Bordick (.264, 8, 44) and Brent Gates (.254, 5, 56).

But there won't be a Rickey Henderson (.300, 9, 54, 32 steals), because he was not re-signed last winter. But if Tartabull, sidelined by a bad back for much of '95, can stay healthy and produce, that will be a huge plus for new manager Art Howe.

PITCHING: The arms got old in a hurry in '95 and, as a result, the '96 Athletics may still be paying the price.

Dave Stewart (3-7, 6.89) was so ineffective he was forced to retire in midseason. Ron Darling (4-7, 6.23) was dropped from the rotation and then just dropped. Steve Ontiveros (9-6, 4.37) broke down after a first half that was so good he was named to the All-Star team and was not re-signed.

Out of the shambles of a '95 season that produced a 12th-ranked 4.93 ERA, the A's will try to resurrect something to keep them in contention. Todd Stottlemyre (14-7, 4.55, 205 Ks) was mostly effective and his blazing fastball will help any staff, which explains why his name surfaced in trade talks last winter. Todd Van Poppel (4-8, 4.88) showed some late-season signs of life. Young Ariel Prieto (2-6, 4.97) should get off to a better start once he has a full spring training.

Re-signed closer Dennis Eckersley (4-6, 4.83, 29 saves) is getting older, but is still effective.

Mark McGwire was reborn Bash Brother with 39 homers.

FIELDING: Steinbach remains one of the AL's most solid catchers defensively. First baseman McGwire is vastly underrated defensively and Gates and Bordick form a respectable pair up the middle.

Overall, the Athletics committed 102 errors in '95, placing them in the middle of the pack defensively in the AL. Without Henderson and Stan Javier, the outfield is in deep trouble, with only the questionable Tartabull and Berroa remaining for flyball duty.

OUTLOOK: This is a vanilla team—reasonably solid, but not solid enough to win. Oakland, 67-77 in '95, could use more pitching for starters, outfield help and more punch in its lineup. And, as always, McGwire's health in particular, remains a key.

ATHLETIC PROFILES

MARK McGWIRE 32 6-5 250 Bats R Throws R

Tied for fourth in AL with 39 home runs, his most since slugging 42 in '92 . . . Spent more time on disabled list in '95, a yearly occurrence for him. But his 104 games played were most since 1992 . . . He played in only 47 games in '94 and 27 in '93 . . . Averaged 38 homers and 105 RBI from 1987-90 . . . Oakland's chances to win AL West usually hinge on his health . . . Made $6.9 million in '95, on third year of a five-year contract . . . With new owners taking over and his contract being expensive, this first baseman said he expects he will finish his career elsewhere . . . Unanimous AL Rookie of the Year pick in 1987, when he debuted with 49 homers, leading league and tying for major-league high with Cubs' Andre Dawson . . . Only second unanimous Rookie of the Year selection. Carlton Fisk was the first, in 1972 . . . Oakland picked him 10th overall in '84 draft . . . Was member of 1984 U.S. Olympic team . . . Born Oct. 1, 1963, in Pomona, Cal.

Year	Club	Pos.	G	AB	R	H	2B	3B	HR	RBI	SB	Avg.
1986	Oakland	3B	18	53	10	10	1	0	3	9	0	.189
1987	Oakland	1B-3B-OF	151	557	97	161	28	4	49	118	1	.289
1988	Oakland	1B-OF	155	550	87	143	22	1	32	99	0	.260
1989	Oakland	1B	143	490	74	113	17	0	33	95	1	.231
1990	Oakland	1B	156	523	87	123	16	0	39	108	2	.235
1991	Oakland	1B	154	483	62	97	22	0	22	75	2	.201
1992	Oakland	1B	139	467	87	125	22	0	42	104	0	.268
1983	Oakland	1B	27	84	16	28	6	0	9	24	0	.333
1994	Oakland	1B	47	135	26	34	3	0	9	25	0	.252
1995	Oakland	1B	104	317	75	87	13	0	39	90	1	.274
	Totals		1094	3659	621	921	150	5	277	747	7	.252

GERONIMO BERROA 31 6-0 195 Bats R Throws R

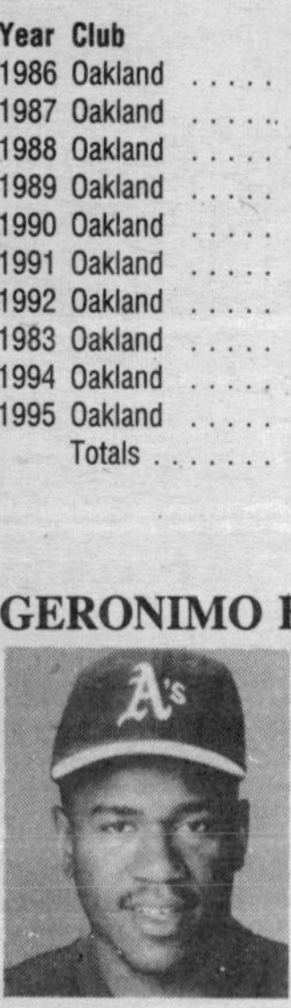

One of baseball's best perseverance stories . . . Is now with his seventh organization since signing as non-drafted free agent with Toronto in September 1983 . . . Had only two complete major-league seasons under his belt going into '95, but guess who led Oakland with 141 games played? . . . Has established himself as a feared hitter who will crush mistake pitches . . . His 22 homers and 88 RBI in '95 were both career highs, by far

Todd Stottlemyre won 14 as A's imported ace.

... Best as designated hitter, because his fielding in outfield is mediocre, at best ... Stopped in seven different minor-league cities before finally reaching majors for first time with Atlanta in 1989 ... Braves selected him in Rule V draft from Toronto, then he was released, signed with Seattle organization, was sold to Cleveland, signed with Cincinnati organization as a free agent, was released, signed with Florida, and finally signed with Oakland as a free agent prior to '94 season ... Whew ... Made $235,000 in '95 ... Born March 18, 1965, in Santo Domingo, D.R.

Year	Club	Pos.	G	AB	R	H	2B	3B	HR	RBI	SB	Avg.
1989	Atlanta	OF	81	136	7	36	4	0	2	9	0	.265
1990	Atlanta	OF	7	4	0	0	0	0	0	0	0	.000
1992	Cincinnati	OF	13	15	2	4	1	0	0	0	0	.267
1993	Florida	OF	14	34	3	4	1	0	0	0	0	.118
1994	Oakland	OF-1B-DH	96	340	55	104	18	2	13	65	7	.306
1995	Oakland	OF	141	546	87	152	22	3	22	88	7	.278
	Totals		252	1075	154	300	46	5	37	162	14	.279

TERRY STEINBACH 34 6-1 195 Bats R Throws R

Getting older, but he remains a steady player, both offensively and defensively ... His 15 homers were his most since hitting 16 in '87 and his 65 RBI were his most since he drove in 67 in '91 ... His .278 batting average was tied for third-highest on team ... Always ranks near top of league among catchers in throwing out would-be base-stealers ... Personable player representative and clubhouse leader ... Made $4.2 million in '95 and is signed through this season ... Batted .333 with a homer and seven RBI in 1992 ALCS vs. Toronto ... Four-time All-Star ... Oakland's ninth-round pick in '83 draft, out of University of Minnesota ... Born March 2, 1962, in New Ulm, Minn.

Year	Club	Pos.	G	AB	R	H	2B	3B	HR	RBI	SB	Avg.
1986	Oakland	C	6	15	3	5	0	0	2	4	0	.333
1987	Oakland	C-3B-1B	122	391	66	111	16	3	16	56	1	.284
1988	Oakland	C-3B-1B-OF	104	351	42	93	19	1	9	51	3	.265
1989	Oakland	C-OF-1B--3B	130	454	37	124	13	1	7	42	1	.273
1990	Oakland	C-1B	114	379	32	95	15	2	9	57	0	.251
1991	Oakland	C-1B	129	456	50	125	31	1	6	67	2	.274
1992	Oakland	C-1B	128	438	48	122	20	1	12	53	2	.279
1993	Oakland	C-1B	104	389	47	111	19	1	10	43	3	.285
1994	Oakland	C-1B	103	369	51	105	21	2	11	57	2	.285
1995	Oakland	C-1B	114	406	43	113	26	1	15	65	1	.278
	Totals		1054	3648	419	1004	180	13	97	495	15	.275

DANNY TARTABULL 33 6-1 204 Bats R Throws R

Here's another guy who became disgusted with life as a Yankee . . . His falling out of Yankee favor crystallized in '95, when he suffered a rib injury that owner George Steinbrenner didn't think was real . . . Outfielder was finally traded to Oakland for another unhappy camper, Ruben Sierra, July 28 . . . Mainly because of those rib troubles, he played in only 83 games . . . It was his second straight disappointing season in New York . . . Got off to a slow start in '94, hitting only .233 and leaving lots of base-runners, until he was temporarily dropped from fourth to sixth in the lineup . . . Then he picked it up and finished at .256 . . . A high fastball hitter . . . Struck out 82 times in 280 at-bats in '95 . . . Made $5.3 million in '95 . . . Born Oct. 30, 1962, in Miami.

Year	Club	Pos.	G	AB	R	H	2B	3B	HR	RBI	SB	Avg.
1984	Seattle	SS-2B	10	20	3	6	1	0	2	7	0	.300
1985	Seattle	SS-3B	19	61	8	20	7	1	1	7	1	.328
1986	Seattle	OF-2B-3B	137	511	76	138	25	6	25	96	4	.270
1987	Kansas City . . .	OF	158	582	95	180	27	3	34	101	9	.309
1988	Kansas City . . .	OF	146	507	80	139	38	3	26	102	8	.274
1989	Kansas City . . .	OF	133	441	54	118	22	0	18	62	4	.268
1990	Kansas City . . .	OF	88	313	41	84	19	0	15	60	1	.268
1991	Kansas City . . .	OF	132	484	78	153	35	3	31	100	6	.316
1992	New York (AL)	OF	123	421	72	112	19	0	25	85	2	.266
1993	New York (AL)	OF	138	513	87	128	33	2	31	102	0	.250
1994	New York (AL)	OF	104	399	68	102	24	1	19	67	1	.256
1995	NY (AL)-Oak. . .	OF	83	280	34	66	16	0	8	35	0	.236
	Totals		1271	4532	696	1246	266	19	235	824	36	.275

MIKE BORDICK 30 5-11 175 Bats R Throws R

Endured poor start, suffering early sprained ankle, but he rebounded nicely . . . His .264 average was his highest since he hit .300 in '92 . . . Slick defensively at shortstop . . . Committed 10 errors in 126 games . . . Made only 13 errors in 112 games at short and one error at second in '94 . . . Was fourth on team in at-bats with 428 in '95 . . . True shortstop who directs the infield . . . Made $1.35 million in '95 . . . Was signed by Oakland as non-drafted free agent in July 1986 . . . Was recalled in June 1991, when Walt Weiss was injured, and ended up starting

81 of 85 games . . . Oakland traded Weiss the next year to clear the way for him . . . Played three years at the University of Maine, appearing in two College World Series . . . Born July 21, 1965, in Marquette, Mich.

Year	Club	Pos.	G	AB	R	H	2B	3B	HR	RBI	SB	Avg.
1990	Oakland	3B-SS-2B	25	14	0	1	0	0	0	0	0	.071
1991	Oakland	SS-2B-3B	90	235	21	56	5	1	0	21	3	.238
1992	Oakland	2B-SS	154	504	62	151	19	4	3	48	12	.300
1993	Oakland	SS-2B	159	546	60	136	21	2	3	48	10	.249
1994	Oakland	SS-2B	114	391	38	99	18	4	2	37	7	.253
1995	Oakland	SS	126	428	46	113	13	0	8	44	11	.264
	Totals		668	2118	227	556	76	11	16	198	43	.263

BRENT GATES 26 6-1 180 Bats S Throws R

Was finally blessed with good health in '95 . . . Played in 136 games after suiting up for only 64 in '94, because of an assortment of injuries . . . Not flashy, but he is solid . . . Should solidify Oakland's second-base situation for at least the next few years . . . Was AL Rookie of the Year candidate in '93, after moving from Huntsville (AA) to Tacoma (AAA) to Oakland in whirlwind five weeks . . . His .290 average in 1990 represents club record for a switch-hitter . . . Made $190,000 in '95 . . . Oakland drafted him 26th overall in '91 . . . Born March 14, 1970, in Grand Rapids, Mich. . . . Along with Terry Steinbach, he is one of two University of Minnesota products on Athletics roster.

Year	Club	Pos.	G	AB	R	H	2B	3B	HR	RBI	SB	Avg.
1993	Oakland	2B	139	535	64	155	29	2	7	69	7	.290
1994	Oakland	2B-1B	64	233	29	66	11	1	2	24	3	.283
1995	Oakland	2B-1B	136	524	60	133	24	4	5	56	3	.254
	Totals		339	1292	153	354	64	7	14	149	13	.274

TODD STOTTLEMYRE 30 6-3 200 Bats L Throws R

Arrived just in time to see end of Oakland's AL West dominance . . . Became one of Oakland's few dependable starters after leaving Blue Jays and signing with Athletics as free agent April 10 of last season . . . Led team with 31 starts and finished second in AL with 205 strikeouts . . . His 14 wins were second-highest total of his career . . . His ERA has been over

4.00 in five of his last six big-league seasons . . . Seven games over .500 record of 14-7 was his best showing since '91 . . . Scouts drool over his stuff and can't figure out why he doesn't dominate more often . . . Throws fastball, change-up, curve and slider . . . Son of former major-league pitcher Mel . . . Attended UNLV . . . Picked by Toronto in secondary phase of '85 draft . . . Made $1.8 million in '95 . . . Born May 20, 1965, in Yakima, Wash.

Year	Club	G	IP	W	L	Pct.	SO	BB	H	ERA
1988	Toronto	28	98	4	8	.333	67	46	109	5.69
1989	Toronto	27	127⅔	7	7	.500	63	44	137	3.88
1990	Toronto	33	203	13	17	.433	115	69	214	4.34
1991	Toronto	34	219	15	8	.652	116	75	194	3.78
1992	Toronto	28	174	12	11	.522	98	63	175	4.50
1993	Toronto	30	176⅔	11	12	.478	98	69	204	4.84
1994	Toronto	26	140⅔	7	7	.500	105	48	149	4.22
1995	Oakland	31	209⅔	14	7	.667	205	80	228	4.55
	Totals	237	1348⅔	83	77	.519	867	494	1410	4.41

DENNIS ECKERSLEY 41 6-2 195 Bats R Throws R

The end is coming closer for one of greatest closers ever . . . Re-signed with Athletics after last season, when he finished seventh in AL with 29 saves . . . That total was improvement over 19 in strike-shortened '94 . . . His ERA was above 4.00 for third consecutive season, at 4.83 . . . Five-year run from 1988-92 was greatest ever by a reliever . . . Won both AL Cy Young and MVP in 1992, when he saved 51 of 54 games. He is one of only five relievers to win those awards in same year . . . Owns AL saves record with 323 . . . What a career . . . Was starter when he broke in with Cleveland in '75 . . . Has pitched a no-hitter, has been a 20-game winner and has battled alcohol addiction . . . Made $2.45 million in '95 . . . Came to Athletics in another legendary bad Cubs trade . . . Oakland got him with Dan Rohn for Dave Wilder, Brian Guinn and Mark Leonette prior to

'87 season . . . Born Oct. 3, 1954, in Oakland . . . Indians drafted him in third round in 1972.

Year	Club	G	IP	W	L	Pct.	SO	BB	H	ERA
1975	Cleveland	34	187	13	7	.650	152	90	147	2.60
1976	Cleveland	36	199	13	12	.520	200	75	155	3.44
1977	Cleveland	33	247	14	13	.519	191	54	214	3.53
1978	Boston	35	268	20	8	.714	162	71	258	2.99
1979	Boston	33	247	17	10	.630	150	59	234	2.99
1980	Boston	30	198	12	14	.462	121	44	188	4.27
1981	Boston	23	154	9	8	.529	79	35	160	4.27
1982	Boston	33	224⅓	13	13	.500	127	43	228	3.73
1983	Boston	28	176⅓	9	13	.409	77	39	223	5.61
1984	Boston	9	64⅔	4	4	.500	33	13	71	5.01
1984	Chicago (NL)	24	160⅓	10	8	.556	81	36	152	3.03
1985	Chicago (NL)	25	169⅓	11	7	.611	117	19	145	3.08
1986	Chicago (NL)	33	201	6	11	.353	137	43	226	4.57
1987	Oakland	54	115⅔	6	8	.429	113	17	99	3.03
1988	Oakland	60	72⅔	4	2	.667	70	11	52	2.35
1989	Oakland	51	57⅔	4	0	1.000	55	3	32	1.56
1990	Oakland	63	73⅓	4	2	.667	73	4	41	0.61
1991	Oakland	67	76	5	4	.556	87	9	60	2.96
1992	Oakland	69	80	7	1	.875	93	11	62	1.91
1993	Oakland	64	67	2	4	.333	80	13	67	4.16
1994	Oakland	45	44⅓	5	4	.556	47	13	49	4.26
1995	Oakland	52	50⅓	4	6	.400	40	11	53	4.83
	Totals	901	3133	192	159	.547	2285	716	2916	3.48

TODD VAN POPPEL 24 6-5 210 Bats R Throws R

He's in the rotation, he's out, he's in . . . Finished last season on a high note . . . Started in 14 of his 36 games . . . His 4-8 record and 4.88 ERA weren't spectacular, but he probably earned another shot at rotation in '96 . . . Control problems have led to disappointing start to career . . . Was 7-10 with 6.09 ERA in '94 . . . Walked more batters (89) than he struck out (83) in '94, but turned that around last year. In 1995, he struck out 122 and walked 56 . . . Should have spent more time in minors . . . His agent's insistence on a major-league contract when he first signed has backfired . . . Made $397,000 in '95 . . . Received stunning $1.2-million deal when Oakland picked him 14th overall in 1990 draft and talked him out of taking scholarship at University of Texas . . . Born Dec. 9, 1971, in Hinsdale, Ill.

Year	Club	G	IP	W	L	Pct.	SO	BB	H	ERA
1991	Oakland	1	4⅔	0	0	.000	6	2	7	9.64
1993	Oakland	16	84	6	6	.500	47	62	76	5.04
1994	Oakland	23	116⅔	7	10	.412	83	89	108	6.09
1995	Oakland	36	138⅓	4	8	.333	122	56	125	4.88
	Totals	76	343⅔	17	24	.415	258	209	316	5.39

TOP PROSPECTS

ARIEL PRIETO 26 6-3 225 Bats R Throws R

Cuban sensation became one of best stories in baseball last year, after gaining citizenship and becoming Oakland's first-round draft pick . . . Joined rotation by August . . . Went 2-6 with 4.97 ERA in nine starts . . . Still has some maturing to do . . . Struck out 37, but walked 32 in 58 innings . . . Throws hard and has ability to become a dominant major-league pitcher soon . . . Born Oct. 22, 1969, in Havana, Cuba.

JASON GIAMBI 25 6-2 200 Bats L Throws R

Got into 54 games with Athletics, many at first base when Mark McGwire was on disabled list, and did well . . . Hit .256 with six homers and 25 RBI for Athletics and .342 with three homers and 41 RBI for Edmonton (AAA) in '95 . . . Can play third base . . . Oakland's second-round pick in '92 draft, out of Long Beach State . . . Born Jan. 8, 1971, in West Covina, Cal.

JOHN WASDIN 23 6-2 190 Bats R Throws R

Went 12-8 with 5.52 ERA for Edmonton (AAA), in hitter-friendly Pacific Coast League in '95 . . . Gave up 193 hits in 174 innings, but struck out 111 and walked only 38 . . . Started two games for Oakland after late-season call-up . . . In five total appearances, he went 1-1 with 4.67 ERA . . . Oakland's first-round pick in '93 draft, out of Florida State . . . Owns good fastball and breaking ball . . . Born Aug. 5, 1972, in Fort Belvoir, Va.

BRIAN LESHER 25 6-5 205 Bats R Throws L

Set a career high with 19 homers for Huntsville (AA) in '95 . . . Outfielder is still a couple of years away . . . Needs more upper-body strength . . . Decent defensively . . . Hit .261 with 71 RBI in 471 at-bats last year . . . Big thing, given his size, is to develop power . . . If he doesn't, he'll never make it to Oakland team that needs more Bash Brothers . . . Born March 5, 1971, in Belgium . . . Athletics drafted him in 25th round in '92, out of University of Delaware.

MANAGER ART HOWE: Named to replace Tony La Russa last fall as 14th manager of Oakland . . . Arrived fresh from batting and first-base coaching role with the Rockies . . . Managed Astros from 1989-93, compiling 392-418 record . . . Best seasons were in 1989 (86-76) and '93 (85-77) . . . As a major-league infielder for a decade with Pittsburgh, Houston and St. Louis, he was a .260 career hitter . . . Played with Astros' first-ever division winner in 1980 . . . His homer, two singles and four RBI led to team's title win over Dodgers in a one-game playoff . . . Born Dec. 15, 1946, in Pittsburgh, he's a graduate of Wyoming, where he starred in baseball and even had a year as a quarterback until a back injury finished his football career . . . After college, he was working as a computer programmer for Westinghouse when a friend convinced him to attend a Pirates tryout camp.

ALL-TIME A's SEASON RECORDS

BATTING: Napoleon Lajoie, .422, 1901
HRs: Jimmie Foxx, 58, 1932
RBI: Jimmie Foxx, 169, 1932
STEALS: Rickey Henderson, 130, 1982
WINS: John Coombs, 31, 1910
Lefty Grove, 31, 1931
STRIKEOUTS: Rube Waddell, 349, 1904

SEATTLE MARINERS

TEAM DIRECTORY: Chairman: John Ellis; Pres.: Chuck Armstrong; VP-Baseball Oper.: Woody Woodward; VP-Scouting and Player Dev.: Roger Jongewaard; Dir. Baseball Adm.: Lee Pelekoudas; Dir. Player Dev.: Larry Beinfest; Dir. Pub. Rel.: David Aust; Trav. Sec.: Craig Detwiler; Mgr.: Lou Piniella; Coaches: Bobby Cuellar, Lee Elia, John McLaren, Sam Mejias, Matt Sinatro, Steve Smith. Home: Kingdome (59,166). Field distances: 331, l.f. line; 389, l.c.; 405, c.f.; 380, r.c.; 312, r.f. line. Spring training: Peoria, Ariz.

SCOUTING REPORT

HITTING: While all the talk centered around the Angels until September, the Mariners proved they pack as potent a lineup as any in the West en route to ranking third in the AL with 796 runs and third with 182 homers.

Knees buckle when The Big Unit is dealing his heat.

With AL batting champ Edgar Martinez (.356, 29, 113), superstar Ken Griffey Jr. (.258, 17, 42) and powerful Jay Buhner (.262, 40, 121) in a tandem, there is no room to pitch around anyone in the heart of the Mariners' order. Joey Cora (.297, 18 steals) and Luis Sojo (.289, 7, 39) pack added punch.

However, newly acquired Russ Davis (.276, 2, 12 with the Yankees) will have to approach his minor-league power numbers to help offset the exiling of Tino Martinez and Mike Blowers, who accounted for 54 homers and 207 RBI last season. Of course, just having Griffey healthy all year might be enough to make these Mariners even more intimidating than the bunch that overcame a 13-game August deficit last year.

PITCHING: Contrary to the Mariners' playoff rotation of Randy Johnson, Johnson and Johnson, Seattle actually has a few other starters—but not enough good ones.

Johnson, of course, is by far the ace of the staff after winning a Cy Young with an 18-2, 2.48 tour de force that featured an AL-leading 294 strikeouts. Otherwise, Chris Bosio (10-8, 4.92) regressed last year and needs to step up in '96. Rookie Rob Wolcott (3-2, 4.42) showed in October that he should be able to help this club this summer. Tim Belcher (10-12, 4.52) and late-season addition Andy Benes were not re-signed. Sterling Hitchcock (11-10, 4.70 with the Yankees) gives Seattle a gifted young lefty for its rotation.

Benny Ayala (6-5, 4.44, 19 saves) was erratic, but Norm Charlton (2-1, 1.51, 14 saves) came to the rescue as a closer for the Mariners. Manager Lou Piniella figures to miss traded setup men Bill Risley (2-1, 3.13) and Jeff Nelson (7-3, 2.17) in '96.

FIELDING: Overall, the Mariners are just average with their gloves, although there are spots where they are better than that. Catcher Dan Wilson is solid defensively. Second baseman Cora's 23 errors don't tell you about his excellent range.

And, of course, Griffey is spectacular in center and Buhner has an exceptionally strong arm in right.

OUTLOOK: After a 79-66 finish and a memorable playoff run to the ALCS in '95, hopes are high in Seattle. And there's good reason. Given their returning players, the Mariners should win their second consecutive AL West title this year. Pitching could be their downfall, but there aren't any better combinations in baseball than Johnson on the mound and this explosive lineup behind him.

MARINER PROFILES

KEN GRIFFEY Jr. 26 6-3 205 Bats L Throws L

Finally got a chance to show his wares in October and he was spectacular . . . Hit .391 with five home runs and seven RBI during Division Series against Yankees, then hit .333 with one homer and two RBI vs. Indians in ALCS . . . Missed nearly three months during '95 because he fractured his wrist crashing into center-field fence against Baltimore May 26 . . . Came back two weeks earlier than expected and finished with respectable numbers considering he had missed 73 games . . . His .258 batting average was lowest mark of his career, but he hit 17 homers . . . Six-time All-Star had to bow out of last year's All-Star Game because of wrist injury . . . Still, he showed up in Texas and hung out with his teammates . . . One of the most popular players in league, among fans and players . . . Entering last year of a four-year, $24-million contract . . . Tied Don Mattingly and Dale Long for major-league record by hitting home runs in eight consecutive games, July 20-28, 1993 . . . Hit first ball off warehouse in Camden Yards' home-run-hitting contest before 1993 All-Star Game . . . Mariners made him first overall pick of '87 draft . . . Earned $7.5 million in '95 . . . Was part of first active father-son team in majors with Ken Sr. . . . Born Nov. 21, 1969, in Donora, Pa. . . . Won sixth straight Gold Glove in '95.

Year	Club	Pos.	G	AB	R	H	2B	3B	HR	RBI	SB	Avg.
1989	Seattle	OF	127	455	61	120	23	0	16	61	16	.264
1990	Seattle	OF	155	597	91	179	28	7	22	80	16	.300
1991	Seattle	OF	154	548	76	179	42	1	22	100	18	.327
1992	Seattle	OF	142	565	83	174	39	4	27	103	10	.308
1993	Seattle	OF-1B	156	582	113	180	38	3	45	109	17	.309
1994	Seattle	OF	111	433	94	140	24	4	40	90	11	.323
1995	Seattle	OF	72	260	52	67	7	0	17	42	4	.258
	Totals		917	3440	570	1039	201	19	189	585	92	.302

EDGAR MARTINEZ 33 5-11 190 Bats R Throws R

Led AL in batting for second time in his career, at .356 . . . His other batting title came when he hit .343 in 1992 . . . Last season was his first healthy season in three years . . . Led AL in on-base percentage (.479) and tied for lead in runs (121) and doubles (52) . . . Was second in hits (182) and walks (116) . . . Isn't much of a third baseman, but, man, this DH

Ken Griffey Jr. is simply thumbthing special.

can hit . . . Had a spectacular Division Series, hitting .571 with two homers and an amazing 10 RBI vs. Yankees . . . Struggled mightily in ALCS against Cleveland, hitting .087 on 2-for-23 with no RBI . . . Became just the seventh right-handed hitter—and the first since Luke Appling (1936 and 1943)—to win at least two batting titles . . . His 52 doubles tied for 22nd-most in history and was fourth-highest total in majors over last 41 years . . . Signed by the Mariners as non-drafted free agent in December 1982 . . . Made $3.56 million in '95 . . . Born Jan. 2, 1963, in New York . . . Mariners exercised $3.5-million option on his contract for '96.

Year	Club	Pos.	G	AB	R	H	2B	3B	HR	RBI	SB	Avg.
1987	Seattle	3B	13	43	6	16	5	2	0	5	0	.372
1988	Seattle	3B	14	32	0	9	4	0	0	5	0	.281
1989	Seattle	3B	65	171	20	41	5	0	2	20	2	.240
1990	Seattle	3B	144	487	71	147	27	2	11	49	1	.302
1991	Seattle	3B	150	544	98	167	35	1	14	52	0	.307
1992	Seattle	3B-1B	135	528	100	181	46	3	18	73	14	.343
1993	Seattle	3B	42	135	20	32	7	0	4	13	0	.237
1994	Seattle	3B	89	326	47	93	23	1	13	51	6	.285
1995	Seattle	3B-1B	145	511	121	182	52	0	29	113	4	.356
	Totals		797	2777	483	868	204	9	91	381	27	.313

Jay Buhner shot to a home-run high of 40.

JAY BUHNER 31 6-3 210 Bats R Throws R

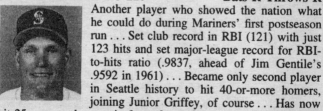

Another player who showed the nation what he could do during Mariners' first postseason run . . . Set club record in RBI (121) with just 123 hits and set major-league record for RBI-to-hits ratio (.9837, ahead of Jim Gentile's .9592 in 1961) . . . Became only second player in Seattle history to hit 40-or-more homers, joining Junior Griffey, of course . . . Has now hit 25-or-more homers in four of past five seasons . . . Only year he missed was strike-shortened '94 season, when he hit 21 . . . Plays well vs. Yankees, as his career .286 batting average with 21 homers and 50 RBI will attest . . . Hit .458 against them during Division Series . . . Hit .304 with three homers and five RBI vs. Indians in ALCS . . . A terrific right fielder whose arm is second to none . . . Made $4.06 million in '95 . . . Obtained by Seattle from Yankees with Rick Balabon and Troy Evers for Ken Phelps,

AL batting champ Edgar Martinez broke Yanks' backs.

July 21, 1988 . . . Pittsburgh's fourth-round pick in January 1984 draft, he was traded to Yankees 11 months later in Steve Kemp deal . . . Born Aug. 13, 1964, in Louisville, Ky.

Year	Club	Pos.	G	AB	R	H	2B	3B	HR	RBI	SB	Avg.
1987	New York (AL)	OF	7	22	0	5	2	0	0	1	0	.227
1988	NY (AL)-Sea. . .	OF	85	261	36	56	13	1	13	38	1	.215
1989	Seattle	OF	58	204	27	56	15	1	9	33	1	.275
1990	Seattle	OF	51	163	16	45	12	0	7	33	2	.276
1991	Seattle	OF	137	406	64	99	14	4	27	77	0	.244
1992	Seattle	OF	152	543	69	132	16	3	25	79	0	.243
1993	Seattle	OF	158	563	91	153	28	3	27	98	2	.272
1994	Seattle	OF	101	358	74	100	23	4	21	68	0	.279
1995	Seattle	OF	126	470	86	123	23	0	40	121	0	.262
	Totals		875	2990	463	769	146	16	169	548	6	.257

DAN WILSON 27 6-3 190 Bats R Throws R

Became regular catcher in his second full season in majors in '95 . . . Set career highs in nearly every offensive category and he is strong behind the plate . . . Has caught 33% of would-be base-stealers during his Seattle career . . . His .278 batting average in '95 was best by any catcher in Mariners history, surpassing Bob Stinson's .269 in 1977 . . . Led AL catchers in putouts (895) and total chances (952) . . . Went 0-for-16 vs. Indians in ALCS . . . Selected by Cincinnati as seventh choice overall in 1990 draft . . . Traded to Seattle with Bobby Ayala for Bret Boone and Erik Hanson prior to '94 season . . . Made $175,000 in '95 . . . Born March 25, 1969, in Arlington Heights, Ill.

Year	Club	Pos.	G	AB	R	H	2B	3B	HR	RBI	SB	Avg.
1992	Cincinnatti	C	12	25	2	9	1	0	0	3	0	.360
1993	Cincinnatti	C	36	76	6	17	3	0	0	8	0	.224
1994	Seattle	C	91	282	24	61	14	2	3	27	1	.216
1995	Seattle	C	119	399	40	111	22	3	9	51	2	.278
	Totals		258	782	72	198	40	5	12	89	3	.253

JOEY CORA 30 5-8 155 Bats S Throws R

Sparkplug gives Seattle action at top or bottom of lineup . . . Hit .297 in '95, more than 30 points better than his career average entering season . . . A smart signing by Mariners, who inked him as a free agent just before late spring training started in '95 and exercised option on '96 after last season . . . Has 43 sacrifices during past two seasons . . . He is no defensive liability at second, either . . . Hit .316 during Division Series against Yankees, but only .174 in ALCS vs. Indians . . . It was best overall year of his career . . . Made $325,000 in '95 . . . San Diego made him first-round pick in 1985 draft, but he spent first full major-league season with White Sox in 1992 . . . Born May 14, 1965, in Caguas, P.R.

Year	Club	Pos.	G	AB	R	H	2B	3B	HR	RBI	SB	Avg.
1987	San Diego	2B-SS	77	241	23	57	7	2	0	13	15	.237
1989	San Diego	SS-3B-2B	12	19	5	6	1	0	0	1	1	.316
1990	San Diego	SS-2B-C	51	100	12	27	3	0	0	2	8	.270
1991	Chicago (AL) . .	2B-SS	100	228	37	55	2	3	0	18	11	.241
1992	Chicago (AL) . .	2B-SS-3B	68	122	27	30	7	1	0	9	10	.246
1993	Chicago (AL) . .	2B-3B	153	579	95	155	15	13	2	51	20	.268
1994	Chicago (AL) . .	2B	90	312	55	86	13	4	2	30	8	.276
1995	Seattle	2B-SS	120	427	64	127	19	2	3	39	18	.297
	Totals		671	2028	318	543	67	25	7	163	91	.268

CHRIS BOSIO 33 6-3 225 Bats R Throws R

Had disappointing season in '95, especially considering he did not lose until his 12th start . . . Ran record to 6-1 before losing next four straight . . . Was forced to leave three games in '95 when he was hit by batted balls . . . Made 31 starts after torn knee cartilage had limited him to 19 in '94 . . . Didn't pitch well in postseason . . . Had 10.57 ERA in Division Series against Yankees, then was 0-1, 3.38 vs. Indians in ALCS . . . Should have had a better season, but he was a victim of blown saves . . . Left 17 of his 31 starts with the lead only to have bullpen blow seven save opportunities . . . Give him Kingdome or give him death . . . Has 17-12 mark with Mariners over past three seasons in 43 Kingdome games, compared to 6-15 mark in road games during that span . . . Made $4.25 million in '95 . . . Born April 3, 1963, in Carmichael, Cal.

Year	Club	G	IP	W	L	Pct.	SO	BB	H	ERA
1986	Milwaukee	10	34⅔	0	4	.000	29	13	41	7.01
1987	Milwaukee	46	170	11	8	.579	150	50	187	5.24
1988	Milwaukee	38	182	7	15	.318	84	38	190	3.36
1989	Milwaukee	33	234⅔	15	10	.600	173	48	225	2.95
1990	Milwaukee	20	132⅔	4	9	.308	76	38	131	4.00
1991	Milwaukee	32	204⅔	14	10	.583	117	58	187	3.25
1992	Milwaukee	33	231⅓	16	6	.727	120	44	223	3.62
1993	Seattle	29	164⅓	9	9	.500	119	59	138	3.45
1994	Seattle	19	125	4	10	.286	67	40	137	4.32
1995	Seattle	31	170	10	8	.556	85	69	211	4.92
	Totals	291	1649⅓	90	89	.503	1020	457	1670	3.89

RANDY JOHNSON 32 6-10 225 Bats R Throws L

"The Big Unit" keeps getting bigger . . . Did outstanding work in postseason, almost single-handedly keeping Mariners from elimination in one-game playoff against California and then in Division Series against Yankees . . . Went 2-0 with 2.70 ERA vs. Yankees, then 0-1 vs. Indians despite 2.35 ERA in ALCS . . . Earned Cy Young by going 18-2 with 2.48 ERA . . . Led AL in strikeouts (294) for fourth consecutive season . . . Biggest difference is he has cut down on his walks, making him even more dominating . . . Became first Seattle pitcher to lead AL in ERA . . . Established new major-league record for best winning percentage in a season (minimum 20 decisions) at .900, breaking Ron Guidry's .893 mark (25-3 in 1978) . . . Has won 20 of his last 22 decisions . . . Has 29-5 record in 44 starts since May 15, 1994 . . . Acquired by Seattle from Montreal with Gene Harris and Brian Holman for Mark Langston and Mike Campbell, May 25, 1989 . . . Made $4.42 million in '95 . . . Born Sept. 10, 1963, in Walnut Creek, Cal.

Year	Club	G	IP	W	L	Pct.	SO	BB	H	ERA
1988	Montreal	4	26	3	0	1.000	25	7	23	2.42
1989	Montreal	7	29⅔	0	4	.000	26	26	29	6.67
1989	Seattle	22	131	7	9	.438	104	70	118	4.40
1990	Seattle	33	219⅔	14	11	.560	194	120	174	3.65
1991	Seattle	33	201⅓	13	10	.565	228	152	151	3.98
1992	Seattle	31	210⅓	12	14	.462	241	144	154	3.77
1983	Seattle	35	255⅓	19	8	.704	308	99	185	3.24
1994	Seattle	23	172	13	6	.684	204	72	132	3.19
1995	Seattle	30	214⅓	18	2	.900	294	65	159	2.48
	Totals	218	1459⅔	99	64	.607	1624	755	1125	3.52

TOP PROSPECTS

ROB WOLCOTT 22 6-0 190 Bats R Throws R

Added to Mariners' postseason roster at last minute and beat Cleveland in Game 1 of AL Championship Series, allowing two runs in seven innings . . . Went 3-2 with 4.42 ERA in seven games, including six starts, for Mariners in '95 . . . Went 7-3 with 2.20 ERA for Port City (AA) and 6-3, 4.08 for Tacoma (AAA) in '95 . . . Turned down a full scholarship to Stanford to sign with Mariners . . . Seattle made him second-round pick in '92 draft . . . Born Sept. 8, 1973, in Huntington Beach, Cal.

RUSS DAVIS 26 6-0 195 Bats R Throws R

Late developer finally gets his chance as Yanks sent him to Mariners in Tino Martinez deal last winter . . . Batted .276 with Yankees in 98 at-bats with two homers and 12 RBI in '95 . . . Third baseman hit .250 with two homers and 15 RBI for Columbus (AAA) . . . Started one game in Division Series for Yankees . . . Born Sept. 13, 1969, in Birmingham, Ala. . . . Yanks' 29th-round pick in 1988 draft hit 20-or-more homers in minors from 1992-94.

DARREN BRAGG 26 5-9 180 Bats L Throws R

Outfielder hit .234 with three homers and 12 RBI in 52 games with Mariners in '95 . . . Hit .307 with four homers and 31 RBI for Tacoma (AAA) last season . . . Mariners made him 22nd-round pick in 1991 draft . . . Attended Georgia Tech and set ACC record with 73 walks in 1989 . . . Played on Team USA in 1990 and participated in Goodwill Games . . . Born Sept. 7, 1969, in Waterbury, Conn.

ARQUIMEDEZ POZO 22 5-10 160 Bats R Throws R

Second baseman hit .300 with 10 homers and 62 RBI for Tacoma (AAA) in '95 and got into one game for Mariners . . . Signed with Mariners as non-drafted free agent in August 1990 . . . Born Aug. 24, 1973, in Santo Domingo, D.R. . . . Best season was 1993, when he hit .342 with 13 homers and 83 RBI for Riverside (A).

DESI RELAFORD 22 5-8 155 Bats S Throws R

A second baseman-type who hit only .239 with two homers and seven RBI for Tacoma (AAA) and .287 with seven homers and 27 RBI for Port City (AA) . . . Has a chance to develop and the switch-hitting should help . . . Mariners made him fourth-round pick in 1991 draft . . . Turned down a full scholarship from University of Tennessee to sign with Seattle . . . Born Sept. 16, 1973, in Valdosta, Ga.

MANAGER LOU PINIELLA: May have recorded his greatest managerial triumph by guiding Mariners back from 11-game August deficit to AL West title, earning AL Manager of the Year honors . . . Delivered first-ever Mariners postseason win . . . Only manager in Mariners history to have a winning percentage over .500 (210-209) . . . Has guided teams to winning records in six of his eight full seasons as major-league manager . . . "Sweet Lou" . . . Manages as much by instinct as by computer-generated statistics . . . Has 689-633 record combined in managerial stops with Yankees (1986-88), Cincinnati (1990-92) and Seattle (1993-95) . . . Left Cincinnati because he had had his fill of tightwad owner Marge Schott and her zany antics . . . Went 179-145 as Yankees manager, but was booted upstairs to GM by owner George Steinbrenner . . . Came back as Yankees manager in June 1988, replacing Billy Martin . . . Batted .291 in 16-plus seasons spent mostly as an outfielder with Royals and Yankees . . . Picked by Seattle Pilots in expansion draft from Cleveland, he was then traded to Royals . . . AL Rookie of the Year in 1969 and AL Manager of the Year in 1995 . . . Born Aug. 28, 1943, in Tampa.

ALL-TIME MARINER SEASON RECORDS

BATTING: Edgar Martinez, .356, 1995
HRs: Ken Griffey Jr., 45, 1993
RBI: Jay Buhner, 121, 1995
STEALS: Harold Reynolds, 60, 1987
WINS: Mark Langston, 19, 1987
Randy Johnson, 19, 1993
STRIKEOUTS: Randy Johnson, 308, 1993

TEXAS RANGERS

TEAM DIRECTORY: General Partners: J. Thomas Schieffer, Edward W. (Rusty) Rose; VP/GM: Doug Melvin; VP-Business Oper.: John McMichael; VP-Adm.: Charles Wangner; Asst. GM-Scouting: Lee MacPhail Jr.; VP-Pub. Rel.: John Blake; Trav. Sec.: Dan Schimek; Mgr.: Johnny Oates; Coaches: Dick Bosman, Bucky Dent, Larry Hardy, Rudy Jaramillo, Ed Napoleon, Jerry Narron. Home: The Ballpark in Arlington (49,292). Field distances: 332, l.f. line; 390, l.c.; 400, c.f.; 377–381, r.c.; 325, r.f. line. Spring training: Port Charlotte, Fla.

SCOUTING REPORT

HITTING: Earl Weaver's old ''play for the big inning'' philosophy is alive and well. The Rangers don't necessarily hit for a high average—their .265 batting average ranked ninth in the AL in '95—but they have plenty of potential pop.

Juan Gonzalez (.295, 27, 82) and Dean Palmer (.336, 9, 24 in 119 at-bats) are two keys this year and their health will be watched as closely as their bats. Gonzalez rebounded from a herniated disc in his back suffered last spring to put together a decent season. Palmer suffered a ruptured biceps tendon in his left arm and played in only 36 games.

Mickey Tettleton (.238, 32, 78) re-signed, but the departure of Otis Nixon (.295, 87 runs, 50 steals) left a large hole in the leadoff spot that Darryl Hamilton (.217, 54 runs, 11 steals with the Brewers) was signed to fill. The Rangers still have Will Clark (.302, 16, 92), Ivan Rodriguez (.303, 12, 67) and Mark McLemore (261, 5, 41, 21 steals).

PITCHING: This is where they're really hurting. Kenny Rogers (17-7, 3.38), one of the best left-handers, was unsigned at press time. The Rangers brought back Bobby Witt (3-4, 4.55 as a Ranger) for a second go-round last year and he has re-signed. With Bob Tewksbury gone via free agency, the Rangers could use improvement from Roger Pavlik (10-10, 4.37).

They've added Ken Hill (6-7, 5.06 with the Cards, 4-1, 3.98 with the Indians).

Manager Johnny Oates had a decent closer in Jeff Russell (1-0, 3.03, 20 saves), but he left via free agency. Ed Vosberg (5-5, 3.00) was the club's most consistent setup man and Matt Whiteside (5-4, 4.08) should help out in that area this season

Will The Thrill's glare is enough to chill any pitcher.

along with Mike Henneman (0-1, 1.53, 18 saves with the Tigers, 0-1, 3.00, 8 saves with the Astros).

FIELDING: Defense isn't going to win this club any championships, but it shouldn't hurt the Rangers too badly, either. Ranked sixth in the AL with 98 errors in '95, this team should be about the same in 1996.

Gold Glove catcher Rodriguez is as good as any behind the plate and first baseman Clark is solid. Flashy Benji Gil makes too many errors at shortstop, but he's young and still improving. Palmer can be a butcher at third. Gonzalez is mediocre in left.

OUTLOOK: As the health of Gonzalez and Palmer goes, so, too, go the Rangers. This club, coming off a 74-70 finish, could challenge if all of the pieces come together properly in '96. The Rangers still need more pitching. But they've been ready to make their move for the past five years and now Seattle has surpassed the Rangers as the team to beat in the AL West.

RANGER PROFILES

JUAN GONZALEZ 26 6-3 235 Bats R Throws R

Saw career flash before his eyes when he was diagnosed with a herniated disc in his back during spring training of '95 . . . Missed beginning of last season and played in only 90 games . . . Still managed 27 homers and 82 RBI and a .594 slugging percentage . . . Had better year than his subpar '94, when he had only 19 homers and 85 RBI . . . He's only a few years removed from a 1993 explosion that featured 46 homers, 118 RBI and a .310 batting average—and he still is only 26 . . . This outfielder ranks fourth in major-league history in homers hit during one season before age of 24 (46) and seventh in major-league history in career homers hit before age of 25 (140) . . . Won AL home-run titles in '92 and '93 . . . Made $5.4 million in 1995 . . . Signed by Texas as non-drafted free agent in May 1986 . . . Born Oct. 16, 1969, in Vega Baja, P.R. . . . Married to sister of Atlanta catcher Javier Lopez.

Year	Club	Pos.	G	AB	R	H	2B	3B	HR	RBI	SB	Avg.
1989	Texas	OF	24	60	6	9	3	0	1	7	0	.150
1990	Texas	OF	25	90	11	26	7	1	4	12	0	.289
1991	Texas	OF	142	545	78	144	34	1	27	102	4	.264
1992	Texas	OF	155	584	77	152	24	2	43	109	0	.260
1993	Texas	OF	140	536	105	166	33	1	46	118	4	.310
1994	Texas	OF	107	422	57	116	18	4	19	85	6	.275
1995	Texas	OF	90	352	57	104	20	2	27	82	0	.295
	Totals		683	2589	391	717	139	11	167	515	14	.277

WILL CLARK 32 6-1 196 Bats L Throws L

Keeps hitting . . . Has now hit .300 or better in four of past five years . . . First baseman's best power years are behind him . . . Has hit only 16, 14, 13 and 16 homers in past four years . . . But his career batting average remains over .300, at .302 . . . Still has that inner fire . . . If you don't believe it, just ask one of the official scorers he has harrassed when he disagreed with a call . . . Good influence in what can be one of baseball's most schizophrenic clubhouses . . . Made only seven errors in '95, after committing 10 the year before . . . Made $5.647 million in '95, second year of a five-year, $30-million deal he signed as free agent . . . Signed with Texas after eight years in San Francisco . . . Giants drafted him No. 2 overall in '85, out of Mississippi State . . . Left the Giants ranking fourth on all-time club hit list with 1,278 . . . Batted .489 with three homers and 11 RBI in two NL Championship Series as a Giant . . . Born March 13, 1964, in New Orleans.

Year	Club	Pos.	G	AB	R	H	2B	3B	HR	RBI	SB	Avg.
1986	San Francisco	1B	111	408	66	117	27	2	11	41	4	.287
1987	San Francisco	1B	150	529	89	163	29	5	35	91	5	.308
1988	San Francisco	1B	162	575	102	162	31	6	29	109	9	.282
1989	San Francisco	1B	159	588	104	196	38	9	23	111	8	.333
1990	San Francisco	1B	154	600	91	177	25	5	19	95	8	.295
1991	San Francisco	1B	148	565	84	170	32	7	29	116	4	.301
1992	San Francisco	1B	144	513	69	154	40	1	16	73	12	.300
1993	San Francisco	1B	132	491	82	139	27	2	14	73	2	.283
1994	Texas	1B	110	389	73	128	24	2	13	80	5	.329
1995	Texas	1B	123	454	85	137	27	3	16	92	0	.302
	Totals		1393	5112	845	1543	300	42	205	881	57	.302

IVAN RODRIGUEZ 24 5-9 205 Bats R Throws R

Has accomplished more by his mid-20s than many do in their entire careers . . . Posted career highs in batting average (.303) and RBI (67) in '95 . . . It marked second year in a row he posted career-high batting average, which means he's still improving . . . Four-time All-Star consistently ranks among game's best defensive catchers . . . Power is in his arm strength . . . "Pudge" . . . Made $2.575 million in '95 . . . Signed as a non-drafted free agent by Rangers in July 1988 . . . Born Nov. 30, 1971, in Vega Baja, P.R., the same hometown as Juan Gonzalez . . . What a send-off: He was married at home plate in Drillers Stadium in Tulsa on the day he was called up to the majors, June 20, 1991 . . . Won fourth Gold Glove last season.

Year	Club	Pos.	G	AB	R	H	2B	3B	HR	RBI	SB	Avg.
1991	Texas	C	88	280	24	74	16	0	3	27	0	.264
1992	Texas	C	123	420	39	109	16	1	8	37	0	.260
1993	Texas	C	137	473	56	129	28	4	10	66	8	.273
1994	Texas	C	99	363	56	108	19	1	16	57	6	.298
1995	Texas	C	130	492	56	149	32	2	12	67	0	.303
	Totals		577	2028	231	569	111	8	49	254	14	.281

MICKEY TETTLETON 35 6-2 212 Bats S Throws R

The free-agent steal of the year in '95 was re-signed to two-year, $5-million deal last winter . . . Signed with Texas last spring for mere $500,000 plus incentives, after attending free-agent camp in Homestead, Fla. . . . Ended up with 32 homers and 78 RBI . . . Had averaged 28 homers and 88 RBI over the previous four seasons with Tigers . . . Ranks as major-league walk leader in '90s with 642 . . . Finished fourth in the AL with 107 walks last season . . . Athletics drafted him in fifth round in 1981 . . . Played at Oklahoma State and was center fielder back then . . . Now he is mostly a DH, although he still plays first base and the outfield on occasion . . . Born Sept. 16, 1960, in Oklahoma City, Okla. . . . Catching days have been over since '94, when he posted AL's lowest percentage of runners caught stealing (14.5%).

Year	Club	Pos.	G	AB	R	H	2B	3B	HR	RBI	SB	Avg.
1984	Oakland	C	33	76	10	20	2	1	1	5	0	.263
1985	Oakland	C	78	211	23	53	12	0	3	15	2	.251
1986	Oakland	C	90	211	26	43	9	0	10	35	7	.204
1987	Oakland	C-1B	82	211	19	41	3	0	8	26	1	.194
1988	Baltimore	C	86	283	31	74	11	1	11	37	0	.261
1989	Baltimore	C	117	411	72	106	21	2	26	65	3	.258
1990	Baltimore	C-1B-OF	135	444	68	99	21	2	15	51	2	.223
1991	Detroit	C-OF-1B	154	501	85	132	17	2	31	89	3	.263
1992	Detroit	C-1B-OF	157	525	82	125	25	0	32	83	0	.238
1993	Detroit	1B-C-OF	152	522	79	128	25	4	32	110	3	.245
1994	Detroit	C-1B-OF	107	339	57	84	18	2	17	51	0	.248
1995	Texas	OF-1B-C	134	429	76	102	19	1	32	78	0	.238
	Totals		1325	4163	628	1007	183	15	218	645	21	.242

DEAN PALMER 27 6-2 195 Bats R Throws R

This will be an important year in his career . . . Was done for the season after he suffered a torn biceps tendon on a swing in a game last June . . . Third baseman was off to a terrific start, too, hitting .336 with nine homers and 24 RBI in only 36 games . . . Had .613 slugging percentage and .448 on-base percentage . . . Could have been the best season in the young career of someone who has not fulfilled his offensive potential . . . Has never hit over .246 in three full major-league seasons and still hasn't had a 100-RBI year . . . Best year was in '93, when he had 33 homers and 96 RBI. He, Juan Gonzalez and Rafael Palmeiro combined to hit 116 homers that year, most of any trio of teammates . . . Made $1.925 million in '95 . . . Earns that money for his offense, because his defense is certainly shaky . . . Selected by Texas in third round of '86 draft . . . Born Dec. 27, 1968, in Tallahassee, Fla.

Year	Club	Pos.	G	AB	R	H	2B	3B	HR	RBI	SB	Avg.
1989	Texas	3B-SS-OF	7	24	4	7	0	1	3	9	0	.292
1991	Texas	3B-OF	81	268	38	50	9	2	15	37	0	.187
1992	Texas	3B	152	541	74	124	25	0	26	72	10	.229
1993	Texas	3B-SS	148	519	88	127	31	2	33	96	11	.245
1994	Texas	3B	93	342	50	84	14	2	19	59	3	.246
1995	Texas	3B	36	119	30	40	6	0	9	24	1	.336
	Totals		517	1803	284	432	85	7	105	297	25	.240

BENJI GIL 23 6-2 182 **Bats R Throws R**

Finally completed slow, painful move into big leagues in '95 . . . Still hit only .219, but he became Rangers regular shortstop, playing in 130 games . . . Sports slick glove and good body frame for a shortstop . . . With experience, he could develop into one of the best . . . Has some untapped power . . . Came up prematurely for two trials in '93 because of injuries and really struggled, batting .123 with zero homers and two RBI in 22 games . . . Spent all of '94 in minors, batting .248 with 10 homers and 55 RBI for Oklahoma City (AAA) . . . Won full-time job with Rangers last spring . . . Made $115,000 in '95 . . . Rangers made him 19th player drafted overall in 1991 . . . Great arm . . . Was promising pitching prospect in high school . . . Born Oct. 6, 1972, in Tijuana, Mexico.

Year	Club	Pos.	G	AB	R	H	2B	3B	HR	RBI	SB	Avg.
1993	Texas	SS	22	57	3	7	0	0	0	2	1	.123
1995	Texas	SS	130	415	36	91	20	3	9	46	2	.219
	Totals		152	472	39	98	20	3	9	48	3	.208

MARK McLEMORE 31 5-11 207 **Bats S Throws R**

Hot start in '95 found him among AL batting leaders for most of first two months . . . Cooled off to .261, but he was a steady player most of year . . . Well-traveled veteran has played with California, Cleveland, Houston, Baltimore and Texas since being selected by Angels in ninth round of '82 draft . . . Versatile . . . Can play second base or outfield adequately . . . His .261 average in '95 was second-highest of his career, behind his .284

mark of '93 . . . Committed only four errors in 129 games . . . Helped Rangers, especially early in year when he subbed for injured Juan Gonzalez . . . Made $825,000 in '95 . . . Rangers signed him as a free agent prior to last season . . . Born Oct. 4, 1964, in San Diego.

Year	Club	Pos.	G	AB	R	H	2B	3B	HR	RBI	SB	Avg.
1986	California	2B	5	4	0	0	0	0	0	0	0	.000
1987	California	12B-SS	138	433	61	102	13	3	3	41	25	.236
1988	California	2B-3B	77	233	38	56	11	2	2	16	13	.240
1989	California	2B	32	103	12	25	3	1	0	14	6	.243
1990	Cal.-Clev.	2B-SS-3B	28	60	6	9	2	0	0	2	1	.150
1991	Houston	2B	21	61	6	9	1	0	0	2	0	.148
1991	Baltimore	2B	101	228	40	56	7	2	0	27	11	.246
1993	Baltimore	OF-2B-3B	148	581	81	165	27	5	4	72	21	.284
1994	Baltimore	2B-OF	104	343	44	88	11	1	3	29	20	.257
1995	Texas	OF-2B	129	467	73	122	20	5	5	41	21	.261
	Totals		783	2513	361	632	95	19	17	244	118	.251

BOBBY WITT 31 6-2 205 Bats R Throws R

Re-signed one-year pact last winter . . . Rangers picked him up from Marlins toward end of last season for their stretch run . . . They didn't make it and he was only mediocre for Texas, going 3-4 with 4.55 ERA for Rangers in 10 starts . . . Worked only 61⅓ innings . . . Started career with Texas, which picked him third overall in '85 draft, out of University of Oklahoma . . . Pitched on 1984 U.S. Olympic team . . . Was 3-0 with 0.36 ERA and 36 strikeouts in 26 innings for Olympic team . . . Rangers traded him to Oakland with Ruben Sierra, Jeff Russell and cash for Jose Canseco, Aug. 31, 1992 . . . Made $1.8 million in '95 . . . Born May 11, 1964, in Arlington, Va.

Year	Club	G	IP	W	L	Pct.	SO	BB	H	ERA
1986	Texas	31	157⅔	11	9	.550	174	143	130	5.48
1987	Texas	26	143	8	10	.444	160	140	114	4.91
1988	Texas	22	174⅓	8	10	.444	148	101	134	3.92
1989	Texas	31	194⅓	12	13	.480	166	114	182	5.14
1990	Texas	33	222	17	10	.630	221	110	197	3.36
1991	Texas	17	88⅔	3	7	.300	82	74	84	6.09
1992	Texas-Oak.	31	193	10	14	.417	125	114	183	4.29
1993	Oakland	35	220	14	13	.519	131	91	226	4.21
1994	Oakland	24	135⅔	8	10	.444	111	70	151	5.04
1995	Florida	19	110⅔	2	7	.222	95	47	104	3.90
1995	Texas	10	61⅓	3	4	.429	46	21	81	4.55
	Totals	279	1700⅔	96	107	.473	1459	1025	1586	4.52

Ivan Rodriguez is at home behind the plate or crossing it.

TOP PROSPECTS

JEFF DAVIS 23 6-0 170 Bats R Throws R

Converted to a starter in '95 after compiling 32 saves in his first two years in Texas organization . . . As a starter, he went 12-7 with 2.89 ERA for Charlotte (A) in '95, striking out 105 and walking only 37 in 165 innings . . . Went 1-0, 0.00 in one start for Tulsa (AA) . . . Texas picked him in 28th round of '93 draft . . . Born Aug. 20, 1972, in Fall River, Mass.

JULIO SANTANA 23 6-0 175 Bats R Throws R

Ran through three minor-league levels in '95, playing for Charlotte (A), Tulsa (AA) and Oklahoma City (AAA) . . . Went 0-3, 3.73 for Charlotte, 6-4, 3.23 for Tulsa and 0-2, 39.00 for Oklahoma City . . . Became a starter in '94, his second pro season . . . Led entire Texas organization in strikeouts in '94 with 148 . . . Signed as non-drafted free agent by Texas in February 1990 . . . Born Jan. 20, 1973, in San Pedro de Macoris, P.R.

ANDREW VESSEL 21 6-3 210 Bats R Throws R

A good-fielding outfielder who is still young . . . Batted .265 with nine homers and 78 RBI for Charlotte (A) in '95 . . . A prep All-American in both football and baseball . . . Texas' third-round pick in '93 draft . . . Born March 11, 1975, in San Leandro, Cal.

EDWIN DIAZ 21 5-11 172 Bats R Throws R

Second baseman had a solid season for Charlotte (A) in '95 . . . Batted .284 with eight homers and 56 RBI . . . Texas' second-round pick in '93 draft . . . Posted .305 batting average in his first year as a pro, for Gulf Coast (R) . . . Born Jan. 15, 1975, in Vega Baja, P.R.

MANAGER JOHNNY OATES: Earned extension through '97

by keeping club in wild-card contention most of '95, but, for whatever reason, Rangers can never seem to get over the hump . . . Missed first few games of his debut season in Texas when he took a leave of absence to tend to his ailing wife . . . Landed in Texas in '95, after being fired in Baltimore by owner Peter Angelos . . . Doug Melvin, former Orioles' GM, hired this guy after becoming GM in Texas . . . Rangers' 74-70 record in '95 leaves his lifetime mark at 365-340 . . . Fired in Baltimore despite Orioles' 63-49 mark in strike-shortened '94 season . . . Was first-base coach with Orioles before replacing Frank Robinson as manager, May 24, 1991 . . . Highly successful minor-league manager who won Southern League championship at Nashville (AA) in 1982, in his first assignment . . . Won regular-season title with Columbus (AAA) in 1983, his second season in Yankees' system . . . Is 14th full-time manager in Texas history, having succeeded Kevin Kennedy . . . Born Jan. 21, 1946, in Sylvia, N.C.

ALL-TIME RANGER SEASON RECORDS

BATTING: Julio Franco, .341, 1991
HRs: Juan Gonzalez, 46, 1993
RBI: Ruben Sierra, 119, 1989
STEALS: Bump Wills, 52, 1987
WINS: Ferguson Jenkins, 25, 1974
STRIKEOUTS: Nolan Ryan, 301, 1989

MAJOR LEAGUE YEAR-BY-YEAR LEADERS

NATIONAL LEAGUE MVP

Year	Player, Club
1931	Frank Frisch, St. Louis Cardinals
1932	Chuck Klein, Philadelphia Phillies
1933	Carl Hubbell, New York Giants
1934	Dizzy Dean, St. Louis Cardinals
1935	Gabby Hartnett, Chicago Cubs
1936	Carl Hubbell, New York Giants
1937	Joe Medwick, St. Louis Cardinals
1938	Ernie Lombardi, Cincinnati Reds
1939	Bucky Walters, Cincinnati Reds
1940	Frank McCormick, Cincinnati Reds
1941	Dolph Camilli, Brooklyn Dodgers
1942	Mort Cooper, St. Louis Cardinals
1943	Stan Musial, St. Louis Cardinals
1944	Marty Marion, St. Louis Cardinals
1945	Phil Cavarretta, Chicago Cubs
1946	Stan Musial, St. Louis Cardinals
1947	Bob Elliott, Boston Braves
1948	Stan Musial, St. Louis Cardinals
1949	Jackie Robinson, Brooklyn Dodgers
1950	Jim Konstanty, Philadelphia Phillies
1951	Roy Campanella, Brooklyn Dodgers
1952	Hank Sauer, Chicago Cubs
1953	Roy Campanella, Brooklyn Dodgers
1954	Willie Mays, New York Giants
1955	Roy Campanella, Brooklyn Dodgers
1956	Don Newcombe, Brooklyn Dodgers
1957	Hank Aaron, Milwaukee Braves
1958	Ernie Banks, Chicago Cubs
1959	Ernie Banks, Chicago Cubs
1960	Dick Groat, Pittsburgh Pirates
1961	Frank Robinson, Cincinnati Reds

Year	Player, Club
1962	Maury Wills, Los Angeles Dodgers
1963	Sandy Koufax, Los Angeles Dodgers
1964	Ken Boyer, St. Louis Cardinals
1965	Willie Mays, San Francisco Giants
1966	Roberto Clemente, Pittsburgh Pirates
1967	Orlando Cepeda, St. Louis Cardinals
1968	Bob Gibson, St. Louis Cardinals
1969	Willie McCovey, San Francisco Giants
1970	Johnny Bench, Cincinnati Reds
1971	Joe Torre, St. Louis Cardinals
1972	Johnny Bench, Cincinnati Reds
1973	Pete Rose, Cincinnati Reds
1974	Steve Garvey, Los Angeles Dodgers
1975	Joe Morgan, Cincinnati Reds
1976	Joe Morgan, Cincinnati Reds
1977	George Foster, Cincinnati Reds
1978	Dave Parker, Pittsburgh Pirates
1979	Keith Hernandez, St. Louis Cardinals
	Willie Stargell, Pittsburgh Pirates
1980	Mike Schmidt, Philadelphia Phillies
1981	Mike Schmidt, Philadelphia Phillies
1982	Dale Murphy, Atlanta Braves
1983	Dale Murphy, Atlanta Braves
1984	Ryne Sandberg, Chicago Cubs
1985	Willie McGee, St. Louis Cardinals
1986	Mike Schmidt, Philadelphia Phillies
1987	Andre Dawson, Chicago Cubs
1988	Kirk Gibson, Los Angeles Dodgers
1989	Kevin Mitchell, San Francisco Giants
1990	Barry Bonds, Pittsburgh Pirates
1991	Terry Pendleton, Atlanta Braves
1992	Barry Bonds, Pittsburgh Pirates
1993	Barry Bonds, San Francisco Giants
1994	Jeff Bagwell, Houston Astros
1995	Barry Larkin, Cincinnati Reds

AMERICAN LEAGUE MVP

Year	Player, Club
1931	Lefty Grove, Philadelphia Athletics
1932	Jimmy Foxx, Philadelphia Athletics
1933	Jimmy Foxx, Philadelphia Athletics
1934	Mickey Cochrane, Detroit Tigers
1935	Hank Greenberg, Detroit Tigers

Year	Player, Club
1936	Lou Gehrig, New York Yankees
1937	Charley Gehringer, Detroit Tigers
1938	Jimmy Foxx, Boston Red Sox
1939	Joe DiMaggio, New York Yankees
1940	Hank Greenberg, Detroit Tigers
1941	Joe DiMaggio, New York Yankees
1942	Joe Gordon, New York Yankees
1943	Spud Chandler, New York Yankees
1944	Hal Newhouser, Detroit Tigers
1945	Hal Newhouser, Detroit Tigers
1946	Ted Williams, Boston Red Sox
1947	Joe DiMaggio, New York Yankees
1948	Lou Boudreau, Cleveland Indians
1949	Ted Williams, Boston Red Sox
1950	Phil Rizzuto, New York Yankees
1951	Yogi Berra, New York Yankees
1952	Bobby Shantz, Philadelphia Athletics
1953	Al Rosen, Cleveland Indians
1954	Yogi Berra, New York Yankees
1955	Yogi Berra, New York Yankees
1956	Mickey Mantle, New York Yankees
1957	Mickey Mantle, New York Yankees
1958	Jackie Jensen, Boston Red Sox
1959	Nellie Fox, Chicago White Sox
1960	Roger Maris, New York Yankees
1961	Roger Maris, New York Yankees
1962	Mickey Mantle, New York Yankees
1963	Elston Howard, New York Yankees
1964	Brooks Robinson, Baltimore Orioles
1965	Zoilo Versalles, Minnesota Twins
1966	Frank Robinson, Baltimore Orioles
1967	Carl Yastrzemski, Boston Red Sox
1968	Dennis McLain, Detroit Tigers
1969	Harmon Killebrew, Minnesota Twins
1970	Boog Powell, Baltimore Orioles
1971	Vida Blue, Oakland A's
1972	Dick Allen, Chicago White Sox
1973	Reggie Jackson, Oakland A's
1974	Jeff Burroughs, Texas Rangers
1975	Fred Lynn, Boston Red Sox
1976	Thurman Munson, New York Yankees
1977	Rod Carew, Minnesota Twins
1978	Jim Rice, Boston Red Sox
1979	Don Baylor, California Angels

Year	Player, Club
1980	George Brett, Kansas City Royals
1981	Rollie Fingers, Milwaukee Brewers
1982	Robin Yount, Milwaukee Brewers
1983	Cal Ripken Jr., Baltimore Orioles
1984	Willie Hernandez, Detroit Tigers
1985	Don Mattingly, New York Yankees
1986	Roger Clemens, Boston Red Sox
1987	George Bell, Toronto Blue Jays
1988	Jose Canseco, Oakland A's
1989	Robin Yount, Milwaukee Brewers
1990	Rickey Henderson, Oakland A's
1991	Cal Ripken Jr., Baltimore Orioles
1992	Dennis Eckersley, Oakland A's
1993	Frank Thomas, Chicago White Sox
1994	Frank Thomas, Chicago White Sox
1995	Mo Vaughn, Boston Red Sox

AMERICAN LEAGUE
Batting Champions

Year	Player, Club	Avg.
1901	Napoleon Lajoie, Philadelphia Athletics	.422
1902	Ed Delahanty, Washington Senators	.376
1903	Napoleon Lajoie, Cleveland Indians	.355
1904	Napoleon Lajoie, Cleveland Indians	.381
1905	Elmer Flick, Cleveland Indians	.306
1906	George Stone, St. Louis Browns	.358
1907	Ty Cobb, Detroit Tigers	.350
1908	Ty Cobb, Detroit Tigers	.324
1909	Ty Cobb, Detroit Tigers	.377
1910	Ty Cobb, Detroit Tigers	.385
1911	Ty Cobb, Detroit Tigers	.420
1912	Ty Cobb, Detroit Tigers	.410
1913	Ty Cobb, Detroit Tigers	.390
1914	Ty Cobb, Detroit Tigers	.368
1915	Ty Cobb, Detroit Tigers	.370
1916	Tris Speaker, Cleveland Indians	.386
1917	Ty Cobb, Detroit Tigers	.383
1918	Ty Cobb, Detroit Tigers	.382
1919	Ty Cobb, Detroit Tigers	.384
1920	George Sisler, St. Louis Browns	.407
1921	Harry Heilmann, Detroit Tigers	.393
1922	George Sisler, St. Louis Browns	.420
1923	Harry Heilmann, Detroit Tigers	.398

Year	Player, Club	Avg.
1924	Babe Ruth, New York Yankees	.378
1925	Harry Heilmann, Detroit Tigers	.393
1926	Heinie Manush, Detroit Tigers	.377
1927	Harry Heilmann, Detroit Tigers	.398
1928	Goose Goslin, Washington Senators	.379
1929	Lew Fonseca, Cleveland Indians	.369
1930	Al Simmons, Philadelphia Athletics	.381
1931	Al Simmons, Philadelphia Athletics	.390
1932	David Alexander, Detroit Tigers-Boston Red Sox	.367
1933	Jimmy Foxx, Philadelphia Athletics	.356
1934	Lou Gehrig, New York Yankees	.365
1935	Buddy Myer, Washington Senators	.349
1936	Lou Appling, Chicago White Sox	.388
1937	Charlie Gehringer, Detroit Tigers	.371
1938	Jimmy Foxx, Boston Red Sox	.349
1939	Joe DiMaggio, New York Yankees	.381
1940	Joe DiMaggio, New York Yankees	.352
1941	Ted Williams, Boston Red Sox	.406
1942	Ted Williams, Boston Red Sox	.356
1943	Luke Appling, Chicago White Sox	.328
1944	Lou Boudreau, Cleveland Indians	.327
1945	Snuffy Stirnweiss, New York Yankees	.309
1946	Mickey Vernon, Washington Senators	.353
1947	Ted Williams, Boston Red Sox	.343
1948	Ted Williams, Boston Red Sox	.369
1949	George Kell, Detroit Tigers	.343
1950	Billy Goodman, Boston Red Sox	.354
1951	Ferris Fain, Philadelphia Athletics	.344
1952	Ferris Fain, Philadelphia Athletics	.327
1953	Mickey Vernon, Washington Senators	.337
1954	Bobby Avila, Cleveland Indians	.341
1955	Al Kaline, Detroit Tigers	.340
1956	Mickey Mantle, New York Yankees	.353
1957	Ted Williams, Boston Red Sox	.388
1958	Ted Williams, Boston Red Sox	.328
1959	Harvey Kuenn, Detroit Tigers	.353
1960	Pete Runnels, Boston Red Sox	.320
1961	Norm Cash, Detroit Tigers	.361
1962	Pete Runnels, Boston Red Sox	.326
1963	Carl Yastrzemski, Boston Red Sox	.321
1964	Tony Oliva, Minnesota Twins	.323
1965	Tony Oliva, Minnesota Twins	.321
1966	Frank Robinson, Baltimore Orioles	.316
1967	Carl Yastrzemski, Boston Red Sox	.326

Year	Player, Club	Avg.
1968	Carl Yastrzemski, Boston Red Sox	.301
1969	Rod Carew, Minnesota Twins	.332
1970	Alex Johnson, California Angels	.329
1971	Tony Oliva, Minnesota Twins	.337
1972	Rod Carew, Minnesota Twins	.318
1973	Rod Carew, Minnesota Twins	.350
1974	Rod Carew, Minnesota Twins	.364
1975	Rod Carew, Minnesota Twins	.359
1976	George Brett, Kansas City Royals	.333
1977	Rod Carew, Minnesota Twins	.388
1978	Rod Carew, Minnesota Twins	.333
1979	Fred Lynn, Boston Red Sox	.333
1980	George Brett, Kansas City Royals	.390
1981	Carney Lansford, Boston Red Sox	.336
1982	Willie Wilson, Kansas City Royals	.332
1983	Wade Boggs, Boston Red Sox	.361
1984	Don Mattingly, New York Yankees	.343
1985	Wade Boggs, Boston Red Sox	.368
1986	Wade Boggs, Boston Red Sox	.357
1987	Wade Boggs, Boston Red Sox	.363
1988	Wade Boggs, Boston Red Sox	.366
1989	Kirby Puckett, Minnesota Twins	.339
1990	George Brett, Kansas City Royals	.329
1991	Julio Franco, Texas Rangers	.341
1992	Edgar Martinez, Seattle Mariners	.343
1993	John Olerud, Toronto Blue Jays	.363
1994	Paul O'Neill, New York Yankees	.359
1995	Edgar Martinez, Seattle Mariners	.356

NATIONAL LEAGUE
Batting Champions

Year	Player, Club	Avg.
1876	Roscoe Barnes, Chicago	.403
1877	James White, Boston	.385
1878	Abner Dalrymple, Milwaukee	.356
1879	Cap Anson, Chicago	.407
1880	George Gore, Chicago	.365
1881	Cap Anson, Chicago	.399
1882	Dan Brouthers, Buffalo	.367
1883	Dan Brouthers, Buffalo	.371
1884	Jim O'Rourke, Buffalo	.350
1885	Roger Connor, New York	.371
1886	Mike Kelly, Chicago	.388

Year	Player, Club	Avg.
1887	Cap Anson, Chicago	.421
1888	Cap Anson, Chicago	.343
1889	Dan Brouthers, Boston	.373
1890	Jack Glassock, New York	.336
1891	Billy Hamilton, Philadelphia	.338
1892	Cupid Childs, Cleveland	.335
	Dan Brouthers, Brooklyn	.335
1893	Hugh Duffy, Boston	.378
1894	Hugh Duffy, Boston	.438
1895	Jesse Burkett, Cleveland	.423
1896	Jesse Burkett, Cleveland	.410
1897	Willie Keeler, Baltimore	.432
1898	Willie Keeler, Baltimore	.379
1899	Ed Delahanty, Philadelphia	.408
1900	Honus Wagner, Pittsburgh	.380
1901	Jesse Burkett, St. Louis Cardinals	.382
1902	C.H. Beaumont, Pittsburgh Pirates	.357
1903	Honus Wagner, Pittsburgh Pirates	.355
1904	Honus Wagner, Pittsburgh Pirates	.349
1905	J. Bentley Seymour, Cincinnati Reds	.377
1906	Honus Wagner, Pittsburgh Pirates	.339
1907	Honus Wagner, Pittsburgh Pirates	.350
1908	Honus Wagner, Pittsburgh Pirates	.354
1909	Honus Wagner, Pittsburgh Pirates	.339
1910	Sherwood Magee, Philadelphia Phillies	.331
1911	Honus Wagner, Pittsburgh Pirates	.334
1912	Heinie Zimmerman, Chicago Cubs	.372
1913	Jake Daubert, Brooklyn Dodgers	.350
1914	Jake Daubert, Brooklyn Dodgers	.329
1915	Larry Dyole, New York Giants	.320
1916	Hal Chase, Cincinnati Reds	.339
1917	Edd Roush, Cincinnati Reds	.341
1918	Zack Wheat, Brooklyn Dodgers	.335
1919	Edd Roush, Cincinnati Reds	.321
1920	Rogers Hornsby, St. Louis Cardinals	.370
1921	Rogers Hornsby, St. Louis Cardinals	.397
1922	Rogers Hornsby, St. Louis Cardinals	.401
1923	Rogers Hornsby, St. Louis Cardinals	.384
1924	Rogers Hornsby, St. Louis Cardinals	.424
1925	Rogers Hornsby, St. Louis Cardinals	.403
1926	Bubbles Hargrave, Cincinnati Reds	.353
1927	Paul Waner, Pittsburgh Pirates	.380
1928	Rogers Hornsby, Boston Braves	.387
1929	Lefty O'Doul, Philadelphia Phillies	.398

Year	Player, Club	Avg.
1930	Bill Terry, New York Giants	.401
1931	Chick Hafey, St. Louis Cardinals	.349
1932	Lefty O'Doul, Brooklyn Dodgers	.368
1933	Chuck Klein, Philadelphia Phillies	.368
1934	Paul Waner, Pittsburgh Pirates	.362
1935	Arky Vaughan, Pittsburgh Pirates	.385
1936	Paul Waner, Pittsburgh Pirates	.373
1937	Joe Medwick, St. Louis Cardinals	.374
1938	Ernie Lombardi, Cincinnati Reds	.342
1939	Johnny Mize, St. Louis Cardinals	.349
1940	Debs Garms, Pittsburgh Pirates	.355
1941	Pete Reiser, Brooklyn Dodgers	.343
1942	Ernie Lombardi, Boston Braves	.330
1943	Stan Musial, St. Louis Cardinals	.330
1944	Dixie Walker, Brooklyn Dodgers	.357
1945	Phil Cavarretta, Chicago Cubs	.355
1946	Stan Musial, St. Louis Cardinals	.376
1947	Harry Walker, St. L. Cardinals-Phila. Phillies	.363
1948	Stan Musial, St. Louis Cardinals	.376
1949	Jackie Robinson, Brooklyn Dodgers	.342
1950	Stan Musial, St. Louis Cardinals	.346
1951	Stan Musial, St. Louis Cardinals	.355
1952	Stan Musial, St. Louis Cardinals	.336
1953	Carl Furillo, Brooklyn Dodgers	.344
1954	Willie Mays, New York Giants	.345
1955	Richie Ashburn, Philadelphia Phillies	.338
1956	Hank Aaron, Milwaukee Braves	.328
1957	Stan Musial, St. Louis Cardinals	.351
1958	Richie Ashburn, Philadelphia Phillies	.350
1959	Hank Aaron, Milwaukee Braves	.328
1960	Dick Groat, Pittsburgh Pirates	.325
1961	Roberto Clemente, Pittsburgh Pirates	.351
1962	Tommy Davis, Los Angeles Dodgers	.346
1963	Tommy Davis, Los Angeles Dodgers	.326
1964	Roberto Clemente, Pittsburgh Pirates	.339
1965	Roberto Clemente, Pittsburgh Pirates	.329
1966	Matty Alou, Pittsburgh Pirates	.342
1967	Roberto Clemente, Pittsburgh Pirates	.357
1968	Pete Rose, Cincinnati Reds	.335
1969	Pete Rose, Cincinnati Reds	.348
1970	Rico Carty, Atlanta Braves	.366
1971	Joe Torre, St. Louis Cardinals	.363
1972	Billy Williams, Chicago Cubs	.333
1973	Pete Rose, Cincinnati Reds	.338

Year	Player, Club	Avg.
1974	Ralph Garr, Atlanta Braves	.353
1975	Bill Madlock, Chicago Cubs	.354
1976	Bill Madlock, Chicago Cubs	.339
1977	Dave Parker, Pittsburgh Pirates	.338
1978	Dave Parker, Pittsburgh Pirates	.334
1979	Keith Hernandez, St. Louis Cardinals	.344
1980	Bill Buckner, Chicago Cubs	.324
1981	Bill Madlock, Pittsburgh Pirates	.341
1982	Al Oliver, Montreal Expos	.331
1983	Bill Madlock, Pittsburgh Pirates	.323
1984	Tony Gwynn, San Diego Padres	.351
1985	Willie McGee, St. Louis Cardinals	.353
1986	Tim Raines, Montreal Expos	.334
1987	Tony Gwynn, San Diego Padres	.370
1988	Tony Gwynn, San Diego Padres	.313
1989	Tony Gwynn, San Diego Padres	.336
1990	Willie McGee, St. Louis Cardinals	.335
1991	Terry Pendleton, Atlanta Braves	.319
1992	Gary Sheffield, San Diego Padres	.330
1993	Andres Galarraga, Colorado Rockies	.370
1994	Tony Gwynn, San Diego Padres	.394
1995	Tony Gwynn, San Diego Padres	.368

NATIONAL LEAGUE
Home Run Leaders

Year	Player, Club	HRs
1900	Herman Long, Boston Nationals	12
1901	Sam Crawford, Cincinnati Reds	16
1902	Tom Leach, Pittsburgh Pirates	6
1903	Jim Sheckard, Brooklyn Dodgers	9
1904	Harry Lumley, Brooklyn Dodgers	9
1905	Fred Odwell, Cincinnati Reds	9
1906	Tim Jordan, Brooklyn Dodgers	12
1907	Dave Brain, Boston Nationals	10
1908	Tim Jordan, Brooklyn Dodgers	12
1909	Jim Murray, New York Giants	7
1910	Fred Beck, Boston Nationals	10
	Frank Schulte, Chicago Cubs	10
1911	Frank Schulte, Chicago Cubs	21
1912	Heinie Zimmerman, Chicago Cubs	14
1913	Gavvy Cravath, Philadelphia Phillies	19
1914	Gavvy Cravath, Philadelphia Phillies	19
1915	Gavvy Cravath, Philadelphia Phillies	24

Year	Player, Club	HRs
1916	Dave Robertson, New York Giants	12
	Cy Williams, Chicago Cubs	12
1917	Gavvy Cravath, Philadelphia Phillies	12
	Dave Robertson, New York Giants	12
1918	Gavvy Cravath, Philadelphia Phillies	8
1919	Gavvy Cravath, Philadelphia Phillies	12
1920	Cy Williams, Philadelphia Phillies	15
1921	George Kelly, New York Giants	23
1922	Rogers Hornsby, St. Louis Cardinals	42
1923	Cy Williams, Philadelphia Phillies	41
1924	Jack Fournier, Brooklyn Dodgers	27
1925	Rogers Hornsby, St. Louis Cardinals	39
1926	Hack Wilson, Chicago Cubs	21
1927	Cy Williams, Philadelphia Phillies	30
	Hack Wilson, Chicago Cubs	30
1928	Jim Bottomley, St. Louis Cardinals	31
	Hack Wilson, Chicago Cubs	31
1929	Chuck Klein, Philadelphia Phillies	43
1930	Hack Wilson, Chicago Cubs	56
1931	Chuck Klein, Philadelphia Phillies	31
1932	Chuck Klein, Philadelphia Phillies	38
	Mel Ott, New York Giants	38
1933	Chuck Klein, Philadelphia Phillies	28
1934	Rip Collins, St. Louis Cardinals	35
	Mel Ott, New York Giants	35
1935	Wally Berger, Boston Braves	34
1936	Mel Ott, New York Giants	33
1937	Joe Medwick, St. Louis Cardinals	31
	Mel Ott, New York Giants	31
1938	Mel Ott, New York Giants	36
1939	Johnny Mize, St. Louis Cardinals	28
1940	Johnny Mize, St. Louis Cardinals	43
1941	Dolph Camilli, Brooklyn Dodgers	34
1942	Mel Ott, New York Giants	30
1943	Bill Nicholson, Chicago Cubs	29
1944	Bill Nicholson, Chicago Cubs	33
1945	Tommy Holmes, Boston Braves	28
1946	Ralph Kiner, Pittsburgh Pirates	23
1947	Ralph Kiner, Pittsburgh Pirates	51
	Johnny Mize, New York Giants	51
1948	Ralph Kiner, Pittsburgh Pirates	40
	Johnny Mize, New York Giants	40
1949	Ralph Kiner, Pittsburgh Pirates	54
1950	Ralph Kiner, Pittsburgh Pirates	47

Year	Player, Club	HRs
1951	Ralph Kiner, Pittsburgh Pirates	42
1952	Ralph Kiner, Pittsburgh Pirates	37
	Hank Sauer, Chicago Cubs	37
1953	Eddie Mathews, Milwaukee Braves	47
1954	Ted Kluszewski, Cincinnati Reds	49
1955	Willie Mays, New York Giants	51
1956	Duke Snider, Brooklyn Dodgers	43
1957	Hank Aaron, Milwaukee Braves	44
1958	Ernie Banks, Chicago Cubs	47
1959	Eddie Mathews, Milwaukee Braves	46
1960	Ernie Banks, Chicago Cubs	41
1961	Orlando Cepeda, San Francisco Giants	46
1962	Willie Mays, San Francisco Giants	49
1963	Hank Aaron, Milwaukee Braves	44
	Willie McCovey, San Francisco Giants	44
1964	Willie Mays, San Francisco Giants	47
1965	Willie Mays, San Francisco Giants	52
1966	Hank Aaron, Atlanta Braves	44
1967	Hank Aaron, Atlanta Braves	39
1968	Willie McCovey, San Francisco Giants	36
1969	Willie McCovey, San Francisco Giants	45
1970	Johnny Bench, Cincinnati Reds	45
1971	Willie Stargell, Pittsburgh Pirates	48
1972	Johnny Bench, Cincinnati Reds	40
1973	Willie Stargell, Pittsburgh Pirates	44
1974	Mike Schmidt, Philadelphia Phillies	36
1975	Mike Schmidt, Philadelphia Phillies	38
1976	Mike Schmidt, Philadelphia Phillies	38
1977	George Foster, Cincinnati Reds	52
1978	George Foster, Cincinnati Reds	40
1979	Dave Kingman, Chicago Cubs	48
1980	Mike Schmidt, Philadelphia Phillies	48
1981	Mike Schmidt, Philadelphia Phillies	31
1982	Dave Kingman, New York Mets	37
1983	Mike Schmidt, Philadelphia Phillies	40
1984	Mike Schmidt, Philadelphia Phillies	36
1984	Dale Murphy, Atlanta Braves	36
1985	Dale Murphy, Atlanta Braves	37
1986	Mike Schmidt, Philadelphia Phillies	37
1987	Andre Dawson, Chicago Cubs	49
1988	Darryl Strawberry, New York Mets	39
1989	Kevin Mitchell, San Francisco Giants	47
1990	Ryne Sandberg, Chicago Cubs	40
1991	Howard Johnson, New York Mets	38

Year	Player, Club	HRs
1992	Fred McGriff, San Diego Padres	35
1993	Barry Bonds, San Francisco Giants	46
1994	Matt Williams, San Francisco Giants	43
1995	Dante Bichette, Colorado Rockies	40

AMERICAN LEAGUE
Home Run Leaders

Year	Player, Club	HRs
1901	Napoleon Lajoie, Philadelphia Athletics	13
1902	Ralph Seybold, Philadelphia Athletics	16
1903	John Freeman, Boston Pilgrims	13
1904	Harry Davis, Philadelphia Athletics	10
1905	Harry Davis, Philadelphia Athletics	8
1906	Harry Davis, Philadelphia Athletics	12
1907	Harry Davis, Philadelphia Athletics	8
1908	Sam Crawford, Detroit Tigers	7
1909	Ty Cobb, Detroit Tigers	9
1910	Garland Stahl, Boston Red Sox	10
1911	Frank (Home Run) Baker, Philadelphia Athletics	9
1912	Frank (Home Run) Baker, Philadelphia Athletics	10
1913	Frank (Home Run) Baker, Philadelphia Athletics	12
1914	Frank (Home Run) Baker, Philadelphia Athletics	8
	Sam Crawford, Detroit Tigers	8
1915	Bob Roth, Cleveland Indians	7
1916	Wally Pipp, New York Yankees	12
1917	Wally Pipp, New York Yankees	9
1918	Babe Ruth, Boston Red Sox	11
	Clarence Walker, Philadelphia Athletics	11
1919	Babe Ruth, Boston Red Sox	29
1920	Babe Ruth, New York Yankees	54
1921	Babe Ruth, New York Yankees	59
1922	Ken Williams, St. Louis Browns	39
1923	Babe Ruth, New York Yankees	41
1924	Babe Ruth, New York Yankees	46
1925	Bob Meusel, New York Yankees	33
1926	Babe Ruth, New York Yankees	47
1927	Babe Ruth, New York Yankees	60
1928	Babe Ruth, New York Yankees	54
1929	Babe Ruth, New York Yankees	46
1930	Babe Ruth, New York Yankees	49
1931	Babe Ruth, New York Yankees	46
	Lou Gehrig, New York Yankees	46
1932	Jimmie Foxx, Philadelphia Athletics	58

Year	Player, Club	HRs
1933	Jimmie Foxx, Philadelphia Athletics	48
1934	Lou Gehrig, New York Yankees	49
1935	Hank Greenberg, Detroit Tigers	36
	Jimmie Foxx, Philadelphia Athletics	36
1936	Lou Gehrig, New York Yankees	46
1937	Joe DiMaggio, New York Yankees	46
1938	Hank Greenberg, Detroit Tigers	58
1939	Jimmy Foxx, Boston Red Sox	35
1940	Hank Greenberg, Detroit Tigers	41
1941	Ted Williams, Boston Red Sox	37
1942	Ted Williams, Boston Red Sox	36
1943	Rudy York, Detroit Tigers	34
1944	Nick Etten, New York Yankees	22
1945	Vern Stephens, St. Louis Browns	24
1946	Hank Greenberg, Detroit Tigers	44
1947	Ted Williams, Boston Red Sox	32
1948	Joe DiMaggio, New York Yankees	39
1949	Ted Williams, Boston Red Sox	43
1950	Al Rosen, Cleveland Indians	37
1951	Gus Zernial, Philadelphia Athletics	33
1952	Larry Doby, Cleveland Indians	32
1953	Al Rosen, Cleveland Indians	43
1954	Larry Doby, Cleveland Indians	32
1955	Mickey Mantle, New York Yankees	37
1956	Mickey Mantle, New York Yankees	52
1957	Roy Sievers, Washington Senators	42
1958	Mickey Mantle, New York Yankees	42
1959	Rocky Colavito, Cleveland Indians	42
	Harmon Killebrew, Washington Senators	42
1960	Mickey Mantle, New York Yankees	40
1961	Roger Maris, New York Yankees	61
1962	Harmon Killebrew, Minnesota Twins	48
1963	Harmon Killebrew, Minnesota Twins	45
1964	Harmon Killebrew, Minnesota Twins	49
1965	Tony Conigliaro, Boston Red Sox	32
1966	Frank Robinson, Baltimore Orioles	49
1967	Carl Yastrzemski, Boston Red Sox	44
	Harmon Killebrew, Minnesota Twins	44
1968	Frank Howard, Washington Senators	44
1969	Harmon Killebrew, Minnesota Twins	49
1970	Frank Howard, Washington Senators	44
1971	Bill Melton, Chicago White Sox	33
1972	Dick Allen, Chicago White Sox	37
1973	Reggie Jackson, Oakland A's	32

Year	Player, Club	HRs
1974	Dick Allen, Chicago White Sox	32
1975	George Scott, Milwaukee Brewers	36
	Reggie Jackson, Oakland A's	36
1976	Graig Nettles, New York Yankees	32
1977	Jim Rice, Boston Red Sox	39
1978	Jim Rice, Boston Red Sox	46
1979	Gorman Thomas, Milwaukee Brewers	45
1980	Ben Oglivie, Milwaukee Brewers	41
	Reggie Jackson, New York Yankees	41
1981	Bobby Grich, California Angels	22
	Eddie Murray, Baltimore Orioles	22
	Dwight Evans, Boston Red Sox	22
	Tony Armas, Oakland A's	22
1982	Reggie Jackson, California Angels	39
	Gorman Thomas, Milwaukee Brewers	39
1983	Jim Rice, Boston Red Sox	39
1984	Tony Armas, Boston Red Sox	43
1985	Darrell Evans, Detroit Tigers	40
1986	Jesse Barfield, Toronto Blue Jays	40
1987	Mark McGwire, Oakland A's	49
1988	Jose Canseco, Oakland A's	42
1989	Fred McGriff, Toronto Blue Jays	36
1990	Cecil Fielder, Detroit Tigers	51
1991	Jose Canseco, Oakland A's	44
	Cecil Fielder, Detroit Tigers	44
1992	Juan Gonzalez, Texas Rangers	43
1993	Juan Gonzalez, Texas Rangers	46
1994	Ken Griffey, Seattle Mariners	40
1995	Albert Belle, Cleveland Indians	50

CY YOUNG AWARD WINNERS

(Prior to 1967 there was a single overall major league award.)

Year	Player, Club
1956	Don Newcombe, Brooklyn Dodgers
1957	Warren Spahn, Milwaukee Braves
1958	Bob Turley, New York Yankees
1959	Early Wynn, Chicago White Sox
1960	Vernon Law, Pittsburgh Pirates
1961	Whitey Ford, New York Yankees
1962	Don Drysdale, Los Angeles Dodgers
1963	Sandy Koufax, Los Angeles Dodgers

Year	Player, Club
1964	Dean Chance, Los Angeles Angels
1965	Sandy Koufax, Los Angeles Dodgers
1966	Sandy Koufax, Los Angeles Dodgers

AL CY YOUNG

Year	Player, Club
1967	Jim Lonborg, Boston Red Sox
1968	Dennis McLain, Detroit Tigers
1969	Mike Cuellar, Baltimore Orioles
	Dennis McLain, Detroit Tigers
1970	Jim Perry, Minnesota Twins
1971	Vida Blue, Oakland A's
1972	Gaylord Perry, Cleveland Indians
1973	Jim Palmer, Baltimore Orioles
1974	Jim Hunter, Oakland A's
1975	Jim Palmer, Baltimore Orioles
1976	Jim Palmer, Baltimore Orioles
1977	Sparky Lyle, New York Yankees
1978	Ron Guidry, New York Yankees
1979	Mike Flanagan, Baltimore Orioles
1980	Steve Stone, Baltimore Orioles
1981	Rollie Fingers, Milwaukee Brewers
1982	Pete Vuckovich, Milwaukee Brewers
1983	LaMarr Hoyt, Chicago White Sox
1984	Willie Hernandez, Detroit Tigers
1985	Bret Saberhagen, Kansas City Royals
1986	Roger Clemens, Boston Red Sox
1987	Roger Clemens, Boston Red Sox
1988	Frank Viola, Minnesota Twins
1989	Bret Saberhagen, Kansas City Royals
1990	Bob Welch, Oakland A's
1991	Roger Clemens, Boston Red Sox
1992	Dennis Eckersley, Oakland A's
1993	Jack McDowell, Chicago White Sox
1994	David Cone, Kansas City Royals
1995	Randy Johnson, Seattle Mariners

NL CY YOUNG

Year	Player, Club
1967	Mike McCormick, San Francisco Giants
1968	Bob Gibson, St. Louis Cardinals

Year	Player, Club
1969	Tom Seaver, New York Mets
1970	Bob Gibson, St. Louis Cardinals
1971	Ferguson Jenkins, Chicago Cubs
1972	Steve Carlton, Philadelphia Phillies
1973	Tom Seaver, New York Mets
1974	Mike Marshall, Los Angeles Dodgers
1975	Tom Seaver, New York Mets
1976	Randy Jones, San Diego Padres
1977	Steve Carlton, Philadelphia Phillies
1978	Gaylord Perry, San Diego Padres
1979	Bruce Sutter, Chicago Cubs
1980	Steve Carlton, Philadelphia Phillies
1981	Fernando Valenzuela, Los Angeles Dodgers
1982	Steve Carlton, Philadelphia Phillies
1983	John Denny, Philadelphia Phillies
1984	Rick Sutcliffe, Chicago Cubs
1985	Dwight Gooden, New York Mets
1986	Mike Scott, Houston Astros
1987	Steve Bedrosian, Philadelphia Phillies
1988	Orel Hershiser, Los Angeles Dodgers
1989	Mark Davis, San Diego Padres
1990	Doug Drabek, Pittsburgh Pirates
1991	Tom Glavine, Atlanta Braves
1992	Greg Maddux, Chicago Cubs
1993	Greg Maddux, Atlanta Braves
1994	Greg Maddux, Atlanta Braves
1995	Greg Maddux, Atlanta Braves

NATIONAL LEAGUE
Rookie of Year

Year	Player, Club
1947	Jackie Robinson, Brooklyn Dodgers
1948	Al Dark, Boston Braves
1949	Don Newcombe, Brooklyn Dodgers
1950	Sam Jethroe, Boston Braves
1951	Willie Mays, New York Giants
1952	Joe Black, Brooklyn Dodgers
1953	Junior Gilliam, Brooklyn Dodgers
1954	Wally Moon, St. Louis Cardinals
1955	Bill Virdon, St. Louis Cardinals
1956	Frank Robinson, Cincinnati Reds
1957	Jack Sanford, Philadelphia Phillies

Year	Player, Club
1958	Orlando Cepeda, San Francisco Giants
1959	Willie McCovey, San Francisco Giants
1960	Frank Howard, Los Angeles Dodgers
1961	Billy Williams, Chicago Cubs
1962	Kenny Hubbs, Chicago Cubs
1963	Pete Rose, Cincinnati Reds
1964	Richie Allen, Philadelphia Phillies
1965	Jim Lefebvre, Los Angeles Dodgers
1966	Tommy Helms, Cincinnati Reds
1967	Tom Seaver, New York Mets
1968	Johnny Bench, Cincinnati Reds
1969	Ted Sizemore, Los Angeles Dodgers
1970	Carl Morton, Montreal Expos
1971	Earl Williams, Atlanta Braves
1972	Jon Matlack, New York Mets
1973	Gary Matthews, San Francisco Giants
1974	Bake McBride, St. Louis Cardinals
1975	John Montefusco, San Francisco Giants
1976	Pat Zachry, Cincinnati Reds
	Butch Metzger, San Diego Padres
1977	Andre Dawson, Montreal Expos
1978	Bob Horner, Atlanta Braves
1979	Rick Sutcliffe, Los Angeles Dodgers
1980	Steve Howe, Los Angeles Dodgers
1981	Fernando Valenzuela, Los Angeles Dodgers
1982	Steve Sax, Los Angeles Dodgers
1983	Darryl Strawberry, New York Mets
1984	Dwight Gooden, New York Mets
1985	Vince Coleman, St. Louis Cardinals
1986	Todd Worrell, St. Louis Cardinals
1987	Benito Santiago, San Diego Padres
1988	Chris Sabo, Cincinnati Reds
1989	Jerome Walton, Chicago Cubs
1990	Dave Justice, Atlanta Braves
1991	Jeff Bagwell, Houston Astros
1992	Eric Karros, Los Angeles Dodgers
1993	Mike Piazza, Los Angeles Dodgers
1994	Raul Mondesi, Los Angeles Dodgers
1995	Hideo Nomo, Los Angeles Dodgers

AMERICAN LEAGUE
Rookie of Year

Year	Player, Club
1949	Roy Sievers, St. Louis Browns

Year	Player, Club
1950	Walt Dropo, Boston Red Sox
1951	Gil McDougald, New York Yankees
1952	Harry Byrd, Philadelphia Athletics
1953	Harvey Kuenn, Detroit Tigers
1954	Bob Grim, New York Yankees
1955	Herb Score, Cleveland Indians
1956	Luis Aparicio, Chicago White Sox
1957	Tony Kubek, New York Yankees
1958	Albie Pearson, Washington Senators
1959	Bob Allison, Washington Senators
1960	Ron Hansen, Baltimore Orioles
1961	Don Schwall, Boston Red Sox
1962	Tom Tresh, New York Yankees
1963	Gary Peters, Chicago White Sox
1964	Tony Oliva, Minnesota Twins
1965	Curt Blefary, Baltimore Orioles
1966	Tommie Agee, Chicago White Sox
1967	Rod Carew, Minnesota Twins
1968	Stan Bahnsen, New York Yankees
1969	Lou Piniella, Kansas City Royals
1970	Thurman Munson, New York Yankees
1971	Chris Chambliss, Cleveland Indians
1972	Carlton Fisk, Boston Red Sox
1973	Al Bumbry, Baltimore Orioles
1974	Mike Hargrove, Texas Rangers
1975	Fred Lynn, Boston Red Sox
1976	Mark Fidrych, Detroit Tigers
1977	Eddie Murray, Baltimore Orioles
1978	Lou Whitaker, Detroit Tigers
1979	John Castino, Minnesota Twins
	Alfredo Griffin, Toronto Blue Jays
1980	Joe Charboneau, Cleveland Indians
1981	Dave Righetti, New York Yankees
1982	Cal Ripken Jr., Baltimore Orioles
1983	Ron Kittle, Chicago White Sox
1984	Alvin Davis, Seattle Mariners
1985	Ozzie Guillen, Chicago White Sox
1986	Jose Canseco, Oakland A's
1987	Mark McGwire, Oakland A's
1988	Walt Weiss, Oakland A's
1989	Gregg Olson, Baltimore Orioles
1990	Sandy Alomar Jr., Cleveland Indians
1991	Chuck Knoblauch, Minnesota Twins
1992	Pat Listach, Milwaukee Brewers

Year	Player, Club
1993	Tim Salmon, California Angels
1994	Bob Hamelin, Kansas City Royals
1995	Marty Cordova, Minnesota Twins

ALL-TIME MAJOR LEAGUE RECORDS

Sandy Koufax owns season K mark for southpaws.

National	American
Batting (Season)	
Average	
.438 Hugh Duffy, Boston, 1894	.422 Napoleon Lajoie, Phila. 1901
.424 Rogers Hornsby, St. Louis, 1924	
At Bat	
701 Juan Samuel, Phila., 1984	705 Willie Wilson, Kansas City, 1980
Runs	
196 William Hamilton, Phila., 1894	177 Babe Ruth, New York, 1921
158 Chuck Klein, Phila., 1930	

Hits

254 Frank J. O'Doul, Phila., 1929	257 George Sisler, St. Louis, 1920
254 Bill Terry, New York, 1930	

Doubles

64 Joseph M. Medwick, St. L., 1936	67 Earl W. Webb, Boston, 1931

Triples

36 J. Owen Wilson, Pitts., 1912	26 Joseph Jackson, Cleve., 1912
	26 Samuel Crawford, Detroit, 1914

Home Runs

56 Hack Wilson, Chicago, 1930	61 Roger Maris, New York, 1961

Runs Batted In

190 Hack Wilson, Chicago, 1930	184 Lou Gehrig, New York, 1931

Stolen Bases

118 Lou Brock, St. Louis, 1974	130 Rickey Henderson, Oakland, 1982

Bases on Balls

148 Eddie Stanky, Brooklyn, 1945	170 Babe Ruth, New York, 1923
148 Jim Wynn, Houston, 1969	

Strikeouts

189 Bobby Bonds, S.F., 1970	186 Rob Deer, Milwaukee, 1987

Pitching (Season)

Games

106 Mike Marshall, L.A., 1974	88 Wilbur Wood, Chicago, 1968

Innings Pitched

434 Joseph J. McGinnity, N.Y., 1903	464 Edward Walsh, Chicago, 1908

Victories

37 Christy Mathewson, N.Y., 1908	41 Jack Chesbro, New York, 1904

Losses

29 Victor Willis, Boston, 1905	26 John Townsend, Wash., 1904
	26 Robert Groom, Wash., 1909

Strikeouts

(Left-hander)

382 Sandy Koufax, Los Angeles, 1965	343 Rube Waddell, Phila., 1904

(Right-hander)

313 J.R. Richard, Houston, 1979	383 Nolan Ryan, Cal., 1973

Bases on Balls

185 Sam Jones, Chicago, 1955	208 Bob Feller, Cleveland, 1938

Earned-Run Average

(Minimum 300 Innings)

1.12 Bob Gibson, St. L., 1968	1.09 Walter Johnson, Washington, 1913

Shutouts

16 Grover C. Alexander, Phila., 1916	13 John W. Coombs, Phila., 1910

WORLD SERIES WINNERS

Year	A.L. Champion	N.L. Champion	World Series Winner
1903	Boston Red Sox	Pittsburgh Pirates	Boston, 5-3
1905	Philadelphia Athletics	New York Giants	New York, 4-1
1906	Chicago White Sox	Chicago Cubs	Chicago (AL), 4-2
1907	Detroit Tigers	Chicago Cubs	Chicago, 4-0-1
1908	Detroit Tigers	Chicago Cubs	Chicago, 4-1
1909	Detroit Tigers	Pittsburgh Pirates	Pittsburgh, 4-3
1910	Philadelphia Athletics	Chicago Cubs	Philadelphia, 4-1
1911	Philadelphia Athletics	New York Giants	Philadelphia, 4-2
1912	Boston Red Sox	New York Giants	Boston, 4-3-1
1913	Philadelphia Athletics	New York Giants	Philadelphia 4-1
1914	Philadelphia Athletics	Boston Braves	Boston, 4-0
1915	Boston Red Sox	Philadelphia Phillies	Boston, 4-1
1916	Boston Red Sox	Brooklyn Dodgers	Boston, 4-1
1917	Chicago White Sox	New York Giants	Chicago, 4-2
1918	Boston Red Sox	Chicago Cubs	Boston, 4-2
1919	Chicago White Sox	Cincinnati Reds	Cincinnati, 5-3
1920	Cleveland Indians	Brooklyn Dodgers	Cleveland, 5-2
1921	New York Yankees	New York Giants	New York (NL), 5-3
1922	New York Yankees	New York Giants	New York (NL), 4-0-1
1923	New York Yankees	New York Giants	New York (AL), 4-2
1924	Washington Senators	New York Giants	Washington, 4-2
1925	Washington Senators	Pittsburgh Pirates	Pittsburgh, 4-3
1926	New York Yankees	St. Louis Cardinals	St. Louis, 4-3
1927	New York Yankees	Pittsburgh Pirates	New York, 4-0
1928	New York Yankees	St. Louis Cardinals	New York, 4-0
1929	Philadelphia Athletics	Chicago Cubs	Philadelphia, 4-2
1930	Philadelphia Athletics	St. Louis Cardinals	Philadelphia, 4-2
1931	Philadelphia Athletics	St. Louis Cardinals	St. Louis, 4-3
1932	New York Yankees	Chicago Cubs	New York, 4-0
1933	Washington Senators	New York Giants	New York, 4-1
1934	Detroit Tigers	St. Louis Cardinals	St. Louis, 4-3
1935	Detroit Tigers	Chicago Cubs	Detroit, 4-2
1936	New York Yankees	New York Giants	New York (AL), 4-2
1937	New York Yankees	New York Giants	New York (AL), 4-1
1938	New York Yankees	Chicago Cubs	New York, 4-0
1939	New York Yankees	Cincinnati Reds	New York, 4-0
1940	Detroit Tigers	Cincinnati Reds	Cincinnati, 4-3
1941	New York Yankees	Brooklyn Dodgers	New York, 4-1
1942	New York Yankees	St. Louis Cardinals	St. Louis, 4-1
1943	New York Yankees	St. Louis Cardinals	New York, 4-1
1944	St. Louis Browns	St. Louis Cardinals	St. Louis (NL), 4-2
1945	Detroit Tigers	Chicago Cubs	Detroit, 4-3
1946	Boston Red Sox	St. Louis Cardinals	St. Louis, 4-3
1947	New York Yankees	Brooklyn Dodgers	New York, 4-3
1948	Cleveland Indians	Boston Braves	Cleveland, 4-2
1949	New York Yankees	Brooklyn Dodgers	New York, 4-1
1950	New York Yankees	Philadelphia Phillies	New York, 4-0
1951	New York Yankees	New York Giants	New York (AL), 4-2
1952	New York Yankees	Brooklyn Dodgers	New York, 4-3

ear	A. L. Champion	N. L. Champion	World Series Winner
953	New York Yankees	Brooklyn Dodgers	New York, 4-2
954	Cleveland Indians	New York Giants	New York, 4-0
955	New York Yankees	Brooklyn Dodgers	Brooklyn, 4-3
956	New York Yankees	Brooklyn Dodgers	New York, 4-3
957	New York Yankees	Milwaukee Braves	Milwaukee, 4-3
958	New York Yankees	Milwaukee Braves	New York, 4-3
959	Chicago White Sox	Los Angeles Dodgers	Los Angeles, 4-2
960	New York Yankees	Pittsburgh Pirates	Pittsburgh, 4-3
961	New York Yankees	Cincinnati Reds	New York, 4-1
962	New York Yankees	San Francisco Giants	New York, 4-3
963	New York Yankees	Los Angeles Dodgers	Los Angeles, 4-0
964	New York Yankees	St. Louis Cardinals	St. Louis, 4-3
965	Minnesota Twins	Los Angeles Dodgers	Los Angeles, 4-0
966	Baltimore Orioles	Los Angeles Dodgers	Baltimore, 4-0
967	Boston Red Sox	St. Louis Cardinals	St. Louis, 4-3
968	Detroit Tigers	St. Louis Cardinals	Detroit, 4-3
969	Baltimore Orioles	New York Mets	New York, 4-1
970	Baltimore Orioles	Cincinnati Reds	Baltimore, 4-1
971	Baltimore Orioles	Pittsburgh Pirates	Pittsburgh, 4-3
972	Oakland A's	Cincinnati Reds	Oakland, 4-3
973	Oakland A's	New York Mets	Oakland, 4-3
974	Oakland A's	Los Angeles Dodgers	Oakland, 4-1
975	Boston Red Sox	Cincinnati Reds	Cincinnati, 4-3
976	New York Yankees	Cincinnati Reds	Cincinnati, 4-0
977	New York Yankees	Los Angeles Dodgers	New York, 4-2
978	New York Yankees	Los Angeles Dodgers	New York, 4-2
979	Baltimore Orioles	Pittsburgh Pirates	Pittsburgh, 4-3
980	Kansas City Royals	Philadelphia Phillies	Philadelphia, 4-2
981	New York Yankees	Los Angeles Dodgers	Los Angeles, 4-2
982	Milwaukee Brewers	St. Louis Cardinals	St. Louis, 4-3
983	Baltimore Orioles	Philadelphia Phillies	Baltimore, 4-1
984	Detroit Tigers	San Diego Padres	Detroit, 4-1
985	Kansas City Royals	St. Louis Cardinals	Kansas City, 4-3
986	Boston Red Sox	New York Mets	New York, 4-3
987	Minnesota Twins	St. Louis Cardinals	Minnesota, 4-3
988	Oakland A's	Los Angeles Dodgers	Los Angeles, 4-1
989	Oakland A's	San Francisco Giants	Oakland, 4-0
990	Oakland A's	Cincinnati Reds	Cincinnati, 4-0
991	Minnesota Twins	Atlanta Braves	Minnesota, 4-3
992	Toronto Blue Jays	Atlanta Braves	Toronto, 4-2
993	Toronto Blue Jays	Philadelphia Phillies	Toronto, 4-2
994	Cancelled due to players' strike		
995	Cleveland Indians	Atlanta Braves	Atlanta, 4-2

1995 WORLD SERIES

ATLANTA BRAVES

PLAYER	AVG	G	AB	R	H	2B	3B	HR	RBI	SH	SF	HB	BB	SO	SB	CS	E
Belliard, R	.000	6	16	0	0	0	0	0	1	2	0	0	0	4	0	0	2
Devereaux, M	.250	5	4	0	1	0	0	0	1	0	0	0	2	1	0	0	1
Grissom, M	.360	6	25	3	9	1	0	0	1	0	0	1	1	3	3	1	0
Jones, C	.286	6	21	3	6	3	0	0	1	0	1	0	4	3	0	0	1
RIGHT	.000	-	3	-	0	0	0	0	0	0	0	0	3	1	-	-	-
LEFT	.333	-	18	-	6	3	0	0	1	0	1	0	1	2	-	-	-
Justice, D	.250	6	20	3	5	1	0	1	5	0	0	0	5	1	0	0	0
Klesko, R	.313	6	16	4	5	0	0	3	4	0	0	0	3	4	0	0	0
Lemke, M	.273	6	22	1	6	0	0	0	0	1	0	0	3	2	0	1	1
RIGHT	.000	-	2	-	0	0	0	0	0	1	0	0	0	0	-	-	-
LEFT	.300	-	20	-	6	0	0	0	0	0	0	0	3	2	-	-	-
Lopez, J	.176	6	17	1	3	2	0	1	3	0	0	1	1	1	0	0	0
McGriff, F	.261	6	23	5	6	2	0	2	3	0	0	0	3	7	1	0	1
Mordecai, M	.333	3	3	0	1	0	0	0	0	1	0	0	0	1	0	0	0
O'Brien, C	.000	2	3	0	0	0	0	0	0	1	0	0	0	1	0	0	0
Polonia, L	.286	6	14	3	4	1	0	1	4	0	0	0	1	3	1	0	0
Smith, D	.500	3	2	0	1	0	0	0	0	0	0	0	1	0	0	0	0
Glavine, T	.000	2	4	0	0	0	0	0	0	0	0	0	1	2	0	0	0
Maddux, G	.000	2	3	0	0	0	0	0	0	0	0	0	0	1	0	0	0

PITCHER		W	L	ERA	G	GS	CG	SHO	SV	IP	H	R	ER	HR	HB	BB	SO	WP
Avery, S	L	1	0	1.50	1	1	0	0	0	6.0	3	1	1	1	0	5	3	0
Borbon, P	L	0	0	0.00	1	0	0	0	1	1.0	0	0	0	0	0	0	2	0
Clontz, B	R	0	0	2.70	2	0	0	0	0	3.1	2	1	1	1	0	0	2	0
Glavine, T	L	2	0	1.29	2	2	0	0	0	14.0	4	2	2	1	0	6	11	1
Maddux, G	R	1	1	2.25	2	2	1	0	0	16.0	9	6	4	1	0	3	8	0
McMichael, G	R	0	0	2.70	3	0	0	0	0	3.1	3	2	1	0	0	2	2	1
Mercker, K	L	0	0	4.50	1	0	0	0	0	2.0	1	1	1	0	0	2	2	0
Pena, A	R	0	1	9.00	2	0	0	0	0	1.0	3	1	1	0	0	2	0	0
Smoltz, J	R	0	0	15.43	1	1	0	0	0	2.1	6	4	4	0	0	2	4	0
Wohlers, M	R	0	0	1.80	4	0	0	0	2	5.0	4	1	1	1	0	3	3	0

Game 1
At ATLANTA
Saturday, October 21 (night)

Cleveland	1 0 0 0 0 0 0 0 1	2 2 0
Atlanta	1 1 0 0 0 0 2 0 x	3 3 2

HERSHISER, Assenmacher (7), Tavarez (7) and Embree (8)
MADDUX
HR: Atlanta (1)-McGriff
Time: 2:37
Att: 51,876

Game 2
At ATLANTA
Sunday, October 22 (night)

Cleveland	0 2 0 0 0 0 1 0 0	3 6 2
Atlanta	0 0 2 0 0 2 0 0 x	4 8 2

MARTINEZ, Embree (6), Poole (7) and Tavarez (8)
GLAVINE, McMichael (7), Pena (7) and Wohlers (S) (8)
HR: Cleveland (1)-Murray; Atlanta (1)-Lopez
Time: 3:17
Att: 51,877

Game 3
At CLEVELAND
Tuesday, October 24 (night)

Atlanta	1 0 0 0 0 1 1 3 0 0 0	6 12 1
Cleveland	2 0 2 0 0 0 1 1 0 0 1	7 12 2

Smoltz, Clontz (3), Mercker (5), McMichael (7), Wohlers (8) and PENA (11)
Nagy, Assenmacher (8), Tavarez (8) and MESA (9)
HR: Atlanta (2)-McGriff, Klesko
Time: 4:09
Att: 43,584

CLEVELAND INDIANS

PLAYER	AVG	G	AB	R	H	2B	3B	HR	RBI	SH	SF	HB	BB	SO	SB	CS	E
Alomar, S	.200	5	15	0	3	2	0	0	1	0	0	0	0	2	0	0	0
Amaro, R	.000	2	2	0	0	0	0	0	0	0	0	0	0	1	0	0	0
RIGHT	.000	-	1	-	0	0	0	0	0	0	0	0	0	0	-	-	-
LEFT	.000	-	1	-	0	0	0	0	0	0	0	0	0	1	-	-	-
Baerga, C	.192	6	26	1	5	2	0	0	4	0	0	0	1	1	0	0	1
RIGHT	.200	-	10	-	2	0	0	0	1	0	0	0	0	0	-	-	-
LEFT	.188	-	16	-	3	2	0	0	3	0	0	0	1	1	-	-	-
Belle, A	.235	6	17	4	4	0	0	2	4	0	0	0	7	5	0	1	1
Espinoza, A	.500	2	2	1	1	0	0	0	0	0	0	0	0	0	0	1	0
Kirby, W	.000	3	1	0	0	0	0	0	0	0	0	0	0	1	0	0	0
Lofton, K	.200	6	25	6	5	1	0	0	0	0	0	0	3	1	6	1	0
Murray, E	.105	6	19	1	2	0	0	1	3	0	0	0	5	4	0	0	0
RIGHT	.167	-	6	-	1	0	0	1	2	0	0	0	4	2	-	-	-
LEFT	.077	-	13	-	1	0	0	0	1	0	0	0	1	2	-	-	-
Pena, T	.167	2	6	0	1	0	0	0	0	0	0	0	0	0	0	0	0
Perry, H	.000	3	5	0	0	0	0	0	0	0	0	0	0	2	0	0	0
Ramirez, M	.222	6	18	2	4	0	0	1	2	0	0	0	4	5	1	0	0
Sorrento, P	.182	6	11	0	2	1	0	0	0	0	0	0	0	4	0	0	1
Thome, J	.211	6	19	1	4	1	0	1	2	0	0	0	2	5	0	0	1
Vizquel, O	.174	6	23	3	4	0	1	0	1	0	0	0	3	5	1	0	0
RIGHT	.000	-	8	-	0	0	0	0	0	0	0	0	2	2	-	-	-
LEFT	.267	-	15	-	4	0	1	0	1	0	0	0	1	3	-	-	-
Hershiser, O	.000	2	2	0	0	0	0	0	0	0	0	0	0	0	0	0	1
Martinez, D	.000	2	3	0	0	0	0	0	0	0	0	0	0	1	0	0	1
Poole, J	.000	2	1	0	0	0	0	0	0	0	0	0	0	0	0	0	0
DH	.091	6	11	0	1	0	0	0	1	0	0	0	3	3	0	0	0
PITCHERS	.000	6	6	0	0	0	0	0	0	0	0	0	0	1	0	0	2

PITCHER		W	L	ERA	G	GS	CG	SHO	SV	IP	H	R	ER	HR	HB	BB	SO	WP
Assenmacher, P	L	0	0	6.75	4	0	0	0	0	1.1	1	2	1	0	0	3	3	0
Embree, A	L	0	0	2.70	4	0	0	0	0	3.1	2	1	1	0	0	2	2	0
Hershiser, O	R	1	1	2.57	2	2	0	0	0	14.0	8	5	4	2	0	4	13	0
Hill, K	R	0	1	4.26	2	1	0	0	0	6.1	7	3	3	1	0	4	1	0
Martinez, D	R	0	1	3.48	2	2	0	0	0	10.1	12	4	4	1	1	8	5	0
Mesa, J	R	1	0	4.50	2	0	0	0	1	4.0	5	2	2	1	0	1	4	0
Nagy, C	R	0	0	6.43	1	1	0	0	0	7.0	8	5	5	2	0	1	4	0
Poole, J	L	0	1	3.86	2	0	0	0	0	2.1	1	1	1	1	0	0	1	0
Tavarez, J	R	0	0	0.00	5	0	0	0	0	4.1	3	0	0	0	1	2	1	0

Game 4
At CLEVELAND
Wednesday, October 25 (night)

Atlanta	000	001	301	5 11 1
Cleveland	000	001	001	2 6 0

AVERY, McMichael (7), Wohlers (9) and Borbon (9) (S)
HILL, Assenmacher (7), Tavarez (8) and Embree (8)
HR: Atlanta (1)-Klesko; Cleveland (2)-Belle, Ramirez
Time: 3:14
Att: 43,578

Game 5
At CLEVELAND
Thursday, October 26 (night)

Atlanta	000	110	002	4 7 0
Cleveland	200	002	01x	5 8 1

MADDUX and Klontz (8)
HERSHISER and Mesa (S) (8)
HR: Atlanta (2)-Polonia, Klesko; Cleveland (2)-Belle, Thome
Time: 2:33
Att: 43,595

Game 6
At ATLANTA
Saturday, October 28 (night)

Cleveland	000	000	000	0 1 1
Atlanta	000	001	00x	1 6 0

Martinez, POOLE (5), Hill (7), Embree (7), Tavarez (8) and Assenmacher (8)
GLAVINE and Wohlers (S) (9)
HR: Atlanta (1)-Justice
Time: 3:02
Att: 51,875

SCORE BY INNINGS

Atlanta	112	115	633	00	23 47 6
Cleveland	522	003	222	01	19 35 6

OFFICIAL 1995 NATIONAL LEAGUE RECORDS

COMPILED BY MLB-IBM BASEBALL INFORMATION SYSTEM
Official Statistician: ELIAS SPORTS BUREAU

FINAL STANDINGS

EASTERN DIVISION	W	L	PCT.	GB
ATLANTA	90	54	.625	-
PHILADELPHIA	69	75	.479	21.0
NEW YORK	69	75	.479	21.0
FLORIDA	67	76	.469	22.5
MONTREAL	66	78	.458	24.0

CENTRAL DIVISION	W	L	PCT.	GB
CINCINNATI	85	59	.590	-
HOUSTON	76	68	.528	9.0
CHICAGO	73	71	.507	12.0
ST. LOUIS	62	81	.434	22.5
PITTSBURGH	58	86	.403	27.0

WESTERN DIVISION	W	L	PCT.	GB
LOS ANGELES	78	66	.542	-
COLORADO	77	67	.535	1.0
SAN DIEGO	70	74	.486	8.0
SAN FRANCISCO	67	77	.465	11.0

FORFEIT GAME—ST. LOUIS AT LOS ANGELES, AUGUST 10

Division Series: Cincinnati defeated Los Angeles, 3 games to 0
Atlanta defeated Colorado, 3 games to 1
Championship Series: Atlanta defeated Cincinnati, 4 games to 0

Batting

Individual Batting Leaders

Batting Average	.368	Gwynn	S.D.
Games	144	Bonds	S.F.
		McGriff	Atl.
		Sosa	Chi.
At-Bats	580	McRae	Chi.
Runs	123	Biggio	Hou.
Hits	197	Bichette	Col.
		Gwynn	S.D.
Total Bases	359	Bichette	Col.
Singles	154	Gwynn	S.D.
Doubles	51	Grace	Chi.
Triples	9	Butler	N.Y.-L.A.
		Young	Col.
Home Runs	40	Bichette	Col.
Runs Batted In	128	Bichette	Col.
Sacrifice Hits	18	B. Jones	N.Y.
Sacrifice Flies	12	Conine	Fla.
Hit by Pitch	22	Biggio	Hou.
Bases on Balls	120	Bonds	S.F.
Intentional Bases on Balls	22	Bonds	S.F.
Strikeouts	146	Galarraga	Col.
Stolen Bases	56	Veras	Fla.
Caught Stealing	21	Veras	Fla.
Grounded Into Double Play	23	Hayes	Phi.
Slugging Percentage	.620	Bichette	Col.
On-Base Percentage	.431	Bonds	S.F.
Longest Batting Streak	23	Bichette	Col. (May 22-June 18)

During the 1995 season 588 players participated in regular season games.

TOP 15 QUALIFIERS FOR BATTING CHAMPIONSHIP

BATTER	TEAM	B	AVG	G	AB	R	H	TB	2B	3B	HR	RBI	SH	SF	HP	BB	IBB	SO	SB	CS	GIDP	SLG	OBP	E
Gwynn, T	SD	L	.368	135	535	82	197	259	33	1	9	90	0	6	1	35	10	15	17	5	20	.484	.404	2
Piazza, M	LA	R	.346	112	434	82	150	263	17	0	32	93	0	1	1	39	10	80	1	0	10	.606	.400	9
Bichette, D	COL	R	.340	139	579	102	197	359	38	2	40	128	0	7	4	22	5	96	13	9	16	.620	.364	3
Bell, D	HOU	R	.334	112	452	63	151	200	21	2	8	86	0	6	8	33	2	71	27	9	10	.442	.385	8
Grace, M	CHI	L	.326	143	552	97	180	285	51	3	16	92	1	7	2	65	9	46	6	2	10	.516	.395	7
Larkin, B	CIN	R	.319	131	496	98	158	244	29	6	15	66	3	4	3	61	2	49	51	5	6	.492	.394	11
Castilla, V	COL	R	.309	139	527	82	163	297	34	2	32	90	4	6	4	30	2	87	2	8	15	.564	.347	15
Segui, D	NY-MON	S	.309	130	456	68	141	210	25	4	12	68	8	3	3	40	5	47	2	7	10	.461	.367	3
Jefferies, G	PHI	S	.306	114	480	69	147	215	31	2	11	56	0	6	0	35	5	26	9	5	15	.448	.349	3
Sanders, R	CIN	R	.306	133	484	91	148	280	36	6	28	99	0	6	8	69	4	122	36	12	9	.579	.397	5
Walker, L	COL	L	.306	131	494	96	151	300	31	5	36	101	0	5	14	49	13	72	16	3	13	.607	.381	3
Caminiti, K	SD	S	.302	143	526	74	159	270	33	0	26	94	0	6	1	69	8	94	12	5	11	.513	.380	27
Conine, J	FLA	R	.302	133	483	72	146	251	26	2	25	105	0	12	1	66	5	94	2	0	13	.520	.379	6
Biggio, C	HOU	R	.302	141	553	123	167	267	30	2	22	77	11	7	22	80	1	85	33	8	6	.483	.406	10
Butler, B	NY-LA	L	.300	129	513	78	154	193	18	9	1	38	10	6	0	67	2	51	32	8	5	.376	.377	2

INDIVIDUAL BATTING

BATTER	TEAM	B	AVG	G	AB	R	H	TB	2B	3B	HR	RBI	SH	SF	HP	BB	IBB	SO	SB	CS	GIDP	SLG	OBP	E
Abbott, K	FLA	R	.255	120	420	60	107	190	18	7	17	60	2	5	5	36	4	110	4	3	6	.452	.318	19
Abbott, K	PHI	L	.500	18	2	1	1	1	0	0	0	0	0	0	0	0	0	1	0	0	0	.500	.500	1
Acevedo, J	COL	R	.056	17	18	0	1	1	0	0	0	0	0	0	0	1	0	6	0	0	2	.056	.105	1
Alfonzo, E	NY	R	.278	101	335	26	93	128	13	5	4	41	4	4	1	12	1	37	1	1	7	.382	.301	7
Alou, M	MON	R	.273	93	344	48	94	158	22	0	14	58	0	4	9	29	6	56	4	3	9	.459	.342	3
Alvarez, C	MON	R	.000	8	12	1	0	0	0	0	0	0	2	0	0	0	0	4	0	0	0	.000	.000	1
Andrews, S	MON	R	.214	84	220	27	47	83	10	1	8	31	1	2	1	17	2	68	1	1	4	.377	.271	7
Anthony, E	CIN	L	.269	47	134	19	36	57	6	0	5	23	0	3	0	13	2	30	2	1	1	.425	.327	4
Aquino, L	MON-SF	R	.250	34	4	0	1	1	0	0	0	0	0	0	0	1	0	2	0	0	0	.250	.400	0
Arias, A	FLA	R	.269	94	216	22	58	80	9	2	3	26	3	3	2	22	1	20	1	0	8	.370	.337	9
Arocha, R	STL	R	.000	41	1	0	0	0	0	0	0	0	0	0	0	0	0	1	0	0	0	.000	.000	0
Ashby, A	SD	R	.163	31	49	2	8	9	1	0	0	3	17	0	0	1	0	24	1	0	0	.184	.180	1

Ashley, B	LA	R	.237	81	215	17	51	80	5	0	8	27	0	2	2	25	4	88	0	0	8	.372	.320	3
Astacio, P	LA	R	.125	48	24	0	3	4	1	0	0	0	2	0	0	1	0	9	0	0	1	.167	.160	0
Aude, R	PIT	R	.248	42	109	10	27	41	8	0	2	19	0	0	0	6	0	20	1	2	4	.376	.287	1
Aurilia, R	SF	R	.474	9	19	4	9	18	3	0	2	4	1	1	0	1	0	2	1	0	1	.947	.476	0
Ausmus, B	SD	R	.293	103	328	44	96	135	16	4	5	34	4	4	2	31	3	56	16	5	6	.412	.353	6
Avery, S	ATL	L	.208	29	53	4	11	20	1	1	2	4	8	1	0	1	0	17	0	0	0	.377	.218	2
Bagwell, J	HOU	R	.290	114	448	88	130	222	29	0	21	87	0	6	6	79	12	102	12	5	9	.496	.399	7
Bailey, R	COL	R	.125	39	16	2	2	2	0	0	0	1	3	0	0	1	0	3	0	0	0	.125	.176	2
Banks, W	CHI-LA-FLA	R	.269	28	26	2	7	8	1	0	0	1	1	0	1	1	0	9	0	0	0	.308	.321	1
Barber, B	STL	R	.125	9	8	0	1	1	0	0	0	0	0	0	0	1	0	2	0	0	0	.125	.222	0
Barry, J	NY	S	.133	15	15	2	2	3	1	0	0	0	0	0	0	1	0	8	0	0	0	.200	.188	0
Barton, S	SF	R	.000	52	0	0	0	0	0	0	0	0	1	0	0	0	0	0	0	0	0	.000	.000	0
Bates, J	COL	S	.267	116	322	42	86	135	17	4	8	46	2	0	2	42	3	70	3	6	4	.419	.355	5
Battle, A	STL	R	.271	61	118	13	32	37	5	0	0	2	3	0	1	15	0	26	3	3	0	.314	.358	1
Bautista, J	SF	R	.000	52	18	0	0	0	0	0	0	0	1	0	0	1	0	9	0	0	0	.000	.053	1
Bean, B	SD	L	.000	4	7	1	0	0	0	0	0	0	0	0	0	1	0	4	0	0	0	.000	.125	1
Beck, R	SF	R	.333	60	3	0	1	1	0	0	0	0	0	0	0	0	0	1	0	0	0	.333	.333	0
Bell, D	STL	R	.250	39	144	13	36	53	7	2	2	19	0	1	2	4	0	25	1	2	0	.368	.278	7
Bell, D	HOU	R	.334	112	452	63	151	200	21	2	8	86	0	6	8	33	2	71	27	9	10	.442	.385	8
Bell, J	PIT	R	.262	138	530	79	139	214	28	4	13	55	3	1	4	55	1	110	2	5	13	.404	.336	14
Belliard, R	ATL	R	.222	75	180	12	40	44	2	1	0	7	4	0	2	6	2	28	2	2	4	.244	.255	1
Benard, M	SF	L	.382	13	34	5	13	18	2	0	1	4	0	0	0	1	0	7	1	0	1	.529	.400	0
Benes, A	SD	R	.150	19	40	2	6	7	1	0	0	3	3	0	0	1	0	18	0	0	1	.175	.171	1
Benes, A	STL	R	.000	3	6	0	0	0	0	0	0	0	0	0	0	0	0	3	0	0	0	.000	.000	0
Benitez, Y	MON	R	.385	14	39	8	15	25	2	1	2	7	0	0	0	1	0	7	0	2	1	.641	.400	1
Benjamin, M	SF	R	.220	68	186	19	41	56	6	0	3	12	7	0	1	8	3	51	11	1	3	.301	.256	4
Bennett, G	PHI	R	.000	1	1	0	0	0	0	0	0	0	0	0	0	0	0	1	0	0	0	.000	.000	0
Benzinger, T	SF	S	.200	9	10	2	2	5	0	0	1	2	0	1	0	2	1	3	0	0	0	.500	.308	0
Berry, S	MON	R	.318	103	314	38	100	166	22	1	14	55	2	5	2	25	1	53	3	8	5	.529	.367	12
Berryhill, D	CIN	S	.183	34	82	6	15	24	3	0	2	11	1	4	0	10	2	19	0	0	3	.293	.260	2
Berumen, A	SD	R	.000	37	1	0	0	0	0	0	0	0	0	0	0	0	0	1	0	0	0	.000	.000	1
Bichette, D	COL	R	.340	139	579	102	197	359	38	2	40	128	0	7	4	22	5	96	13	9	16	.620	.364	3
Biggio, C	HOU	R	.302	141	553	123	167	267	30	2	22	77	11	7	22	80	1	85	33	8	6	.483	.406	10
Birkbeck, M	NY	R	.333	4	6	1	2	2	0	0	0	0	1	0	1	1	0	1	0	0	0	.333	.500	0
Blair, W	SD	R	.000	40	24	2	0	0	0	0	0	1	4	0	0	1	0	17	0	0	0	.000	.040	2
Blauser, J	ATL	R	.211	115	431	60	91	147	16	2	12	31	2	2	12	57	2	107	8	5	6	.341	.319	15
Bochtler, D	SD	R	.000	34	2	0	0	0	0	0	0	0	0	0	0	0	0	0	0	0	0	.000	.000	0
Bogar, T	NY	R	.290	78	145	17	42	52	7	0	1	21	2	1	0	9	0	25	1	0	2	.359	.329	6
Bonds, B	SF	L	.294	144	506	109	149	292	30	7	33	104	0	4	5	120	22	83	31	10	12	.577	.431	6

BATTER	TEAM	B	AVG	G	AB	R	H	TB	2B	3B	HR	RBI	SH	SF	HP	BB	IBB	SO	SB	CS	GIDP	SLG	OBP	E
Bonilla, B	NY	S	.325	80	317	49	103	190	25	4	18	53	0	2	1	31	10	48	0	3	11	.599	.385	14
Boone, B	CIN	R	.267	138	513	63	137	220	34	2	15	68	5	5	6	41	0	84	5	1	14	.429	.326	4
Borbon, P	ATL	R	.000	41	1	0	0	0	0	0	0	0	0	0	0	0	0	0	0	0	0	.000	.000	0
Borders, P	HOU	R	.114	11	35	1	4	4	0	0	0	0	0	0	0	2	1	7	0	0	2	.114	.162	1
Borland, T	PHI	R	.200	50	5	1	1	1	0	0	0	1	0	1	0	0	0	1	0	0	0	.200	.167	2
Bottalico, R	PHI	L	.000	62	5	0	0	0	0	0	0	0	1	0	0	0	0	4	0	0	0	.000	.000	0
Bowen, R	FLA	R	.333	4	6	1	2	2	0	0	0	0	0	0	0	0	0	3	0	0	0	.333	.333	0
Bradshaw, T	STL	L	.227	19	44	6	10	13	1	1	0	2	0	0	0	2	0	10	1	2	0	.295	.261	1
Branson, J	CIN	L	.260	122	331	43	86	144	18	2	12	45	1	6	2	44	14	69	2	1	9	.435	.345	9
Brantley, J	CIN	R	.000	56	3	0	0	0	0	0	0	0	0	0	0	0	0	1	0	0	0	.000	.000	0
Brewington, J	SF	R	.217	14	23	3	5	5	0	0	0	1	4	0	0	0	0	7	0	0	0	.217	.217	0
Brito, J	COL	R	.216	18	51	5	11	14	3	0	0	7	1	0	1	2	0	17	1	0	1	.275	.259	1
Brocail, D	HOU	L	.250	37	16	3	4	6	0	1	0	1	4	0	0	0	0	5	0	0	0	.375	.250	0
Brogna, R	NY	L	.289	134	495	72	143	240	27	2	22	76	2	2	2	39	7	111	0	0	10	.485	.342	3
Browne, J	FLA	S	.255	77	184	21	47	54	4	0	1	17	9	1	1	25	0	20	1	1	7	.293	.346	3
Brumfield, J	PIT	R	.271	116	402	64	109	148	23	2	4	26	0	1	5	37	0	71	22	12	3	.368	.339	8
Brumley, M	HOU	S	.056	18	18	1	1	4	0	0	1	2	0	0	0	0	0	6	1	0	0	.222	.056	1
Buechele, S	CHI	R	.189	32	106	10	20	25	2	0	1	9	1	0	0	11	0	19	0	0	1	.236	.265	5
Buford, D	NY	R	.235	44	136	24	32	49	5	0	4	12	0	2	5	19	0	28	7	7	3	.360	.346	2
Bullett, S	CHI	L	.273	104	150	19	41	69	5	7	3	22	1	0	1	12	2	30	8	3	4	.460	.331	2
Bullinger, J	CHI	R	.128	25	47	1	6	9	3	0	0	5	8	2	0	5	0	16	0	0	1	.191	.204	0
Burba, D	SF-CIN	R	.067	52	15	2	1	1	0	0	0	0	4	0	0	3	0	9	0	0	0	.067	.222	0
Burkett, J	FLA	R	.106	31	66	3	7	8	1	0	0	3	4	0	1	2	0	23	0	0	1	.121	.145	0
Burks, E	COL	R	.266	103	278	41	74	138	10	6	14	49	1	1	2	39	0	72	7	3	7	.496	.359	5
Busch, M	LA	R	.235	13	17	3	4	13	0	0	3	6	0	0	0	0	0	7	0	0	0	.765	.235	1
Butler, B	NY-LA	L	.300	129	513	78	154	193	18	9	1	38	10	6	0	67	2	51	32	8	5	.376	.377	2
Byrd, P	NY	R	1.000	17	1	0	1	1	0	0	0	0	0	0	0	0	0	0	0	0	0	1.000	1.000	1
Caminiti, K	SD	S	.302	143	526	74	159	270	33	0	26	94	0	6	1	69	8	94	12	5	11	.513	.380	27
Candiotti, T	LA	R	.109	30	55	2	6	6	0	0	0	2	5	0	0	3	0	16	0	0	1	.109	.155	1
Cangelosi, J	HOU	S	.318	90	201	46	64	79	5	2	2	18	2	1	4	48	2	42	21	5	3	.393	.457	5
Caraballo, R	STL	S	.202	34	99	10	20	32	4	1	2	3	2	0	3	6	0	33	3	2	1	.323	.269	6
Carr, C	FLA	R	.227	105	308	54	70	96	20	0	2	20	7	2	2	46	1	49	25	11	2	.312	.330	3
Carrasco, H	CIN	R	.000	64	7	0	0	0	0	0	0	0	0	0	0	0	0	4	0	0	0	.000	.000	2
Carreon, M	SF	R	.301	117	396	53	119	194	24	0	17	65	0	3	4	23	1	37	0	1	7	.490	.343	7
Carter, A	PHI	L	1.000	4	1	0	1	1	0	0	0	0	0	0	0	0	0	0	0	0	0	1.000	1.000	0
Casian, L	CHI	R	.000	42	2	0	0	0	0	0	0	0	0	0	0	0	0	1	0	0	0	.000	.000	0

Castilla, V	COL	R	.309	139	527	82	163	297	34	2	32	90	4	6	4	30	2	87	2	8	15	.564	.347	15
Castillo, A	NY	R	.103	13	29	2	3	3	0	0	0	0	0	0	1	3	0	9	1	0	0	.103	.212	2
Castillo, F	CHI	R	.102	29	59	1	6	6	0	0	0	1	7	0	0	3	0	25	0	0	0	.102	.145	2
Castro, J	LA	R	.250	11	4	0	1	1	0	0	0	0	0	0	0	1	0	1	0	0	0	.250	.400	0
Cedeno, A	SD	R	.210	120	390	42	82	120	16	2	6	31	0	1	5	28	7	92	5	3	12	.308	.271	17
Cedeno, R	LA	S	.238	40	42	4	10	12	2	0	0	3	0	1	0	3	0	10	1	0	1	.286	.283	1
Charlton, N	PHI	S	1.000	25	1	0	1	2	1	0	0	1	0	0	0	0	0	0	0	0	0	2.000	1.000	0
Christiansen, J	PIT	R	.000	63	1	0	0	0	0	0	0	0	0	0	0	0	0	1	0	0	0	.000	.000	2
Cianfrocco, A	SD	R	.263	51	118	22	31	53	7	0	5	31	0	1	2	11	1	28	0	2	3	.449	.333	3
Clark, D	PIT	L	.281	77	196	30	55	73	6	0	4	24	0	2	1	24	1	38	3	3	9	.372	.359	4
Clark, P	SD	R	.216	75	97	12	21	30	3	0	2	7	0	2	1	8	1	18	0	2	3	.309	.278	0
Clayton, R	SF	R	.244	138	509	56	124	174	29	3	5	58	4	3	3	38	1	109	24	9	7	.342	.298	20
Clontz, B	ATL	R	.000	59	2	0	0	0	0	0	0	0	0	0	0	0	0	0	0	0	0	.000	.000	0
Colbrunn, G	FLA	R	.277	138	528	70	146	239	22	1	23	89	0	4	6	22	4	69	11	3	15	.453	.311	5
Coles, D	STL	R	.225	63	138	13	31	47	7	0	3	16	0	1	3	16	1	20	0	0	1	.341	.316	3
Conine, J	FLA	R	.302	133	483	72	146	251	26	2	25	105	0	12	1	66	5	94	2	0	13	.520	.379	6
Cooper, S	STL	L	.230	118	374	29	86	117	18	2	3	40	0	4	3	49	3	85	0	3	9	.313	.321	18
Cordero, W	MON	R	.286	131	514	64	147	216	35	2	10	49	1	4	9	36	4	88	9	5	11	.420	.341	22
Cornelius, R	MON-NY	R	.100	18	20	0	2	2	0	0	0	0	0	0	0	0	0	7	0	0	0	.100	.100	1
Counsell, C	COL	L	.000	3	1	0	0	0	0	0	0	0	0	0	0	1	0	0	0	0	0	.000	.500	0
Cromer, T	STL	R	.226	105	345	36	78	112	19	0	5	18	1	5	4	14	2	66	0	0	14	.325	.261	17
Cummings, J	LA	L	.000	35	3	0	0	0	0	0	0	0	0	0	0	0	0	1	0	0	0	.000	.000	0
Cummings, M	PIT	L	.243	59	152	13	37	52	7	1	2	15	0	0	0	13	3	30	1	0	1	.342	.303	1
Daulton, D	PHI	L	.249	98	342	44	85	137	19	3	9	55	0	2	5	55	2	52	3	0	4	.401	.359	4
Dawson, A	FLA	R	.257	79	226	30	58	98	10	3	8	37	0	3	8	9	1	45	0	0	7	.434	.305	8
Decker, S	FLA	R	.226	51	133	12	30	43	2	1	3	13	0	2	0	19	1	22	1	0	1	.323	.318	5
DeLeon, J	MON	R	.000	7	0	0	0	0	0	0	0	0	1	0	0	1	0	0	0	0	0	.000	1.000	0
DeLucia, R	STL	R	.200	56	10	1	2	2	0	0	0	0	1	0	0	1	0	3	0	0	1	.200	.273	2
Deshaies, J	PHI	L	.000	2	1	0	0	0	0	0	0	0	0	0	0	0	0	1	0	0	0	.000	.000	0
DeShields, D	LA	L	.256	127	425	66	109	157	18	3	8	37	3	1	1	63	4	83	39	14	6	.369	.353	11
Devereaux, M	ATL	R	.255	29	55	7	14	20	3	0	1	8	0	0	0	2	0	11	2	0	1	.364	.281	0
Dewey, M	SF	R	.000	27	1	0	0	0	0	0	0	0	0	0	0	0	0	1	0	0	0	.000	.000	1
Diaz, M	FLA	R	.230	49	87	5	20	26	3	0	1	6	1	0	0	1	0	12	0	0	4	.299	.239	2
DiPoto, J	NY	R	.000	58	5	0	0	0	0	0	0	0	1	0	0	0	0	3	0	0	0	.000	.000	3
Dishman, G	SD	R	.200	19	30	4	6	6	0	0	0	4	2	1	1	0	0	13	0	0	0	.200	.219	0
Donnels, C	HOU	L	.300	19	30	4	9	9	0	0	0	2	0	0	0	3	2	6	0	0	1	.300	.364	2
Dougherty, J	HOU	R	.125	56	8	1	1	1	0	0	0	0	1	0	0	0	0	2	0	0	0	.125	.125	0
Drabek, D	HOU	R	.233	33	60	4	14	17	3	0	0	8	8	0	0	2	0	17	0	0	0	.283	.258	2
Duncan, M	PHI-CIN	R	.287	81	265	36	76	112	14	2	6	36	1	5	1	5	0	62	1	3	7	.423	.297	11

BATTER	TEAM	B	AVG	G	AB	R	H	TB	2B	3B	HR	RBI	SH	SF	HP	BB	IBB	SO	SB	CS	GI DP	SLG	OBP	E
Dunston, S	CHI	R	.296	127	477	58	141	225	30	6	14	69	7	3	6	10	3	75	10	5	8	.472	.317	17
Dyer, M	PIT	R	.571	55	7	1	4	4	0	0	0	1	1	0	0	0	0	2	0	0	0	.571	.571	0
Dykstra, L	PHI	L	.264	62	254	37	67	90	15	1	2	18	0	2	3	33	2	28	10	5	1	.354	.353	2
Eischen, J	LA	L	.000	17	1	0	0	0	0	0	0	0	0	0	0	0	0	1	0	0	0	.000	.000	0
Eisenreich, J	PHI	L	.316	129	377	46	119	175	22	2	10	55	2	5	1	38	4	44	10	0	7	.464	.375	0
Elster, K	PHI	R	.208	26	53	10	11	20	4	1	1	9	2	2	1	7	1	14	0	0	1	.377	.302	1
Encarnacion, A	PIT	R	.226	58	159	18	36	53	7	2	2	10	3	0	0	13	5	28	1	1	3	.333	.285	7
Ericks, J	PIT	R	.097	19	31	2	3	4	1	0	0	1	6	0	0	0	0	12	0	0	0	.129	.097	3
Estes, S	SF	R	.000	3	5	0	0	0	0	0	0	0	0	0	0	0	0	2	0	0	1	.000	.000	0
Eusebio, T	HOU	R	.299	113	368	46	110	151	21	1	6	58	1	5	3	31	1	59	0	2	12	.410	.354	5
Everett, C	NY	S	.260	79	289	48	75	126	13	1	12	54	1	0	2	39	2	67	2	5	11	.436	.352	3
Eversgerd, B	MON	R	.000	25	1	0	0	0	0	0	0	0	0	0	0	0	0	0	0	0	0	.000	.000	1
Faneyte, R	SF	R	.198	46	86	7	17	23	4	1	0	4	1	0	0	11	0	27	1	0	2	.267	.289	1
Fassero, J	MON	L	.070	30	57	6	4	4	0	0	0	1	8	0	0	5	0	29	0	0	0	.070	.145	4
Fernandez, S	PHI	L	.043	11	23	1	1	1	0	0	0	1	1	0	0	1	0	15	0	0	0	.043	.083	1
Finley, S	SD	L	.297	139	562	104	167	236	23	8	10	44	4	2	3	59	5	62	36	12	8	.420	.366	7
Fletcher, D	MON	L	.286	110	350	42	100	156	21	1	11	45	1	2	4	32	1	23	0	1	15	.446	.351	4
Flora, K	PHI	R	.213	24	75	12	16	25	3	0	2	7	2	0	0	4	0	22	1	0	0	.333	.253	0
Florence, D	NY	R	.000	14	1	0	0	0	0	0	0	0	0	0	0	0	0	1	0	0	0	.000	.000	0
Florie, B	SD	R	.000	47	2	0	0	0	0	0	0	0	0	0	0	0	0	2	0	0	0	.000	.000	1
Floyd, C	MON	L	.130	29	69	6	9	13	1	0	1	8	0	0	1	7	0	22	3	0	1	.188	.221	3
Foley, T	MON	L	.208	11	24	2	5	7	2	0	0	2	0	0	0	2	0	4	1	0	2	.292	.269	0
Fonville, C	MON-LA	S	.278	102	320	43	89	97	6	1	0	16	6	0	1	23	1	42	20	7	3	.303	.328	11
Fordyce, B	NY	R	.500	4	2	1	1	2	1	0	0	0	0	0	0	1	0	0	0	0	0	1.000	.667	0
Foster, K	CHI	R	.250	33	60	7	15	21	1	1	1	9	5	0	0	3	0	16	2	0	0	.350	.286	0
Franco, M	CHI	L	.294	16	17	3	5	6	1	0	0	1	0	0	0	0	0	4	0	0	0	.353	.294	0
Frascatore, J	STL	R	.000	14	7	0	0	0	0	0	0	0	1	0	0	1	0	6	0	0	0	.000	.125	0
Fraser, W	MON	R	.000	22	2	0	0	0	0	0	0	0	0	0	0	0	0	0	0	0	0	.000	.000	0
Frazier, L	MON	S	.190	35	63	6	12	14	2	0	0	3	0	1	2	8	0	12	4	0	1	.222	.297	1
Freeman, M	COL	R	.087	22	23	2	2	5	0	0	1	4	6	0	0	1	0	16	0	0	0	.217	.125	3
Frey, S	SF-PHI	L	.000	18	1	0	0	0	0	0	0	0	0	0	0	0	0	1	0	0	0	.000	.000	1
Galarraga, A	COL	R	.280	143	554	89	155	283	29	3	31	106	0	5	13	32	6	146	12	2	14	.511	.331	13
Gallagher, D	PHI	R	.318	62	157	12	50	65	12	0	1	12	2	1	0	16	0	20	0	0	5	.414	.379	0
Gant, R	CIN	R	.276	119	410	79	113	227	19	4	29	88	1	5	3	74	5	108	23	8	11	.554	.386	3
Garces, R	CHI-FLA	R	.000	18	1	0	0	0	0	0	0	0	0	0	0	0	0	0	0	0	0	.000	.000	0
Garcia, F	PIT	R	.140	42	57	5	8	11	1	1	0	1	1	0	0	8	0	17	0	1	0	.193	.246	1
Garcia, C	PIT	R	.294	104	367	41	108	154	24	2	6	50	5	3	2	25	5	55	8	4	4	.420	.340	15

Garcia, K	LA	L	.200	13	20	1	4	4	0	0	0	0	0	0	0	0	0	4	0	0	0	.200	.200	0
Gardner, M	FLA	R	.190	39	21	1	4	4	0	0	0	1	4	0	0	0	0	6	0	0	0	.190	.190	2
Giannelli, R	STL	L	.091	9	11	0	1	1	0	0	0	0	0	0	0	3	0	4	0	0	0	.091	.286	0
Gibralter, S	CIN	R	.333	4	3	0	1	1	0	0	0	0	0	0	0	0	0	0	0	0	0	.333	.333	0
Gilkey, B	STL	R	.298	121	480	73	143	235	33	4	17	69	1	3	5	42	3	70	12	6	17	.490	.358	3
Giovanola, E	ATL	L	.071	13	14	2	1	1	0	0	0	0	0	0	0	3	0	5	0	0	1	.071	.235	0
Girardi, J	COL	R	.262	125	462	63	121	166	17	2	8	55	12	1	2	29	0	76	3	3	15	.359	.308	10
Glavine, T	ATL	L	.222	29	63	6	14	18	1	0	1	8	8	0	1	2	0	15	0	0	0	.286	.258	1
Goff, J	HOU	L	.154	12	26	2	4	9	2	0	1	3	0	0	0	4	0	13	0	0	1	.346	.267	0
Gomez, P	SF	L	.000	18	1	0	0	0	0	0	0	0	0	0	0	0	0	1	0	0	0	.000	.000	0
Gonzalez, L	HOU-CHI	L	.276	133	471	69	130	214	29	8	13	69	1	6	6	57	8	63	6	8	16	.454	.357	6
Gott, J	PIT	R	.000	25	1	0	0	0	0	0	0	0	0	0	0	0	0	1	0	0	0	.000	.000	1
Grace, M	PHI	R	.000	2	2	0	0	0	0	0	0	0	2	0	0	0	0	2	0	0	0	.000	.000	0
Grace, M	CHI	L	.326	143	552	97	180	285	51	3	16	92	1	7	2	65	9	46	6	2	10	.516	.395	7
Grahe, J	COL	R	.417	17	12	1	5	6	1	0	0	2	6	0	0	0	0	3	0	0	0	.500	.417	1
Green, T	PHI	R	.182	27	44	2	8	16	5	0	1	5	8	0	0	0	0	16	0	1	0	.364	.182	1
Greene, T	PHI	R	.000	11	8	0	0	0	0	0	0	0	1	0	0	2	0	3	0	0	0	.000	.200	0
Greene, W	CIN	L	.105	8	19	1	2	2	0	0	0	0	0	0	0	3	0	7	0	0	1	.105	.227	0
Greer, K	SF	R	.000	8	1	0	0	0	0	0	0	0	0	0	0	0	0	1	0	0	0	.000	.000	1
Gregg, T	FLA	L	.237	72	156	20	37	60	5	0	6	20	0	2	2	16	1	33	3	1	3	.385	.313	1
Grissom, M	ATL	R	.258	139	551	80	142	207	23	3	12	42	1	4	3	47	4	61	29	9	8	.376	.317	2
Grudzielanek, M	MON	R	.245	78	269	27	66	85	12	2	1	20	3	0	7	14	4	47	8	3	7	.316	.300	10
Gunderson, E	NY	R	.000	30	0	1	0	0	0	0	0	0	0	0	1	0	0	0	0	0	0	.000	1.000	0
Guthrie, M	LA	S	.000	24	1	0	0	0	0	0	0	0	0	0	0	0	0	0	0	0	0	.000	.000	0
Gutierrez, R	HOU	R	.276	52	156	22	43	49	6	0	0	12	1	1	1	10	3	33	5	0	4	.314	.321	8
Gwynn, C	LA	L	.214	67	84	8	18	28	3	2	1	10	0	1	1	6	1	23	0	0	5	.333	.272	0
Gwynn, T	SD	L	.368	135	535	82	197	259	33	1	9	90	0	6	1	35	10	15	17	5	20	.484	.404	2
Habyan, J	STL	R	.000	31	2	0	0	0	0	0	0	0	0	0	0	0	0	1	0	0	0	.000	.000	0
Hajek, D	HOU	R	.000	5	2	0	0	0	0	0	0	0	2	0	0	1	0	1	1	0	0	.000	.333	0
Hamilton, J	SD	R	.108	31	65	4	7	9	2	0	0	3	5	1	0	2	0	38	0	0	1	.138	.132	6
Hammond, C	FLA	L	.271	25	48	7	13	18	2	0	1	4	5	0	0	7	0	16	0	0	1	.375	.364	1
Hampton, M	HOU	R	.146	24	48	7	7	7	0	0	0	0	4	0	1	4	0	14	0	0	0	.146	.226	3
Haney, T	CHI	R	.411	25	73	11	30	44	8	0	2	6	1	0	0	7	0	11	0	0	0	.603	.463	2
Hansen, D	LA	L	.287	100	181	19	52	65	10	0	1	14	0	1	1	28	4	28	0	0	4	.359	.384	7
Harnisch, P	NY	R	.091	18	33	0	3	3	0	0	0	0	3	0	0	0	0	6	0	0	0	.091	.091	2
Harris, G	MON	S	.333	45	3	0	1	2	1	0	0	0	0	0	0	0	0	1	0	0	0	.667	.333	2
Harris, L	CIN	L	.208	101	197	32	41	61	8	3	2	16	3	1	0	14	0	20	10	1	6	.310	.259	4
Hartgraves, D	HOU	R	.000	40	2	0	0	0	0	0	0	0	1	0	0	0	0	1	0	0	0	.000	.000	0
Hayes, C	PHI	R	.276	141	529	58	146	215	30	3	11	85	0	6	4	50	2	88	5	1	22	.406	.340	14

BATTER	TEAM	B	AVG	G	AB	R	H	TB	2B	3B	HR	RBI	SH	SF	HP	BB	IBB	SO	SB	CS	GI DP	SLG	OBP	E
Hemond, S	STL	R	.144	57	118	11	17	27	1	0	3	9	1	1	2	12	0	31	0	0	8	.229	.233	3
Henke, T	STL	R	.000	52	1	0	0	0	0	0	0	0	0	0	0	0	0	0	0	0	0	.000	.000	0
Henry, B	MON	L	.048	21	42	1	2	2	0	0	0	1	5	0	0	0	0	11	0	0	0	.048	.048	0
Henry, D	NY	R	1.000	51	1	1	1	1	0	0	0	0	1	0	0	0	0	0	0	0	0	1.000	1.000	1
Heredia, G	MON	R	.182	40	33	1	6	6	0	0	0	2	5	0	0	1	0	3	0	0	0	.182	.206	0
Hernandez, C	LA	R	.149	45	94	3	14	21	1	0	2	8	1	0	1	7	0	25	0	0	5	.223	.216	4
Hernandez, J	FLA	R	.000	7	1	0	0	0	0	0	0	0	0	0	0	0	0	0	0	0	0	.000	.000	0
Hernandez, J	CHI	R	.245	93	245	37	60	118	11	4	13	40	8	2	0	13	3	69	1	0	8	.482	.281	9
Hernandez, X	CIN	L	.000	59	8	0	0	0	0	0	0	0	0	0	0	0	0	4	0	0	0	.000	.000	0
Hickerson, B	CHI-COL	L	.667	56	3	1	2	4	0	1	0	3	1	0	0	1	0	0	0	0	0	1.333	.750	0
Hill, G	SF	R	.264	132	497	71	131	240	29	4	24	86	0	2	1	39	4	98	25	5	11	.483	.317	10
Hill, K	STL	R	.194	18	31	1	6	6	0	0	0	3	5	1	0	2	0	10	0	0	0	.194	.235	1
Hoffman, T	SD	R	.500	55	2	1	1	2	1	0	0	2	0	0	0	0	0	1	0	0	0	1.000	.500	0
Holbert, R	SD	R	.178	63	73	11	13	23	2	1	2	5	3	0	2	8	1	20	4	0	3	.315	.277	5
Hollandsworth, T	LA	L	.233	41	103	16	24	41	2	0	5	13	0	1	1	10	2	29	2	1	1	.398	.304	4
Hollins, D	PHI	S	.229	65	205	46	47	84	12	2	7	25	0	4	5	53	4	38	1	1	4	.410	.393	7
Holmes, D	COL	R	.000	68	1	0	0	0	0	0	0	0	3	0	0	0	0	0	0	0	0	.000	.000	1
Hook, C	SF	R	.000	45	3	0	0	0	0	0	0	0	0	0	0	0	0	2	0	0	0	.000	.000	0
Howard, T	CIN	S	.302	113	281	42	85	113	15	2	3	26	1	1	1	20	0	37	17	8	3	.402	.350	2
Hubbard, M	CHI	R	.174	15	23	2	4	4	0	0	0	1	0	0	0	2	0	2	0	0	1	.174	.240	1
Hubbard, T	COL	R	.310	24	58	13	18	31	4	0	3	9	1	0	0	8	0	6	2	1	2	.534	.394	0
Hudek, J	HOU	S	1.000	19	1	0	1	1	0	0	0	2	0	0	0	0	0	0	0	0	0	1.000	1.000	0
Hulett, T	STL	R	.182	4	11	0	2	2	0	0	0	0	0	0	0	0	0	3	0	0	0	.182	.182	2
Hundley, T	NY	S	.280	90	275	39	77	133	11	0	15	51	1	3	5	42	5	64	1	0	4	.484	.382	7
Hunter, B	HOU	R	.302	78	321	52	97	127	14	5	2	28	2	3	2	21	0	52	24	7	2	.396	.346	9
Hunter, B	CIN	R	.215	40	79	9	17	26	6	0	1	9	0	2	1	11	1	21	2	1	2	.329	.312	3
Huskey, B	NY	R	.189	28	90	8	17	27	1	0	3	11	1	1	0	10	0	16	1	0	3	.300	.267	6
Hyers, T	SD	L	.000	6	5	0	0	0	0	0	0	0	0	0	0	0	0	1	0	0	1	.000	.000	0
Ingram, G	LA	R	.200	44	55	5	11	13	2	0	0	3	2	0	0	9	0	8	3	0	0	.236	.313	8
Isringhausen, J	NY	R	.148	14	27	2	4	5	1	0	0	0	4	0	1	2	0	10	0	0	1	.185	.233	2
Jackson, D	STL	R	.161	19	31	1	5	7	2	0	0	2	4	0	0	1	0	16	0	0	0	.226	.188	3
Jackson, M	CIN	R	.250	40	4	0	1	1	0	0	0	0	0	0	0	0	0	0	0	0	0	.250	.250	0
Jacome, J	NY	L	.000	5	7	0	0	0	0	0	0	0	1	0	0	0	0	6	0	0	0	.000	.000	1
Jarvis, K	CIN	L	.143	19	21	2	3	4	1	0	0	0	1	0	1	0	0	8	0	0	0	.190	.182	2
Jefferies, G	PHI	S	.306	114	480	69	147	215	31	2	11	56	0	6	0	35	5	26	9	5	15	.448	.349	3
Johnson, B	SD	R	.251	68	207	20	52	70	9	0	3	29	1	4	1	11	2	39	0	0	2	.338	.287	4

Johnson, C............	FLA	R	.251	97	315	40	79	129	15	1	11	39	4	2	4	46	2	71	0	2	11	.410	.351	6
Johnson, H	CHI	S	.195	87	169	26	33	60	4	1	7	22	0	2	1	34	0	46	1	1	2	.355	.330	7
Johnson, M............	PIT	L	.208	79	221	32	46	93	6	1	13	28	0	1	2	37	2	66	5	2	2	.421	.326	8
Jones, B	NY	R	.161	30	56	3	9	9	0	0	0	2	18	0	0	1	0	25	0	0	0	.161	.175	6
Jones, C................	ATL	S	.265	140	524	87	139	236	22	3	23	86	1	4	0	73	1	99	8	4	10	.450	.353	25
Jones, C................	NY	R	.280	79	182	33	51	85	6	2	8	31	2	3	1	13	1	45	2	1	2	.467	.327	2
Jones, T................	HOU	L	.200	68	5	1	1	2	1	0	0	0	0	0	0	0	0	1	0	0	0	.400	.200	1
Jordan, B	STL	R	.296	131	490	83	145	239	20	4	22	81	0	2	11	22	4	79	24	9	5	.488	.339	1
Jordan, K	PHI	R	.185	24	54	6	10	17	1	0	2	6	0	0	1	2	1	9	0	0	0	.315	.228	1
Juden, J	PHI	R	.056	13	18	1	1	4	0	0	1	4	3	0	0	0	0	12	0	0	0	.222	.056	0
Justice, D..............	ATL	L	.253	120	411	73	104	197	17	2	24	78	0	5	2	73	5	68	4	2	5	.479	.365	4
Karros, E	LA	R	.298	143	551	83	164	295	29	3	32	105	0	4	4	61	4	115	4	4	14	.535	.369	7
Kelly, M	ATL	R	.190	97	137	26	26	43	6	1	3	17	2	1	2	11	0	49	7	3	2	.314	.258	4
Kelly, R	MON-LA	R	.278	136	504	58	140	188	23	2	7	57	0	7	6	22	6	79	19	10	14	.373	.312	6
Kent, J	NY	R	.278	125	472	65	131	219	22	3	20	65	1	4	8	29	3	89	3	3	9	.464	.327	10
Kile, D..................	HOU	R	.111	25	36	1	4	5	1	0	0	6	5	0	0	4	0	20	0	0	1	.139	.200	3
King, J	PIT	R	.265	122	445	61	118	203	27	2	18	87	0	8	1	55	5	63	7	4	10	.456	.342	17
Kingery, M...........	COL	L	.269	119	350	66	94	144	18	4	8	37	6	1	0	45	1	40	13	5	7	.411	.351	5
Klesko, R..............	ATL	L	.310	107	329	48	102	200	25	2	23	70	0	3	2	47	10	72	5	4	8	.608	.396	8
Kmak, J	CHI	R	.245	19	53	7	13	19	3	0	1	6	0	1	1	6	0	12	0	0	2	.358	.328	0
Kowitz, B	ATL	L	.167	10	24	3	4	5	1	0	0	3	1	0	1	2	0	5	0	1	0	.208	.259	0
Laker, T	MON	R	.234	64	141	17	33	52	8	1	3	20	1	1	1	14	4	38	0	1	5	.369	.306	7
Lampkin, T	SF	L	.276	65	76	8	21	26	2	0	1	9	0	0	1	9	1	8	2	0	1	.342	.360	0
Lankford, R...........	STL	L	.277	132	483	81	134	248	35	2	25	82	0	5	2	63	6	110	24	8	10	.513	.360	3
Lansing, M	MON	R	.255	127	467	47	119	183	30	2	10	62	1	3	3	28	2	65	27	4	14	.392	.299	6
Larkin, B..............	CIN	R	.319	131	496	98	158	244	29	6	15	66	3	4	3	61	2	49	51	5	6	.492	.394	11
Ledesma, A	NY	R	.242	21	33	4	8	8	0	0	0	3	0	0	0	6	1	7	0	0	2	.242	.359	2
Lee, M	STL	S	1.000	1	1	1	1	1	0	0	0	0	0	0	0	0	0	0	0	0	0	1.000	1.000	1
Leiper, D	MON	L	.000	26	1	0	0	0	0	0	0	0	0	0	0	0	0	0	0	0	0	.000	.000	0
Leiter, M	SF	R	.098	30	61	2	6	6	0	0	0	5	9	0	0	4	0	33	0	0	2	.098	.154	4
Lemke, M..............	ATL	S	.253	116	399	42	101	142	16	5	5	38	7	3	0	44	4	40	2	2	17	.356	.325	5
Leonard, M............	SF	L	.190	14	21	4	4	8	1	0	1	4	0	0	0	5	1	2	0	0	0	.381	.346	0
Leskanic, C	COL	R	.143	76	7	1	1	1	0	0	0	0	2	0	0	0	0	1	0	0	1	.143	.143	0
Lewis, D................	SF-CIN	R	.250	132	472	66	118	140	13	3	1	24	12	1	8	34	0	57	32	18	9	.297	.311	2
Lewis, M	CIN	R	.339	81	171	25	58	82	13	1	3	30	0	2	0	21	2	33	0	3	1	.480	.407	4
Lewis, R	FLA	R	.000	21	1	0	0	0	0	0	0	0	0	0	0	1	0	1	0	0	0	.000	.500	2
Lieber, J................	PIT	L	.048	21	21	0	1	1	0	0	0	0	0	0	0	0	0	14	0	0	1	.048	.048	1
Lieberthal, M	PHI	R	.255	16	47	1	12	14	2	0	0	4	2	0	0	5	0	5	0	0	1	.298	.327	1
Liriano, N..............	PIT	S	.286	107	259	29	74	103	12	1	5	38	1	3	2	24	3	34	2	2	2	.398	.347	5

BATTER	TEAM	B	AVG	G	AB	R	H	TB	2B	3B	HR	RBI	SH	SF	HP	BB	IBB	SO	SB	CS	GIDP	SLG	OBP	E
Livingstone, S	SD	L	.337	99	196	26	66	96	15	0	5	32	0	2	0	15	1	22	2	1	3	.490	.380	3
Loaiza, E	PIT	R	.192	33	52	4	10	13	1	1	0	2	7	1	0	1	0	11	0	0	1	.250	.204	0
Lomon, K	NY	R	.000	6	0	0	0	0	0	0	0	0	1	0	0	0	0	0	0	0	0	.000	.000	1
Longmire, T	PHI	L	.356	59	104	21	37	53	7	0	3	19	0	1	1	11	1	19	1	1	1	.510	.419	0
Lopez, J	ATL	R	.315	100	333	37	105	166	11	4	14	51	0	3	2	14	0	57	0	1	13	.498	.344	8
Mabry, J	STL	L	.307	129	388	35	119	157	21	1	5	41	0	4	2	24	5	45	0	3	6	.405	.347	4
Maddux, G	ATL	R	.153	28	72	8	11	13	2	0	0	0	6	0	0	3	0	22	0	0	0	.181	.187	0
Magadan, D	HOU	L	.313	127	348	44	109	139	24	0	2	51	1	2	0	71	9	56	2	1	9	.399	.428	18
Manwaring, K	SF	R	.251	118	379	21	95	126	15	2	4	36	4	4	10	27	6	72	1	0	8	.332	.314	7
Manzanillo, R	PIT	L	.000	5	1	0	0	0	0	0	0	0	0	0	0	0	0	1	0	0	0	.000	.000	0
Marsh, T	PHI	R	.294	43	109	13	32	46	3	1	3	15	0	1	0	4	0	25	0	1	1	.422	.316	3
Martin, A	PIT	L	.282	124	439	70	124	194	25	3	13	41	1	0	2	44	6	92	20	11	5	.442	.351	5
Martinez, P	HOU	L	.000	25	0	1	0	0	0	0	0	0	0	0	0	1	0	0	0	0	0	.000	1.000	0
Martinez, P	MON	R	.111	30	63	2	7	7	0	0	0	2	5	2	2	0	0	30	0	0	1	.111	.134	2
Martinez, R	LA	L	.172	30	64	2	11	15	4	0	0	4	13	0	0	1	0	19	0	0	0	.234	.185	3
Mathews, T	FLA	L	.462	57	13	2	6	8	2	0	0	3	0	0	0	0	0	4	0	0	1	.615	.462	0
Mathews, T	STL	R	.000	23	2	0	0	0	0	0	0	0	0	0	0	0	0	1	0	0	0	.000	.000	1
Mauser, T	SD	R	.000	5	1	0	0	0	0	0	0	0	0	0	0	0	0	1	0	0	0	.000	.000	0
May, D	HOU	L	.301	78	206	29	62	103	15	1	8	41	0	3	1	19	0	24	5	0	4	.500	.358	2
McCarty, D	SF	R	.250	12	20	1	5	6	1	0	0	2	0	0	0	2	0	4	1	0	0	.300	.318	1
McCracken, Q	COL	S	.000	3	1	0	0	0	0	0	0	0	0	0	0	0	0	1	0	0	0	.000	.000	0
McCurry, J	PIT	R	.000	55	3	0	0	0	0	0	0	0	0	0	0	0	0	1	0	0	0	.000	.000	0
McDavid, R	SD	L	.176	11	17	2	3	3	0	0	0	0	0	0	0	2	0	6	1	1	1	.176	.263	0
McElroy, C	CIN	L	.000	44	3	0	0	0	0	0	0	0	0	0	0	0	0	0	0	0	0	.000	.000	0
McGriff, F	ATL	L	.280	144	528	85	148	258	27	1	27	93	0	6	5	65	6	99	3	6	19	.489	.361	5
McMichael, G	ATL	R	.000	67	6	0	0	0	0	0	0	0	0	0	0	1	0	4	0	0	0	.000	.143	1
McMurtry, C	HOU	R	.000	11	1	0	0	0	0	0	0	0	0	0	0	0	0	1	0	0	0	.000	.000	0
McRae, B	CHI	S	.288	137	580	92	167	255	38	7	12	48	3	1	7	47	1	92	27	8	12	.440	.348	3
Mejia, R	COL	R	.154	23	52	5	8	12	1	0	1	4	0	1	1	0	0	17	0	1	1	.231	.167	2
Merced, O	PIT	L	.300	132	487	75	146	228	29	4	15	83	0	5	1	52	9	74	7	2	9	.468	.365	6
Mercker, K	ATL	L	.104	29	48	1	5	8	3	0	0	5	6	0	0	0	0	17	0	0	0	.167	.104	1
Miceli, D	PIT	R	.000	58	1	0	0	0	0	0	0	0	0	0	0	0	0	1	0	0	0	.000	.000	0
Miller, O	HOU	R	.262	92	324	36	85	122	20	1	5	36	4	0	5	22	8	71	3	4	7	.377	.319	15
Mimbs, M	PHI	L	.143	35	35	2	5	6	1	0	0	2	8	0	0	0	0	12	0	0	0	.171	.143	1
Minor, B	NY	R	.000	35	2	0	0	0	0	0	0	0	0	0	0	0	0	0	0	0	0	.000	.000	0
Mintz, S	SF	L	.000	14	3	0	0	0	0	0	0	0	0	0	0	0	0	3	0	0	0	.000	.000	0

Mlicki, D	NY	R	.051	29	39	2	2	2	0	0	0	2	12	0	0	8	0	12	0	0	0	.051	.213	1
Mondesi, R	LA	R	.285	139	536	91	153	266	23	6	26	88	0	7	4	33	4	96	27	4	7	.496	.328	6
Morandini, M	PHI	L	.283	127	494	65	140	206	34	7	6	49	4	1	9	42	3	80	9	6	11	.417	.350	7
Mordecai, M	ATL	R	.280	69	75	10	21	36	6	0	3	11	2	1	0	9	0	16	0	0	0	.480	.353	0
Morgan, M	CHI-STL	R	.053	21	38	2	2	2	0	0	0	0	4	0	0	3	0	20	0	0	0	.053	.122	1
Morman, R	FLA	R	.278	34	72	9	20	33	2	1	3	7	0	0	1	3	0	12	0	0	5	.458	.316	1
Morris, H	CIN	L	.279	101	359	53	100	162	25	2	11	51	1	1	1	29	7	58	1	1	10	.451	.333	5
Mouton, J	HOU	R	.262	104	298	42	78	112	18	2	4	27	3	1	4	25	1	59	25	8	5	.376	.326	0
Mulholland, T	SF	R	.102	30	49	3	5	11	1	1	1	3	3	1	0	1	0	22	0	0	1	.224	.118	3
Munoz, B	PHI	R	.000	3	5	0	0	0	0	0	0	0	0	0	0	0	0	2	0	0	0	.000	.000	1
Munoz, M	COL	L	.500	64	2	1	1	2	1	0	0	1	0	0	0	2	0	1	0	0	0	1.000	.750	0
Munoz, N	LA	R	.000	2	1	0	0	0	0	0	0	0	0	0	0	0	0	0	0	0	0	.000	.000	0
Murphy, R	LA-FLA	L	1.000	14	1	0	1	1	0	0	0	0	0	0	0	0	0	0	0	0	0	1.000	1.000	0
Murray, M	ATL	L	.500	4	2	0	1	1	0	0	0	0	0	0	0	0	0	0	0	0	0	.500	.500	0
Myers, R	CHI	L	.000	57	0	0	0	0	0	0	0	1	0	0	0	1	0	0	0	0	0	.000	1.000	0
Nabholz, C	CHI	L	.000	34	1	0	0	0	0	0	0	0	0	0	0	0	0	0	0	0	0	.000	.000	0
Natal, R	FLA	R	.233	16	43	2	10	20	2	1	2	6	1	1	0	1	0	9	0	0	0	.465	.244	1
Navarro, J	CHI	R	.185	29	65	0	12	17	5	0	0	7	8	0	0	1	0	25	0	0	0	.262	.197	1
Neagle, D	PIT	L	.122	32	74	5	9	15	3	0	1	8	5	0	0	4	0	26	0	0	0	.203	.167	1
Nevin, P	HOU	R	.117	18	60	4	7	8	1	0	0	1	1	0	1	7	1	13	1	0	2	.133	.221	3
Newfield, M	SD	R	.309	21	55	6	17	27	5	1	1	7	0	0	0	2	0	8	0	0	3	.491	.333	0
Nieves, M	SD	S	.205	98	234	32	48	98	6	1	14	38	1	3	5	19	0	88	2	3	9	.419	.276	2
Nitkowski, C	CIN	L	.200	9	10	1	2	2	0	0	0	1	0	0	0	0	0	6	0	0	0	.200	.200	1
Nokes, M	COL	L	.182	10	11	1	2	3	1	0	0	0	0	0	0	1	1	4	0	0	1	.273	.250	1
Nomo, H	LA	R	.091	28	66	2	6	6	0	0	0	4	5	1	0	0	0	33	0	0	1	.091	.090	3
O'Brien, C	ATL	R	.227	67	198	18	45	79	7	0	9	23	0	0	6	29	2	40	0	1	8	.399	.343	4
Ochoa, A	NY	R	.297	11	37	7	11	12	1	0	0	0	0	0	0	2	0	10	1	0	1	.324	.333	0
Offerman, J	LA	S	.287	119	429	69	123	161	14	6	4	33	10	0	3	69	0	67	2	7	5	.375	.389	35
Oliva, J	ATL-STL	R	.142	70	183	15	26	52	5	0	7	20	0	1	2	12	0	46	0	0	5	.284	.202	7
Olivares, O	COL-PHI	R	.222	17	9	1	2	6	1	0	1	2	1	0	0	1	0	4	0	0	0	.667	.300	0
Oquendo, J	STL	S	.209	88	220	31	46	66	8	3	2	17	4	1	0	35	3	21	1	1	1	.300	.316	6
Orsulak, J	NY	L	.283	108	290	41	82	108	19	2	1	37	1	6	1	19	2	35	1	3	3	.372	.323	4
Osborne, D	STL	L	.161	19	31	1	5	8	3	0	0	4	3	0	1	3	0	15	0	0	0	.258	.257	0
Osuna, P	LA	R	.000	39	2	0	0	0	0	0	0	0	0	0	0	0	0	0	0	0	0	.000	.000	0
Otero, R	NY	S	.137	35	51	5	7	9	2	0	0	1	1	0	0	3	0	10	2	1	1	.176	.185	0
Owens, E	CIN	R	1.000	2	2	0	2	2	0	0	0	1	1	0	0	0	0	0	0	0	0	1.000	1.000	0
Owens, J	COL	R	.244	18	45	7	11	25	2	0	4	12	0	1	1	2	0	15	0	0	0	.556	.286	1
Pagnozzi, T	STL	R	.215	62	219	17	47	69	14	1	2	15	0	1	1	11	0	31	0	1	9	.315	.254	2
Painter, L	COL	L	.111	33	9	0	1	2	1	0	0	0	1	0	0	1	0	4	0	0	0	.222	.200	0

BATTER	TEAM	B	AVG	G	AB	R	H	TB	2B	3B	HR	RBI	SH	SF	HP	BB	IBB	SO	SB	CS	GIDP	SLG	OBP	E
Palacios, V	STL	R	.167	20	6	1	1	1	0	0	0	0	1	0	0	0	0	4	0	0	0	.167	.167	0
Parent, M	PIT-CHI	R	.234	81	265	30	62	127	11	0	18	38	1	0	0	26	2	69	0	0	6	.479	.302	4
Park, C	LA	R	.000	2	1	0	0	0	0	0	0	0	0	0	0	0	0	1	0	0	0	.000	.000	0
Parker, R	LA	R	.276	27	29	3	8	8	0	0	0	4	2	0	0	2	0	4	1	1	1	.276	.323	0
Parra, J	LA	R	.000	8	0	0	0	0	0	0	0	0	2	0	0	0	0	0	0	0	0	.000	.000	0
Parrett, J	STL	R	.500	59	2	0	1	1	0	0	0	0	0	0	0	0	0	1	0	0	0	.500	.500	2
Parris, S	PIT	R	.250	15	28	2	7	9	2	0	0	4	1	0	0	0	0	10	0	0	0	.321	.250	0
Patterson, J	SF	S	.205	95	205	27	42	56	5	3	1	14	6	0	12	14	1	41	4	2	7	.273	.294	4
Pegues, S	PIT	R	.246	82	171	17	42	68	8	0	6	16	0	3	1	4	0	36	1	2	3	.398	.263	4
Pena, A	FLA-ATL	R	.000	27	1	0	0	0	0	0	0	0	0	0	0	0	0	1	0	0	0	.000	.000	0
Pena, G	STL	S	.267	32	101	20	27	38	6	1	1	8	4	2	1	16	1	30	3	2	2	.376	.367	3
Pendleton, T	FLA	S	.290	133	513	70	149	225	32	1	14	78	0	4	2	38	7	84	1	2	7	.439	.339	18
Pennington, B	CIN	L	.000	6	2	0	0	0	0	0	0	0	0	0	0	0	0	1	0	0	0	.000	.000	1
Perez, C	MON	L	.133	28	45	1	6	12	1	1	1	5	4	0	0	4	0	21	0	0	0	.267	.204	2
Perez, E	ATL	R	.308	7	13	1	4	8	1	0	1	4	0	0	0	0	0	2	0	0	0	.615	.308	0
Perez, M	CHI	R	.000	68	4	1	0	0	0	0	0	0	1	0	0	2	0	4	0	0	0	.000	.333	1
Perez, Y	FLA	S	.000	69	2	0	0	0	0	0	0	0	0	0	0	0	0	1	0	0	0	.000	.000	0
Perry, G	STL	L	.165	65	79	4	13	17	4	0	0	5	0	0	0	6	0	12	0	0	2	.215	.224	0
Person, R	NY	R	.667	3	3	1	2	2	0	0	0	0	0	0	0	0	0	0	0	0	0	.667	.667	0
Petagine, R	SD	L	.234	89	124	15	29	46	8	0	3	17	2	0	0	26	2	41	0	0	2	.371	.367	1
Petkovsek, M	STL	R	.081	26	37	4	3	3	0	0	0	2	3	1	0	5	0	11	0	0	0	.081	.186	0
Phillips, J	SF	L	.195	92	231	27	45	81	9	0	9	28	2	0	0	19	2	69	1	1	3	.351	.256	4
Piazza, M	LA	R	.346	112	434	82	150	263	17	0	32	93	0	1	1	39	10	80	1	0	10	.606	.400	9
Plantier, P	HOU-SD	L	.255	76	216	33	55	88	6	0	9	34	0	3	1	28	3	48	1	1	3	.407	.339	4
Plesac, D	PIT	L	.250	58	4	0	1	1	0	0	0	0	0	0	0	0	0	3	0	0	0	.250	.250	0
Polonia, L	ATL	L	.264	28	53	6	14	21	7	0	0	2	1	0	0	3	0	9	3	0	0	.396	.304	0
Portugal, M	SF-CIN	R	.138	31	58	5	8	13	5	0	0	5	8	0	0	5	0	13	0	0	1	.224	.206	1
Powell, R	HOU-PIT	L	.000	27	3	0	0	0	0	0	0	0	1	0	0	0	0	1	0	0	0	.000	.000	0
Pratt, T	CHI	R	.133	25	60	3	8	10	2	0	0	4	0	1	0	6	1	21	0	0	1	.167	.209	3
Pride, C	MON	L	.175	48	63	10	11	12	1	0	0	2	1	0	0	5	0	16	3	2	2	.190	.235	2
Prince, T	LA	R	.200	18	40	3	8	15	2	1	1	4	0	0	0	4	0	10	0	0	0	.375	.273	1
Pugh, T	CIN	R	.143	29	28	2	4	6	2	0	0	1	4	0	0	1	0	12	0	0	1	.214	.172	1
Pulliam, H	COL	R	.400	5	5	1	2	6	1	0	1	3	0	0	0	0	0	2	0	0	0	1.200	.400	0
Pulsipher, W	NY	L	.105	17	38	4	4	6	2	0	0	4	4	2	0	5	0	19	0	0	0	.158	.200	0
Pye, E	LA	R	.000	7	8	0	0	0	0	0	0	0	0	0	0	0	0	4	0	0	0	.000	.000	0
Quantrill, P	PHI	L	.105	33	57	5	6	6	0	0	0	0	7	0	0	3	0	24	0	0	1	.105	.150	1
Rapp, P	FLA	R	.107	28	56	1	6	7	1	0	0	5	9	0	0	0	0	25	0	0	1	.125	.107	1

Reed, J	SF	L	.265	66	113	12	30	32	2	0	0	9	1	0	0	20	3	17	0	0	3	.283	.376	1
Reed, J	SD	R	.256	131	445	58	114	146	18	1	4	40	3	3	5	59	1	38	6	4	9	.328	.348	4
Reed, R	CIN	R	.000	4	3	0	0	0	0	0	0	0	2	0	0	0	0	0	0	0	0	.000	.000	0
Reed, S	COL	R	.333	71	3	0	1	1	0	0	0	0	0	0	0	0	0	1	0	0	0	.333	.333	1
Rekar, B	COL	R	.038	15	26	1	1	1	0	0	0	0	4	0	0	3	0	15	0	1	2	.038	.138	1
Remlinger, M	NY-CIN	L	.000	7	1	0	0	0	0	0	0	0	0	0	0	0	0	0	0	0	0	.000	.000	0
Reynolds, S	HOU	R	.127	31	63	4	8	9	1	0	0	1	10	0	0	1	0	30	0	0	2	.143	.141	1
Reynoso, A	COL	R	.133	20	30	1	4	4	0	0	0	0	2	0	0	1	0	11	0	0	2	.133	.161	2
Rhodes, K	CHI	L	.125	13	16	2	2	2	0	0	0	2	0	1	0	0	0	4	0	0	1	.125	.118	1
Rijo, J	CIN	R	.136	14	22	1	3	4	1	0	0	3	2	0	0	0	0	3	0	0	0	.182	.136	0
Ritz, K	COL	R	.188	31	48	3	9	10	1	0	0	2	11	0	2	2	0	20	1	1	1	.208	.250	0
Roberson, K	CHI	S	.184	32	38	5	7	20	1	0	4	6	0	0	1	6	0	14	0	1	1	.526	.311	0
Roberts, B	SD	S	.304	73	296	40	90	110	14	0	2	25	1	0	2	17	1	36	20	2	2	.372	.346	4
Rodriguez, H	LA-MON	L	.239	45	138	13	33	45	4	1	2	15	0	1	0	11	2	28	0	1	5	.326	.293	1
Rojas, M	MON	R	.000	59	6	0	0	0	0	0	0	0	2	0	0	0	0	4	0	0	0	.000	.000	0
Roper, J	CIN-SF	R	.000	3	1	0	0	0	0	0	0	0	1	0	0	0	0	0	0	0	0	.000	.000	0
Rosselli, J	SF	R	.200	9	10	1	2	2	0	0	0	1	1	0	0	0	0	3	0	0	0	.200	.200	0
Rueter, K	MON	L	.000	9	16	0	0	0	0	0	0	1	2	0	0	0	0	6	0	0	0	.000	.000	0
Ruffin, B	COL	S	.000	37	2	0	0	0	0	0	0	0	0	0	0	0	0	2	0	0	0	.000	.000	0
Ruffin, J	CIN	R	.000	10	2	0	0	0	0	0	0	0	0	0	0	0	0	0	0	0	0	.000	.000	0
Saberhagen, B	NY-COL	R	.102	25	49	3	5	6	1	0	0	0	5	0	0	2	0	12	0	0	0	.122	.137	1
Sabo, C	STL	R	.154	5	13	0	2	3	1	0	0	3	0	0	0	1	0	2	1	0	1	.231	.214	1
Sager, A	COL	R	.000	10	3	0	0	0	0	0	0	0	0	0	0	0	0	1	0	0	0	.000	.000	0
Sanchez, R	CHI	R	.278	114	428	57	119	154	22	2	3	27	8	2	1	14	2	48	6	4	9	.360	.301	7
Sanders, D	CIN-SF	L	.268	85	343	48	92	137	11	8	6	28	3	2	4	27	0	60	24	9	1	.399	.327	5
Sanders, R	CIN	R	.306	133	484	91	148	280	36	6	28	99	0	6	8	69	4	122	36	12	9	.579	.397	5
Sanders, S	SD	R	.296	17	27	2	8	9	1	0	0	4	3	0	0	1	0	3	1	0	0	.333	.321	0
Santangelo, F	MON	S	.296	35	98	11	29	39	5	1	1	9	1	0	2	12	0	9	1	1	0	.398	.384	1
Santiago, B	CIN	R	.286	81	266	40	76	129	20	0	11	44	0	2	4	24	1	48	2	2	7	.485	.351	2
Sasser, M	PIT	L	.154	14	26	1	4	5	1	0	0	0	0	0	0	0	0	0	0	0	0	.192	.154	0
Scarsone, S	SF	R	.266	80	233	33	62	111	10	3	11	29	3	1	6	18	0	82	3	2	2	.476	.333	11
Schall, G	PHI	R	.231	24	65	2	15	17	2	0	0	5	0	0	1	6	1	16	0	0	1	.262	.306	2
Scheid, R	FLA	L	.000	6	1	0	0	0	0	0	0	0	0	0	0	0	0	0	0	0	0	.000	.000	0
Schilling, C	PHI	R	.175	17	40	3	7	9	2	0	0	3	5	0	0	0	0	15	0	0	1	.225	.175	1
Schmidt, J	ATL	R	.200	9	5	0	1	1	0	0	0	0	1	0	0	1	0	2	0	0	0	.200	.333	0
Schofield, D	LA	R	.100	9	10	0	1	1	0	0	0	0	0	0	0	1	0	3	0	0	0	.100	.182	0
Schourek, P	CIN	L	.220	29	59	7	13	15	2	0	0	4	12	0	0	0	0	12	0	0	1	.254	.220	1
Scott, T	MON	R	.250	62	4	0	1	1	0	0	0	0	0	0	0	0	0	2	0	0	0	.250	.250	0

BATTER	TEAM	B	AVG	G	AB	R	H	TB	2B	3B	HR	RBI	SH	SF	HP	BB	IBB	SO	SB	CS	GI DP	SLG	OBP	E
Seanez, R	LA	R	.000	37	1	0	0	0	0	0	0	0	0	0	0	0	0	1	0	0	0	.000	.000	1
Sefcik, K	PHI	R	.000	5	4	1	0	0	0	0	0	0	0	0	0	0	0	2	0	0	0	.000	.000	0
Segui, D	NY-MON	S	.309	130	456	68	141	210	25	4	12	68	8	3	3	40	5	47	2	7	10	.461	.367	3
Servais, S	HOU-CHI	R	.265	80	264	38	70	131	22	0	13	47	2	3	3	32	8	52	2	2	9	.496	.348	12
Service, S	SF	R	.000	28	1	0	0	0	0	0	0	0	0	0	0	0	0	1	0	0	0	.000	.000	0
Sharperson, M	ATL	R	.143	7	7	1	1	2	1	0	0	2	0	0	0	0	0	2	0	0	0	.286	.143	0
Shaw, J	MON	R	.000	50	6	2	0	0	0	0	0	0	0	0	0	2	0	4	0	0	0	.000	.250	0
Sheaffer, D	STL	R	.231	76	208	24	48	75	10	1	5	30	0	1	0	23	2	38	0	0	8	.361	.306	3
Sheffield, G	FLA	R	.324	63	213	46	69	125	8	0	16	46	0	2	4	55	8	45	19	4	3	.587	.467	7
Shipley, C	HOU	R	.263	92	232	23	61	80	8	1	3	24	1	2	2	8	3	28	6	1	13	.345	.291	3
Siddall, J	MON	L	.300	7	10	4	3	3	0	0	0	1	0	0	1	3	0	3	0	0	0	.300	.500	2
Silvestri, D	MON	R	.264	39	72	12	19	31	6	0	2	7	1	1	0	9	0	27	2	0	2	.431	.341	1
Simms, M	HOU	R	.256	50	121	14	31	62	4	0	9	24	0	1	3	13	0	28	1	2	3	.512	.341	1
Slaught, D	PIT	R	.304	35	112	13	34	40	6	0	0	13	1	0	1	9	2	8	0	0	5	.357	.361	1
Slocumb, H	PHI	R	.000	61	1	0	0	0	0	0	0	0	0	0	0	0	0	0	0	0	0	.000	.000	1
Smiley, J	CIN	L	.164	28	55	6	9	16	1	0	2	5	6	1	0	4	0	26	0	0	1	.291	.217	0
Smith, D	ATL	L	.252	103	131	16	33	54	8	2	3	21	0	1	2	13	1	35	0	3	2	.412	.327	2
Smith, O	STL	S	.199	44	156	16	31	38	5	1	0	11	5	2	2	17	0	12	4	3	6	.244	.282	7
Smith, P	CIN	R	.000	11	3	0	0	0	0	0	0	0	0	0	0	2	0	2	0	0	0	.000	.400	0
Smoltz, J	ATL	R	.107	29	56	5	6	6	0	0	0	1	6	0	0	7	0	25	0	0	0	.107	.206	2
Sosa, S	CHI	R	.268	144	564	89	151	282	17	3	36	119	0	2	5	58	11	134	34	7	8	.500	.340	13
Spehr, T	MON	R	.257	41	35	4	9	17	5	0	1	3	3	0	0	6	0	7	0	0	0	.486	.366	1
Spiers, B	NY	L	.208	63	72	5	15	19	2	1	0	11	1	2	0	12	1	15	0	1	0	.264	.314	7
Springer, D	PHI	R	.125	4	8	0	1	1	0	0	0	0	0	0	0	0	0	3	0	0	0	.125	.125	1
Springer, R	PHI	R	.000	14	1	0	0	0	0	0	0	0	1	0	0	0	0	1	0	0	0	.000	.000	0
Stankiewicz, A	HOU	R	.115	43	52	6	6	7	1	0	0	7	1	0	0	12	2	19	4	2	1	.135	.281	1
Stinnett, K	NY	R	.219	77	196	23	43	65	8	1	4	18	0	0	6	29	3	65	2	0	3	.332	.338	7
Stocker, K	PHI	S	.218	125	412	42	90	113	14	3	1	32	10	3	9	43	9	75	6	1	7	.274	.304	17
Sullivan, S	CIN	R	.000	3	1	0	0	0	0	0	0	0	0	0	0	0	0	1	0	0	0	.000	.000	0
Sweeney, M	STL	L	.273	37	77	5	21	29	2	0	2	13	1	2	0	10	0	15	1	1	3	.377	.348	2
Swift, B	COL	R	.194	19	36	5	7	11	1	0	1	4	5	0	0	2	0	5	1	0	0	.306	.237	1
Swindell, G	HOU	R	.240	34	50	4	12	15	3	0	0	5	6	0	0	3	0	9	0	0	1	.300	.283	1
Tabaka, J	SD-HOU	R	.000	34	1	0	0	0	0	0	0	0	1	0	0	0	0	0	0	0	0	.000	.000	0
Tapani, K	LA	R	.176	13	17	0	3	4	1	0	0	2	3	0	0	0	0	7	0	0	0	.235	.176	1
Tarasco, T	MON	L	.249	126	438	64	109	177	18	4	14	40	3	1	2	51	12	78	24	3	2	.404	.329	5
Tatum, J	COL	R	.235	34	34	4	8	11	1	1	0	4	0	0	0	1	0	7	0	0	1	.324	.257	0
Taubensee, E	CIN	L	.284	80	218	32	62	107	14	2	9	44	1	1	2	22	2	52	2	2	2	.491	.354	6

Telgheder, D	NY	R	.333	7	6	1	2	2	0	0	0	1	1	0	0	0	0	3	0	0	0	.333	.333	0
Thompson, M	HOU	L	.220	92	132	14	29	44	9	0	2	19	2	1	1	14	3	37	4	2	3	.333	.297	1
Thompson, M	COL	R	.385	21	13	2	5	5	0	0	0	0	1	0	0	0	0	7	0	0	0	.385	.385	0
Thompson, R	SF	R	.223	95	336	51	75	114	15	0	8	23	9	0	4	42	1	76	1	2	3	.339	.317	3
Thompson, R	NY	R	.251	75	267	39	67	101	13	0	7	31	0	4	4	19	1	77	3	1	12	.378	.306	3
Timmons, O	CHI	R	.263	77	171	30	45	81	10	1	8	28	0	1	0	13	2	32	3	0	8	.474	.314	2
Torres, S	SF	R	.000	4	1	0	0	0	0	0	0	0	0	0	0	0	0	0	0	0	0	.000	.000	0
Trachsel, S	CHI	R	.265	30	49	3	13	15	2	0	0	4	6	1	0	2	0	17	0	0	0	.306	.288	1
Treadway, J	LA-MON	L	.209	58	67	6	14	18	2	1	0	13	0	0	0	5	1	4	0	1	0	.269	.264	0
Tucker, S	HOU	R	.286	5	7	1	2	5	0	0	1	1	0	0	0	0	0	0	0	0	0	.714	.286	0
Urbani, T	STL	L	.316	24	19	3	6	10	1	0	1	3	2	0	0	3	0	6	0	0	0	.526	.409	0
Urbina, U	MON	R	.333	7	6	0	2	2	0	0	0	0	0	0	0	0	0	4	0	0	0	.333	.333	0
Valdes, I	LA	R	.097	33	62	2	6	6	0	0	0	1	7	0	0	1	0	26	1	0	0	.097	.111	1
Valdes, M	FLA	R	.000	3	2	0	0	0	0	0	0	0	0	0	0	0	0	0	0	0	0	.000	.000	0
Valdez, C	SF	R	.000	11	1	0	0	0	0	0	0	0	0	0	0	0	0	1	0	0	0	.000	.000	0
Valdez, S	SF	R	.095	13	21	1	2	2	0	0	0	1	3	0	0	0	0	9	0	0	0	.095	.095	2
Valenzuela, F	SD	L	.250	29	32	3	8	15	1	0	2	8	3	0	0	0	0	6	0	0	0	.469	.250	0
Vander Wal, J	COL	L	.347	105	101	15	35	60	8	1	5	21	0	1	0	16	5	23	1	1	2	.594	.432	2
VanLandingham, W	SF	R	.152	18	46	1	7	12	2	0	1	3	1	0	0	0	0	24	0	0	1	.261	.152	1
Van Slyke, A	PHI	L	.243	63	214	26	52	75	10	2	3	16	0	2	2	28	1	41	7	0	6	.350	.333	2
Varsho, G	PHI	L	.252	72	103	7	26	29	1	1	0	11	0	1	2	7	1	17	2	0	1	.282	.310	2
Veras, Q	FLA	S	.261	124	440	86	115	164	20	7	5	32	7	2	9	80	0	68	56	21	7	.373	.384	9
Veres, D	HOU	R	.000	72	5	0	0	0	0	0	0	0	1	0	0	0	0	4	0	0	0	.000	.000	1
Veres, R	FLA	R	.000	47	3	0	0	0	0	0	0	0	0	0	0	0	0	0	0	0	0	.000	.000	1
Villone, R	SD	L	.000	19	1	0	0	0	0	0	0	0	0	0	0	0	0	0	0	0	0	.000	.000	0
Viola, F	CIN	L	.167	3	6	0	1	2	1	0	0	0	0	0	0	0	0	1	0	0	0	.333	.167	0
Vizcaino, J	NY	S	.287	135	509	66	146	186	21	5	3	56	13	3	1	35	4	76	8	3	14	.365	.332	10
Wagner, P	PIT	R	.214	34	42	5	9	10	1	0	0	4	6	0	0	4	0	11	0	0	1	.238	.283	0
Walker, L	COL	L	.306	131	494	96	151	300	31	5	36	101	0	5	14	49	13	72	16	3	13	.607	.381	3
Walker, M	CHI	R	.000	42	3	0	0	0	0	0	0	0	0	0	0	0	0	1	0	0	0	.000	.000	1
Wall, D	HOU	R	.000	6	5	0	0	0	0	0	0	0	3	0	0	0	0	2	0	0	0	.000	.000	1
Wallach, T	LA	R	.266	97	327	24	87	140	22	2	9	38	0	4	4	27	4	69	0	0	11	.428	.326	5
Walton, J	CIN	R	.290	102	162	32	47	85	12	1	8	22	3	2	4	17	0	25	10	7	0	.525	.368	2
Watson, A	STL	L	.417	21	36	5	15	19	4	0	0	5	3	0	0	2	0	7	0	0	1	.528	.447	0
Weathers, D	FLA	R	.154	28	26	1	4	4	0	0	0	1	5	0	0	0	0	17	0	0	0	.154	.154	2
Webster, L	PHI	R	.267	49	150	18	40	61	9	0	4	14	1	0	0	16	0	27	0	0	4	.407	.337	3
Webster, M	LA	S	.179	54	56	6	10	16	1	1	1	3	2	0	1	4	1	14	0	0	1	.286	.246	0
Wehner, J	PIT	R	.308	52	107	13	33	39	0	3	0	5	4	2	0	10	1	17	3	1	2	.364	.361	0

BATTER	TEAM	B	AVG	G	AB	R	H	TB	2B	3B	HR	RBI	SH	SF	HP	BB	IBB	SO	SB	CS	GI DP	SLG	OBP	E
Weiss, W	COL	S	.260	137	427	65	111	137	17	3	1	25	6	1	5	98	8	57	15	3	7	.321	.403	16
Wells, D	CIN	L	.143	11	28	2	4	4	0	0	0	0	1	0	0	0	0	5	0	0	0	.143	.143	0
Wendell, T	CHI	L	.000	43	7	0	0	0	0	0	0	0	0	0	0	1	0	5	0	0	0	.000	.125	1
West, D	PHI	L	.125	8	8	1	1	4	0	0	1	3	6	0	0	1	0	4	0	0	1	.500	.222	1
White, G	MON	L	.000	19	3	0	0	0	0	0	0	0	1	0	0	0	0	3	0	0	0	.000	.000	0
White, R	PIT	R	.067	15	15	1	1	2	1	0	0	1	2	0	0	0	0	3	0	0	0	.133	.067	1
White, R	MON	R	.295	130	474	87	140	220	33	4	13	57	0	4	6	41	1	87	25	5	11	.464	.356	4
Whiten, M	PHI	S	.269	60	212	38	57	102	10	1	11	37	0	0	1	31	1	63	7	0	4	.481	.365	4
Whitmore, D	FLA	L	.190	27	58	6	11	16	2	0	1	2	1	1	0	5	0	15	0	0	1	.276	.250	1
Wilkins, R	CHI-HOU	L	.203	65	202	30	41	65	3	0	7	19	0	2	1	46	2	61	0	0	9	.322	.351	4
Williams, B	SD	R	.071	44	14	1	1	2	1	0	0	0	0	0	0	0	0	4	0	0	1	.143	.071	0
Williams, E	SD	R	.260	97	296	35	77	126	11	1	12	47	0	2	4	23	0	47	0	0	21	.426	.320	7
Williams, M	SF	R	.336	76	283	53	95	183	17	1	23	65	0	3	2	30	8	58	2	0	8	.647	.399	10
Williams, M	PHI	R	.125	33	16	0	2	3	1	0	0	1	7	0	0	1	0	5	0	0	0	.188	.176	1
Williams, R	LA	S	.091	15	11	2	1	1	0	0	0	1	0	0	0	2	0	3	0	0	0	.091	.231	0
Williams, T	LA	R	.500	16	2	0	1	1	0	0	0	0	0	0	0	0	0	0	0	0	0	.500	.500	0
Wilson, G	PIT	R	.000	10	0	0	0	0	0	0	0	0	1	0	0	0	0	0	0	0	0	.000	.000	0
Wilson, N	CIN	L	.000	5	7	0	0	0	0	0	0	0	0	0	0	0	0	4	0	0	0	.000	.000	0
Wilson, T	SF	L	.233	19	30	1	7	8	1	0	0	3	3	0	0	0	0	8	0	0	0	.267	.233	1
Witt, B	FLA	R	.063	21	32	0	2	3	1	0	0	2	4	1	0	1	0	10	0	0	0	.094	.088	0
Wohlers, M	ATL	R	.000	65	3	0	0	0	0	0	0	0	0	0	0	0	0	3	0	0	0	.000	.000	0
Woodall, B	ATL	S	1.000	9	1	0	1	1	0	0	0	1	0	0	0	0	0	0	0	0	0	1.000	1.000	0
Worrell, T	SD	R	.000	9	1	0	0	0	0	0	0	0	0	0	0	0	0	0	0	0	0	.000	.000	0
Worrell, T	LA	R	.000	59	2	0	0	0	0	0	0	0	0	0	0	0	0	2	0	0	0	.000	.000	0
Worthington, C	CIN	R	.278	10	18	1	5	9	1	0	1	2	0	0	0	2	0	1	0	0	0	.500	.350	0
Young, A	CHI	R	.667	32	3	2	2	2	0	0	0	0	0	0	0	0	0	0	0	0	0	.667	.667	2
Young, E	COL	R	.317	120	366	68	116	173	21	9	6	36	3	1	5	49	3	29	35	12	4	.473	.404	11
Young, K	PIT	R	.232	56	181	13	42	69	9	0	6	22	1	3	2	8	0	53	1	3	5	.381	.268	12
Zeile, T	STL-CHI	R	.246	113	426	50	105	169	22	0	14	52	4	5	4	34	1	76	1	0	13	.397	.305	19
Zosky, E	FLA	R	.200	6	5	0	1	1	0	0	0	0	0	0	0	0	0	0	0	0	0	.200	.200	1

CLUB BATTING

CLUB	AVG	G	AB	R	OR	H	TB	2B	3B	HR	GS	RBI	SH	SF	HP	BB	IBB	SO	SB	CS	GI DP	LOB	SHO	SLG	OBP
COLORADO	.282	144	4994	785	783	1406	2351	259	43	200	3	749	82	31	56	484	47	943	125	59	118	1017	11	.471	.350
HOUSTON	.275	144	5097	747	674	1403	2034	260	22	109	3	694	78	47	69	566	58	992	176	60	114	1153	4	.399	.353
SAN DIEGO	.272	144	4950	668	672	1345	1964	231	20	116	9	618	56	38	35	447	45	872	124	46	125	998	6	.397	.334
CINCINNATI	.270	144	4903	747	623	1326	2156	277	35	161	1	694	62	50	40	519	42	946	190	68	92	1001	3	.440	.342
NEW YORK	.267	144	4958	657	618	1323	1984	218	34	125	4	617	92	43	42	446	44	994	58	39	105	1041	8	.400	.330
CHICAGO	.265	144	4963	693	671	1315	2134	267	39	158	2	648	71	35	34	440	46	953	105	37	110	956	5	.430	.327
LOS ANGELES	.264	144	4942	634	609	1303	1976	191	31	140	4	593	68	35	30	468	46	1023	127	45	99	1049	12	.400	.329
PHILADELPHIA	.262	144	4950	615	658	1296	1901	263	30	94	2	576	77	41	46	497	38	884	72	25	107	1114	9	.384	.332
FLORIDA	.262	143	4886	673	673	1278	1982	214	29	144	7	636	69	48	49	517	36	916	131	53	105	1028	9	.406	.335
PITTSBURGH	.259	144	4937	629	736	1281	1955	245	27	125	3	587	51	33	24	456	45	972	84	55	88	1010	8	.396	.323
MONTREAL	.259	144	4905	621	638	1268	1935	265	24	118	5	572	58	32	56	400	43	901	120	49	107	970	8	.394	.320
SAN FRANCISCO	.253	144	4971	652	776	1256	2007	229	33	152	2	610	79	24	57	472	55	1060	138	46	92	1046	8	.404	.323
ATLANTA	.250	144	4814	645	540	1202	1970	210	27	168	2	618	56	34	40	520	37	933	73	43	106	988	4	.409	.326
ST. LOUIS	.247	143	4779	563	658	1182	1789	238	24	107	1	533	48	40	46	436	31	920	79	46	110	957	19	.374	.314
TOTALS	.263	1007	69049	9329	9329	18184	28138	3367	418	1917	48	8745	947	531	624	6668	613	13309	1602	671	1478	14328	114	.408	.331

Pitching

Individual Pitching Leaders

Games Won	19	Maddux	Atl.
Games Lost	16	Wagner	Pit.
Won-Lost Percentage	.905	Maddux	Atl. (19-2)
Earned Run Average	1.63	Maddux	Atl.
Games	76	Leskanic	Col.
Games Started	31	Ashby	S.D.
		Drabek	Hou.
		Loaiza	Pit.
		Neagle	Pit.
		Portugal	S.F.-Cin.
Complete Games	10	Maddux	Atl.
Games Finished	54	Nen	Fla.
		Slocumb	Phi.
Shutouts	3	Maddux	Atl.
		Nomo	L.A.
Saves	38	Myers	Chi.
Innings	209.2	Maddux	Atl.
		Neagle	Pit.
Hits	221	Neagle	Pit.
Batsmen Faced	876	Neagle	Pit.
Runs	115	Loaiza	Pit.
Earned Runs	99	Loaiza	Pit.
Home Runs	32	Foster	Chi.
Sacrifice Hits	19	Fassero	Mon.
Sacrifice Flies	9	Loaiza	Pit.
Hit Batsmen	17	Leiter	S.F.
Bases on Balls	81	Martinez	L.A.
Intentional Bases on Balls	17	Jones	Hou.
Strikeouts	236	Nomo	L.A.
Wild Pitches	19	Nomo	L.A.
Balks	5	Nomo	L.A.
Games Won, Consecutive	10	Maddux	Atl. (May 23-Aug. 4)
Games Lost, Consecutive	9	Jackson	St.L. (April 27-July 2
		Mulholland	S.F. (May 11-July 29)

During the 1995 season 290 pitchers participated in regular season games.

PITCHER	TEAM	T	W	L	ERA	G	GS	CG	SHO	GF	SV	IP	H	TBF	R	ER	HR	SH	SF	HB	BB	IBB	SO	WP	BK	OPP AVG
Maddux, G	ATL	R	19	2	1.63	28	28	10	3	0	0	209.2	147	785	39	38	8	9	1	4	23	3	181	1	0	.197
Nomo, H	LA	R	13	6	2.54	28	28	4	3	0	0	191.1	124	780	63	54	14	11	4	5	78	2	236	19	5	.182
Ashby, A	SD	R	12	10	2.94	31	31	2	2	0	0	192.2	180	800	79	63	17	10	4	11	62	3	150	7	0	.253
Glavine, T	ATL	L	16	7	3.08	29	29	3	1	0	0	198.2	182	822	76	68	9	7	5	5	66	0	127	3	0	.246
Hamilton, J	SD	R	6	9	3.08	31	30	2	2	1	0	204.1	189	850	89	70	17	12	4	11	56	5	123	2	0	.246
Smoltz, J	ATL	R	12	7	3.18	29	29	2	1	0	0	192.2	166	808	76	68	15	13	5	4	72	8	193	13	0	.232
Castillo, F	CHI	R	11	10	3.21	29	29	2	2	0	0	188.0	179	795	75	67	22	11	3	6	52	4	135	3	1	.248
Schourek, P	CIN	L	18	7	3.22	29	29	2	0	0	0	190.1	158	754	72	68	17	4	4	8	45	3	160	1	1	.228
Navarro, J	CHI	R	14	6	3.28	29	29	1	1	0	0	200.1	194	837	79	73	19	2	3	3	56	7	128	1	0	.251
Hampton, M	HOU	L	9	8	3.35	24	24	0	0	0	0	150.2	141	641	73	56	13	11	5	4	49	3	115	3	1	.247
Neagle, D	PIT	L	13	8	3.43	31	31	5	1	0	0	209.2	221	876	91	80	20	13	6	3	45	3	150	6	0	.273
Rapp, P	FLA	R	14	7	3.44	28	28	3	2	0	0	167.1	158	716	72	64	10	8	0	7	76	2	102	7	0	.253
Smiley, J	CIN	L	12	5	3.46	28	27	1	0	0	0	176.2	173	724	72	68	11	17	5	4	39	3	124	5	1	.263
Reynolds, S	HOU	R	10	11	3.47	30	30	3	2	0	0	189.1	196	792	87	73	15	8	0	2	37	6	175	7	1	.263
Candiotti, T	LA	R	7	14	3.50	30	30	1	1	0	0	190.1	187	812	93	74	18	7	5	9	58	2	141	7	0	.255

INDIVIDUAL PITCHING

PITCHER	TEAM	T	W	L	ERA	G	GS	CG	SHO	GF	SV	IP	H	TBF	R	ER	HR	SH	SF	HB	BB	IBB	SO	WP	BK	OPP AVG
Abbott, K	PHI	L	2	0	3.81	18	0	0	0	3	0	28.1	28	122	12	12	3	0	1	0	16	0	21	2	1	.267
Acevedo, J	COL	R	4	6	6.44	17	11	0	0	0	0	65.2	82	291	53	47	15	4	2	6	20	2	40	2	1	.317
Adams, T	CHI	R	1	1	6.50	18	0	0	0	7	1	18.0	22	86	15	13	0	0	0	0	10	1	15	1	0	.289
Alvarez, C	MON	R	1	5	6.75	8	8	0	0	0	0	37.1	46	173	30	28	2	1	0	3	14	0	17	1	0	.297
Aquino, L	MON-SF	R	0	3	5.10	34	0	0	0	9	2	42.1	57	199	34	24	6	1	1	3	13	2	26	3	0	.315
Arocha, R	STL	R	3	5	3.99	41	0	0	0	13	0	49.2	55	216	24	22	6	8	2	3	18	4	25	2	0	.297
Ashby, A	SD	R	12	10	2.94	31	31	2	2	0	0	192.2	180	800	79	63	17	10	4	11	62	3	150	7	0	.253
Astacio, P	LA	R	7	8	4.24	48	11	1	1	7	0	104.0	103	436	53	49	12	5	3	4	29	5	80	5	0	.261
Avery, S	ATL	L	7	13	4.67	29	29	3	1	0	0	173.1	165	724	92	90	22	6	4	6	52	4	141	3	0	.252
Bailey, P	STL	R	0	0	7.36	3	0	0	0	0	0	3.2	2	15	3	3	0	0	0	0	2	1	5	1	0	.154
Bailey, R	COL	R	7	6	4.98	39	6	0	0	9	0	81.1	88	360	49	45	9	7	2	1	39	3	33	7	1	.283
Banks, W	CHI-LA-FLA	R	2	6	5.66	25	15	0	0	2	0	90.2	106	430	71	57	14	6	3	2	58	7	62	9	1	.294

PITCHER	TEAM	T	W	L	ERA	G	GS	CG	SHO	GF	SV	IP	H	TBF	R	ER	HR	SH	SF	HB	BB	IBB	SO	WP	BK	OPP AVG
Barber, B	STL	R	2	1	5.22	9	4	0	0	2	0	29.1	31	130	17	17	4	0	3	0	16	0	27	3	0	.279
Barton, S	SF	L	4	1	4.26	52	0	0	0	11	1	44.1	37	181	22	21	3	1	3	2	19	1	22	0	1	.237
Bautista, J	SF	R	3	8	6.44	52	6	0	0	19	0	100.2	120	451	77	72	24	8	5	5	26	3	45	1	2	.295
Beck, R	SF	R	5	6	4.45	60	0	0	0	52	33	58.2	60	255	31	29	7	4	3	2	21	3	42	2	0	.267
Bedrosian, S	ATL	R	1	2	6.11	29	0	0	0	7	0	28.0	40	129	21	19	6	1	2	1	12	2	22	0	0	.354
Benes, A	STL	R	1	2	8.44	3	3	0	0	0	0	16.0	24	76	15	15	2	1	0	1	4	0	20	3	0	.343
Benes, A	SD	R	4	7	4.17	19	19	1	1	0	0	118.2	121	518	65	55	10	3	4	4	45	3	126	3	0	.262
Berumen, A	SD	R	2	3	5.68	37	0	0	0	17	1	44.1	37	207	29	28	3	1	3	3	36	3	42	6	0	.226
Birkbeck, M	NY	R	0	1	1.63	4	4	0	0	0	0	27.2	22	104	5	5	2	2	0	0	2	0	14	3	1	.220
Blair, W	SD	R	7	5	4.34	40	12	0	0	11	0	114.0	112	485	60	55	11	8	2	2	45	3	83	4	0	.262
Bochtler, D	SD	R	4	4	3.57	34	0	0	0	11	1	45.1	38	181	18	18	5	2	1	0	19	0	45	1	0	.239
Borbon, P	ATL	L	2	2	3.09	41	0	0	0	19	2	32.0	29	143	12	11	2	3	1	1	17	4	33	0	1	.240
Borland, T	PHI	R	1	3	3.77	50	0	0	0	18	6	74.0	81	339	37	31	3	3	2	5	37	7	59	12	0	.277
Bottalico, R	PHI	R	5	3	2.46	62	0	0	0	20	1	87.2	50	350	25	24	7	3	1	4	42	3	87	1	0	.167
Bowen, R	FLA	R	2	0	3.78	4	3	0	0	0	0	16.2	23	85	11	7	3	1	2	0	12	2	15	0	0	.329
Brantley, J	CIN	R	3	2	2.82	56	0	0	0	49	28	70.1	53	283	22	22	11	2	3	1	20	3	62	2	2	.206
Brewington, J	SF	R	6	4	4.54	13	13	0	0	0	0	75.1	68	334	38	38	8	4	4	4	45	6	45	3	0	.245
Brocail, D	HOU	R	6	4	4.19	36	7	0	0	12	1	77.1	87	339	40	36	10	1	1	4	22	2	39	1	1	.280
Bruske, J	LA	R	0	0	4.50	9	0	0	0	3	1	10.0	12	45	7	5	0	0	0	1	4	0	5	1	0	.300
Bullinger, J	CHI	R	12	8	4.14	24	24	1	1	0	0	150.0	152	665	80	69	14	12	5	9	65	7	93	5	1	.265
Burba, D	SF-CIN	R	10	4	3.97	52	9	1	1	7	0	106.2	90	451	50	47	9	4	1	0	51	3	96	5	0	.228
Burgos, E	SF	L	0	0	8.64	5	0	0	0	2	0	8.1	14	44	8	8	1	0	0	1	6	0	12	2	0	.378
Burkett, J	FLA	R	14	14	4.30	30	30	4	0	0	0	188.1	208	810	95	90	22	10	0	6	57	5	126	2	1	.282
Byrd, P	NY	R	2	0	2.05	17	0	0	0	6	0	22.0	18	91	6	5	1	0	2	1	7	1	26	1	2	.222
Candiotti, T	LA	R	7	14	3.50	30	30	1	1	0	0	190.1	187	812	93	74	18	7	5	9	58	2	141	7	0	.255
Cangelosi, J	HOU	L	0	0	0.00	1	0	0	0	1	0	1.0	0	4	0	0	0	0	0	0	1	0	0	0	0	.000
Carrasco, H	CIN	R	2	7	4.12	64	0	0	0	28	5	87.1	86	391	45	40	1	2	6	2	46	5	64	15	0	.257
Carter, A	PHI	L	0	0	6.14	4	0	0	0	1	0	7.1	4	28	5	5	3	0	1	1	2	1	6	0	0	.167
Casian, L	CHI	L	1	0	1.93	42	0	0	0	5	0	23.1	23	107	6	5	1	1	2	0	15	6	11	2	0	.258
Castillo, F	CHI	R	11	10	3.21	29	29	2	2	0	0	188.0	179	795	75	67	22	11	3	6	52	4	135	3	1	.248
Charlton, N	PHI	L	2	5	7.36	25	0	0	0	5	0	22.0	23	102	19	18	2	1	1	3	15	3	12	1	0	.280
Christiansen, J	PIT	L	1	3	4.15	63	0	0	0	13	0	56.1	49	255	28	26	5	6	3	3	34	9	53	4	1	.234
Clark, T	ATL	R	0	0	4.91	3	0	0	0	1	0	3.2	3	18	2	2	0	0	0	0	5	0	2	1	0	.231
Clontz, B	ATL	R	8	1	3.65	59	0	0	0	14	4	69.0	71	295	29	28	5	3	2	4	22	4	55	0	0	.269
Cornelius, R	MON-NY	R	3	7	5.54	18	10	0	0	1	0	66.2	75	301	44	41	11	4	3	3	30	5	39	2	1	.288
Courtright, J	CIN	L	0	0	9.00	1	0	0	0	0	0	1.0	2	5	1	1	[illegible]	[illegible]	[illegible]	[illegible]	[illegible]	[illegible]	[illegible]	[illegible]	[illegible]	[illegible]

Cummings, J	LA	L	3	1	3.00	35	0	0	0	11	0	39.0	38	165	16	13	3	2	1	0	10	4	21	1	0	.250
Daal, O	LA	L	4	0	7.20	28	0	0	0	0	0	20.0	29	100	16	16	1	1	1	1	15	4	11	0	1	.354
DeLeon, J	MON	R	0	1	7.56	7	0	0	0	1	0	8.1	7	40	7	7	2	0	2	1	7	0	12	0	0	.233
DeLucia, R	STL	R	8	7	3.39	56	1	0	0	8	0	82.1	63	342	38	31	9	5	2	3	36	2	76	5	0	.213
Deshaies, J	PHI	L	0	1	20.25	2	2	0	0	0	0	5.1	15	32	12	12	3	0	0	0	1	0	6	0	0	.484
Dewey, M	SF	R	1	0	3.13	27	0	0	0	5	0	31.2	30	137	12	11	2	1	1	0	17	6	32	1	0	.254
DiPoto, J	NY	R	4	6	3.78	58	0	0	0	26	2	78.2	77	330	41	33	2	6	3	4	29	8	49	3	1	.267
Dishman, G	SD	L	4	8	5.01	19	16	0	0	1	0	97.0	104	421	60	54	11	6	3	4	34	1	43	3	1	.278
Dougherty, J	HOU	R	8	4	4.92	56	0	0	0	11	0	67.2	76	294	37	37	7	3	3	3	25	1	49	1	0	.292
Drabek, D	HOU	R	10	9	4.77	31	31	2	1	0	0	185.0	205	797	104	98	18	4	3	8	54	4	143	8	1	.282
Dunbar, M	FLA	L	0	1	11.57	8	0	0	0	1	0	7.0	12	45	9	9	0	2	0	1	11	3	5	1	0	.387
Dyer, M	PIT	R	4	5	4.34	55	0	0	0	15	0	74.2	81	327	40	36	9	3	1	5	30	3	53	4	1	.281
Edens, T	CHI	R	1	0	6.00	5	0	0	0	1	0	3.0	6	18	3	2	0	0	0	0	3	0	2	0	0	.400
Eischen, J	LA	L	0	0	3.10	17	0	0	0	8	0	20.1	19	95	9	7	1	0	0	2	11	1	15	1	0	.232
Elliott, D	SD	R	0	0	0.00	1	0	0	0	1	0	2.0	2	9	0	0	0	0	0	0	1	0	3	0	0	.250
Ericks, J	PIT	R	3	9	4.58	19	18	1	0	0	0	106.0	108	472	59	54	7	5	5	2	50	4	80	11	1	.263
Estes, S	SF	L	0	3	6.75	3	3	0	0	0	0	17.1	16	76	14	13	2	0	0	1	5	0	14	4	0	.229
Eversgerd, B	MON	L	0	0	5.14	25	0	0	0	5	0	21.0	22	95	13	12	2	1	2	1	9	2	8	1	0	.268
Fassero, J	MON	L	13	14	4.33	30	30	1	0	0	0	189.0	207	833	102	91	15	19	7	2	74	3	164	7	1	.283
Fernandez, S	PHI	L	6	1	3.34	11	11	0	0	0	0	64.2	48	263	25	24	11	1	0	1	21	0	79	0	1	.200
Fletcher, P	PHI	R	1	0	5.40	10	0	0	0	1	0	13.1	15	64	8	8	2	1	1	1	9	2	10	2	0	.288
Florence, D	NY	L	3	0	1.50	14	0	0	0	3	0	12.0	17	57	3	2	0	1	0	0	6	0	5	0	0	.340
Florie, B	SD	R	2	2	3.01	47	0	0	0	10	1	68.2	49	290	30	23	8	5	1	4	38	3	68	7	2	.202
Fossas, T	STL	L	3	0	1.47	58	0	0	0	20	0	36.2	28	145	6	6	1	2	1	1	10	3	40	1	0	.214
Foster, K	CHI	R	12	11	4.51	30	28	0	0	1	0	167.2	149	703	90	84	32	4	6	6	65	4	146	2	2	.240
Franco, J	NY	L	5	3	2.44	48	0	0	0	41	29	51.2	48	213	17	14	4	4	1	0	17	2	41	0	0	.251
Frascatore, J	STL	R	1	1	4.41	14	4	0	0	3	0	32.2	39	151	19	16	3	1	1	2	16	1	21	0	0	.298
Fraser, W	MON	R	2	1	5.61	22	0	0	0	6	2	25.2	25	114	17	16	6	1	0	3	9	1	12	2	0	.248
Freeman, M	COL	R	3	7	5.89	22	18	0	0	0	0	94.2	122	437	64	62	15	7	3	2	41	1	61	5	1	.318
Frey, S	SF-PHI	L	0	1	2.12	18	0	0	0	4	1	17.0	10	65	7	4	2	2	1	0	4	1	7	0	0	.172
Garces, R	CHI-FLA	R	0	2	4.44	18	0	0	0	7	0	24.1	25	108	15	12	1	1	0	0	11	2	22	0	0	.260
Gardner, M	FLA	R	5	5	4.49	39	11	1	1	7	1	102.1	109	456	60	51	14	7	0	5	43	5	87	3	1	.272
Glavine, T	ATL	L	16	7	3.08	29	29	3	1	0	0	198.2	182	822	76	68	9	7	5	5	66	0	127	3	0	.246
Gomez, P	SF	L	0	0	5.14	18	0	0	0	3	0	14.0	16	70	8	8	2	0	0	0	12	1	15	0	1	.276
Gott, J	PIT	R	2	4	6.03	25	0	0	0	12	3	31.1	38	147	26	21	2	1	1	1	12	2	19	3	0	.288
Grace, M	PHI	R	1	1	3.18	2	2	0	0	0	0	11.1	10	47	4	4	0	1	0	0	4	0	7	0	0	.238
Grahe, J	COL	R	4	3	5.08	17	9	0	0	0	0	56.2	69	265	42	32	6	3	3	3	27	2	27	3	2	.301
Green, T	PHI	R	8	9	5.31	26	25	4	2	0	0	140.2	157	623	86	83	15	5	6	4	66	3	85	9	2	.290
Greene, T	PHI	R	0	5	8.29	11	6	0	0	3	0	33.2	45	167	32	31	6	2	1	3	20	0	24	3	1	.319

PITCHER	TEAM	T	W	L	ERA	G	GS	CG	SHO	GF	SV	IP	H	TBF	R	ER	HR	SH	SF	HB	BB	IBB	SO	WP	BK	OPP AVG
Greer, K	SF	R	0	2	5.25	8	0	0	0	1	0	12.0	15	61	12	7	3	2	1	1	5	2	7	0	0	.288
Groom, B	FLA	L	1	2	7.20	14	0	0	0	5	0	15.0	26	71	12	12	2	0	0	0	6	0	12	0	0	.400
Grott, M	CIN	L	0	0	21.60	2	0	0	0	0	0	1.2	6	11	4	4	1	0	0	0	0	0	2	0	0	.545
Gunderson, E	NY	L	1	1	3.70	30	0	0	0	7	0	24.1	25	103	10	10	2	0	1	1	8	3	19	1	0	.269
Guthrie, M	LA	L	0	2	3.66	24	0	0	0	7	0	19.2	19	91	11	8	1	2	0	1	9	2	19	2	0	.241
Habyan, J	STL	R	3	2	2.88	31	0	0	0	9	0	40.2	32	165	18	13	0	4	1	1	15	4	35	2	3	.222
Hamilton, J	SD	R	6	9	3.08	31	30	2	2	1	0	204.1	189	850	89	70	17	12	4	11	56	5	123	2	0	.246
Hammond, C	FLA	L	9	6	3.80	25	24	3	2	0	0	161.0	157	683	73	68	17	7	7	9	47	2	126	3	1	.256
Hampton, M	HOU	L	9	8	3.35	24	24	0	0	0	0	150.2	141	641	73	56	13	11	5	4	49	3	115	3	1	.247
Hancock, L	PIT	L	0	0	1.93	11	0	0	0	3	0	14.0	10	54	3	3	0	0	0	0	2	0	6	2	0	.196
Hansell, G	LA	R	0	1	7.45	20	0	0	0	7	0	19.1	29	93	17	16	5	1	1	2	6	1	13	0	0	.349
Harnisch, P	NY	R	2	8	3.68	18	18	0	0	0	0	110.0	111	462	55	45	13	4	6	3	24	4	82	0	1	.261
Harris, G	PHI	R	2	2	4.26	21	0	0	0	5	0	19.0	19	82	9	9	2	1	0	0	8	0	9	0	0	.260
Harris, G	MON	R	2	3	2.61	45	0	0	0	12	0	48.1	45	204	18	14	6	3	0	1	16	1	47	3	0	.245
Hartgraves, D	HOU	L	2	0	3.22	40	0	0	0	11	0	36.1	30	150	14	13	2	1	1	0	16	2	24	1	0	.227
Harvey, B	FLA	R	0	0	....	1	0	0	0	0	0	0.0	2	3	3	3	1	0	0	0	1	0	0	0	0	.000
Henke, T	STL	R	1	1	1.82	52	0	0	0	47	36	54.1	42	221	11	11	2	2	0	0	18	0	48	1	0	.209
Henneman, M	HOU	R	0	1	3.00	21	0	0	0	18	8	21.0	21	87	7	7	1	0	2	2	4	1	19	3	0	.266
Henry, B	MON	L	7	9	2.84	21	21	1	1	0	0	126.2	133	524	47	40	11	7	3	2	28	3	60	0	1	.275
Henry, D	NY	R	3	6	2.96	51	0	0	0	20	4	67.0	48	273	23	22	7	3	2	1	25	6	62	6	1	.198
Heredia, G	MON	R	5	6	4.31	40	18	0	0	5	1	119.0	137	509	60	57	7	9	4	5	21	1	74	1	0	.291
Hermanson, D	SD	R	3	1	6.82	26	0	0	0	6	0	31.2	35	151	26	24	8	3	0	1	22	1	19	3	0	.280
Hernandez, J	FLA	R	0	0	11.57	7	0	0	0	3	0	7.0	12	36	9	9	2	1	1	1	3	1	5	0	0	.400
Hernandez, X	CIN	R	7	2	4.60	59	0	0	0	19	3	90.0	95	391	47	46	8	6	2	4	31	1	84	7	0	.273
Hickerson, B	CHI-COL	L	3	3	8.57	56	0	0	0	13	1	48.1	69	239	52	46	8	2	0	1	28	5	40	5	1	.332
Hill, K	STL	R	6	7	5.06	18	18	0	0	0	0	110.1	125	493	71	62	16	9	2	0	45	4	50	3	0	.286
Hoffman, T	SD	R	7	4	3.88	55	0	0	0	51	31	53.1	48	218	25	23	10	0	0	0	14	3	52	1	0	.235
Holmes, D	COL	R	6	1	3.24	68	0	0	0	33	14	66.2	59	286	26	24	3	5	3	1	28	3	61	7	1	.237
Hook, C	SF	R	5	1	5.50	45	0	0	0	14	0	52.1	55	239	33	32	7	3	3	3	29	3	40	2	0	.274
Hope, J	PIT	R	0	0	30.86	3	0	0	0	0	0	2.1	8	21	8	8	0	0	1	3	4	0	2	0	0	.615
Hudek, J	HOU	R	2	2	5.40	19	0	0	0	16	7	20.0	19	83	12	12	3	1	0	0	5	0	29	2	0	.247
Isringhausen, J	NY	R	9	2	2.81	14	14	1	0	0	0	93.0	88	385	29	29	6	3	3	2	31	2	55	4	1	.254
Jackson, D	STL	L	2	12	5.90	19	19	2	1	0	0	100.2	120	467	82	66	10	10	7	6	48	1	52	6	0	.303
Jackson, M	CIN	R	6	1	2.39	40	0	0	0	10	2	49.0	38	200	13	13	5	1	1	1	19	1	41	1	1	.213
Jacome, J	NY	L	0	4	10.29	5	5	0	0	0	0	21.0	33	110	24	24	3	1	1	1	15	0	11	1	0	.359
Jarvis, K	CIN	R	3	4	5.70	19	11	1	1	2	0	79.0	91	354	56	50	13	2	5	3	32	2	33	2	0	.292
Johnstone, J	FLA	R	0	0	3.86	4	0	0	0	0	0	4.2	7	23	2	2	1	0	0	0	2	1	3	0	0	.333

Jones, B	NY	R	10	10	4.19	30	30	3	1	0	0	195.2	209	839	107	91	20	11	6	7	53	6	127	2	1	.274
Jones, T	HOU	R	6	5	3.07	68	0	0	0	40	15	99.2	89	442	38	34	8	5	4	6	52	17	96	5	0	.237
Juden, J	PHI	R	2	4	4.02	13	10	1	0	0	0	62.2	53	271	31	28	6	5	4	5	31	0	47	4	1	.235
Karp, R	PHI	L	0	0	4.50	1	0	0	0	0	0	2.0	1	10	1	1	0	0	0	0	3	0	2	1	0	.143
Kile, D	HOU	R	4	12	4.96	25	21	0	0	1	0	127.0	114	570	81	70	5	7	3	12	73	2	113	11	1	.240
Konuszewski, D	PIT	R	0	0	54.00	1	0	0	0	0	0	0.1	3	5	2	2	0	1	0	0	1	0	0	0	0	.000
Kroon, M	SD	R	0	1	10.80	2	0	0	0	1	0	1.2	1	7	2	2	0	0	0	0	2	0	2	0	0	.200
Krueger, B	SD	L	0	0	7.04	6	0	0	0	0	0	7.2	13	41	6	6	1	2	0	0	4	1	6	2	0	.371
Leiper, D	MON	L	0	2	2.86	26	0	0	0	7	2	22.0	16	88	8	7	2	2	0	0	6	0	12	0	1	.200
Leiter, M	SF	R	10	12	3.82	30	29	7	1	0	0	195.2	185	817	91	83	19	10	6	17	55	4	129	9	3	.254
Leskanic, C	COL	R	6	3	3.40	76	0	0	0	27	10	98.0	83	406	38	37	7	3	2	0	33	1	107	6	1	.226
Lewis, R	FLA	R	0	1	3.75	21	1	0	0	6	0	36.0	30	152	15	15	9	2	0	1	15	5	32	1	2	.224
Lieber, J	PIT	R	4	7	6.32	21	12	0	0	3	0	72.2	103	327	56	51	7	5	6	4	14	0	45	3	0	.346
Loaiza, E	PIT	R	8	9	5.16	32	31	1	0	0	0	172.2	205	762	115	99	21	10	9	5	55	3	85	6	1	.300
Lomon, K	NY	R	0	1	6.75	6	0	0	0	1	0	9.1	17	47	8	7	0	0	0	0	5	1	6	0	0	.405
Maddux, G	ATL	R	19	2	1.63	28	28	10	3	0	0	209.2	147	785	39	38	8	9	1	4	23	3	181	1	0	.197
Maddux, M	PIT	R	1	0	9.00	8	0	0	0	1	0	9.0	14	42	9	9	0	0	0	0	3	1	4	1	0	.359
Mantei, M	FLA	R	0	1	4.73	12	0	0	0	3	0	13.1	12	64	8	7	1	1	1	0	13	0	15	1	0	.245
Manzanillo, J	NY	R	1	2	7.88	12	0	0	0	4	0	16.0	18	73	15	14	3	0	1	0	6	2	14	5	0	.273
Manzanillo, R	PIT	L	0	0	4.91	5	0	0	0	0	0	3.2	3	16	3	2	0	0	0	1	2	0	1	0	0	.231
Martinez, P	MON	R	14	10	3.51	30	30	2	2	0	0	194.2	158	784	79	76	21	7	3	11	66	1	174	5	2	.227
Martinez, P	HOU	L	0	0	7.40	25	0	0	0	3	0	20.2	29	109	18	17	3	2	1	2	16	1	17	0	1	.330
Martinez, R	LA	R	17	7	3.66	30	30	4	2	0	0	206.1	176	859	95	84	19	7	5	5	81	5	138	3	0	.231
Mathews, T	STL	R	1	1	1.52	23	0	0	0	12	2	29.2	21	120	7	5	1	4	0	0	11	1	28	2	0	.200
Mathews, T	FLA	R	4	4	3.38	57	0	0	0	14	3	82.2	70	332	32	31	9	5	1	1	27	4	72	3	0	.235
Mauser, T	SD	R	0	1	9.53	5	0	0	0	1	0	5.2	4	30	6	6	0	0	0	0	9	0	9	0	0	.190
May, D	ATL	L	0	0	11.25	2	0	0	0	1	0	4.0	10	21	5	5	0	0	1	0	0	0	1	0	0	.500
McCurry, J	PIT	R	1	4	5.02	55	0	0	0	10	1	61.0	82	282	38	34	9	4	0	5	30	4	27	2	0	.337
McElroy, C	CIN	L	3	4	6.02	44	0	0	0	11	0	40.1	46	178	29	27	5	1	3	1	15	3	27	1	0	.291
McMichael, G	ATL	R	7	2	2.79	67	0	0	0	16	2	80.2	64	337	27	25	8	5	0	0	32	9	74	3	0	.213
McMurtry, C	HOU	R	0	1	7.84	11	0	0	0	3	0	10.1	15	56	11	9	0	2	2	1	9	1	4	2	0	.357
Mercker, K	ATL	L	7	8	4.15	29	26	0	0	1	0	143.0	140	622	73	66	16	8	7	3	61	2	102	6	2	.258
Miceli, D	PIT	R	4	4	4.66	58	0	0	0	51	21	58.0	61	264	30	30	7	2	4	4	28	5	56	4	0	.270
Mimbs, M	PHI	L	9	7	4.15	35	19	2	1	6	1	136.2	127	603	70	63	10	6	8	6	75	2	93	9	0	.250
Minor, B	NY	R	4	2	3.66	35	0	0	0	10	1	46.2	44	192	21	19	6	4	0	1	13	1	43	3	0	.253
Mintz, S	SF	R	1	2	7.45	14	0	0	0	3	0	19.1	26	96	16	16	4	2	1	2	12	3	7	0	0	.329
Mlicki, D	NY	R	9	7	4.26	29	25	0	0	1	0	160.2	160	696	82	76	23	8	5	4	54	2	123	5	1	.256
Morel, R	PIT	R	0	1	2.84	5	0	0	0	0	0	6.1	6	23	2	2	0	1	0	0	2	1	3	0	0	.300
Morgan, M	CHI-STL	R	7	7	3.56	21	21	1	0	0	0	131.1	133	548	56	52	12	12	5	6	34	2	61	6	0	.271

PITCHER	TEAM	T	W	L	ERA	G	GS	CG	SHO	GF	SV	IP	H	TBF	R	ER	HR	SH	SF	HB	BB	IBB	SO	WP	BK	OPP AVG
Mulholland, T	SF	L	5	13	5.80	29	24	2	0	2	0	149.0	190	666	112	96	25	11	6	4	38	1	65	4	0	.313
Munoz, B	PHI	R	0	2	5.74	3	3	0	0	0	0	15.2	15	70	13	10	2	0	2	3	9	0	6	0	0	.268
Munoz, M	COL	L	2	4	7.42	64	0	0	0	19	2	43.2	54	208	38	36	9	2	2	1	27	0	37	5	0	.307
Murphy, R	LA-FLA	L	1	2	10.95	14	0	0	0	1	0	12.1	14	58	16	15	3	2	0	0	8	1	7	1	0	.292
Murray, M	ATL	R	0	2	6.75	4	1	0	0	1	0	10.2	10	46	8	8	3	1	0	1	5	0	3	0	0	.256
Myers, M	FLA	L	0	0	0.00	2	0	0	0	2	0	2.0	1	9	0	0	0	0	0	0	3	0	0	0	0	.167
Myers, R	CHI	L	1	2	3.88	57	0	0	0	47	38	55.2	49	240	25	24	7	2	3	0	28	1	59	0	0	.237
Nabholz, C	CHI	L	0	1	5.40	34	0	0	0	4	0	23.1	22	104	15	14	4	1	2	0	14	3	21	2	0	.253
Navarro, J	CHI	R	14	6	3.28	29	29	1	1	0	0	200.1	194	837	79	73	19	2	3	3	56	7	128	1	0	.251
Neagle, D	PIT	L	13	8	3.43	31	31	5	1	0	0	209.2	221	876	91	80	20	13	6	3	45	3	150	6	0	.273
Nen, R	FLA	R	0	7	3.29	62	0	0	0	54	23	65.2	62	279	26	24	6	0	1	1	23	3	68	2	0	.244
Nichols, R	ATL	R	0	0	5.40	5	0	0	0	0	0	6.2	14	38	11	4	3	0	0	0	5	1	3	0	0	.424
Nied, D	COL	R	0	0	20.77	2	0	0	0	0	0	4.1	11	27	10	10	2	0	0	0	3	0	3	0	0	.458
Nitkowski, C	CIN	L	1	3	6.12	9	7	0	0	0	0	32.1	41	154	25	22	4	2	1	2	15	1	18	1	2	.306
Nomo, H	LA	R	13	6	2.54	28	28	4	3	0	0	191.1	124	780	63	54	14	11	4	5	78	2	236	19	5	.182
Olivares, O	COL-PHI	R	1	4	6.91	16	6	0	0	4	0	41.2	55	195	34	32	5	2	2	3	23	0	22	4	0	.333
Osborne, D	STL	L	4	6	3.81	19	19	0	0	0	0	113.1	112	477	58	48	17	8	3	2	34	2	82	0	0	.260
Osuna, P	LA	R	2	4	4.43	39	0	0	0	8	0	44.2	39	186	22	22	5	2	1	1	20	2	46	1	0	.241
Painter, L	COL	L	3	0	4.37	33	1	0	0	7	1	45.1	55	198	23	22	9	0	0	2	10	0	36	4	1	.296
Palacios, V	STL	R	2	3	5.80	20	5	0	0	3	0	40.1	48	184	29	26	7	2	1	2	19	1	34	1	0	.300
Park, C	LA	R	0	0	4.50	2	1	0	0	0	0	4.0	2	16	2	2	1	0	0	0	2	0	7	0	1	.143
Parra, J	LA	R	0	0	4.35	8	0	0	0	0	0	10.1	10	47	8	5	2	0	1	1	6	1	7	0	1	.256
Parrett, J	STL	R	4	7	3.64	59	0	0	0	17	0	76.2	71	328	33	31	8	5	2	1	28	5	71	7	0	.243
Parris, S	PIT	R	6	6	5.38	15	15	1	1	0	0	82.0	89	360	49	49	12	3	2	7	33	1	61	4	0	.283
Pena, A	FLA-ATL	R	2	0	2.61	27	0	0	0	6	0	31.0	22	121	9	9	3	0	0	0	7	1	39	0	0	.193
Pennington, B	CIN	L	0	0	5.59	6	0	0	0	2	0	9.2	9	47	8	6	0	0	2	1	11	0	7	3	0	.273
Perez, C	MON	L	10	8	3.69	28	23	2	1	2	0	141.1	142	592	61	58	18	6	1	5	28	2	106	8	4	.257
Perez, M	CHI	R	2	6	3.66	68	0	0	0	18	2	71.1	72	308	30	29	8	5	3	4	27	8	49	4	0	.268
Perez, Y	FLA	L	2	6	5.21	69	0	0	0	11	1	46.2	35	205	29	27	6	2	1	2	28	4	47	2	0	.203
Person, R	NY	R	1	0	0.75	3	1	0	0	0	0	12.0	5	44	1	1	1	0	0	0	2	0	10	0	0	.119
Petkovsek, M	STL	R	6	6	4.00	26	21	1	1	1	0	137.1	136	569	71	61	11	4	4	6	35	3	71	1	1	.262
Plesac, D	PIT	L	4	4	3.58	58	0	0	0	16	3	60.1	53	259	26	24	3	4	3	1	27	7	57	1	0	.237
Portugal, M	SF-CIN	R	11	10	4.01	31	31	1	0	0	0	181.2	185	775	91	81	17	9	1	4	56	2	96	7	0	.262
Powell, J	FLA	R	0	0	1.08	9	0	0	0	1	0	8.1	7	38	2	1	0	1	0	2	6	1	4	0	0	.241
Powell, R	HOU-PIT	L	0	2	6.98	27	3	0	0	6	0	29.2	36	148	26	23	6	3	1	2	21	4	20	4	0	.298
Pugh, T	CIN	R	6	5	3.84	28	12	0	0	4	0	98.1	100	413	46	42	13	2	2	1	32	2	38	3	1	.267
Pulsipher, W	NY	L	5	7	3.98	17	17	2	0	0	0	126.2	122	530	58	56	11	2	1	4	45	0	81	2	1	.255

Quantrill, P	PHI	R	11	12	4.67	33	29	0	0	1	0	179.1	212	784	102	93	20	9	6	6	44	3	103	0	3	.295
Rapp, P	FLA	R	14	7	3.44	28	28	3	2	0	0	167.1	158	716	72	64	10	8	0	7	76	2	102	7	0	.253
Reed, R	CIN	R	0	0	5.82	4	3	0	0	1	0	17.0	18	70	12	11	5	1	0	0	3	0	10	0	0	.273
Reed, S	COL	R	5	2	2.14	71	0	0	0	15	3	84.0	61	327	24	20	8	3	1	1	21	3	79	0	2	.203
Rekar, B	COL	R	4	6	4.98	15	14	1	0	0	0	85.0	95	375	51	47	11	7	4	3	24	2	60	3	2	.282
Remlinger, M	NY-CIN	L	0	1	6.75	7	0	0	0	4	0	6.2	9	34	6	5	1	1	0	0	5	0	7	0	0	.321
Reynolds, S	HOU	R	10	11	3.47	30	30	3	2	0	0	189.1	196	792	87	73	15	8	0	2	37	6	175	7	1	.263
Reynoso, A	COL	R	7	7	5.32	20	18	0	0	0	0	93.0	116	418	61	55	12	8	2	5	36	3	40	2	0	.316
Ricci, C	PHI	R	1	0	1.80	7	0	0	0	3	0	10.0	9	40	2	2	0	1	2	1	3	0	9	0	0	.273
Rijo, J	CIN	R	5	4	4.17	14	14	0	0	0	0	69.0	76	295	33	32	6	3	3	0	22	1	62	3	0	.285
Ritz, K	COL	R	11	11	4.21	31	28	0	0	3	2	173.1	171	743	91	81	16	8	5	6	65	3	120	6	0	.259
Rivera, R	CHI	L	0	0	5.40	7	0	0	0	2	0	5.0	8	23	3	3	1	0	0	0	2	0	2	0	0	.381
Rodriguez, F	LA	R	1	1	2.53	11	0	0	0	5	0	10.2	11	45	3	3	2	0	0	0	5	0	5	0	0	.275
Rodriguez, R	STL	L	0	0	0.00	1	0	0	0	0	0	1.2	0	4	0	0	0	0	0	0	0	0	0	0	0	.000
Rojas, M	MON	R	1	4	4.12	59	0	0	0	48	30	67.2	69	302	32	31	2	2	1	7	29	4	61	6	0	.262
Roper, J	CIN-SF	R	0	0	12.38	3	2	0	0	0	0	8.0	15	44	12	11	3	1	1	0	6	0	6	0	1	.417
Rosselli, J	SF	L	2	1	8.70	9	5	0	0	0	0	30.0	39	140	29	29	5	2	4	0	20	2	7	0	1	.342
Rueter, K	MON	L	5	3	3.23	9	9	1	1	0	0	47.1	38	184	17	17	3	4	0	1	9	0	28	0	0	.224
Ruffin, B	COL	L	0	1	2.12	37	0	0	0	19	11	34.0	26	140	8	8	1	4	0	0	19	1	23	1	0	.222
Ruffin, J	CIN	R	0	0	1.35	10	0	0	0	6	0	13.1	4	54	3	2	0	0	0	0	11	0	11	3	0	.093
Saberhagen, B	NY-COL	R	7	6	4.18	25	25	3	0	0	0	153.0	165	658	78	71	21	7	3	10	33	3	100	3	0	.273
Sager, A	COL	R	0	0	7.36	10	0	0	0	2	0	14.2	19	70	16	12	1	2	0	0	7	1	10	0	0	.311
Sanders, S	SD	R	5	5	4.30	17	15	1	0	0	0	90.0	79	383	46	43	14	2	2	2	31	4	88	6	1	.228
Scheid, R	FLA	L	0	0	6.10	6	0	0	0	1	0	10.1	14	50	7	7	1	1	1	0	7	0	10	1	0	.341
Schilling, C	PHI	R	7	5	3.57	17	17	1	0	0	0	116.0	96	473	52	46	12	5	2	3	26	2	114	0	1	.220
Schmidt, C	MON	R	0	0	6.97	11	0	0	0	0	0	10.1	15	54	8	8	1	1	0	2	9	0	7	0	0	.357
Schmidt, J	ATL	R	2	2	5.76	9	2	0	0	1	0	25.0	27	119	17	16	2	2	4	1	18	3	19	1	0	.287
Schourek, P	CIN	L	18	7	3.22	29	29	2	0	0	0	190.1	158	754	72	68	17	4	4	8	45	3	160	1	1	.228
Scott, T	MON	R	2	0	3.98	62	0	0	0	15	2	63.1	52	268	30	28	6	4	1	6	23	2	57	4	0	.222
Seanez, R	LA	R	1	3	6.75	37	0	0	0	12	3	34.2	39	159	27	26	5	3	0	1	18	3	29	0	0	.285
Service, S	SF	R	3	1	3.19	28	0	0	0	6	0	31.0	18	129	11	11	4	3	2	2	20	4	30	3	0	.176
Shaw, J	MON	R	1	6	4.62	50	0	0	0	17	3	62.1	58	268	35	32	4	6	1	3	26	4	45	0	0	.250
Slocumb, H	PHI	R	5	6	2.89	61	0	0	0	54	32	65.1	64	289	26	21	2	4	0	1	35	3	63	3	0	.257
Small, A	FLA	R	1	0	1.42	7	0	0	0	1	0	6.1	7	32	2	1	1	0	0	0	6	0	5	0	0	.269
Smiley, J	CIN	L	12	5	3.46	28	27	1	0	0	0	176.2	173	724	72	68	11	17	5	4	39	3	124	5	1	.263
Smith, P	CIN	R	1	2	6.66	11	2	0	0	3	0	24.1	30	106	19	18	8	1	3	1	7	1	14	1	0	.319
Smoltz, J	ATL	R	12	7	3.18	29	29	2	1	0	0	192.2	166	808	76	68	15	13	5	4	72	8	193	13	0	.232
Springer, D	PHI	R	0	3	4.84	4	4	0	0	0	0	22.1	21	94	15	12	3	2	0	1	9	1	15	1	0	.256
Springer, R	PHI	R	0	0	3.71	14	0	0	0	3	0	26.2	22	112	11	11	5	1	2	2	10	3	32	1	0	.227

PITCHER	TEAM	T	W	L	ERA	G	GS	CG	SHO	GF	SV	IP	H	TBF	R	ER	HR	SH	SF	HB	BB	IBB	SO	WP	BK	OPP AVG
Stanton, M	ATL	L	1	1	5.59	26	0	0	0	10	1	19.1	31	94	14	12	3	2	1	1	6	2	13	1	1	.369
Sturtze, T	CHI	R	0	0	9.00	2	0	0	0	0	0	2.0	2	9	2	2	1	0	0	0	1	0	0	0	0	.250
Sullivan, S	CIN	R	0	0	4.91	3	0	0	0	1	0	3.2	4	17	2	2	0	1	0	0	2	0	2	0	0	.286
Swartzbaugh, D	CHI	R	0	0	0.00	7	0	0	0	2	0	7.1	5	27	2	0	0	0	0	0	3	1	5	0	0	.208
Swift, B	COL	R	9	3	4.94	19	19	0	0	0	0	105.2	122	463	62	58	12	6	1	1	43	2	68	2	0	.296
Swindell, G	HOU	L	10	9	4.47	33	26	1	1	3	0	153.0	180	659	86	76	21	4	8	2	39	2	96	3	0	.297
Tabaka, J	SD-HOU	L	1	0	3.23	34	0	0	0	6	0	30.2	27	128	11	11	2	0	0	0	17	1	25	1	0	.243
Tapani, K	LA	R	4	2	5.05	13	11	0	0	0	0	57.0	72	255	37	32	8	3	2	1	14	2	43	1	0	.306
Telgheder, D	NY	R	1	2	5.61	7	4	0	0	2	0	25.2	34	118	18	16	4	3	1	0	7	3	16	0	1	.318
Thobe, J	MON	R	0	0	9.00	4	0	0	0	2	0	4.0	6	21	4	4	0	0	0	0	3	0	0	1	0	.333
Thobe, T	ATL	L	0	0	10.80	3	0	0	0	1	0	3.1	7	17	4	4	0	0	0	0	0	0	2	0	0	.412
Thompson, M	COL	R	2	3	6.53	21	5	0	0	3	0	51.0	73	240	42	37	7	4	4	1	22	2	30	2	0	.349
Torres, S	SF	R	0	1	9.00	4	1	0	0	2	0	8.0	13	40	8	8	4	0	0	0	7	0	2	0	0	.394
Trachsel, S	CHI	R	7	13	5.15	30	29	2	0	0	0	160.2	174	722	104	92	25	12	5	0	76	8	117	2	1	.277
Urbani, T	STL	L	3	5	3.70	24	13	0	0	2	0	82.2	99	354	40	34	11	6	0	2	21	4	52	5	0	.305
Urbina, U	MON	R	2	2	6.17	7	4	0	0	0	0	23.1	26	109	17	16	6	2	0	0	14	1	15	2	0	.280
Valdes, I	LA	R	13	11	3.05	33	27	6	2	1	1	197.2	168	804	76	67	17	10	5	1	51	5	150	1	3	.228
Valdes, M	FLA	R	0	0	14.14	3	3	0	0	0	0	7.0	17	49	13	11	1	1	1	1	9	0	2	1	0	.459
Valdez, C	SF	R	0	1	6.14	11	0	0	0	3	0	14.2	19	69	10	10	1	0	1	1	8	1	7	1	1	.322
Valdez, S	SF	R	4	5	4.75	13	11	1	0	0	0	66.1	78	290	43	35	12	5	3	3	17	3	29	2	1	.298
Valenzuela, F	SD	L	8	3	4.98	29	15	0	0	5	0	90.1	101	395	53	50	16	10	2	0	34	2	57	4	0	.289
VanLandingham, W	SF	R	6	3	3.67	18	18	1	0	0	0	122.2	124	523	58	50	14	6	5	2	40	2	95	5	4	.264
Veres, D	HOU	R	5	1	2.26	72	0	0	0	15	1	103.1	89	418	29	26	5	6	8	4	30	6	94	4	0	.241
Veres, R	FLA	R	4	4	3.88	47	0	0	0	15	1	48.2	46	215	25	21	6	5	4	1	22	7	31	2	0	.251
Villone, R	SD	L	2	1	4.21	19	0	0	0	8	1	25.2	24	111	12	12	5	0	1	0	11	0	37	2	0	.242
Viola, F	CIN	L	0	1	6.28	3	3	0	0	0	0	14.1	20	64	11	10	3	0	1	0	3	1	4	1	0	.333
Wade, T	ATL	L	0	1	4.50	3	0	0	0	0	0	4.0	3	18	2	2	1	0	0	0	4	0	3	1	0	.214
Wagner, B	HOU	L	0	0	0.00	1	0	0	0	0	0	0.1	0	1	0	0	0	0	0	0	0	0	0	0	0	.000
Wagner, P	PIT	R	5	16	4.80	33	25	3	1	1	1	165.0	174	725	96	88	18	7	2	7	72	7	120	8	0	.273
Walker, M	CHI	R	1	3	3.22	42	0	0	0	12	1	44.2	45	206	22	16	2	4	4	0	24	3	20	3	1	.259
Walker, P	NY	R	1	0	4.58	13	0	0	0	10	0	17.2	24	79	9	9	3	0	1	0	5	0	5	0	0	.329
Wall, D	HOU	R	3	1	5.55	6	5	0	0	0	0	24.1	33	110	19	15	5	0	2	0	5	0	16	1	0	.320
Watson, A	STL	L	7	9	4.96	21	19	0	0	1	0	114.1	126	491	68	63	17	2	1	5	41	0	49	2	2	.285
Weathers, D	FLA	R	4	5	5.98	28	15	0	0	0	0	90.1	104	419	68	60	8	7	3	5	52	3	60	3	0	.295
Wells, D	CIN	L	6	5	3.59	11	11	3	0	0	0	72.2	74	300	34	29	6	4	1	0	16	4	50	1	1	.265
Wendell, T	CHI	R	3	1	4.92	43	0	0	0	17	0	60.1	71	270	35	33	11	3	3	2	24	4	50	1	0	.298
[illegible]	[illegible]	[illegible]	[illegible]	[illegible]	3.79	8	8	0	0	0	0	38.0	34	163	17	16	5	2	0	1	19	0	25	1	0	.241

White, R	PIT	R	2	3	4.75	15	9	0	0	2	0	55.0	66	247	33	29	3	3	3	2	18	0	29	2	0	.299
Williams, B	SD	R	3	10	6.00	44	6	0	0	7	0	72.0	79	337	54	48	3	7	1	8	38	4	75	7	1	.279
Williams, M	PHI	R	3	3	3.29	33	8	0	0	7	0	87.2	78	367	37	32	10	5	3	3	29	2	57	7	0	.239
Williams, T	LA	R	2	2	5.12	16	0	0	0	5	0	19.1	19	83	11	11	3	3	1	0	7	2	8	0	0	.264
Wilson, G	PIT	R	0	1	5.02	10	0	0	0	1	0	14.1	13	61	8	8	2	0	0	2	5	0	8	1	0	.241
Wilson, T	SF	L	3	4	3.92	17	17	0	0	0	0	82.2	82	354	42	36	8	5	2	4	38	1	38	0	1	.269
Witt, B	FLA	R	2	7	3.90	19	19	1	0	0	0	110.2	104	472	52	48	8	5	3	2	47	1	95	2	0	.251
Wohlers, M	ATL	R	7	3	2.09	65	0	0	0	49	25	64.2	51	269	16	15	2	2	0	1	24	3	90	4	0	.211
Woodall, B	ATL	L	1	1	6.10	9	0	0	0	3	0	10.1	13	52	10	7	1	1	1	0	8	1	5	1	0	.310
Worrell, T	SD	R	1	0	4.73	9	0	0	0	4	0	13.1	16	63	7	7	2	1	0	1	6	0	13	1	0	.291
Worrell, T	LA	R	4	1	2.02	59	0	0	0	53	32	62.1	50	249	15	14	4	1	2	1	19	2	61	2	0	.221
Young, A	CHI	R	3	4	3.70	32	1	0	0	8	2	41.1	47	181	20	17	5	1	0	3	14	2	15	6	0	.288

CLUB PITCHING

CLUB	W	L	ERA	G	CG	SHO	REL	SV	IP	H	R	ER	HR	HB	BB	IBB	SO	WP	BK	OPP AVG
ATLANTA	90	54	3.44	144	18	11	339	34	1291.2	1184	540	494	107	32	436	46	1087	38	4	.244
LOS ANGELES	78	66	3.66	144	16	11	355	37	1295.0	1188	609	526	125	37	462	45	1060	49	12	.243
NEW YORK	69	75	3.88	144	9	9	298	36	1291.0	1296	618	556	133	35	401	48	901	39	12	.262
CINCINNATI	85	59	4.03	144	8	10	330	38	1289.1	1270	623	578	131	31	424	32	903	58	10	.260
HOUSTON	76	68	4.06	144	6	8	394	32	1320.1	1357	674	596	118	50	460	52	1056	53	6	.266
ST. LOUIS	62	81	4.09	143	4	6	377	38	1265.2	1290	658	575	135	40	445	37	842	51	6	.268
MONTREAL	66	78	4.11	144	7	9	396	42	1283.2	1286	638	586	128	59	416	26	950	45	9	.262
CHICAGO	73	71	4.13	144	6	12	414	45	1301.0	1313	671	597	162	34	518	68	926	38	6	.262
SAN DIEGO	70	74	4.13	144	6	10	337	35	1284.2	1242	672	590	142	51	512	37	1047	60	5	.255
PHILADELPHIA	69	75	4.21	144	8	8	341	41	1290.1	1241	658	603	134	55	538	36	980	57	10	.254
FLORIDA	67	76	4.27	143	12	7	400	29	1286.0	1299	673	610	139	46	562	54	994	36	5	.264
PITTSBURGH	58	86	4.70	144	11	7	391	29	1275.1	1407	736	666	130	57	477	50	871	65	4	.283
SAN FRANCISCO	67	77	4.86	144	12	5	381	34	1293.2	1368	776	699	173	56	505	51	801	43	15	.275
COLORADO	77	67	4.97	144	1	1	456	43	1288.1	1443	783	711	160	41	512	31	891	62	13	.286
TOTALS	1007	1007	4.18	1007	124	114	5209	513	18056.0	18184	9329	8387	1917	624	6668	613	13309	694	117	.263

OFFICIAL 1995 AMERICAN LEAGUE RECORDS

COMPILED BY MLB-IBM BASEBALL INFORMATION SYSTEM
Official Statistician: ELIAS SPORTS BUREAU

FINAL STANDINGS

AMERICAN LEAGUE EAST

CLUB	W.	L.	PCT.	GB
BOSTON	86	58	.597	
NEW YORK	79	65	.549	7.0
BALTIMORE	71	73	.493	15.0
DETROIT	60	84	.417	26.0
TORONTO	56	88	.389	30.0

AMERICAN LEAGUE CENTRAL

CLUB	W.	L.	PCT.	GB
CLEVELAND	100	44	.694	
KANSAS CITY	70	74	.486	30.0
CHICAGO	68	76	.472	32.0
MILWAUKEE	65	79	.451	35.0
MINNESOTA	56	88	.389	44.0

AMERICAN LEAGUE WEST

CLUB	W.	L.	PCT.	GB
SEATTLE	79	66	.545	
CALIFORNIA	78	67	.538	1.0
TEXAS	74	70	.514	4.5
OAKLAND	67	77	.465	11.5

NOTE: Chicago and New York played a 6½-inning tie game on July 17.

Division Series: Seattle defeated New York, 3 games to 2
Cleveland defeated Boston, 3 games to 0
Championship Series: Cleveland defeated Seattle, 4 games to 2

Batting

Individual Batting Leaders

Batting Average	.356	E. Martinez	Sea.
Games	145	F. Thomas	Chi.
		E. Martinez	Sea.
At-Bats	607	Johnson	Chi.
Runs	121	Belle	Cle.
		E. Martinez	Sea.
Hits	186	Johnson	Chi.
Total Bases	377	Belle	Cle.
Singles	151	Nixon	Tex.
Doubles	52	Belle	Cle.
		E. Martinez	Sea.
Triples	13	Lofton	Cle.
Home Runs	50	Belle	Cle.
Runs Batted In	126	Belle	Cle.
		Vaughn	Bos.
Sacrifice Hits	14	Goodwin	K.C.
Sacrifice Flies	12	F. Thomas	Chi.
Hit by Pitch	15	Sprague	Tor.
Bases on Balls	136	F. Thomas	Chi.
Intentional Bases on Balls	29	F. Thomas	Chi.
Strikeouts	150	Vaughn	Bos.
Stolen Bases	54	Lofton	Cle.
Caught Stealing	21	Nixon	Tex.
Grounded Into Double Play	24	Belle	Cle.
Slugging Percentage	.690	Belle	Cle.
On-Base Percentage	.479	E. Martinez	Sea.
Longest Batting Streak	23	Edmonds	Cal. (June 4-29)

During the 1995 season 604 players participated in regular season games.

TOP 15 QUALIFIERS FOR BATTING CHAMPIONSHIP

BATTER	TEAM	B	AVG	G	AB	R	H	TB	2B	3B	HR	RBI	SH	SF	HP	BB	IBB	SO	SB	CS	GIDP	SLG	OBP	E
Martinez, E	SEA	R	.356	145	511	121	182	321	52	0	29	113	0	4	8	116	19	87	4	3	11	.628	.479	2
Knoblauch, C	MIN	R	.333	136	538	107	179	262	34	8	11	63	0	3	10	78	3	95	46	18	15	.487	.424	10
Salmon, T	CAL	R	.330	143	537	111	177	319	34	3	34	105	0	4	6	91	2	111	5	5	9	.594	.429	4
Boggs, W	NY	L	.324	126	460	76	149	194	22	4	5	63	0	7	0	74	5	50	1	1	13	.422	.412	5
Murray, E	CLE	S	.323	113	436	68	141	225	21	0	21	82	0	5	0	39	5	65	5	1	12	.516	.375	3
Surhoff, B	MIL	L	.320	117	415	72	133	204	26	3	13	73	2	4	4	37	4	43	7	3	7	.492	.378	5
Davis, C	CAL	S	.318	119	424	81	135	218	23	0	20	86	0	9	0	89	12	79	3	3	12	.514	.429	0
Belle, A	CLE	R	.317	143	546	121	173	377	52	1	50	126	0	4	6	73	5	80	5	2	24	.690	.401	6
Baerga, C	CLE	S	.314	135	557	87	175	252	28	2	15	90	0	5	3	35	6	31	11	2	15	.452	.355	19
Thome, J	CLE	L	.314	137	452	92	142	252	29	3	25	73	0	3	5	97	3	113	4	3	8	.558	.438	16
Puckett, K	MIN	R	.314	137	538	83	169	277	39	0	23	99	0	5	3	56	18	89	3	2	15	.515	.379	4
Seitzer, K	MIL	R	.311	132	492	56	153	207	33	3	5	69	5	3	6	64	2	57	2	0	13	.421	.395	10
Palmeiro, R	BAL	L	.310	143	554	89	172	323	30	2	39	104	0	5	3	62	5	65	3	1	12	.583	.380	4
Lofton, K	CLE	L	.310	118	481	93	149	218	22	13	7	53	4	3	1	40	6	49	54	15	6	.453	.362	8
Joyner, W	KC	L	.310	131	465	69	144	208	28	0	12	83	5	9	2	69	10	65	3	2	10	.447	.394	3

INDIVIDUAL BATTING

BATTER	TEAM	B	AVG	G	AB	R	H	TB	2B	3B	HR	RBI	SH	SF	HP	BB	IBB	SO	SB	CS	GIDP	SLG	OBP	E
Aldrete, M	OAK-CAL	L	.268	78	149	19	40	60	8	0	4	24	0	3	1	19	1	31	0	0	4	.403	.349	3
Alexander, M	BAL	R	.236	94	242	35	57	77	9	1	3	23	4	0	2	20	0	30	11	4	2	.318	.299	10
Alicea, L	BOS	S	.270	132	419	64	113	157	20	3	6	44	13	9	7	63	0	61	13	10	10	.375	.367	16
Allanson, A	CAL	R	.171	35	82	5	14	26	3	0	3	10	1	0	1	7	0	12	0	1	0	.317	.244	1
Alomar, S	CLE	R	.300	66	203	32	61	97	6	0	10	35	4	1	3	7	0	26	3	1	8	.478	.332	2
Alomar, R	TOR	S	.300	130	517	71	155	232	24	7	13	66	6	7	0	47	3	45	30	3	16	.449	.354	4
Amaral, R	SEA	R	.282	90	238	45	67	91	14	2	2	19	1	0	1	21	0	33	21	2	3	.382	.342	1
Amaro, R	CLE	S	.200	28	60	5	12	18	3	0	1	7	2	0	2	4	0	6	1	3	1	.300	.273	0
Anderson, B	BAL	L	.262	143	554	108	145	246	33	10	16	64	4	2	10	87	4	111	26	7	3	.444	.371	3
Anderson, G	CAL	L	.321	106	374	50	120	189	19	1	16	69	2	4	1	19	4	65	6	2	8	.505	.352	5
Baerga, C	CLE	S	.314	135	557	87	175	252	28	2	15	90	0	5	3	35	6	31	11	2	15	.452	.355	19
Baines, H	BAL	L	.299	127	385	60	115	208	19	1	24	63	0	4	0	70	13	45	0	2	17	.540	.403	0
Barberie, B	BAL	S	.241	90	237	32	57	77	14	0	2	25	6	3	6	36	0	50	3	3	6	.325	.351	7

Bass, K	BAL	S	.244	111	295	32	72	99	12	0	5	32	4	2	2	24	0	47	8	8	15	.336	.303	2
Battle, H	TOR	R	.200	9	15	3	3	3	0	0	0	0	0	0	0	4	0	8	1	0	0	.200	.368	0
Bautista, D	DET	R	.203	89	271	28	55	85	9	0	7	27	6	0	0	12	0	68	4	1	6	.314	.237	2
Becker, R	MIN	S	.237	106	392	45	93	116	15	1	2	33	6	2	4	34	0	95	8	9	9	.296	.303	4
Bell, D	CLE	R	.000	2	2	0	0	0	0	0	0	0	0	0	0	0	0	0	0	0	0	.000	.000	0
Bell, J	BOS	S	.154	17	26	7	4	9	2	0	1	2	0	1	0	2	0	10	0	0	0	.346	.207	3
Belle, A	CLE	R	.317	143	546	121	173	377	52	1	50	126	0	4	6	73	5	80	5	2	24	.690	.401	6
Beltre, E	TEX	R	.217	54	92	7	20	28	8	0	0	7	3	0	0	4	0	15	0	0	1	.304	.250	5
Berroa, G	OAK	R	.278	141	546	87	152	246	22	3	22	88	0	6	1	63	2	98	7	4	12	.451	.351	4
Blowers, M	SEA	R	.257	134	439	59	113	208	24	1	23	96	3	3	0	53	0	128	2	1	18	.474	.335	16
Boggs, W	NY	L	.324	126	460	76	149	194	22	4	5	63	0	7	0	74	5	50	1	1	13	.422	.412	5
Bonilla, B	BAL	S	.333	61	237	47	79	129	12	4	10	46	0	2	1	23	0	31	0	2	11	.544	.392	5
Borders, P	KC	R	.231	52	143	14	33	55	8	1	4	13	0	0	0	7	1	22	0	0	1	.385	.267	0
Bordick, M	OAK	R	.264	126	428	46	113	150	13	0	8	44	7	3	5	35	2	48	11	3	8	.350	.325	10
Brady, D	CHI	S	.190	12	21	4	4	5	1	0	0	3	0	0	0	2	0	4	0	1	1	.238	.261	0
Bragg, D	SEA	L	.234	52	145	20	34	50	5	1	3	12	1	2	4	18	1	37	9	0	2	.345	.331	1
Brito, B	MIN	R	.200	5	5	1	1	4	0	0	1	1	0	0	1	0	0	3	0	0	1	.800	.333	0
Brosius, S	OAK	R	.262	123	389	69	102	176	19	2	17	46	1	4	8	41	0	67	4	2	5	.452	.342	15
Brown, J	BAL	R	.148	18	27	2	4	5	1	0	0	1	3	0	0	7	0	9	1	1	0	.185	.324	0
Buechele, S	TEX	R	.125	9	24	0	3	3	0	0	0	0	0	0	0	4	1	3	0	0	0	.125	.250	0
Buford, D	BAL	R	.063	24	32	6	2	2	0	0	0	2	3	1	0	6	0	7	3	1	0	.063	.205	0
Buhner, J	SEA	R	.262	126	470	86	123	266	23	0	40	121	2	6	1	60	7	120	0	1	15	.566	.343	2
Burnitz, J	CLE	L	.571	9	7	4	4	5	1	0	0	0	0	0	0	0	0	0	0	0	0	.714	.571	0
Caceres, E	KC	S	.239	55	117	13	28	41	6	2	1	17	3	1	1	8	0	15	2	2	3	.350	.291	1
Cameron, M	CHI	R	.184	28	38	4	7	12	2	0	1	2	3	0	0	3	0	15	0	0	0	.316	.244	0
Canseco, J	BOS	R	.306	102	396	64	121	220	25	1	24	81	0	5	7	42	4	93	4	0	9	.556	.378	0
Carter, J	TOR	R	.253	139	558	70	141	239	23	0	25	76	0	5	3	37	5	87	12	1	11	.428	.300	7
Cedeno, D	TOR	S	.236	51	161	18	38	58	6	1	4	14	1	0	2	10	0	35	0	1	3	.360	.289	3
Chamberlain, W	BOS	R	.119	19	42	4	5	9	1	0	1	1	0	0	0	3	0	11	1	0	2	.214	.178	1
Cirillo, J	MIL	R	.277	125	328	57	91	145	19	4	9	39	1	4	4	47	0	42	7	2	8	.442	.371	15
Clark, J	MIN	R	.339	36	109	17	37	60	8	3	3	15	0	1	1	2	0	11	3	0	5	.550	.354	0
Clark, T	DET	S	.238	27	101	10	24	40	5	1	3	11	0	0	0	8	0	30	0	0	2	.396	.294	4
Clark, W	TEX	L	.302	123	454	85	137	218	27	3	16	92	0	11	4	68	6	50	0	1	7	.480	.389	7
Cole, A	MIN	L	.342	28	79	10	27	37	3	2	1	14	2	0	1	8	0	15	1	3	0	.468	.409	3
Coleman, V	KC-SEA	S	.288	115	455	66	131	181	23	6	5	29	5	1	2	37	2	80	42	16	8	.398	.343	4
Cookson, B	KC	R	.143	22	35	2	5	6	1	0	0	5	1	0	0	2	0	7	1	0	0	.171	.189	0
Coomer, R	MIN	R	.257	37	101	15	26	46	3	1	5	19	0	0	1	9	0	11	0	1	9	.455	.324	2
Cora, J	SEA	S	.297	120	427	64	127	159	19	2	3	39	13	4	6	37	0	31	18	7	8	.372	.359	23
Cordova, M	MIN	R	.277	137	512	81	142	249	27	4	24	84	0	5	10	52	1	111	20	7	10	.486	.352	5

BATTER	TEAM	B	AVG	G	AB	R	H	TB	2B	3B	HR	RBI	SH	SF	HP	BB	IBB	SO	SB	CS	GI DP	SLG	OBP	E
Correia, R	CAL	R	.238	14	21	3	5	8	1	1	0	3	1	0	0	0	0	5	0	0	1	.381	.238	5
Cruz, F	OAK	R	.217	8	23	0	5	5	0	0	0	5	2	2	0	3	0	5	1	1	1	.217	.286	1
Curtis, C	DET	R	.268	144	586	96	157	255	29	3	21	67	0	7	7	70	3	93	27	15	12	.435	.349	3
Cuyler, M	DET	S	.205	41	88	15	18	27	1	4	0	5	2	0	0	8	0	16	2	1	0	.307	.271	4
Dalesandro, M	CAL	R	.100	11	10	1	1	2	1	0	0	0	0	0	0	0	0	2	0	0	0	.200	.100	0
Damon, J	KC	L	.282	47	188	32	53	83	11	5	3	23	2	3	1	12	0	22	7	0	2	.441	.324	1
Davis, C	CAL	S	.318	119	424	81	135	218	23	0	20	86	0	9	0	89	12	79	3	3	12	.514	.429	0
Davis, R	NY	R	.276	40	98	14	27	42	5	2	2	12	0	0	1	10	0	26	0	0	0	.429	.349	2
Delgado, C	TOR	L	.165	37	91	7	15	27	3	0	3	11	0	2	0	6	0	26	0	0	1	.297	.212	0
Devarez, C	BAL	R	.000	6	4	0	0	0	0	0	0	0	1	0	0	0	0	0	0	0	0	.000	.000	0
Devereaux, M	CHI	R	.306	92	333	48	102	155	21	1	10	55	0	3	0	25	3	51	6	6	10	.465	.352	3
Diaz, A	SEA	S	.248	103	270	44	67	90	14	0	3	27	5	2	2	13	2	27	18	8	3	.333	.286	2
DiSarcina, G	CAL	R	.307	99	362	61	111	166	28	6	5	41	7	3	2	20	0	25	7	4	10	.459	.344	6
Donnels, C	BOS	L	.253	40	91	13	23	35	2	2	2	11	0	1	0	9	0	18	0	0	1	.385	.317	4
Dunn, S	MIN	L	.000	5	6	0	0	0	0	0	0	0	0	0	0	1	0	3	0	0	0	.000	.143	0
Durham, R	CHI	S	.257	125	471	68	121	181	27	6	7	51	5	4	6	31	2	83	18	5	8	.384	.309	15
Easley, D	CAL	R	.216	114	357	35	77	107	14	2	4	35	6	4	6	32	1	47	5	2	11	.300	.288	10
Edmonds, J	CAL	L	.290	141	558	120	162	299	30	4	33	107	1	5	5	51	4	130	1	4	10	.536	.352	1
Eenhoorn, R	NY	R	.143	5	14	1	2	3	1	0	0	2	0	0	0	1	0	3	0	0	1	.214	.200	1
Elster, K	NY	R	.118	10	17	1	2	3	1	0	0	0	0	0	0	1	0	5	0	0	0	.176	.167	0
Espinoza, A	CLE	R	.252	66	143	15	36	46	4	0	2	17	2	2	1	2	0	16	0	2	3	.322	.264	5
Fabregas, J	CAL	L	.247	73	227	24	56	69	10	0	1	22	3	1	0	17	0	28	0	2	9	.304	.298	6
Fermin, F	SEA	R	.195	73	200	21	39	45	6	0	0	15	8	1	4	6	0	6	2	0	7	.225	.232	6
Fernandez, T	NY	S	.245	108	384	57	94	133	20	2	5	45	3	5	4	42	4	40	6	6	14	.346	.322	10
Fielder, C	DET	R	.243	136	494	70	120	233	18	1	31	82	0	4	5	75	8	116	0	1	17	.472	.346	5
Flaherty, J	DET	R	.243	112	354	39	86	143	22	1	11	40	8	2	3	18	0	47	0	0	8	.404	.284	11
Fletcher, S	DET	R	.231	67	182	19	42	57	10	1	1	17	4	1	3	19	0	27	1	0	2	.313	.312	0
Flora, K	CAL	R	.000	2	1	1	0	0	0	0	0	0	0	0	0	0	0	1	0	0	0	.000	.000	0
Fox, E	TEX	S	.000	10	15	2	0	0	0	0	0	0	1	0	0	3	0	4	0	0	0	.000	.167	0
Frazier, L	TEX	S	.212	49	99	19	21	23	2	0	0	8	3	0	2	7	0	20	9	1	2	.232	.278	2
Frye, J	TEX	R	.278	90	313	38	87	118	15	2	4	29	8	4	5	24	0	45	3	3	7	.377	.335	11
Fryman, T	DET	R	.275	144	567	79	156	232	21	5	15	81	0	7	3	63	4	100	4	2	18	.409	.347	14
Gaetti, G	KC	R	.261	137	514	76	134	266	27	0	35	96	3	6	8	47	6	91	3	3	7	.518	.329	16
Gagne, G	KC	R	.256	120	430	58	110	161	25	4	6	49	7	5	2	38	2	60	3	5	11	.374	.316	18
Gallagher, D	CAL	R	.188	11	16	1	3	4	1	0	0	0	0	0	0	2	0	1	0	0	0	.250	.278	0
Gallego, M	OAK	R	.233	43	120	11	28	28	0	0	0	8	2	0	1	9	0	24	0	1	3	.233	.292	5
Gates, B	OAK	S	.254	136	524	60	133	180	24	4	5	56	4	11	0	46	2	84	3	3	15	.344	.308	12

Giambi, J	OAK	L	.256	54	176	27	45	70	7	0	6	25	1	2	3	28	0	31	2	1	4	.398	.364	4
Gibson, K	DET	L	.260	70	227	37	59	102	12	2	9	35	0	2	3	33	3	61	9	2	6	.449	.358	0
Gil, B	TEX	R	.219	130	415	36	91	144	20	3	9	46	10	2	1	26	0	147	2	4	5	.347	.266	17
Giles, B	CLE	L	.556	6	9	6	5	8	0	0	1	3	0	0	0	0	0	1	0	0	0	.889	.556	0
Gomez, C	DET	R	.223	123	431	49	96	153	20	2	11	50	3	4	3	41	0	96	4	1	13	.355	.292	15
Gomez, L	BAL	R	.236	53	127	16	30	47	5	0	4	12	0	2	2	18	1	23	0	1	0	.370	.336	2
Gonzales, R	CAL	R	.333	30	18	1	6	10	1	0	1	3	0	0	0	0	0	4	0	0	1	.556	.333	0
Gonzalez, A	TOR	R	.243	111	367	51	89	146	19	4	10	42	9	4	1	44	1	114	4	4	7	.398	.322	19
Gonzalez, J	TEX	R	.295	90	352	57	104	209	20	2	27	82	0	5	0	17	3	66	0	0	15	.594	.324	0
Goodwin, C	BAL	L	.263	87	289	40	76	96	11	3	1	24	7	3	2	15	0	53	22	4	5	.332	.301	2
Goodwin, T	KC	L	.288	133	480	72	138	172	16	3	4	28	14	0	5	38	0	72	50	18	7	.358	.346	3
Grebeck, C	CHI	R	.260	53	154	19	40	55	12	0	1	18	4	0	3	21	0	23	0	0	4	.357	.360	7
Green, S	TOR	L	.288	121	379	52	109	193	31	4	15	54	0	3	3	20	3	68	1	2	4	.509	.326	6
Greenwell, M	BOS	L	.297	120	481	67	143	221	25	4	15	76	0	4	2	38	4	35	9	5	18	.459	.349	6
Greer, R	TEX	L	.271	131	417	58	113	177	21	2	13	61	2	3	1	55	1	66	3	1	9	.424	.355	6
Griffey, K	SEA	L	.258	72	260	52	67	125	7	0	17	42	0	2	0	52	6	53	4	2	4	.481	.379	2
Grotewold, J	KC	L	.278	15	36	4	10	14	1	0	1	6	0	0	0	9	0	7	0	0	2	.389	.422	1
Guillen, O	CHI	L	.248	122	415	50	103	132	20	3	1	41	4	1	0	13	1	25	6	7	11	.318	.270	12
Hale, C	MIN	L	.262	69	103	10	27	37	4	0	2	18	0	0	0	11	1	20	0	0	6	.359	.333	0
Hall, J	DET	R	.133	7	15	2	2	2	0	0	0	0	0	0	0	2	0	3	0	0	1	.133	.235	0
Hamelin, B	KC	L	.168	72	208	20	35	65	7	1	7	25	0	1	6	26	1	56	0	1	6	.313	.278	0
Hamilton, D	MIL	L	.271	112	398	54	108	155	20	6	5	44	8	3	3	47	3	35	11	1	9	.389	.350	3
Hammonds, J	BAL	R	.242	57	178	18	43	66	9	1	4	23	1	2	1	9	0	30	4	2	3	.371	.279	1
Hare, S	TEX	L	.250	18	24	2	6	7	1	0	0	2	0	0	0	4	0	6	0	0	1	.292	.357	0
Harper, B	OAK	R	.000	2	7	0	0	0	0	0	0	0	0	0	0	0	0	1	0	0	0	.000	.000	0
Haselman, B	BOS	R	.243	64	152	22	37	60	6	1	5	23	0	3	2	17	0	30	0	2	4	.395	.322	3
Hatcher, B	TEX	R	.083	6	12	2	1	2	1	0	0	0	0	0	0	1	0	1	0	0	0	.167	.154	0
Hatteberg, S	BOS	L	.500	2	2	1	1	1	0	0	0	0	0	0	0	0	0	0	0	0	1	.500	.500	0
Helfand, E	OAK	L	.163	38	86	9	14	18	2	1	0	7	3	0	1	11	0	25	0	0	2	.209	.265	1
Henderson, R	OAK	R	.300	112	407	67	122	182	31	1	9	54	1	3	4	72	2	66	32	10	8	.447	.407	2
Herrera, J	OAK	L	.243	33	70	9	17	22	1	2	0	2	0	1	0	6	0	11	1	3	1	.314	.299	2
Hiatt, P	KC	R	.204	52	113	11	23	41	6	0	4	12	2	0	0	9	0	37	1	0	3	.363	.262	3
Higginson, R	DET	L	.224	131	410	61	92	161	17	5	14	43	2	7	5	62	3	107	6	4	5	.393	.329	4
Hocking, D	MIN	S	.200	9	25	4	5	9	0	2	0	3	1	0	0	2	1	2	1	0	1	.360	.259	1
Hoiles, C	BAL	R	.250	114	352	53	88	162	15	1	19	58	0	3	4	67	3	80	1	0	11	.460	.373	3
Hollins, D	BOS	S	.154	5	13	2	2	2	0	0	0	1	0	0	0	4	0	7	0	0	0	.154	.353	0
Horn, S	TEX	L	.111	11	9	0	1	1	0	0	0	0	0	0	0	1	0	6	0	0	0	.111	.200	0
Hosey, D	BOS	S	.338	24	68	20	23	42	8	1	3	7	1	0	0	8	0	16	6	0	0	.618	.408	0
Howard, D	KC	S	.243	95	255	23	62	83	13	4	0	19	6	1	1	24	1	41	6	1	7	.325	.310	6

BATTER	TEAM	B	AVG	G	AB	R	H	TB	2B	3B	HR	RBI	SH	SF	HP	BB	IBB	SO	SB	CS	GIDP	SLG	OBP	E
Hudler, R	CAL	R	.265	84	223	30	59	93	16	0	6	27	2	1	5	10	1	48	13	0	2	.417	.310	4
Huff, M	TOR	R	.232	61	138	14	32	46	9	1	1	9	5	2	1	22	0	21	1	1	4	.333	.337	2
Hulse, D	MIL	L	.251	119	339	46	85	117	11	6	3	47	2	5	0	18	2	60	15	3	3	.345	.285	3
Huson, J	BAL	L	.248	66	161	24	40	51	4	2	1	19	2	1	1	15	1	20	5	4	4	.317	.315	1
Ingram, R	MIN	R	.125	4	8	0	1	1	0	0	0	1	0	0	0	2	0	1	0	0	1	.125	.300	0
Jaha, J	MIL	R	.313	88	316	59	99	183	20	2	20	65	0	1	4	36	0	66	2	1	8	.579	.389	2
James, C	KC-BOS	R	.268	42	82	8	22	32	4	0	2	8	2	2	1	7	0	14	1	0	2	.390	.326	0
James, D	NY	L	.287	85	209	22	60	74	6	1	2	26	0	2	0	20	2	16	4	1	5	.354	.346	1
Javier, S	OAK	S	.278	130	442	81	123	171	20	2	8	56	5	4	4	49	3	63	36	5	8	.387	.353	0
Jefferson, R	BOS	L	.289	46	121	21	35	58	8	0	5	26	0	2	0	9	1	24	0	0	3	.479	.333	0
Jeter, D	NY	R	.250	15	48	5	12	18	4	1	0	7	0	0	0	3	0	11	0	0	0	.375	.294	2
Johnson, L	CHI	L	.306	142	607	98	186	258	18	12	10	57	2	3	1	32	2	31	40	6	7	.425	.341	3
Jose, F	KC	S	.133	9	30	2	4	5	1	0	0	1	0	0	0	2	0	9	0	0	1	.167	.188	0
Joyner, W	KC	L	.310	131	465	69	144	208	28	0	12	83	5	9	2	69	10	65	3	2	10	.447	.394	3
Karkovice, R	CHI	R	.217	113	323	44	70	125	14	1	13	51	9	6	5	39	0	84	2	3	5	.387	.306	6
Kelly, P	NY	R	.237	89	270	32	64	90	12	1	4	29	10	2	5	23	0	65	8	3	5	.333	.307	7
Kirby, W	CLE	L	.207	101	188	29	39	56	10	2	1	14	1	2	1	13	0	32	10	3	4	.298	.260	1
Knoblauch, C	MIN	R	.333	136	538	107	179	262	34	8	11	63	0	3	10	78	3	95	46	18	15	.487	.424	10
Knorr, R	TOR	R	.212	45	132	18	28	45	8	0	3	16	1	0	0	11	0	28	0	0	5	.341	.273	8
Kreuter, C	SEA	S	.227	26	75	12	17	25	5	0	1	8	1	0	2	5	0	22	0	0	0	.333	.293	4
Kruk, J	CHI	L	.308	45	159	13	49	62	7	0	2	23	0	3	0	26	0	33	0	1	5	.390	.399	1
LaValliere, M	CHI	L	.245	46	98	7	24	33	6	0	1	19	0	2	0	9	0	15	0	0	3	.337	.303	1
Lawton, M	MIN	L	.317	21	60	11	19	28	4	1	1	12	0	0	3	7	0	11	1	1	1	.467	.414	1
Leius, S	MIN	R	.247	117	372	51	92	130	16	5	4	45	0	4	2	49	3	54	2	1	14	.349	.335	14
Levis, J	CLE	L	.333	12	18	1	6	8	2	0	0	3	1	2	0	1	0	0	0	0	1	.444	.333	0
Leyritz, J	NY	R	.269	77	264	37	71	104	12	0	7	37	0	1	8	37	2	73	1	1	4	.394	.374	3
Lind, J	KC-CAL	R	.236	44	140	9	33	38	5	0	0	7	1	0	0	6	0	12	0	1	5	.271	.267	1
Listach, P	MIL	S	.219	101	334	35	73	85	8	2	0	25	7	1	2	25	0	61	13	3	6	.254	.276	6
Lockhart, K	KC	L	.321	94	274	41	88	131	19	3	6	33	1	7	4	14	2	21	8	1	2	.478	.355	8
Lofton, K	CLE	L	.310	118	481	93	149	218	22	13	7	53	4	3	1	40	6	49	54	15	6	.453	.362	8
Loretta, M	MIL	R	.260	19	50	13	13	19	3	0	1	3	1	0	1	4	0	7	1	1	1	.380	.327	1
Lyons, B	CHI	R	.266	27	64	8	17	34	2	0	5	16	1	1	0	4	0	14	0	0	0	.531	.304	2
Maas, K	MIN	L	.193	22	57	5	11	18	4	0	1	5	0	0	0	7	2	11	0	0	4	.316	.281	3
Macfarlane, M	BOS	R	.225	115	364	45	82	147	18	1	15	51	0	4	14	38	0	78	2	1	9	.404	.319	5
Mahay, R	BOS	L	.200	5	20	3	4	9	2	0	1	3	0	0	1	1	0	6	0	0	0	.450	.273	0
Maldonado, C	TOR-TEX	R	.263	74	190	28	50	93	16	0	9	30	0	3	2	32	0	50	1	2	6	.489	.370	1
Manto, J	BAL	R	.256	89	254	31	65	125	9	0	17	38	0	0	2	24	0	69	0	3	6	.492	.325	6

Martin, N	CHI	R	.269	72	160	17	43	64	7	4	2	17	2	3	1	3	0	25	5	0	5	.400	.281	7
Martinez, A	TOR	L	.241	62	191	12	46	64	12	0	2	25	0	1	1	7	0	45	0	0	1	.335	.270	5
Martinez, C	CAL	R	.180	26	61	7	11	15	1	0	1	9	0	0	1	6	2	7	0	0	2	.246	.265	1
Martinez, D	CHI	L	.307	119	303	49	93	132	16	4	5	37	9	4	1	32	2	41	8	2	6	.436	.371	3
Martinez, E	SEA	R	.356	145	511	121	182	321	52	0	29	113	0	4	8	116	19	87	4	3	11	.628	.479	2
Martinez, T	SEA	L	.293	141	519	92	152	286	35	3	31	111	2	6	4	62	15	91	0	0	10	.551	.369	8
Marzano, J	TEX	R	.333	2	6	1	2	2	0	0	0	0	0	0	0	0	0	0	0	0	0	.333	.333	0
Masteller, D	MIN	L	.237	71	198	21	47	68	12	0	3	21	1	1	1	18	0	19	1	2	7	.343	.303	2
Matheny, M	MIL	R	.247	80	166	13	41	52	9	1	0	21	1	0	2	12	0	28	2	1	3	.313	.306	4
Mattingly, D	NY	L	.288	128	458	59	132	189	32	2	7	49	0	8	1	40	7	35	0	2	17	.413	.341	7
May, D	MIL	L	.248	32	113	15	28	36	3	1	1	9	0	0	1	5	0	18	0	1	1	.319	.286	2
Mayne, B	KC	L	.251	110	307	23	77	100	18	1	1	27	11	1	3	25	1	41	0	1	16	.326	.313	3
McCarty, D	MIN	R	.218	25	55	10	12	17	3	1	0	4	0	1	1	4	0	18	0	1	1	.309	.279	1
McGee, W	BOS	S	.285	67	200	32	57	80	11	3	2	15	5	3	0	9	0	41	5	2	5	.400	.311	3
McGinnis, R	KC	R	.000	3	5	1	0	0	0	0	0	0	0	0	0	1	0	1	0	0	0	.000	.167	0
McGwire, M	OAK	R	.274	104	317	75	87	217	13	0	39	90	0	6	11	88	5	77	1	1	9	.685	.441	12
McLemore, M	TEX	S	.261	129	467	73	122	167	20	5	5	41	10	3	3	59	6	71	21	11	10	.358	.346	4
Meares, P	MIN	R	.269	116	390	57	105	168	19	4	12	49	4	5	11	15	0	68	10	4	17	.431	.311	18
Mercedes, H	KC	R	.256	23	43	7	11	13	2	0	0	9	1	2	1	8	0	13	0	0	0	.302	.370	1
Merullo, M	MIN	L	.282	76	195	19	55	74	14	1	1	27	1	3	3	14	0	27	0	1	5	.379	.335	3
Mieske, M	MIL	R	.251	117	267	42	67	118	13	1	12	48	0	5	4	27	0	45	2	4	8	.442	.323	4
Miller, K	KC	R	.333	9	15	2	5	8	0	0	1	3	0	0	0	2	0	4	0	0	1	.533	.412	0
Molitor, P	TOR	R	.270	130	525	63	142	222	31	2	15	60	3	4	5	61	1	57	12	0	10	.423	.350	0
Mota, J	KC	S	.000	2	2	0	0	0	0	0	0	0	0	0	0	0	0	0	0	0	0	.000	.000	0
Mouton, L	CHI	R	.302	58	179	23	54	85	16	0	5	27	0	1	2	19	0	46	1	0	7	.475	.373	1
Munoz, P	MIN	R	.301	104	376	45	113	184	17	0	18	58	0	2	3	19	0	86	0	3	14	.489	.338	5
Murray, E	CLE	S	.323	113	436	68	141	225	21	0	21	82	0	5	0	39	5	65	5	1	12	.516	.375	3
Myers, G	CAL	L	.260	85	273	35	71	114	12	2	9	38	1	2	1	17	3	49	0	1	4	.418	.304	4
Naehring, T	BOS	R	.307	126	433	61	133	194	27	2	10	57	4	2	4	77	5	66	0	2	16	.448	.415	16
Nevin, P	DET	R	.219	29	96	9	21	32	3	1	2	12	0	0	3	11	0	27	0	0	3	.333	.318	2
Newfield, M	SEA	R	.188	24	85	7	16	28	3	0	3	14	0	0	1	3	1	16	0	0	2	.329	.225	0
Newson, W	CHI-SEA	L	.261	84	157	34	41	62	2	2	5	15	0	0	1	39	0	45	2	1	3	.395	.411	2
Nilsson, D	MIL	L	.278	81	263	41	73	123	12	1	12	53	0	5	2	24	4	41	2	0	9	.468	.337	2
Nixon, O	TEX	S	.295	139	589	87	174	199	21	2	0	45	6	3	0	58	1	85	50	21	6	.338	.357	4
Nokes, M	BAL	L	.122	26	49	4	6	13	1	0	2	6	0	1	0	4	0	11	0	0	2	.265	.185	1
Norman, L	KC	R	.225	24	40	6	9	11	0	1	0	4	1	0	0	6	0	6	0	1	0	.275	.326	1
Nunnally, J	KC	L	.244	119	303	51	74	143	15	6	14	42	4	0	2	51	5	86	6	4	4	.472	.357	6
Obando, S	BAL	R	.263	16	38	0	10	11	1	0	0	3	0	1	0	2	0	12	1	0	0	.289	.293	1
O'Leary, T	BOS	L	.308	112	399	60	123	196	31	6	10	49	3	2	1	29	4	64	5	3	8	.491	.355	5

BATTER	TEAM	B	AVG	G	AB	R	H	TB	2B	3B	HR	RBI	SH	SF	HP	BB	IBB	SO	SB	CS	GI DP	SLG	OBP	E
Olerud, J	TOR	L	.291	135	492	72	143	199	32	0	8	54	0	1	4	84	10	54	0	0	17	.404	.398	4
Oliver, J	MIL	R	.273	97	337	43	92	148	20	0	12	51	2	0	3	27	1	66	2	4	11	.439	.332	8
O'Neill, P	NY	L	.300	127	460	82	138	242	30	4	22	96	0	11	1	71	8	76	1	2	25	.526	.387	3
Ortiz, L	TEX	R	.231	41	108	10	25	37	5	2	1	18	0	1	0	6	0	18	0	1	7	.343	.270	8
Owen, S	CAL	S	.229	82	218	17	50	68	9	3	1	28	1	0	0	18	1	22	3	2	7	.312	.288	6
Pagliarulo, M	TEX	L	.232	86	241	27	56	84	16	0	4	27	2	3	1	15	2	49	0	0	10	.349	.277	7
Palmeiro, O	CAL	L	.350	15	20	3	7	7	0	0	0	1	0	0	0	1	0	1	0	0	0	.350	.381	0
Palmeiro, R	BAL	L	.310	143	554	89	172	323	30	2	39	104	0	5	3	62	5	65	3	1	12	.583	.380	4
Palmer, D	TEX	R	.336	36	119	30	40	73	6	0	9	24	0	1	4	21	1	21	1	1	2	.613	.448	5
Paquette, C	OAK	R	.226	105	283	42	64	118	13	1	13	49	3	5	1	12	0	88	5	2	5	.417	.256	8
Parrish, L	TOR	R	.202	70	178	15	36	57	9	0	4	22	6	2	1	15	0	52	0	0	4	.320	.265	0
Pemberton, R	DET	R	.300	12	30	3	9	14	3	1	0	3	0	0	1	1	0	5	0	0	3	.467	.344	0
Pena, T	CLE	R	.262	91	263	25	69	99	15	0	5	28	1	0	1	14	1	44	1	0	9	.376	.302	7
Penn, S	DET	S	.333	3	9	0	3	3	0	0	0	0	0	0	0	1	0	2	0	0	2	.333	.400	3
Perez, E	CAL	R	.169	29	71	9	12	21	4	1	1	7	0	1	2	12	0	9	0	2	3	.296	.302	7
Perez, R	TOR	R	.188	17	48	2	9	14	2	0	1	3	0	0	0	0	0	5	0	0	1	.292	.188	0
Perez, T	TOR	S	.245	41	98	12	24	32	3	1	1	8	0	1	0	7	0	18	0	1	6	.327	.292	5
Perry, H	CLE	R	.315	52	162	23	51	75	13	1	3	23	3	2	4	13	0	28	1	3	5	.463	.376	0
Phillips, T	CAL	S	.261	139	525	119	137	241	21	1	27	61	1	1	3	113	6	135	13	10	5	.459	.394	20
Pichardo, H	KC	R	.000	44	2	0	0	0	0	0	0	0	0	0	0	0	0	0	0	0	0	.000	.000	0
Pirkl, G	SEA	R	.235	10	17	2	4	4	0	0	0	0	0	0	0	1	0	7	0	0	0	.235	.278	0
Polonia, L	NY	L	.261	67	238	37	62	83	9	3	2	15	2	4	0	25	1	29	10	4	3	.349	.326	0
Pozo, A	SEA	R	.000	1	1	0	0	0	0	0	0	0	0	0	0	0	0	0	0	0	0	.000	.000	0
Puckett, K	MIN	R	.314	137	538	83	169	277	39	0	23	99	0	5	3	56	18	89	3	2	15	.515	.379	4
Raabe, B	MIN	R	.214	6	14	4	3	3	0	0	0	1	0	0	0	1	0	0	0	0	0	.214	.267	0
Raines, T	CHI	S	.285	133	502	81	143	212	25	4	12	67	3	3	3	70	3	52	13	2	8	.422	.374	4
Ramirez, M	CLE	R	.308	137	484	85	149	270	26	1	31	107	2	5	5	75	6	112	6	6	13	.558	.402	5
Randa, J	KC	R	.171	34	70	6	12	17	2	0	1	5	0	0	0	6	0	17	0	1	2	.243	.237	3
Reboulet, J	MIN	R	.292	87	216	39	63	86	11	0	4	23	2	0	1	27	0	34	1	2	3	.398	.373	4
Rhodes, K	BOS	L	.080	10	25	2	2	3	1	0	0	1	0	0	0	3	0	4	0	0	1	.120	.179	1
Ripken, C	BAL	R	.262	144	550	71	144	232	33	2	17	88	1	8	2	52	6	59	0	1	15	.422	.324	7
Ripken, B	CLE	R	.412	8	17	4	7	13	0	0	2	3	0	0	0	0	0	3	0	0	0	.765	.412	0
Rivera, R	NY	R	.000	5	1	0	0	0	0	0	0	0	0	0	0	0	0	1	0	0	0	.000	.000	0
Rodriguez, A	SEA	R	.232	48	142	15	33	58	6	2	5	19	1	0	0	6	0	42	4	2	0	.408	.264	8
Rodriguez, C	BOS	S	.333	13	30	5	10	12	2	0	0	5	3	0	1	2	0	2	0	0	0	.400	.394	1
Rodriguez, I	TEX	R	.303	130	492	56	149	221	32	2	12	67	0	5	4	16	2	48	0	2	11	.449	.327	8
Rodriguez, S	BOS-DET	R	.179	18	39	5	7	8	1	0	0	0	1	0	0	6	0	10	2	2	1	.205	.289	2

Rowland, R	BOS	R	.172	14	29	1	5	6	1	0	0	1	0	0	0	0	0	11	0	0	0	.207	.172	1
Sabo, C	CHI	R	.254	20	71	10	18	26	5	0	1	8	2	2	2	3	1	12	2	0	0	.366	.295	1
Salmon, T	CAL	R	.330	143	537	111	177	319	34	3	34	105	0	4	6	91	2	111	5	5	9	.594	.429	4
Samuel, J	DET-KC	R	.263	91	205	31	54	102	10	1	12	39	1	0	2	29	1	49	6	4	3	.498	.360	9
Schofield, D	CAL	R	.250	12	20	1	5	5	0	0	0	2	2	0	0	4	0	2	0	0	1	.250	.375	0
Seitzer, K	MIL	R	.311	132	492	56	153	207	33	3	5	69	5	3	6	64	2	57	2	0	13	.421	.395	10
Shumpert, T	BOS	R	.234	21	47	6	11	14	3	0	0	3	0	0	0	4	0	13	3	1	0	.298	.294	2
Sierra, R	OAK-NY	S	.263	126	479	73	126	215	32	0	19	86	0	8	0	46	4	76	5	4	8	.449	.323	5
Silvestri, D	NY	R	.095	17	21	4	2	5	0	0	1	4	0	1	1	4	0	9	0	0	1	.238	.259	0
Singleton, D	MIL	L	.065	13	31	0	2	2	0	0	0	0	0	0	0	1	0	10	1	0	0	.065	.094	0
Smith, M	BAL	R	.231	37	104	11	24	38	5	0	3	15	2	1	1	12	2	22	3	0	4	.365	.314	0
Snopek, C	CHI	R	.324	22	68	12	22	29	4	0	1	7	0	0	0	9	0	12	1	0	2	.426	.403	2
Snow, J	CAL	S	.289	143	544	80	157	253	22	1	24	102	5	2	3	52	4	91	2	1	16	.465	.353	4
Sojo, L	SEA	R	.289	102	339	50	98	141	18	2	7	39	6	1	1	23	0	19	4	2	9	.416	.335	9
Sorrento, P	CLE	L	.235	104	323	50	76	165	14	0	25	79	0	4	0	51	6	71	1	1	10	.511	.336	7
Sprague, E	TOR	R	.244	144	521	77	127	212	27	2	18	74	1	7	15	58	3	96	0	0	19	.407	.333	17
Stahoviak, S	MIN	L	.266	94	263	28	70	98	19	0	3	23	0	2	1	30	1	61	5	1	3	.373	.341	5
Stairs, M	BOS	L	.261	39	88	8	23	35	7	1	1	17	1	1	1	4	0	14	0	1	4	.398	.298	2
Stanley, M	NY	R	.268	118	399	63	107	192	29	1	18	83	0	9	5	57	1	106	1	1	14	.481	.360	5
Steinbach, T	OAK	R	.278	114	406	43	113	186	26	1	15	65	1	4	3	25	4	74	1	3	15	.458	.322	6
Steverson, T	DET	R	.262	30	42	11	11	17	0	0	2	6	0	2	0	6	0	10	2	0	0	.405	.340	0
Stewart, S	TOR	R	.211	12	38	2	8	8	0	0	0	1	0	0	1	5	0	5	2	0	0	.211	.318	1
Stottlemyre, T	OAK	L	.000	31	1	0	0	0	0	0	0	0	0	0	0	0	0	1	0	0	0	.000	.000	2
Strange, D	SEA	S	.271	74	155	19	42	61	9	2	2	21	1	0	2	10	0	25	0	3	3	.394	.323	5
Strawberry, D	NY	L	.276	32	87	15	24	39	4	1	3	13	0	0	2	10	1	22	0	0	0	.448	.364	2
Stubbs, F	DET	L	.250	62	116	13	29	46	11	0	2	19	0	1	1	19	1	27	0	1	3	.397	.358	5
Stynes, C	KC	R	.171	22	35	7	6	7	1	0	0	2	0	0	0	4	0	3	0	0	3	.200	.256	1
Surhoff, B	MIL	L	.320	117	415	72	133	204	26	3	13	73	2	4	4	37	4	43	7	3	7	.492	.378	5
Sweeney, M	KC	R	.250	4	4	1	1	1	0	0	0	0	0	0	0	0	0	0	0	0	0	.250	.250	1
Tartabull, D	NY-OAK	R	.236	83	280	34	66	106	16	0	8	35	0	4	1	43	1	82	0	2	9	.379	.335	0
Tettleton, M	TEX	S	.238	134	429	76	102	219	19	1	32	78	1	3	7	107	5	110	0	0	8	.510	.396	3
Tewksbury, B	TEX	R	.000	22	1	0	0	0	0	0	0	0	0	0	0	0	0	1	0	0	0	.000	.000	1
Thomas, F	CHI	R	.308	145	493	102	152	299	27	0	40	111	0	12	6	136	29	74	3	2	14	.606	.454	7
Thome, J	CLE	L	.314	137	452	92	142	252	29	3	25	73	0	3	5	97	3	113	4	3	8	.558	.438	16
Thurman, G	SEA	R	.320	13	25	3	8	10	2	0	0	3	0	1	0	1	0	3	5	2	0	.400	.333	0
Tingley, R	DET	R	.226	54	124	14	28	50	8	1	4	18	5	1	0	15	0	38	0	1	1	.403	.307	2
Tinsley, L	BOS	S	.284	100	341	61	97	137	17	1	7	41	9	1	1	39	1	74	18	8	8	.402	.359	5
Tomberlin, A	OAK	L	.212	46	85	15	18	30	0	0	4	10	2	0	0	5	0	22	4	1	2	.353	.256	1
Trammell, A	DET	R	.269	74	223	28	60	78	12	0	2	23	3	2	0	27	4	19	3	1	8	.350	.345	5

BATTER	TEAM	B	AVG	G	AB	R	H	TB	2B	3B	HR	RBI	SH	SF	HP	BB	IBB	SO	SB	CS	GI DP	SLG	OBP	E
Tremie, C	CHI	R	.167	10	24	0	4	4	0	0	0	0	1	0	0	1	0	2	0	0	0	.167	.200	1
Tucker, M	KC	L	.260	62	177	23	46	68	10	0	4	17	2	0	1	18	2	51	2	3	3	.384	.332	1
Tucker, S	CLE	R	.000	17	20	2	0	0	0	0	0	0	1	0	1	5	0	4	0	0	0	.000	.231	1
Turner, C	CAL	R	.100	5	10	0	1	1	0	0	0	1	0	0	0	0	0	3	0	0	0	.100	.100	0
Unroe, T	MIL	R	.250	2	4	0	1	1	0	0	0	0	0	0	0	0	0	0	0	0	0	.250	.250	0
Valentin, J	BOS	R	.298	135	520	108	155	277	37	2	27	102	4	6	10	81	2	67	20	5	7	.533	.399	18
Valentin, J	MIL	S	.219	112	338	62	74	136	23	3	11	49	7	4	0	37	0	83	16	8	0	.402	.293	15
Valle, D	TEX	R	.240	36	75	7	18	21	3	0	0	5	1	0	1	6	0	18	1	0	2	.280	.305	1
Van Slyke, A	BAL	L	.159	17	63	6	10	20	1	0	3	8	0	0	0	5	1	15	0	0	1	.317	.221	1
Vaughn, G	MIL	R	.224	108	392	67	88	160	19	1	17	59	0	4	0	55	3	89	10	4	10	.408	.317	0
Vaughn, M	BOS	L	.300	140	550	98	165	316	28	3	39	126	0	4	14	68	17	150	11	4	17	.575	.388	11
Velarde, R	NY	R	.278	111	367	60	102	144	19	1	7	46	3	3	4	55	0	64	5	1	9	.392	.375	10
Ventura, R	CHI	L	.295	135	492	79	145	245	22	0	26	93	1	8	1	75	11	98	4	3	8	.498	.384	19
Vina, F	MIL	L	.257	113	288	46	74	104	7	7	3	29	4	2	9	22	0	28	6	3	6	.361	.327	8
Vitiello, J	KC	R	.254	53	130	13	33	58	4	0	7	21	0	0	4	8	0	25	0	0	4	.446	.317	1
Vizquel, O	CLE	S	.266	136	542	87	144	190	28	0	6	56	10	10	1	59	0	59	29	11	4	.351	.333	9
Voigt, J	BAL-TEX	R	.175	36	63	9	11	20	3	0	2	8	0	1	0	10	0	14	0	0	2	.317	.284	1
Walbeck, M	MIN	S	.257	115	393	40	101	124	18	1	1	44	1	2	1	25	2	71	3	1	11	.316	.302	6
Ward, T	MIL	S	.264	44	129	19	34	51	3	1	4	16	1	1	1	14	1	21	6	1	2	.395	.338	1
Whitaker, L	DET	L	.293	84	249	36	73	129	14	0	14	44	0	3	2	31	4	41	4	0	6	.518	.372	4
White, D	DET	R	.188	39	48	3	9	11	2	0	0	2	0	0	0	0	0	7	1	0	1	.229	.188	2
White, D	TOR	S	.283	101	427	61	121	184	23	5	10	53	1	3	5	29	1	97	11	2	5	.431	.334	3
Whiten, M	BOS	S	.185	32	108	13	20	26	3	0	1	10	0	1	0	8	0	23	1	0	5	.241	.239	0
Widger, C	SEA	R	.200	23	45	2	9	12	0	0	1	2	0	1	0	3	0	11	0	0	0	.267	.245	0
Williams, B	NY	S	.307	144	563	93	173	274	29	9	18	82	2	3	5	75	1	98	8	6	12	.487	.392	8
Williams, G	OAK	S	.291	29	79	13	23	39	5	1	3	14	0	2	2	11	2	21	0	0	1	.494	.383	3
Williams, G	NY	R	.247	100	182	33	45	85	18	2	6	28	0	3	1	22	1	34	4	2	4	.467	.327	1
Wilson, D	SEA	R	.278	119	399	40	111	166	22	3	9	51	5	1	2	33	1	63	2	1	12	.416	.336	5
Winfield, D	CLE	R	.191	46	115	11	22	33	5	0	2	4	0	0	1	14	2	26	1	0	5	.287	.285	0
Worthington, C	TEX	R	.221	26	68	4	15	25	4	0	2	6	2	0	0	7	0	8	0	0	6	.368	.293	1
Young, E	OAK	R	.200	26	50	9	10	19	3	0	2	5	0	0	0	8	0	12	0	0	1	.380	.310	2
Zaun, G	BAL	S	.260	40	104	18	27	41	5	0	3	14	2	0	0	16	0	14	1	1	2	.394	.358	3

TOP 15 DESIGNATED HITTERS
(Minimum: 100 At-Bats)

BATTER	TEAM	B	AVG	G	AB	R	H	TB	2B	3B	HR	RBI	SH	SF	HP	BB	IBB	SO	SB	CS	GIDP	SLG	OBP
Martinez, E	SEA	R	.360	138	491	115	177	314	50	0	29	110	0	3	8	108	17	84	4	3	11	.640	.480
Murray, E	CLE	S	.344	95	363	61	125	195	19	0	17	75	0	4	0	36	4	50	5	1	10	.537	.400
Puckett, K	MIN	R	.336	28	107	15	36	47	8	0	1	17	0	0	1	11	4	25	1	0	2	.439	.403
James, D	NY	L	.327	27	101	12	33	40	4	0	1	13	0	1	0	5	0	7	3	1	2	.396	.355
Davis, C	CAL	S	.318	119	424	81	135	218	23	0	20	86	0	9	0	89	12	79	3	3	12	.514	.429
Kruk, J	CHI	L	.318	42	154	13	49	62	7	0	2	23	0	3	0	25	0	31	0	1	4	.403	.407
Canseco, J	BOS	R	.306	101	392	62	120	218	24	1	24	81	0	5	7	41	4	91	4	0	9	.556	.378
Munoz, P	MIN	R	.303	77	290	39	88	141	11	0	14	46	0	2	3	15	0	68	0	2	10	.486	.342
Gonzalez, J	TEX	R	.300	83	333	57	100	203	20	1	27	78	0	5	0	17	3	62	0	0	14	.610	.330
Baines, H	BAL	L	.297	122	381	60	113	206	19	1	24	63	0	4	0	69	13	44	0	2	17	.541	.401
Berroa, G	OAK	R	.277	72	289	51	80	129	11	1	12	48	0	4	0	32	2	44	2	3	3	.446	.345
Thomas, F	CHI	R	.271	54	177	27	48	82	7	0	9	35	0	7	2	45	9	27	1	1	7	.463	.411
Molitor, P	TOR	R	.270	129	525	63	142	222	31	2	15	60	3	4	5	60	1	57	12	0	10	.423	.348
Gibson, K	DET	L	.253	63	221	35	56	96	12	2	8	28	0	1	3	33	3	60	8	2	6	.434	.357
Sierra, R	OAK-NY	S	.252	53	206	33	52	89	13	0	8	46	0	4	0	22	3	33	0	0	6	.432	.319

CLUB BATTING

CLUB	AVG	G	AB	R	OR	H	TB	2B	3B	HR	GS	RBI	SH	SF	HP	BB	IBB	SO	SB	CS	GIDP	LOB	SHO	SLG	OBP
CLEVELAND	.291	144	5028	840	607	1461	2407	279	23	207	5	803	31	48	35	542	40	766	132	53	128	1018	3	.479	.361
CHICAGO	.280	145	5060	755	758	1417	2181	252	37	146	6	712	46	56	32	576	54	767	110	39	106	1155	6	.431	.354
BOSTON	.280	144	4997	791	698	1399	2272	286	31	175	7	754	45	49	65	560	38	923	99	44	129	1084	1	.455	.357
MINNESOTA	.279	144	5005	703	889	1398	2096	270	34	120	2	662	18	36	58	471	32	916	105	57	152	1025	6	.419	.346
CALIFORNIA	.277	145	5019	801	697	1390	2250	252	25	186	3	761	33	38	36	564	40	889	58	39	115	1056	7	.448	.352
NEW YORK	.276	145	4947	749	688	1365	2079	280	34	122	4	709	20	68	39	625	36	851	50	30	139	1126	7	.420	.357
SEATTLE	.276	145	4996	796	708	1377	2239	276	20	182	10	767	52	34	39	549	53	871	110	41	109	1033	2	.448	.350
MILWAUKEE	.266	144	5000	740	747	1329	2046	249	42	128	10	700	41	42	46	502	20	800	105	40	105	1012	8	.409	.336
TEXAS	.265	144	4913	691	720	1304	2013	247	24	138	4	651	49	45	33	526	28	877	90	47	112	1031	8	.410	.338
OAKLAND	.264	144	4916	730	761	1296	2067	228	18	169	7	694	32	58	45	565	25	911	112	46	108	1049	8	.420	.341
BALTIMORE	.262	144	4837	704	640	1267	2069	229	27	173	6	668	40	41	39	574	36	803	92	45	119	1022	8	.428	.342
KANSAS CITY	.260	144	4903	629	691	1275	1942	240	35	119	2	578	66	39	43	475	33	849	120	53	105	1018	7	.396	.328
TORONTO	.260	144	5036	642	777	1309	2058	275	27	140	4	613	33	45	44	492	27	906	75	16	119	1079	10	.409	.328
DETROIT	.247	144	4865	654	844	1204	1967	228	29	159	5	619	35	43	41	551	30	987	73	36	121	1017	9	.404	.327
TOTALS	.270	1010	69522	10225	10225	18791	29686	3591	406	2164	75	9691	541	642	595	7572	492	12116	1331	586	1667	14725	90	.427	.344

Pitching

Individual Pitching Leaders

Games Won	19	Mussina	Bal.
Games Lost	15	Bere	Chi.
		Gross	Tex.
		Moore	Det.
Won-Lost Percentage	.900	Johnson	Sea. (18-2)
Earned Run Average	2.48	Johnson	Sea.
Games	65	Orosco	Bal.
Games Started	33	Gubicza	K.C.
Complete Games	8	McDowell	N.Y.
Games Finished	57	Hernandez	Chi.
		Mesa	Cle.
Shutouts	4	Mussina	Bal.
Saves	46	Mesa	Cle.
Innings	229.1	Cone	Tor.-N.Y.
Hits	236	Hentgen	Tor.
Batsmen Faced	954	Cone	Tor.-N.Y.
Runs	129	Hentgen	Tor.
Earned Runs	114	Hentgen	Tor.
Home Runs	32	Radke	Min.
Sacrifice Hits	11	Langston	Cal.
Sacrifice Flies	12	Sparks	Mil.
Hit Batsmen	14	Clemens	Bos.
Bases on Balls	108	Leiter	Tor.
Intentional Bases on Balls	12	Boever	Det.
Strikeouts	294	Johnson	Sea.
Wild Pitches	14	Leiter	Tor.
Balks	3	B. Anderson	Cal.
		Fortugno	Chi.
Games Won, Consecutive	10	Wakefield	Bos. (June 29-Aug. 13)
Games Lost, Consecutive	10	Moore	Det. (June 29-Aug. 31)

During the 1995 season 295 pitchers participated in regular season games.

TOP 15 QUALIFIERS FOR EARNED RUN AVERAGE CHAMPIONSHIP

PITCHER	TEAM	T	W	L	ERA	G	GS	CG	SHO	GF	SV	IP	H	TBF	R	ER	HR	SH	SF	HB	BB	IBB	SO	WP	BK	OPP AVG
Johnson, R	SEA	L	18	2	2.48	30	30	6	3	0	0	214.1	159	866	65	59	12	2	1	6	65	1	294	5	2	.201
Wakefield, T	BOS	R	16	8	2.95	27	27	6	1	0	0	195.1	163	804	76	64	22	3	7	9	68	0	119	11	0	.227
Martinez, D	CLE	R	12	5	3.08	28	28	3	2	0	0	187.0	174	771	71	64	17	4	4	12	46	2	99	3	0	.247
Mussina, M	BAL	R	19	9	3.29	32	32	7	4	0	0	221.2	187	882	86	81	24	2	2	1	50	4	158	2	0	.226
Rogers, K	TEX	L	17	7	3.38	31	31	3	1	0	0	208.0	192	877	87	78	26	3	5	2	76	1	140	8	1	.243
Cone, D	TOR-NY	R	18	8	3.57	30	30	6	2	0	0	229.1	195	954	95	91	24	2	3	6	88	2	191	11	1	.228
Brown, K	BAL	R	10	9	3.60	26	26	3	1	0	0	172.1	155	706	73	69	10	5	2	9	48	1	117	3	0	.241
Leiter, A	TOR	L	11	11	3.64	28	28	2	1	0	0	183.0	162	805	80	74	15	6	4	6	108	1	153	14	0	.238
Abbott, J	CHI-CAL	L	11	8	3.71	30	30	4	1	0	0	196.3	209	842	93	81	14	8	4	2	64	1	86	1	0	.274
Gubicza, M	KC	R	12	14	3.76	33	33	3	2	0	0	213.1	222	898	97	89	21	9	6	6	62	2	81	4	1	.272
Fernandez, A	CHI	R	12	8	3.80	30	30	5	2	0	0	203.2	200	858	98	86	19	4	6	0	65	7	159	3	0	.255
Hershiser, O	CLE	R	16	6	3.87	26	26	1	1	0	0	167.1	151	683	76	72	21	3	4	5	51	1	111	3	0	.244
Appier, K	KC	R	15	10	3.89	31	31	4	1	0	0	201.1	163	832	90	87	14	3	3	8	80	1	185	5	0	.221
McDowell, J	NY	R	15	10	3.93	30	30	8	2	0	0	217.2	211	927	106	95	25	8	6	5	78	1	157	9	1	.254
Pettitte, A	NY	L	12	9	4.17	31	26	3	0	1	0	175.0	183	745	86	81	15	4	5	1	63	3	114	8	1	.272

INDIVIDUAL PITCHING

PITCHER	TEAM	T	W	L	ERA	G	GS	CG	SHO	GF	SV	IP	H	TBF	R	ER	HR	SH	SF	HB	BB	IBB	SO	WP	BK	OPP AVG
Abbott, J	CHI-CAL	L	11	8	3.70	30	30	4	1	0	0	197.0	209	842	93	81	14	8	4	2	64	1	86	1	0	.274
Acre, M	OAK	R	1	2	5.71	43	0	0	0	10	0	52.0	52	236	35	33	7	1	2	2	28	2	47	2	1	.256
Aguilera, R	MIN-BOS	R	3	3	2.60	52	0	0	0	51	32	55.1	46	223	16	16	6	1	4	1	13	1	52	0	0	.225
Ahearne, P	DET	R	0	2	11.70	4	3	0	0	0	0	10.0	20	55	13	13	2	0	0	0	5	1	4	1	0	.400
Alberro, J	TEX	R	0	0	7.40	12	0	0	0	7	0	20.2	26	101	18	17	2	0	1	1	12	1	10	2	0	.299
Alvarez, W	CHI	L	8	11	4.32	29	29	3	0	0	0	175.0	171	769	96	84	21	6	5	2	93	4	118	1	2	.258
Anderson, B	CAL	L	6	8	5.87	18	17	1	0	0	0	99.2	110	433	66	65	24	5	5	3	30	2	45	1	3	.282
Anderson, S	KC	R	1	0	5.33	6	4	0	0	0	0	25.1	29	109	15	15	3	0	0	1	8	0	6	0	0	.290
Andujar, L	CHI	R	2	1	3.26	5	5	0	0	0	0	30.1	26	128	12	11	4	0	0	1	14	2	9	0	0	.230
Appier, K	KC	R	15	10	3.89	31	31	4	1	0	0	201.1	163	832	90	87	14	3	3	8	80	1	185	5	0	.221
Assenmacher, P	CLE	L	6	2	2.82	47	0	0	0	12	0	38.1	32	160	13	12	3	1	2	3	12	3	40	1	0	.225
Ausanio, J	NY	R	2	0	5.73	28	0	0	0	10	1	37.2	42	173	24	24	9	1	2	0	23	0	36	3	0	.286

PITCHER	TEAM	T	W	L	ERA	G	GS	CG	SHO	GF	SV	IP	H	TBF	R	ER	HR	SH	SF	HB	BB	IBB	SO	WP	BK	OPP AVG
Ayala, B	SEA	R	6	5	4.44	63	0	0	0	50	19	71.0	73	320	42	35	9	2	3	6	30	4	77	3	0	.262
Baker, S	OAK	L	0	0	9.82	1	0	0	0	0	0	3.2	5	22	4	4	0	0	1	1	5	0	3	0	0	.333
Baldwin, J	CHI	R	0	1	12.89	6	4	0	0	0	0	14.2	32	81	22	21	6	0	0	0	9	1	10	1	0	.444
Bankhead, S	NY	R	1	1	6.00	20	1	0	0	8	0	39.0	44	175	26	26	9	0	1	0	16	0	20	1	0	.278
Bark, B	BOS	L	0	0	0.00	3	0	0	0	2	0	2.1	2	8	0	0	0	0	0	0	1	0	0	0	0	.286
Belcher, T	SEA	R	10	12	4.52	28	28	1	0	0	0	179.1	188	802	101	90	19	4	5	5	88	5	96	6	0	.269
Belinda, S	BOS	R	8	1	3.10	63	0	0	0	30	10	69.2	51	285	25	24	5	0	4	4	28	3	57	2	0	.205
Benes, A	SEA	R	7	2	5.86	12	12	0	0	0	0	63.0	72	291	42	41	8	1	4	2	33	2	45	2	0	.287
Benitez, A	BAL	R	1	5	5.66	44	0	0	0	18	2	47.2	37	221	33	30	8	2	3	5	37	2	56	3	1	.213
Bennett, E	CAL	R	0	0	0.00	1	0	0	0	1	0	0.1	0	1	0	0	0	0	0	0	0	0	0	0	0	.000
Bere, J	CHI	R	8	15	7.19	27	27	1	0	0	0	137.2	151	668	120	110	21	4	7	6	106	6	110	8	0	.277
Bergman, S	DET	R	7	10	5.12	28	28	1	1	0	0	135.1	169	630	95	77	19	5	3	4	67	8	86	13	0	.307
Bertotti, M	CHI	L	1	1	12.56	4	4	0	0	0	0	14.1	23	80	20	20	6	0	3	3	11	0	15	2	1	.365
Bielecki, M	CAL	R	4	6	5.97	22	11	0	0	2	0	75.1	80	334	56	50	15	2	5	3	31	1	45	3	0	.273
Black, B	CLE	L	4	2	6.85	11	10	0	0	0	0	47.1	63	219	42	36	8	1	3	0	16	2	34	1	1	.317
Blomdahl, B	DET	R	0	0	7.77	14	0	0	0	5	1	24.1	36	115	21	21	5	1	0	0	13	0	15	2	0	.356
Boehringer, B	NY	R	0	3	13.75	7	3	0	0	0	0	17.2	24	99	27	27	5	0	1	1	22	1	10	3	0	.320
Boever, J	DET	R	5	7	6.39	60	0	0	0	27	3	98.2	128	463	74	70	17	7	8	3	44	12	71	1	1	.319
Bohanon, B	DET	L	1	1	5.54	52	10	0	0	7	1	105.2	121	474	68	65	10	0	5	4	41	5	63	3	0	.285
Bolton, R	CHI	R	0	2	8.18	8	3	0	0	2	0	22.0	33	109	23	20	4	0	1	0	14	1	10	1	0	.351
Bones, R	MIL	R	10	12	4.63	32	31	3	0	0	0	200.1	218	877	108	103	26	3	11	4	83	2	77	5	2	.281
Borowski, J	BAL	R	0	0	1.23	6	0	0	0	3	0	7.1	5	30	1	1	0	0	0	0	4	0	3	0	0	.192
Bosio, C	SEA	R	10	8	4.92	31	31	0	0	0	0	170.0	211	766	98	93	18	5	11	5	69	3	85	10	0	.313
Boskie, S	CAL	R	7	7	5.64	20	20	1	0	0	0	111.2	127	494	73	70	16	4	6	7	25	0	51	4	0	.281
Brandenburg, M	TEX	R	0	1	5.93	11	0	0	0	5	0	27.1	36	123	18	18	5	0	1	1	7	1	21	0	1	.316
Brewer, B	KC	L	2	4	5.56	48	0	0	0	13	0	45.1	54	209	28	28	9	1	0	2	20	1	31	5	1	.290
Briscoe, J	OAK	R	0	1	8.35	16	0	0	0	7	0	18.1	25	99	17	17	4	2	2	2	21	1	19	1	0	.347
Bronkey, J	MIL	R	0	0	3.65	8	0	0	0	4	0	12.1	15	56	6	5	0	2	0	0	6	0	5	1	0	.313
Brown, K	BAL	R	10	9	3.60	26	26	3	1	0	0	172.1	155	706	73	69	10	5	2	9	48	1	117	3	0	.241
Browning, T	KC	L	0	2	8.10	2	2	0	0	0	0	10.0	13	49	9	9	2	1	0	0	5	0	3	0	0	.302
Bunch, M	KC	R	1	3	5.63	13	5	0	0	3	0	40.0	42	175	25	25	11	0	0	0	14	1	19	6	0	.261
Burrows, T	TEX	L	2	2	6.45	28	3	0	0	6	1	44.2	60	207	37	32	11	0	0	2	19	0	22	4	0	.323
Butcher, M	CAL	R	6	1	4.73	40	0	0	0	13	0	51.1	49	227	28	27	7	1	3	1	31	2	29	3	0	.257
Campbell, K	MIN	R	0	0	4.66	6	0	0	0	1	0	9.2	8	39	5	5	0	0	0	0	5	0	5	1	0	.235
Carmona, R	SEA	R	2	4	5.66	15	3	0	0	6	1	47.2	55	230	31	30	9	1	5	2	34	1	28	3	1	.293
Carrara, G	TOR	R	2	4	7.21	12	7	1	0	2	0	48.2	64	229	46	39	10	1	2	1	25	1	27	1	0	.322

Castillo, T	TOR	L	1	5	3.22	55	0	0	0	31	13	72.2	64	298	27	26	7	3	5	3	24	1	38	0	0	.243
Charlton, N	SEA	L	2	1	1.51	30	0	0	0	22	14	47.2	23	182	12	8	2	3	1	1	16	0	58	5	1	.143
Christopher, M	DET	R	4	0	3.82	36	0	0	0	11	1	61.1	71	262	28	26	8	1	2	2	14	2	34	5	0	.292
Clark, M	CLE	R	9	7	5.27	22	21	2	0	0	0	124.2	143	552	77	73	13	3	6	4	42	0	68	8	0	.288
Clark, T	BAL	R	2	5	3.46	38	0	0	0	12	1	39.0	40	166	15	15	3	4	1	1	15	5	18	1	0	.276
Clemens, R	BOS	R	10	5	4.18	23	23	0	0	0	0	140.0	141	623	70	65	15	2	3	14	60	0	132	9	0	.259
Cone, D	TOR-NY	R	18	8	3.57	30	30	6	2	0	0	229.1	195	954	95	91	24	2	3	6	88	2	191	11	1	.228
Converse, J	SEA-KC	R	1	3	6.56	15	1	0	0	4	1	23.1	28	109	17	17	2	2	0	0	16	2	14	2	0	.308
Cook, D	CLE-TEX	L	0	2	4.53	46	1	0	0	10	2	57.2	63	255	32	29	9	4	5	2	26	3	53	1	0	.289
Cormier, R	BOS	L	7	5	4.07	48	12	0	0	3	0	115.0	131	488	60	52	12	6	2	3	31	2	69	4	0	.294
Cornett, B	TOR	R	0	0	9.00	5	0	0	0	2	0	5.0	9	25	6	5	1	0	0	1	3	0	4	1	0	.429
Corsi, J	OAK	R	2	4	2.20	38	0	0	0	7	2	45.0	31	187	14	11	2	5	1	2	26	1	26	0	0	.203
Cox, D	TOR	R	1	3	7.40	24	0	0	0	7	0	45.0	57	218	40	37	4	1	3	1	33	4	38	7	0	.317
Crabtree, T	TOR	R	0	2	3.09	31	0	0	0	19	0	32.0	30	141	16	11	1	0	1	2	13	0	21	2	0	.240
Cummings, J	SEA	L	0	0	11.81	4	0	0	0	0	0	5.1	8	30	8	7	0	1	2	0	7	2	4	4	1	.400
Darling, R	OAK	R	4	7	6.23	21	21	1	0	0	0	104.0	124	484	79	72	16	7	8	4	46	2	69	5	0	.296
Darwin, D	TOR-TEX	R	3	10	7.45	20	15	1	0	0	0	99.0	131	448	87	82	25	3	5	4	31	3	58	2	0	.323
Davis, T	SEA	L	2	1	6.38	5	5	0	0	0	0	24.0	30	117	21	17	2	0	1	0	18	2	19	0	0	.306
Davison, S	SEA	R	0	0	6.23	3	0	0	0	3	0	4.1	7	21	3	3	1	0	0	0	1	0	3	0	0	.350
Dedrick, J	BAL	R	0	0	2.35	6	0	0	0	1	0	7.2	8	35	2	2	1	0	2	1	6	0	3	0	0	.308
DeLeon, J	CHI	R	5	3	5.19	38	0	0	0	4	0	67.2	60	293	41	39	10	2	5	6	28	2	53	2	1	.238
DeSilva, J	BAL	R	1	0	7.27	2	2	0	0	0	0	8.2	8	41	7	7	3	1	1	1	7	0	1	0	0	.258
Dettmer, J	TEX	R	0	0	27.00	1	0	0	0	0	0	0.1	2	4	1	1	0	0	1	0	0	0	0	0	0	.667
Dibble, R	CHI-MIL	R	1	2	7.18	31	0	0	0	8	1	26.1	16	143	21	21	2	3	6	3	46	2	26	8	0	.188
Doherty, J	DET	R	5	9	5.10	48	2	0	0	18	6	113.0	130	499	66	64	10	3	2	6	37	10	46	0	0	.288
Eckersley, D	OAK	R	4	6	4.83	52	0	0	0	48	29	50.1	53	212	29	27	5	1	2	1	11	0	40	0	0	.269
Eddy, C	OAK	L	0	0	7.36	6	0	0	0	0	0	3.2	7	22	3	3	0	2	0	2	2	0	2	1	0	.438
Edenfield, K	CAL	R	0	0	4.26	7	0	0	0	3	0	12.2	15	56	7	6	1	0	1	0	5	0	6	3	0	.300
Eiland, D	NY	R	1	1	6.30	4	1	0	0	1	0	10.0	16	51	10	7	1	0	1	1	3	1	6	1	0	.348
Eldred, C	MIL	R	1	1	3.42	4	4	0	0	0	0	23.2	24	104	10	9	4	1	0	1	10	0	18	1	1	.261
Embree, A	CLE	L	3	2	5.11	23	0	0	0	8	1	24.2	23	111	16	14	2	2	2	0	16	0	23	1	0	.253
Erickson, S	MIN-BAL	R	13	10	4.81	32	31	7	2	1	0	196.1	213	836	108	105	18	3	3	5	67	0	106	3	2	.281
Eshelman, V	BOS	L	6	3	4.85	23	14	0	0	4	0	81.2	86	356	47	44	3	0	3	1	36	0	41	4	0	.272
Fajardo, H	TEX	R	0	0	7.80	5	0	0	0	1	0	15.0	19	67	13	13	2	0	0	1	5	0	9	3	0	.311
Farrell, J	CLE	R	0	0	3.86	1	0	0	0	0	0	4.2	7	21	4	2	0	1	1	0	0	0	4	0	0	.368
Fermin, R	OAK	R	0	0	13.50	1	0	0	0	1	0	1.1	4	9	2	2	0	0	0	0	1	0	0	1	0	.500
Fernandez, A	CHI	R	12	8	3.80	30	30	5	2	0	0	203.2	200	858	98	86	19	4	6	0	65	7	159	3	0	.255
Fernandez, S	BAL	L	0	4	7.39	8	7	0	0	1	0	28.0	36	137	26	23	9	1	1	0	17	2	31	0	0	.305

PITCHER	TEAM	T	W	L	ERA	G	GS	CG	SHO	GF	SV	IP	H	TBF	R	ER	HR	SH	SF	HB	BB	IBB	SO	WP	BK	OPP AVG
Fetters, M	MIL	R	0	3	3.38	40	0	0	0	34	22	34.2	40	163	16	13	3	2	1	0	20	4	33	5	0	.286
Finley, C	CAL	L	15	12	4.21	32	32	2	1	0	0	203.0	192	880	106	95	20	4	5	7	93	1	195	13	1	.249
Fleming, D	SEA-KC	L	1	6	5.96	25	12	1	0	3	0	80.0	84	374	61	53	19	3	4	2	53	4	40	5	0	.269
Fortugno, T	CHI	L	1	3	5.59	37	0	0	0	11	0	38.2	30	163	24	24	7	1	2	0	19	2	24	5	3	.213
Frey, S	SEA	L	0	3	4.76	13	0	0	0	3	0	11.1	16	56	7	6	0	3	1	1	6	1	7	0	0	.356
Gardiner, M	DET	R	0	0	14.59	9	0	0	0	1	0	12.1	27	66	20	20	5	3	2	0	2	1	7	1	0	.458
Givens, B	MIL	L	5	7	4.95	19	19	0	0	0	0	107.1	116	481	71	59	11	1	1	3	54	0	73	3	2	.275
Gohr, G	DET	R	1	0	0.87	10	0	0	0	1	0	10.1	9	41	1	1	0	1	0	0	3	0	12	1	0	.243
Gordon, T	KC	R	12	12	4.43	31	31	2	0	0	0	189.0	204	843	110	93	12	7	11	4	89	4	119	9	0	.279
Grimsley, J	CLE	R	0	0	6.09	15	2	0	0	2	1	34.0	37	165	24	23	4	1	2	2	32	1	25	7	0	.289
Groom, B	DET	L	1	3	7.52	23	4	0	0	6	1	40.2	55	203	35	34	6	2	2	2	26	4	23	3	0	.322
Gross, K	TEX	R	9	15	5.54	31	30	4	0	0	0	183.2	200	825	124	113	27	5	7	8	89	8	106	5	0	.279
Guardado, E	MIN	L	4	9	5.12	51	5	0	0	10	2	91.1	99	410	54	52	13	6	5	0	45	2	71	5	1	.280
Gubicza, M	KC	R	12	14	3.75	33	33	3	2	0	0	213.1	222	898	97	89	21	9	6	6	62	2	81	4	1	.272
Guetterman, L	SEA	L	0	0	6.88	23	0	0	0	3	1	17.0	21	85	13	13	1	1	0	3	11	0	11	0	0	.300
Gunderson, E	BOS	L	2	1	5.11	19	0	0	0	1	0	12.1	13	58	7	7	0	2	1	2	9	1	9	0	0	.295
Guthrie, M	MIN	L	5	3	4.46	36	0	0	0	7	0	42.1	47	181	22	21	5	2	0	1	16	3	48	3	1	.290
Guzman, J	TOR	R	4	14	6.32	24	24	3	0	0	0	135.1	151	619	101	95	13	3	2	3	73	6	94	8	0	.281
Habyan, J	CAL	R	1	2	4.13	28	0	0	0	7	0	32.2	36	146	16	15	2	2	2	1	12	0	25	2	0	.279
Hall, D	TOR	R	0	2	4.41	17	0	0	0	11	3	16.1	21	77	9	8	2	0	0	0	9	0	11	0	0	.309
Hammaker, A	CHI	L	0	0	12.79	13	0	0	0	2	0	6.1	11	38	9	9	2	1	0	1	8	1	3	0	0	.393
Haney, C	KC	L	3	4	3.65	16	13	1	0	0	0	81.1	78	338	35	33	7	1	4	2	33	0	31	2	0	.262
Hanson, E	BOS	R	15	5	4.24	29	29	1	1	0	0	186.2	187	800	94	88	17	6	8	1	59	0	139	5	0	.258
Harikkala, T	SEA	R	0	0	16.20	1	0	0	0	1	0	3.1	7	18	6	6	1	0	0	0	1	0	1	0	0	.412
Harkey, M	OAK-CAL	R	8	9	5.44	26	20	1	0	1	0	127.1	155	573	78	77	24	4	4	4	47	2	56	2	0	.302
Harris, G	BAL	R	0	0	4.50	3	0	0	0	0	0	4.0	4	17	2	2	0	1	0	0	1	0	4	2	0	.267
Harris, G	MIN	R	0	5	8.82	7	6	0	0	0	0	32.2	50	160	35	32	5	1	2	0	16	0	21	3	0	.355
Hartley, M	BOS-BAL	R	1	0	5.14	8	0	0	0	2	0	14.0	13	58	8	8	1	2	2	2	3	0	6	0	0	.265
Hawkins, L	MIN	R	2	3	8.67	6	6	1	0	0	0	27.0	39	131	29	26	3	0	3	1	12	0	9	1	1	.339
Haynes, J	BAL	R	2	1	2.25	4	3	0	0	0	0	24.0	11	94	6	6	2	1	0	0	12	1	22	0	0	.136
Helling, R	TEX	R	0	2	6.57	3	3	0	0	0	0	12.1	17	62	11	9	2	0	2	2	8	0	5	0	0	.340
Henneman, M	DET	R	0	1	1.53	29	0	0	0	26	18	29.1	24	118	5	5	0	1	0	0	9	1	24	2	0	.222
Henry, D	DET	R	1	0	6.23	10	0	0	0	6	5	8.2	11	47	6	6	0	1	0	0	10	2	9	1	0	.306
Hentgen, P	TOR	R	10	14	5.11	30	30	2	0	0	0	200.2	236	913	129	114	24	2	1	5	90	6	135	7	2	.290
Heredia, W	TEX	R	0	1	3.75	6	0	0	0	0	0	12.0	9	58	5	5	2	2	1	0	15	2	6	0	0	.225
Hernandez, R	CHI	R	3	7	3.92	60	0	0	0	57	32	59.2	63	272	30	26	9	4	0	3	28	4	84	1	0	.266

Hershiser, O	CLE	R	16	6	3.87	26	26	1	1	0	0	167.1	151	683	76	72	21	3	4	5	51	1	111	3	0	.244
Hill, K	CLE	R	4	1	3.98	12	11	1	0	0	0	74.2	77	324	36	33	5	3	1	1	32	0	48	3	0	.268
Hitchcock, S	NY	L	11	10	4.70	27	27	4	1	0	0	168.1	155	719	91	88	22	5	9	5	68	1	121	5	2	.245
Holzemer, M	CAL	L	0	1	5.40	12	0	0	0	5	0	8.1	11	45	6	5	1	1	0	1	7	1	5	0	0	.306
Honeycutt, R	OAK-NY	L	5	1	2.96	52	0	0	0	6	2	45.2	39	180	16	15	6	3	1	1	10	0	21	0	0	.236
Horsman, V	MIN	L	0	0	7.00	6	0	0	0	3	0	9.0	12	43	8	7	2	2	1	0	4	1	4	0	0	.333
Howard, C	TEX	L	0	0	0.00	4	0	0	0	1	0	4.0	3	15	0	0	0	0	1	0	1	0	2	1	0	.231
Howe, S	NY	L	6	3	4.96	56	0	0	0	20	2	49.0	66	230	29	27	7	3	2	4	17	3	28	1	0	.324
Hudson, J	BOS	R	0	1	4.11	39	0	0	0	11	1	46.0	53	205	21	21	2	3	1	2	23	1	29	6	0	.301
Huisman, R	KC	R	0	0	7.45	7	0	0	0	2	0	9.2	14	44	8	8	2	1	0	0	1	0	12	0	0	.333
Hurtado, E	TOR	R	5	2	5.45	14	10	1	0	0	0	77.2	81	345	50	47	11	2	3	5	40	3	33	11	0	.275
Ignasiak, M	MIL	R	4	1	5.90	25	0	0	0	2	0	39.2	51	186	27	26	5	1	3	2	23	3	26	1	0	.325
Jacome, J	KC	L	4	6	5.36	15	14	1	0	0	0	84.0	101	364	52	50	15	2	3	1	21	2	39	0	1	.300
James, M	CAL	R	3	0	3.88	46	0	0	0	11	1	55.2	49	237	27	24	6	2	0	3	26	2	36	1	0	.238
Johns, D	OAK	L	5	3	4.61	11	9	1	1	1	0	54.2	44	229	32	28	5	2	1	5	26	1	25	5	1	.226
Johnson, R	SEA	L	18	2	2.48	30	30	6	3	0	0	214.1	159	866	65	59	12	2	1	6	65	1	294	5	2	.201
Johnston, J	BOS	R	0	1	11.25	4	0	0	0	0	0	4.0	2	18	5	5	1	0	0	1	3	0	4	0	0	.143
Jones, D	BAL	R	0	4	5.01	52	0	0	0	47	22	46.2	55	211	30	26	6	1	0	2	16	2	42	0	0	.286
Jordan, R	TOR	L	1	0	6.60	15	0	0	0	3	1	15.0	18	76	11	11	3	0	2	2	13	1	10	1	0	.305
Kamieniecki, S	NY	R	7	6	4.01	17	16	1	0	1	0	89.2	83	391	43	40	8	1	0	3	49	1	43	4	0	.246
Karchner, M	CHI	R	4	2	1.69	31	0	0	0	10	0	32.0	33	137	8	6	2	0	4	1	12	2	24	1	0	.275
Karl, S	MIL	L	6	7	4.14	25	18	1	0	3	0	124.0	141	548	65	57	10	3	3	3	50	6	59	0	0	.288
Key, J	NY	L	1	2	5.64	5	5	0	0	0	0	30.1	40	134	20	19	3	3	1	0	6	1	14	1	0	.323
Keyser, B	CHI	R	5	6	4.97	23	10	0	0	0	0	92.1	114	404	53	51	10	0	2	2	27	1	48	1	1	.306
Kiefer, M	MIL	R	4	1	3.44	24	0	0	0	7	0	49.2	37	209	20	19	6	0	0	0	27	2	41	4	0	.203
King, K	SEA	L	0	0	12.27	2	0	0	0	0	0	3.2	7	20	5	5	0	0	1	1	1	0	3	1	0	.412
Klingenbeck, S	BAL-MIN	R	2	4	7.12	24	9	0	0	4	0	79.2	101	373	65	63	22	3	1	4	42	0	42	7	0	.314
Krivda, R	BAL	L	2	7	4.54	13	13	1	0	0	0	75.1	76	319	40	38	9	0	4	4	25	1	53	2	2	.266
Krueger, B	SEA	L	2	1	5.85	6	5	0	0	1	0	20.0	37	96	17	13	4	1	0	0	4	1	10	1	0	.407
Langston, M	CAL	L	15	7	4.63	31	31	2	1	0	0	200.1	212	859	109	103	21	11	3	3	64	1	142	5	1	.272
Lee, M	BAL	L	2	0	4.86	39	0	0	0	7	1	33.1	31	148	18	18	5	1	2	1	18	3	27	0	0	.246
Leiper, D	OAK	L	1	1	3.57	24	0	0	0	3	0	22.2	23	103	10	9	3	0	0	1	13	1	10	0	0	.258
Leiter, A	TOR	L	11	11	3.64	28	28	2	1	0	0	183.0	162	805	80	74	15	6	4	6	108	1	153	14	0	.238
Lilliquist, D	BOS	L	2	1	6.26	28	0	0	0	6	0	23.0	27	103	17	16	7	2	3	0	9	2	9	1	0	.303
Lima, J	DET	R	3	9	6.11	15	15	0	0	0	0	73.2	85	320	52	50	10	2	1	4	18	4	37	5	0	.288
Linton, D	KC	R	0	1	7.25	7	2	0	0	0	0	22.1	22	98	21	18	4	0	0	2	10	1	13	0	0	.256
Lira, F	DET	R	9	13	4.31	37	22	0	0	7	1	146.1	151	635	74	70	17	4	9	8	56	7	89	5	1	.271
Lloyd, G	MIL	L	0	5	4.50	33	0	0	0	14	4	32.0	28	127	16	16	4	1	4	0	8	2	13	3	0	.246

PITCHER	TEAM	T	W	L	ERA	G	GS	CG	SHO	GF	SV	IP	H	TBF	R	ER	HR	SH	SF	HB	BB	IBB	SO	WP	BK	OPP AVG
Looney, B	BOS	L	0	1	17.36	3	1	0	0	0	0	4.2	12	29	9	9	1	1	2	0	4	1	2	0	0	.545
Lopez, A	CLE	R	0	0	3.13	6	2	0	0	0	0	23.0	17	92	8	8	4	0	1	1	7	1	22	2	0	.205
Lorraine, A	CHI	L	0	0	3.38	5	0	0	0	2	0	8.0	3	30	3	3	0	0	0	1	2	0	5	0	0	.111
MacDonald, B	NY	L	1	1	4.86	33	0	0	0	5	0	46.1	50	202	25	25	7	2	0	1	22	0	41	1	0	.282
Maddux, M	BOS	R	4	1	3.61	36	4	0	0	6	1	89.2	86	367	40	36	5	1	1	2	15	3	65	5	0	.247
Magnante, M	KC	L	1	1	4.23	28	0	0	0	7	0	44.2	45	190	23	21	6	2	2	2	16	1	28	2	0	.268
Mahomes, P	MIN	R	4	10	6.37	47	7	0	0	16	3	94.2	100	423	74	67	22	3	2	2	47	1	67	6	0	.271
Manzanillo, J	NY	R	0	0	2.08	11	0	0	0	4	0	17.1	19	81	4	4	1	2	0	2	9	2	11	1	0	.279
Marquez, I	CHI	R	0	1	6.75	7	0	0	0	2	0	6.2	9	31	5	5	3	1	0	0	2	0	8	0	0	.321
Martinez, D	CHI	L	0	0	0.00	1	0	0	0	1	0	1.0	0	5	0	0	0	0	0	0	2	0	0	0	0	.000
Martinez, D	CLE	R	12	5	3.08	28	28	3	2	0	0	187.0	174	771	71	64	17	4	4	12	46	2	99	3	0	.247
Maxcy, D	DET	R	4	5	6.88	41	0	0	0	14	0	52.1	61	247	48	40	6	3	3	2	31	7	20	6	2	.293
McAndrew, J	MIL	R	2	3	4.71	10	4	0	0	2	0	36.1	37	153	21	19	2	1	0	1	12	2	19	0	0	.266
McCaskill, K	CHI	R	6	4	4.89	55	1	0	0	17	2	81.0	97	365	50	44	10	3	3	5	33	4	50	10	0	.302
McDonald, B	BAL	R	3	6	4.16	14	13	1	0	1	0	80.0	67	342	40	37	10	0	2	3	38	3	62	4	2	.224
McDowell, J	NY	R	15	10	3.93	30	30	8	2	0	0	217.2	211	927	106	95	25	8	6	5	78	1	157	9	1	.254
McDowell, R	TEX	R	7	4	4.02	64	0	0	0	26	4	85.0	86	362	39	38	5	6	5	6	34	7	49	1	1	.277
Meacham, R	KC	R	4	3	4.98	49	0	0	0	26	2	59.2	72	262	36	33	6	1	4	1	19	5	30	0	0	.304
Mecir, J	SEA	R	0	0	0.00	2	0	0	0	1	0	4.2	5	21	1	0	0	0	0	0	2	0	3	0	0	.263
Menhart, P	TOR	R	1	4	4.92	21	9	1	0	6	0	78.2	72	350	49	43	9	3	4	6	47	4	50	6	0	.248
Mercedes, J	MIL	R	0	1	9.82	5	0	0	0	0	0	7.1	12	42	9	8	1	0	2	0	8	0	6	1	0	.375
Mesa, J	CLE	R	3	0	1.13	62	0	0	0	57	46	64.0	49	250	9	8	3	4	2	0	17	2	58	5	0	.216
Mills, A	BAL	R	3	0	7.43	21	0	0	0	1	0	23.0	30	118	20	19	4	0	1	2	18	4	16	1	0	.309
Miranda, A	MIL	L	4	5	5.23	30	10	0	0	5	1	74.0	83	339	47	43	8	1	4	0	49	2	45	5	1	.291
Mohler, M	OAK	L	1	1	3.04	28	0	0	0	6	1	23.2	16	100	8	8	0	1	0	0	18	1	15	1	0	.198
Monteleone, R	CAL	R	1	0	2.00	9	0	0	0	2	0	9.0	8	36	2	2	1	1	2	0	3	0	5	0	0	.267
Montgomery, J	KC	R	2	3	3.43	54	0	0	0	46	31	65.2	60	275	27	25	7	5	5	2	25	4	49	1	1	.252
Moore, M	DET	R	5	15	7.53	25	25	1	0	0	0	132.2	179	632	118	111	24	4	4	2	68	3	64	8	0	.323
Moyer, J	BAL	L	8	6	5.21	27	18	0	0	3	0	115.2	117	483	70	67	18	5	3	3	30	0	65	0	0	.265
Munoz, O	MIN	R	2	1	5.60	10	3	0	0	4	0	35.1	40	164	28	22	6	0	1	1	17	0	25	0	0	.276
Murray, M	BOS	R	0	1	18.90	2	1	0	0	0	0	3.1	11	24	10	7	1	0	0	0	3	0	1	0	0	.524
Mussina, M	BAL	R	19	9	3.29	32	32	7	4	0	0	221.2	187	882	86	81	24	2	2	1	50	4	158	2	0	.226
Myers, M	DET	L	1	0	9.95	11	0	0	0	3	0	6.1	10	33	7	7	1	0	1	2	4	0	4	0	0	.385
Nagy, C	CLE	R	16	6	4.55	29	29	2	1	0	0	178.0	194	771	95	90	20	2	5	6	61	0	139	2	0	.278
Nelson, J	SEA	R	7	3	2.17	62	0	0	0	24	2	78.2	58	318	21	19	4	5	3	6	27	5	96	1	0	.209
Nichting, C	TEX	R	0	0	7.03	13	0	0	0	3	0	24.1	36	122	19	19	1	1	2	1	13	1	6	3	0	.343

Nitkowski, C	DET	L	1	4	7.09	11	11	0	0	0	0	39.1	53	184	32	31	7	0	3	3	20	2	13	1	0 .335
Ogea, C	CLE	R	8	3	3.05	20	14	1	0	3	0	106.1	95	442	38	36	11	0	5	1	29	0	57	3	1 .234
Oliver, D	TEX	L	4	2	4.22	17	7	0	0	2	0	49.0	47	222	25	23	3	5	1	1	32	1	39	4	0 .257
Olson, G	CLE-KC	R	3	3	4.09	23	0	0	0	12	3	33.0	28	141	15	15	4	1	2	0	19	2	21	1	0 .235
Ontiveros, S	OAK	R	9	6	4.37	22	22	2	1	0	0	129.2	144	558	75	63	12	2	6	4	38	0	77	5	0 .283
Oquist, M	BAL	R	2	1	4.17	27	0	0	0	2	0	54.0	51	255	27	25	6	1	4	2	41	3	27	2	0 .246
Orosco, J	BAL	L	2	4	3.26	65	0	0	0	23	3	49.2	28	200	19	18	4	2	4	1	27	7	58	2	1 .169
Parra, J	MIN	R	1	5	7.59	12	12	0	0	0	0	61.2	83	292	59	52	11	0	3	2	22	0	29	3	0 .313
Patterson, B	CAL	L	5	2	3.04	62	0	0	0	20	0	53.1	48	212	18	18	6	2	1	1	13	3	41	0	1 .246
Patterson, J	NY	R	0	0	2.70	3	0	0	0	3	0	3.1	3	16	1	1	1	0	0	0	3	0	3	0	0 .231
Pavlas, D	NY	R	0	0	3.18	4	0	0	0	1	0	5.2	8	24	2	2	0	0	0	0	0	0	3	0	0 .333
Pavlik, R	TEX	R	10	10	4.37	31	31	2	1	0	0	191.2	174	819	96	93	19	4	5	4	90	5	149	10	1 .243
Pena, A	BOS	R	1	1	7.40	17	0	0	0	5	0	24.1	33	117	23	20	5	0	0	0	12	2	25	0	0 .314
Pennington, B	BAL	L	0	1	8.10	8	0	0	0	2	0	6.2	3	33	7	6	1	0	0	0	11	1	10	1	0 .136
Percival, T	CAL	R	3	2	1.95	62	0	0	0	16	3	74.0	37	284	19	16	6	4	1	1	26	2	94	2	2 .147
Perez, M	NY	R	5	5	5.58	13	12	1	0	1	0	69.1	70	304	46	43	10	1	3	1	31	2	44	4	0 .261
Pettitte, A	NY	L	12	9	4.17	31	26	3	0	1	0	175.0	183	745	86	81	15	4	5	1	63	3	114	8	1 .272
Phoenix, S	OAK	R	0	0	32.40	1	0	0	0	0	0	1.2	3	11	6	6	1	1	0	0	3	0	3	0	0 .429
Pichardo, H	KC	R	8	4	4.36	44	0	0	0	16	1	64.0	66	287	34	31	4	3	1	4	30	7	43	4	1 .265
Pierce, J	BOS	R	0	3	6.60	12	0	0	0	2	0	15.0	16	72	12	11	0	1	1	0	14	4	12	0	0 .286
Pittsley, J	KC	R	0	0	13.50	1	1	0	0	0	0	3.1	7	17	5	5	3	0	0	0	1	0	0	0	0 .438
Plunk, E	CLE	R	6	2	2.67	56	0	0	0	22	2	64.0	48	263	19	19	5	2	2	4	27	2	71	3	0 .211
Poole, J	CLE	L	3	3	3.75	42	0	0	0	9	0	50.1	40	206	22	21	7	1	2	2	17	0	41	2	1 .217
Prieto, A	OAK	R	2	6	4.97	14	9	1	0	1	0	58.0	57	258	35	32	4	3	2	5	32	1	37	4	1 .264
Radinsky, S	CHI	L	2	1	5.45	46	0	0	0	10	1	38.0	46	171	23	23	7	1	4	0	17	4	14	0	0 .309
Radke, B	MIN	R	11	14	5.32	29	28	2	1	0	0	181.0	195	772	112	107	32	2	9	4	47	0	75	4	0 .275
Rasmussen, D	KC	L	0	1	9.00	5	1	0	0	1	0	10.0	13	51	10	10	3	0	0	0	8	2	6	2	0 .302
Reyes, A	MIL	R	1	1	2.43	27	0	0	0	13	1	33.1	19	138	9	9	3	1	2	3	18	2	29	0	0 .167
Reyes, C	OAK	R	4	6	5.09	40	1	0	0	19	0	69.0	71	306	43	39	10	4	0	5	28	4	48	5	0 .264
Rhodes, A	BAL	L	2	5	6.21	19	9	0	0	3	0	75.1	68	336	53	52	13	4	0	0	48	1	77	3	1 .239
Righetti, D	CHI	L	3	2	4.20	10	9	0	0	1	0	49.1	65	221	24	23	6	1	2	0	18	0	29	0	0 .325
Rightnowar, R	MIL	R	2	1	5.40	34	0	0	0	13	1	36.2	35	160	23	22	3	5	3	5	18	3	22	1	0 .271
Risley, B	SEA	R	2	1	3.13	45	0	0	0	5	1	60.1	55	249	21	21	7	2	3	1	18	1	65	2	0 .244
Rivera, M	NY	R	5	3	5.51	19	10	0	0	2	0	67.0	71	301	43	41	11	0	2	2	30	0	51	0	1 .266
Roa, J	CLE	R	0	1	6.00	1	1	0	0	0	0	6.0	9	28	4	4	1	1	0	0	2	0	0	0	0 .360
Roberson, S	MIL	L	6	4	5.76	26	13	0	0	8	0	84.1	102	379	55	54	16	0	2	8	37	3	40	3	0 .307
Robertson, R	MIN	L	2	0	3.83	25	4	1	0	8	0	51.2	48	228	28	22	4	5	2	0	31	4	38	0	1 .253
Robinson, K	TOR	R	1	2	3.69	21	0	0	0	9	0	39.0	25	167	21	16	7	1	2	2	22	1	31	1	0 .179

PITCHER	TEAM	T	W	L	ERA	G	GS	CG	SHO	GF	SV	IP	H	TBF	R	ER	HR	SH	SF	HB	BB	IBB	SO	WP	BK	OPP AVG
Rodriguez, F	BOS-MIN	R	5	8	6.13	25	18	0	0	1	0	105.2	114	478	83	72	11	1	4	5	57	1	59	9	0	.277
Rogers, J	TOR	R	2	4	5.70	19	0	0	0	9	0	23.2	21	110	15	15	4	3	1	0	18	4	13	0	0	.239
Rogers, K	TEX	L	17	7	3.38	31	31	3	1	0	0	208.0	192	877	87	78	26	3	5	2	76	1	140	8	1	.243
Ruffcorn, S	CHI	R	0	0	7.88	4	0	0	0	0	0	8.0	10	46	7	7	0	1	0	2	13	0	5	0	0	.333
Russell, J	TEX	R	1	0	3.03	37	0	0	0	32	20	32.2	36	139	12	11	3	0	0	0	9	1	21	1	0	.277
Ryan, K	BOS	R	0	4	4.96	28	0	0	0	20	7	32.2	34	153	20	18	4	1	0	1	24	6	34	1	0	.268
Sanderson, S	CAL	R	1	3	4.12	7	7	0	0	0	0	39.1	48	170	23	18	6	1	2	2	4	1	23	0	1	.298
Sanford, M	MIN	R	0	0	5.30	11	0	0	0	6	0	18.2	16	89	11	11	7	0	0	2	16	0	17	1	0	.225
Scanlan, B	MIL	R	4	7	6.59	17	14	0	0	1	0	83.1	101	389	66	61	9	0	6	7	44	3	29	3	0	.304
Schullstrom, E	MIN	R	0	0	6.89	37	0	0	0	16	0	47.0	66	225	36	36	8	2	1	1	22	1	21	5	0	.332
Sele, A	BOS	R	3	1	3.06	6	6	0	0	0	0	32.1	32	146	14	11	3	1	1	3	14	0	21	3	0	.252
Shaw, J	CHI	R	0	0	6.52	9	0	0	0	1	0	9.2	12	41	7	7	2	1	0	1	1	0	6	0	0	.316
Shepherd, K	BOS	R	0	0	36.00	2	0	0	0	0	0	1.0	4	9	4	4	0	0	0	0	2	0	0	0	0	.571
Shuey, P	CLE	R	0	2	4.26	7	0	0	0	3	0	6.1	5	28	4	3	0	2	0	0	5	0	5	1	0	.238
Simas, W	CHI	R	1	1	2.57	14	0	0	0	4	0	14.0	15	66	5	4	1	0	0	1	10	2	16	1	0	.273
Sirotka, M	CHI	L	1	2	4.19	6	6	0	0	0	0	34.1	39	152	16	16	2	1	3	0	17	0	19	2	0	.298
Slusarski, J	MIL	R	1	1	5.40	12	0	0	0	6	0	15.0	21	73	11	9	3	1	1	2	6	1	6	0	0	.333
Smith, L	CAL	R	0	5	3.47	52	0	0	0	51	37	49.1	42	209	19	19	3	3	3	1	25	4	43	1	0	.237
Smith, Z	BOS	L	8	8	5.61	24	21	0	0	0	0	110.2	144	484	78	69	7	0	5	1	23	1	47	0	1	.316
Sodowsky, C	DET	R	2	2	5.01	6	6	0	0	0	0	23.1	24	112	15	13	4	1	0	0	18	0	14	1	1	.258
Sparks, S	MIL	R	9	11	4.63	33	27	3	0	2	0	202.0	210	875	111	104	17	5	12	5	86	1	96	5	1	.274
Springer, R	CAL	R	1	2	6.10	19	6	0	0	3	1	51.2	60	238	37	35	11	1	0	5	25	1	38	1	0	.290
Stanton, M	BOS	L	1	0	3.00	22	0	0	0	12	0	21.0	17	84	9	7	3	0	0	0	8	0	10	1	0	.224
Stevens, D	MIN	R	5	4	5.07	56	0	0	0	34	10	65.2	74	302	40	37	14	4	5	1	32	1	47	2	0	.285
Stewart, D	OAK	R	3	7	6.89	16	16	0	0	0	0	81.0	101	381	65	62	11	6	3	2	39	1	58	8	1	.305
Stottlemyre, T	OAK	R	14	7	4.55	31	31	2	0	0	0	209.2	228	920	117	106	26	4	4	6	80	7	205	11	0	.276
Suppan, J	BOS	R	1	2	5.96	8	3	0	0	1	0	22.2	29	100	15	15	4	1	1	0	5	1	19	0	0	.312
Tapani, K	MIN	R	6	11	4.92	20	20	3	1	0	0	133.2	155	579	79	73	21	3	3	4	34	2	88	3	0	.290
Tavarez, J	CLE	R	10	2	2.44	57	0	0	0	15	0	85.0	76	350	36	23	7	0	2	3	21	0	68	3	2	.235
Taylor, S	TEX	R	1	2	9.39	3	3	0	0	0	0	15.1	25	71	16	16	6	0	0	0	5	0	10	0	0	.379
Tewksbury, B	TEX	R	8	7	4.58	21	21	4	1	0	0	129.2	169	561	75	66	8	6	3	3	20	4	53	4	0	.319
Thomas, L	CHI	L	0	0	1.32	17	0	0	0	5	0	13.2	8	54	2	2	1	0	0	0	6	1	12	1	0	.167
Thomas, M	MIL	L	0	0	0.00	1	0	0	0	0	0	1.1	2	7	0	0	0	0	0	0	1	0	0	0	0	.333
Timlin, M	TOR	R	4	3	2.14	31	0	0	0	19	5	42.0	38	179	13	10	1	3	0	2	17	5	36	3	1	.242
Torres, D	KC	R	1	2	6.09	24	2	0	0	7	0	44.1	56	198	30	30	6	0	0	1	17	2	28	1	0	.311
Torres, S	SEA	R	3	8	6.00	16	13	1	0	2	0	72.0	87	344	53	48	12	1	0	2	42	3	45	1	2	.291

Trombley, M	MIN	R	4	8	5.62	20	18	0	0	0	0	97.2	107	442	68	61	18	3	2	3	42	1	68	4	0	.273
Vanegmond, T.....	BOS	R	0	1	9.45	4	1	0	0	1	0	6.2	9	35	7	7	2	0	0	0	6	0	5	1	0	.310
Van Poppel, T......	OAK	R	4	8	4.88	36	14	1	0	10	0	138.1	125	582	77	75	16	3	6	4	56	1	122	4	0	.244
Villone, R	SEA	L	0	2	7.91	19	0	0	0	7	0	19.1	20	101	19	17	6	3	0	1	23	0	26	1	0	.270
Vosberg, E	TEX	L	5	5	3.00	44	0	0	0	20	4	36.0	32	154	15	12	3	2	3	0	16	1	36	3	2	.241
Wakefield, T........	BOS	R	16	8	2.95	27	27	6	1	0	0	195.1	163	804	76	64	22	3	7	9	68	0	119	11	0	.227
Ward, D...............	TOR	R	0	1	27.00	4	0	0	0	0	0	2.2	11	25	10	8	0	0	0	1	5	0	3	2	0	.579
Ware, J................	TOR	R	2	1	5.47	5	5	0	0	0	0	26.1	28	124	18	16	2	1	0	1	21	0	18	2	0	.277
Wasdin, J	OAK	R	1	1	4.67	5	2	0	0	3	0	17.1	14	69	9	9	4	0	0	1	3	0	6	0	0	.215
Watkins, S	MIN	L	0	0	5.40	27	0	0	0	7	0	21.2	22	94	14	13	2	1	3	0	11	1	11	0	0	.278
Wegman, B..........	MIL	R	5	7	5.35	37	4	0	0	17	2	70.2	89	314	45	42	14	3	2	3	21	2	50	1	0	.312
Wells, B...............	SEA	R	4	3	5.75	30	4	0	0	3	0	76.2	88	358	51	49	11	1	5	3	39	3	38	1	0	.284
Wells, D...............	DET	L	10	3	3.04	18	18	3	0	0	0	130.1	120	539	54	44	17	3	2	2	37	5	83	6	1	.242
Wengert, D..........	OAK	R	1	1	3.34	19	0	0	0	10	0	29.2	30	129	14	11	3	1	1	1	12	2	16	1	0	.263
Wetteland, J	NY	R	1	5	2.93	60	0	0	0	56	31	61.1	40	233	22	20	6	1	2	0	14	2	66	1	0	.185
Whiteside, M	TEX	R	5	4	4.08	40	0	0	0	18	3	53.0	48	223	24	24	5	2	3	1	19	2	46	4	0	.242
Whiteside, S	DET	L	0	0	14.73	2	0	0	0	0	0	3.2	7	22	6	6	1	0	2	0	4	1	2	1	0	.438
Wickander, K	DET-MIL	L	0	0	1.93	29	0	0	0	9	1	23.1	19	99	6	5	1	1	2	1	12	5	11	1	1	.229
Wickman, B	NY	R	2	4	4.05	63	1	0	0	14	1	80.0	77	347	38	36	6	4	1	5	33	3	51	2	0	.253
Williams, M.........	CAL	L	1	2	6.75	20	0	0	0	3	0	10.2	13	65	10	8	1	0	1	2	21	0	9	2	1	.317
Williams, W.........	TOR	R	1	2	3.69	23	3	0	0	10	0	53.2	44	232	23	22	6	2	0	2	28	1	41	0	0	.220
Willis, C..............	MIN	R	0	0	94.50	3	0	0	0	0	0	0.2	5	12	7	7	0	1	0	0	5	0	0	0	0	.833
Witt, B.................	TEX	R	3	4	4.55	10	10	1	0	0	0	61.1	81	276	35	31	4	2	2	1	21	1	46	5	0	.324
Wojciechowski, S	OAK	L	2	3	5.18	14	7	0	0	3	0	48.2	51	219	28	28	7	1	2	1	28	1	13	0	0	.273
Wolcott, B	SEA	R	3	2	4.42	7	6	0	0	0	0	36.2	43	164	18	18	6	0	3	2	14	0	19	0	0	.297

CLUB PITCHING

CLUB	W	L	ERA	G	CG	SHO	REL	SV	IP	H	R	ER	HR	HB	BB	IBB	SO	WP	BK	OPP AVG
CLEVELAND	100	44	3.83	144	10	10	335	50	1301.0	1261	607	554	135	45	445	16	926	48	5	.255
BALTIMORE	71	73	4.31	144	19	10	336	29	1267.0	1165	640	607	149	37	523	40	930	30	9	.245
BOSTON	86	58	4.39	144	7	9	370	39	1292.2	1338	698	631	127	46	476	28	888	57	1	.268
KANSAS CITY	70	74	4.49	144	11	10	308	37	1288.0	1323	691	642	142	38	503	38	763	45	5	.268
SEATTLE	79	66	4.50	145	9	8	324	39	1289.1	1343	708	644	149	47	591	37	1068	50	7	.268
CALIFORNIA	78	67	4.52	145	8	9	368	42	1284.1	1310	697	645	163	43	486	23	901	42	10	.265
NEW YORK	79	65	4.56	145	18	5	302	35	1284.2	1286	688	651	159	32	535	21	908	50	5	.261
TEXAS................	74	70	4.66	144	14	4	310	34	1285.0	1385	720	665	152	36	514	38	838	60	6	.278
MILWAUKEE......	65	79	4.82	144	7	4	321	31	1286.0	1391	747	689	146	47	603	39	699	45	7	.280
CHICAGO	68	76	4.85	145	12	4	373	36	1284.2	1374	758	693	164	39	617	47	892	45	8	.275
TORONTO	56	88	4.88	144	16	8	265	22	1292.2	1336	777	701	145	51	654	42	894	73	4	.268
OAKLAND..........	67	77	4.93	144	8	4	358	34	1273.0	1320	761	698	153	53	556	26	890	56	4	.269
DETROIT	60	84	5.49	144	5	3	366	38	1275.0	1509	844	778	170	45	536	79	729	67	7	.296
MINNESOTA	56	88	5.76	144	7	2	336	27	1272.2	1450	889	815	210	36	533	18	790	52	4	.287
TOTALS...........	1009	1009	4.71	1010	151	90	4672	493	17976.0	18791	10225	9413	2164	595	7572	492	12116	720	82	.270

AL hit-by-pitch leader: Toronto's Ed Sprague (15).

1996 ATLANTA SCHEDULE

HOME		AWAY	
Apr. 1, 3-4	San Francisco	Apr. 8-10	Los Angeles
Apr. 5-7	St. Louis	Apr. 11-14	San Diego
Apr. 16-18	Florida	Apr. 24-25	San Francisco
Apr. 19-21	San Diego	Apr. 26-28	St. Louis
Apr. 22-23	Los Angeles	Apr. 30-May 1	Houston
May 3-5	Philadelphia	May 10-12	Philadelphia
May 6-8	Colorado	May 24-26	Pittsburgh
May 13-15	Pittsburgh	May 27-29	Chicago
May 17-19	Cincinnati	May 31, June 1-2	Cincinnati
May 20-22	Chicago	June 7-9	Colorado
June 3-5	New York	June 10-12	New York
June 13-16	Los Angeles	June 28-30	Florida
June 17-19	San Diego	July 1-3	Montreal
June 21-23	San Francisco	July 18-21	Houston
June 24-27	St. Louis	July 22-24	St. Louis
July 4-7	Houston	July 25-28	San Francisco
July 11-14	Florida	July 30-31, Aug. 1	San Diego
July 15-16	Montreal	Aug. 2-4	Los Angeles
Aug. 6-8	Philadelphia	Aug. 12-15	Philadelphia
Aug. 9-11	Colorado	Aug. 27-29	Pittsburgh
Aug. 16-18	Pittsburgh	Aug. 30-31, Sept. 1	Chicago
Aug. 20-22	Cincinnati	Sept. 2-4	Cincinnati
Aug. 23-25	Chicago	Sept. 10-12	Colorado
Sept. 6-8	New York	Sept. 13-16	New York
Sept. 17-18	Houston	Sept. 24-26	Florida
Sept. 19-23	Montreal	Sept. 27-29	Montreal

1996 CHICAGO CUBS SCHEDULE

HOME		AWAY	
Apr. 1, 3	San Diego	Apr. 8, 10	Colorado
Apr. 4-7	Los Angeles	Apr. 12-14	San Francisco
Apr. 15-17	Cincinnati	Apr. 24-25	San Diego
Apr. 18-21	San Francisco	Apr. 26-29	Los Angeles
Apr. 22-23	Colorado	May 6-8	Montreal
Apr. 30-May 1	St. Louis	May 10-12	New York
May 3-5	New York	May 20-22	Atlanta
May 13-16	Houston	May 24-26	Houston
May 17-19	Florida	May 31-June 2	Florida
May 27-29	Atlanta	June 10-12	Philadelphia
June 3-5	Philadelphia	June 20-23	San Diego
June 7-9	Montreal	June 25-26	Los Angeles
June 13-16	San Diego	June 28-30	Cincinnati
June 17-19	Los Angeles	July 1-3	Pittsburgh
July 4-7	Cincinnati	July 18-21	St. Louis
July 11-14	St. Louis	July 22-24	San Francisco
July 15-17	Pittsburgh	July 25-28	Colorado
July 30-31	San Francisco	Aug. 9-11	Montreal
Aug. 1-4	Colorado	Aug. 12-14	New York
Aug. 5-7	New York	Aug. 23-25	Atlanta
Aug. 16-18	Houston	Aug. 27-29	Houston
Aug. 19-21	Florida	Sept. 2-4	Florida
Aug. 30-Sept. 1	Atlanta	Sept. 5-8	Philadelphia
Sept. 9-11	Montreal	Sept. 17-19	St. Louis
Sept. 13-15	Philadelphia	Sept. 20-23	Pittsburgh
Sep. 27-29	Pittsburgh	Sept. 24-26	Cincinnati

1996 CINCINNATI SCHEDULE

HOME		AWAY	
Apr. 1, 3-4	Montreal	Apr. 5-7	Philadelphia
Apr. 8-10	New York	Apr. 15-17	Chicago
Apr. 11-14	Houston	Apr. 19-21	Houston
Apr. 26-28	Philadelphia	Apr. 22-23	New York
Apr. 30-May 1	Pittsburgh	Apr. 24-25	Montreal
May 7-8	Los Angeles	May 3-5	San Francisco
May 10-12	San Diego	May 17-19	Atlanta
May 14-15	Colorado	May 23-26	Colorado
May 20-22	Florida	May 27-29	Florida
May 31-June 2	Atlanta	June 7-9	Los Angeles
June 3-6	San Francisco	June 10-12	San Diego
June 14-16	Montreal	June 17-19	Houston
June 24-26	Philadelphia	June 20-23	New York
June 28-30	Chicago	July 1-3	St. Louis
July 11-14	Pittsburgh	July 4-7	Chicago
July 15-17	St. Louis	July 18-21	Pittsburgh
July 26-28	New York	July 22-24	Philadelphia
July 29-31	Houston	Aug. 1-4	Montreal
Aug. 9-12	Los Angeles	Aug. 5-7	San Francisco
Aug. 13-15	San Diego	Aug. 20-22	Atlanta
Aug. 16-19	Colorado	Aug. 23-25	Florida
Aug. 30-Sept. 1	Florida	Aug. 26-28	Colorado
Sept. 2-4	Atlanta	Sept. 9-11	Los Angeles
Sept. 6-8	San Francisco	Sept. 13-15	San Diego
Sept. 20-23	St. Louis	Sept. 17-19	Pittsburgh
Sept. 24-26	Chicago	Sept. 27-29	St. Louis

1996 COLORADO SCHEDULE

HOME		AWAY	
Apr. 8, 10	Chicago	Apr. 1, 3-4	Philadelphia
Apr. 11-14	New York	Apr. 5-7	Montreal
Apr. 15-17	San Diego	Apr. 19-21	New York
Apr. 24-25	Philadelphia	Apr. 22-23	Chicago
Apr. 26-28	Montreal	Apr. 30-May 1	Los Angeles
May 3-5	Florida	May 6-8	Atlanta
May 17-19	St. Louis	May 9-12	Florida
May 20-22	Pittsburgh	May 14-15	Cincinnati
May 23-26	Cincinnati	May 27-29	St. Louis
June 7-9	Atlanta	May 31-June 3	Pittsburgh
June 10-12	Houston	June 4-6	Houston
June 13-16	Philadelphia	June 21-23	Philadelphia
June 17-19	Montreal	June 24-26	New York
June 27-30	Los Angeles	July 1-3	San Francisco
July 11-14	San Diego	July 4-7	Los Angeles
July 15-17	San Francisco	July 18-21	San Diego
July 23-24	New York	July 29-31	Montreal
July 25-28	Chicago	Aug. 1-4	Chicago
Aug. 5-7	Florida	Aug. 9-11	Atlanta
Aug. 20-22	St. Louis	Aug. 13-15	Florida
Aug. 23-25	Pittsburgh	Aug. 16-19	Cincinnati
Aug. 26-28	Cincinnati	Aug. 30-Sept. 1	St. Louis
Sept. 10-12	Atlanta	Sept. 2, 4	Pittsburgh
Sept. 13-15	Houston	Sept. 6-9	Houston
Sept. 16-18	Los Angeles	Sept. 19-22	San Francisco
Sept. 27-29	San Francisco	Sept. 24-25	San Diego

1996 FLORIDA SCHEDULE

HOME		AWAY	
Apr. 1-2,4	Pittsburgh	Apr. 8-10	San Diego
Apr. 5-7	San Francisco	Apr. 11-14	Los Angeles
Apr. 19-21	Los Angeles	Apr. 16-18	Atlanta
Apr. 22-23	San Diego	Apr. 24-25	Pittsburgh
Apr. 30-May 2	Philadelphia	Apr. 26-28	San Francisco
May 6-8	New York	May 3-5	Colorado
May 9-12	Colorado	May 17-19	Chicago
May 13-15	St. Louis	May 20-22	Cincinnati
May 27-29	Cincinnati	May 24-26	St. Louis
May 31-June 2	Chicago	June 7-9	New York
June 4-5	Montreal	June 10-12	Montreal
June 21-23	Pittsburgh	June 13-16	Pittsburgh
June 24-26	San Francisco	June 17-19	San Francisco
June 28-30	Atlanta	July 1-3	Houston
July 15-17	Houston	July 4-7	Philadelphia
July 18-21	Philadelphia	July 11-14	Atlanta
July 23-25	Los Angeles	July 30-Aug. 1	Los Angeles
July 26-29	San Diego	Aug. 2-4	San Diego
Aug. 8-11	New York	Aug. 5-7	Colorado
Aug. 13-15	Colorado	Aug. 19-21	Chicago
Aug. 16-18	St. Louis	Aug. 27-29	St. Louis
Aug. 23-25	Cincinnati	Aug. 30-Sept. 1	Cincinnati
Sept. 2-4	Chicago	Sept. 9-11	New York
Sept. 5-8	Montreal	Sept. 12-15	Montreal
Sept. 20-22	Houston	Sept. 17-18	Philadelphia
Sept. 23-25	Atlanta	Sept. 27-29	Houston

1996 HOUSTON SCHEDULE

HOME		AWAY	
Apr. 1-3	Los Angeles	Apr. 11-14	Cincinnati
Apr. 5-7	San Diego	Apr. 16-17	New York
Apr. 8-10	San Francisco	Apr. 22-23	San Francisco
Apr. 19-21	Cincinnati	Apr. 24-25	Los Angeles
Apr. 30-May 1	Atlanta	Apr. 26-29	San Diego
May 3-5	Montreal	May 6-8	Philadelphia
May 17-19	Pittsburgh	May 9-12	Montreal
May 20-22	St. Louis	May 13-16	Chicago
May 24-26	Chicago	May 27-29	Pittsburgh
June 4-6	Colorado	May 31, June 1-2	St. Louis
June 7-9	Philadelphia	June 10-12	Colorado
June 17-19	Cincinnati	June 13-16	San Francisco
June 28-30	New York	June 20-23	Los Angeles
July 1-3	Florida	June 25-26	San Diego
July 18-21	Atlanta	July 4-7	Atlanta
July 22-24	San Diego	July 11-14	New York
July 26-28	Los Angeles	July 15-17	Florida
Aug. 2-4	San Francisco	July 29-31	Cincinnati
Aug. 6-8	Montreal	Aug. 9-11	Philadelphia
Aug. 19-22	Pittsburgh	Aug. 12-14	Montreal
Aug. 23-26	St. Louis	Aug. 16-18	Chicago
Sept. 6-9	Colorado	Aug. 30-31, Sept. 1	Pittsburgh
Sept. 10-12	Philadelphia	Sept. 2-4	St. Louis
Sept. 24-26	New York	Sept. 13-15	Colorado
Sept. 27-29	Florida	Sept. 17-18	Atlanta
		Sept. 20-22	Florida

1996 LOS ANGELES SCHEDULE

HOME		AWAY	
Apr. 8-10	Atlanta	Apr. 1-3	Houston
Apr. 11-14	Florida	Apr. 4-7	Chicago
Apr. 24-25	Houston	Apr. 16-17	San Francisco
Apr. 26-29	Chicago	Apr. 19-21	Florida
Apr. 30-May 1	Colorado	Apr. 22-23	Atlanta
May 13-15	Montreal	May 3-6	Pittsburgh
May 16-19	Philadelphia	May 7-8	Cincinnati
May 20-22	New York	May 10-12	St. Louis
June 4-6	Pittsburgh	May 24-26	Montreal
June 7-9	Cincinnati	May 28-30	Philadelphia
June 10-11	St. Louis	May 31-June 2	New York
June 20-23	Houston	June 13-16	Atlanta
June 25-26	Chicago	June 17-19	Chicago
July 4-7	Colorado	June 27-30	Colorado
July 11-14	San Francisco	July 1-3	San Diego
July 15-17	San Diego	July 18-21	San Francisco
July 30-Aug. 1	Florida	July 23-25	Florida
Aug. 2-4	Atlanta	July 26-28	Houston
Aug. 16-18	Montreal	Aug. 6-7	Pittsburgh
Aug. 20-22	Philadelphia	Aug. 9-12	Cincinnati
Aug. 23-25	New York	Aug. 13-15	St. Louis
Sept. 6-8	Pittsburgh	Aug. 27-29	Montreal
Sept. 9-11	Cincinnati	Aug. 30-Sept. 1	Philadelphia
Sept. 12-15	St. Louis	Sept. 2-4	New York
Sept. 24-26	San Francisco	Sept. 16-18	Colorado
Sept. 27-29	San Diego	Sept. 19-22	San Diego

1996 MONTREAL SCHEDULE

HOME		AWAY	
Apr. 5-7	Colorado	Apr. 1, 3-4	Cincinnati
Apr. 16-18	Philadelphia	Apr. 8, 10	St. Louis
Apr. 19-21	Pittsburgh	Apr. 11-14	Pittsburgh
Apr. 22-23	St. Louis	Apr. 26-28	Colorado
Apr. 24-25	Cincinnati	Apr. 29-May 1	New York
May 6-8	Chicago	May 3-5	Houston
May 9-12	Houston	May 13-15	Los Angeles
May 24-26	Los Angeles	May 17-19	San Diego
May 27-29	San Diego	May 20-22	San Francisco
May 31-June 2	San Francisco	June 4-5	Florida
June 10-12	Florida	June 7-9	Chicago
June 20-23	St. Louis	June 14-16	Cincinnati
June 24-26	Pittsburgh	June 17-19	Colorado
July 1-3	Atlanta	June 28-30	Philadelphia
July 4-7	New York	July 15-16	Atlanta
July 11-14	Philadelphia	July 18-21	New York
July 29-31	Colorado	July 23-24	Pittsburgh
Aug. 1-4	Cincinnati	July 25-28	St. Louis
Aug. 9-11	Chicago	Aug. 6-8	Houston
Aug. 12-14	Houston	Aug. 16-18	Los Angeles
Aug. 27-29	Los Angeles	Aug. 19-21	San Diego
Aug. 30-Sept. 1	San Diego	Aug. 22-25	San Francisco
Sept. 2-4	San Francisco	Sept. 5-8	Florida
Sept. 12-15	Florida	Sept. 9-11	Chicago
Sept. 17-18	New York	Sept. 19-23	Atlanta
Sept. 27-29	Atlanta	Sept. 24-25, 27	Philadelphia

1996 NEW YORK METS SCHEDULE

HOME

Apr. 1, 3-4	St. Louis
Apr. 5-7	Pittsburgh
Apr. 16-17	Houston
Apr. 19-21	Colorado
Apr. 22-23	Cincinnati
Apr. 29-May 1	Montreal
May 10-12	Chicago
May 24-26	San Diego
May 28-30	San Francisco
May 31-June 2	Los Angeles
June 7-9	Florida
June 10-12	Atlanta
June 20-23	Cincinnati
June 24-26	Colorado
July 11-14	Houston
July 15-17	Philadelphia
July 18-21	Montreal
July 29-Aug. 1	Pittsburgh
Aug. 2-4	St. Louis
Aug. 12-14	Chicago
Aug. 27-29	San Diego
Aug. 30-Sept. 1	San Francisco
Sept. 2-4	Los Angeles
Sept. 9-11	Florida
Sept. 13-16	Atlanta
Sept. 27-29	Philadelphia

AWAY

Apr. 8-10	Cincinnati
Apr. 11-14	Colorado
Apr. 24-25	St. Louis
Apr. 26-28	Pittsburgh
May 3-5	Chicago
May 6-8	Florida
May 13-16	San Diego
May 17-19	San Francisco
May 20-22	Los Angeles
June 3-5	Atlanta
June 13-16	St. Louis
June 17-19	Pittsburgh
June 28-30	Houston
July 1-3	Philadelphia
July 4-7	Montreal
July 23-24	Colorado
July 26-28	Cincinnati
Aug. 5-7	Chicago
Aug. 8-11	Florida
Aug. 16-18	San Diego
Aug. 19-21	San Francisco
Aug. 23-25	Los Angeles
Sept. 6-8	Atlanta
Sept. 17-18	Montreal
Sept. 19-22	Philadelphia
Sept. 24-26	Houston

1996 PHILADELPHIA SCHEDULE

HOME

Apr. 1, 3-4	Colorado
Apr. 5-7	Cincinnati
Apr. 19-21	St. Louis
Apr. 22-23	Pittsburgh
May 6-8	Houston
May 10-12	Atlanta
May 13-15	San Francisco
May 28-30	Los Angeles
May 31-June 2	San Diego
June 10-12	Chicago
June 21-23	Colorado
June 28-30	Montreal
July 1-3	New York
July 4-7	Florida
July 22-24	Cincinnati
July 30-Aug. 1	St. Louis
Aug. 2-5	Pittsburgh
Aug. 9-11	Houston
Aug. 12-15	Atlanta
Aug. 16-18	San Francisco
Aug. 30-Sept. 1	Los Angeles
Sept. 2-4	San Diego
Sept. 5-8	Chicago
Sept. 17-18	Florida
Sept. 19-22	New York
Sept. 24-26	Montreal

AWAY

Apr. 8, 10	Pittsburgh
Apr. 11-14	St. Louis
Apr. 16-18	Montreal
Apr. 24-25	Colorado
Apr. 26-28	Cincinnati
Apr. 30-May 2	Florida
May 3-5	Atlanta
May 16-19	Los Angeles
May 21-23	San Diego
May 24-26	San Francisco
June 3-5	Chicago
June 7-9	Houston
June 13-16	Colorado
June 18-19	St. Louis
June 24-26	Cincinnati
July 11-14	Montreal
July 15-17	New York
July 18-21	Florida
July 25-28	Pittsburgh
Aug. 6-8	Atlanta
Aug. 20-22	Los Angeles
Aug. 23-25	San Diego
Aug. 26-28	San Francisco
Sept. 10-12	Houston
Sept. 13-15	Chicago
Sept. 27-29	New York

1996 PITTSBURGH SCHEDULE

HOME		AWAY	
Apr. 8,10	Philadelphia	Apr. 1, 3-4	Florida
Apr. 11-14	Montreal	Apr. 5-7	New York
Apr. 24-25	Florida	Apr. 15-18	St. Louis
Apr. 26-28	New York	Apr. 19-21	Montreal
May 3-6	Los Angeles	Apr. 22-23	Philadelphia
May 7-9	San Diego	Apr. 30-May 1	Cincinnati
May 10-12	San Francisco	May 13-15	Atlanta
May 24-26	Atlanta	May 17-19	Houston
May 27-29	Houston	May 20-22	Colorado
May 31-June 3	Colorado	June 4-6	Los Angeles
June 13-16	Florida	June 7-9	San Diego
June 17-19	New York	June 10-11	San Francisco
July 1-3	Chicago	June 21-23	Florida
July 4-7	St. Louis	June 24-26	Montreal
July 18-21	Cincinnati	June 28-30	St. Louis
July 23-24	Montreal	July 11-14	Cincinnati
July 25-28	Philadelphia	July 15-17	Chicago
Aug. 6-7	Los Angeles	July 29-Aug. 1	New York
Aug. 8-11	San Diego	Aug. 2-5	Philadelphia
Aug. 13-15	San Francisco	Aug. 16-18	Atlanta
Aug. 27-29	Atlanta	Aug. 19-22	Houston
Aug. 30-Sept. 1	Houston	Aug. 23-25	Colorado
Sept. 2, 4	Colorado	Sept. 6-8	Los Angeles
Sept. 17-19	Cincinnati	Sept. 9-11	San Diego
Sept. 20-23	Chicago	Sept. 12-15	San Francisco
Sept. 24-25	St. Louis	Sept. 27-29	Chicago

1996 ST. LOUIS SCHEDULE

HOME		AWAY	
Apr. 8, 10	Montreal	Apr. 1, 3-4	New York
Apr. 11-14	Philadelphia	Apr. 5-7	Atlanta
Apr. 15-18	Pittsburgh	Apr. 19-21	Philadelphia
Apr. 24-25	New York	Apr. 22-23	Montreal
Apr. 26-28	Atlanta	Apr. 30-May 1	Chicago
May 7-9	San Francisco	May 3-5	San Diego
May 10-12	Los Angeles	May 13-15	Florida
May 27-29	Colorado	May 17-19	Colorado
May 31-June 2	Houston	May 20-22	Houston
June 13-16	New York	May 24-26	Florida
June 18-19	Philadelphia	June 3-5	San Diego
June 28-30	Pittsburgh	June 7-9	San Francisco
July 1-3	Cincinnati	June 10-11	Los Angeles
July 18-21	Chicago	June 20-23	Montreal
July 22-24	Atlanta	June 24-27	Atlanta
July 25-28	Montreal	July 4-7	Pittsburgh
Aug. 5-7	San Diego	July 11-14	Chicago
Aug. 8-11	San Francisco	July 15-17	Cincinnati
Aug. 13-15	Los Angeles	July 30-Aug. 1	Philadelphia
Aug. 16-18	Florida	Aug. 2-4	New York
Aug. 27-29	Florida	Aug. 20-22	Colorado
Aug. 30-Sept. 1	Colorado	Aug. 23-26	Houston
Sept. 2-4	Houston	Sept. 9-11	San Francisco
Sept. 6-8	San Diego	Sept. 12-15	Los Angeles
Sept. 17-19	Chicago	Sept. 20-23	Cincinnati
Sept. 27-29	Cincinnati	Sept. 24-25	Pittsburgh

1996 SAN DIEGO SCHEDULE

HOME		AWAY	
Apr. 8-10	Florida	Apr. 2-3	Chicago
Apr. 11-14	Atlanta	Apr. 5-7	Houston
Apr. 24-25	Chicago	Apr. 15-17	Colorado
Apr. 26-29	Houston	Apr. 19-21	Atlanta
Apr. 30-May 1	San Francisco	Apr. 22-23	Florida
May 3-5	St. Louis	May 7-9	Pittsburgh
May 13-16	New York	May 10-12	Cincinnati
May 17-19	Montreal	May 24-26	New York
May 21-23	Philadelphia	May 27-29	Montreal
June 3-5	St. Louis	May 31-June 2	Philadelphia
June 7-9	Pittsburgh	June 13-16	Chicago
June 10-12	Cincinnati	June 17-19	Atlanta
June 20-23	Chicago	June 27-30	San Francisco
June 25-26	Houston	July 11-14	Colorado
July 1-3	Los Angeles	July 15-17	Los Angeles
July 4-7	San Francisco	July 22-24	Houston
July 18-21	Colorado	July 26-29	Florida
July 30-Aug. 1	Atlanta	Aug. 5-7	St. Louis
Aug. 2-4	Florida	Aug. 8-11	Pittsburgh
Aug. 16-18	New York	Aug. 13-15	Cincinnati
Aug. 19-21	Montreal	Aug. 27-29	New York
Aug. 23-25	Philadelphia	Aug. 30-Sept. 1	Montreal
Sept. 9-11	Pittsburgh	Sept. 2-4	Philadelphia
Sept. 13-15	Cincinnati	Sept. 6-8	St. Louis
Sept. 19-22	Los Angeles	Sept. 16-18	San Francisco
Sept. 24-25	Colorado	Sept. 27-29	Los Angeles

1996 SAN FRANCISCO SCHEDULE

HOME		AWAY	
Apr. 12-14	Chicago	Apr. 1, 3-4	Atlanta
Apr. 16-17	Los Angeles	Apr. 5-7	Florida
Apr. 22-23	Houston	Apr. 8-10	Houston
Apr. 24-25	Atlanta	Apr. 18-21	Chicago
Apr. 26-28	Florida	Apr. 30-May 1	San Diego
May 3-5	Cincinnati	May 7-9	St. Louis
May 17-19	New York	May 10-12	Pittsburgh
May 20-22	Montreal	May 13-15	Philadelphia
May 24-26	Philadelphia	May 28-30	New York
June 7-9	St. Louis	May 31-June 2	Montreal
June 10-11	Pittsburgh	June 3-6	Cincinnati
June 13-16	Houston	June 21-23	Atlanta
June 17-19	Florida	June 24-26	Florida
June 27-30	San Diego	July 4-7	San Diego
July 1-3	Colorado	July 11-14	Los Angeles
July 18-21	Los Angeles	July 15-17	Colorado
July 22-24	Chicago	July 30-31	Chicago
July 25-28	Atlanta	Aug. 2-4	Houston
Aug. 5-7	Cincinnati	Aug. 8-11	St. Louis
Aug. 19-21	New York	Aug. 13-15	Pittsburgh
Aug. 22-25	Montreal	Aug. 16-18	Philadelphia
Aug. 26-28	Philadelphia	Aug. 30-Sept. 1	New York
Sept. 9-11	St. Louis	Sept. 2-4	Montreal
Sept. 12-15	Pittsburgh	Sept. 6-8	Cincinnati
Sept. 16-18	San Diego	Sept. 24-26	Los Angeles
Sept. 19-22	Colorado	Sept. 27-29	Colorado

1996 BALTIMORE SCHEDULE

HOME		AWAY	
Apr. 1, 3-4	Kansas City	Apr. 5-7	Minnesota
Apr. 9-10	Cleveland	Apr. 19-21	Texas
Apr. 12-14	Minnesota	Apr. 22-23	Cleveland
Apr. 16-18	Boston	Apr. 24-25	Kansas City
Apr. 26-29	Texas	May 7-9	Chicago
Apr. 30-May 1	New York	May 10-12	Milwaukee
May 3-5	Milwaukee	May 13-15	Oakland
May 17-19	Seattle	May 28-29	Seattle
May 20-22	California	May 31-June 2	California
May 24-26	Oakland	June 10-12	Detroit
June 4-6	Detroit	June 13-16	Kansas City
June 7-9	Chicago	June 24-26	Texas
June 17-19	Texas	June 27-30	New York
June 21-23	Kansas City	July 1-3	Toronto
July 4-7	Boston	July 18-21	Boston
July 11-14	New York	July 30-Aug. 1	Minnesota
July 15-17	Toronto	Aug. 2-5	Cleveland
July 22-24	Minnesota	Aug. 6-8	Milwaukee
July 25-28	Cleveland	Aug. 9-11	Chicago
Aug. 12-14	Milwaukee	Aug. 15-18	Oakland
Aug. 20-22	Seattle	Aug. 29-Sept. 1	Seattle
Aug. 23-25	California	Sept. 2-4	California
Aug. 26-28	Oakland	Sept. 13-15	Detroit
Sept. 6-9	Detroit	Sept. 17-19	New York
Sept. 10-12	Chicago	Sept. 24-26	Boston
Sept. 20-22	Toronto	Sept. 27-29	Toronto

1996 BOSTON SCHEDULE

HOME		AWAY	
Apr. 8, 10-11	Minnesota	Apr. 1, 3-4	Texas
Apr. 12-15	Cleveland	Apr. 5-7	Kansas City
Apr. 24-25	Texas	Apr. 16-18	Baltimore
Apr. 26-28	Kansas City	Apr. 19-21	Cleveland
Apr. 30-May 1	Detroit	Apr. 22-23	Minnesota
May 3-5	Toronto	May 7-9	Milwaukee
May 14-15	California	May 10-12	Toronto
May 17-20	Oakland	May 24-26	California
May 21-23	Seattle	May 27-29	Oakland
June 4-6	Chicago	May 30-June 2	Seattle
June 7-9	Milwaukee	June 10-12	Chicago
June 13-16	Texas	June 18-20	Cleveland
June 25-26	Cleveland	June 21-23	Texas
June 27-30	Detroit	July 1-3	New York
July 15-17	New York	July 4-7	Baltimore
July 18-21	Baltimore	July 11-14	Detroit
July 22-24	Kansas City	July 25-28	Minnesota
Aug. 2-4	Minnesota	July 30-Aug. 1	Kansas City
Aug. 5-8	Toronto	Aug. 9-11	Milwaukee
Aug. 16-19	California	Aug. 12-14	Toronto
Aug. 20-22	Oakland	Aug. 26-28	California
Aug. 23-25	Seattle	Aug. 30-Sept. 1	Oakland
Sept. 9-11	Milwaukee	Sept. 2-4	Seattle
Sept. 13-15	Chicago	Sept. 6-8	Chicago
Sept. 24-25	Baltimore	Sept. 17-19	Detroit
Sept. 26-29	New York	Sept. 20-22	New York

1996 CALIFORNIA SCHEDULE

HOME		AWAY	
Apr. 2-3	Milwaukee	Apr. 9-11	Toronto
Apr. 5-7	Chicago	Apr. 12-14	Detroit
Apr. 17-18	Toronto	Apr. 15-16	Seattle
Apr. 19-22	Detroit	Apr. 24-25	Milwaukee
May 3-5	Minnesota	Apr. 26-29	Chicago
May 6-9	Kansas City	Apr. 30, May 1-2	Oakland
May 10-12	Cleveland	May 14-15	Boston
May 24-26	Boston	May 17-19	New York
May 27-29	New York	May 20-22	Baltimore
May 31, June 1-2	Baltimore	June 3-5	Minnesota
June 13-16	Toronto	June 7-9	Cleveland
June 17-19	Chicago	June 10-12	Kansas City
June 27-30	Oakland	June 20-23	Milwaukee
July 1-3	Texas	June 24-25	Chicago
July 18-21	Seattle	July 4-7	Oakland
July 22-23	Detroit	July 11-14	Seattle
July 25-28	Milwaukee	July 15-17	Texas
Aug. 6-8	Minnesota	July 30-31, Aug. 1	Detroit
Aug. 9-11	Kansas City	Aug. 2-4	Toronto
Aug. 12-14	Cleveland	Aug. 16-19	Boston
Aug. 26-28	Boston	Aug. 20-22	New York
Aug. 29-31, Sept. 1	New York	Aug. 23-25	Baltimore
Sept. 2-4	Baltimore	Sept. 6-8	Minnesota
Sept. 17-18	Oakland	Sept. 9-12	Cleveland
Sept. 20-22	Texas	Sept. 13-15	Kansas City
Sept. 23-25	Seattle	Sept. 26-29	Texas

1996 CHICAGO WHITE SOX SCHEDULE

HOME		AWAY	
Apr. 9, 11	Texas	Mar. 31, Apr. 2-3	Seattle
Apr. 12-14	Oakland	Apr. 5-7	California
Apr. 24-25	Seattle	Apr. 15-17	Kansas City
Apr. 26-29	California	Apr. 19-21	Oakland
May 7-9	Baltimore	Apr. 22-23	Texas
May 10-12	New York	Apr. 29-May 1	Cleveland
May 21-22	Toronto	May 2-5	New York
May 24-26	Milwaukee	May 13-16	Milwaukee
May 30-June 2	Detroit	May 17-19	Detroit
June 10-12	Boston	May 27-29	Toronto
June 20-23	Seattle	June 4-6	Boston
June 24-25	California	June 7-9	Baltimore
June 27-30	Cleveland	June 14-16	Seattle
July 1-3	Minnesota	June 17-19	California
July 18-21	Kansas City	July 4-7	Cleveland
July 22-24	Oakland	July 11-14	Kansas City
July 25-28	Texas	July 15-17	Minnesota
Aug. 9-11	Baltimore	July 30-Aug. 1	Oakland
Aug. 12-14	New York	Aug. 2-5	Texas
Aug. 22-25	Toronto	Aug. 6-8	New York
Aug. 26-28	Milwaukee	Aug. 16-18	Milwaukee
Sept. 2-4	Detroit	Aug. 19-21	Detroit
Sept. 6-8	Boston	Aug. 30-Sept. 1	Toronto
Sept. 16-18	Cleveland	Sept. 10-12	Baltimore
Sept. 19-22	Minnesota	Sept. 13-15	Boston
Sept. 24-25	Kansas City	Sept. 27-29	Minnesota

1996 CLEVELAND SCHEDULE

HOME		AWAY	
Apr. 1, 3-4	New York	Apr. 9-10	Baltimore
Apr. 5-7	Toronto	Apr. 12-15	Boston
Apr. 19-21	Boston	Apr. 16-17	Minnesota
Apr. 22-23	Baltimore	Apr. 24-25	New York
Apr. 30-May 1	Chicago	Apr. 26-28	Toronto
May 14-16	Detroit	May 2-5	Seattle
May 17-19	Texas	May 6-8	Oakland
May 21-23	Milwaukee	May 10-12	California
June 4-6	Seattle	May 24-26	Detroit
June 7-9	California	May 27-29	Texas
June 10-12	Oakland	May 30-June 2	Milwaukee
June 18-20	Boston	June 13-16	New York
June 21-23	New York	June 25-26	Boston
July 1-3	Kansas City	June 27-30	Chicago
July 4-7	Chicago	July 11-14	Minnesota
July 18-21	Minnesota	July 15-17	Kansas City
July 30-Aug. 1	Toronto	July 22-24	Toronto
Aug. 2-5	Baltimore	July 25-28	Baltimore
Aug. 16-18	Detroit	Aug. 6-8	Seattle
Aug. 19-21	Texas	Aug. 9-11	Oakland
Aug. 23-25	Milwaukee	Aug. 12-14	California
Sept. 6-8	Seattle	Aug. 26-28	Detroit
Sept. 9-12	California	Aug. 30-Sept. 1	Texas
Sept. 13-15	Oakland	Sept. 2-4	Milwaukee
Sept. 19-22	Kansas City	Sept. 16-18	Chicago
Sept. 23-25	Minnesota	Sept. 27-29	Kansas City

1996 DETROIT SCHEDULE

HOME		AWAY	
Apr. 9, 11	Seattle	Apr. 1-3	Minnesota
Apr. 12-14	California	Apr. 4-7	Oakland
Apr. 24-25	Minnesota	Apr. 15-16	Toronto
Apr. 26-28	Oakland	Apr. 17-18	Seattle
May 2-5	Texas	Apr. 19-22	California
May 17-19	Chicago	Apr. 30-May 1	Boston
May 21-22	Kansas City	May 6-9	New York
May 24-26	Cleveland	May 10-12	Texas
June 7-9	New York	May 14-16	Cleveland
June 10-12	Baltimore	May 27, 29	Kansas City
June 17-19	Oakland	May 30-June 2	Chicago
June 20-23	Minnesota	June 4-6	Baltimore
July 1-3	Milwaukee	June 14-16	Minnesota
July 4-7	Toronto	June 24-25	Oakland
July 11-14	Boston	June 27-30	Boston
July 30-Aug. 1	California	July 15-17	Milwaukee
Aug. 2-5	Seattle	July 18-21	Toronto
Aug. 6-8	Texas	July 22-23	California
Aug. 19-21	Chicago	July 25-28	Seattle
Aug. 26-28	Cleveland	Aug. 9-11	New York
Aug. 29-Sept. 1	Kansas City	Aug. 12-14	Texas
Sept. 10-12	New York	Aug. 16-18	Cleveland
Sept. 13-15	Baltimore	Aug. 22-25	Kansas City
Sept. 17-19	Boston	Sept. 2-4	Chicago
Sept. 23-25	Toronto	Sept. 6-9	Baltimore
Sept. 27-29	Milwaukee	Sept. 20-22	Milwaukee

1996 KANSAS CITY SCHEDULE

HOME		AWAY	
Apr. 5-7	Boston	Apr. 1, 3-4	Baltimore
Apr. 15-17	Chicago	Apr. 9, 11	New York
Apr. 18-21	Milwaukee	Apr. 12-14	Milwaukee
Apr. 22-23	New York	Apr. 26-28	Boston
Apr. 24-25	Baltimore	Apr. 29-30, May 1	Minnesota
May 3-5	Oakland	May 6-9	California
May 17-20	Toronto	May 10-12	Seattle
May 22-25	Texas	May 13-15	Texas
May 27, 29	Detroit	May 21-22	Detroit
June 7-9	Seattle	May 31, June 1-2	Toronto
June 10-12	California	June 3-5	Oakland
June 13-16	Baltimore	June 17-19	Milwaukee
June 25-27	Milwaukee	June 21-23	Baltimore
June 28-30	Minnesota	July 1-3	Cleveland
July 11-14	Chicago	July 4-7	Minnesota
July 15-17	Cleveland	July 18-21	Chicago
July 30-31, Aug. 1	Boston	July 22-24	Boston
Aug. 2-5	New York	July 25-28	New York
Aug. 6-8	Oakland	Aug. 9-11	California
Aug. 19-21	Toronto	Aug. 12-14	Seattle
Aug. 22-25	Detroit	Aug. 16-18	Texas
Aug. 27-28	Texas	Aug. 29-31, Sept. 1	Detroit
Sept. 10-12	Seattle	Sept. 2-4	Toronto
Sept. 13-15	California	Sept. 6-8	Oakland
Sept. 16-18	Minnesota	Sept. 19-22	Cleveland
Sept. 27-29	Cleveland	Sept. 24-25	Chicago

1996 MILWAUKEE SCHEDULE

HOME		AWAY	
Apr. 9, 11	Oakland	Apr. 2-3	California
Apr. 12-14	Kansas City	Apr. 5-7	Seattle
Apr. 16-17	New York	Apr. 18-21	Kansas City
Apr. 24-25	California	Apr. 22-23	Oakland
Apr. 26-29	Seattle	Apr. 30-May 2	Toronto
May 7-9	Boston	May 3-5	Baltimore
May 10-12	Baltimore	May 17-20	Minnesota
May 13-16	Chicago	May 21-23	Cleveland
May 28-29	Minnesota	May 24-26	Chicago
May 30-June 2	Cleveland	June 7-9	Boston
June 3-5	Texas	June 10-12	Texas
June 13-16	Oakland	June 25-27	Kansas City
June 17-19	Kansas City	June 28-30	Toronto
June 20-23	California	July 1-3	Detroit
July 11-14	Toronto	July 4-7	New York
July 15-17	Detroit	July 22-24	Seattle
July 18-21	New York	July 25-28	California
July 30-Aug. 1	Seattle	Aug. 2-5	Oakland
Aug. 6-8	Baltimore	Aug. 12-14	Baltimore
Aug. 9-11	Boston	Aug. 19-21	Minnesota
Aug. 16-18	Chicago	Aug. 23-25	Cleveland
Aug. 29-Sept. 1	Minnesota	Aug. 26-28	Chicago
Sept. 2-4	Cleveland	Sept. 9-11	Boston
Sept. 6-8	Texas	Sept. 12-15	Texas
Sept. 17-18	Toronto	Sept. 24-25	New York
Sept. 20-22	Detroit	Sept. 27-29	Detroit

1996 MINNESOTA SCHEDULE

HOME		AWAY	
Apr. 1-3	Detroit	Apr. 8, 10-11	Boston
Apr. 5-7	Baltimore	Apr. 12-14	Baltimore
Apr. 16-17	Cleveland	Apr. 24-25	Detroit
Apr. 19-21	New York	Apr. 26-28	New York
Apr. 22-23	Boston	May 3-5	California
Apr. 29-30, May 1	Kansas City	May 6-8	Seattle
May 14-16	Toronto	May 10-12	Oakland
May 17-20	Milwaukee	May 23-26	Toronto
May 21-22	Texas	May 28-29	Milwaukee
June 3-5	California	May 31, June 1-2	Texas
June 7-8(2), 9	Oakland	June 17-19	New York
June 10-12	Seattle	June 20-23	Detroit
June 14-16	Detroit	June 28-30	Kansas City
June 24-26	New York	July 1-3	Chicago
July 4-7	Kansas City	July 18-21	Cleveland
July 11-14	Cleveland	July 22-24	Baltimore
July 15-17	Chicago	Aug. 2-4	Boston
July 25-28	Boston	Aug. 6-8	California
July 30-31, Aug. 1	Baltimore	Aug. 9-11	Seattle
Aug. 16-18	Toronto	Aug. 12-14	Oakland
Aug. 19-21	Milwaukee	Aug. 26-28	Toronto
Aug. 22-25	Texas	Aug. 29-31, Sept. 1	Milwaukee
Sept. 6-8	California	Sept. 2-4	Texas
Sept. 9-12	Oakland	Sept. 16-18	Kansas City
Sept. 13-15	Seattle	Sept. 19-22	Chicago
Sept. 27-29	Chicago	Sept. 23-25	Cleveland

1996 NEW YORK YANKEES SCHEDULE

HOME		AWAY	
Apr. 9, 11	Kansas City	Apr. 1, 3-4	Cleveland
Apr. 12-14	Texas	Apr. 5-7	Texas
Apr. 24-25	Cleveland	Apr. 16-17	Milwaukee
Apr. 26-28	Minnesota	Apr. 19-21	Minnesota
May 2-5	Chicago	Apr. 22-23	Kansas City
May 6-9	Detroit	Apr. 30-May 1	Baltimore
May 14-15	Seattle	May 10-12	Chicago
May 17-19	California	May 24-26	Seattle
May 21-23	Oakland	May 27-29	California
June 4-6	Toronto	May 31-June 2	Oakland
June 13-16	Cleveland	June 7-9	Detroit
June 17-19	Minnesota	June 10-12	Toronto
June 27-30	Baltimore	June 21-23	Cleveland
July 1-3	Boston	June 24-26	Minnesota
July 4-7	Milwaukee	July 11-14	Baltimore
July 22-24	Texas	July 15-17	Boston
July 25-28	Kansas City	July 18-21	Milwaukee
Aug. 6-8	Chicago	July 30-Aug. 1	Texas
Aug. 9-11	Detroit	Aug. 2-5	Kansas City
Aug. 16-19	Seattle	Aug. 12-14	Chicago
Aug. 20-22	California	Aug. 26-28	Seattle
Aug. 23-25	Oakland	Aug. 29-Sept. 1	California
Sept. 6-8	Toronto	Sept. 2-4	Oakland
Sept. 17-19	Baltimore	Sept. 10-12	Detroit
Sept. 20-22	Boston	Sept. 13-16	Toronto
Sept. 24-25	Milwaukee	Sept. 26-29	Boston

1996 OAKLAND SCHEDULE

HOME		AWAY	
Apr. 1, 3	Toronto	Apr. 9, 11	Milwaukee
Apr. 4-7	Detroit	Apr. 12-14	Chicago
Apr. 19-21	Chicago	Apr. 15-17	Texas
Apr. 22-23	Milwaukee	Apr. 24-25	Toronto
Apr. 30-May 2	California	Apr. 26-28	Detroit
May 6-8	Cleveland	May 3-5	Kansas City
May 10-12	Minnesota	May 17-20	Boston
May 13-15	Baltimore	May 21-23	New York
May 27-29	Boston	May 24-26	Baltimore
May 31-June 2	New York	June 7, 8 (2), 9	Minnesota
June 3-5	Kansas City	June 10-12	Cleveland
June 20-23	Toronto	June 13-16	Milwaukee
June 24-25	Detroit	June 17-19	Detroit
July 4-7	California	June 27-30	California
July 11-14	Texas	July 1-3	Seattle
July 15-17	Seattle	July 18-21	Texas
July 30-Aug. 1	Chicago	July 22-24	Chicago
Aug. 2-5	Milwaukee	July 25-28	Toronto
Aug. 9-11	Cleveland	Aug. 6-8	Kansas City
Aug. 12-14	Minnesota	Aug. 20-22	Boston
Aug. 15-18	Baltimore	Aug. 23-25	New York
Aug. 30-Sept. 1	Boston	Aug. 26-28	Baltimore
Sept. 2-4	New York	Sept. 10-12	Minnesota
Sept. 6-8	Kansas City	Sept. 13-15	Cleveland
Sept. 23-24	Texas	Sept. 17-18	California
Sept. 26-29	Seattle	Sept. 20-22	Seattle

1996 SEATTLE SCHEDULE

HOME		AWAY	
Mar. 31, Apr. 2-3	Chicago	Apr. 9-11	Detroit
Apr. 5-7	Milwaukee	Apr. 12-14	Toronto
Apr. 15-16	California	Apr. 24-25	Chicago
Apr. 17-18	Detroit	Apr. 26-29	Milwaukee
Apr. 19-22	Toronto	Apr. 30-May 1	Texas
May 2-5	Cleveland	May 14-15	New York
May 6-8	Minnesota	May 17-19	Baltimore
May 10-12	Kansas City	May 21-23	Boston
May 24-26	New York	June 4-6	Cleveland
May 28-29	Baltimore	June 7-9	Kansas City
May 30-June 2	Boston	June 10-12	Minnesota
June 14-16	Chicago	June 20-23	Chicago
June 18-19	Toronto	June 25-27	Toronto
June 28-30	Texas	July 4-7	Texas
July 1-3	Oakland	July 15-17	Oakland
July 11-14	California	July 18-21	California
July 22-24	Milwaukee	July 30-Aug. 1	Milwaukee
July 25-28	Detroit	Aug. 2-4	Detroit
Aug. 6-8	Cleveland	Aug. 16-19	New York
Aug. 9-11	Minnesota	Aug. 20-22	Baltimore
Aug. 12-14	Kansas City	Aug. 23-25	Boston
Aug. 26-28	New York	Sept. 6-8	Cleveland
Aug. 29-Sept. 1	Baltimore	Sept. 10-12	Kansas City
Sept. 2-4	Boston	Sept. 13-15	Minnesota
Sept. 16-19	Texas	Sept. 23-25	California
Sept. 20-22	Oakland	Sept. 27-29	Oakland

1996 TEXAS SCHEDULE

HOME		AWAY	
Apr. 1, 3-4	Boston	Apr. 9, 11	Chicago
Apr. 5-7	New York	Apr. 12-14	New York
Apr. 15-17	Oakland	Apr. 24-25	Boston
Apr. 19-21	Baltimore	Apr. 26-29	Baltimore
Apr. 22-23	Chicago	May 2-5	Detroit
Apr. 30-May 1	Seattle	May 17-19	Cleveland
May 7-9	Toronto	May 21-22	Minnesota
May 10-12	Detroit	May 23-26	Kansas City
May 13-15	Kansas City	June 3-5	Milwaukee
May 27-29	Cleveland	June 13-16	Boston
May 31-June 2	Minnesota	June 17-19	Baltimore
June 7-9	Toronto	June 28-30	Seattle
June 10-12	Milwaukee	July 1-3	California
June 21-23	Boston	July 11-14	Oakland
June 24-26	Baltimore	July 22-24	New York
July 4-7	Seattle	July 25-28	Chicago
July 15-17	California	Aug. 6-8	Detroit
July 18-21	Oakland	Aug. 9-11	Toronto
July 30-Aug. 1	New York	Aug. 19-21	Cleveland
Aug. 2-5	Chicago	Aug. 22-25	Minnesota
Aug. 12-14	Detroit	Aug. 27-28	Kansas City
Aug. 16-18	Kansas City	Sept. 6-8	Milwaukee
Aug. 30-Sept. 1	Cleveland	Sept. 9-11	Toronto
Sept. 2-4	Minnesota	Sept. 16-19	Seattle
Sept. 12-15	Milwaukee	Sept. 20-22	California
Sept. 26-29	California	Sept. 23-24	Oakland

1996 TORONTO SCHEDULE

HOME		AWAY	
Apr. 9-11	California	Apr. 1, 3	Oakland
Apr. 12-14	Seattle	Apr. 5-7	Cleveland
Apr. 15-16	Detroit	Apr. 17-18	California
Apr. 24-25	Oakland	Apr. 19-22	Seattle
Apr. 26-28	Cleveland	May 3-5	Boston
Apr. 30-May 2	Milwaukee	May 7-9	Texas
May 10-12	Boston	May 14-16	Minnesota
May 23-26	Minnesota	May 17-20	Kansas City
May 27-29	Chicago	May 21-22	Chicago
May 31-June 2	Kansas City	June 4-6	New York
June 10-12	New York	June 7-9	Texas
June 25-27	Seattle	June 13-16	California
June 28-30	Milwaukee	June 18-19	Seattle
July 1-3	Baltimore	June 20-23	Oakland
July 18-21	Detroit	July 4-7	Detroit
July 22-24	Cleveland	July 11-14	Milwaukee
July 25-28	Oakland	July 15-17	Baltimore
Aug. 2-4	California	July 30-Aug. 1	Cleveland
Aug. 9-11	Texas	Aug. 5-8	Boston
Aug. 12-14	Boston	Aug. 16-18	Minnesota
Aug. 26-28	Minnesota	Aug. 19-21	Kansas City
Aug. 30-Sept. 1	Chicago	Aug. 22-25	Chicago
Sept. 2-4	Kansas City	Sept. 6-8	New York
Sept. 9-11	Texas	Sept. 17-18	Milwaukee
Sept. 13-16	New York	Sept. 20-22	Baltimore
Sept. 27-29	Baltimore	Sept. 23-25	Detroit

ALL-TIME LEADERS

BATTING AVERAGE
(4,000 at-bats minimum)

1. Ty Cobb	.367	11. Pete Browning	.341
2. Rogers Hornsby	.358	12. Willie Keeler	.341
3. Joe Jackson	.356	13. Bill Terry	.341
4. Ed Delahanty	.346	14. George Sisler	.340
5. Tris Speaker	.345	15. Lou Gehrig	.340
6. Ted Williams	.344	16. Jesse Burkett	.338
7. Billy Hamilton	.344	17. Nap Lajoie	.338
8. Dan Brouthers	.342	18. Riggs Stephenson	.336
9. Babe Ruth	.342	19. Tony Gwynn	.336
10. Harry Heilmann	.342	20. Wade Boggs	.334

HITS

1. Pete Rose	4,256	11. Nap Lajoie	3,242
2. Ty Cobb	4,189	12. George Brett	3,154
3. Hank Aaron	3,771	13. Paul Waner	3,152
4. Stan Musial	3,630	14. Robin Yount	3,142
5. Tris Speaker	3,514	15. Dave Winfield	3,110
6. Carl Yastrzemski	3,419	16. Eddie Murray	3,071
7. Cap Anson	3,415	17. Rod Carew	3,053
Honus Wagner	3,415	18. Lou Brock	3,023
9. Eddie Collins	3,312	19. Al Kaline	3,007
10. Willie Mays	3,283	20. Roberto Clemente	3,000

DOUBLES

1. Tris Speaker	792	11. Robin Yount	583
2. Pete Rose	746	12. Cap Anson	582
3. Stan Musial	725	13. Charlie Gehringer	574
4. Ty Cobb	724	14. Harry Heilmann	542
5. George Brett	665	15. Rogers Hornsby	541
6. Nap Lajoie	657	16. Joe Medwick	540
7. Carl Yastrzemski	646	17. Dave Winfield	540
8. Honus Wagner	640	18. Al Simmons	539
9. Hank Aaron	624	19. Lou Gehrig	534
10. Paul Waner	605	20. Eddie Murray	532

Ty Cobb spiked his batting average to all-time .367.

TRIPLES

1.	Sam Crawford	309
2.	Ty Cobb	295
3.	Honus Wagner	252
4.	Jake Beckley	243
5.	Roger Connor	233
6.	Tris Speaker	222
7.	Fred Clarke	220
8.	Dan Brouthers	205
9.	Joe Kelley	194
10.	Paul Waner	191
11.	Bid McPhee	188
12.	Eddie Collins	186
13.	Ed Delahanty	185
14.	Sam Rice	184
15.	Jesse Burkett	182
16.	Edd Roush	182
17.	Ed Konetchy	181
18.	Buck Ewing	178
19.	Stan Musial	177
	Rabbit Maranville	177

HOME RUNS

1.	Hank Aaron	755
2.	Babe Ruth	714
3.	Willie Mays	660
4.	Frank Robinson	586
5.	Harmon Killebrew	573
6.	Reggie Jackson	563
7.	Mike Schmidt	548
8.	Mickey Mantle	536
9.	Jimmie Foxx	534
10.	Ted Williams	521
	Willie McCovey	521
12.	Ernie Banks	512
	Eddie Mathews	512
14.	Mel Ott	511
15.	Lou Gehrig	493
16.	Eddie Murray	479
17.	Stan Musial	475
	Willie Stargell	475
19.	Dave Winfield	465
20.	Carl Yastrzemski	452

RUNS BATTED IN

1.	Hank Aaron	2,297
2.	Babe Ruth	2,213
3.	Lou Gehrig	1,995
4.	Cap Anson	1,981
5.	Stan Musial	1,951
6.	Ty Cobb	1,937
7.	Jimmie Foxx	1,922
8.	Willie Mays	1,903
9.	Mel Ott	1,860
10.	Carl Yastrzemski	1,844
11.	Ted Williams	1,839
12.	Dave Winfield	1,833
13.	Al Simmons	1,827
14.	Eddie Murray	1,820
15.	Frank Robinson	1,812
16.	Honus Wagner	1,732
17.	Reggie Jackson	1,702
18.	Tony Perez	1,652
19.	Ernie Banks	1,636
20.	Goose Goslin	1,609

Hank Aaron went from historic 715th to 755 home runs.

SLUGGING AVERAGE
(4,000 at-bats minimum)

1.	Babe Ruth	.690
2.	Ted Williams	.634
3.	Lou Gehrig	.632
4.	Jimmie Foxx	.609
5.	Hank Greenberg	.605
6.	Joe DiMaggio	.579
7.	Rogers Hornsby	.577
8.	Johnny Mize	.562
9.	Stan Musial	.559
10.	Willie Mays	.557
	Mickey Mantle	.557
12.	Hank Aaron	.555
13.	Ralph Kiner	.548
14.	Hack Wilson	.545
15.	Chuck Klein	.543
17.	Duke Snider	.540
18.	Frank Robinson	.537
19.	Al Simmons	.535
20.	Dick Allen	.534
	Earl Averill	.534

ON-BASE PERCENTAGE
(4,000 at-bats minimum)

1.	Ted Williams	.483
2.	Babe Ruth	.474
3.	John McGraw	.465
4.	Billy Hamilton	.455
5.	Lou Gehrig	.447
6.	Rogers Hornsby	.434
7.	Ty Cobb	.433
8.	Jimmie Foxx	.428
	Tris Speaker	.428
	Wade Boggs	.428
11.	Ferris Fain	.425
12.	Eddie Collins	.424
13.	Joe Jackson	.423
	Mickey Mantle	.423
	Dan Brouthers	.423
	Max Bishop	.423
17.	Mickey Cochrane	.419
18.	Stan Musial	.418
19.	Cupid Childs	.416
20.	Jesse Burkett	.415

STOLEN BASES

1.	Rickey Henderson	1,149
2.	Lou Brock	938
3.	Billy Hamilton	912
4.	Ty Cobb	891
5.	Tim Raines	777
6.	Eddie Collins	744
7.	Vince Coleman	740
8.	Arlie Latham	739
9.	Max Carey	738
10.	Honus Wagner	722
11.	Joe Morgan	689
12.	Willie Wilson	668
13.	Tom Brown	657
14.	Bert Campaneris	649
15.	George Davis	616
16.	Dummy Hoy	594
17.	Maury Wills	586
18.	George Van Haltren	583
19.	Hugh Duffy	574
20.	Ozzie Smith	573

Nobody has stolen more bases than Rickey Henderson.

RUNS SCORED

1.	Ty Cobb	2,246	11.	Frank Robinson	1,829
2.	Babe Ruth	2,174	12.	Eddie Collins	1,821
	Hank Aaron	2,174	13.	Carl Yastrzemski	1,816
4.	Pete Rose	2,165	14.	Ted Williams	1,798
5.	Willie Mays	2,062	15.	Charlie Gehringer	1,774
6.	Cap Anson	1,996	16.	Jimmie Foxx	1,751
7.	Stan Musial	1,949	17.	Honus Wagner	1,736
8.	Lou Gehrig	1,888	18.	Jim O'Rourke	1,732
9.	Tris Speaker	1,882	19.	Jesse Burkett	1,720
10.	Mel Ott	1,859	20.	Willie Keeler	1,719

WALKS

1.	Babe Ruth	2,056	11.	Harmon Killebrew	1,559
2.	Ted Williams	2,019	12.	Rickey Henderson	1,550
3.	Joe Morgan	1,865	13.	Lou Gehrig	1,508
4.	Carl Yastrzemski	1,845	14.	Mike Schmidt	1,507
5.	Mickey Mantle	1,733	15.	Eddie Collins	1,499
6.	Mel Ott	1,708	16.	Willie Mays	1,464
7.	Eddie Yost	1,614	17.	Jimmie Foxx	1,452
8.	Darrell Evans	1,605	18.	Eddie Mathews	1,444
9.	Stan Musial	1,599	19.	Frank Robinson	1,420
10.	Pete Rose	1,566	20.	Hank Aaron	1,402

GAMES

1.	Pete Rose	3,562	11.	Al Kaline	2,834
2.	Carl Yastrzemski	3,308	12.	Eddie Collins	2,826
3.	Hank Aaron	3,298	13.	Reggie Jackson	2,820
4.	Ty Cobb	3,035	14.	Eddie Murray	2,819
5.	Stan Musial	3,026	15.	Frank Robinson	2,808
6.	Willie Mays	2,992	16.	Honus Wagner	2,792
7.	Dave Winfield	2,966	17.	Tris Speaker	2,789
8.	Rusty Staub	2,951	18.	Tony Perez	2,777
9.	Brooks Robinson	2,896	19.	Mel Ott	2,730
10.	Robin Yount	2,856	20.	George Brett	2,707

Farewell to Mickey Mantle, No. 4 in all-time walks.

WINS

1.	Cy Young	511	11.	Eddie Plank	326
2.	Walter Johnson	417	12.	Nolan Ryan	324
3.	Pete Alexander	373		Don Sutton	324
	Christy Mathewson	373	14.	Phil Niekro	318
5.	Jim Galvin	364	15.	Gaylord Perry	314
6.	Warren Spahn	363	16.	Tom Seaver	311
7.	Kid Nichols	361	17.	Charley Radbourn	309
8.	Tim Keefe	342	18.	Mickey Welch	307
9.	Steve Carlton	329	19.	Early Wynn	300
10.	John Clarkson	328		Lefty Grove	300

WINNING PERCENTAGE

(1,500 innings minimum)

1.	Al Spalding	.796	11.	Dick McBride	.656
2.	Dave Foutz	.690	12.	Sandy Koufax	.655
3.	Whitey Ford	.690	13.	Johnny Allen	.654
4.	Bob Caruthers	.688	14.	Ron Guidry	.651
5.	Lefty Grove	.680	15.	Lefty Gomez	.649
6.	Vic Raschi	.667		Roger Clemens	.649
7.	Larry Corcoran	.665		Dwight Gooden	.649
	Christy Mathewson	.665	18.	John Clarkson	.648
9.	Sam Leever	.660		Mordecai Brown	.648
10.	Sal Maglie	.657	20.	Dizzy Dean	.644

EARNED-RUN AVERAGE

1.	Ed Walsh	1.82		Ed Reulbach	2.28
2.	Addie Joss	1.89	12.	Jim Scott	2.30
3.	Mordecai Brown	2.06	13.	Tommy Bond	2.31
4.	John Ward	2.10	14.	Eddie Plank	2.35
5.	Christy Mathewson	2.13	15.	Larry Corcoran	2.36
6.	Al Spalding	2.14	16.	Ed Killian	2.38
7.	Rube Waddell	2.16		Eddie Cicotte	2.38
8.	Walter Johnson	2.17		George McQuillan	2.38
9.	Orval Overall	2.23	19.	Doc White	2.39
10.	Will White	2.28	20.	George Bradley	2.42

Warren Spahn tops the moderns in wins.

STRIKEOUTS

1. Nolan Ryan	5,714	11. Jim Bunning	2,855
2. Steve Carlton	4,136	12. Mickey Lolich	2,832
3. Bert Blyleven	3,701	13. Cy Young	2,803
4. Tom Seaver	3,640	14. Frank Tanana	2,773
5. Don Sutton	3,574	15. Warren Spahn	2,583
6. Gaylord Perry	3,534	16. Bob Feller	2,581
7. Walter Johnson	3,509	17. Jerry Koosman	2,556
8. Phil Niekro	3,342	18. Tim Keefe	2,545
9. Fergie Jenkins	3,192	19. Christy Mathewson	2,502
10. Bob Gibson	3,117	20. Don Drysdale	2,486

SHUTOUTS

1. Walter Johnson	110	11. Ed Walsh	57
2. Pete Alexander	90	Jim Galvin	57
3. Christy Mathewson	79	13. Bob Gibson	56
4. Cy Young	76	14. Mordecai Brown	55
5. Eddie Plank	69	Steve Carlton	55
6. Warren Spahn	63	16. Gaylord Perry	53
7. Nolan Ryan	61	Jim Palmer	53
Tom Seaver	61	18. Juan Marichal	52
9. Bert Blyleven	60	19. Rube Waddell	50
10. Don Sutton	58	Vic Willis	50

SAVES

1. Lee Smith	471	11. Randy Myers	243
2. Jeff Reardon	367	12. Doug Jones	239
3. Rollie Fingers	341	13. Sparky Lyle	238
4. Dennis Eckersley	323	14. Hoyt Wilhelm	227
5. Tom Henke	311	15. Gene Garber	218
6. Rich Gossage	310	Jeff Montgomery	218
7. Bruce Sutter	300	17. Dave Smith	216
8. John Franco	295	18. Rick Aguilera	211
9. Dave Righetti	252	19. Bobby Thigpen	201
10. Dan Quisenberry	244	20. Roy Face	193

Can anyone ever top Nolan Ryan's 5,714 strikeouts?

COMPLETE GAMES

1. Cy Young	749	11. Jim McCormick	466
2. Jim Galvin	646	12. Gus Weyhing	448
3. Tim Keefe	554	13. Pete Alexander	437
4. Kid Nichols	531	14. Christy Mathewson	434
Walter Johnson	531	15. Jack Powell	422
6. Bobby Mathews	525	16. Eddie Plank	410
Mickey Welch	525	17. Will White	394
8. Charley Radbourn	489	18. Amos Rusie	392
9. John Clarkson	485	19. Vic Willis	388
10. Tony Mullane	468	20. Tommy Bond	386

GAMES PITCHED

1. Hoyt Wilhelm	1,070	11. Jim Kaat	898
2. Kent Tekulve	1,050	12. Jeff Reardon	880
3. Rich Gossage	1,002	13. Don McMahon	874
4. Lindy McDaniel	987	14. Phil Niekro	864
5. Rollie Fingers	944	15. Charlie Hough	858
6. Lee Smith	943	16. Roy Face	848
7. Gene Garber	931	17. Tug McGraw	824
8. Cy Young	906	18. Nolan Ryan	807
9. Dennis Eckersley	901	19. Walter Johnson	802
10. Sparky Lyle	899	20. Gaylord Perry	777

FEWEST WALKS PER NINE INNINGS

(Minimum 1,500 innings)

1. Al Spalding	0.49	11. Jim Whitney	1.06
Candy Cummings	0.49	12. Jim Galvin	1.12
Tommy Bond	0.49	13. Deacon Phillippe	1.25
4. George Bradley	0.60	14. Will White	1.26
5. George Zettlein	0.61	15. Babe Adams	1.29
6. Terry Larkin	0.71	16. Jack Lynch	1.38
7. Dick McBride	0.74	17. Addie Joss	1.41
8. John Ward	0.92	18. Cy Young	1.49
9. Fred Goldsmith	0.96	19. Guy Hecker	1.51
10. Bobby Mathews	0.97	20. Lee Richmond	1.53

Goose Gossage ranks third in games pitched.

GAMES STARTED

1.	Cy Young	815
2.	Nolan Ryan	773
3.	Don Sutton	756
4.	Phil Niekro	716
5.	Steve Carlton	709
6.	Tommy John	700
7.	Gaylord Perry	690
8.	Jim Galvin	689
9.	Bert Blyleven	685
10.	Walter Johnson	666
11.	Warren Spahn	665
12.	Tom Seaver	647
13.	Jim Kaat	625
14.	Frank Tanana	616
15.	Early Wynn	612
16.	Robin Roberts	609
17.	Pete Alexander	599
18.	Fergie Jenkins	594
19.	Tim Keefe	593
20.	Bobby Mathews	568

INNINGS PITCHED

1.	Cy Young	7,355.1
2.	Jim Galvin	6,003.1
3.	Walter Johnson	5,915.0
4.	Phil Niekro	5,404.1
5.	Nolan Ryan	5,386.0
6.	Gaylord Perry	5,350.1
7.	Don Sutton	5,282.1
8.	Warren Spahn	5,243.2
9.	Steve Carlton	5,217.1
10.	Pete Alexander	5,190.0
11.	Kid Nichols	5,056.1
12.	Tim Keefe	5,047.1
13.	Bert Blyleven	4,970.0
14.	Bobby Mathews	4,956.1
15.	Mickey Welch	4,802.0
16.	Tom Seaver	4,782.2
17.	Christy Mathewson	4,780.2
18.	Tommy John	4,710.1
19.	Robin Roberts	4,688.2
20.	Early Wynn	4,564.0

Ageless Phil Niekro: No. 4 in innings pitched.

No wall is too high for acrobatic Kenny Lofton to climb.

Cheers for Craig Biggio, who remains in Astroland.